WORLD HERITAGE

911 Cultural and Natural Heritage Monuments selected by UNESCO

WORLD HERITAGE

The Pyramids of Ancient Egypt, the Acropolis in Athens, the Serengeti in Tanzania, the Taj Mahal in India, the Temple of Heaven in Beijing, the Inca town of Machu Picchu in Peru and the Grand Canyon in the United States all have one thing in common: They are unique cultural and natural sites protected by UNESCO. The Convention Concerning the Protection of World Cultural and Natural Heritage was agreed upon and put into effect in 1972, creating a list of sites possessing extraordinary and universal importance whose preservation would be the responsibility of all humankind. This effort has become more important than ever in the face of threats to unique ecosystems and cultural sites. In this book we provide detailed texts and pictures of the sites that have so far been

included in the world heritage list, all arranged by continent and country. Within those they are organized in geographical sequence from north to south. The images are accompanied by texts on cultural history and natural geography as well as maps with locations to make it easy to find them quickly. Join us on a journey to the world's most fascinating centers of natural and human culture.

PREFACE

This page: Views of Florence's most beautiful structures unfold from the Piazzale Michelangelo: Ponte Vecchio, Palazzo Vecchio, the cathedral (Duomo) and the Basilica of Santa Croce (from left).
Title page: Huge anthropomorphic stone sculptures dating from the pre-Columbian era are the main attractions at the San Agustín Archaeological Park in southern Colombia.
Pages 2/3: The giant stone heads of King Antiochus I of Commagene (69–36 BC) and sculptures of deities line the plateau on top of Nemrut Dağ in south-eastern Turkey.
Pages 4/5: A human figure seems tiny in front of the colossal sandstone columns decorated with hieroglyphics in the Hypostyle Hall in Karnak, Egypt.

CONTENTS

World Heritage Sites that straddle national boundaries are described in a single entry as long as the respective countries follow one another in the book; otherwise they are portrayed by multiple entries in the chapters of each respective country. In the case of the "Struve Geodetic Arc" World Heritage Site, which straddles ten countries, the entry is cross-referenced.

Carcassonne (below) is one of the best-preserved fortified medieval towns in France. In the foreground is the Pont Vieux, a bridge over the Aude River that was built in 1320.

The Acropolis (right) is an ancient stronghold built on top of a rock in the middle of Athens. The Parthenon is the impressive structure at its center.

Iceland / Norway

THINGVELLIR NATIONAL PARK

Thingvellir on the Reykjanes Peninsula in south-western Iceland is a place of great importance both historically and geologically.

Icelandic people called their assemblies of free men the Thing or Althing, a term that originated from Old Norse. They were open-air meetings where the men consulted on legal and other matters. Starting in 930, the Thingvellir, literally the "Valley of the Thing", was the assembly site for all free men in Iceland.

First, the law of the time was recited by the "law speaker". They then made amendments or changes that affected the entire country. One of the most important of these changes was the acceptance of Christianity in 1000. The last official Althing took place in 1798, but Thingvellir has retained its mythical significance.

It was here in 1944 that the country became an independent republic, and the valley, located in the geologically active Icelandic expansion zone, was declared a national park back in 1928. The Althing was convened for all those years in the roughly 5-km-long (3-mi) Almannagjá escarpment, or "All Men's Gorge", because its steep walls actually amplified speech without creating a disruptive echo. This World Heritage Site also includes a stretch of Lake Thingvallavatn and its population of arctic char.

In some areas, the Thingvellir opens out into a valley characterized by its arctic tundra vegetation.

VOLCANIC ISLAND OF SURTSEY

The island about 32 km (20 mi) off the south coast of Iceland was formed by volcanic eruptions beneath the ocean surface between 1963–1967. This natural laboratory now serves as a research center for the study of colonization.

Surtsey is off-limits to the regular public. From the beginning it has been used for scientific purposes in order to allow animal and plant life to develop naturally – i.e., without human interference. The island, named after the Nordic fire giant Surtr, was made into a nature reserve in 1965, but before that mosses and lichens had taken hold, followed by more highly developed plants such as European sea-rocket, European marram grass and oysterleaf, whose seeds had been washed ashore by the sea.

Birds and insects also reached the island in the first years of its life. Today, Surtsey is populated by 335 invertebrate and 89 bird species. However, time and the elements are eroding more and more of its mass. The consolidation of tephra, which forms the base, and the compaction of sediment beneath the island cause its surface area to continuously diminish.

Within 100 years, the island will have lost most of its landmass. However, Surtsey is not expected to disappear completely – its core will remain as a mighty rock in the ocean.

Surtsey emerged in 1963 as a result of powerful volcanic eruptions. The southernmost of the Vestmannaeyjar chain, the island is like a giant nature laboratory.

ROCK ART OF ALTA

The rock art of Alta is considered important evidence of early human settlement in northern Europe after the last Ice Age. It also provides information on how the first humans lived in the region.

The Alta region is located north of the Arctic Circle, at the sheltered end of a fjord. Thanks to the North Atlantic Current, it is not glaciated and therefore habitable.

In 1973, no fewer than 3,000 rock drawings were discovered accidentally here in an area covering more than 40 sites in all. The images were most probably drawn between about 4200 and 500 BC.

Chiseled several centimeters (inches) deep into the stone, the well-preserved pictures portray elks, reindeer and bears as well as depict scenes from everyday life: people fishing or navigating boats, hunting, and performing religious rituals and ceremonies. The drawings give a surprisingly vivid impression of the life of prehistoric people in northern Europe while also portraying their relationship with nature and spirituality.

More recent excavations near these sites have now unearthed settlements that were inhabited at around the same time as the rock drawings were made, thus helping us to understand the lifestyle and habits of people from that time.

The inhabitants of the far north once hunted with spears and bow and arrow.

Struve Geodetic Arc see page 124

THE VEGA ARCHIPELAGO (VEGAØYAN)

For 1,500 years the people of the Vega Archipelago just south of the Arctic Circle lived off fishing and harvesting the soft and highly desirable eider down.

The Vega Archipelago comprises several dozen islands grouped around the main island of Vega. The region is a breeding ground of the eider duck, which upholsters its nest with the famously fine eider down.

For 1,500 years, the inhabitants of the islands lived mainly from fishing and the trade in eider down. By fencing the eider ducks in, they eventually domesticated the mostly wild birds. The settlements of the island's inhabitants bear testimony to the establishment of a sustainable economy and the development of a distinctive lifestyle despite the harsh conditions of this far northern latitude. These days eider down feathers are used in the textile industry to make warm clothing, blankets and sleeping bags. Two-thirds of the nest feathers are harvested while one-third is left intact to guarantee the survival of the species. The World Heritage Site includes the fishing villages, the quays and warehouses, and the agricultural land, beacons and lighthouses.

Eider ducks call the dramatic and barren landscape of the Vega Archipelago home. They forms part of the Norwegian Sør Helgeland region.

RØROS MINING TOWN

The best-preserved mining town in Norway owes its existence to copper deposits that were discovered here as early as the 17th century. Today, tourism is the most important source of income for the roughly 5,000 inhabitants.

Røros is located in the quite sizable Skanden mountain range at an altitude of 628 m (2,060 ft) above sea level. For exactly 333 years, from 1644 until 1977, copper was mined in Røros and its surrounding areas before smelting ultimately came to an end in 1953.

The meticulously preserved historic center of the town, which was rebuilt after being destroyed by Swedish troops in the Scanian War in 1679, features quaint wooden houses that are grouped around inner courtyards. The pits and smelting works as well as some of the miners' homes have been put under heritage protection and today form part of an open-air museum that nicely portrays the history of copper mining in Norway.

The mining museum of Røros was established in a former smelting works in 1990. Also worth seeing is the baroque church completed in 1784, the only stone structure in the entire town center of Røros.

Wooden houses up to 250 years old were originally built as homes for the miners. They are clustered around the church in the upper part of town.

URNES STAVE CHURCH

Arguably the oldest stave church in Norway, Urnes is an outstanding example of Scandinavian timber construction from the end of the Viking period.

Norway's medieval stave churches are unique among Christian buildings. The framework of the structures consists of wooden posts reminiscent of ships' masts – they are also known as central mast churches.

The interior of these stave churches is usually very plain. The main space is considered the architectural successor of the ancient Norwegian great hall of the king. Aside from Viking influences, the architecture of the stave churches also features elements from Romanesque and Celtic building traditions. The steeply pitched, stacked roofs, the open arcades as well as the narthex (entrance) are all typical features of these churches.

Among the thirty or so preserved stave churches in Norway, the one in Urnes on a spit of land in the Lusterfjord is thought to be the oldest. Built in the 12th century, it features exquisite carvings in the Viking style depicting mythical creatures, dragon heads, densely interlaced animal sculptures and snakelike shapes. The carvings can be seen on the cubiform capitals in the interior as well as the powerful reliefs on the portals.

The Vikings crossed the Lusterfjord by boat to reach the spit of land (above left) where the elaborate nave of the Urnes stave church awaited them (below left).

Norway

BRYGGEN

Bergen's former merchant district is testimony to a time when this Hanseatic city flourished as the center of the entire Nordic fishing trade.

From the 14th to the 16th centuries, business in the trading and port town of Bergen was largely controlled by German Hanseatic merchants who had a stranglehold on trade in salt, which made it possible to preserve the fish caught in the Norwegian Sea. The fish was then sold to countries as far away as the Mediterranean.

It was thanks to the fishing trade that Bergen rose to become one of the most important commercial towns of the Hanseatic League. The gabled façades of the warehouses on the wharfs, known as "Tyskebryggen" (German Bridge) because of the Hanseatic merchants who used them,

A view of the row of houses at night across Vågen Bay with the marina on the north shore (top). Some 300 traditional warehouses (bottom) line the waterfront.

still testify to the former prosperity of the settlement. Of the preserved buildings in the district, sixty-two are part of the World Heritage Site despite the fact that they do not actually date back to the Middle Ages – they were rebuilt using the original construction methods after the fire of 1702. Fires have frequently caused devastation on the wharf, the last one being in 1955. Bergen is still one of Norway's most important ports.

The marina and the Old Town (right) are the main attractions in this Norwegian city on the Byfjord.

Bergen's port is dominated by the wooden clerk houses which typically consisted of two parallel rows with open, covered passageways. Goods, in particular stockfish (dried cod) from the Lofoten Islands in the north, were stored in the lower sections of the houses. Some façades are decorated with badges in animal shapes.

This clerk house, rebuilt after the fire of 1702, is the only one in Bergen from the Hanseatic days with its original furnishings. It offers a glimpse of the everyday life of merchants at that time and is now the Hanseatic Museum.

Norway

GEIRANGER-FJORD AND NÆRØYFJORD IN WESTERN NORWAY

Norway is the land of the fjords. Among the longest, deepest and most beautiful are the Geirangerfjord and the Nærøyfjord, both in the south of the country.

"Fjord" is a Norwegian word for valleys initially formed by rivers and then shaped by glaciers during the Ice Age. The U-shaped gorges were cut deeply into the coastal mountains extending far into Norway's interior before sea levels rose at the end of the Ice Age and flooded the valleys. Typical of the fjords are their dramatically steep cliffs and the coarse rubble left at the bottom.

Geirangerfjord and Nærøyfjord are about 120 km (75 mi) away from each other and the glacial masses that formed them carved their way into 1,900-m-high (6,234-ft) mountains.

In some places, the Nærøyfjord is no more than 250 m (820 ft) wide.

The waterways can be up to 500 m (1,640 ft) deep and one or two kilometers (1/2 to 1 miles) wide. Impressive mountains then rise beyond the steep cliffs. Torvløysa Mountain, for example, which is part of the Geirangerfjord region, rises to a mighty 1,850 m (6,070 ft) in height while Stiganosi Mountain on the Nærøyfjord hits 1,761 m (5,778 ft).

The Geirangerfjord Mountains are more alpine than the Nærøyfjord Mountains, which have low summits in comparison. Rivers, which flow in hanging valleys from the nearby mountains into the fjord, often form beautiful waterfalls that spill down the cliffs. These torrents at Geirangerfjord and Nærøyfjord are not yet used to produce hydroelectric energy, which is common in Norway. Both fjords run parallel to the coast before merging with another fjord system.

At the end of the Geirangerfjord lies Geiranger, a village of 250 people (top). A cruise up the fjord takes visitors to the Seven Sisters Waterfall, which is 300 m (984 ft) high (right).

THE ARCTIC LAPONIAN AREA

The expansive cultivated landscape of northern Sweden is the native land of the Lapps, or Sámi. Thanks to their nomadic lifestyle, this ethnic group can make optimum use of the sparse natural resources.

The Sámi, also known as the Saami or Samek (meaning "swamp people"), have inhabited the northern regions of Scandinavia for more than 2,000 years. With their giant herds of reindeer they trek across the thinly populated expanses, covering hundreds of miles each year in the process.

Many Sámi still lead traditional lives although they no longer survive exclusively from fishing and reindeer breeding. Tourism and the preservation of the countryside have become additional sources of employment. Crafts have always flourished here as well. Weaving, wood and bone carving as well as the preparation of animal furs are some of the traditional trades, and the brightly colored local garb is also still widely available.

Covered by tundra vegetation, the Laponian areas extend from the lower woodland fringes to the coast of the Norwegian Sea. Aside from elks, the regions are also home to wolves and brown bears.

The Laponian landscape is dominated by mountains, fjords and scree.

THE CHURCH VILLAGE OF GAMMELSTAD IN LULEÅ

Gammelstad is the best-preserved church village in Sweden. It still offers temporary accommodation to the faithful, who come from far and wide to celebrate mass or or other festivities.

Gammelstad, with its 424 wooden cabins, is approximately 10 km (6 mi) north of the city of Luleå on the Gulf of Bothnia. If the journey there and back home for a particular mass or an important celebration cannot be made within a day because of the great distances, visitors may spend the night in one of the old wooden cabins. This has remained a practical and popular institution even today since the northern reaches of Sweden are so sparsely populated and the cold winters here often last more than 200 days.

The first small houses here were probably built around the middle of the 16th century while the church was constructed in the early 15th century from red and white granite. The interior features the Antwerp Altar from 1520 as well as magnificent frescoes from around 1480. Clustered around the church are some thirty dwellings from the Middle Ages.

The church is the center of Gammelstad. From the steeple you can see the wooden cabins that surround it and provide basic shelter for the faithful.

ENGELSBERG IRONWORKS

One of the most important Swedish mining villages is in the iron ore region of Norberg. Iron ore was worked here as early as the Viking period.

Engelsberg, once the most important mining settlement for iron ore in Sweden, is near the town of Fagersta in the mining region of Högbyn. In fact, ore was being mined, smelted and processed here as early as the 6th century, and at the end of the 17th century the enormous ironworks in Engelsberg needed just a few decades to become one of the foremost smelting operations in Sweden.

The large deposits and high quality of Swedish iron created the basis for the country's rise as an international power. The heyday of furnaces and forging hammers lasted until the end of the 19th century, after which the competition became too great and the industry began to decline – the mine was closed in 1920. Despite that, Sweden is still one of the top producers and processors of iron ore in the world today.

Many of the old buildings in Engelsberg were restored according to original designs including an operating blast furnace from 1778, now used to demonstrate old smelting processes. Some sections of the tunnel network have even been reopened and visitors can explore these on guided tours.

The Engelsberg Ironworks were operational until 1920. Today they house an open-air museum and large parts have been opened up for visitors.

Sweden

MINING AREA OF THE GREAT COPPER MOUNTAIN IN FALUN

The copper mine in Falun is Sweden's oldest industrial complex. In the 17th century, two-thirds of the world's copper was produced here.

Roughly 1,000 years ago a copper vein was discovered on what was then dubbed Great Copper Mountain. The provincial capital of Falun owes its existence to the metal.

The Stora Kopparberget copper mining company was founded in 1284, becoming the oldest limited liability company in history. In 1650, most of the world's copper production was extracted by Stora and for more than two centuries it wielded great influence on mining technology in Europe. Sadly, the Great Copper Mountain was worked in a rather haphazard way, which led to a catastrophe in 1687 in which several shafts and galleries collapsed. The hole can still be seen on the edge of Falun's historic center. What was the Stora Stöten (or "large mine") is 100 m (328 ft) deep. Next to it is the Kopparberg Museum, with exhibits on copper mining.

The provincial capital was built on a rectangular grid based on plans from 1646 that included Sweden's first owner-occupied housing estates for the miners.

At the edge of the Falun town center is the "Störa Stöten", or large mine, site of the 1687 mining disaster.

Struve Geodetic Arc see page 124

ROCK CARVINGS IN TANUM

The rock drawings near Tanum, in Bohuslän Province on the Skagerrak, make this one of the most significant prehistoric sites in Scandinavia. A Bronze Age village was also reconstructed in the commune.

Thousands of years ago, the inhabitants of the area around what is now Tanum created what some of the most significant archeological finds in Scandinavia. They offer visitors superb insight into the Bronze Age world of northern Europe. They were most likely created at the end of the second century BC.

The carvings possess great artistic quality, depicting objects and scenes from the lives of Bronze Age Scandinavians including their rites, rituals and religious notions. Carved into the granite rock with elaborate detail, the rock drawings of Tanum also show hunting and battle scenes, dancing people, horses and bears, weapons and tools, cult figures and even jewelry. Of particularly interest is the large number of ships depicted.

Based on the remains that have been studied, the drawings were likely produced in different colors. This World Heritage Site includes finds in Fossum, Torsbo, Litsleby, Aspeberget and Vitlycke. During excavations nearby, runic stones and Neolithic rock graves were also discovered.

Battle scenes, rituals and even boats make up a sizable portion of the roughly 10,000 rock carvings in Tanum.

ROYAL DOMAIN OF DROTTNINGHOLM

Drottningholm Palace was built between 1662 and 1670 as a summer residence for the Swedish kings. It was enlarged on several occasions thereafter.

Drottningholm Palace (or "Queen's Island") stands elegantly on Lovö Island in Lake Mälar on the site of a previous building from the 16th century. The castle, which was not completed until 1700, is the largest baroque castle complex in Sweden. It was commissioned in 1662 by Queen Dowager Hedwig Eleonora, widow of the late King Charles X Gustav. It is the most important work by architect Nicodemus Tessin the Elder.

The palace was enlarged in 1750, when many of the rooms were given lavish rococo furnishings. After 1777, the palace was also used for state functions, which led to a remodeling of some rooms in the elegant neoclassical style.

King Gustav III of Sweden (1771–92) commissioned an English garden where visitors today are especially attracted by the Chinese Pavilion and the Drottningholm Theater, one of the few baroque stages in Europe still in use.

Situated in the lovely environs of Lake Mälar, Drottningholm Palace possesses a graceful harmony between nature and culture. It is still the summer residence of the Swedish royal family.

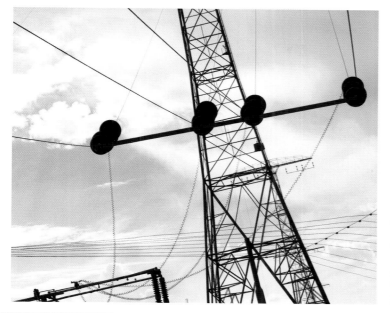

VARBERG RADIO STATION

Varberg Radio Station near Grimeton is an unusual technological monument. The station was put into operation in 1924 and provided a radio link with North America until the end of the 20th century.

In 1895, The Italian physicist Guglielmo Marconi invented wireless radio telegraphy. Soon after, radio stations all over the world began making use of his new technology.

During the course of World War I, the Swedish parliament decided to build a long-wave transmitter and receiving station for telegraphy communication. It was essential that the location that was ultimately selected would make it possible for radio waves to reach New York across the open ocean.

Massive Varberg Radio Station was finally built between 1922 and 1924. The most important part of the station is the alternating current generator built by Ernst Alexanderson. The six steel-lattice transmitter towers are each 127 m (417 ft) high, with 46-m-long (151-ft) horizontal arms that carry the eight copper wires.

The Neoclassical main buildings were built by Carl Åkerblad. Of twenty similar stations around the world, only the one in Grimeton is still operating in its original manifestation.

The transmitter tower of the Swedish radio station at Grimeton neat Varberg juts 127 m (417 ft) high into the sky. The steel framework is reminiscent of electricity pylons today.

BIRKA AND HOVGÅRDEN VIKING SETTLEMENTS

Bishop Ansgar consecrated Scandinavia's first church in the middle of the 9th century in the town of Birka on an island in Lake Mälar. At the time, Birka was the main trading hub between eastern and western Europe.

Bishop Ansgar of Bremen reported on his missionary travels to Birka in 830 and 853, but his reports were also confirmed by archaeological finds in the year 1871. Around 3,000 graves as well as the remains of enormous fortifications on Björkö Island testify to the former political and commercial importance of Birka and nearby Hovgården on Adelsö Island.

Commodities from western Europe, Russia, Byzantium and even Arabia were traded here, the main carriers on the long-distance routes being the Vikings, who transported goods by sea between east and west. As early as 975, however, the trade routes were relocated and Birka basically disappeared from the map until its discovery in the 19th century. One reason for the shift in commerce was probably the fact that the lake was cut off from the sea. With that development, Birka lost the link that was so essential to its survival.

There are still archaeological excavations underway in Birka today. The finds can be viewed in an exhibition at the museum.

NAVAL PORT OF KARLSKRONA

Monumental parade grounds and historic streets characterize Karlskrona, Sweden's largest naval port, and its extensive harbor and park complexes convey the ambience of a metropolis.

Karlskrona, the capital of the Blekinge District, is located on an island off the south-eastern coast of the Swedish mainland and has roughly 33,000 inhabitants. In 1680, King Charles XI ordered the establishment of a naval port for the country's sizable Baltic fleet.

Generously proportioned streets and squares were eventually built according to plans by architects Nicodemus Tessin and Erik Dahlberg. The fleet, at that time comprising ten frigates and 38 battleships, dominated the Baltic Sea until the collapse of the reign of King Charles XIII. This base of the technologically advanced Swedish navy has been continuously enlarged over the years and with its industrial complexes and fishing harbor, Karlskrona has become a flourishing port with the atmosphere of a cosmopolitan city. The Marine Museum features weapons, ship models, navigational instruments and old maps to illustrate Sweden's seafaring history.

Karlskrona's naval base is omnipresent – everywhere sailors and officers amble through its historic streets.

Sweden

HANSEATIC TOWN OF VISBY

Visby on Gotland Island is one of the most important Hanseatic towns in Scandinavia, and large areas of the historic Old Town have been very well preserved. The fortifications, ramparts and towers have all largely survived the passing centuries.

Documents show that this town on the north-western coast of Gotland Island was settled as early as the Stone Age. In the 12th century, German merchants even used Visby, initially as a stopover for the extremely lucrative trade with Novgorod in the Russian interior, and soon after as a base for expanding the mighty Hanseatic League into the east. The Baltic cities of Riga, Reval, Gdansk and Dorpat were ultimately brought into the fold from here.

In the 13th century, Visby was probably the most important trading town

Old Visby was a town of churches. St Mary's (above) dates from the 13th century, but only ruins remain of many of the other churches.

in northern Europe aside from Lübeck. The town even coined its own money and became a legislative center for international marine law that held sway in the entire Baltic Sea region. Visby's relatively short heyday ended in 1361, however, when Danish King Valdemar IV conquered Gotland. But the powerful town walls, up to 9 m (30 ft) high in places and 3.4 km (2 mi) long, still testify to the city's former prosperity. All told, thirty-eight historic towers still stand watch. The numerous merchant houses from the 12th and 13th centuries line narrow medieval alleyways and reinforce Visby's reputation as one of the best-preserved Hanseatic towns in Europe.

The port of Visby is more like a quaint pond these days (top), but the town walls (middle and bottom) are still pretty impressive. They are 3.4 km (2 mi) long and crowned by thirty-eight wonderfully preserved watchtowers.

AGRICULTURAL LANDSCAPE OF SOUTHERN ÖLAND

The southern portion of Öland Island in the Baltic Sea has a unique agrarian landscape that bears testimony to our ability to adapt to extreme conditions.

Öland, the second-largest island in Sweden after Gotland, has a unique geological composition that limits agricultural activities. Only the southeastern end with its moraine soil can be cultivated. Elsewhere sandstone, slate and limestone dominate the island's southern plateau.

Despite this and the obvious climatic challenges of the region, humans have lived in southern Öland for at least 5,000 years. Numerous Iron Age burial grounds and several ringforts from the Migration Period even indicate permanent settlement. Eketorp Castle, now a museum, offered shelter and protection to people here between AD 400 and 1300. The oldest runic stone, from the 10th century, stands on a burial mound south of Kalmarsund Bridge.

Especially noteworthy is the 5-km-long (3-mi) wall erected across the island by King Charles X Gustav in 1653. The agricultural landscape here is evidence that humans were able to effectively exploit natural even in the Bronze Age.

The large stones, probably marking graves, are indications of a late Iron Age settlement.

SKOGSKYRKOGÅRDEN

This cemetery complex south of Stockholm harmoniously combines architecture, sculpture and landscape design.

In 1912, the Stockholm City Council decided to create a woodland cemetery in the city's Enskede District. They invited tenders for the design in 1914, which were won by the architects Erik Gunnar Asplund and Sigurd Lewerentz. From 1917 to 1920 the cemetery was built in an area measuring more than 100 ha (247 acres). It was further extended until 1940.

Asplund and Lewerentz incorporated numerous buildings into their landscape design. In 1920, Asplund constructed a square wooden chapel with an open narthex (entrance). Another chapel, designed by Lewerentz, was then dedicated in 1925. Asplund was also responsible for the crematorium with its three chapels (1937–1940) and the large freestanding cross.

The designers at Skogskyrkogården Cemetery were able to achieve a harmonious blend of natural and architectural elements. Landscape formations were integrated into the complex, with tall trees lining the paths and lawns, and their work ultimately had a profound and lasting influence on funerary architecture around the world. When Asplund died in 1940, he was of course laid to rest in Skogskyrkogården.

The crematorium at Skogskyrkogården is a modern structure.

HIGH COAST AND THE KVARKEN ARCHIPELAGO

The High Coast is a fascinating skerry landscape shaped over millennia by glacial movements. Since the addition of the Finnish part of the Kvarken Archipelago in 2006, the area has become a transnational natural heritage site.

These rolling landscapes in the Gulf of Bothnia were shaped by the last ice age, which began about 80,000 years ago and ended in Scandinavia about 9,600 years ago. When the giant ice sheets melted, sea levels rose by some 115 m (380 feet). As a result, massive swathes of land were left below sea level. Freed from the weight of the glaciers bearing down upon it, the land gradually rose, and skerries (rock islands) emerged from the sea.

To date, the region has risen by 285 m (935 ft), and the process is still in motion. In fact, the subsoil is rising at a rate of around 93 cm (37 in) every century. The hills of the hinterland are now up to 350 m (1,150 ft) high.

It is a largely untamed landscape with rich, chalky soil and many lakes. Combined with the brackish water of the shallow coastal estuaries and the open waters of the Baltic, the small High Coast region still boasts three geologically and biologically significant water systems.

Ice Age relics: Beautiful lakes and forested hills are typical of the High Coast region.

Denmark (Greenland)

ILULISSAT ICEFJORD

The ice of the Sermeq Kujalleq glacier is transported from Greenland's vast interior. It reaches the sea at the Ilulissat icefjord where the glacier calves and releases large numbers of icebergs into the North Atlantic.

The Sermeq Kujalleq glacier flows from the Greenland ice cap, which is up to 3,000 m (9,900 ft) thick in places, into the North Atlantic. With a daily flow rate of between 19 and 22 m (63–72 ft), the Sermeq Kujalleq is one of the fastest and most active glaciers in the world. As it reaches the water, giant blocks of ice break off and crash into the sea with dramatic and deafening sounds. These icebergs then float slowly south, where they can become a danger to ships (e.g. the Titanic).

The Sermeq Kujalleq calves roughly 35 sq km (14 sq mi) of ice every year and is thus responsible for ten percent of the icebergs formed in Greenland,

These icebergs calved from the Sermeq Kujalleq glacier and tower like vertical walls out of the cold North Atlantic.

far more than any other glacier outside the Antarctic.

The Ilulissat and its glacier have been the subject of scientific investigation for more than 250 years and have yielded copious data regarding local geomorphology, glaciology, and general climate change. This calving glacier and the tall icebergs in the fjord are a fascinating sight, but because of the icebergs, the trip to the glacier is not without its dangers. Off the Greenland coast, the icebergs can reach a height of 100 m (330 ft) above the water. Many of them do not melt until they are just north of New York.

The icy cold sea is in fact teeming with life and is a fishing ground for many Danish trawlers (right). The ice formations of Greenland were studied long before concerns about climate change arose.

ROSKILDE CATHEDRAL

Scandinavia's oldest Romanesque-Gothic brick church is the burial place of Danish kings, who have been laid to rest here since the 15th century. The country's former capital, Roskilde still has symbolic significance for the Danes.

Until the Reformation in the 16th century, Denmark's ecclesiastical focal point was in Roskilde, a town on Sjælland Island about 30 km (19 mi) west of the capital, Copenhagen. Before 1443, Roskilde was also the royal residence and capital of the country. Bishop Absalon, the architect of the first Romanesque-Gothic brick church in Scandinavia, was also the founder of Copenhagen. He commissioned the building in 1170, on the foundations of two smaller churches that once stood here. The objective was to give the royal residence a dignified place of worship that was worthy of its august patrons.

The cathedral was essentially given its present appearance when the two large towers were built in the 14th century. It is considered an important example of Danish religious architecture. The interior of the cathedral, which was enlarged later in the 19th century using ante-structures and side chapels, contains the richly adorned graves of thirty-seven Danish kings and queens, who were buried here in artfully decorated sarcophagi starting in the 15th century.

The cathedral towers over Roskilde's Old Town. It was begun in the Romanesque and completed in Gothic style.

JELLING BURIAL MOUNDS, RUNIC STONES AND CHURCH

An impressive royal grave with runic stones, large burial mounds and relics as well as an historic church in Jelling near Vejle in the east of Jutland all tell the tale of the Christianization of Denmark.

Denmark's most impressive royal burial site can be found in front of Jelling Church, and the burial gifts found here document the might of the Vikings, who had gained dominion over the northern sea routes in the early Middle Ages.
The complex also includes two enormous burial mounds 60 and 77 m (197 and 253 ft) across, respectively, and a boat-shaped stone setting with a church between them and two runic stones. It is an historic monument to the Christianization of the Danish people, which basically marks the

country's entry into the history of European states.
Pagan King Gorm (end of 9th century) and his wife Tyra were originally buried in the more northerly of the two tumuli. Their son, Harald Blåtand, Denmark's first Christian king, later had their bones reburied in the new church. The larger of the runic stones, from around 980, carries the oldest depiction of Christ in Scandinavia.

The inscription (left) on one of the large runic stones in Jelling was dedicated by King Gorm to his wife.

KRONBORG CASTLE NEAR HELSINGØR

This Renaissance castle on the Öresund was built in the 16th century and reconstructed in the 17th century following a fire. The castle became world-famous as Elsinore in William Shakespeare's tragedy "Hamlet".

Its commanding location overlooking the Öresund, the narrowest stretch of water between Denmark and Sweden, gave this royal residence immense strategic importance. Kronborg Castle controlled the vital sound as early as the late Middle Ages, levying toll payments on passing ships.
In addition to the castle's beauty, it is primarily this strategic significance that has remained in the psyche of the Danish people – it represents the former power and glory of the kingdom. King Frederick II, who ruled from 1559 until 1588, had the four-sided

castle complex built in the Dutch Renaissance style. The site had already been used for a previous fortification, but this time the bastions were strengthened according to the contemporary theories of military architecture. The castle of "Hamlet" fame was then rebuilt after a fire in 1629. The extensive casemates were later added in 1700.

Kronborg Castle is not only the fictional setting for Shakespeare's "Hamlet". The mighty Renaissance structure also controlled the narrows of the Öresund.

Finland

PETÄJÄVESI OLD CHURCH

This distinctive red wooden church in Petäjävesi to the west of Jyväskylä in central Finland is one of the most attractive places of worship in the country and a typical example of Scandinavian church architecture.

This historic village church on a small peninsula between Lake Jämsänvesi and Lake Petäjävesi was finally completed in the year 1765 by architect Jaakko Klementinpoika Leppänen. The villagers had been waiting for two years for the building permit.

The wooden structure elegantly blends elements of the Renaissance and the Gothic with the distinctive styles of traditional eastern Scandinavian woodwork and architecture. Modeled on the centrally planned edifices of the Renaissance, Petajavesi's church is cruciform in its layout, with arms of equal length. High pine vaults cover the transepts, and an octagonal dome rises above the central crossing. The altarpiece and the depictions of Martin Luther and Moses on the pulpit date from the year 1843.

The church's exterior features a shingled hipped roof displaying Gothic elements. Overall, the structure bears witness to the religious faith of the village inhabitants while gracefully portraying the technical and artistic skills of its builders.

The altar – like the whole interior of the church – is quite simple, but a number of paintings, woodcarvings and statues give it a cozy feel.

Struve Geodetic Arc see page 124

OLD RAUMA

Rauma, one of Finland's most important villages until 1550, has a charming Old Town built on a medieval plan with traditional low wooden houses. Also noteworthy is the even older Church of the Holy Cross.

When Franciscan monks settled in this trading post in what is now southwestern Finland in around 1400, it had likely been there for quite some time already. Of their monastery complex, which stood here until 1538, only the Church of the Holy Cross remains today. Built in 1449, it boasts valuable ceiling frescoes.

The monastery formed the focal point of a settlement that eventually became the town of Rauma. It is one of only a few medieval villages in Finland and, after a devastating fire in 1682, it is still classified today as a medieval complex despite having been rebuilt later with the old street layout.

Some of the houses in the Old Town feature richly ornamented paneled façades dating from the 18th and 19th centuries, when Rauma boasted the largest merchant fleet in Finland. They form one of the most extensive ensembles of wooden structures in Scandinavia. The two-storey Old Town Hall, completed in 1777, now houses a museum that documents the craft of tatting introduced by the Franciscan monks.

The heart of Rauma's Old Town consists of a unified ensemble of buildings featuring one- and two-story wooden houses interspersed with gardens.

BRONZE AGE BURIAL SITE OF SAMMALLAHDENMÄKI

The more than thirty stone burial cairns in south-western Finland are mostly more than 3,000 years old. Their number, state of preservation and size are all proof of highly developed funerary practices in Bronze Age northern Europe.

The cults of the sun typical of Finland's coastal regions were many, but their activities took place far from established settlements, high up on remote cliffs where special emphasis was placed on the mystic relationship between the sun and sea. Despite evidence of their existence, however, scientists have not been able to explain the meaning of the cairns.

Of the Sammallahdenmäki graves in the Satakunta area east of Rauma, twenty-eight can be dated back to the Bronze Age. The stone piles lie in groups along the slopes of a narrow, 700-m-long (2,297-ft) ridge. Several types of Bronze Age stone graves were found here: small, low, round cairns, large burial mounds and graves ringed by a wall. Inside they feature burial chambers lined with stone slabs. Archaeological excavations have so far unearthed only a few burned bones and some charcoal.

This aerial view gives a good idea of the extent of the burial area. The mounds consist of piled stones and rocks.

FORTRESS OF SUOMENLINNA

This impressive fortified complex extends across six islands and was built to protect the port of Helsinki from attack. With its mighty walls, it still looks a powerful defensive structure today.

The Swedes, who ruled Finland for many centuries, built Sveaborg fortress at the entrance to the port of Helsinki in the middle of the 18th century. When the Russians took the fortifications without a fight in 1808, the Swedes began their withdrawal from Finland. Czar Alexander I, who ruled from 1801 to 1825, then made Helsingfors the capital of the newly founded Grand Duchy of Finland. An Orthodox church, wooden houses and a garrison headquarters are all that remain from the time of the Russian occupation. During the Crimean War in 1855, Suomenlinna, as the fortress is now called, was bombed by a fleet led by Great Britain and parts of it were badly damaged.

After 1918, when Finland became an independent nation, the fortress was used as a prison for communist soldiers and leaders, many of whom lost their lives in Suomenlinna's dungeons. Today, a museum of the history of the fortress provides visitors with more detailed information. Suomenlinna is an important example of European military architecture.

Suomenlinna is a popular attraction for visitors. The complex is vast, straddling several islands with its defensive walls and numerous buildings.

VERLA GROUNDWOOD AND BOARD MILL

This complex of mills in southern Finland 150 km (93 mi) north-east of Helsinki is one of the most significant monuments to the Finnish timber industry. Paper and cellulose are still important products here.

Scandinavia and northern Russia's abundant forest resources formed the foundation for a flourishing paper industry that began in earnest in the second half of the 19th century. It was a time when the forests of Canada and the north-eastern United States brought about similar developments. However, only very few of the then numerous industrial complexes still exist today.

The paper mill established in Verla in 1882, along with the adjacent cardboard factory and workers' tenement estates, are located in the middle of a park on the banks of the small river that runs past the site. The entire ensemble impresses with its geometric brick architecture. The factory owes its preservation to the fact that it was in operation until 1964. Today it houses a museum recounting the history of the Finnish timber industry.

The giant pulp machines of the Verla paper mill still work, despite the mill closing in 1964, and even look as if they could take up the production of board again at a moment's notice.

HISTORIC CENTER (OLD TOWN) OF TALLINN

This town on the Baltic Sea was originally founded by the Danes in the Middle Ages before becoming a power center of the Hanseatic League. Many merchant homes and churches still bear witness to Tallinn's former prosperity.

After sustaining serious damage in World War II, the historic center of the Estonian capital was rebuilt in the style of the 18th century. The nucleus of the Old Town, known as Reval by Hanseatic Germans, is located on Cathedral Hill. In 1920, Reval became the capital of the Republic of Estonia and was renamed Tallinn. Today, the mighty towers and walls of the former fortifications still stand strong. St Mary's Cathedral, begun in about 1230, holds art treasures from numerous periods. The Church of the Holy Ghost, from the 12th/13th centuries, is a chapel and poorhouse typical of the Baltic region. It was later furnished with elaborate woodcarvings and now boasts remarkable pulpits – just like St Nicholas Church from the 13th/14th centuries.

The center of Tallinn's Old Town is dominated by the Town Hall Square with its many historic buildings and the 14th-century Gothic town hall.

Cathedral Hill offers superb views over the city with its many churches, including St Olav's Church, and the watchtowers of the Old Town ramparts.

Struve Geodetic Arc see page 124

HISTORIC CENTER OF RIGA

The historic Old Town of the Latvian capital boasts a number of medieval churches and merchant houses as well as one of the most beautiful clusters of Art Nouveau buildings in Europe.

Riga is located at the mouth of the Daugava River on the Baltic Sea. Outstanding among its many important places of worship are the cathedral, begun in 1211 and completed in its present form in 1775, as well as the octagonal wooden steeple of the Lutheran Jesus Church (1819–1822). Of the once mighty city fortifications, the Powder Tower (14th century) and Ramer's Tower (13th century) have been faithfully preserved; the Citadel was begun in 1760 under Swedish rule, and the Swedish Gate also dates back to this period. The Great Guild Hall is the only administrative building that has been preserved while the Small Guild Hall, built in the middle of the 14th century, is one of the most prestigious structures in the city. The Riga Stock Exchange was built between 1852 and 1855 in the style of a Venetian palace. The city's other historically significant houses include magnificent structures such as the Reutern House, begun in 1683.

Views of the Old Town with its many turrets unfold across the Daugava (top). The House of Blackheads on Town Hall Square was built in 1334 and is the largest of its kind anywhere (right).

Struve Geodetic Arc see page 124

KERNAVÉ ARCHAEOLOGICAL SITE

In Kernavé, north-west of Vilnius, an archaeological site provides information on life in the Baltic region from the Paleolithic Age to modern times. Of particular importance here are the hill forts from the pre-Christian period.

The Kernavé Archaeological Site provides visitors with evidence of human settlement dating back approximately 10,000 years. The oldest finds are from the Stone Age while the youngest come from the Middle Ages. Seen together, the World Heritage Site is an ensemble of elements extending over nearly 200 hectares and comprising the town itself along with fortresses, unfortified settlements and burial sites. Its is especially easy to see the relationship between pagan and Christian funerary traditions here. Indications of how the land was formerly used in the Neris River valley are also visible, as are the remains of five hill forts, each part of a remarkably extensive system of defences. In the Middle Ages, Kernavé was an important town with five powerful castles. First mentioned in 1279, it is considered the first capital of Lithuania. In the late 14th century, Teutonic Knights destroyed the duchy.

The complex of Kernavé in the Neris Valley still has great symbolic meaning for Lithuanians (right a family at a midsummer picnic).

VILNIUS HISTORIC CITY CENTER

The Old Town in the merchant settlement of Vilnius sprawls along the Neris Valley at the foot of Vilnius Castle. During its heyday in the 15th and 16th centuries it mediated between Russian towns and the Hanseatic League.

Vilnius was the political center of the Grand Duchy of Lithuania from the 13th through the 18th centuries. As a hub of culture amidst diverse European traditions, it left its mark on the rich architectural fabric of eastern Europe. Gothic, baroque and Renaissance styles all exist side by side in this beautiful city.

Particularly outstanding among the older buildings are some of the late-Gothic churches such as St Anne, St Nicholas and the Bernardine Church, as well as some baroque palaces of former nobility. The Church of Ss Peter & Paul from the 17th century is also baroque in appearance.

At the heart of the Old Town, however, is St Stanislaus Cathedral, which was given its present appearance between the years 1783 and 1801. With its neoclassical style it rather resembles a Greek temple.

Vilnius Cathedral (left, with the separate bell tower, and below with a view of the altar) was dedicated in 1801. The (City) Gate of Dawn (below left) features a gate superstructure built in the Renaissance style.

Struve Geodetic Arc see page 124

CURONIAN SPIT

Since the Neolithic Age, a narrow stretch of dunes called the Curonian Spit has extended between the Baltic Sea and the Curonian Lagoon, connecting Lithuania with the Russian enclave of Kaliningrad.

When the Baltic Sea broke against the 80-m-thick (262-ft) ground moraine left behind by the Ice Age glaciers, only two islands still rose from the sea, near the present-day villages of Rybackiy and Zelenogradsk. Wind and waves drove sand from the Sambian coast against these islands, which grew each year by up to 6 m (20 ft) towards the north-east.

You might think you were on the edge of the Sahara, such is the effect of the mighty shifting sands. It is home to one of Europe's largest dunes, the Great Dune of Nida, which has a plateau at an altitude of 60 m (197 ft). The sands only shift in a small area here; for all other dunes this process was stopped by a planting program begun in the 19th century. Archaeological digs confirm that the dune landscape has been settled since the fourth century BC. Since that time the Curonian Spit has developed through the interplay of natural forces and human intervention. The picturesque fishing villages in the area are also part of the World Cultural Heritage Site.

The Curonian Spit is almost 100 km long (62 mi) and only a few hundred meters wide with dunes up to 60 m (197 ft) high.

United Kingdom

ST KILDA

Located around 175 km (110 mi) off the west coast of Scotland, Britain's most isolated and remote archipelago provides an ideal nesting place for the world's largest colony of northern gannets.

Spared from glaciation during the last ice age, the St Kilda volcanic archipelago managed to retain its characteristic landscape. This group of islands "at the end of the world" comprises Dun, Soay, Boreray, and Hirta. The residents of Hirta were resettled in 1930, and the island has been uninhabited ever since – given over entirely to nature. Its impressive, steep cliff faces provide optimal nesting conditions for rare birds, notably for the large numbers of gannets who have taken refuge here. Despite the harsh climate on these islands, humans still decided to settle here some two thousand years ago.

Their most notable buildings are the so-called "cleits", of which there are 1,260 on Hirta Island alone, and over 170 more spread about on the other islands. They are small structures built of dry stone walls and covered with a grassed earth roof. Their primary purpose was as storage space – the lack of mortar in the walls guaranteed the constant circulation of fresh air, a necessity since they were mainly used to store bird's eggs, feathers, peat and turf.

Most of these natural stone houses can be found on the main island of Hirta.

HEART OF NEOLITHIC ORKNEY

The monuments on Mainland, the main island of the Orkneys off the north coast of Scotland, document human cultural achievement in northern Europe from the period between 3,000 and 2,000 BC.

Most of the Orkney Islands, located off the north-easterly tip of Scotland, are uninhabited. About three-quarters of the total population lives on the main island, appropriately called Mainland, which features a number of Stone-Age relics. Maes Howe is a large chambered tomb about 15 km (9 mi) from the capital of Kirkwall. It dates from around 2,500 BC and has a sizable diameter of more than 30 m (98 ft). The remains of the Stenness Stone Circle also date from prehistoric times. Not far from here stands the Ring of

Brodgar, which has stones up to 4.5 m (15 ft) in height positioned in a circle of about 100 m (328 ft) in diameter. Particularly impressive is the Stone-Age settlement of Skara Brae, which was uncovered by a massive storm only about 150 years ago. It is considered the best-preserved neolithic settlement in Europe.

Of the originally sixty stones in the Ring of Brodgar, twenty-seven are still standing today. This neolithic stone circle was presumably used as a temple for sun worship.

NEW LANARK

Despite being derided by some as a "social revolutionary", industrialist Robert Owen built this town around what was once the largest cotton mill in Great Britain in an effort to make his utopian vision of society a reality.

In 1783, in a valley some 40 km (25 mi) from Glasgow, Scotland, Richard Arkwright and Welsh entrepreneur David Dale built a mighty cotton mill. The working conditions were similar to other factories during the Industrial Revolution: child labor and other abuses were commonplace. Things were about to change, however. In 1799, Robert Owen became Dale's son-in-law and joined the company's board in 1800. Owen, who was somewhat of a revolutionary in his time, had managed to publish his ideas in numerous publications and they had gained traction all around Europe. He was finally able

to make his dreams a reality in New Lanark. He reduced working hours, rebuilt the dwellings of his 2,500 workers, set up a free health service, and established child nurseries and leisure facilities as well as the first schools for working-class children in Great Britain. Thanks to its architecture and social institutions, this model industrial community, restored in the 1980s, is regarded as a milestone in social and industrial history.

Visitors to New Lanark can now explore the village and its production facilities as well as the living quarters of the industrialist Robert Owen.

FRONTIERS OF THE ROMAN EMPIRE

Hadrian's Wall and the Antonine Wall are part of the World Heritage Site "Frontiers of the Roman Empire", which includes the Roman Limes in Germany.

In order to strengthen the defenses of the Roman Empire against the "wild" peoples of the north, walls were built in the second century that extended some 5,000 km (3,107 mi) across Europe. Sections particularly worthy of protection were Hadrian's Wall, added to the list of World Heritage Sites in 1987, the Upper Germanic-Rhaetian Limes in Germany, added in 2005, and the Antonine Wall in Scotland, added in 2008.

Hadrian's Wall stretches from Newcastle through Carlisle near the English-Scottish border up to Bowness-on-Solway on the Irish Sea, 120 km (75 mi) away. The wall was built using a mixture of earth and stone. After the Romans withdrew from the islands in around AD 410, the fortifications soon fell into disrepair.

About 150 km (93 mi) farther north, the Antonine Wall extends approximately 60 km (37 mi) from the Firth of Forth to the Firth of Clyde. This fortified border and its nineteen Roman forts were built in AD 140 under Emperor Antoninus Pius but abandoned only a few decades later.

Hadrian's Wall, built mostly of stone, is located in northern England.

THE OLD AND NEW TOWNS OF EDINBURGH

The character of the Scottish capital is defined by the unique architectural contrast between the medieval Old Town and the carefully planned Georgian New Town.

Edinburgh Castle is an awe-inspiring edifice that dates back to the 11th century in its oldest parts. St Margaret's Chapel, dedicated in 1090, is also up on Castle Rock, below which the Royal Mile begins. The Old Town has tiny alleyways and back courtyards where aristocratic villas such as Gladstone's Land sit side by side with churches like the late-Gothic St Giles' Cathedral.

At the eastern end of the Royal Mile is the Palace of Holyroodhouse, built in 1128 as an Augustine monastery and later the residence of the Scottish monarchs. Opposite the palace is the new Scottish Parliament building.

Despite its decline in political significance since joining England in 1707, Edinburgh remained an important cultural center. Toward the end of the 18th century, the Georgian New Town was built in a rectangular grid on a north-south axis.

Edinburgh is famous for its magnificent buildings. Top left and right: Edinburgh Castle and St Giles' Cathedral. Left: the 17th-century Parliament.

United Kingdom

DURHAM CASTLE AND CATHEDRAL

Durham is located in the county of the same name in north-eastern England. The Norman Castle and the city's three-storey Anglo-Norman Cathedral testify to its former importance and the power of the bishops.

The fortress-like Castle of the prince-bishops of Durham sits high above the River Wear where a Norman castle complex was built in 1072, as a bulwark against the Picts of Scotland. It later became the center of a settlement of Benedictine monks and the residence of the prince-bishops, who until 1536 also wielded secular power in the region.

Begun in 1093, the cathedral was to house the relics of the Venerable Bede and St Cuthbert. Erected by the Normans, who conquered much of what is now the United Kingdom, it is considered one of the most beautiful edifices from the transition between the Romanesque and the Gothic.

The relatively low and elongated nave is a typical feature of the English Gothic style. The cross-ribbed vaulting above the transepts is the oldest preserved vaulting of its kind, assuring the cathedral an important place in the history of European architecture.

Durham Cathedral is one of the most important places of worship in England. It was built in 1093, in the Norman Romanesque and early Gothic styles.

SALTAIRE INDUSTRIAL VILLAGE

Saltaire is the largest completely preserved model village of the early industrial age. It reflects the philanthropic paternalism of the Victorian Era, when factory owners began to develop a sense of social responsibility for their workers.

On September 20, 1853, industrialist Sir Titus Salt built his factory on the River Aire in West Yorkshire county. Wool of all kinds was teased, spun and woven here on approximately 1,200 weaving looms on which workers produced some seventeen miles of fabric a day. The building was as long as St Paul's Cathedral in London. Even more unusual was the settlement that Salt established around his factory: an industrial village boasting well-equipped housing estates for workers, a church, a school, a hospital, a park, a temple-like bath house and an institute with a library, assembly rooms and a gym – all available to the workers. Pubs could not be found in Saltaire, for Salt was of the opinion that discussions should take place not at the bar but in the specially designated public rooms.

Saltaire, an example of forward-thinking, worker-friendly industrialization, is now a monument whose architecture considerably influenced the conception and development of the garden cities of our future.

The houses in the workers' village of Saltaire in West Yorkshire were designed by architects from Bradford using the latest social and sanitary standards of the day.

LIVERPOOL – MARITIME MERCANTILE CITY

Six areas in the historic center and port of Liverpool have been declared a World Cultural Heritage Site. With its impressive buildings and docks, the city bears testimony to Great Britain's rise as an industrial and world power.

Liverpool's municipal charter was issued back in 1207, but it remained a small fishing village for another 500 years before the lucrative slave trade eventually led to the first dock being built in 1715. The city ultimately played an important role in the "Triangle Trade" in which weapons, alcohol, salt and textiles were shipped from England in exchange for slaves in West Africa, who were then taken to the New World. The ships were then loaded with tobacco, cotton and sugar for transport back to Liverpool. After the abolition of slavery in 1807, still more docks were built, this time designed primarily to transport emigrants to America. The docks were in use until the middle of the 20th century, when the economic decline of Liverpool began in earnest. With the help of EU finance the city was able to restore the historic center and the docks. Today, Liverpool boasts shops, bars, restaurants and museums.

The Three Graces – the Royal Liver Building, the Port of Liverpool Building and the Cunard Building – dominate the Pier Head in Liverpool's port.

BLAENAVON INDUSTRIAL LANDSCAPE

This industrial complex in South Wales features the world's best-preserved ironworks from the early Industrial Revolution at the end of the 18th century.

In 1789, three English industrialists came and built three blast furnaces in the mountains of South Wales, near the village of Blaenavon. They utilized steam power and the latest technologies of the day to produce iron ore. All the necessary raw materials were mined on site and the blast furnaces were built directly into the slope so they could be fed from above.

In 1788, a workers' village for the miners was also established here, with plain stone houses that were reminiscent of traditional cottages. On the edge of the former industrial area was one of the largest collieries, known as the "Big Pit". It was here that the coal needed to operate the blast furnaces was extracted.

Toward the end of the 20th century, with the decline of iron ore production, the area fell into disrepair. The downturn did not stop until 1975 when a restoration program began.

The "Big Pit" became the Big Pit Mining Museum in 1983. A guided underground tour takes visitors through the forge and to the pits themselves.

IRONBRIDGE GORGE INDUSTRIAL MONUMENTS

Ironbridge Gorge and the village of Coalbrookdale, located in Telford near Birmingham, are pioneering sites of the Industrial Age.

Ironbridge Gorge owes its name to the bridge built here by ironworks proprietor Abraham Darby in 1779. It is the so-called "Stonehenge of the Industrial Revolution". Spanning the Severn Valley near Coalbrookdale, it was the first bridge in history to be made of cast iron. It is still in use by pedestrians.

The nearby mines and the cokery can also be visited, as can the numerous railway lines, which were added later and enabled transport around the country. The well-preserved installations today form an extensive museum landscape that vividly documents the beginnings of the industrial age in England.

The complex comprises, among other features, a blast furnace that was also built as early as the 18th century, Blists Hill Victorian Town, with exhibitions relating to the Victorian Age, and a workshop once dedicated to the manufacture of roof tiles.

The porcelain factory founded in 1796 by John Rose in Coalport is at the eastern end of a number of industrial monuments in the valley of Ironbridge. It is now a museum.

STUDLEY ROYAL PARK AND RUINS OF FOUNTAINS ABBEY

The royal gardens in Studley in North Yorkshire surround the impressive ruins of Fountains Abbey, a once prosperous Cistercian monastery and one of England's largest and best-preserved complexes of this kind.

Monks from York originally founded the Cistercian Fountains Abbey. The abbey experienced great prosperity until the Dissolution of the Monasteries in 1539, a result of the separation of the Church of England from papal authority. Sheep breeding and the trade in wool made it one of the largest and richest monasteries in the country.

The complex includes the 123-m-long (404-ft) church (pictured below), the 55-m-high (180-ft) bell tower above the northern transept, and the immediately adjacent abbey building with its cloisters, featuring impressive Norman-Romanesque arches.

After the Dissolution of the Monasteries in England by Henry VIII in the early-16th century, the complex was largely ignored until it became part of Studley Royal in the 18th century. The Georgian Park from 1727, with its Octagon Tower, the Temple of Piety and the Half Moon Pond, is one of the most magnificent gardens in England.

The ruins of Fountains Abbey feature the remains of an earlier Cistercian abbey.

BLENHEIM PALACE

Blenheim Palace near Woodstock in Oxfordshire is one of the most beautiful and powerful examples of baroque architecture in England. It is located in the middle of a park designed according to the ideals of Romanticism.

England gifted this superb residence in Oxfordshire to John Churchill, the first Duke of Marlborough, in a gesture of gratitude for his successful campaign against French and Bavarian troops in the Battle of Blenheim on the Danube in 1704. The palace was built between 1705 and 1722, under the supervision of Sir John Vanbrugh, one of England's most highly regarded architects.

The three wings of the two-storey baroque palace feature towers and arcades set around a massive courtyard. The extensive gardens have been remodeled several times over the years. Initially designed by Henry

Wise based on the model of Versailles, the park was re-naturalized by landscape gardener Lancelot "Capability" Brown and transformed into a more romantic environment by adding a number of waterfalls and a lake, both popular features of the time. The ensemble of palace and park reflects some of the primary concerns of Romanticism: a return to nature and to the country's roots.

When Blenheim was being built, the Duchess of Marlborough tried in vain to persuade the architect, Sir John Vanbrugh, to adopt a more modest design.

DERWENT VALLEY MILLS (INDUSTRIAL LANDSCAPE)

The first cotton factories and spinning mills in England were set up in the 18th century along the River Derwent. The industrial landscape of the Derwent Valley quickly became the heartland of the textile industry.

In 1769, Richard Arkwright invented the water frame spinning machine. His innovation not only fundamentally changed the production process but also the organization of the work processes and the lives of people connected with it. It was first put to use in the factories of Cromford and marked the start of the Industrial Revolution.

The industrial area of the Derwent Valley extends for 24 km (15 mi) along the River Derwent, from Masson Mill via Matlock Bath to Lombe's Silk Mill in Derby. The silk mill has been turned into a museum. Also part of this cultural monument is the industrial village of Darley Abbey with its factories, workers' houses, a church and a park. Machines and buildings date back to the 18th and 19th centuries and are of great technological and historical interest. The ensemble eventually became a model for modern industrial towns around the world.

This World Cultural Heritage Site comprises the historic workers' village of Darley Abbey as well as various production sites.

United Kingdom

WESTMINSTER ABBEY AND PALACE

Westminster Abbey and Westminster Palace – the latter better known as the Houses of Parliament – dominate the west bank of the Thames in central London. This World Heritage Site also includes nearby St Margaret's Church.

The building of Westminster Palaces and Abbey was begun under Edward the Confessor (1003–1066). The associated church, which was replaced by a Gothic cathedral in the 13th century, would eventually serve as a burial site for the king and subsequent rulers until 1760. It is still the coronation church of the monarchs, and royal weddings and funerals are also held here. Nearby is Saint Margaret's Church, the parish church of parliament. The present structure was built from 1486 to 1523. Particularly noteworthy are its Flemish glass windows and the sundial.

Two of the most distinctive parts of the Palace of Westminster are St Stephen's Tower, better known as Big Ben, and the Victoria Tower.

Westminster Palace was begun by Edward the Confessor and enlarged in 1097 by William II. After 1547, it became the seat of the English parliament, but the fire of 1834 destroyed all of it except Westminster Hall and the Crypt of St Stephen's Chapel. The complex was rebuilt in its present form between 1840 and 1870 based on plans by Charles Barry. He chose to adopt the neo-Gothic style in order to match the façades of nearby Westminster Abbey. Westminster Palace is dominated on its north side by the clock tower "Big Ben".

Just under 100 m (328 ft) in height, Big Ben was built in 1858 by Benjamin Hall and is today one of London's most famous landmarks (top). The Royal Gallery in Westminster Abbey (center) is a popular sight. The Choir (bottom) was designed in the neo-Gothic style.

TOWER OF LONDON

In the 11th century, William the Conqueror built a fortress on the Thames in London. The symbol of the Norman conquest of England, it served both to protect and control the capital.

William the Conqueror commissioned the White Tower in the style of Norman military architecture to serve as a fortified residential castle and a station to control shipping on the Thames. The fortress was given its current appearance in the 13th century and the Tower remained the residence of English monarchs until the fortress was transformed into the state prison in 1509. Many famous prisoners were incarcerated here, including Thomas More, two of Henry VIII's wives and the future Queen of England, Elizabeth I.

At present, the historic structure is primarily a museum featuring sizable collections relating to European military history. The Crown Jewels of the English monarchs are also kept in the Jewel House. Also part of the complex built around the White Tower is the Norman St John's Chapel, which dates from the year 1080 – London's oldest church. Those who were executed in the Tower, including the wives of Henry VIII, were laid to rest in the Chapel Royal of St Peter, which was restored after a fire in 1512.

The White Tower, built during the 11th century by William the Conqueror and enlarged several times over the years, is one of the oldest buildings in London.

ROYAL BOTANIC GARDENS IN KEW

The botanic garden in Kew shows the development of English landscape gardens from the 18th to the 20th centuries. The gardens contain the largest collection of its kind in the world as well as some famous monuments.

An herb garden established in 1759 marked the beginning of the Royal Botanic Gardens in Kew, but there was a garden and a park here even earlier that contained a number of buildings, including Kew Palace (1631), built in the Dutch style. The garden did not become a scientific institution until 1770, when famous botanist Sir Joseph Banks took over the directorship.

Kew's most famous landmark is the Palm House, completed in 1848 by architects Richard Turner and Decimus Burton. Made from wrought iron, steel and glass and standing 20 m (65 ft) high, the greenhouse contains one of the largest collections of palm trees in the world. The Herbarium of Kew Gardens holds some eight million herbals, forming a remarkable library. In addition there are some 70,000 living plants, which today play an increasingly important role as a genetic resource.

The Botanic Garden is particularly famous for its Palm House (left top). Left is the Temperate House with its subterranean heating system.

MARITIME GREENWICH

No other name symbolizes England's scientific endeavours of the 17th and 18th centuries quite like this place, which gained international fame as a baseline for the measurement of longitude.

This World Heritage Site in Greenwich, an eastern district of London, includes a number of buildings and institutions that are all closely linked with the nautical exploration and history of the Royal Navy. The park on the south bank of the Thames was designed by André Le Nôtre and features one of the most important complexes of historical buildings in England.

The Queen's House, the royal "villa", was built in 1616 to 1635 by Inigo Jones (1573–1652). In 1694, architect Sir Christopher Wren was commissioned with the transformation and enlargement of one part of the palaces originally constructed for King Charles II as the Royal Naval Hospital. Starting in 1873, the four vast buildings finally housed the Royal Naval College. Located on a hill, all other buildings are dominated by the Royal Observatory, founded by Charles II in 1675 and built by Wren. Astronomical research has now been conducted here for over three centuries, including the classification of the stars for navigational purposes.

The telescope in Flamsteed House, the oldest part of the Observatory, was instrumental in defining the Prime Meridian in 1884.

United Kingdom

CITY OF BATH

With the most elegant buildings in southern England, Bath is a testimony to the creativity of its architects. It often feels like a giant open-air museum.

Bath is located in the county of Somerset, not far from Bristol. The Romans recognized its beauty early on, building recreational spa and bath complexes around the natural hot springs. The remains of a temple also testify to the city's rich history, known to the Romans as Aquae Sulis. In the 10th century, Bath became a bishops' see and the center of the wool trade throughout the Middle Ages.

In the 17th century, it became the most popular spa town in England as well as the most important high-society hotspot outside London. The city acquired its Georgian appearance at the end of the 18th century, in particular thanks to the monumental ensembles by architect John Wood as well as efforts by Ralph Allen and Richard "Beau" Nash. The crescents, terraces and squares lead to neoclassical masterpieces like the Assembly Rooms, the Royal Crescent or Pulteney Bridge, designed in 1770. Bath is a prime example of the departure from strictly geometric Renaissance towns, stressing the links between architecture and the surrounding landscape, which became a dominant concept in the 19th century.

The Abbey Church in Bath was completed in 1156. In a bad state of repair during the 13th century, it was lovingly restored in the 16th century.

CORNWALL AND WEST DEVON MINING LANDSCAPE

In the 19th century, two-thirds of the world's copper was mined in southern England. Between 1700 and 1914, the economy, the landscape and social structure of Cornwall were significantly influenced by mining.

The trade in copper, tin and arsenic was dependent on a functioning infrastructure that included trams, canals, trains and ports, all of which still testify to early industrial enterprise in Devon and Cornwall. In addition to the machines, equipment and structural remains of the mines, both mansions and workers' holdings with beautiful ornamental gardens have also been preserved.

Since several companies were involved in the extraction of copper, and the nature of the copper deposits varied from one place to another, different technological processes were developed and used here. This expertise was then exported from Great Britain to other mining centers around the world. Landowners and private entrepreneurs set up mines in the area that developed into foundry towns with the typical rows of terraced dwellings for workers and their families. Ten mining areas are now part of this World Heritage Site.

This abandoned colliery in Cornwall is an example of a cultural landscape shaped by early industrialization.

THE COASTS OF DORSET AND EAST DEVON

The cliff formations along England's "Jurassic coast" bear witness to 185 million years of geological history. For 300 years now, fossils from the Triassic, Jurassic and Cretaceous periods have been found in the area.

The 150-km (90-mi) long coastline between Old Harry Rocks near Swanage in Dorset and Orcombe Point in Devon is known as the "Jurassic Coast". The geology in this area spans the entire Mesozoic era, with rock formations from the Triassic, Jurassic and Cretaceous periods displayed in the layers of soil.

Geomorphologists first became aware of the importance of this stretch of coastline in 1810, when an 11-year-old girl came across what she described as a "dragon" in the cliffs. What she had discovered was the first complete fossil of an ichthyosaur. There has been a constant stream of new finds along this coast ever since, without even the need to excavate. The ongoing erosion of the cliffs means that the landscape here changes at a breathtaking pace. A stroll along the beach can quickly become a journey of discovery of the earth's geological history.

Portland Island can only be reached on a narrow landbridge (top right). Right: The Durdle Door arch.

STONEHENGE, AVEBURY AND ASSOCIATED SITES

The meaning of the neolithic monuments of Stonehenge and nearby Avebury is still unclear. In addition to being religious sites, they may have served in the observation of the stars.

A 114-m-wide (374-ft) ditch encircles the sanctuary of Stonehenge, a world-famous circle of monoliths whose origins date back as far as 3000 BC. The rocks measure up to 7 m (23 ft) in height and were brought here from hundreds of miles away. Apparently aligned with specific stars, the ring probably served cultic and astronomical purposes.

The remains of three other stone circles can also be found in an area of about 15 ha (37 acres) in and around the village of Avebury, near Bath in the county of Wiltshire. Silbury Hill, roughly 40 m (131 ft) in height, was built in about 2800 BC with an effort that must have been almost superhuman. Measuring about 180 m (591 ft) in diameter, it is the largest tumulus from European prehistory.

Also in the vicinity is the 113-m-long (371-ft) West Kenneth Long Barrow. Excavations there indicate that the complex served as a burial place and a sanctuary.

The menhirs of Stonehenge are arranged as columnar stones bridged by capstones (above). Left: The stone circle of Avebury.

CANTERBURY

One of England's oldest towns, in the county of Kent, is home to the Archbishopric of Canterbury, the Anglican world's leading body. The town gained a note of infamy when Archbishop Thomas Becket was murdered here.

Canterbury has been at the heart of English ecclesiastical history from the beginning, and two of the sacred sites that have been declared World Heritage Sites here have witnessed nearly all of it. One is Martin's Church outside the city center, dating back to the fourth century (possibly even back to the time of the Roman occupation) and the oldest church in England still in use today. The other is the ruin of the Benedictine Abbey, founded in 597 by St Augustine, who evangelized the people of Britannia. It became the center of the newly created diocese of Canterbury and was destroyed later under Henry VIII.

Canterbury Cathedral was built in 1070 as a Norman structure. Archbishop Thomas Becket was murdered here by royalist knights in 1170. His shrine in the church then became a popular destination for pilgrims. After a fire in 1174, the cathedral was rebuilt by William of Sens, heralding the introduction of the Gothic style to England. The tombs of King Henry IV of England and of Edward, the Black Prince, are also in the cathedral.

The cloisters built between 1396 and 1420 and the vaulting under the tower are of an almost unearthly beauty.

United Kingdom

CASTLES AND TOWN WALLS OF KING EDWARD IN GWYNEDD

The various castles built for Edward I in Wales are important testimonies to medieval military architecture and to the colonization of this neighboring country by the English crown.

Gwynedd, an inhospitable region in northern Wales, had been ruled by small aristocratic dynasties for many centuries until Edward I (1239–1307) brought the area under crown rule. The English king was able to secure his position in Wales, which he managed to subjugate by 1284, by commissioning three strongholds close to the English border.
Conwy, begun in 1283 and completed within just four and a half years, is a masterpiece of medieval military architecture. Its master builder, James of St George, was a leading architect

of fortifications who also supervised the work on Caernarfon and Harlech castles, which were begun in the same year. Together with the fortresses at Aberystwyth, Beaumaris and Flint, they formed a chain of defenses along the northern Welsh coast. Conwy Castle thus became a monument of English rule in Wales.

King Edward I had nine castles built for himself after conquering Wales in the 13th century. Conwy Castle was the first of these. The swing bridge (right) leading to the castle dates from 1826.

PONTCYSYLLTE AQUEDUCT AND CANAL

The Pontcysyllte Aqueduct was built as a navigable trough bridge across the valley of the River Dee in north-eastern Wales and is an engineering masterpiece. Also part of the World Heritage Site is an 18-km (11-mi) stretch of the associated canal, which is can be navigated entirely without locks.

The United Kingdom seems to have recognized the commercial potential of waterways and canals far earlier than other countries. An outstanding example is the Pontcysyllte Aqueduct about 65 km (40 mi) south of Liverpool: 307 m (1,007 ft) long and about 38 m (125 ft) high, it is the largest structure of its kind in Great Britain. Soon after the inauguration of the aqueduct, built between 1795 and 1805 by Thomas Telford and William Jessop, its construction method, an elegant combination of cast-iron and

stone, became a model for similar structures around the world. At this dizzying height, it is still an amazing experience to cross the aqueduct, celebrated as the "waterway in the sky". The trough-shaped channel on top of the bridge leads you across the chasm while a tow path once used by horses to tow the boats runs next to you.

The Pontcysyllte Aqueduct is an outstanding example of the engineering feats of Europe's Industrial Revolution.

GIANT'S CAUSEWAY AND THE CAUSEWAY COAST

The basalt columns of the Giant's Causeway span 5 km (3 mi) of the northern Irish coastline. Their emergence is the stuff of legends and the geology still manages to baffle scientists.

Not far from the fishing village of Ballycastle in County Antrim, some 40,000 basalt columns rise majestically out of the sea. Mostly hexagonal, the columns are believed to be about sixty million years old and together they create a 5-km (3-mi) path along the rocky coastline.
Formed by the crystallization of molten lava as it met with the cold seawater, the tallest columns are up to 6 m (20 ft) high. The name "Giant's Causeway" comes from one of the many legends to which this wonder of the natural world has been attrib-

uted. According to the story, Irish warrior Finn MacCool, challenged by his Scottish rival, the giant Benandonner, built the causeway to cross the Irish Sea to Scotland.
Research performed here over the last three hundred years has contributed greatly to the geological sciences.

The Giant's Causeway looks like a huge, man-made staircase. Though most of the basalt columns are six-sided, closer inspection reveals stones with four, five, seven, and even eight edges.

GOUGH AND INACCESSIBLE ISLANDS

The largely untouched volcanic island of Gough in the southern Atlantic Ocean is a habitat for one of the largest seabird colonies in the world. The World Heritage Site also encompasses nearby Inaccessible Island.

Discovered in the 16th century by Portuguese sailors, the island belongs to the Tristan da Cunha archipelago, a group of islands located halfway between the most southerly tips of Africa and South America. Aside from a weather station, the volcanic island is uninhabited. The special significance of the island of Gough lies in its untouched flora and fauna: The steep cliffs are a habitat for various species of seal and provide nesting areas for Gough's huge colonies of seabirds. Two endemic bird species live here – a distinctive type of moorhen, the gallinule and the Gough rowettie –, as well as 12 endemic species of plants. In 2004, the World Heritage Site was enlarged by the volcanic Inaccessible Island, situated south-west of Tristan da Cunha and measuring around 14 sq km (sq miles). Lush vegetation, waterfalls and numerous rare species of animals and plants make this island, too, one of the last natural paradises.

The steep rocks of the volcanic island of Gough in the South Atlantic provide shelter and living space for numerous rare species of birds and plants.

ST GEORGE AND ITS FORTIFICATIONS, BERMUDA

The historic buildings and fortifications in and around St George, the capital of the island of the same name in Bermuda, impressively document the beginning of British colonial power in the newly discovered territories.

The first settlers on the islands of Bermuda were English colonists en route to Virginia who were stranded on the island after a shipwreck in 1609. St George's became the seat of parliament for these mid-Atlantic islands as early as 1612, and as such the first English town founded in the New World.

The center of the town is King's Square with the Town Hall. In 1713, St Peter's Church was built in the style typical of the island group, on the site of an older wooden church. Limestone and cedar wood were the construction materials. Many other buildings reflect in their architecture a piece of colonial history. The numerous fortifications in the surroundings of St George are remarkable. The largest among them is the 17th-century Fort St Catherine, which was upgraded several times over the years and today houses a museum.

Many of the well-preserved colonial-style houses are painted in pastels and have shiny white roofs, lending St George's Town its characteristic flair.

HENDERSON ISLAND, PITCAIRN ISLANDS

At 10 km (6 mi) in length and 5 km (3 mi) in width, Henderson is the largest member of the Pitcairn Islands British Overseas Territory. It is one of the only atolls in the world that has remained largely untouched.

Until the 18th century, this remote and virtually impenetrable island was largely spared from any human interference. As a result, the animal and plant life on this towering atoll, with its dramatic cliffs and breathtaking beauty, was able to develop unhindered by outside influences.

The island's dense bush forest has revealed eleven plant species unique to Henderson, among them a special type of sandalwood. Over twenty land and seabirds as well as a number of insect and snail species are also found only here – and that is most certainly not all of the species still waiting to be discovered here.

Because of its isolated location, Henderson is also an ideal setting for scientific research into the biological process of species evolution, in particular natural selection and the development of traits unique to islands.

Henderson Island is a paradise for numerous native plants and rare birds including the English fairy tern (left) with its white feathers and black ring around the eyes.

BEND OF THE BOYNE

One of the largest and most significant archaeological finds in Europe has not yet been fully exposed and will probably still pose a few more riddles to archaeologists in the future.

About 50 km (31 mi) north of Dublin, in an area measuring roughly 780 ha (1,927 acres) near the villages of Knowth, Dowth and Newgrange, mausoleums and tombs have been discovered hidden beneath the grassy hills. The burial mound in Knowth, for example, contains a princely tomb from the fourth millennium BC. Nearby, some fifteen smaller tumuli are expected to be found that might reveal even more of these ancient graves.

The most famous of the Boyne graves is the royal tomb of Newgrange, which was opened for the first time as early as 1699. It comprises a mighty stone-and-earth mound, around which

twelve large monoliths have been placed. The circular central hall in the middle is surrounded by side chambers arranged in a cloverleaf pattern. Archaeologists from University College in Cork reconstructed parts of the complex in the 1960s and 1970s.

Decorated stones and long passageways can be found inside the mounds. Archaeologists believe the impressive monuments served as cult and burial sites, but they might have also had social and economic functions.

The largest burial mound of Knowth, with a diameter of 95 m (312 ft), is surrounded by more than fifteen smaller mounds.

SKELLIG MICHAEL

The well-preserved structures of this medieval monastic settlement on a small pyramid-shaped rock island in the Atlantic Ocean illustrates the austere lifestyle of the early Irish Christians.

About 12 km (7 mi) off the Irish coast, a rocky island called Skellig Michael rises proudly from the Atlantic. It is here that one of Ireland and Europe's most important archaeological sites can be found.

Legend has it that the monastery here was founded as early as the sixth century, but the first documents mentioning its existence date from the eighth century. Records from around 1000 AD already confirm that the complex, which was inhabited without interruption until the 12th century, was dedicated to Archangel Michael. Changes in the climate eventually forced the hardy monks to abandon

their spartan existence and resettle on the nearby mainland. The walls of the prayer and monks' cells were joined together without mortar into beehive-like structures in the manner typical of early Irish architecture.

Aside from the remains of a 12th-century church, a staircase with about 500 steps has also been preserved. It served to help pilgrims reach the highest point of the island.

At its highest point, Skellig Michael rises 289 m (948 ft) above sea level. The monastery complex with its beehive-shaped stone huts can be reached via a small surfaced path.

WADDEN SEA

The western end of the Wadden Sea World Heritage Site, which covers about 9,700 sq km (3,780 sq mi), belongs to the Netherlands. Combined with the German portion of the overall area, it is one of the last intact ecosystems along the northern coastal region of Europe.

The northern end of the North Sea Wadden starts near Blåvandshuk in Denmark and stretches for 450 km (280 mi) to Den Helder in the Netherlands, across tidal flats that can reach 40 km (25 miles) across. About one-third of the area, which emerged after the last ice age, is under Dutch administration. The most obvious features of the region are the five West Frisian islands of Texel, Vlieland, Terschelling, Ameland und Schiermonnikoog.

The coastal landscape here is characterized by sand dunes, salt marshes, mudflats and mussel beds. The so-called "priele", watercourses that remain full

even at low tide, provide a rich habitat for some 10,000 plant and animal species, ranging from the simple mudworm to the gray seal. Millions of migratory birds also come to rest on the mudflats every year.

The Wadden Sea's tidal ecosystem is one of the few great remaining landscapes in densely populated Europe where natural processes have been allowed to continue more or less undisturbed for centuries.

The Wadden Sea experiences dramatic tidal swings. Here, an image of the coast off the island of Schiermonnikoog.

WOUDA PUMPING STATION

On the shores of the Ijsselmeer in the Netherlands is the largest steam pumping station in the world. Wouda is testimony to the great feats of Dutch architects, who were early to recognize and exploit the importance of steam.

More than eighty years on, the largest steam pumping station ever built is still in operation. Five or six times a year it pumps six per cent of the surplus water in Friesland into the Ijsselmeer (Lake Ijssel), thus protecting the population from an ever-present threat of flooding.

This installation in north-western Netherlands was built between 1917 and 1918 based on plans by architect Dirk Frederik Wouda. The station was put into service two years after construction began and it has been supplying energy ever since. Right away, Wouda set the standard for steam pumping stations around the world.

Comprising a boiler house and a turbine building, the station boasts a particularly impressive design. Four giant floodgates that open toward the Ijsselmeer dominate the brick structure. The machinery inside the powerhouse includes two centrifugal pumps and four double steam engines, each with a capacity of 500 horsepower. The interior design of the machine hall follows practical as well as aesthetic principles.

The Wouda Steam Pumping Station was consecrated by Queen Wilhelmina of the Netherlands in October 1920.

SCHOKLAND POLDER LANDSCAPE

The cultural landscape of the Ijsselmeer is unique evidence to a battle that the Netherlands (lit. "low" countries) have been fighting since time immemorial: against the mighty forces of water.

Starting as far back as the fourth century, Frisians living in the low-lying region around the Zuiderzee have built dykes to protect their agricultural lands from the destructive forces of the North Sea. Nevertheless, the relentless tides continued their encroachment and eventually formed what is now the Zuiderzee in the 13th century.

Areas known as "polders", reclaimed marshes surrounded by dykes, were protected from floodwaters, yet they had to be frequently re-drained. Still the sea continued to rise on the Dutch coast and by the 19th century so much of Schokland was below sea level that the island's population had to be evacuated in 1859.

A plan to reclaim the land was put into action between 1927 and 1932, and today Schokland symbolizes an effort to wrest land back from the sea. Excavations have revealed some of the methods used in land reclamation since prehistoric times.

Schokland's churches were dismantled down to their foundations and then rebuilt on the mainland.

BEEMSTER POLDER

The cultural landscape around the Beemster Polder, which dates from the early 17th century, is a masterpiece of land reclamation and landscape architecture.

More than one quarter of the surface area of the Netherlands is actually below sea level and must be drained and protected from the threat of flooding by a complex system of dykes, mills and pumping stations. The reclaimed land, which is now protected by miles of flood barriers that boast previously unavailable technologies, had to be wrested by force from the North Sea over the course of many centuries. The Beemster Polder is the oldest of these man-made landscapes.

Under the direction of Jan Adriaansz Leeghwater, Beemster was drained for the first time in 1609. However, the dykes were not able to withstand the highest storm tides, making it impossible to reclaim the land fully until 1612 – and not without the help of forty-seven mills.

In the decades that followed, innovative housing concepts were put in place in the newly created landscape and gradually settled. Now a tangled network of canals, waterways, paths and dykes criss-crosses the fields and meadows, interrupted only by farmhouses, hamlets and small towns.

Canals, dykes and mills all help to maintain the Beemster Polder.

Netherlands

WINDMILLS AT KINDERDIJK-ELSHOUT

The historic Kinderdijk-Elshout windmill region near Rotterdam demonstrates the outstanding land reclamation technologies developed over centuries of water management in the Netherlands.

The landscape around Kinderdijk-Elshout is characterized by reservoirs, dykes, pumping stations, administrative buildings and by the numerous and lovingly preserved windmills, some of which have been continuously in operation since the 18th century. As early as the beginning of the 17th century, Belgian engineer Simon Stevin had perfected a technique to drain polders, or reclaimed marsh areas. By arranging windmills in rows along the Kinderdijk, his ingenious concept consisted of "grinding the water" in two phases: first from a lower-lying canal to a higher-lying canal, and then into a weir for evacuation. Visitors can find out how the system really works in one of the historic mills that has been converted into an interesting museum.

On the canal between the village of Kinderdijk and the Alblasserdam to the south of it, 19 windmills are lined up one after the other in a row, forming the largest and best-preserved collection of historic mills in the country in a landscape so typical for the Netherlands.

DEFENSE LINE OF AMSTERDAM

"De Stelling" is a defensive ring of fortifications around Amsterdam with an ingenious flooding system and forty-five strongholds. It illustrates some advanced skills in Dutch military architecture.

Construction on the defensive ring that encircles Amsterdam for 135 km (84 mi) was begun in 1883. In addition to the firing positions and casemates, the defense system also comprises locks with which the Dutch were able to regulate the water supply as well as flooding the area around the city if the situation called for it. Hydraulics in this case would be ingeniously employed for defensive purposes. The area would be flooded just deep enough to prevent soldiers from wading through on foot while simultaneously keeping ships from passing – between half and one meter (1 1/2 and 3 ft) of water.

Despite some clever ideas, however, construction was not complete until 1920, and with the rise of aerial warfare the system quickly lost its importance. The wall itself links forty-five strongholds. One of the best-known sections of the ring is the mighty fortress island of Pampus, built to protect the mouth of the River Ij from enemy attack.

Fort Pampus is part of the fortifications encircling Amsterdam.

RIETVELD SCHRÖDER HOUSE IN UTRECHT

This house on the outskirts of Utrecht, built in 1924 by Dutch architect Gerrit Rietveld for his client Truus Schröder-Schräder, is considered a sort of manifesto of the "De Stijl" artists' group.

The De Stijl movement, which began in 1917 in Leiden and was associated with the German Bauhaus, included artists such as Piet Mondrian and Theo van Doesburg. In its time, De Stijl combined painting, architecture and design to develop its very own geometric-abstract language of form. Influenced by Cubism and by Wassily Kandinsky's writings on the theory of art, the movement in many ways found a perfect manifestation of its goals in the Rietveld Schröder House. In terms of its construction, this is a conventional brick building with a wooden beam ceiling whose foundations, cellar and balconies are made of concrete. The upper story was designed as an open continuum of space with sliding walls that were an element of the client's wishes. The furnishings correspond in their shape and color with the purist appearance of the house.

Almost immediately after its completion, Experts hailed the Rietveld Schröder House in Utrecht as one of the architectural highlights of classical Modernism.

HISTORIC CENTER AND HARBOR OF WILLEMSTAD, CURAÇAO

Willemstad on the island of Curaçao in the Netherlands Antilles was once the Dutch West India Company's most important port. Today many buildings still testify to the splendor of that time.

The Dutch sailors who had come here on a quest for salt to preserve herrings, quickly recognized the potential of the natural harbor linked to the sea by a narrow canal. Without much further ado they founded the village of Willemstad as the capital of the Netherlands Antilles. Thanks to a lucrative trade in slaves from Africa and the transshipment of goods from plantations in South America, the town soon flourished as a center of regional and transcontinental commerce. Despite frequent raids and attacks in the wars between England and the Netherlands, many historic Dutch buildings in the center of Willemstad managed to survive. Among the most attractive of these is the Dutch Reformed Church.

The Mikvé Israel-Emanuel Synagogue of 1732 is the oldest, continuously inhabited Jewish community in the New World. As far back as the 16th century, Sephardic Jews had emigrated from Portugal to Curaçao.

The Willemstad harbor front boasts remarkable houses with brightly painted façades built in the Dutch style.

HISTORIC BRUGGE

A perfectly preserved ensemble of buildings in the historic center of the old trading town of Bruges is evidence of a prosperous past.

In the Middle Ages, much of the lucrative trade in cloth between England and the European continent was conducted via Bruges. At its height, merchants from seventeen countries had trading posts here.

Thanks to the patronage of Jan van Eyck and Hans Memling, Bruges became a city of art and culture with few rivals. The town experienced its heyday in the 15th century, when the dukes of Burgundy, more or less the standard bearers of late-Gothic court culture, resided within its walls. Soon after, however, international trade began a relatively rapid decline as the River Zwin silted up and blocked access to the sea.

To access the town you follow numerous charming canals and long streets with rows of gable-fronted houses.

The Bruges Belfry affords superb views over the Old Town.

Laid out on an oval plan, the patrician homes, counting houses of the merchants and the richly decorated Town Hall, where the counts of Flanders granted the commune its municipal charters, speak of the former glory and power of the city.

Its proudest symbol is the belfry of the Cloth Hall. Large-scale building projects also bear witness to the social activities of the community, for example the Godshuizen hospices and St John's Hospital complex, which now houses the Memling Museum.

Among Bruges' many churches, the tall towers and naves of the St Salvator Cathedral and the Church of Our Lady dominate the irresistably picturesque townscape.

Cloth was once traded in the market halls of Bruges, bringing prosperity to the town. The famous belfry was begun in 1240. Top left: The Rozenhoedkaai. Left: The market square with the 14th-century Stadthuis, one of the oldest town halls in Flanders.

Belgium

PLANTIN-MORETUS HOUSE-WORKSHOPS MUSEUM COMPLEX

More than 2,450 books were printed in Christophe Plantin's workshops from 1555 to 1598 – an average of fifty-seven books per year. Plantin was one of the leading publishers in the 16th century and made a decisive contribution to Humanism, disseminating knowledge of the sciences and humanities.

In the 16th century, Antwerp was one of Europe's three largest publishing centers. The most important of the printing presses here was the Officina Plantiniana, founded by the humanist Christophe Plantin.

A total of eighty people worked at the presses, including twenty-two typesetters, thirty-two printers and three editors. Plantin's son-in-law Jan Moretus took over the company in 1689, which then stayed in the same family until 1867. The press now illustrates how the urban upper class was able to combine work, family life and business.

The World Heritage Site includes not only the building itself but also the furnishings, which date from various periods, the living area, the workshops, the presses and the collections of valuables. Aside from early printed works, the museum also exhibits some 15,000 wooden printing blocks.

The Plantin-Moretus Printing Museum is home to the oldest printing press in the world.

FLEMISH BÉGUINAGES

This World Heritage Site recognizes thirteen institutions in Flanders to which, starting in the 13th century, unmarried women withdrew in order to lead a life of religious commitment.

The Béguine movement started in many cities of northern Europe in the late 12th and early 13th centuries. The so-called béguinages were founded by young, unmarried women hoping to lead a life of spirituatliy without having to join one of the official and often overcrowded convents.

These semi-monastic communities often consisted of detached or terraced houses arranged around a green inner courtyard, and included a church with ancillary buildings. A wall protected them from the outside world, creating self-contained islands within a town. For a long time, life here did not follow strict monastic discipline, however. The women had to take chastity and obedience vows upon entering the community, of course, but they were allowed to return to a secular life at any point if they so chose. Alas, the church disapproved, accusing the movement of heresy and even banning it at times.

Many béguinages were economically independent, through the production of cloth, lace and other items, and dedicated themselves to social causes such as the care of the elderly.

One of the most beautiful Flemish béguinages is the one in Bruges, founded as early as 1245.

MAJOR TOWN HOUSES OF THE ARCHITECT VICTOR HORTA

Victor Horta's townhouses and mansions in Brussels represent a fine collection of early Art Nouveau architecture that is unique in Europe.

Hôtel Tassel (1893–1895), Hôtel Solvay (1894–1898) and Hôtel van Eetvelde (1895 bis 1897) as well as the Maison & Atelier (1898–1901) of Belgian architect Victor Horta (1861–1947) are all early examples of townhouses in which he articulated the design concepts of Art Nouveau in refreshingly new variations.

The characteristic features of these buildings include their open layout, with individual rooms arranged and furnished according to their specific function; bright stairwells, illuminated from above, forming the inner core and assuring quick and practical access to the various floors; and the use of modern materials such as iron, steel and glass for interior and exterior elements, which was revolutionary for its day.

For his interior designs, Horta liked to incorporate as many genres of the visual arts as possible, from architecture and painting to sculpture and handicrafts. In this way his buildings themselves became a veritable synthesis of the arts.

The former home and studio of Belgian architect Victor Horta now houses the Horta Museum.

LA GRAND-PLACE IN BRUSSELS

The market square, or Grand-Place, in Brussels is a unique collection of public and private buildings and one of the most beautiful squares in the world. Victor Hugo called the square "a real marvel".

The Grand-Place in the Belgian capital measures a mere 110 m (361 ft) in length and 68 m (223 ft) in width, but its Town Hall is surrounded by magnificent guild houses all tightly packed together to make it one of the most attractive architectural complexes in all of Europe.

In the 15th century, when the wealthy guilds of Brussels replaced the traditional aristocrats of the city's administration, they built a monument for themselves: La Grand-Place, featuring stunning guild houses. At the center of the square stands the seven-storey Town Hall. The Maison des Ducs de Brabant, so-called after the busts of nineteen dukes that adorn its façade, consists of six guild houses all linked by a continuous, monumental pilaster façade. Vivid scenes also adorn the portals and façades of the other splendid guildhalls that can be admired as you wander the square.

The Grand-Place is lined by a series of magnificent houses including the narrow guild halls, built in the baroque style and featuring intricately bold façades (above). The Italianate façade of the Maison des Ducs de Brabant (left), completed in 1698 and renovated in the 19th century, conceals six guild houses, each with its own entrance door.

STOCLET HOUSE IN BRUSSELS

Regarded as one of the most important works of art of the Viennese Secession, the Stoclet House in Brussels is the only structure by the Wiener Werkstätten still in its original state today.

Between 1905 and 1911, Belgian art collector and banker Adolf Stoclet commissioned Austrian architect Josef Hoffmann – a founding member and one of the main proponents of the Wiener Werkstätten – to build his private residence. Money was apparently no object, and the house soon turned into a palace.

The interior furnishings of the Stoclet House alone are worth an estimated 30 million euros and include works by artists like Gustav Klimt and Kolo Moser – another founding member of the Wiener Werkstätten. With this building, Hoffmann realized his dream of combining visual arts, architecture and design into one harmonious ensemble. The best materials, including bronze, marble and copper were only just good enough for the appointments. The abundance of natural light in the rooms on the upper floor demonstrates, however, that he also took into account the latest concepts of healthy living. Stoclet was seemingly very fond of the 60-m-long (197-ft) house and gardens very much – it has remained unchanged to this day.

The Stoclet House in Brussels is a jewel of the Viennese Secession that features stately marble façades and an unusual tower construction.

Belgium

NOTRE-DAME CATHEDRAL IN TOURNAI

Five towers adorn this cathedral, which was begun in the early 12th century. Among its other distinctive features are the unusually large Romanesque central nave and the contrasting Gothic choir.

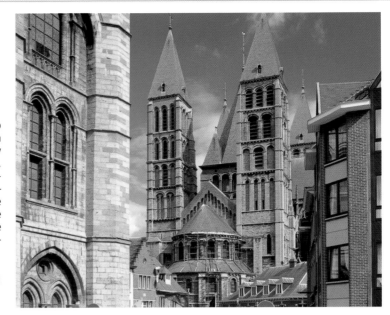

The eventful history of the Cathedral of Tournai began in 1171, the year the Romanesque pillar basilica was dedicated. The accompanying choir and transept were then remodeled, a task that lasted until 1325.

Immediately after its consecration, work began on an early-Gothic transept that was completed by 1223. It was enclosed on both sides by a conch, each flanked by two towers. The central crossing tower and the four bell towers at the corners create a monumental five-tower structure that still dominates the city visually.

A mighty Gothic choir was added to the already gigantic structure from 1243 to 1325, which in length roughly corresponds to the Romanesque nave. Architecturally speaking, the enormous dimensions of the Cathedral – 134 m high, 83 m high, 67 m wide (440 ft, 272 ft, 220 ft) – demonstrate that it stood in competition with the other monumental ecclesiastic buildings of the day.

Four corner towers and a central crossing tower adorn the Romanesque-Gothic Notre-Dame Cathedral of Tournai.

NEOLITHIC FLINT MINES AT SPIENNES

The area around Spiennes boasts not only the most extensive but also the oldest cluster of ancient mines in Europe. It also documents a decisive phase in the technological development of the Neolithic Age.

More than 6,000 years ago, the first settlers on the limestone plateau near Spiennes, in the province of Hainaut, began extracting flint from opencast mines. The Michelsberg farmers, so named after an important excavation site on Michelsberg in Baden-Württemberg, Germany, then sank vertical shafts 5 to 16 m (16 and 52 ft) deep and built a widely branched system of galleries.

Mining continued in Spiennes until the end of the Bronze Age, in about 750 BC. Excavations have now unearthed the remains of a settlement that existed up to the time of the Roman occupation and provides proof that the settlers worked the flint into weapons (such as hand axes) as well as trading the valuable raw material. The earthworks typical of the Michelsberg culture still pose some riddles for scientists, but their main purpose was probably defensive.

During construction of a train line in the 19th century, flint mines were discovered near Spiennes that date from the Neolithic Age. The shafts extend over an area of about 100 ha (247 acres).

THE FOUR LIFTS ON THE CANAL DU CENTRE

Boat lifts on a section of the historic Canal du Centre are a masterpiece of 19th-century European engineering.

Originally, the Canal du Centre was constructed to connect the Condé-Mons Canal, opened in 1818, with a branch of the old Brussels-Charleroi Canal. The two waterways, which were used mainly to transport coal, had already been widened in 1885, in order to accommodate the steadily growing commercial traffic.

In 1888, after four years of construction, King Leopold II inaugurated the first of the four lifts. Flooding then halted the expansion work until 1908, only to be further delayed by the outbreak of World War I. In 1918, the Canal du Centre was finally fully operational again, this time with all four of its hydraulic lifts.

Today, these four unique industrial monuments divide the roughly 19-km (12-mi) stretch of the canal – now an historic section – into four separate sections, each with a drop in height of about 16 m (52 ft) and negotiating an overall difference in height of 66 m (217 ft).

Four hydraulic boat lifts once served to overcome the immense difference in height on the commercially vital Canal du Centre, between the region around Mons and the North Sea.

CITY OF LUXEMBOURG: OLD QUARTERS AND FORTIFICATIONS

Luxembourg, the largest town and also the capital of the Grand Duchy of the same name, is characterized by an astonishing range of architectural styles.

In 963, Count Sigefroi Luxembourg founded the fortress of Lucilinburhuc, or Luxembourg, on top of the steep and strategically located Bock Hill. The town at the base of the hill began to grow in earnest in the Middle Ages, and the fortress was continuously enlarged until the 14th century, when Henry VII of Luxembourg became the Holy Roman Emperor.

Three fortification rings served to defend the city. The innermost consisted of bastions, the second of fifteen forts and the third of nine external forts. A great network of underground strongholds, galleries and casemates was then blasted into the rock and traverses the entire city.

Other notable buildings are the Palace of the Grand Dukes, the City Palace of the grand ducal family in the middle of the Old Town, St Michael's Church, the oldest sacred building in Luxembourg, and the Cathedral to the Blessed Virgin (Notre-Dame).

The towers of St Michael's Church and the Cathedral to Our Lady rise from a sea of houses in the ancient city (top). The Cathedral combines elements from both the late-Gothic and the Renaissance eras (left).

BELFRIES OF BELGIUM AND FRANCE

The belfries of the cities of Flanders, Wallonia and northern France were once a symbol of bourgeois pride in the face of an overly dominant nobility.

The increasingly powerful bourgeoisie in France and Belgium used ostentatiously magnificent belfries to set themselves apart from the power structure traditionally dominated by the nobility and the church. The most famous of these "melodic skyscrapers of the Middle Ages" are in Ghent and Bruges.

The cities of Kortrijk, Mechelen and Antwerp also have several belfries while in Tongeren and Mechelen the towers of the main churches act as both the church bell tower and the town belfry. The fine municipal tower of Aalst dates back to 1225. The Cloth Hall and the Belfry of Ypres were rebuilt after being badly damaged during World War I. Wallonia's Art Deco Belfry of Charleroi stands out with a carillon from 1936. The imposing belfry of Tournai, from 1187, has forty-three bells.

In 2005, the World Heritage Site was extended to include twenty-three belfries in northern France – in Artois and Picardy provinces. The most famous French belfries are in Amiens, Arras, Boulogne, Calais, Dunkirk and Lille.

The Belfry of Ghent was begun in 1313 and completed in 1380.

France

PARIS, BANKS OF THE SEINE

Paris, one of the world's truly cosmopolitan cities, boasts an incredible abundance of historic buildings and cultural highlights. The stretch of the Seine between Pont de Sully and Pont d'Iéna, which has been declared a World Heritage Site in and of itself, is particularly steeped in history.

The heritage section of the Seine starts at the Île Saint-Louis, where the statue of St Geneviève, Paris's patron saint, overlooks the river. The Île de la Cité, farther to the west, is the heart of religious Paris with the Gothic Cathedral of Notre-Dame and La Sainte-Chapelle, a filigree masterpiece of High Gothic.
Farther along is the Conciergerie, once part of the medieval royal palace and the state prison. Opposite that is the Louvre, the Renaissance palace of the French kings, which house one of world's most outstanding collections

From the Pont de Sully, views open out to the two Seine islands, Île Saint-Louis and Île de la Cité, with the Gothic cathedral Notre-Dame de Paris (top). The Pont Alexandre III (bottom) was built for the Paris Exposition Universelle of 1900. It spans the Seine in a single 6-m-high (20-ft) steel arch – without any intermediate supports.

of art. Down river is the Musée d'Orsay, the Grand and the Petit Palais and the National Assembly. The site ends with the Eiffel Tower, a steel structure that was revolutionary in its day.

Paris's Notre-Dame Cathedral was built in the Gothic style starting in 1163 on the Île de la Cité island in the Seine. Innovative construction elements in the Cathedral of Our Lady include the transepts with spectacular rose windows and the flying buttresses above the side aisle roofs.

During the French Revolution, as many as 1,200 prisoners were incarcerated at the Conciergerie on the west end of the Île de la Cité, once part of the royal palace and then a prison. Marie Antoinette, Danton and Robespierre awaited death by guillotine there.

La Sainte-Chapelle, once the palatine chapel of the former royal residence on the Île de la Cité, was regarded by the faithful of the Middle Ages as the "Gate of Heaven". It comprises the Lower and Upper Chapel (top). The latter contains a superb ensemble of 12-m-high (23-ft) stained-glass windows.

La Sainte-Chapelle (here the Lower Chapel) was built by Pierre de Montreuil in what is thought to have been less than thirty-three months. Completed in 1248, It is hailed as a "miracle of the High Gothic". Louis IX commissioned the double chapel to house relics of the Passion of Christ, which he had bought from the Emperor of Constantinople.

France

The Louvre houses one of the most important collections of antiquities in the world.

The most famous exhibit in the Louvre is Leonardo da Vinci's "Mona Lisa", painted in 1503. According to research by the art historian Roberto Zapperi, it might be the portrait of Pacifica Brandani, the (unmarried) mistress of Giuliano de' Medici, who bore him an illegitimate son.

Also exhibited in the Louvre is the monumental painting "The Coronation of Napoléon I" by Jacques-Louis David.

The glass and steel pyramid by Ieoh Ming Pei, an American architect of Chinese descent, has marked the main entrance to the Musée du Louvre since 1989.

France

Inside Garnier's Opera House is where the building reveals its true beauty.

The Avenue des Champs-Élysées is Paris' most famous boulevard. It begins at the Place de la Concorde and ends at the Place Charles de Gaulle with the Arc de Triomphe (top), which was built between 1806 and 1836 as a glorious tribute to the Napoleonic army.

Completed in 1889 for the Paris Exposition, the Eiffel Tower is now the most recognizable icon of the Paris cityscape.

The two bronze fountains (right) on Place de la Concorde were created by Cologne architect Jakob Ignaz Hittorf (1792–1867).

France

PALACE AND PARK OF VERSAILLES

The Palace of Versailles outside Paris is the prototype of an absolutist ruler's residence and as such became the ideal model for many European palaces. The lavish baroque complex built for Louis XIV, the "Sun King", is also surrounded by a vast park.

King Louis XIV of France (1638–1715) is widely considered the ultimate representative of absolutist rule. His grandiose display of power, the excessive splendor of his court and the exaggerated glamour of Versailles had a formative effect on an entire epoch. Starting in 1661, he converted his father Louis XIII's former hunting lodge into a palace that was later to become the permanent seat of his government. Architects Le Vau and Hardouin-Mansart created a truly extravagant complex comprising roughly 700 rooms surrounded by a massive

A view across the forecourt of Versailles toward the wings, embellished with porticoes and flanking the equestrian statue of Louis XIV.

palace park – a unified work of art consisting of plants, fountains and sculptures as well as the garden palaces of the Petit and the Grand Trianon. Versailles was the political center of France for the next 100 years. At its height, 5,000 people lived at the palace, including a considerable number of French nobles. As many as 14,000 soldiers also lived in the various outbuildings and the village of Versailles itself.

Of the many magnificent rooms in Versailles, the Hall of Mirrors is historically the most significant. It is where the German Emperor Wilhelm was crowned in 1871, and where the Versailles Treaty was signed in 1919. The seventeen mirrors reflect the light from the windows opposite them.

Right, from top: View of the Palace Chapel in the north wing; the Hall of Mirrors, measuring 73 by 11 m (240 by 36 ft); the Versailles Opera House.

PALACE AND PARK OF FONTAINEBLEAU

The Palace of Fontainebleau about 60 km (37 mi) south of Paris is the ancestral home of the kings of France. Over centuries it was rebuilt and remodeled on several occasions by numerous architects and artists. The park around the palace is particularly worth exploring.

In the 12th century, King Louis VII commissioned a small hunting lodge in the forest of Fontainebleau. After being abandoned, however, it was rebuilt in 1528 on the orders of Francis I. Only one of the building's original towers was spared demolition in the process.

Italian artists like Rosso Fiorentino and Francesco Primaticcio were commissioned to furnish the interior. Their work ultimately came to represent a version of Mannerism known as the "School of Fontainebleau".

In 1645, landscape designer André Le Nôtre designed the Grand Parterre in the park of the Palace of Fontainebleau, a terraced garden area used for state functions. It is famous for its topiary and the geometrical layout of the paths.

The palace was later remodeled many more times, in particular under Henry IV and Napoleon. Today it houses a number of outstanding works from the Italian and French Baroque, Rococo and Neoclassicism.

Among the most impressive structures in the Palace of Fontainebleau, which over time has been expanded to include five different inner courtyards, are the horseshoe-shaped staircase and the majestic ballroom. The extensive gardens surrounding the palace were created in the 17th century by André Le Nôtre, the designer of the park at Versailles.

Left, from top: The 80-m-long (262-ft) Diana's Gallery, which since 1851 has been home to Napoleon III's library; the Palace Chapel; and the neoclassical Throne Room.

France

AMIENS CATHEDRAL

The Cathédrale Notre-Dame d'Amiens is one of the greatest church buildings of the French High Gothic. Its dimensions are vast, covering a total area of 7,700 sq m (82,852 sq ft). In fact, the Cathedral of Our Lady in the capital of the region of Picardy is the largest church in France.

The first church that was built in Amiens went up in 1137 and was located on the site where today the mighty Cathedral of Our Lady rises majestically above the sea of houses. Two years after being destroyed by a massive fire in 1218, Bishop Évrard de Fouilloy decided to lay the foundations for a new cathedral that would be 145 m (476 ft) long.

Most of the structure was completed quite quickly – by the end of the 13th century – based on plans by Robert de Luzarches. The Cathedral consists of a triple-aisled nave that reaches an impressive height of 42.3 m (139 ft).

The west façade features three portals and is crowned by two wide towers. It boasts a large rose window and elegant detailing. The portals are embellished with three large scenes from the Old and New Testaments that are considered some of the best medieval sculptures in Europe.

Amiens Cathedral boasts an impressive western façade with two towers and richly ornamented portals. The church is famous for its impressive spatial relations as well as for its rich decorative figures. It is stabilized by a total of 126 flying buttresses.

REIMS

The city from where the Christianization of Gaul began has been a bulwark of the Catholic Church for centuries. Three structures here are World Heritage Sites: the Notre-Dame Cathedral, the archiepiscopal Palace of Tau and the former Abbey of Saint-Remi with its basilica.

Reims is located in the heart of the Champagne region and looks back on a very rich history. Clovis was anointed King of the Franks here by St Remigius in around 500. The archbishop's bones are kept in the Abbey Church of Saint Remi, built in the 11th century. The narrow central nave from the ninth century is attached to an early-Gothic choir and the windows date from the 12th century.

The Gothic Notre-Dame Cathedral was once the coronation church of French kings and was built in 1211 on the site of an earlier church that had burned down. The structure is adorned with expressive stone sculptures and stained-glass windows that have been lovingly restored. Some were done by Marc Chagall and are vivid masterpieces of light and color.

The Archbishops' Palace of Tau, built around 1500, once served as a temporary residence for the French kings. It features magnificent tapestries.

The high-Gothic Notre-Dame Cathedral (right) has impressive reliefs and a west front richly adorned with sculptures. The nave of the Basilica of Saint-Remi (below) emphasizes the structure's vertical dimensions.

CHARTRES CATHEDRAL

Notre-Dame de Chartres is the undisputed mother of all high-Gothic structures. Unlike many other cathedrals, it has retained almost all of its original furnishings. Its elegance and simplicity embody the triumph of Gothic art.

The triple-aisled basilica with transept and five-aisled choir is one of the very first purely Gothic edifices and quickly became a model for the cathedrals of Reims and Amiens. Construction here began early in the 12th century and the church was consecrated in 1260. As if by some miracle, the early-Gothic west façade from 1140 managed to survive the fire of 1194. Below the choir is St Fulbert's crypt from 1024. At a length of 108 m (354 ft), it is the largest Romanesque crypt in France.

A number of new architectural techniques were employed during the construction of Chartres, for example the flying buttresses, which made it possible to interrupt the long walls with large windows.

The colorful stained-glass windows from the 12th and 13th centuries provide the interior with a unique light and the rich sculptures and reliefs of the portals were groundbreaking. The Royal Portal, in particular, was long regarded as a model of harmony in sculpture and architecture.

The differing towers of Notre Dame de Chartres date from the 12th (left) and 15th (right) centuries. Vertical dimensions are especially emphasized in the design here. Below: The ambulatory.

BOURGES CATHEDRAL

In the former capital of the dukes of Berry it is the five-aisled cathedral dedicated to St Stephen that stands out among the architectural gems. The west front is particularly impressive. With its five large portals, the concept of the church as a gateway to heaven found its strongest expression here.

St Stephen's Cathedral was built in two stages: The choir and apse were built between 1195 and 1215, while the nave and the main façade went up between 1225 and 1260. Two asymmetric towers rise proudly above the church. The north tower collapsed in 1506 and was rebuilt by 1542.

Parts of the Gothic structure such as the southern side portal date from the Romanesque period. The sculptures adorning the west front, which contains five portals that correspond with the aisles, are of particular significance. Biblical subjects such as the Last Judgment as well as legends from the life of St Stephen (Saint-Étienne) are depicted here. The interior is illuminated by natural light falling through the intricate stained-glass windows that date from the 13th century.

The room under the choir, erroneously called the "crypt" despite not being underground, is the resting place of Duke John of Berry (1340–1416), the brother of King Charles V. In fact, this room, created in 1195, is its own church with its own liturgical functions.

The west façade of the high-Gothic cathedral at Bourges is in the heart of a densely built-up town.

France

THE LOIRE VALLEY FROM SULLY-SUR-LOIRE TO CHALONNES

One of Europe's most fascinating cultural landscapes extends along the mostly unregulated Loire River. It features an incredible array of spectacular châteaux and abbeys.

The stretch of the Loire between Sully-sur-Loire in the east and Chalonnes a few miles downriver from Angers is approximately 200 km (124 mi) long. It is where France's longest river meanders its way eastward toward the Atlantic, through the historic regions of the Orléanais, Blésois, Touraine and Anjou, an area that boasts an abundance of cultural monuments.

The rise of settlements on the Loire began with St Martin, Bishop of Tours from 371 to 397 and patron saint of the Franks, whose tomb in Tours became an important pilgrimage site. In 848, Charles the Bald was crowned king in Orléans and the river valley became the preferred residence for the Capetian dynasty in the 10th and 11th centuries.

There are important Romanesque structures here: the abbey churches of Saint-Benoît-sur-Loire with its narthex and crypt dating from the 11th century; Germigny-des-Prés with its 12th-century mosaic; frescoes in Liget and Tavant; and the Church of Notre-Dame in Cunault.

One of Europe's largest monastic complexes is the Fontevraud Abbey with the burial church of the Plantagenets. When Henry Plantagenets was coronated as king of England in 1154, a vast empire was created with centers in Angers and Chinon. It was here that Joan of Arc took on Charles VII during the Hundred-Years' War, in 1429, before setting off to liberate Orléans from English troops.

Under Francis I, a number of castles were rebuilt or remodeled here: the splendid Château of Azay-le-Rideau (1527), built on an island as the Loire's archetypal Renaissance castle; Château de Chenonceau; the Château de Chambord (a World Heritage Site in its own right) and the châteaux of Blois and Amboise.

The châteaux of Villandry and Saumur are also worth a visit and feature vineyards lining the Loire with its islands, sandbanks and colorful meadows.

Francis I built Chambord, the Loire's largest château, as a hunting lodge in 1619. Its distinctive towers and chimneys rise above more than 400 rooms that accommodated up to 10,000 guests.

It is not difficult to surmise that the Château Sully-sur-Loire was originally built as a fortress.

The Loire also has some impressive religious buildings, like the Cathedral Sainte-Croix in Orléans.

The Château of Blois overlooks the Loire from the center of town. During the reign of Louis XII, it was even the capital of France for a few years after 1498.

Château d'Amboise – built from 1490 on the foundations of a former medieval castle – sits high on a rock above Amboise on the Loire.

France

The main attraction at Château de Villandry is its stunning Renaissance garden, completed in 1536 and located just 15 km (9 mi) west of Tours.

Château de Saumur achieved world fame when it was depicted on a calendar page in the Duke of Berry's book of hours, "Les Très Riches Heures".

Angers sits at the confluence of the Maine and Loire rivers – here the Maine Bridge and Saint Maurice Cathedral. The Château is home to the famous Tapestry of the Apocalypse cycle (1373–1377).

Château de Chenonceau (right) is famous for its extraordinary location. The two-story gallery was built above the modest River Cher during the time of Catherine de' Medici (1519–89).

MONT-SAINT-MICHEL AND ITS BAY

On a rocky islet in the English Channel, about 1 km (1/2 mi) off the Normandy coast, is the former Benedictine Abbey of Mont-Saint-Michel, an important station on the Way of St James.

The history of the Abbey of Mont-Saint-Michel begins with a vision that Bishop Aubert, who was residing in nearby Avranches at the time, is said to have had in 708 while out on this tidal island on the border with Brittany. According to the story, the Archangel Michael appeared three times to Aubert, each time demanding that he build a memorial in his name. The bishop, who was later canonized, proceeded to build a small prayer hall for pilgrims on a rock that had earlier served as a pagan and early-Christian place of worship.

Between the 11th and the 16th centuries, this oratory developed into the present Benedictine abbey. A settlement soon developed at the foot of the abbey as well. Some of the houses dating from the 14th century are still preserved today.

The World Heritage Site also includes the surrounding bay, which is to be saved from silting up by a costly restoration project.

The island fortress of Mont-Saint-Michel with its famous abbey is situated at the mouth of the River Couesnon (top). The Monastic Fraternities of Jerusalem handle the administration and support of pilgrims. They also conduct services in the Gothic abbey church (left).

FORTIFICATIONS OF VAUBAN

The defense installations of Vauban, named after the master builder, are outstanding examples of Western European military architecture. They were copied all over the continent, in America and even the Middle East.

Sébastien le Prestre de Vauban (1633–1707) was an architect, town planner and a pioneering fortress designer under Louis XIV. He was responsible for no fewer than thirty-three new fortresses and more than 160 battlements, and conducted more than fifty sieges as a commander. In 1678, he became the General Commissar of Fortifications and was promoted to Marshall of France in 1703. Fortifications of his have been chosen as World Heritage Sites in twelve places and represent the best of his architectural efforts at the seaside, in the mountains and next to rivers. They are situated on the western,

northern and eastern borders of France, and they are all still in virtually original condition.

Vauban's architectural prowess in the face of geophysically challenging locations can be admired in places like Arras, Longwy, Neuf-Brisach, Besançon, Briançon, Mont-Dauphin, Villefranche-de-Conflent, Mont-Louis, Cussac-Fort-Medoc / Blaye, Saint-Martin-de-Ré, Camaret-sur-Mer and Saint-Vaast-La-Hougue.

The fortifications of Besançon, capital of the Franche-Comté Region, extend over a total area of 195 ha (482 acres). The citadel is at the center.

LE HAVRE

The port city of Le Havre, which had been transformed into an Atlantic fortress during World War II, was largely destroyed by bombs in September 1944. The "Atelier de Réconstruction" was given the task of rebuilding the city.

Auguste Perret, one of the pioneers of reinforced concrete construction, originally wanted to rebuild Le Havre, on the mouth of the River Seine, on a concrete platform 3 m (11 ft) above the rubble. It was an inpracticable plan, however.

During the reconstruction, between 1946 and 1964, the few preserved buildings were incorporated into the new layout, and the course of the old roads was also partly maintained. Unique is the consistency with which a grid of squares, measuring 100 m (328 ft) on each side was mapped onto the construction area, and precast components with a uniform edge length of 6 m (20 ft) were used without the results being too monotonous. The individual concrete slabs are not plastered, and it is possible to see how the skeleton structures of the buildings were assembled. The social concept underlying the new Le Havre is also new. Population density was reduced from 2,000 to 800 people per hectare (from 800 to 324 per acre), and the apartments became co-operative dwellings.

St Joseph's Church (far left) was designed by Auguste Perret. The market halls (left) were the work of André la Donné, Charles Fabre and Jean Le Soudier.

PROVINS

The authentically medieval town architecture of Provins, a small town between Paris and Troyes, epitomizes the political, social and economic structure of a flourishing community in the 12th and 13th centuries.

Provins, once part of the territory of the counts of Champagne, stood at the intersection of the trading routes between the North Sea and the Mediterranean, between Flanders and Italy. No fewer than nine major as well as eleven minor trade routes ran through here.

As a result, in the 12th and 13th centuries Provins became a major international trade fair town where goods of all kinds were exchanged. Among the best-known events were the annual cloth and leather fairs. When a count brought a damask rose back from the crusades, Provins also became a center for the cultivation of roses.

At the base of the Tour César, a 12th-century octagonal watchtower that was later also used as a prison, is a superb example of a beautifully-preserved medieval town. It encompasses the ancient town ramparts and gates, underground galleries, the Romanesque churches of Saint Quiriace and Saint Ayoul as well as the 13th-century Grange aux Dîmes, a tithe barn serving as a covered market square.

The building of the collegiate church of Saint Quiriace was begun in around 1160. Its choir already anticipates elements of the Gothic style.

NANCY

Stanislas Leszczynski, the deposed King of Poland, nominally became the Duke of Lorraine in 1737, and it is to him that Nancy owes its matchless squares. Three of these were awarded World Heritage Site status: Place Stanislas, Place de la Carrière and Place d'Alliance.

Place Stanislas was meant to be an architectural bridge between the Old Town and the New Town to the south. As Place Royale it was to become the new center of Nancy. Designed and built in 1752 to 1755 under the supervision of the architect Emmanuel Héré de Corny, the square's most prominent building is the Hôtel de Ville (town hall) on the south side. Its interior was lavishly decorated, and the staircase seems even larger than it is thanks to a trompe-l'oeil painting on the back wall. The pavilions on the west and east side of the square were designed in a similar style.

The square is crowned by a triumphal arch, on the other side of which is the long Place de la Carrière. This square was built in the 16th century and completed under Stanislas.

The Palais de Justice and the Bourse des Marchands opposite were also designed by Héré. Work on the Place d'Alliance began in 1753. It is particularly impressive thanks to the uniform façades of its houses.

Wrought-iron latticework by Jean Lamour and the Neptune Fountain by Barthélemy Guibal adorn the north side of the generously proportioned Place Stanislas.

France

ABBEY OF FONTENAY

The remarkably well-preserved buildings of the Cistercian Abbey of Fontenay, built by Bernard of Clairvaux in 1119, are an exceptionally vivid illustration of medieval monastic life.

The Abbey of Fontenay, dedicated by Pope Eugene III in 1147, lies about 50 km (31 mi) north-west of Dijon. Although it was partially replaced by new buildings in the 18th century, the original layout of the Cistercian abbey is still clearly visible.

The Cistercian order goes back to a reformist movement within the Benedictine community. They lived solely from the harvest they themselves could reap and in decidedly modest dwellings. Their plain and harmonious abbey complex is surrounded by a high wall. The church and abbey form a strictly closed, largely unadorned unit. The abbey church, for its part, was originally intended only for the devotions of the monastic community, which is why stairs connect it directly with the dormitory.

Several ancillary buildings are loosely grouped around the twin structures, between green spaces and trees. A forge and a mill dating from the 12th century have also been lovingly preserved here.

The church of Fontenay is bound by strict Cistercian ideals. There are no benches inside – only a beaten-earth floor. The choir (right) contains the gravestones of noblemen from Burgundy.

VÉZELAY ABBEY CHURCH AND CITY HILL

The Basilica of St Mary Magdalene is perched on a hilltop above the Old Town of Vézelay, which is surrounded by mighty ramparts. The largest abbey church in France, it is a masterpiece of the French Romanesque style.

The 9th-century church of the abbey located about 100 km (62 mi) west of Dijon allegedly holds the relics of St Mary Magdalene. Needless to say, it didn't take long before the church was unable to accommodate the seemingly endless stream of pilgrims, and in 1096 a new building was begun.

During the Crusades, Vézelay developed as an important spiritual center. However, in 1279, when the reputedly genuine bones of the penitent were found in Provence, it brought about sudden decline in significance of the abbey.

The church's barrel vaulting, which reaches 18 m (59 ft) in height and 62 m (203 ft) in length, is unique in Romanesque architecture and the plain furnishings of the bright interior were enlivened by the use of colored blocks. The statues above the main portal were restored in the 19th century; they are the most sophisticated from the Middle Ages.

Vézelay Abbey Church is perched on top of City Hill (top left). Some parts of it were built much later than the Romanesque central nave (right). The capitals and the tympanum of the narthex are particularly lavish in their designs (above right).

STRASBOURG: GRANDE ÎLE

The medieval Old Town of Strasbourg is located on the Grande Île (big island), in the River Ill, which runs through the city. The historic center contains a high concentration of beautifully preserved buildings.

The main landmark of Strasbourg is its Minster, one of the most important religious buildings of the Middle Ages. Begun in 1015, the Minster was originally Romanesque, but since construction extended over several centuries, it also features Gothic elements. Particularly interesting is the western façade, praised for its proportions as well as its portals, which are bedecked with elaborate stone sculptures. Having taken on the financing of the vast structure in 1286, the citizens of Strasbourg built the cathedral as much as

The four towers of the Ponts Couverts (top) are the last of eighty towers in the ramparts of the former imperial city of Strasbourg. La Petite France (above), the former tanners' district in the Old Town, is full of nooks and crannies and half-timbered houses.

a place of worship as a monument to their own efforts. Other highlights in the church are the magnificent stained-glass windows and the astronomical clock.

The Minster square is lined by rows of five-storey half-timbered houses like the Maison Kammerzell and the Palais Rohan, built in about 1740 in the style of Louis XV. Also worth seeing are the picturesque tanners' district La Petite France from the 16th and 17th centuries, the Ponts Couverts (formerly covered bridges) and the Vauban weir.

Seen from the Rue Mercière, the western façade with its central portal, rose window and the north tower.

France

GREAT SALTWORKS OF SALINS-LES-BAINS AND ROYAL SALTWORKS OF ARC-ET-SENANS

Inextricably linked by 7,000 years of salt production in the Franche-Comté region, two saltworks now form a combined monument that impressively illustrates the history of "white gold" in eastern France: the Royal Saltworks of Arc-et-Senans, dating from the 18th century and a World Heritage Site since 1982, and the medieval Great Saltworks of Salins-les-Bains, inducted in 2009.

The Royal Saltworks of Arc-et-Senans, built on the orders of King Louis XV, were linked with the Saltworks of Salins-les-Bains by a 21-km-long (13-mi) road along which workers transported as much as 135,000 ltr (29,700 gal) of brine every day.

Aside from the architecture of the saltworks themselves, the techniques used here for producing salt were also innovative: The brine was artificially heated until the water evaporated.

The director's house in the Royal Salt-works in Arc-et-Senans is symbolic of the social hierarchy: The entire complex was custom-made for his person.

HISTORIC SITE OF LYON

The history of this former Roman colony founded at the confluence of the Saône and Rhône rivers is reflected brilliantly in the numerous buildings dating from different periods.

Thanks to its abundant silk mills and print works, Lyon developed as one of Europe's foremost fair towns in the 16th century. In 1506, France's first stock exchange was established here as well.

Narrow, winding alleyways and fabulous medieval buildings characterize the oldest part of the city, Fourvière, adapted from the Roman "forum vetus" (old forum). St John's Cathedral (12th–15th centuries) stands here with its early-Gothic stained-glass windows and an astronomical clock from the 14th century.

On a hill above the River Saône, where the Romans founded the city is the pilgrims' basilica of Notre-Dame de Fourvière (19th century). On the 5-km (3-mi) peninsula between the two rivers are the 17th-century town hall, the Palais des Arts (a former Benedictine abbey), the Stock Exchange and several late-medieval churches. The center of Lyon is the Place Bellecour. South of here is the Church of Saint-Martin-d'Ainay (12th century), which dates back to a 6th-century basilica.

The Place des Terreaux is home to sixty-nine fountains and the town hall (above), whose façade was designed by Jules Hardouin-Mansart Right: The Romanesque-Gothic Saint John's Cathedral.

ORANGE: AMPHITHEATER AND TRIUMPHAL ARCH

The Romans founded Arausio on the site of a Celtic settlement they had conquered in the Rhône Valley. The remains of their buildings can still be seen here, including one of the best-preserved amphitheaters in Europe.

The façade of the Théâtre Romain is 103 m (338 ft) long and 37 m (121 ft) high. It was one of the largest theaters in Antiquity. Because of its spectacular location on a hill in the city center, some corridors had to be dug directly out of the rock.

As many as 10,000 spectators were able to marvel at the performances and the magnificently decorated backdrop. After centuries of decay, as well as use as a quarry and a prison, renovations began in the 19th century to restore the location as a venue for festival performances.

The "Triumphal Arch", completed in about AD 25, is the best and most completely preserved Roman arch in what was known then as Gaul. The structure, which is 20 m (66 ft) wide, 18 m (59 ft) high and 8.5 m (28 ft) deep, marks the entrance to the city on the Via Agrippa. It has three arches, the central passage being larger then the two side passages.

The Roman Theater of Orange was built shortly after the birth of Christ and features an impressive stage wall adorned by a statue of Augustus.

PONT DU GARD

This bridge aqueduct across the River Gard is a masterpiece of Roman engineering. It was part of an approximately 50-km-long (31-mi) water supply channel extending from the source of the River Eure to Nîmes.

During the reigns of Emperors Claudius and Nero, between roughly AD 40 and 60, a bridge aqueduct was built over the rocky valley of the River Gard. It was a daring feat at the time in terms of its construction methods. The purpose of this engineering marvel was to supply the fast-growing ancient town of Nemausus (present-day Nîmes) with water.

The row of arcades on three levels were slightly offset from each other, the uppermost level measuring 275 m (902 ft) in length. The lowest level has six arches, varying in width from 15 to 24 m (49 to 79 ft) while the middle level has a total of eleven arches.

Water was transported on the top level, supported by thirty-five smaller arches each 5 m (16 ft) in width. The structure was built using limestone blocks without any mortar.

The aqueduct began to decay in the fourth century. In the Middle Ages, the pillars on the middle level were tapered so they could be used as a road. The structure was not restored until the 18th century.

The Pont du Gard is 50 m (164 ft) high and once transported 40,000 cu m (1,412,586 cu ft) of water to Nîmes. The installation has a slight incline, which allowed the water to flow.

ARLES

The Romans selected Arles for its strategic location on the Rhône canal. Aside from remarkable remains from Roman times, there are also important French Romanesque structures to be admired.

Among the oldest Roman structures in Arles are the subterranean passages of the Cryptoporticus below the Forum. These vast corridors, more than 100 m (328 ft) long and about 70 m (230 ft) wide, likely served as grain storage silos.

Two amphitheaters built in the first and second centuries are also Roman. One of them, Les Arènes, is 136 m (446 ft) wide and 107 m (351 ft) long, making it the largest ancient open-air stage still standing. Its vast arena is now used for bullfights. The Thermae on the right bank of the Rhône are from late Roman times and were part of a 200-m-long (656-ft) palace.

Thanks to its well-preserved sarcophagi, the necropolis of Alyscamps gives us insight into some of the funerary methods from early- and pre-Christian times. Saint-Trophime Cathedral, with a nave from the 11th/12th centuries, is one of France's most remarkable Romanesque buildings. It is home to an exquisite portal and magnificent cloisters.

Arles also entered art history as the place where Vincent van Gogh painted some of his most famous pictures.

Les Arènes, one of two amphitheaters in Arles, had room for 20,000 spectators.

France

The Popes in Avignon

The "Babylonian Captivity of the Church" (1309–1376) refers to a time when seven popes in succession – all of French origin – resided in Avignon. It is considered the lowest point in the history of the papacy, when the Church came under the influence of the French monarchy, thereby endangering its supranational identity.

It all began with Pope Clement V, a Frenchman, who after his election did not even move to chaotic Rome but instead stayed in his home country. The kings of France offered protection and money in return for support from succeeding popes, for example during the suppression of the Order of the Knights Templar.

The Avignon popes ultimately lost the respect of the community due to their avarice: levies were increased, ecclesiastical offices were systematically sold for money, and they reputed the Christian rejection of greed as heresy. Pope John XXII refused to recognize Ludwig the Bavarian as king of Germany and excommunicated him.

AVIGNON

This World Heritage Site on the Rhône, where the popes resided for sixty-seven years in the 14th century, includes the Old Town with its fortified Papal Palace, the surrounding Episcopal Ensemble and the Pont d'Avignon.

The Palais des Papes consists of the Old and New Palaces. On the north side is connected to the 12th-century Romanesque Cathedral of Notre-Dame des Doms. Also part of the Episcopal district, on the west side of the Place du Palais, is the Petit Palais, built in 1317, which was given to the bishop in recompense for the demolition of his former palace.

Since the 14th century, the town had been encircled by almost 5 km (3 mi) of ramparts, reinforced by defense installations and watchtowers including the Tour des Chiens and the Tour du Châtelet. The latter controlled access to the Saint Bénézet Bridge, also known as the Pont d'Avignon, which today is only a rump jutting halfway into the river.

The Papal Palace, built in 1334 during the papacies of Benedict XII and Clement VI, is one of the greatest Gothic palaces in the world. It also contains liturgical rooms such as Saint John's Chapel, with magnificent paintings by Matteo Giovanetti (above).

"Sur le Pont d'Avignon" is the song that made the Saint Bénézet Bridge at the foot of the Papal Palace (above right and right) famous around the world. In the year 1660, half the bridge was washed away by floods, and today only four of its arches are still standing. At the level of the second pillar is the two-story Saint Nicolas Chapel from the 14th century.

Ludwig for his part organized the election of an antipope in 1328, who quickly crowned him as emperor but soon disappeared.

The return of the popes to Rome must be credited on the one hand to the influence of St Catherine of Siena, on the other hand to the crisis in France during the Hundred Years War. When marauding soldiers attacked the fortified Papal Palace, it became clear that the French king could no longer afford the protection he needed.

Not one of the seven popes who resided in Avignon was buried in the Papal Palace but there are burial sculptures here for other ecclesiastical dignitaries.

France

ROUTES OF SANTIAGO DE COMPOSTELA IN FRANCE

The Way of St James actually consists of a dense network of trails that cover the continent, converging into four main routes in south-western France before continuing into Spain.

The alleged grave of St James in north-western Spain is one of the most important pilgrimage destinations in the Christian world. Four main routes traverse France before crossing the border: Via Turonensis starts in Paris and continues via Tours, Poitiers and Bordeaux to Ostabat, where it merges with the Via Lemovicensis from Vézelay and the Via Podiensis from Le Puy. These routes cross the Pyrenees together.

The Via Tolosana starts in Arles and continues via Toulouse and the Somport Pass to Jaca and Puente la Reina.

The scallop shell, here set into the pavement in Périgueux, is the symbol of the Apostle James and a signpost for pilgrims on the Way of St James.

There, all routes combine as Camino Francés, which ends in Santiago de Compostela.

Medieval pilgrimages were certainly comparable to modern tourism. To draw pilgrims into the villages along the route, impressive sacred buildings were erected along the way. Becoming popular destinations in their own right thanks to the valuable relics collected, they now feature some of the most remarkable works of medieval architecture. The Way of St James thus gained great importance in the evolution of Romanesque art and inspired individual centers in return.

In art historical terms, Via Turonensis is the most impressive route on the Way of St James. Churches themselves became attractions. Here, the crypt in Tours with the grave of St Martin.

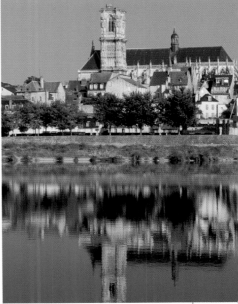

From Vézelay, the pilgrimage goes via Nevers (above: the Romanesque-Gothic Saint-Cyr-et-Sainte-Juliette Cathedral) on the Loire to the junction at Ostabat.

One of the oldest pilgrimage routes on the Way of St James, mentioned in the 12th-century Codex Calixtinus, begins at Le Puy-en-Velay.

Saint-Guilhem-le-Désert is a popular post in the Languedoc-Roussillon region.

France

ABBEY CHURCH OF SAINT-SAVIN SUR GARTEMPE

With its 11th- and 12th-century frescoes, the "Sistine Chapel of the Romanesque" holds the greatest Romanesque cycle of paintings in France.

As if by a miracle, this abbey church was spared from destruction and looting over the centuries, but it began to decay after the French Revolution. In 1836, writer Prosper Mérimée, who became the Inspector of Historic Monuments in France in 1831, discovered it some 35 km (22 mi) east of Poitiers and immediately placed it on the list of protected buildings. The cycle of paintings was rescued thanks to restoration work in the 1970s.

On a surface area of more than 400 sq m (4,304 sq ft), the images preserved in the vaults of the central nave represent a self-contained Old Testament cycle from Genesis to the Exodus. The wall frescoes in the rood loft and narthex depict the Life of Christ and the Apocalypse of John. The images of the saints in the crypt are less elaborate in their execution.

Aside from these invaluable wall paintings, the abbey church also boasts precious Romanesque altars.

The frescoes of the Abbey Church of Saint-Savin (right: the painted barrel vaulting) attemped to use popular images to introduce the contents of the Bible to the faithful, who were mostly illiterate.

VÉZÈRE VALLEY PREHISTORIC SITES AND DECORATED CAVES

Concentrated along an approximately 40-km-long (25-mi) stretch of the Vézère Valley in the Périgord Region is a series of prehistoric sites and caves with rock paintings that give us valuable insights into human life during the Paleolithic and the Neolithic Ages.

This World Heritage Region comprises an impressive 147 sites and twenty-five caves with rock paintings that were discovered over the course of the 19th and 20th centuries. The most important sites in this treasure trove of early humanity are all in a row on a hill above the Vézère River: Le Moustier, La Madeleine, Lascaux and Cro-Magnon.

At Cro-Magnon, five skeletons dating from the late Paleolithic Age were found. They are the origin of the name given to the type of homo sapiens. In the cave at Lascaux about 100 paintings dating back roughly 15,000 years display remarkably realistic hunting scenes while finds in other caves confirm that the hunters and gatherers, who settled in southern France during the Ice Age, were responsible for the first works of art in Europe as far back as 30,000 years ago.

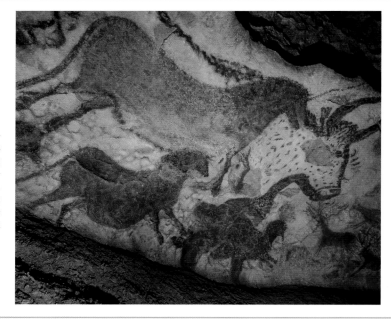

In the "Great Hall of the Bulls" in the cave of Lascaux we encounter a partial representation of a bull in the middle of a group of horses.

SAINT-ÉMILION

This is the first time a historic wine-growing area was given the coveted status of World Heritage Site. The Jurisdiction of Saint-Émilion and another seven surrounding communities are about 30 km (19 mi) east of Bordeaux.

It was the Romans who originally introduced viticulture to the fertile Aquitaine Region. Today, this protected territory includes – aside from Saint-Émilion itself – the municipalities of Saint-Christophe des Bardes, Saint-Étienne-de-Lisse, Saint-Hippolyte, Saint-Laurent-des-Combes, Saint-Pey-d'Armens, Vignonet and Saint-Sulpice-de-Faleyrens.

Saint-Émilion rose around the grotto in which the Breton monk Émilion lived in seclusion in the 8th century. Later a subterranean church, the triple-aisled Église Monolithe was hewn into the rock next to the hermitage. A direct passageway links the church with the catacombs, where St Émilion is said to be buried. Other historic buildings worth seeing in Saint-Émilion are the magnificent Cloître de la Collégiale and the Chapelle de la Trinité. The latter was built in the 13th century to honor St Émilion, the patron saint of vintners. Thanks to its location on the pilgrimage route to Santiago de Compostela, many monasteries, churches and hospices were built in the region starting in the 11th century.

Saint-Émilion, its bell tower rising high above the rock church, is the leading wine village of the Bordeaux region.

HISTORIC BORDEAUX ("PORT OF THE MOON")

The Old Town of Bordeaux hugs the left bank of the Garonne River, which flows through in the shape of a sickle and gives Bordeaux its epithet "Port of the Moon". With the exception of Paris, there are more historic monuments in Bordeaux from the time of the Enlightenment than in any other French city.

Bordeaux has been a port since Roman times. One of its most important commercial products is the wine for which the town and its environs are still world-famous today. Until the early 18th century, Bordeaux was still medieval in character, but the Enlightenment paved the way for an intellectual movement that transformed the city into a neoclassical gem.
First, Jacques Gabriel designed the Place de la Bourse in about 1730.

Louis-Urbain Aubert, the marquis von Tournay and administrator of the local community from 1743 to 1757, then played a key role in the restructuring of Bordeaux, replacing the medieval gates with neoclassical structures. The old port on the left bank, however, remained unchanged.

In the middle of the half-moon-shaped Place de la Bourse stands the Fountain of the Three Graces, built in 1864.

MONT PERDU, PYRENEES

The extraordinary mountain landscape around 3,352-m (11,000-ft) Mont Perdu – in Spanish, Monte Perdido – straddles the French-Spanish border in the Pyrenees and was granted Natural as well as Cultural Heritage status because of the impressive geological formations and its unique local population.

The 300 sq km (11.5 sq mi) world heritage site around Mt Perdu includes parts of the Spanish Parque Nacional de Ordesa y Monte Perdido and the French Parc National de Pyrénées. In 1999, the site was extended to include the French commune of Gèdre.
Añisclo and Ordesa canyons – two of Europe's largest – are the main attractions on the Spanish side of the border while the three valleys of Troumouse, Estaubé, and Gavarnie belong to the French administrative department of Hautes-Pyrénées. The U-shaped valleys were formed by glaciers and are among the most beautiful in Europe.

The most striking feature of this imposing landscape is its unspoilt state. Focused on pastoral farming, life here has remained virtually unchanged for centuries, and the trappings of modern living have failed to leave any real mark on the villages, farms and fields that are still connected by old mountain roads. The landscape bears testimony to a mountain lifestyle that has long since ceased to exist in other parts of Europe.

The Grande Cascade in Cirque de Gavarnie is one of the highest waterfalls in Europe at 423 m (1,400 ft).

CANAL DU MIDI

The Canal du Midi links Toulouse (and thus, via the Garonne River, the Atlantic Ocean) with the Mediterranean. It is one of the greatest achievements of engineering from the Absolutist period.

Together with its various auxiliary channels like the Canal de la Robine, this man-made waterway was completed with amazing swiftness – fourteen years, from 1667 to 1681 – and extends over an impressive length of about 350 km (217 mi). It also features over 300 structures including locks, aqueducts, tunnels and bridges. On the roughly 50-km-long (31-mi) long stretch between Toulouse and its highest point near Naurouze, the canal has to overcome a difference in height of 63 m (207 ft) with the help of 26 locks. Dozens of additional locks are then needed to master the descent of 190 m (623 ft) down to its estuary

at the Mediterranean near Agde. And yet the riskiest undertaking by engineer Pierre-Paul Riquet was the construction of the 150-m-long (492-ft) Malpas Tunnel near Béziers, where for the first time explosives were used to clear a path.
The Canal led to a great boom in the Languedoc Region, where shipping traffic did not decline until the rise of the railroads. Today, the Canal is used mostly by houseboats.

Today it is possible to cruise down the Canal du Midi in all manner of craft, enjoying the Languedoc landscape at a leisurely pace.

France

CARCASSONNE

The fortified Old Town of Carcassonne, with its double ring of ramparts and numerous gates and towers, is one of the most impressive examples of medieval European fortification architecture.

People from Iberia had already settled in Roman times on the hill above the River Aude, along the old trading routes between the Mediterranean and the Atlantic. In 418, Gallo-Roman Carcasso was conquered by the Visigoths, who built the inner ramparts in 485. In 725, the Moors took over, and in 759 they were followed by the Franks. In 1229, Carcassonne finally came under the control of the French Crown.

The impressive Romanesque Basilica of Saint-Nazaire was built during the town's expansion in the Middle Ages, roughly between 1096 to 1150, before being remodeled later in the Gothic style in the 13th century. The stunning stained-glass windows date from the 14th to 16th centuries.

In the Middle Ages, the towers and bastions of Carcassonne were an almost insurmountable bulwark.

Around 1125, the Château Comtal was integrated into the fortifications of the inner complex. Toward the end of the 13th century, construction began on the outer ramparts and watchtowers. In the process, the inner ramparts also acquired an impressive gate, the Porte Narbonnaise. The Pont Vieux is also from the 12th century.

Starting roughly in 1660, the fortifications were no longer needed and began to fall into disrepair. In 1844, a decision was made to reconstruct the medieval city, but the historic quarter had long since become a slum. Master builder and art historian Eugène Viollet-le-Duc (1814 to 1879), a pioneer of modern restoration, supervised the restoration work on the ancient ramparts and the Cathedral, which took until 1960 to complete.

The illuminated fortifications recall notions of fairy-tale romance.

GULF OF PORTO

This World Natural Heritage Site along the middle of the west coast of Corsica includes the coastal region around the Gulf of Porto as well as local underwater habitats and the islands of Elbo and Gargallo.

In 2006, the official name of this site was changed to "Gulf of Porto: Calanche of Piana, Gulf of Girolata, Scandola Reserve". The inclusion of the names of the two bays and peninsulas reflected the full extent of the land covered by this protected area. It was listed not only for the beauty of its landscape, but also for its flora and fauna, and the traditional methods of agricultural and pasture management used by the inhabitants.

The nature reserve is part of a larger Corsican regional park. It provides an ideal nesting and breeding ground for many seabirds including seagulls, cormorants and the now rare sea eagle.

The rocky peninsula of La Girolata is largely covered in wild forests, and there are large areas of typically Mediterranean maquis. Dense eucalyptus forests line the sandy yellow beaches, and the waters around the bays and coves along the deeply fissured rocky cliffs are alive with flora and fauna the likes of which are hard to find anywhere else. Rare algae are just one example of the underwater life that has survived here.

Both rough and smooth rock formations can be found on the Scandola peninsula. Below is the Gulf of Porto between Ota and Eviso.

THE LAGOONS OF NEW CALEDONIA

The lagoons of New Caledonia are home to a great variety of animal and plant life. Between clumps of marine grass lie unique reefs which cannot be found anywhere else in the world and which offer a habitat for endangered species of fish, turtles and mammals. The World Heritage Site encompasses six ecosystems with a total surface area of almost 16,000 sq km (6,200 sq mi).

New Caledonia covers an area of some 18,600 sq km (7,240 sq mi) and includes both the eponymous main island and several smaller coral and volcanic islands. The group came under French rule in 1853 and is now a French Overseas Territory. Geographically it is part of Melanesia.

The main island and the islands to its south are surrounded by one of the largest coral reef systems in the world – along with the Australian Great Barrier Reef. The untouched mangrove forests are home to a variety of animal life and lush vegetation, while numerous species of rare fish live in the largely intact lagoon ecosystem. Extensive fields of sea grass provide sustenance for the world's third-largest population of sea cows and ancient fossil remains in the lagoons provide a rich source of information for natural history scientists studying the Pacific.

The New Caledonian Barrier Reef (left, with shipwreck) is home to numerous species of rare coral and fish.

Germany

THE WADDEN SEA

The Wadden Sea is one of the largest tidal-dependent, coastal ecosystems on earth and is home to a great variety of wildlife. It is also one of the last pristine natural landscapes left in Central Europe.

Between Blåvandshuk in Denmark and Den Helder in Holland, there is a 450-km (280-mi) stretch of tidal flats along the North Sea coast that sometimes reach 40 km (25 mi) in width. Dominated by the ebb and flow of the tides, about two-thirds of this unique biotope for plants, animals and humans was declared a World Heritage Site in 2009. The site encompasses the Wadden Sea National Parks of Schleswig-Holstein and Lower Saxony as well as the North, West and East Frisian islands.

This coastal landscape is characterized by expansive beaches, sand dunes, fields of seagrass and vast mudflats.

The funnel-shaped estuaries, called "priele" (watercourses that remain full even at low tide), are also typical of the area and provide a rich habitat for some 10,000 plant and animal species, of which the common porpoise is one of the most popular. The Wadden Sea is also one of the main stopovers for millions of migratory birds who come to rest in the mudflats every year. It is one of the last areas in Europe in which nature is allowed to run its course unhindered.

Schleswig-Holstein (here the Westerhever lighthouse) was the first German state to put the Wadden Sea under protection.

HANSEATIC CITY OF LÜBECK

The Hanseatic League, marzipan, the Mann family – these are the things that are generally associated with Lübeck. The main attraction of this once mighty Hanseatic city, however, is its medieval city center, whose trend-setting brick Gothic buildings have been almost entirely preserved, despite the devastation of World War II.

Lübeck was founded as a mercantile settlement in the year 1143 by Count Graf Adolf II of Holstein. When it was awarded the status of a free imperial city in 1226, the town gained a large degree of economic independence for its merchants and artisan guilds.

An aptitude for trade and hard work soon made the city on the Trave River in the Baltic hinterland the "Queen City of the Hanseatic League", and as early as the late 12th century it assumed a leading position within this powerful league of cities.

Lübeck was also very important as the spiritual center of the Oldenburg bishopric, something that visitors to the Old Town will notice right away. The Cathedral, built in the 13th century and later remodeled in the Gothic style, speaks of the influence of the bishops while the twin-towered Church of St Mary shows the council's willingness to fund such projects.

Another important church here is the Museum Church of St Catherine, from the early 14th century. It contains sculptures by Ernst Barlach and Gerhard Marcks as well as a painting by Tintoretto. The Town Hall, one of the largest from the Middle Ages, and the Hospital of the Holy Spirit, donated in the year 1280, illustrate the prosperity of the merchants, as do numer-

ous proud patrician and guild houses. Of the five mighty city gates, only the Holsten Gate remains. It was built between 1464 and 1478 by Lübeck master builder Hinrich Helmstede as an emblem of the city.

The Buddenbrooks House on Mengstrasse commemorates the novelist brothers Heinrich and Thomas Mann, who were born in Lübeck.

Restored sailing vessels and merchants' homes in the Lübeck Museum Port testify to the Hanseatic city's former importance (top). Equally impressive are the façades of the Hospital of the Holy Spirit (right) and the Town Hall.

TOWN HALL AND ROLAND ON THE MARKETPLACE OF BREMEN

The Town Hall and its statue of Roland bear witness to the self-confidence of this venerable Hanseatic City on the River Weser, as do the numerous merchants' houses and lovely churches.

In 787, Charlemagne declared this settlement on the banks of the Weser a bishopric. A century later, the town was awarded a market license and in 1200 received a town charter. In 1358 Bremen joined the Hanseatic League. The Gothic Town Hall was built between 1405 and 1410 and renewed in the style of the Weser Renaissance between 1609 and 1612. It stands as a symbol for the development of the town as part of the mighty Hanseatic League. The lower hall in the Town Hall remained essentially Gothic in style, whereas the upper floors feature Renaissance elements. One particular gem is the Golden Chamber in the aldermen's festival hall, where confidential meetings were once held in the richly adorned surroundings.

In front of the Town Hall, the "petrified Roland" measures almost 10 m (33 ft) in height. The Song of Roland is part of a cycle of legends relating to Charlemagne. In the late Middle Ages, Roland had become an emblem of a city's liberation and independence.

Town Hall and statue of Roland, a magnificent setting for the market square.

HISTORIC CENTERS OF STRALSUND AND WISMAR

The two Baltic towns of Wismar and Stralsund form a combined World Heritage Site representing typical examples of the cultural legacy of the Hanseatic League.

Both of these cities boast complete medieval or early-modern Old Town districts that feature the beautiful brick buildings typical of northern Germany. As a result, their historic centers were restored in exemplary fashion in the 1990s.

Its location on Wismar Bay as well as on the ancient trading route from Lübeck to the Baltic states made Wismar a preferred trading hub early on. First mentioned as a town in 1229, it joined the Hanseatic League in 1259. Stralsund, a member of the Hanseatic League since 1293, became one of the most important cities in the Baltic region in the 14th century. The lavishly designed merchants' houses in the Old Town, located on an island between the Strelasund and the lakes dammed in the 13th century, testify to the pride of its prosperous citizens.

St Nicholas' Church and the town hall with its gables dominate the Old Market Square in Stralsund (left). The preeminent building on Wismar's Market Square is the Wasserkunst (water art), built in 1602, which supplied the city with water until 1897 (top).

Germany

ST MARY'S CATHEDRAL AND ST MICHAEL'S CHURCH AT HILDESHEIM

Hildesheim, in the foothills of the Harz Mountains, has not just one but two important religious buildings: St Michael's Church and St Mary's Cathedral. Both originally date from the 11th century and are outstanding examples of Romanesque architecture. The cathedral was destroyed in World War II but faithfully rebuilt based on the original between 1950 and 1960.

Bishop Bernward's bronze door, with eight reliefs cast as a single piece, is probably the most significant work of art in Hildesheim Cathedral. Bernward's Easter Column, also cast in bronze, is only partially preserved and illustrates the life of Jesus. The Ottonian Church of St Michael, built during Bernward's time in office between 1010 and 1033, held the imperial relic of the True Cross, which led to the founding of the bishopric of Hildesheim in 815. Its ancient and medieval motifs are unique, and the monumental central nave ceiling painting is considered a masterpice.

The showpiece at St Michael's is the fresco on the ceiling above the central nave. It depicts the family tree of Jesus, in 1,300 individual pieces, a unique example of Romanesque monumental art.

COLLEGIATE CHURCH, CASTLE AND OLD TOWN OF QUEDLINBURG

Quedlinburg, located in the northern part of the Harz foothills, is an outstanding example of a European medieval town.

Henry I built his Quitilingaburg residence on the foundations of a palace from the Carolingian period. The Abbey was built in 936 on the castle hill and its church was dedicated to St Servatius in 1129.

A portal with Gothic columns adorned the entrance to the crypt, which was embellished with Romanesque frescoes. King Henry I and his wife were buried here. Quedlinburg palace was built next to the Collegiate Church, on the foundations of earlier Romanesque structures, and shows a variety of style elements mainly from the 16th and 17th centuries.

The Old Town below the hill lies within mighty ramparts and is particularly charming, with half-timbered houses and narrow alleyways that carry visitors back to the Middle Ages. The market square features the town hall (1613 to 1615) with its early-baroque portal and a statue of Roland (1427).

Quedlinburg's Old Town is dominated by the Collegiate Church of St Servatius and the Renaissance castle (right).

MINES OF RAMMELSBERG AND HISTORIC TOWN OF GOSLAR

Goslar owes its imperial status and the moniker "Rome of the North" to its silver mines. The historic mines of Rammelsberg are also part of this World Heritage Site, as is the ensemble of half-timbered houses in the Old Town.

The first documented mention of Rammelsberg, which was mined for ore as far back as Roman times, was in 968. In the 11th century, Emperor Henry II then commissioned an extravagant palace close to the rich silver and copper deposits.

Goslar was granted its town charter in 1100 and became the seat of a royal bailiwick before developing into a flourishing imperial city and a religious center of Germany. The convent church of St Mary in the Garden, now the Newark Church, was dedicated in 1186, but has managed to preserve its Romanesque style to an astonishing degree, and the murals in the town hall's Hall of Homage offer a fine example of late-Gothic styling.

The 16th-century miners' village in the Frankenberg region depicts the everyday life of a miner. After more than 1,000 years of exploitation, these mines were finally shut down in 1988. The museum here is one of the most important of its kind in Europe.

Houses like the "Kaiserworth", the tailors' guildhall built in 1494, testify to the former glory of Goslar.

PALACES AND PARKS OF POTSDAM AND BERLIN

The Prussian palaces and parks in Potsdam by Berlin are an extraordinary ensemble of buildings and gardens. The site comprises Sanssouci Palace and Park, Babelsberg with its Observatory, Lindstedt, Sacrow, Glienicke, the New Garden with Cecilienhof Palace, Pfingstberg with the Belvedere, and Peacock Island.

"Sanssouci" (lit. "without worries") is how Frederick the Great wanted to live in his summer palace at Potsdam. Starting in 1745, he had a one-storey palace built by Georg Wenzeslaus von Knobelsdorff on these terraced vineyards. He designed part of it himself. With its sculptures and rich furnishings, Sanssouci Palace is an outstanding example of German rococo. The same architect also designed the

In 1824, Glienicke Palace was remodeled to designs by Schinkel in the style of a Roman villa.

parks, and a number of other structures were added including the Picture Gallery, the New Chambers and the vast New Palace.

During Frederick William IV's reign, the most famous master builders and landscape architects of the day spent time here. A former manor house became Charlottenhof Palace based on plans by Schinkel while Lenné designed the park in Romanesque style. By 1860, Roman baths, the Orangery and the Peace Church were also built. The World Heritage Site also includes the village of Little Glienicke, the Bornstedt Crown Estate and the Russian Colony Alexandrovka in Potsdam.

The façade of the palace of Sanssouci is adorned with caryatids and atlases in the shape of male and female bacchants (top left). The sumptuous figures create a thematic link with the vineyard that was planted here by Frederick the Great. The Chinese House (bottom left) is an example of the Chinese fashion typical of court culture in the 18th century.

Germany

MUSEUM ISLAND, BERLIN

Museum Island is located between the Spree and the Kupfergraben Canal. In an area of less than 1 sq km (247 acres), visitors are greeted here by an ensemble of five museums that is unique in the world. Together they represent more than 5,000 years of human history.

One of Germany's first museums, the Altes Museum (Old Museum) was built here between 1824 and 1828, based on plans by Schinkel. The monumental complex represented the citizens' equivalent of the most important structure in the town at the time, the Königliches Residenzschloss (Royal

The showpiece at the refurbished Neues Museum is the bust of Nefertiti.

Residence). Boasting attractively laid out neoclassical rooms, the museum's exhibits featured classical paintings and sculptures over two floors. When the available space was no longer sufficient, Frederick William IV ordered the remaining parts of the island to be reserved for the exhibition of works of art. He then commissioned two more buildings.

From 1843 until 1855, the Neues Museum (New Museum) was built based on plans by Schinkel's student Friedrich

August Stüler. It documented the arts from ancient Egypt to the Renaissance. After World War II, the building was in ruins and the museum could not be reopened until October 2009.

The Alte Nationalgalerie (Old National Gallery), built between 1866 and 1876, was at the time dedicated to contemporary painting and sculpture. Since reopening in 2001, many of the 19th-century works are back on display in their original locations.

The Bode Museum (formerly the Kaiser Friedrich Museum), at the tip of the island, features a domed staircase and was inaugurated in 1904. After comprehensive restoration, the Collection of Sculptures, the Museum of Byzantine Art and the Coin Cabinet again reside here today.

The last one of the five museums, the neoclassical Pergamon Museum, was added between 1912 and 1930, and is the first architecture museum in the world. It was built specifically to display giant archaeological finds from Asia Minor, which are now shown here as impressive reconstructions. Berlin's most visited museum also houses the Collection of Antiquities and the Museum of Islamic Art.

Right from top to bottom: The Altes Museum by Schinkel is one of the most important neoclassical buildings in the world. The Bode Museum has sculptures from the early Middle Ages to the 18th century, one of the most significant of such collections. Friedrich August Stüler built the Alte Nationalgalerie in the form of a Roman temple.

BERLIN MODERNISM HOUSING ESTATES

With their clear minimalist shapes, these six ensembles built in Berlin in 1913 and 1934 by architects such as Bruno Taut, Hans Scharoun and Walter Gropius represent a strong connection to classic modernism.

In the Germany of the Weimar Republic, the focus on a harmonious synthesis between form and function was accompanied by utopian sociopolitical ideals of creating a new architecture to complement a new city and a new society. The housing estates of the Berlin Modernism World Heritage Site comprise six complexes – Gartenstadt Falkenberg, Siedlung Schillerpark, Großsiedlung Britz, Wohnstadt Carl Legien, Weiße Stadt and Großsiedlung Siemensstadt – and appropriately reflect this period of architectural and social turmoil.

In them, modernist architecture is combined with the idea of social housing as an answer to the growing population. The poorer strata of society were to be given a higher standard of living.

Thanks to their clear design, the quality of their architectural compositions and their urban shapes the estates of Berlin Modernism (right: the horseshoe-shaped Großsiedlung Britz) exerted a lasting influence on the development of 20th-century architecture.

LUTHER MEMORIALS IN EISLEBEN AND WITTENBERG

These towns are home to numerous relics of the great reformer Martin Luther (1483–1546). The memorials are in Eisleben – the house where Luther was born and last resided – and in Wittenberg – the Luther House, the Stadtkirche (City Church), the Schlosskirche (Castle Church) and Melanchthon House.

"Out of love and concern for the truth, and with the objective of eliciting it" – this is the start of Luther's Ninety-five Theses of the Reformation. Today they are written in golden letters on the bronze door of the Castle Church. The Reformer's tomb can be found inside as well, before the pulpit. Luther preached at the City Church for more than 30 years all the while encouraging liturgical reform.
The Luther House in the former Augustinian Monastery of Wittenberg university courtyard was his home and place of work for more than 40 years. The Luther Room on the top floor even features some of his original furniture. Today, the Luther House is home to a museum on the history of the Reformation. In Eisleben, the house where Martin Luther was born and the house where he died are also memorials to the life and work of this influential man. Both have been restored in exemplary fashion.

St Mary's Church and Luther's statue on the market square in Wittenberg.

WARTBURG CASTLE

Thanks to its location and architecture, Wartburg Castle high above the Thuringian town of Eisenach is much more than the just a castle. Like no other fortress, it is an outstanding symbol of German history.

"Wait, mountain – you shall become a castle for me!", Ludwig the Leaper is said to have exclaimed in 1067, upon seeing Wartberg mountain. The Wartburg Castle was first mentioned in 1080. The town of Eisenach developed quickly under its protection and soon became the center of the Landgraviate of Thuringia. Landgrave Hermann I (d. 1217) turned the fortress into a grand castle.
The "Sängerkrieg" – a collection of 13th-century Middle High German poems about an alleged minstrels' contest at Wartburg Castle – inspired many poets and musicians including composer Richard Wagner for his opera "Tannhäuser". Martin Luther lived at the castle under the protection of Elector Frederick the Wise from 1521 to 1522, disguised as "Squire Jörg". He began his translation of the New Testament from the Greek here. By the time of the Wartburg Castle Festival in 1817, when German fraternities began gathering there, the castle had become largely derelict and wasn't to be restored until the second half of the 19th century.

The mixture of styles is plain to see to the left here. On the far left in the picture are the Romanesque palace and the castle keep.

BAUHAUS SITES IN WEIMAR AND DESSAU

The Bauhaus was one of Germany's eminent design schools. Most of the Bauhaus sites are in Dessau while only two buildings remain in Weimar.

"Architects, sculptors and painters, we all must return to the crafts", wrote Walter Gropius in 1919, as new director of the State Bauhaus in Weimar. Indeed, the unity of artistic design and craftsmanship that he posited is reflected in the name: "Bauhaus" (building house) was reminiscent of the tradition of the cathedral workshops, which built the great cathedrals of the Middle Ages.
Artists like Paul Klee and Wassily Kandinsky accepted the call to Weimar. Due to political circumstances, however, they were forced to transfer to the more liberal town of Dessau in 1925, where Gropius erected the Bauhaus building, a monument to early industrial design.
The Masters' Houses were also built there. After 1923, the Haus am Horn in Weimar became a model for the residential homes of the future. In 1933, the National Socialists closed the Bauhaus, and many of the artists left for the United States, where the traditions of modernism lived on in the "New Bauhaus".

Of the seven Masters' Houses in Dessau, five remain and have been restored, including the Muche House seen here.

GARDEN KINGDOM OF DESSAU-WÖRLITZ

This World Heritage Site is an "outstanding example of the application of the philosophical principles of the Age of the Enlightenment to the design of a landscape", where six palaces and seven parks form a grand, harmonious ensemble.

In 1764, Duke Leopold III Frederick Franz of Anhalt-Dessau ordered that a large park in the style of English landscape gardens be built on the banks of a former tributary of the Elbe near Wörlitz. The lead garden architect was Johann Friedrich Eyserbeck.

Friedrich Wilhelm von Erdmannsdorff designed the various structures scattered around the landscape based on models of famous buildings from Roman Antiquity, the Italian late-Renaissance and English Classicism. The main building is the Garden Palace of Wörlitz, built between 1769 and 1773, and has been called the cradle

of German classicism. Like other structures in the park – the Flora Temple, synagogue and Gothic house, for example – it creates an interplay with the surrounding gardens.

The Garden Kingdom also includes the palaces and parks Großkühnau, Georgium, Luisium, Sieglitzer Berg, Mosigkau and Oranienbaum.

A number of structures were built among the 112 ha (277 acres) of exotic flowers, shrubs and trees in Wörlitz, for example the Wörlitz Palace (above) and the library (right), which no longer contains any books).

MUSKAUER PARK / PARK MUŻAKOWSKI

A showcase project of German-Polish cultural cooperation as well as a supranational World Heritage Site, Muskauer Park/Park Mużakowski was created in the years 1815 to 1844 by Prince Hermann von Pückler-Muskau. In a vast garden realm, he "painted with nature" using living plants.

Prince Hermann von Pückler-Muskau (1785–1871) was an idiosyncratic figure: a bon-vivant and womanizer, an adventurer and a writer, but above all a garden artist. He was inspired to create a park in the English style after a sojourn in England in 1815. Today, his park straddles the Neisse River, with one-third in Germany and two-thirds in Poland. Visitors can move between the countries via a bridge. The German side features Castle Park, Bathing Park and Mountain Park, while the Polish side boasts

Upper Park, Arboretum and the Braunsdorfer Fields. Also part of the park are structures that harmonize with the landscape such as the Old and New Castles, an orangery built by Semper, a tropical house and a church ruins. The Muskauer Park/Park Mużakowski became a model for landscape architecture in Europe and America.

The Muskauer Park/Park Mużakowski is an idyllic realm of woods, meadows and flowerbeds. From the "meadow of tears", views unfold of the New Castle.

CLASSICAL WEIMAR

Weimar, a small town in Thuringia on the River Ilm, was the epicenter of one of the most significant periods of European culture, "Weimar Classicism", of which Goethe and Schiller are the main representatives.

Goethe's home on the Frauenplan was originally built in around 1709 by a hosiery manufacturer. Goethe moved in as a tenant in 1782, living there until 1786 and again from 1789, after returning from Italy. During this time, the famous poet had the building converted in an Italian style. The "most famous garden house in the world", where the poet lived from 1776 until 1782, is in a park on the River Ilm.

The baroque Herder House was built in 1726. It is named after its occupant, Johann Gottfried von Herder, who lived there with his family from 1776 to 1803. He was the court preacher at the late-Gothic City Church.

Belvedere Palace presents itself in flamboyant rococo style.

Weimar's art collections are housed in the City palace with its distinctive tower. In 1774, Duchess Anna Amalia moved into the Wittums Palace, which was the scene of regular round table discussions. The duchess also turned the Tiefurt manor into a notable meeting place for Weimar society.

Ettersburg Castle, at the northern end of Ettersberg mountain, was the duke's summer residence during Goethe's time. The park was designed based on ideas of Prince Pückler-Muskau. The rococo Belvedere Palace (begun in 1724) was initially planned as a hunting lodge for the dukes.

The Duchess Anna Amalia Library in the Green Castle (1563), which contains one of the most valuable book collections of German classicism, was badly damaged by a fire in 2004, but the historic library with its magnificent rococo hall reopened to the public in late 2007.

One of the most beautiful library spaces in the world: the oval rococo room of the Duchess Anna Amalia Library, which extends over three floors.

Germany

AACHEN CATHEDRAL

Aachen Cathedral is an outstanding example of Carolingian architecture and an important symbolic site in German history: Between 936 and 1531, thirty-one German emperors were crowned here. Charlemagne laid the foundation for the cathedral when he built the palace chapel.

The Palace Chapel, dedicated in about 800, was based on designs by Odo von Metz with an octagonal layout. A two-level ambulatory encircles the vast space beneath its dome, which was later embellished with mosaics. The furnishings in the cathedral are oriented on Roman as well as Byzantine models, an indication of the vastness of Charlemagne's empire.

In subsequent centuries, several extensions and conversions became necessary in order to create space for the coronation ceremonies and pilgrims who thronged to Charlemagne's grave. Particularly impressive are the monumental windows of the Gothic hall choir, which was consecrated in the 15th century.

In the middle of the choir is the precious Shrine of Charlemagne, created in 1200 to 1215. The Chapel itself has largely managed to preserve its appearance since 1200. The Aachen Cathedral treasury holds the most valuable reliquary north of the Alps.

The interior furnishings of Aachen Cathedral are spectacular. The octagonal central structure, for example, is influenced by Byzantine styles (right). Starting in 936, German emperors were crowned on the Emperor's Throne in the western gallery above the octagon (below).

AUGUSTUSBURG AND FALKEN-LUST CASTLES AT BRÜHL

The Archbishop-Elector's Augustusburg Castle and Falkenlust Hunting Lodge are seminal structures of the late baroque and rococo in the Rhineland. Many famous artists from Austria, Bavaria, Italy and France worked on the design of these grand buildings, including Balthasar Neumann.

Augustusburg Castle, located between Bonn and Cologne, was built as a residence for the Archbishop-Elector Clemens August. Construction begain in 1725.

In this building, Johann Conrad Schlaun, François de Cuvilliés and Dominique Girard created a convincing synthesis of the arts that impressively documents a transition in style from baroque to rococo.

The furnishings in the sumptuous staterooms are of the most exquisite quality, and all of the rooms open out to the gardens, bestowing on the residence the character of a maison de plaisance.

Falkenlust Castle, which was begun in 1729 based on plans by Cuvilliés and Leveilly, served as the Archbishop-Elector's falconry lodge. The premises are more intimate in character, yet their furnishings are just as splendid.

The Castle of Augustusburg reveals its full charm and beauty in the harmonious interplay of the baroque gardens.

COLOGNE CATHEDRAL

The Cathedral St Peter and Our Lady in Cologne possesses a purity of High Gothic style despite the 600 years it took to complete it. The world's third-largest cathedral was not finished until 1880.

Cologne Cathedral, 145 m (476 ft) long, 45 m (148 ft) wide and in the central nave 43 m (141 ft) high, is one of the great churches of Christendom and boasts one of the richest treasuries in Germany. Its ambulatories and dimensions were planned for the many pilgrims who came to see the Shrine of the Three Kings.

The plans for the monumental western façade date from 1310 and by 1559, the choir, transept, nave and the base of the southern tower were completed. The cathedral was given its present appearance between 1842 and 1880. The interior of the five-aisled basilica with an ambulatory choir and a wreath of chapels is more than 6,000 sq m (64,560 sq ft); fifty-six pillars carry the roof.

The Shrine of the Three Kings by Nicholas of Verdun is a masterpiece of Rhenish gold work. In the ambulatory is the famous triptych of the Altar of the City Patrons by Stefan Lochner (1440) and the Romanesque Gero Crucifix (10th century). The choir with 104 seats is from the 13th century.

The 157-m (515-ft) spires of Cologne Cathedral near the banks of the Rhine, dominate the Old Town (top). A view over the Hohenzollern Bridge (left) with the equestrian statue of Emperor William II.

ZOLLVEREIN COAL MINE INDUSTRIAL COMPLEX IN ESSEN

Today, mining and heavy industry are mainly a thing of the past in the Ruhr. What remain are the giant shaft towers, machine halls and blast furnaces. One of the most imposing monuments is the former Zollverein Coal Mine in Essen.

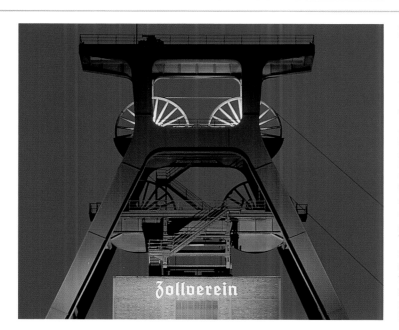

Designed by Fritz Schupp and Martin Kremmer, in its day this mine was the largest and most modern hard coal conveying complex in the world. It was finally shut down in 1986. After the decline of the steel industry, the adjacent coking plant was also closed down in 1993.

The entire industrial complex is now a monument and is used for exhibitions and concerts. The Zollverein Foundation was set up in 1998 with the aim of preserving the monument. A museum route takes visitors through the buildings of the former screening and coal washing plants, and past the machines and conveyor belts that demonstrate the once arduous work done here. The Ruhr Museum, opened in 2009 in the former coal washery, is a "memory and showcase of the new Ruhr metropolis". Transformed by star architect Lord Norman Foster, the former boiler house now features contemporary design at the "Red Dot Design Museum".

The emblem of the Zollverein coal mine is the characteristic Doppelbock winding tower of Shaft XII.

Germany

UPPER MIDDLE RHINE VALLEY

The Upper Middle Rhine Valley is a "cultural landscape of great diversity and beauty", an overall impression created not only by the picturesque river landscape but also by an extraordinary wealth of cultural and historic monuments spanning centuries.

The Upper Middle Rhine Valley is delineated in the south by Bingen on the left bank and Rüdesheim on the right bank, and in the north by Koblenz. This 65-km (40-mi) section of the romantic Rhine gorge features an abundance of well preserved historic buildings that is unlike any other area in Germany. It also has a long wine-growing tradition thanks to its unusually mild climate.

The Rhine Valley has been one of the most important trading routes in Europe for two thousand years. It has also been a vein of cultural exchange between the Mediterranean regions and northern Europe.

Katz Castle, above St Goarshausen.

With its vine-covered slopes, quaint villages and small towns tucked in along the narrow banks, and a large number of hilltop castles this section of the Rhine is considered the apogee of the river's romantic scenery. It has inspired literary figures, painters and musicians for hundreds of years, in particular in the 19th century.

Highlights are Bingen with its Mouse Tower (13th century) at the mouth of the Nahe River, above the Binger Hole; the well-preserved historic cityscapes of the ancient wine villages Rüdesheim and Bacharach; mighty Lorelei rock; the former imperial free city of Boppard with Germany's best-preserved Roman camp; Koblenz, on the confluence of the Rhine and Mosel rivers; and the Rheinstein, Reichenstein, Marksburg, Rheinfels, Katz and Pfalzgrafenstein castles, the latter built on an island in near Kaub.

Castles, palaces and romantic villages characterize the scenery of the Upper Middle Rhine Valley. Right, from the top: the wine village of Bacharach, the Bingen Mouse Tower, and Pfalzgrafenstein Castle near Kaub.

TRIER

Germany's oldest town was founded by Roman Emperor Augustus in about 16 BC and is home to some of the best-preserved ancient buildings north of the Alps. Ancient Trier was one of the largest cities in the Roman Empire, with 80,000 inhabitants. The World Heritage Site comprises Roman monuments as well as the cathedral and the adjacent Church of Our Dear Lady.

The most recognizable landmark of Trier is the Porta Nigra, a colossal city gate with two protruding semicircular towers dating back to the second century. Remnants from ancient Trier, or "Augusta Treverorum", once the capital of the Roman province of Belgica Prima, include the imperial and Barbara thermal baths and the ruins of the amphitheater, built to accommodate 20,000 spectators.

Emperor Constantine the Great took up residence at the Aula Palatina, once part of the imperial palace, from 306 to 312. The Romanesque St Peter Cathedral east of the market square dates back to the fourth century in its oldest parts, making it one of the oldest churches in Germany. Its treasury also boasts some significant pieces of Ottonian art.

Next to the cathedral is the Basilica of Our Dear Lady, completed in 1270 and a jewel of early-Gothic architecture.

In the 11th/12th centuries, the ancient northern gate in the Roman walls of Trier was transformed into the Church of St Simeon. Its name, Porta Nigra ("Black Gate"), dates back to the Middle Ages.

VÖLKLINGEN IRONWORKS

The Völklingen Ironworks are an impressive monument of the industrial age and a memorial to the era of steel and iron production in Saarland. Founded in 1881 by entrepreneur Carl Röchling, it set technological benchmarks in iron smelting for a century until it was finally shut down in 1986.

The principal structure at this "cathedral of the industrial age", the only complete and mostly original ironworks in the world, are the massive blast furnaces that were built between 1882 and 1916. Each of them was once able to produce up to 1,000 tons of raw iron a day.

The ore and the coal were then transported on an extensive network of tracks that traversed an area of more than 7 ha (17 acres). The coking plant, which was set up in 1897, supplied the coke for operating the blast furnaces. Particularly impressive are the colossal blowers here, which chased compressed air heated to more than 1,500°C (2,732°F) into the blast furnaces.

Also worth seeing are the Handwerkergasse (craftsmen's alley) and the Völklingen Ironworks Station of 1893.

In the 19th and 20th centuries, the Völklingen Ironworks were one of the technologically most advanced ironworks in Europe. In the Blower Hall, blower machines with gigantic flywheels once produced enormous amounts of wind for the blast furnaces, which made it possible to increase the furnace temperature to melting point.

MESSEL PIT FOSSIL SITE

Messel Pit, the first UNESCO Natural Heritage Site in Germany, is considered one of the world's most important fossil sites. The sedimentation and lack of oxygen in the water-filled volcanic crater have led to the preservation of fossils dating back some fifty million years.

This 65-hectare (161-acre) pit near Darmstadt features layers of oil shale that contain numerous well-preserved fossils. Together they provide an almost complete picture of the climate, biology, and geology of this area during the Eocene epoch – a period of natural history between sixty and thirty-six million years ago when, after the dinosaurs died out, plants and animals gradually began developing into the flora and fauna we know today. Messel Pit thus provides a unique insight into the early evolution of mammals.

Among the most spectacular finds here are the remains of over seventy early horses, with more than thirty complete skeletons. The skeletons of other vertebrates, meanwhile, were preserved with some soft body parts and even the intact contents of the animals' stomachs.

The finds allowed scientists to draw conclusions about things such as continental drift, land bridges, sedimentation and biospheric evolution.

Preserved in the oil shales of Messel Pit are fossils of primeval insects, reptiles, birds and mammals, some fifty million years old. The primeval horses found here are of particular interest (above).

ABBEY AND ALTENMÜNSTER OF LORSCH

The entrance hall of the former Benedictine Abbey of Lorsch, also known as the "Royal Hall", is the only completely preserved historic building from the Carolingian Empire. Not far from this structure, which dates back to the ninth century, are the remains of the original monastic complex excavated in Altenmünster.

The magnificent entrance hall in this small village between Darmstadt and Worms, as well as the ruins of a 70-m-long (230-ft) Romanesque basilica und other ruins, are all that remain of one of the largest abbeys in the Frankish Empire. Founded by Count Cancor and his mother Williswinda during the reign of Pepin the Short (751–768), the abbey became the burial place of the kings of the East Carolingian Empire. Destroyed by fire in 1090 and rebuilt in the 12th century, the abbey had by the 13th century become one of the wealthiest monastic centers of the late Middle Ages. After its takeover by the archbishopric of Mainz, the abbey lost most of its privileges. It finally closed in 1557, during the Reformation.

Remains of the original abbey were found in Altenmünster, first mentioned in 764, and transferred to Lorsch three years later. A provost was set up here in the 11th century.

The colorful façade of the entrance hall has survived the centuries.

Germany

SPEYER CATHEDRAL

Speyer Cathedral, built during the reign of Emperor Conrad II, was the largest church in the Western Christian world at the time of its construction. The burial place of many rulers from the Salian, Staufen and Habsburg dynasties, the Romanesque basilica also has a great symbolic status.

The history of this ancient imperial city goes back to the Romans, who founded it in the first century before it became an episcopal see in the sixth or seventh century. At the beginning of the 11th century, Emperor Conrad II commissioned Speyer Cathedral as the burial church of the Salians.

The Cathedral Basilica of the Assumption and St Stephen, which boasts six towers, was consecrated in 1061, the year of Conrad's death, by his grandson, Henry IV. The latter had by then enlarged the church considerably in order to demonstrate his claim to political power vis-à-vis the Pope – a conflict that eventually led to the Investiture Controversy. The crypt, completed in 1039, allows access to sixteen tombs of rulers, including the tombs of four Salian emperors.

The Palatinate War of Succession in 1689 brought with it serious destruction, but Napoleon rescued the church from total demolition. Reconstruction began in 1772, but only after World War II was the dignity of the cathedral fully restored.

The crypt of Speyer Cathedral is an imposing hall of columns with groined vaults of yellow and red sandstone.

MONASTIC ISLAND OF REICHENAU

The monastery complex on Reichenau, in Lake Constance, is a unique reminder of clerical culture in the early Middle Ages. The simplicity of the Romanesque buildings is particularly moving within this somewhat melancholic landscape.

The first abbey on Reichenau Island goes back to the itinerant bishop and abbot St Pirmin, who in 724 founded a Benedictine settlement here that became a major spiritual center in Europe. The remains of this first complex indicate a simple hall church with monastic buildings to the north.

The saga of the monastery church of St Mary and St Marcusin Reichenau-Mittelzell began during the Carolingian period. It was first consecrated by Abbot Heito in 816 and was remodeled repeatedly until the 11th century. In its present state it is a strict pillar basilica with twin transepts and an imposing west-facing structure.

St George's abbey church in Oberzell is a plain columned basilica from late-Carolingian times featuring valuable murals from the 10th century. The abbey church of Sts Peter and Paul in Niederzell, built between 1080 and 1134, is a columned basilica with no transept and a choir with three apses.

The late-Carolingian St George's Basilica in Oberzell on Reichenau Island features unique Ottonian wall frescoes with scenes from the life of Jesus Christ.

FRONTIERS OF THE ROMAN EMPIRE

The Upper Germanic and Rhaetian Limes, Hadrian's Wall close to the present-day border between Scotland and England, and the Antonine Wall, which runs across the Scottish Lowlands, form the supranational World Heritage Site "Frontiers of the Roman Empire".

In the first century AD, the Romans began building a fortified border that stretched from the Rhine (near present-day Neuwied) via Bad Ems, Saalburg, Seligenstadt, Miltenberg, Lorch, Aalen and Weißenburg up to the Danube (today's Neustadt in Bavaria). To construct the Upper Germanic and Rhaetian Limes, swathes of forest were cleared, ditches dug, palisade fences built and (up to) 3-m-high (10-ft) walls erected along with 120 Roman forts and 900 watchtowers. The World Heritage Site comprises this frontier line and the adjacent military installations, including nearby civilian sites. Of course settlements developed in these areas and eventually became towns where Roman culture mingled with Celtic and Germanic traditions. The frontier lasted until 260, when it fell under the onslaught of the Alemanii.

Hundreds of towers once guarded the Upper Germanic and Rhaetian Limes. Remains of the walls and reconstructed watchtowers and milestones still indicate the course of the frontier today.

MAULBRONN MONASTERY

Maulbronn is one of the most completely preserved medieval monasteries north of the Alps. According to the legend, a mule is said to have quenched its thirst at a spring here. The monks saw this as a sign from above and founded their abbey near that very spot.

Twelve monks from the Alsace region once began the construction of an abbey here, in the isolation of the Salzach valley near Karlsruhe. Its design was based on Cistercian abbeys in Burgundy. The monks of the order lived and worked here for almost 400 years, erecting one of the most beautiful monasteries in Germany. Their return to traditional monastic ideals brought about new architectural solutions that aimed to omit any form of pageantry or extravagance.

The buildings in the complex combine both Romanesque and Gothic style elements. The triple-aisled, columned basilica, for example, was consecrated in 1178 and later enlarged with late-Gothic vaulting in the 15th century. The adjacent cloister, whose southern section dates back to the 13th century, features a fountain chapel from the 14th century with an interesting fresco in the vault. The abbey's narthex, known as "paradise", was completed in 1220, during the transition from Romanesque to Gothic.

The richly carved choir stalls in the central nave of the abbey church, built in the first half of the 15th century, offered seating for ninety-two monks.

WÜRZBURG RESIDENCE

The Würzburg Residence with Court Gardens and Residence Square is the "synthesis of European baroque". Furnished by the most renowned artists of the day and surrounded by stunning gardens, it is one of the most splendid royal complexes in Europe.

Prince-Bishop Johann Philipp Franz von Schönborn first commissioned the residence's construction in 1720. Responsible for its conception and design was Balthasar Neumann (1687–1753); its construction was taken on by a number of other important contemporary master builders and artists.

The heart of the palace is the Imperial Hall, which features frescoes and

A round basin with a monolith made of tuff dominates the southern garden, which leads to the Court Garden.

Marble putti and stuccowork adorn the magnificent interior of the Court Chapel and its curved gallery, designed by Balthasar Neumann.

monumental ceiling paintings above the staircase by Tiepolo. The central painting measures 18 x 30 m (59 x 98 ft), one of the largest single frescoes ever painted. The restored Hall of Mirrors is also a gem.

The prince-bishops used the vast cellars to store up to 1.4 million liters (370,000 US gallons) of wine. Outside, the beautiful Court Garden was laid out by the court gardener Johann Prokop Mayer in the late 18th century.

Venetian Giovanni Battista Tiepolo's ceiling fresco above the staircase by Balthasar Neumann depicts four continents.

Germany

HISTORIC BAMBERG

The old episcopal and imperial city built on seven hills boasts the largest completely preserved Old Town in Germany. Idyllically situated between branches of the River Regnitz, Bamberg's historic buildings cover virtually all style epochs – from the Middle Ages to the present – and boast a density that is difficult to top.

First documented in 902, Bamberg became an episcopal see in 1007, during the reign of Emperor Henry II. The episcopal church that was built above the ancient castle at the time was later replaced by a four-towered cathedral in the 13th century. It is one of Europe's most attractive buildings from the Middle Ages.

Among its many treasures, the cover on the tomb of Henry II and his wife stands out. It was created by Tilman Riemenschneider. The world-famous Bamberg Rider was sculpted in around 1240, and the western choir houses

The Bamberg Rider in the Cathedral was created by unknown masters from France. It probably depicts King Stephen I of Hungary.

the marble tomb of Pope Clement II, the only papal tomb in Germany. The bishop's palace was the former Alte Hofhaltung (old palace), also built on the cathedral hill between 1571 and 1576.

The garden of the Benedictine abbey, which was founded in 1009 on the Michaelsberg, was designed by Balthasar Neumann in 1742. You enter the "people's town" in the valley through the old town hall, remodeled in the 18th century, or via the Upper Bridge across the Regnitz River. The half-timbered houses of the former fishermen's colony of "Little Venice" are particularly attractive as well.

With its four-towered Cathedral and the Benedictine Michaelsberg Abbey in the background, Bamberg boasts a lively cityscape (top). The old town hall is in the middle of the Regnitz (right).

OLD TOWN OF REGENSBURG WITH STADTAMHOF

The Old Town of Regensburg and the once independent village of Stadtamhof, which is linked with the Old Town by the Steinerne Brücke, is an outstanding example of a central European medieval trading town.

Regensburg developed from the ruins of a Roman fort, the Castra Regina, in the Middle Ages when Prince Arnulf of Bavaria had the entire western suburb and the area around St Emmeram's Abbey encircled by ramparts in 920. The first post-Roman town walls north of the Alps initially excluded the craftsmen's district, but at the end of the 13th century this too was enclosed by fortifications.

The Steinerne Brücke (Stone Bridge), completed by 1146, was for a long time the only stone bridge over the Danube between Ulm and Vienna, a fact that secured Regensburg's rank as an important trading center. The many Romanesque and Gothic patrician mansions that have been preserved here as well as the sizable residential complexes with dynastic towers are examples of an architecture that is unique in its density and condition north of the Alps. Aside from its abundance of early stone buildings, Regensburg also boasts Johannes Kepler's house. Built in 1250, it is the oldest completely preserved wooden house in Germany.

The large Romanesque and Gothic churches and monasteries in Regensburg are outstanding artistic achievements of their time and include places like St Emmeram's Abbey, built on the grave of a saint; the Old Chapel; Niedermünster Abbey; the Benedictine Abbey of St James, founded by Irish monks in 1090; and the cathedral, which is the only church in Bavaria influenced by the French Gothic cathedral styles. The churches of the mendicant orders of Minorites and Dominicans are early architectural examples of a change in religious attitudes in the late Middle Ages.

An important political center in the Holy Roman Empire of the German Nation, this imperial city actually converted to Protestantism in 1542 and fought as a garrison town against Bavaria during the Thirty Years' War. It was plundered and suffered economically, but was largely spared any greater catastrophes over its history. The "Old Town of Regensburg with Stadtamhof" roughly corresponds to the city's size after the final medieval expansion around 1320.

An important criteria for World Heritage status in Regensburg was that the continuous stages of historic development were still intact. Today the "Old Town of Regensburg with Stadtamhof" also includes 984 individual monuments.

The cathedral and the Steinerne Brücke (left) – the only bridge over the Danube here for about 800 years – are the main landmarks of Regensburg.

PILGRIMAGE CHURCH OF WIES

The "Pilgrimage Church of the Scourged Saviour of Wies" is about 20 km (13 mi) north-east of Füssen and an outstanding example of Bavarian rococo architecture. Commonly known as "The Wies" or "Wieskirche", it boasts a stunning location near Steingaden with the Ammergau Alps as a backdrop.

In 1730, the monks of the Premonstratensian Monastery in Steingaden produced a sculpture of Christ for the Good Friday procession. It was later placed on the family altar of a farm near the hamlet of Wies, which belonged of the monastery. When the Savior on the Scourging Column suddenly began to shed tears, the miracle brought about a rush of pilgrims, so the monastery's abbot commissioned the construction of what was to become one of the most beautiful rococo churches in Germany.

The contract was given to architect Dominikus Zimmermann, who had already built the pilgrimage church in Steinhausen. Zimmermann was aided by his brother Johann Baptist, who painted the interior. The successful combination of architecture and decoration achieved a fabulous effect of light and space. The ceiling frescoes are extraordinarily beautiful. Together with the outstanding stuccowork they frame the two-level altar containing the miraculous sculpture.

The stuccowork in the Church of Wies was done by master builder Dominikus Zimmermann (1685–1766) from Wessobrunn.

Switzerland

CONVENT OF ST GALL

The heyday of the Benedictine Convent of St Gall began when it became an imperial abbey in the ninth century. It was also the cornerstone for the convent's famous library, which helped the establishment develop into a renowned place of learning known throughout Europe.

The buildings that make up the Convent of St Gall, which closed in 1805, date mainly from its third era of prosperity in the 17th century (after the "golden" and the "silver" ages from the ninth to the 11th centuries). The oldest remaining part of the original monastic complex is the crypt, which dates from the 10th century and contains the tombs of the bishops of St Gall.

The Abbey Church of St Gallus and St Otmar, a baroque building with a central rotunda, was built between 1755 and 1765 and features a magnificent eastern façade. When the

The rococo library hall in the Convent of St Gall was designed by Caspar Moosbrugger and built in 1758 by Peter Thumb, who also built the abbey church. The glorious rooms hold about 2,000 valuable medieval manuscripts.

twin bishoprics of Chur and St Gall were founded in 1824, the abbey church became a cathedral.

The west wing of the convent is home to the convent's renowned library, with roughly 170,000 books and other articles. Among its medieval treasures is a copy of the "Song of the Nibelungs". The two-level rococo library room with its ceiling frescoes and stuccowork is one of the most stunning athenaeums in the world.

Baroque stuccowork and trompe-l'oeil ceiling paintings are a highlight of the abbey church, whose choir stalls were made by Joseph Anton Feichtmayr.

LAVAUX, VINEYARD TERRACES

Grapes have been cultivated in the terraced landscape of the Lavaux on Lake Geneva for at least 1,000 years. Many of the villages here reflect the development of viticulture over centuries and the landscape is considered one of the most charming in Switzerland.

The Lavaux region extends for about 30 km (19 mi) on the north shore of Lake Geneva, from the eastern suburbs of Lausanne to the Château de Chillon. The World Heritage Site itself comprises the slopes nearest the lake, mostly located between the villages and the lakeshore.

Three suns, say the locals, warm the grapes here: the glowing sun of the day; the reflection of the sun's rays on the glistening surface of the lake; and the warmth of the sun that is stored during the day by the stone walls, which release their energy again at night.

The present-day stone terraces actually go back to the Benedictine and Cistercian monks of the 11th and 12th centuries. Their estimated total length is roughly 400 to 450 km (249 to 280 mi). Of its core area, which measures almost 900 ha (2,240 acres), about 570 ha (1,408 acres) are vineyards. The fourteen communes of the Lavaux produce white wine with the appellations contrôlées Villette, Saint-Saphorin, Dézaley, Epesses and Chardonne.

Lake Geneva and the Alps – a grandiose backdrop for the Lavaux wine terraces.

CASTLES OF BELLINZONA

The three castelli in the charming Old Town of Bellinzona in the canton of Ticino are a unique example of medieval fortress building, bestowing a singular character on the appearance of the village.

The reason for building these fortresses was the fact that several routes connecting northern Europe with Italy passed through the narrow Ticino River gorge in the southern Alps. The largest of the three castles, Castelgrande, is on a hill within the town and was built in the 13th century before being enlarged between 1486 and 1489 by the Sforza Dukes of Milan in order to block the advance of the Swiss Confederates.

The smaller Castello di Montebello, perched on the side of a hill, was given its present look in the second half of the 15th century. Castello di Sasso Corbaro was built in just six months in 1479 on the ridge of a mountain in the south-east, 230 m (755 ft) above the town.

The strategic defense system was complemented by the Murata, a city wall up to 5 m (16 ft) thick with twin galleries stacked on top of each other and extending all the way down to the river. Despite the fortifications, however, Bellinzona eventually fell to the Swiss Confederation in 1516, after fierce fighting.

The largest of the three castles in Bellinzona, the Castelgrande, was built on a hill within the city walls in the 13th century and later enlarged.

MONTE SAN GIORGIO

Pyramid-shaped Monte San Giorgio is one of the world's richest depositories of fossils from the Triassic period – 245–230 million years ago. The fossilized remains of numerous marine animals have even been found here, among them saurians measuring up to 6 m (20 feet) in length.

Nowhere else in Switzerland have such well-preserved fossils been found as in this remote region around the 1,096-m (3,596-ft) Monte San Giorgio. The most spectacular finds are predominantly marine reptiles such as the Ticinosuchus and Ceresiosaurus ("Ceresio" being the local name for Lake Lugano). The finds were made in five successive layers of earth, together documenting a complete chapter of our planet's history. This relatively short period in geological terms actually witnessed such great evolution with regard to flora and fauna that to speak of an eruption in species types is no exag-geration. Because the lagoon in which these animals lived was separated from the open sea by a reef but still close to the mainland, Monte San Giorgio has also yielded fossils of land-based plants and animals. Furthermore, the fossils are completely intact and exceptionally well preserved. Some of the most beautiful examples are on display in the small museum at Meride town hall.

Around 20 cm (8 in) long, this Pachy-pleurosaurus, a Triassic sea saurian, is just one of the specimens found at Monte San Giorgio.

Switzerland

LA CHAUX-DE-FONDS / LE LOCLE: WATCHMAKING TOWN PLANNING

La Chaux-de-Fonds and Le Locle, twin cities located at an altitude of 1,000 m (3,281 ft) in the Swiss Canton of Neuchâtel, are prime examples of town planning and architecture dedicated entirely to the needs of the growing watchmaking industry, which gained international renown in just a few decades.

La-Chaux-de-Fonds and Le Locle to the north became twin towns due to their comparable political, economic and social situations as well as their geographic proximity.

As early as the 18th century, at the same time agriculture began its rise in importance, artisan businesses also experienced strong development in the Neuchâtel Jura – in particular watchmaking. Le Locle is known as the cradle of the Swiss watchmaking industry.

Both towns had to be rebuilt after fires in the 18th and 19th centuries, but their development illustrates an important chapter in Swiss industrial history.

When La Chaux-de-Fonds fell victim to fire, new workshops, factories and housing for artisans went up, all laid out on a rectangular grid. The setup guaranteed the rationality, efficiency and profitability expected for the precision production of watches.

BENEDICTINE CONVENT OF ST JOHN AT MÜSTAIR

The largest preserved cycle of paintings from the Carolingian Age can be found deep in the Grisons Alps.

The Convent of St John is located in the Val Müstair at an altitude of 1,240 m (4,068 ft). Founded by Charlemagne in about 785, it is a superb example of Carolingian architecture.

The convent buildings, mostly dating from the Middle Ages, are grouped around two inner courtyards. The heart of the complex is the roughly 1,200-year-old Abbey Church of St John, which was remodeled at the end of the 15th century as a late-Gothic hall church. Inside, it boasts original frescoes from the time of the convent's founding. They extend around the interior as five friezes depicting scenes

from the life of King David and Jesus Christ. The Last Judgment is illustrated on the western wall. The three apses and the eastern wall of the church were painted over in 1165 and 1180, with the unknown artist adopting the themes of the Carolingian frescoes.

The fresco in the central apse of the Convent Church of Müstair (above right) is the most famous motif in the cycle of paintings created in this church around 800 (above). It illustrates Salome dancing at Herod's feast and the head of John the Baptist. Right is the cemetery near the Holy Cross Chapel.

RHAETIAN RAILWAY IN THE ALBULA / BERNINA LANDSCAPES

This cross-border World Heritage Site straddling Switzerland and Italy features the historic Albula and Bernina railway lines as monuments to technological achievements and includes the surrounding landscapes.

More than 100 years old, these historic railway lines are superlative examples of the successful opening up of the alpine region. The 62-km (39-mi) Albula line was put into service in 1904, and runs from Thusis in Grisons to St Moritz, surmounting a difference in elevation of about 1,000 m (3,281 ft). The trains run on one of the architecturally most sophisticated narrow-gauge lines in the world, navigating 144 viaducts and bridges as well as forty-two galleries and tunnels on their route, including the 6-km (3.5-mi) Albula Tunnel. The 61-km (38-mi) Bernina line was completed in 1910, linking St Moritz with the Italian town of Tirano. It runs across the Bernina Pass at an elevation of 2,253 m (7,392 ft), navigating thirteen tunnels and galleries and fifty-two bridges and viaducts on grades of up to seven degrees.

The red cars of the Bernina and Albula railways snake their way across dizzying viaducts (left, the Landwasser Viaduct; below, en route to the Albula Pass).

SWISS TECTONIC ARENA SARDONA

The region around the 3,056-m (10,026-ft) Piz Sardona on the borders of the cantons of St Gallen, Glarus and Grisons is an example of a collision of continental plates and the dramatic effects of tectonic forces.

The Glarus Overthrust is the central feature of this protected area covering a region of 328 ha (810 acres) and including seven peaks above 3,000 m (9,900 ft). Twenty or thirty million years ago, a layer of rock about 15 km (9 mi) thick was pushed up from the Anterior Rhine Valley over younger rock strata. Along the thrust line, 250 to 300 million-year-old green and brown verrucano rock lies on top of 35 to 50 million-year-old brownish-grey flysch. The overlap begins in the valley of the Anterior Rhine and culminates in the 3,000-m (9,900-ft) Haus-stock, Sardona and Ringelspitz chain of peaks before sinking away to the north. The Tectonic Arena Sardona also includes important biotopes such as high moorland, flood plains and the oldest colony of resettled ibexes in Switzerland. Other geotopes here are the Martinsloch in the Tschingelhorn range, the copper mine on the Mürtschenalp, and the Segnesboden, a floodplain in the Murgtal formed by glaciers in the Ice Age.

The Piz Sardona is highest point in the tectonic area of the same name.

Austria

Johann Bernhard Fischer von Erlach

The son of a sculptor, Fischer von Erlach (1656–1723) virtually grew up with the art form. Following a stay in Rome, where he became acquainted with sculptor and master builder Gian Lorenzo Bernini, Erlach devoted himself to architecture, becoming one of the most prominent architects of the Austrian baroque. He was responsible for the original design of Schönbrunn Palace – though little is left after various renovations – and he participated in building several churches in Salzburg (Trinity, Ursuline, Collegiate, St John's Hospital churches) as well as several city palaces in Vienna (Strattmann, Batthyány, Trautson, Schwarzenberg palaces, Winter Palace

HISTORIC CITY CENTER OF VIENNA

In many European cities the historic buildings, and in particular those from the years of rapid industrial expansion, had to make room for large-scale building projects. Not so in Vienna, where the splendid architectural legacy has remained largely untouched by modernization.

The abundance of stunning buildings and monuments in Vienna's historic center reflects three periods of European cultural and political development: the Middle Ages, the baroque and the Gründerzeit (the period of rapid industrial expansion in the late 19th century). The World Heritage Site also includes the Ringstrasse, which contains the heart of the city, with its grand buildings from the late 19th century, and a so-called "buffer zone" in the suburbs.

As both the royal residence of the Habsburg dynasty and the capital of the Austro-Hungarian dual monarchy, the metropolis on the Danube was for many centuries a political, intellectual and cultural center – for literature, theater, fine art, music and even psychoanalysis. When World War I began, Vienna had more inhabitants than it does today. It was one of the largest cities in the world.

The imperial layout is also reflected in numerous historic buildings and art treasures. Worth mentioning here are St Stephen's Cathedral, the Hofburg Palace, the Museum of Art History, Josephsplatz with the massive Austrian National Library, the Augustinian Church with the Capuchins' Crypt, the Spanish Riding School, St Charles's Church, the Secession, the Vienna State Opera, the Burgtheater and Belvedere Palace. Last but not least, Vienna is a city of coffee houses, and has been ever since the Turkish Siege of 1683.

St Stephen's Cathedral, rising high above the cityscape, is one of the preeminent Gothic buildings in Austria. In the foreground is the mighty dome of St Peter's Church.

of Prince Eugene). The 80-m-long (262-ft) and 20-m-high (66-ft) Grand Hall of the National Library in the Hofburg Palace is a jewel of baroque room design and also his work.

St Charles's Church in Vienna, built from 1716 to 1737, is regarded as Fischer's masterpiece. With its strictly composed shapes and elements bor-

rowed from antiquity, Romanesque baroque and baroque classicism, the cupola structure reveals a brand new version of the baroque. It clearly dissociates itself from the buoyant shapes of his contemporary, Lukas von Hildebrandt, and with its monumental lines it has become the symbol of the Habsburgs' display of power.

The Grand Hall of the Austrian National Library in Hofburg Palace was built by Fischer von Erlach. The largest baroque library in Europe, it houses more than 200,000 volumes as well as an historical collection of globes.

Far left: Johann Bernhard Fischer von Erlach in a copper engraving created in 1719 by Johann Adam Delsenbach.

St Charles's Church, designed by Johann Bernhard Fischer von Erlach with a dome, triumphal columns and side towers, is one of the most important baroque structures in Vienna.

The State Opera House, built on the Ring between 1861 and 1869 in neo-Renaissance style, is one of the world's most famous opera houses.

Other grand buildings on the Ring include the parliament with the Pallas Athena Fountain and allegorical figures of the legislature and executive branches.

Austria

HISTORIC CITY CENTER OF VIENNA

Hofburg Palace was once the city residence of the Habsburgs. It was continuously enlarged with additional tracts and wings.

The Austrian National Library (above: the Grand Hall) was commissioned by Emperor Charles VI in 1722 and built by Johann Bernhard Fischer von Erlach and his son.

The Spanish Riding School was not opened to the general public until after World War I. It is one of the oldest institutions for classic dressage.

Hofburg Palace, seen here in the evening light, still bears witness to the power of the Habsburg rulers, who filled their capital with elegant buildings until the end of the monarchy in 1918.

SCHÖNBRUNN PALACE

Schönbrunn Palace, the former summer residence of the Habsburgs, illustrates in its monumental dimensions the wealth and power of this important dynasty.

Emperor Charles VI commissioned architect Johann Bernhard Fischer von Erlach with the project of designing Schönbrunn. Erlach originally came up with a giant complex that would far surpass even Versailles. Empress Maria Theresa had the still incomplete building converted into her residence starting in 1744, and it was ultimately completed by Nikolaus Pacassi in the neoclassical style.

The transformation left little of the original structures intact. By 1737, the flat roof, which was concealed behind a balustrade richly adorned with statues, was replaced by the current roofs.

The paths in Schönbrunn Palace Park are lined by countless baroque statues.

In 1744, the clerestory window was installed above the central risalit, and the balconies and the stairs were put in place, but Fischer's domed central structure was destroyed in the process. Of the interior decorations, only the "Blue Stairs" remain.

Commissioned with furnishing the palace interior, Johann Hetzendorf also expanded and transformed the park that had been laid out by Jean Trehet as early as 1695. The Palace Chapel, state and private rooms, mirror galleries and cabinets therefore display the finest decorations of the late rococo.

The forecourt of Schönbrunn is truly imperial in its dimensions (top right). The Gloriette, an early-neoclassical colonnaded structure with a central section resembling a triumphal arch, sits atop Schönbrunn Mountain – a hill above Schönbrunn Palace Park (right).

WACHAU CULTURAL LANDSCAPE

The Wachau is a water gap in the Danube between the Benedictine Abbey of Melk and the town of Krems. The river and hills, vineyards and orchards, medieval villages and small towns, and castles and abbeys create a cultural landscape reminiscent of the Mediterranean.

The attractions along this stretch of the steep, narrow valley of the Wachau begin in the west with the grand baroque Melk Abbey and the mighty twin towers of the domed cathedral – the "jewel" of the area. On the way, villages of fruit orchards and vineyards, picturesque castles, fortress ruins, palaces and churches line the river.

The little village of Willendorf is also here, a place that became famous far beyond national borders thanks to one of the most significant finds from

On a rocky promontory, Melk Abbey rises high above the Danube with its magnificent baroque church and the famous abbey library.

the Paleolithic Age: the so-called Venus of Willendorf. Passing through the popular wine-growing villages of Spitz and Weißenkirchen, visitors arrive in Dürnstein, where the steep banks require sturdy shoes to reach the abbey below the castle ruins. The abbey's slender, late-baroque tower is one of the most elegant of its kind. Beyond Dürnstein, the water gap widens, affording views right up to Krems, a medieval town with the Gothic structures of the Gozzo Palace, the Dominican Church und the Piarist Church. The Abbey of Göttweig, a solemn complex of buildings saluting from on high forms the serene finish of any Wachau excursion.

An emblem of the Wachau Valley is Dürnstein with its castle ruins, Renaissance palace, baroque abbey and the former convent of Poor Clares (top left). Only a few miles away is the vineyard town of Weißenkirchen (left).

Austria

HISTORIC CITY CENTER OF SALZBURG

Salzburg's Old Town is a baroque jewel, where prince-bishops made fabulous fortunes mining salt and built magnificent churches and palaces throughout the 17th and 18th centuries.

Numerous religious buildings still testify to the reign of the lords spiritual who once ruled Salzburg. In the 17th century, two archbishops were primarily responsible for shaping the image of the town, which hugs the Mönchsberg and Kapuzinerberg mountains where the Hohensalzburg fortress is perched: Wolf Dietrich von Raitenau and Johann Ernst von Thun. Salzburg owes its baroquification to Raitenau. He called in master builders from Italy, including Vincenzo Scamozzi, a student under Palladio, and Santino Solari, who built Salzburg's St Rupert's Cathedral, whose bright

Wrought-iron symbols of various guilds hang above the businesses in the famous Getreidegasse. On January 27, 1756, composer Wolfgang Amadeus Mozart was born here.

façade and octagonal dome still dominate the city's skyline. Thun called Fischer von Erlach to Salzburg to build the Collegiate, Ursuline and Trinity churches here.
Stunning secular mansions were also built, including Mirabell Palace with its orangery, and Hellbrunn Palace, which boasts beautifully painted interiors. Characteristic of the Old Town are also the nested inner courtyards and alleyways, the so-called "through houses".

"The heart of the heart of Europe" is how Hugo von Hofmannsthal once described the capital of the Salzburger Land. Hohensalzburg fortress, one of the largest and most imposing in Europe, was built back in the 11th century and enlarged many times over the years. It looks down over the cathedral and other towers of the city on the Salzach River.

The Mirabell Garden surrounding Mirabell Palace was designed by Fischer von Erlach. In 1730, it was transformed into a baroque garden, emphasizing its longitudinal axis, which oriented the park toward the Cathedral and Hohensalzburg fortress (in the background). Its characteristic elements are a central fountain and groups of sculptures, including historical gnomes.

Hellbrunn Palace was commissioned in 1612 by Count Markus Sittikus of Hohenems, cousin and successor of Salzburg's Archbishop Wolf Dietrich of Raitenau, who wanted a "villa suburbana". It was completed in 1615 in the district of Morzg. One of the wall paintings in the music room, known as "Octagon", boasts beautiful frescoes by Donato Mascagni. They are said to depict the archbishop as Knight of the Carnation (top). Above is the stunning park with its extensive water gardens and fountains.

Austria

FERTÖ / NEUSIEDLERSEE CULTURAL LANDSCAPE

The region around Lake Neusiedl on the Austria-Hungary border is a unique biosphere reserve and an ancient agricultural landscape.

Lake Neusiedl, of which three-quarters belong to Austria and one-quarter to Hungary, was on the ancient trading route between the Adriatic and the Baltic. As such it was a meeting point of cultures. Relics of these times are archaeological monuments, ancient sanctuaries, vineyards and palaces. An agricultural landscape was created here by deforesting, draining and grazing the land. Economic gain in harmony with the preservation of natural habitats was the objective.

The slightly saline lake located at the rim of the small Hungarian lowland region is completely encircled by a belt of reeds and salt marshes up to 3 km (2 mi) wide in places. The shallow waters here are rich in fish stocks, offering a habitat to rare species of birds and serving as a resting place for migratory birds.

Since 2001, the two national parks of Neusiedler See/Seewinkel in Austria and Fertö-Hanság in Hungary, plus several Austrian communes and the Hungarian Esterházy Palace in Fertöd have formed a single supranational World Heritage property.

These huts are hidden in Rust Bay by the dense belt of reeds.

HALLSTATT-DACHSTEIN / SALZKAMMERGUT CULTURAL LANDSCAPE

The little village of Hallstatt in the Salzkammergut region gave its name to an entire culture, when excavations from 1846 to 1899 uncovered a well-stocked burial site from the early Iron Age (800–500 BC). The World Heritage Site, however, also encompasses the grandiose mountain landscape as well as the important cultural and architectural monuments of the region.

When Johann Georg Ramsauer began his first excavations on the prehistory of Central Europe at the foot of the Dachstein Mountains in 1846, tens of thousands of invaluable artifacts were unearthed that documented the transition from the European Bronze Age to the early Iron Age.

The so-called Hallstatt Culture ranged from south-eastern Europe through the alpine region and southern and western Germany as far as southern France. It was based around rock salt mining and the mining and smelting of vast deposits of iron ore. Prosperous economic centers flourished out of these prehistoric villages tucked high in the mountain range.

Hallstatt, where early Iron-Age artifacts were excavated, became the name of the prehistoric culture discovered here.

SEMMERING RAILWAY

The Semmering Railway is a masterpiece from the pioneering days of railway construction. It was the first in the world to traverse a mountain pass, and was soon regarded as a harmonious synthesis of technology and nature.

The easternmost and lowest of all the great alpine passes is the Semmering, between Styria and Lower Austria. After the opening of the first railway line between Vienna and Gloggnitz, back in May 1842, an extension was ordered by imperial decree to cross the Semmering up to Mürzzuschlag.

Carl Ritter von Ghega plotted the more than 41-km-long (25-mi) route and its construction began in 1848. Because the master builder vehemently rejected structures made of steel and iron, the entire track was built on about sixty-five million bricks and stone blocks. At the climax of the construction period, up to 20,000 people were employed here every day. After first trial runs, scheduled operation of trains across the Semmering was ceremonially inaugurated on July 17, 1854. From then on, trains steamed at a speed of about 6 km/h (4 mph) across the pass carrying hundreds of tourists. Excursions over the Semmering soon became a popular leisure activity for the Viennese.

The course of the track reaches its highest altitude (898 m/2,946 ft) in the 1,430-m-long (4,692-ft) main tunnel. The fifteen tunnels have a total length of 5,420 m (17,783 ft) and the sixteen viaducts cover 1,502 m (4,928 ft).

HISTORIC GRAZ

The Habsburgs certainly left their mark on the historic heart of the Styrian capital, where local traditions meld with influences from the surrounding regions.

Graz – Austria's second-largest city – boasts one of the best-preserved historic Old Towns in Central Europe. Slovenes originally built a castle on top of 473-m-high (1,552-ft) Castle Mountain in 800. Today, only the clock tower from 1561 (the clock dates from 1712) recalls a later Renaissance fortress that was destroyed by Napoleon.

At the south-eastern foot of Castle Mountain is the old town of Graz with its sea of red-tiled roofs. Buildings from various centuries characterize this part of the city. The Gothic St Agidius Cathedral, for example, and the Kaiserburg (Imperial Castle), with its superb late-Gothic double spiral staircase, date back to the 15th cen-

The Gemaltes Haus (painted house) – also known as Herzogshof – in Herrengasse features superb frescoes.

tury. The Landhaus, with its magnificent arcaded courtyard, was built in 1567 by Domenico dell'Aglio as an assembly house for Styrian estates. It is now the seat of the Styrian state parliament and one of the most important Renaissance structures outside Italy.

The Landeszeughaus, built by Antonio Solar in 1643/44 as an arms depot to fend off Turkish incursions, boasts a still complete arsenal of weapons with the largest collection of its kind in the world. The University of the Styrian capital was founded in 1586. It was from here that the Counter-Reformation began in Austria.

Tradition and modernity stand side by side in Graz. Top left: A view from the Franciscan church to the Castle Mountain. Middle: Herrengasse. Bottom: The floating shell island in the River Mur, a unified work of art by New York artist Vito Acconci held in place by steel cables and accessible via a jetty.

Poland

CASTLE OF THE TEUTONIC ORDER IN MALBORK

Situated in the beautiful Polish county of Malbork, this castle was the headquarters of the influential knights of the Teutonic Order between 1309 and 1466. The brick complex on the Nogat River is one of the most impressive medieval castles in Europe.

In 1276 the knights of the Teutonic Order began work expanding an old Prussian castle about 60 km (37 mi) south-east of present-day Gdańsk. Malbork then became the monastic headquarters in 1280. It was from this base that the knights began their conquest and conversion of Prussia, equipped with a range of papal and imperial privileges. When the seat of the Grand Master was moved from Venice to Malbork in 1309, the Teutonic Order's territory already reached far into the Baltic states and as far as southern and central Germany. During the Reformation it was converted into a hereditary duchy under Polish rule. Following severe damage during World War II, reconstruction work was carried out in the 1960s and 1970s using old drawings. Today the halls, chapels, corridors and courtyards contain extensive museums with valuable medieval treasures.

After 700 years and a number of extensions and conversions, Malbork is now the largest brick castle in the world.

MEDIEVAL TOWN OF TORUŃ

This city on the Vistula River owes its origins to the Teutonic Order, which built a magnificent castle complex here in the 13th century. Toruń also joined the Hanseatic League towards the end of that century.

The knights of the Teutonic Order built a castle here in the 13th century that ultimately developed into a flourishing centre of trade in the 14th century with its own merchant fleet for commerce with the Netherlands. The First and the Second Peace agreements of Toruń, between the Teutonic Order and Poland, were concluded here in 1411 and 1466, respectively, but residents of Toruń had burnt down the Teutonic Order's castle in 1454 (the ruins of which remain today), and the town finally became an independent city-state under the sovereignty of the Polish king. The town has continually changed its appearance over the centuries, as is evidenced by the Gothic patrician houses, the baroque and classical town houses and the prestigious palatial residences dating from the 19th century.
Construction of the Old Town Hall began in 1259. The birthplace of Nicolaus Copernicus (1473–1543) dating from the 15th century also survived the years. Churches such as St John's Cathedral (1260–1480) and St Mary's Church are among the town's other worthy attractions.

The Catholic St Mary's Church was built in the 14th century and is just one of the town's many impressive churches.

MUSKAUER PARK / PARK MUŻAKOWSKI

The supranational World Heritage Site Muskau Park sits directly on the Neisse River, which forms the border between Germany and Poland. Created by Prince Hermann von Pückler-Muskau in the mid-19th century, it is one of the loveliest landscaped parks in Europe.

About two-thirds of the park's 700 ha (1730 acres) lies on the east bank of the Neisse River in the Polish municipality of Leknica. The Polish part was linked in 2003 with the German section in Bad Muskau on the other side of the river by the lovingly restored historical double bridge. The bridge once again links territories separated by the Iron Curtain since 1945, as the park was originally intended to do by its designer.
Prince von Pückler-Muskau was a passionate landscape gardener who built this unique park here between 1815 and 1844. He had been influenced by English horticulture during a visit to England between 1826 and 1829. Unlike other comparable parks of the age, this one was not meant to be reminiscent of an exotic landscape but to emphasize the character of the local countryside, hence the predominantly European selection of plants.

Architecture and nature in harmony – the viaduct over Sarah's Walk surrounded by old oak trees in the Polish section.

CENTENNIAL HALL IN WROCŁAW

The Wrocław Centennial Hall by Max Berg is one of the most important examples of modernist architecture. Built out of reinforced concrete between 1911 and 1913, it was the largest hall of its kind in the world when it was completed – its dome spans 65 m (201 ft).

The Centennial Hall was built to commemorate the Battle of Leipzig in 1813, a decisive battle against the forces of Napoleon that led to a hasty retreat of the French troops. Its functional construction marks a departure from the more elaborate shapes of Historicism. As was the intention of architect Max Berg (1870–1947), this conference and exhibition hall makes a sober and austere impression. It has four entrances that lead to the central area which features the grandiose 42-m (138-ft) dome.
Critics initially derided the hall as a "cardboard box", while it's advocates compared it with the Pantheon or the Hagia Sophia. In addition to its symbolic significance as a war memorial, the hall had a more tangible social purpose as well: providing a venue for sporting, cultural and social events for a large section of the population.

The Centennial Hall with its magnificent dome can accommodate 6,000 people. It is situated in the Exhibition Grounds.

HISTORIC CENTER OF WARSAW

Poland's capital was largely destroyed during World War II, but a campaign for the meticulous reconstruction of the historic center took place between 1949 and 1963. The whole country contributed to the program.

By the time of its liberation in 1945, more than three-quarters of the buildings in the Polish capital had been turned to rubble by the Germans, but the Polish population began swiftly with the enormous efforts required to reconstruct it. They started with the restoration of countless historic buildings from the Gothic to the classical eras in the historic Old Town (Stare Miasto) and New Town (Nowe Miasto) districts. The historic city center once again features the traditional covered marketplace and the building façades are adorned with elaborate Renaissance and baroque elements.

Warsaw's Royal Castle with its 60-m-high (199-ft) clock tower was given its early-baroque character between 1598 and 1619.

Warsaw's early-baroque Royal Castle, the reconstruction of which began in 1971, dominates the Castle Square with its Zygmunt's Column from 1644. In addition to a number of other reconstructed historical buildings, the adjoining New Town with its restored 15th-century edifices is home to the elegant baroque Krasiński Palace. The New Town market is dominated by the 17th-century Church of St Casimir.

The market square in Warsaw's Old Town (above left) dates from the 13th century and the patrician houses around it were built following a fire that destroyed the city in 1607. The interior of Warsaw's Royal Castle (left: the Great Hall) exhibits classical style elements.

Poland

Veit Stoss

Originally from the German town of Horb am Neckar, Veit Stoss (ca. 1448–1533) settled in Cracow in 1477 following sojourns in Swabia and the Upper Rhine area as a wandering apprentice. It was here that this important German late-Gothic sculptor was given the opportunity to exhibit the extent of his masterful skills.

CRACOW CITY CENTER

Due to its importance as a distribution center for cloth, Cracow became Poland's richest city during the Middle Ages. It was also an important center of culture.

Cracow was the capital of Poland until 1596 as well as the venue for the coronation of kings from the 11th to the 18th centuries. The Royal Castle and the cathedral perch atop Wawel Hill as testimony to that era.

During its heyday between the 12th and 17th centuries, the historic center was given its shape by master builders and artists from all over Europe. The market square, for example, is one of the largest medieval squares in Europe. It features the 13th-century cloth halls as well as the Gothic St Mary's

Wawel Cathedral combines a variety of styles from different eras. The main Gothic section is surrounded by twenty-one chapels that display Renaissance and baroque style elements.

Basilica, which dates from the 14th century. Some of the greatest minds of the Middle Ages also taught at the university here, founded in the 14th century and boasting a precious Gothic cloister. They made Cracow one of the intellectual and cultural centers of Europe. Numerous Gothic, Renaissance, and baroque churches and monasteries bear witness to the city's rich history. The Kazimierz district, once home to a thriving Jewish population, has several synagogues and Jewish cemeteries that have survived.

Right: City hall tower, the Cloth Halls, and St Mary's Basilica.

The high altar in Cracow's St Mary's Church was his first masterpiece. The altarpiece alone, with two inner and two outer panels, set a new standard for the time with its magnificent dimensions: 11 m/35 ft wide and 13 m /43 ft high. The dynamic gestures and intense expressions of the figures, the realistic details, and the narrative impact of the scenes are all testimony to the superior artistic quality of the work. Veit Stoss spent twelve years completing the altar and its carved centerpiece.

Cracow's St Mary's Church also houses the earliest monumental crucifix by this master sculptor, thought to have been created after 1496 while he was living in St Sebald, Nuremberg — apparently trying to make money through more dubious means. As a result of his activities during this time he was tainted as a fraudster by 1503, but his artistic fame outlived his disgrace. Veit Stoss produced other outstanding works while in Nuremberg, including the lovely piece "Angel's Greeting" in the St Lorenz Church.

Veit Stoss created the high altar (far left) in the presbytery of St Mary's Church in Cracow between 1477 and 1489. The centerpiece depicts The Death of the Virgin, surrounded by the twelve Apostles. When opened, the side panels portray six scenes from the Joys of the Virgin; the closed panels feature twelve scenes from the Sorrows of the Virgin.

Poland

THE CHURCHES OF PEACE IN JAWOR AND ŚWIDNICA

The Protestant Churches of Peace in Jawor and Świdnica are the largest half-timbered religious buildings in Europe.

The Peace of Westphalia brought an end to the Thirty Years' War in 1648, after which the Protestants in Habsburg-ruled Silesia were permitted to build their churches under specific conditions. They had to be situated outside of the town walls and were to be built of wood, clay, sand and straw only. Bell towers were forbidden. The followers of the new faith adhered to these exterior constraints, the interior decorations being all the more magnificent as a result.

The plain façade of the Church of Peace in Świdnica boasts valuable ceiling paintings from the late 17th century and houses a large organ. The baroque high altar was added in 1752. The interior of the church, including the two- and three-storey galleries and boxes for the aristocracy, was able to accommodate up to 7,500 people. The interior of the Church of Peace in Jawor is also breathtaking in its beauty.

The paintings on the galleries of the Church of Peace in Jawor (above) depict scenes from the Old and New Testaments. The elaborate pulpit from 1729 in the Church of Peace in Świdnica is by Gottfried August Hoffmann (right).

AUSCHWITZ BIRKENAU: GERMAN NAZI CONCENTRATION AND EXTERMINATION CAMP (1940–1945)

This site's walls, platforms, barbed wire fences, gas chambers and cremation ovens are a monument to the appalling crimes once committed by the Germans.

The construction of the Auschwitz I concentration camp was ordered in April 27, 1940, with the first Polish prisoners arriving by June. The camp was later known as Auschwitz Birkenau following completion of the extensions a year later.

Starting in 1941 this was the site of the extermination camps that were to put the "Final Solution" into effect, namely the complete extermination of Europe's Jews. Auschwitz III, built in 1942 close to the village of Dwory, served as a labor camp from which the German company I.G. Farben recruited those prisoners deemed healthy and fit enough to work.

When the troops of the Red Army reached the Auschwitz camps on January 27, 1945, they found roughly 7,650 inmates there. Approximately one million people were murdered in Auschwitz alone.

Many of those deported to Auschwitz were led off to the gas chambers, referred to as the "bath facilities", directly after their arrival.

KALWARIA ZEBRZYDOWSKA

After construction of a monastery at the beginning of the 17th century, Kalwaria Zebrzydowska became a place of great spiritual significance as a pilgrimage destination. It has remained virtually unchanged to this day.

In 1600, Cracow's Voivode Nikolaj Zebrzydowski (a duke) had a small Church of the Crucifixion built on a hill close to Wadowice, the birthplace of the later Pope John Paul II (1920–2005). It was based on the example of the Basilica of the Holy Cross in Jerusalem and was accompanied by the founding of a Bernardine monastery. A community of pilgrims, named after Zebrzydowski, quickly developed here thereafter.

Zebrzydowski's intention was to recreate the holy sites of Jerusalem in Poland. Designed by Giovanni Bernardoni and Paul Baudarth, forty-two churches and chapels were built between Mount Lanckorona and the "Zar" hill. It was thus Poland's first replica of Mount Calvary near Jerusalem. Extensions were made to the monastery in 1655 and the monastery church between 1692 and 1720 to accommodate the tremendous number of pilgrims coming to Kalwaria Zebrzydowska.

The Franciscan monastery Kalwaria Zebrzydowska is a late-baroque and rococo construction. The organ is one of the most impressive decorative elements in the monastery church.

WIELICZKA SALT MINE

The first of over 200 mining operations in the foothills of the Carpathians were dug back in the Middle Ages. More than 25 million cubic meters (33 million cubic yds) of "white gold" have been mined here since the mid-13th century.

The Polish kings owed the greater part of their wealth to the abundant salt deposits at Wieliczka in southern Little Poland, around 15 km (9 mi) southeast of Cracow. The massive underground galleries in Europe's oldest salt mine extend over a total of nearly 300 km (186 mi) at depths of up to 315 m (1,034 ft) on more than nine levels.

A museum comprising several subterranean spaces displays both excavated finds as well as the historic machinery and technology used by the miners. The highlight of the site, however, which also included a health center for the treatment of respiratory disease, is without doubt the 13th-century Chapel of Saint Kinga, wife of Bolelaw the Chaste. Built at an impressive depth of 101 m (331 ft), this and two other chapels feature altars and sculptures carved out of salt by the miners. A ventilation system protects the valuable sculptures from damage by moisture.

Mass is still held in the Chapel of St Kinga, carved out of salt by the miners on the second of nine main underground levels. They also created reliefs portraying biblical themes.

THE WOODEN CHURCHES OF SOUTHERN LITTLE POLAND

The nine churches in Little Poland are rectangular constructions built out of horizontal logs. The technique was common in Eastern Europe but what is unusual is its use in the construction of Roman Catholic churches.

The wooden churches in the villages of Binarowa, Blizne, D'bno, Haczów, Lachowice, Lipnica Murowana, Orawka, S´kowa and Szalowa in southern Little Poland were once commissioned by aristocratic families. With just one exception, they all date from the late 15th and the 16th centuries. The best craftsmen and artists of the age were involved in their construction and decoration, which was intended to continue medieval church-building tradition.

The churches are complex in design and very well maintained, with interiors featuring elaborate ornamentation and paintings. They were initially built without towers but these were added later as the churches became status symbols for their benefactors. Extensions were also made regularly to the churches over later centuries, with the interiors in particular being adapted to match contemporary tastes.

Although different in their architectural design and generally very modest in their outward appearance, the interior of the churches – as here that in Haczów – feature meticulous decorative detail.

OLD TOWN OF ZAMOŚĆ

Designed by Italian master builder Bernardo Morando on orders of the Grand Chancellor and Commander Jan Zamoyski, Zamość was meant to be the "Padua of the North". Construction began in 1580, and by its heyday in the 17th century, Zamość had become one of Europe's first planned cities.

Planning for Zamość, in the present-day south-eastern Polish administrative district of Lublin, took as many aspects of urban life into account as possible. The result was the development of a diverse, multinational community that met with an unfortunately appalling end during World War II at the hands of the Germans, who murdered or deported many Poles and nearly all of the Jews living here.

The impressive town houses lining the squares feature arcades and ornamental façades while the city hall, built between 1639 and 1651, was given a monumental baroque staircase in the 18th century. The collegiate Church of St Thomas was built between 1587 and 1598 and is considered one of the loveliest late-Renaissance churches in Poland.

The interior of the former synagogue, built between 1610 and 1620, boasts magnificent stucco work. The birthplace of Rosa Luxemburg can be visited at ul. Staszica 37 just a short distance from the city museum.

The Old Town of Zamość is made up of the main market (Rynek Wielki) and the eye-catching city hall with its sweeping staircase and octagonal clock tower.

BIAŁOWIEŻA NATIONAL PARK / BELOVEZHSKAYA PUSHCHA

For hundreds of years this wetland and primeval forest region on the Polish-Belarus border was a hunting ground for Polish kings.

Despite extreme temperatures, which often drop to -40 °C (-40 °F) in winter, an astonishing diversity of species has developed inside this supranational World Heritage Site.

There are some 3,000 variety of fungus and more than a dozen species of orchid here. The tallest trees in Europe – 55-m (180-ft) spruce trees and 40-m (131-ft) ashes – also grow inside the strictly protected core of the park. In the 1920s, the Polish government even began to breed wisent (bison) from zoo stocks, and starting in 1952, they were then reintroduced into the wild. Toward the end of the 19th century, these ancient cattle had been hunted to near extinction. The wild horses that were once native to all of Eurasia have also found refuge in this sanctuary. Aside from bears, moose, lynxes and wolves, more than 220 species of bird also live here.

More than 300 wisents have been reintroduced to this expansive forest and heath region. They are the European relatives of the North American bison.

Czech Republic

HISTORIC CENTER OF PRAGUE

The "Golden City" on the Vltava River is one of the oldest capital cities in Europe. Its historic center constitutes a comprehensive display of Gothic and baroque buildings.

The city of Prague is dominated by the colossal Hradčany castle complex, which developed from a Slavic settlement founded back in the 9th century. The highest point is marked by the tower of the St Vitus Cathedral, the largest church in Prague and the burial place of emperors and kings that also houses the royal insignia. Construction of the famous Charles Bridge began in 1357, with baroque statues being added between 1707 and 1714. It links the Lesser Quarter, the district beneath Hradčany, with the Old Town by way of the Vtlava River. The winding alleyways of the Old Town feature many Renaissance and baroque buildings, some of which were originally Gothic in style.

Letná Park in Prague affords wonderful views of the Vltava River with the Mánesûv, Charles and Most Legii bridges in the Old Town.

The Jesuit Collegium Clementinum was built between 1578 and 1722 and was the second-largest complex in the city. The Teyn Church (1365–1511) is also in the center of the Old Town along with the Charles University building, founded in 1348 by King Charles I (later Emperor Charles IV), which was renovated in the baroque style in the 17th century. The Astronomical Clock was added to the 14th-century city hall at the beginning of the 15th century while the old Jewish quarter, Josefov, dates from the 13th century. The New Town, which developed 100 years later, features Wenceslas Square and Charles Square with the New Town Hall.

Construction of the over 500-m-long (1,700-ft) Charles Bridge was begun in 1357 under Charles IV. Master builder Peter Parler based his work on the stone bridge in Regensburg, Germany.

Czech Republic

The Hradčany and St Vitus Cathedral tower over Prague. The castle complex has been the country's political and cultural center for more than 1,000 years and is now the official residence of the president.

The Old Town Square is about 9,000 sq m (96,840 sq ft) in size and served as the main marketplace. It was a feature on the Bohemian kings' coronation route as well as a place of execution.

The famous Astronomical Clock is on the south side of Prague's Old City Hall. It displays hours and minutes, but also the phases of the moon, the position of the sun and planetary constellations.

The Clementinum, a complex of scholarly buildings built around five courtyards between 1578 and 1726, now houses the national library.

Czech Republic

KUTNÁ HORA: HISTORIC TOWN CENTER WITH CHURCH OF ST BARBARA AND CATHEDRAL OF OUR LADY AT SEDLEC

The historic center of Kutná Hora, around 70 km (43 mi) east of Prague, is characterized by Gothic, Renaissance, and baroque buildings.

In around 1300, at the behest of King Wenceslas II, Florentine coiners began minting the "Prague groschen" at the castle in Kutná Hora. It marked the beginning of Kutná Hora's rise as one of Bohemia wealthiest towns.

The castle was also the royal residence and later underwent a number of transformations. The St Wenceslas Chapel dates from the 15th century while the Church of St Barbara was built between 1388 and 1585. It was commissioned by the mine owners and dedicated to the patron saint of miners. The Cathedral of Our Lady, part of the former Cistercian abbey at nearby Sedlec, was the first in Bohemia to be built in the style of the French Gothic. It was later renovated by Giovanni Santini-Aichel in baroque-Gothic style between 1699 and 1707.

The Church of St Barbara in Kutná Hora incorporates French influences.

PILGRIMAGE CHURCH AT ZELENÁ HORA

The pilgrimage church dedicated to St John of Nepomuk was designed by architect Giovanni Santini and is one of the most important baroque-Gothic buildings in the Bohemia region of the Czech Republic.

The Pilgrimage Church of St John of Nepomuk is near Zelená Hora (The Green Mountain) and close to the little town of Žďár nad Sázavou, north-west of Brno. It was built in the Bohemian baroque-Gothic style and completed in 1722. The design was based on plans by Jan Blažej Santini-Aichel, a local Bohemian architect with Italian heritage who was also responsible for the renovation of the adjoining monastery church. It was to be his final masterpiece.

The pilgrimage church has an unusual star-shaped layout and is also fully enclosed by an outer ring of buildings comprising five chapels and entrances. The interior, which has remained more or less unchanged since its construction, includes impressive features like the elaborate high altar depicting St John of Nepomuk in paradise.

The number five played a key role in the construction of the pilgrimage church at Zelená Hora. Its layout is that of a five-pointed star, it has five entrances and the altar is decorated with five stars and five angels.

HISTORIC CENTER OF ČESKÝ KRUMLOV

This castle built in the 13th century on the cliffs above the Vltava River was surpassed in size only by the Hradčany in Prague. The Old Town on the opposite bank is one of the loveliest in Central Europe.

The narrow streets of the Latrán district form a labyrinth beneath the imposing castle complex. In the actual Old Town of Český Krumlov, the "Pearl of the Bohemian Forest" on the other side of the Vltava River, the winding alleys alternate with large squares, small artisan houses and magnificent residences, all dominated by the Church of St Vitus (1407–1439).

The former town brewery, which was built in 1578, now commemorates the illustrator and painter Egon Schiele who lived here for several months in 1911 (before he had to leave town again because of his nude portraits). The lovely former Jesuit monastery in a Renaissance building is now a hotel. The illusionist wall paintings in the Hall of Masks are particularly worth seeing. They are inside the magnificent castle, where construction originally began in 1250 and which was extended over the centuries with additional state rooms, reception halls and a rococo theater.

Covering an area of seven ha (17 acres), the castle complex at Český Krumlov is one of the largest in Central Europe.

HOLAŠOVICE HISTORICAL VILLAGE RESERVATION

This picturesque village close to České Budějovice in the southern Bohemian lowlands boasts just 140 residents but its architecture includes some of the finest examples of South Bohemian Folk Baroque.

In 1292, Bohemian King Wenceslas II gifted a number of villages to the monastery of Vyšší Brod, including the little village of Holašovice, which eventually retained close links to the monastery over the course of five centuries. The monastery records indicate that both Germans and Czechs lived in Holašovice during this time. The first stone buildings were erected on the village's medieval layout at the beginning of the 19th century but it was only between 1840 and 1880 that the buildings were given their present-day look.

It is not known where the master builders came from or who they were, but their work survives to this day and features some of the finest works of South Bohemian Folk Baroque architecture. The style combines different baroque, rococo and neoclassical elements and cleverly adapts them to the rural surroundings.

There are twenty-two farmsteads grouped around the Holašovice village square, a majority of them dating from the second half of the 19th century.

HISTORIC CENTER OF TELČ

Telč was rebuilt in the aftermath of several devastating fires – the whole western half of the market square, including the church and the town hall, burnt down in 1386 – and is today a comprehensive example of a Renaissance town.

Telč owes its present-day appearance to the influence of Prince Zacharias of Hradec during the second half of the 16th century. The prince was a Renaissance enthusiast and had the Gothic fortress, which is thought to have been built after 1354, converted into a magnificent castle, adding a number of Renaissance-style buildings in the process. Later, wealthy merchants and some of the town's prosperous citizens also began converting their Gothic houses with decorated and blind gables, or building new ones in the style of the day.
The long market square is the town's highlight, lined with arcades beneath

the gabled roofs of continuous rows of stepped and curved Renaissance town houses. The eastern section of the market square features St Mary's column dating from 1717 as well as two baroque fountains.

The town of Telč, with its long market square, was given a facelift by Prince Zacharias of Hradec in the 16th century. Above: The statue of St Margaret at the lower fountain. Left: The twin towers of the Jesuit St Jacob's Church, and a corner tower of the castle walls in the background.

Czech Republic

TŘEBÍČ

The World Heritage site in this town in south-western Moravia includes the Jewish Quarter, the Jewish cemetery, and the Basilica of St Procopius on the northern banks of the Jihlava River. The buildings are a refreshing reminder of the coexistence of Jewish and Christian cultures from the Middle Ages through to the 20th century.

A Benedictine monastery was founded on the northern banks of the Jihlava River in 1101. This resulted in the development of a market attracting throngs of traders, some of whom were Jews. It was the beginning of a rich history in the town of Třebíč.

The Basilica of St Procopius was built in the mid-13th century, only to be renovated and restored on a repeated basis over the course of centuries. The Jewish Quarter comprises two main streets on a hilltop linked by alleyways and bridged by gatehouses. Its buildings have retained their simplicity, usually featuring a vaulted ground floor and one or two upper floors with wooden ceilings. The mix of styles is a common feature: one house with a medieval entrance, for instance, an 18th-century façade, Renaissance vaults, and stucco work from the 1930s. Jews were forced to live in the Jewish Quarter until 1875 when residential restrictions were lifted. The Jewish cemetery is elsewhere.

The Basilica of St Procopius and the Jewish Quarter on the banks of the Jihlava River.

LITOMYŠL CASTLE

This elaborate Renaissance castle in eastern Bohemia was built in the 16th century based on Italian design influences, but the impressive building also features a number of local style elements.

Construction of this luxurious Renaissance castle was commissioned by the Pernštejn family, to whom the entire town belonged at the time. Bohemian Chancellor Vratislav Pernštejn was granted the town and its associated estates in 1567. He died in 1582, the year the castle was completed.

Giovanni Battista and Ulrico Aostalli, in cooperation with other northern Italian artists, were involved in its design and construction. The square building is impressive in its wealth of decoration and lovely arcades.

High baroque features were added to the castle in the 18th century, and the complex was also given a small theater – one of the first theaters in the country at the time of its construction.

Famous Czech composer Bedřich Smetana (1824–1884) was born in the brewery, built in 1630, which is also located on the castle grounds. Renowned for its music festivals, the castle also houses a small museum dedicated to Smetana and to Czech music in general.

Litomyšl Castle's uniform façade is interspersed with arches, Renaissance gables and sundials.

HOLY TRINITY COLUMN IN OLOMOUC

The Holy Trinity Column in Olomouc is the most monumental example of the tradition of Virgin Mary and Holy Trinity Columns popular in southern Germany, Austria and the Czech Republic in the 18th century.

The magnificent Holy Trinity Column, consecrated in 1754 in the presence of Empress Maria Theresa, towers above its central location on Peace Square adjacent to the town hall. The column is the work of local Olomouc stonemason Wenzel Reder and German sculptor Andreas Zahner. Goldsmith Simon Forstner created the magnificent gilded Holy Trinity group that crowns the monumental column. The largest and most elaborate of its kind north of the Alps, the monument is divided into a tiered base section featuring pedestals and steps, a compact pyramid-shaped lower section, and a towering pilaster column.

The mostly life-sized figures are distributed across all sides of each level. The highlight of the sculptural decoration is the group of golden Holy Trinity statues based on Romanesque high baroque style traditions.

The various artists responsible for this masterpiece spent three decades working on the 35-m (115-ft) Holy Trinity Column on Peace Square.

TUGENDHAT VILLA IN BRNO

The Tugendhat Villa in Brno built in 1930 by Ludwig Mies van der Rohe is an outstanding example of modernist architecture's "international Style" that developed at the beginning of the 1920s.

This villa is regarded as the last major work completed in Europe by German architect Ludwig Mies van der Rohe, born in Aachen in 1886, before he became director of the Bauhaus school in Dessau in 1930 and ultimately emigrated to America in 1937.

The typical characteristics of the "international style" that Mies van der Rohe played a key role in defining, included asymmetrical ground plans and elevations, cubic shapes, steel frame constructions as well as a visible lack of ornamentation and distinct forms. The style incorporated the prevalent use of glass, steel, reinforced concrete and even chrome. It was here that Mies van der Rohe implemented these new compositional features for the first time into a residential building.

The steel frame construction with cross-shaped, chromium-plated supports allowed him to design the interior with an open plan, essentially doing away with load-bearing walls. Huge glass walls, retractable at the press of a button – a novelty at the time – reinforced this unique impression of open space.

The Tugendhat Villa in Brno is a quintessential modernist work lauded for its "simplicity of construction, clarity of tectonic means, and purity of materials".

GARDENS AND CASTLE AT KROMĚŘÍŽ

The castle and gardens in Kroměříž in eastern Moravia are among the best preserved examples of a baroque princely residence.

This town on the Morava River dates back to 1110. After being completely destroyed during the Thirty Years' War, Kroměříž was rebuilt on orders of the artistically-inclined Bishop Karl Liechtenstein, who also inaugurated the reconstruction of the magnificent baroque bishop's residence in 1686. Bishop Leopold von Egk then commissioned more restoration work following a major fire in 1752 that destroyed valuable sections of the castle's interior. He hired some of the leading late-baroque artists from Austria to take part in the projects. In fact, the Austrian parliament met in the assembly hall here during their revolution of 1848/1849. Today it is the setting for classical concerts.

The interiors of the luxurious living quarters and staterooms are among the most valuable in Central Europe. A collection of paintings comprising key works by old masters is a major attraction for art fans from all over the world, and the castle also boasts an extensive park that is well worth a casual stroll.

The lovely park in Kroměříž features playful elements such as fountains, rotundas, pavilions and grottos.

LEDNICE-VALTICE CULTURAL LANDSCAPE

This stretch of land in southern Moravia boasts two magnificent castles and is one of the most extensive historical landscape complexes in the world. Today the parks serve as a bird sanctuary.

The creation of this unique cultural landscape can largely be attributed to the dukes of Liechtenstein, who had two impressive castles built within their sizable domains. Austrian architect Johann Bernhard Fischer von Erlach, for his part, was commissioned to build a magnificent baroque riding school in Lednice between 1688 and 1690. A castle housing valuable art collections was then built here in the mid-19th century.

An avenue leads from here to adjoining Valtice, also the site of a splendid castle from the 17th century. The two castle complexes are surrounded by a park landscape based primarily on English principles of landscape architecture that cover a total of 200 sq km (77 sq mi).

Between gently rolling hills and wooded plains on the border between the Czech Republic and Austria is a harmonious artistic ensemble combining nature and architecture (left: Lednice Castle). It was created by the dukes of Liechtenstein, whose predecessors had been resident in the Lednice and Valtice area since the 14th century.

Slovakia

VLKOLÍNEC

Vlkolínec is a settlement comprising forty-five wooden buildings constructed in the style typical of central Slovakia. Today this village close to Ružomberok on the north-western edge of the Low Tatras is an open-air museum.

On a sweeping plateau set against the backdrop of Sidorovo mountain is the farming village of Vlkolínec. The name is derived from "vlk", meaning "wolf" in Slovak, and there are indeed still wolves and bears in this region of eastern Slovakia between the Low and the High Tatras.

Far removed from the hustle and bustle of modern towns, the 19th-century wooden architecture of the "wolf village" has remained surprisingly intact. It is in fact the largest surviving ensemble of this type of traditional log houses characteristic of Slovak mountain settlements. The properties comprise the living quarters along the road with the stables and barns at the back. Only the living room of the clay plastered cottages has a wooden floor. The village also provides insight into the lives of the people in the remote mountain regions of Eastern Europe during the Middle Ages. Although the village has long been an open-air museum, Vlkolínec still has a number of permanent residents, most of whom are elderly folks.

The brightly painted walls of the farmhouses in Vlkolínec are made of wood and clay. They rest on stone foundations and support what are mostly wood shingle roofs.

HISTORIC BANSKÁ ŠTIAVNICA AND THE TECHNICAL MONUMENTS IN ITS VICINITY

Banská Štiavnica was one of the most important mining towns in the Kingdom of Hungary between the 14th and 16th centuries. Gold and silver had been mined here even in prehistoric times.

The landmark of this town tucked away in the Carpathian Mountains just 20 km (12 mi) from Zvolen is the historic castle, built during the 16th century through the fortification of an existing Gothic church. The buildings around Trinity Square once belonged to wealthy residents. Some of them date from the 14th and 15th centuries but were converted during the Renaissance and baroque eras. The headquarters of the chamber of mines, for example, is now a prestigious Renaissance building. The mines here were leased and expanded by the Fuggers in the 16th century, and Banská Štiavnica made history in the 17th and 18th centuries when gunpowder was first used to extend the tunnels in 1627, and steam engines were used to pump out water in 1732. The academy founded in 1735 was closed in 1918 with the shutdown of the mines.

The baroque column on Trinity Square in the old mining town of Banská Štiavnica.

WOODEN CHURCHES OF THE SLOVAK PART OF THE CARPATHIAN MOUNTAIN AREA

These eight wooden churches in the Slovak part of the Carpathian Mountains are testimony to the local tradition of religious architecture at the crossroads between Western European and Byzantine cultures.

These wooden churches in the northwestern Carpathian Mountains testify to centuries of peaceful coexistence between different confessions, beliefs and peoples. The Roman Catholic churches in Hervartov and Tvrdošín were both built in about 1500 in a Gothic style. The Protestant "articular" churches in Leštiny (1688), Kežmarok (1687, converted 1717), and Hronsek (1726), on the other hand, represent a different style. The Ruthenian Greek-Catholic Church, a uniate church, is represented by the three wooden churches in Bodružal (1658), Ladomirová (1742), and Ruská Bystrá (1720–1730). Their interiors largely date from the 18th century. All of them feature elaborately painted walls and ceilings.

Protestants (above), Catholics and Orthodox Greeks built wooden churches in the Slovak part of the Carpathian Mountains, all of them varying according to religious practice.

LEVOČA, SPIŠSKÝ HRAD AND CULTURAL MONUMENTS

Together with the Spišské Podhrahie, Spišská Kapitula and the Church at Žehra, the ruins of the Spišsky Hrad – one of the largest castles in Slovakia and once the capital of the Royal Hungarian administrative county – make up the World Heritage Site that was expanded in 2009 to include the historic center of Levoča and the works of Master Paul in Spiš.

The medieval Spišsky Hrad developed from an early Slavic fortress in Zips, an area and series of former administrative units in and around the foothills of the High Tatras. It was from here that Spišsky Podhrahie and Spišská Kapitula (the latter being the provost's residence) were founded just a short distance away. They all boast important architectural monuments including a baroque monastery and numerous Renaissance structures. The cultural monuments associated with the Spišsky Hrad also include the early Gothic Church of the Holy Spirit in Žehra. The town of Levoča was first mentioned in 1249 as the "shining jewel in the crown of Spišsky Hrad". It is home to the parish church of St James with the highest (19 m/61 ft) Gothic altar in the world carved from linden timber between 1507 and 1517 by Master Paul from Levoča.

Spišsky Hrad towers high atop a 634-m-high (2,080-ft) limestone cliff.

BARDEJOV TOWN CONSERVATION RESERVE

The historic town of Bardejov in Slovakia still has the air of a medieval trading town. It is representative of the type of urbanization that took place in eastern-central Europe between the 14 and 16th centuries.

Bardejov was founded as an imperial free town at the beginning of the 14th century along the former trade routes with Poland. The town reached its cultural peak in the 15th and 16th centuries, including the founding of the country's first public library.

The town's elongated layout is arranged in grid fashion. The center of the long market square features the late-Gothic town hall with its steep gables and oriel as well as a Renaissance staircase. Meanwhile, the Church of St Aegidius was given its present design in the second half of the 15th century. The town's overall appearance is characterized by the many Gothic and Renaissance town houses. There is also the small Jewish quarter surrounding the 18th-century synagogue.

The well-preserved market place in Bardejov was developed in the 14th century. It is lined on three sides by magnificent 16th-century town houses (above) and is dominated by the Basilica of St. Aegidius. The city hall (left) is situated in the middle of the square.

PRIMEVAL BEECH FORESTS OF THE CARPATHIANS

Europe's most beautiful and untouched beech forests are located along the border of Slovakia and Ukraine. The World Natural Heritage Site comprises ten protected areas along a 185 km axis from the Rakhiv Mountains in the Ukraine to the Vihorlat Mountains in Slovakia.

Deciduous trees and mixed deciduous forests once covered most of Central Europe, and beech trees were particularly prevalent. Alongside the tree's ability to adapt to a variety of different environments, its survival can also be put down to constantly spreading seeds that then impede the development of other trees.

The World Natural Heritage Site comprises the following areas: in Slovakia Havešová (tallest specimens in the world), Rožok, Stužica, Bukovské Vrch und Vihorlat; in the Ukraine Tschorna Hora, Kusij-Tribuschanij, Marmarosch, Stuschicja-Uschok, Swydowez und Uholka/Schirokij Luh. In addition to that there are nearly 1,100 species of flowering plant, about 100 species of bird and seventy mammal species.

The red beech (Fagus sylvatica) grows in many parts of Europe, but pure beech forests and other beech-dominated woodlands are now only found in the Ukrainian and Slovakian Carpathians. Some of the trees here grow as tall as 55 m (180 ft).

CAVES OF AGGTELEK KARST AND SLOVAK KARST

The Hungarian karst region is in the foothills of the Ore Mountains of Slovakia. The area has several hundred caves spread across both sides of the border and featuring magnificent stalactites and stalagmites.

Aggtelek National Park is located roughly 600 m (1,970 ft) above sea level in the karst region of the low mountain ranges of northern Hungary and south-eastern Slovakia. The World Heritage Site takes in parts of both countries and includes an extensive cave network that goes down several hundred meters below the surface. It can be accessed via several entrances. The highlight of the guided tours is the huge Baradla Cave, where the history of the earth is displayed in a breathtaking manner in an incredible landscape of stalactites and stalag-mites. In some of the other chambers, meanwhile, fossils and evidence of the caves' Paleolithic inhabitants have been found.

In 1965, the Béke Cave – the second biggest in the Aggtelek karst – was officially declared a "healing cave". Its moist atmosphere is particularly beneficial for people who suffer from severe asthma. It is also occasionally used as a concert hall.

The network of dripstone caves in the Hungarian part of the Aggtelek karst region is 17 km (11 mi) long.

Hungary

BUDAPEST

The independent cities of Buda and Pest merged in 1872 to form the new capital of what was then the Kingdom of Hungary. The World Heritage Site in Budapest includes the Buda Castle Quarter, the banks of the Danube and Andrássy Avenue.

The medieval structure of the royal castle town of Buda has been attentively preserved and its narrow streets are lined with Gothic and baroque buildings. Trinity Square marks the center of Castle Hill, part of the town since the 17th century, which is dominated by the Church of Our Lady, originally built in 1250 and converted to the neo-Gothic style in the 19th century. The church's southern portal features a tympanum relief comprised of pieces from the original High-Gothic building. To the south of Castle Hill is the Royal Buda Castle, construction of which began in 1749 to replace the previous building destroyed in 1686.

In Óbuda visitors will find the excavated sites of the ancient Roman city

The Fisherman's Bastion was built on the site of the former fish market in Buda between 1895 and 1902. The architect Frigyes Schulek's conical towers on this building are reminiscent of the tents of the Magyar people. The Bastion offers a wonderful view of the Danube and the parliament building.

of Aquincum with an amphitheater that accommodates 13,000 people. The monumental neoclassical synagogue here dates from 1820.

On the eastern side of the Danube is Pest, an independent trading town in the 19th century. It is considered the more intellectual and upmarket area. The town houses and aristocratic palaces lining the main ring road here are testimony to the former importance of the Pest side.

It is the oldest and the best-known of Budapest's nine bridges: the Chain Bridge, built between 1839 and 1849, supported by two triumphal arch-like buttresses.

St Matthew's Church was used as a mosque when the Ottomans ruled the region but its interior decoration dates from the 19th-century neo-Gothic conversion by Frigyes Schulek.

St Stephen's Basilica close to the Chain Bridge was consecrated in 1905 and accommodates around 8,500 people.

The parliament building with its magnificent staircase was built between 1885 and 1904 based on plans by Imre Steindl.

The roof of the Gellért Baths – opened in 1918 – can be opened above the main interior pool when the weather is nice.

Hungary

FERTÖ / NEUSIEDLER SEE CULTURAL LANDSCAPE

Fertö Hanság National Park was founded on the Hungarian side of Lake Neusiedl in 1991 – two years ahead of its counterpart on the Austrian side.

As part of the former north-south trade route connecting the Adriatic and the Baltic seas, Neusiedl Lake on the Little Hungarian Plain bordering Austria has been a cultural meeting place for eight thousand years. The region continues to exhibit unusual ethnic and commercial diversity.

Logging, drainage, hunting, and grazing around this Pannonic steppe lake have created a cultural landscape in which economic utilization and the preservation of natural habitats are largely in harmony with one another – the importance of which is also being more greatly appreciated.

The Austrian side of this cross-border World Heritage Site comprises the Neusiedlersee / Seewinkel National Park as well as a number of other villages. On the Hungarian side it includes Fertö Hanság National Park and Esterhazy Castle. The rich floral diversity of this slightly salty steppe lake is remarkable, and it is encircled by a belt of reeds and salt flats that are up to 3 km (2 mi) in width.

The traditional draw wells and reed huts typical of the region can be seen all around the lake.

MILLENARY BENEDICTINE ABBEY OF PANNONHALMA

The former St Martin's Benedictine abbey in Pannonhalma, around 30 km (19 mi) south-east of Györ, is one of the main centers from which Christianity spread across Hungary. It is still occupied by monks to this day.

The founding of the abbey here dates back to Prince Géza (940–997). It was later made an archabbey under King Stephan I (the Holy) and has been the center of the Benedictine order in Hungary ever since.

The oldest part of the complex is the collegiate church, consecrated in 1225 and built upon the remains of two previous buildings. The crypt beneath the elevated choir was probably built on the foundations of the original church. In addition to lovely baroque stuccowork and neoclassical features, the collegiate church also contains a great number of Romanesque and Gothic works of art. The sculptures in the vaults of the late-Gothic cloister, for example, are intended to symbolize human vices and virtues.

The 55-m (180-ft) west tower was only built in 1830 during the neoclassical conversion of the complex. A particular gem from this era is the stateroom of the neoclassical library built between 1824 and 1832. It is home to valuable manuscripts and incunabula.

Prince Géza founded Pannonhalma in 996 as the Benedictine order's archabbey.

OLD VILLAGE OF HOLLÓKÖ AND ITS SURROUNDINGS

The historic center of Hollókö has managed to retain its medieval character, with houses characterized by wooden porches and ground level cellars.

Situated in picturesque surroundings, Hollókö is tucked in amongst the hills of the Cserhát Mountains about 100 km (62 mi) from Budapest. The village with its row of medieval homes is situated below the ruins of Hollókö Castle, which has towered high up on the cliff since the 13th century but was destroyed at the beginning of the 18th century. The houses managed to survive both war and fire and remain almost unchanged to this day.

In the center of the village is the shingled Catholic church from 1889 with its wooden steeple. The houses are built in a style typical of the Palóc people here. Because they are mostly built on slopes, the houses' ground level cellars are accessible from the road. At the gabled end is the courtyard surrounded by a narrow hipped-roof porch.

Elaborate carvings on the wooden porches complete the medieval ensemble in one of Hungary's loveliest villages. The majority of the farmhouses are still inhabited and one of them contains the village museum.

Formerly inhabited by the Palóc people, the church in Hollókö was built in the rural Gothic style.

TOKAJ WINE REGION CULTURAL LANDSCAPE

This region at the foot of the Zemplin Mountains is defined by the viticultural tradition that has been practiced here for a thousand years.

The Tokaj-Hegyalja wine-growing region spreads through the northern foothills of the Puszta, close to the border with Slovakia and Ukraine. It encompasses a total of twenty-six localities, the largest and best-known of which is the pretty little town of Tokaj on the banks of the Tisza River. The wine referred to by the "Sun King" Louis XIV as "Vinum regum, rex vinorum" (wine of kings, king of wines) was named after this town. A dessert wine, Tokaj wine, made primarily from the Furmint grape variety, and to a lesser extent from varieties like Hárslevlı, Sárga Muskotály and Zéta is indeed one of the country's oldest wine types. This town in northern Hungary around 200 km (124 mi) east of the capital Budapest is its home. Wine-growing has always influenced the region, its traditions and its settlement patterns. This has resulted in a cultural landscape that lives from and with wine, and the quality of the products is subject to strict controls.

Not only did the small town of Tokaj give its name to the famous Hungarian white wine, it also has an attractive historic center (left: the charming town hall, Városháza).

HORTOBÁGY NATIONAL PARK – THE "PUSZTA"

The "Puszta" is an austere landscape that is largely dedicated to agricultural purposes. Hortobágy National Park is intended to help preserve its unique character and traditions.

The landscape known today as the "Puszta", or "desolate, lonely place", used to be forested – before the Mongol hordes and later the Turks burnt down both the villages and forests. The reintroduction of livestock breeding then led to overgrazing and salination, which resulted in the current landscape. In addition to Hortobágy Puszta, the national park also comprises a large part of Nagykunság. Traditional forms of land use are still practiced in Hortobágy National Park, which was established in 1973. In addition to grazing animals – which now includes the protection of historic domestic breeds threatened by extinction – the national park also boasts a tremendous wealth of local flora and fauna. The many stretches of water in the park ultimately necessitated the construction of several bridges, such as the Nine Arch Bridge near the village of Hortobágy. It spans the river of the same name.

Historic Hungarian domestic animals such as Hungarian Gray Cattle are kept in the "Puszta", Europe's largest continuous area of natural grasslands.

EARLY-CHRISTIAN NECROPOLIS OF PÉCS

As one of the towns founded in the Roman province of Pannonia, Pécs, formerly known as Sopianae, developed into an important trading and commercial center.

This late-Roman cemetery is southwest of the Pécs town center. Archaeological excavations have unearthed sixteen burial chambers here to date, revealing several thousand graves as well as the burial items found in them. A majority of these 4th-century Christian graves in fact used to be above ground. One burial chamber discovered as early as 1780 is worthy of special mention. The two-storey structure is decorated with well-preserved wall paintings depicting the apostles Peter and Paul, Mary, Jonas, Noah and other biblical figures as well as one of the earliest naked portraits of Adam and Eve after the Fall of Man. The most important architectural find to date has been the remains of two memorial chapels: one of the chapels (decorated with intricate frescoes and featuring three apses) and the small mausoleum dating from the 5th or 6th century. The early Christian cemetery at Pécs is an important monumental ensemble not only for Hungary but for all of Europe.

Three of the early-Christian chapels and burial chambers (left) in Pécs are open regularly to visitors.

Belarus

BELOVEZHSKAYA PUSHCHA / BIAŁOWIEŻA FOREST

One of the last primeval forests in Europe with unique flora and fauna stretches from western Belarus to the border with Poland.

Initially, only the Białowieża National Park in Poland was designated a World Heritage Site while the larger Belovezhskaya Pushcha section in Belarus was only added in 1992. Together they cover some 1,000 sq km (386 sq mi), making it the largest transnational UNESCO World Heritage Site.

Recognized primarily for its densely mixed virgin forest – the only woods of their kind in Europe – the heavily protected core of the park is home to spruce, pine, black alder, hornbeam, oak, birch, ash, lime, maple and poplar trees. Some of the individual trees are even natural monuments in their own right. There are also hundreds of species of fungi, lichen and vascular plants.

The park is most famous, however, for its wisents. The animals – cousins of the North American bison – came close to extinction but were reintroduced to the wild in 1952 using zoo stock bred in the 1920s. Now around 300 of them roam the vast forest once more with bears, elk, wolves, lynx and otters. There are also more than 220 species of bird including the black stork.

The last sizable population of wisents (bison) in Europe lives in these vast primeval forests.

Struve Geodetic Arc see page 124

MIR CASTLE COMPLEX

This castle on the Miranka River some 80 km (50 mi) south-west of Minsk in present-day Belarus has various stylistic elements that make it prime example of Magnate architecture from the era of Polish-Lithuanian rule.

The little town of Mir was initially part of the Grand Duchy of Lithuania, then part of the czardom of Russia, then Poland, then the Soviet Union, and is currently part of Belarus. Mir was also once a typical Eastern European shtetl (Yiddish for small city) until 1,500 Jews were killed here by the German army on November 9, 1941.

In the early 16th century, the quadrangle-shaped citadel was constructed with protective walls and five towers. In 1568, ownership of the fort fell to Prince Radziwill and in the 16th and 17th centuries it became an aristocratic residence after the construction of a two-winged castle.

The fort, with its stout brick towers, was built on a square ground plan with sides 75 m (246 ft) in length. The hefty brickwork and series of embrasures demonstrate the military nature of the complex while the representational purpose is evident in the rich decoration of the tower façades. Red-brick sections alternate with white plastered sections and, together with the bulky towers, ensure the construction makes an imposing impression even from a great distance.

The façade of Mir Castle is dominated by the squat, red-brick towers.

ARCHITECTURAL COMPLEX OF THE RADZIWILL FAMILY

Nesvizh, the former residence of the aristocratic Radziwill family, is located in south-western Belarus and symbolizes the merging and mutual enrichment of Western and Eastern European cultures. The unique architectural and cultural legacy of the Radziwills is now listed as a UNESCO World Heritage Site.

Belarus long acted as an intermediary between Eastern and Western Europe. The members of the Radziwill family, who owned the residence until 1939, played an important role in political and cultural life, and are often referred to as "the Medicis of Belarus". They played many roles in society, from church leaders and proponents of the Enlightenment to patrons of the arts, collectors, writers, composers and business moguls, and had ruled Rzeczpospolita, present-day Belarus, since the 15th century.

The oldest parts of the complex date back to about 1500, when Prince Nicholas had a manor built here. It now comprises ten buildings around a hexagonal courtyard within an English-style park. The World Heritage site includes the church, with graves of members of the family. The building's appearance was shaped by Polish, German, Italian and Belorussian architects hired by Michael Radziwill.

Nesvizh Castle fell into a state of visible disrepair during the 20th century.

L'VIV – THE ENSEMBLE OF THE HISTORIC CENTER

L'viv was for centuries the administrative and economic center of Galicia (Eastern Europe). Its historic center is home to a unique ensemble of magnificent buildings from the 14th to the 18th century.

Founded in the 13th century by Prince Daniil Romanovich on the site of a former Slavic settlement, L'viv experienced a rapid rise as the center of Galicia. However, its strategic location on the important east-west trade routes and passes of the Carpathian Mountains resulted in a turbulent history for this multiethnic city.

In 1349, L'viv became part of Poland, and in 1356 was given the status of a free city. In 1648, it was conquered by the Cossacks, and in 1704 it fell under Swedish rule. In the first division of Poland, the city became part of Austria in 1772, and was the capital of Austrian Galicia under the name of Lemberg until 1918.

After the Russian occupation during World War I, a Ukrainian national movement emerged here in 1918, but was defeated by Polish troops. After German troops had taken over during World War II, the city became part of the Soviet Union (as Lvov) in 1945. Today, L'viv is the centre and communications hub of western Ukraine.

The Krushelnyzka Opera from 1900 is modeled on the Vienna Opera House.

SAINT-SOPHIA CATHEDRAL AND MONASTIC BUILDINGS

This World Heritage Site symbolizes the Kievan Rus' quest for equality with Byzantium. It is considered the cradle of the Orthodox proselytization of Russia.

Kiev, the capital of Ukraine, was first mentioned in chronicles in about 860. By 1037, Yaroslav the Wise had laid the foundations for the ambitious Saint-Sophia Cathedral, a five-aisled cross-in-square church with thirteen domes symbolizing Jesus with the Apostles. The design was modeled on the Hagia Sophia in Constantinople. The cathedral was later reconstructed on several occasions, but the 55-m-wide (180-ft), 37-m-long (121-ft) and 29-m-high (95-ft) interior retained its original Byzantine character.

The Pechersk Lavra monastery on the banks of the Dnieper River also dates back to the 11th century. It was founded by hermits who in 1050 submitted to a monastic order and soon began constructing a solid building above the cave system. The caves then served as a burial site for the monks. Three different churches have been preserved from the 12th century here, the most magnificent in the monastery complex being the Cathedral of the Assumption, which was rebuilt after World War II.

Thanks to magnificent buildings like Saint-Sophia Cathedral, Kiev was once considered a "rival of the scepter of Constantinople".

PRIMEVAL BEECH FORESTS OF THE CARPATHIANS

This transnational World Heritage Site consists of the largest primeval beech forests in Europe, covering the southern slopes of the northern Carpathians and eastern Slovakia.

This protected site comprises ten areas along the nearly 200-km-long (124-mi) axis from the Rakhiv and Chornohirskyi Ranges in the Ukraine via the Polonynian Ridge up to the Bukovské Vrchy and the Vihorlat Mountains in Slovakia. Altogether, the protected terrain covers roughly 300 sq km (116 sq mi), with additional buffer zones of roughly 500 sq km (193 sq mi). The Carpathians are an ancient refuge of the beech tree and, combined with the Dinaric Alps, the only region in Europe where it was able to survive the Ice Age.

From here, it managed to spread once again across the temperate zones of the continent. The largest reservation on Ukrainian territory is the primeval forest of Uholka. Some sixty-five different forest biomes exist here, where the European beech (Fagus sylvatica) attains heights of up to 55 m (180 ft). There are also three other nature reserves in Ukraine: Chorna Hora, Kuziy-Trybushany, Maramarosh and Stuzhytsia–Uzhok, Svydovets.

Magnificent beech forests in the Ukrainian sections of the Carpathians.

Moldova

STRUVE GEODETIC ARC

People have long been investigating methods for precisely measuring the circumference of the earth. In the 19th century, the triangulation method was so far advanced that it was frequently used in land surveying, and only further developed using very sophisticated instruments. The Struve Geodetic Arc is an excellent example of how this method was applied.

The term "triangulation" comes from the Latin word "triangulum" (triangle). Put simply, this method involves measuring angles to a third point, based on a straight line with two fixed endpoints (whereby the length between the points must be known), and using them to construct a triangle. Using trigonometric formulas, the distance to a faraway object or point can then be calculated. With a network of measurement triangles, the distances between towns can be determined relatively accurately.

Friedrich Georg Wilhelm von Struve (1793–1864) is the intellectual originator of the arc of geodesic measurement points between Fuglenes and Stara Nekrasivka. The arc is named after him.

Led by German-Russian astronomer Friedrich Georg Wilhelm von Struve between 1816 and 1855, 258 main triangles with 265 main and sixty subordinate measurement points were constructed between Fuglenes, near Hammerfest, in Norway and Stara Nekrasivka on the Black Sea in what is now Ukraine. They covered a distance of 2,822 km (1,754 mi) and traversed what are now ten countries. The measurement served to calculate the length of the Tartu Prime Meridian (26°43′), i.e. the degree of longitude that runs through Tartu. Thirty-four of the measurement points were ultimately selected. They represent the importance of the Struve Geodetic Arc in the development of geodesy.

The thirty-four red points, including that of Rudi in Moldova, are part of a supranational World Heritage Site.

CURONIAN SPIT

The Curonian Spit is a sandy peninsula almost 100 km (62 mi) long and only one or 2 km (up to 1 mi) wide that stretches along the Russian-Lithuanian Baltic Sea coast. It is a supranational World Heritage Site.

The Curonian Spit starts in Lesnoye, north of Kaliningrad, a Russian enclave sandwiched between Poland and Lithuania, and ends just before the port town of Klaipeda in Lithuania, where a passage only a few hundred feet wide leads from the Baltic Sea to the Curonian Lagoon, which is hemmed in by the spit. The Russian-Lithuanian border runs down the middle of the headland. The Curonian Spit was formed by sand washed ashore some 7,000 years ago. Humans later intervened and made some momentous changes. In the 16th century, for example, the dense woodlands were almost completely cleared, leaving the sand by the sea to pile up.

The sand near the lagoon then formed dunes, which shifted and overwhelmed the villages. The dunes were only brought to a halt through systematic planting. Visitors can now climb the highest of them, which is not far from the Russian-Lithuanian border. The villages by the lagoon are still home to some traditional fishermen's houses. Many artists (Corinth, Pechstein, Kirchner) once spent the summer at the main town of Nida; Thomas Mann's summer house is today a museum.

The Curonian Spit, with its dunes up to 70 m (230 ft) high, is known as the "Sahara of the Baltic Sea".

CULTURAL AND HISTORIC ENSEMBLE OF THE SOLOVETSKY ISLANDS

The six islands of Solovetsky Archipelago lie off the coast of Onega Bay in the White Sea. At the center of this World Heritage Site is Solovetsky Monastery, founded by the ascetics German and Savvati.

These islands were once covered in forests and swamps and were settled as early as the 5th century BC. They did not become historically significant until the monastery was built on the main island. Founded in 1429 as a hermitage, it quickly assumed a more monastic character. Between 1584 and 1594, the complex was turned into a fort that withstood many attacks, and a jail for political prisoners was also built there under the tsars. Until it was confiscated by the Soviets in

1922, the monastery was one of the country's richest convents and greatly influenced the economic and cultural development of northern Russia. After the Bolsheviks took power, the islands and monastery were converted into a labor camp and became one of the main islands in the Gulag Archipelago. Up to 70,000 prisoners were detained here before its closure in 1933. It became an Orthodox Church in 1991.

The Solovetsky fort complex.

Struve Geodesic Arc see opposite page

KIZHI POGOST

Kizhi, an island in Lake Onega, is home to some outstanding examples of Russian wooden architecture including two churches and a monumental bell tower that can be admired in an open-air museum.

Lake Onega has a surface area of 9,720 sq km (3,752 sq mi) and is up to 127 m (417 ft) deep. It is also covered in ice from November to mid-May and is Europe's second-largest lake after Lake Ladoga. During ice-free months a ferry crosses the river from Petrozavodsk, the most important port in the area, to Kizhi, an island famous for its prominent wooden structures.

The Preobrazhensky church, or Church of the Transfiguration, is a traditional wooden structure built in 1774 – not a single nail was used. Its twenty-two domes demonstrate the great artistry and craftsmanship of Russian carpenters. Pokrov church, or the Church of

the Intercession of Our Lady, was built in 1764 using the same methods. The complex's octagonal bell tower was erected in 1862.

All the historic buildings in the open-air museum are impressive in the way they are harmoniously embedded into the landscape. Dismantled at their original location and relocated here, they document centuries of Russian wood architecture.

In the Church of the Transfiguration (above) as well as the Church of the Intercession of Our Lady, an iconostasis separates the faithful from the altar area, where the priest leads ceremonies.

VIRGIN KOMI FORESTS

The Virgin Komi Forests in north-eastern Europe are one of the last remaining vestiges of the boreal vegetation that originally occurred only in the northern reaches of Europe, Asia and North America. These vast woodlands are dominated by conifers, aspen and birch trees.

The area protected by this World Natural Heritage site covers roughly 32,800 sq km (12,660 sq mi) of the Komi Republic, which is named after the original Finnish-Ugric inhabitants of the area. Large parts of these forests have barely been touched by humans, and are therefore an extremely valuable resource for natural historians.

The protected area stretches from the seemingly endless plains of the Taiga all the way into the mighty Ural Mountains. It includes the Pechoro-Ilychsky Nature Reserve – founded in 1930 specifically for scientific research

and only accessible to authorized personnel – and Yugyd Va National Park, which is freely accessible except for a few select zones. The landscape features rivers, moors and hundreds of lakes alongside alpine and subalpine pastures that merge with the tundra. The forests are home to a wide variety of both European and Asian animal species including bears, wolves, polar foxes, deer, reindeer, elk, beavers, otters, and squirrels.

The flora and fauna of Komi's vast primeval birch forests are typical of their northern location.

Russia

Peter the Great

Peter the Great was the first Russian tsar to travel abroad – even including forays to learn from more advanced nations. Indeed, as a slightly backward country still stuck in the Middle Ages, Russia needed to have closer contact with the rest of Europe. Pyotr Alexeyevich Romanov (1672–1725), known as Peter the Great, thus be-

came the great modernizer of Russia. He reformed the economy, army, government and the church and built a new capital from scratch – St Petersburg – that was "more European" than Moscow and had vital access to the sea. The construction of a completely new city where the Neva opens out into the Baltic Sea is con-

ST PETERSBURG

Tsar Peter the Great followed a very precise plan when constructing his new capital, which is characterized by hundreds of baroque and neoclassical buildings. The World Heritage Site here includes the historic centre as well as the forts and palaces of Kronstadt, Peterhof, Tsarskoe-Selo (Pushkin), Pavlovsk and Lomonosov, all of which are outside the city.

After wresting control of coastal lands along the Gulf of Finland from Swedish King Charles XII, Peter the Great had gained his long-desired access to the Baltic Sea – and thus the West. He wanted his new capital to outshine other European metropolises in terms of splendor and even today it still impresses visitors with the harmony of its baroque and neoclassical architecture, magnificent squares and canals with over 400 bridges.

The Orthodox Peter and Paul Cathedral, with its golden spire above, was built from 1712 to 1733 on the location of a fort of the same name.

Nevsky Prospekt is lined with prestigious buildings such as the Anichkov and Stroganov Palaces, but the city's most recognizable buildings are the baroque Winter Palace and the Hermitage. The World Heritage Site comprises roughly 2,400 buildings: the various palaces, churches, cathedrals, monasteries, museums, theaters, train stations and military buildings such as the Peter and Paul Fortress and the Admiralty.

The Hermitage is one of the world's most important art museums comprising the Winter Palace (right, the magnificent Jordan Staircase), the Small Hermitage, the New Hermitage and the Old Hermitage, and the Hermitage Theater.

sidered the most ambitious project carried out by the tsar, who ruled from 1682 until he died in 1725. His reign was ruthless, having taken place during the Great Northern War, and though Peter the Great was a dynamic, open-minded ruler he was by no means a "good king". Taxes were raised and farmers were forced

to build roads, quays, houses and churches to drain swampland. They lived and worked in primitive conditions and thousands died in order to fulfil the tsar's goals. "Beautiful St Petersburg is built on human bones", the saying goes. Peter the Great propelled Russia out of the Middle Ages, but the price paid was high.

From 1703, Peter the Great (far left, a portrait painted around 1700 by Pierre Gobert) had a new capital city built virtually from scratch where the Neva River opens out into the Baltic Sea. Work had progressed well within just a few years, as this contemporary copper engraving by Johann Baptist Homann shows (left).

Nevsky Prospekt is almost 5 km (3 mi) long and crosses several bridges (here, the Anichkov Bridge over the Fontanka).

The Winter Palace was built directly on the Neva starting in 1754. It was based on plans by Bartolomeo Rastrelli.

The Cathedral of the Resurrection of Christ on Griboedov Canal recalls St Basil's on Red Square in Moscow.

The baroque Smolny Cathedral, with its central dome and four corner towers was built by Bartolomeo Rastrelli.

Russia

The Peterhof residence with its artistic gardens was built in 1714 and is the most elegant of the tsars' palaces around St Petersburg.

The suburb of Lomonosov is home to the Oranienbaum estate, a complex of beautiful palaces and parks built in the 18th century. It was later converted into the tsars' summer residence.

Pavlovsk dates back to Tsar Paul I, whose wife, Maria Fyodorovna, was responsible for expanding the complex (above: hallway to the State Bedroom).

The Amber Room was reconstructed at Catherine Palace in Pushkin near St Petersburg in 2003.

The vast Catherine Palace, with its 300-m-long (984-ft) façade, is the centrepiece of the castle and park complex in Pushkin (Tsarskoe Selo).

Russia

ENSEMBLE OF THE FERRAPONTOV MONASTERY

The lovingly preserved Ferrapontov Monastery complex in the district of Vologda in north-west Russia is a pristine example of monastic life in the Russian Orthodox community.

After the fire of 1488, the buildings on the hill by the White Sea were not rebuilt until the 17th century. The main church, the Cathedral of the Nativity of the Blessed Virgin Mary, owes its iconic status to the murals inside – the final work by painter Dionisy and his sons in the early 16th century.

The church of the same name is a cubicle cross-in-square brick building erected in 1490 topped with a cylindrical tambour and a characteristic onion dome. The exterior is adorned with clear brick patterns while the interior walls, vaults and support columns are adorned with paintings by Dionisy that accentuate elegant lines and refrain from any three-dimensional elements. The cheerful and light colors give the room an easy feel by emphasizing the vertical thrust of the spatial structure.

Adjoining the cathedral is St Martinian's Church with a pyramidal pinnacle atop simple double arching on the first floor. The refectory is followed by the Church of the Annunciation.

Three churches and a bell tower form the backdrop of the Ferrapontov Monastery.

HISTORIC CENTER OF THE CITY OF YAROSLAVL

The layout of Yaroslavl embodies the progressive urban planning introduced by Catherine the Great. Its large number of old churches is also of interest.

The focal point of Yaroslavl, one of the cities on the Golden Ring some 300 km (186 mi) north-east of Moscow, is a wooden fort complex near to where the Spasky and Petrovsky monasteries were established on the Kotorosl and Volga rivers in the 12th century. The two religious centers would later become the residence of a grand duke and develop into a stronghold of the Russian Orthodox Church – fifty new churches were built here in the 17th century alone.

The city had to be rebuilt in the 18th century after several devastating fires, and the reconstruction was based on the ideal city envisioned by Catherine the Great. In 1763 she had enacted an urban development reform that applied to the whole country. Yaroslavl was thus given a facelift between 1770 and 1830. The Church of the Prophet Elias (1650) became the city's new focal point. Roads radiated out from it and the city formed a semicircle. The older churches were incorporated into the plan as well, which is why some twenty churches have been preserved from the 17th century.

Magnificent frescoes adorn the Church of the Prophet Elias, built in 1650.

HISTORIC MONUMENTS OF NOVGOROD AND SURROUNDINGS

Novgorod, or "new city", was first officially mentioned in 859, which makes it one of the oldest cities in Russia. It was once the center of a kingdom that stretched from the Baltic Sea to the Arctic Ocean.

The kremlin, or citadel, was just a wooden fortress reinforced with stone ramparts in the 11th century. It was also the historic center of Novgorod, a city about 150 km (93 mi) south-east of St Petersburg that has been known as "Veliky Novgorod" since Gorky was renamed "Nizhny Novgorod" in 1991.

The city wall here is nearly 1,400 m (4,593 ft) long, has twelve towers and dates back to the 15th century, when Grand Duke Ivan III of Moscow took control of the city. The oldest and most beautiful building inside the kremlin is Saint Sophia Cathedral, a five-aisled cross-in-square church with three apses completed in 1052 at the behest of Prince Vladimir.

On the opposite bank of the Volkhov is the Church of the Redeemer (1378) with murals by Theophanes the Greek. The style of frescoes and icons created in Novgorod and its environs are now referred to as "Novgorod School".

The Saint Sophia Cathedral with its gilded main dome is the most striking building in the Kremlin on the left bank of the Volkhov River in Novgorod.

KREMLIN AND RED SQUARE, MOSCOW

Since the 13th century, all major historical and political events in Russia have been inextricably linked with Moscow's Kremlin, the headquarters of the tsars and bishops.

The Kremlin had already reached its present-day size when Grand Duke Ivan IV, known as Ivan the Terrible, had himself crowned tsar in 1547. The city's defensive wall, which was built of wood in the 14th century, was first mentioned in 1147. Ivan the Terrible, for his part, commissioned leading Italian and Russian master builders of his time to then construct magnificent buildings and renovate the city's walls and churches. These buildings were actually still being expanded and modified in the 20th

An entire ensemble of fortress and church towers defines the vista of the Kremlin at Red Square in Moscow.

century. Today, they house priceless works of art.

Red Square, spanning an area of 500 by 150 m (1640 by 492 ft), was built towards the end of the 15th century as a market and gathering place – and a place of execution. The famous St Basil's Cathedral was built at the behest of Ivan the Terrible after the victory over the Golden Horde, and consecrated in 1561. It is considered a masterpiece of Old Russian architecture. Eight chapels are arranged on a cross-shaped floorplan around a central church beneath the tower. The extension of the original chapel gave the complex its cathedral status. The central building with its pavilion roof is topped with nine different domes and the Kremlin is still the seat of Russia's government.

Red Square is bordered by the Kremlin wall, St Basil's Cathedral, GUM department store and the History Museum (top left). Terem Palace (center) houses the chambers of Peter the Great. The Cathedral of the Assumption (left) was the coronation site of the tsars.

Russia

ENSEMBLE OF THE NOVODEVICHY CONVENT

Novodevichy is one in the ring of convents around Moscow that also served to defend the city. The main church dates back to around 1525, while the remaining buildings are products of Moscow's baroque age in the second half of the 17th century. The tsars had a close relationship with the convent.

Novodevichy Convent, or "New Virgin Convent", was founded by Vasily III, who was fulfilling a vow he had taken in 1514 during the war against Lithuania. The convent, strategically located at a bend in the Moskva River 4 km (2.5 mi) from Moscow's city center, was part of a defensive line to protect the city against attacks from the southwest. The cathedral dedicated to the icon of the Holy Mother of Smolensk was completed in about 1525, a cross-in-square church with six cross-shaped columns, three apses and five domes.

Its iconography has been carefully preserved and includes Russian rulers, scenes from the Bible and Byzantine history as a way of proving the rulers' identities. The gilded five-row iconostasis was created in around 1685. The convent was fortified and endowed with a palace and churches in the Moscow Baroque style towards the end of the 17th century.

The former military significance of Novodevichy Convent south-west of Moscow is unmistakable.

THE TRINITY SERGIUS LAVRA IN SERGIEV POSAD

The monastery at Sergiev Posad, formerly Sagorsk, on the Golden Ring 70 km (43 mi) north-east of Moscow was once a very important cultural and religious center of the Muscovite Empire.

As one of the defensive monasteries on the Golden Ring, Sergius Lavra was founded in 1340 by St Sergius of Radonezh and is surrounded by immense fortifications that were built between the 15th and 18th centuries. Peter the Great even hid from rebellious palace guards in one of the fortress towers during the Streltsy Uprising. The monastery soon became a place of pilgrimage and one of the most important centers of the Russian Orthodox Church.

The Cathedral of the Assumption forms the heart of the monastery. The oldest place of worship, however, is the Trinity Cathedral from 1422 with the gravesite of Tsar Boris Godunov. The church is also home to the copy (the original is in the Tretyakov Gallery in Moscow) of an iconostasis with works by Andrei Rublyov, the most important icon painter of his time. St Sergius' church and the refectory are the most impressive buildings at this monastery complex.

Nine churches stand on the grounds of the Trinity Sergius Lavra. The bishop once also resided here in a palace.

CHURCH OF THE ASCENSION, KOLOMENSKOYE

The Church of the Ascension is unique in Russia, towering atop a hill by the Moskva River on the outskirts of Moscow. An interesting museum complex has been built just nearby.

When the long-awaited heir apparent, Ivan, later known as "Ivan the Terrible", was born in 1530, his father, Vasily III, ordered a church to be built to express his gratitude. Construction on the white stone Church of the Ascension (also known as the Church of the Resurrection), began in 1532, and has since assumed a distinguished position in Russian architecture. It was one of the first places of worship to have a tent-shaped roof. Other prominent buildings (which are not part of the World Heritage site) were erected in the area around the church as well.

For some decades the site was home to an imperial summer residence made from wood; only one wooden and one stone entrance gate and the Kazanskaya Church remain of it. Also worth seeing are the 17th-century Church of the Holy Mother of Kazan, with its blue domes, and the Church of St John the Baptist from the 16th century, which became the model for Moscow's St Basil Cathedral.

Kolomenskoye's Church of the Ascension features an octagonal tower tapering upwards into a tent-shaped roof.

WHITE MONUMENTS OF VLADIMIR AND SUZDAL

The cities of Vladimir and Suzdal about 200 km (124 mi) north-east of Moscow were the center of their own grand duchy from the 12th to the 14th centuries. The World Heritage Site includes several white stone constructions in Vladimir and the historic town of Suzdal as well as the Church of Boris and Gleb in Kideksha, just a few miles away.

Vladimir, which had been the capital of the Grand Duchy of Vladimir-Suzdal since 1157, hosted master builders, painters and stuccoworkers from all over Europe while they created structures like the magnificent Cathedral of the Assumption (with frescoes by Andrei Rublyov), the Church of the Protection of the Holy Virgin, the Cathedral of St Demetrios, the Bogolyubovo Convent and the Golden Gate.

Until the political center was relocated to Vladimir, Suzdal was the residence of the Grand Prince of Kiev at the end of the 11th century. The kremlin here is home to the city's most beautiful place of worship, the Cathedral of the Nativity of the Blessed Virgin Mary, begun in 1100. The elaborate Convent of the Deposition of the Robe and the Spaso-Yevfimiev Monastery have been partially restored. In Kideksha, only the Cathedral of Boris and Gleb remain.

The Monastery of St Euthymius is one of Suzdal's most imposing buildings.

HISTORIC AND ARCHITECTURAL COMPLEX OF KAZAN KREMLIN

The Kazan Kremlin, on the middle reaches of the Volga, dates back to the time of Ivan the Terrible (Grand Prince from 1533, Tsar from 1547). It is significant because of the 60-m (197-ft) Syuyumbike Tower, allegedly the only major building to survive from the time of the "Golden Horde".

The Khanate of Kazan, founded in 1438, was conquered by Tsar Ivan IV the Terrible in 1552. That same year, he ordered the construction of the citadel which, with its stone walls and elegant towers, was given a new look under the direction of master builder Postnik Yakovlev, also responsible for Moscow's Kremlin.

The old Tartar fortress is symbolized by the great main tower, a seven-storey brick construction with a square base that tapers into an octagonal peak. The entire kremlin complex has been gradually expanded since the 16th century, making it a kaleidoscope of Russian architectural styles. The most important buildings are the Syuyumbike Tower, as well as the Annunciation Cathedral, the Governor's Palace, the military cadet school and the Kul Sharif Mosque.

The Kazan Kremlin watches over this city on the Volga. The skyline is dominated by the spires of the Annunciation Cathedral, the Kul Sharif Mosque, and the Syuyumbike Tower.

WESTERN CAUCASUS

With regard to biodiversity, the region of the Western Caucusus is not just unique in Russia but in the world. It is the largest continuous nature reserve in Europe and Western Asia and contains a vast number of ecosystems that have thus far been spared any significant intervention by human civilization.

The Western Caucasus is about 50 km (30 mi) from the Black Sea coast and covers an area of nearly 3,000 sq km (1,200 sq mi). It stretches some 130 km (80 mi) from west to east and some 50 km (30 mi) from north to south.

The heart of the Natural Heritage Site is made up of large swathes of the Caucasus biosphere reserve and its buffer zone as well as Sochi National Park and several smaller nature reserves. The landscape ranges from lowland areas to the pastures and forests of the region's subalpine sectors, and on into its mountainous regions whose highest peaks reach altitudes of over 3,000 m (9,800 ft). The site is home to over 6,000 registered species of animals and plants, many of them native to the region and many of which are threatened with extinction. The area also provides a wonderful refuge for a vast number of birds and some severely endangered mammals.

The karst-like Lagonaki mountains, in the Republic of Adygea, are situated in the northern part of the protected area and feature roughly 130 caves.

CITADEL, ANCIENT CITY AND FORTRESS BUILDINGS OF DERBENT

The northern ramparts of the Persian Sassanid Empire once ran close to this city in present-day Dagestan, on the border with Azerbaijan.

Derbent is the second-largest city in Dagestan, and one of the oldest in the Russian Federation. The earliest archaeological findings date back to the 3rd millennium BC. The first urban settlement here was established in the 9th century BC while the first fort of significance was built by the Sassanids (224-651), who thus controlled the north-south passage on the western shores of the Caspian Sea until they were overthrown by the Arabs. All subsequent occupiers of the city continued to use the original defense fortifications and the city itself ultimately developed within those walls.

The ancient city is home to baths, cisterns, old cemeteries, a caravanserai, a mausoleum, an Armenian church and a number of mosques. The Juma Mosque was built on the site of a 6th-century Christian basilica and is unique in the region. Derbent was also a hub for the spread of Christianity in the Caucasus. It was part of Russia after 1813 and remained of strategic importance until around 1900.

The 4-ha (10-acre) citadel is perched atop a cliff high above Derbent. Its walls are reinforced with merlons and towers and are up to 3 m (10 ft) thick.

GOLDEN MOUNTAINS OF ALTAI

The Altai mountains of central Asia straddle the borders of Russia, Kazakhstan, China and Mongolia. More than 16,000 sq km (6,200 sq mi) of the Altai World Natural Heritage Site is within Russian territory and is home to numerous rare, native species of plants and animals.

Russia's Altai mountains in southern Siberia form part of an Asian range that includes the Mongolian and Gobi Altai mountains. The World Natural Heritage Site in the Russian Republic of Altai comprises three distinct areas: the Altai reserve and buffer zone around 80-km-long (50-mi) Lake Teletskoye, the Katunsky reserve and buffer zone around Mount Belukha, and the Ukok Quiet Zone.

From the steppe to its alpine areas, the Altai features the most entire sequence of vegetation zones in Central Siberia; the variety of plant life is enormous. Over 2,000 genera have been identified thus far, 212 of which are found only here. The area's animal population, meanwhile, is typical of its Siberian forest environment: over seventy mammal, 300 bird, eleven reptile and amphibian, and more than twenty fish species. Some of them are on the IUCN's Red List of Threatened Species.

Mountain peaks reflected on Lake Ak-Kem on the border of Russia and Kazakhstan.

Russia

UVS NUUR BASIN

This transnational World Heritage Site encompasses twelve protected areas in north-west Mongolia and the Russian republic of Tuva.

The Uvs Nuur is a so-called endorehic basin that covers an area of roughly 10,000 sq km (3,900 sq mi) and is surrounded by a stunning mountain landscape. The basin takes its name from the saline lake at its base. The region is notable for its wide range of ecosystems, which represent all of the landscapes and vegetation zones that occur over 1,000 km (600 mi) of neighboring Siberia, for example, – from vast snowfields, lakes, marshlands and steppe to deserts, semi-deserts, tundra and taiga – all within a 100-km (60-mi) stretch of land from Uvs Nuur Lake at 750 m (2,400 ft) to the nearby peaks at 4,000 m (13,500 ft).

The Uvs Nuur salt lake and the other freshwater lakes in the area are an important refuge for a number of local bird species as well as some migratory birds rest here on their way through. In the desert and mountain regions there are also still some very rare species of animal running around including the Mongolian Gerbil, the beautiful snow leopard, Steppe polecats, wild sheep and the Asian ibex.

The western foothills of the World Heritage Site are home to impressive plateaus. Here: The Charchira mountains of the Mongolian Altai.

LAKE BAIKAL

Lake Baikal is the world's lake of lakes. It is not only the deepest freshwater lake in the world with the greatest volume of water, but also the oldest, dating back twenty-five million years.

Lake Baikal is roughly 650 km (400 mi) long and on average just under 50 km (30 mi) wide. It is situated in southern Siberia not far from the city of Irkutsk. Geologically, this is a highly active region, meaning it experiences relatively frequent earthquakes. The mineral hot springs dotted along the banks of the lake have led to the establishment of numerous spa and recreation resorts.

In the Buryat language, Lake Baikal means "rich lake", and the lake and its surroundings are indeed home to a great diversity of plant and animal life. Over 1,200 animal species have been identified in the water alone,

and most of these – like the Baikal seal or the live-bearing golomyanka fish – are native to the area. Some 600 plant species grow on the lake's surface and its shores.

Lake Baikal is surrounded by high mountain ranges including the Baikal Mountains, the Stanovoy Highlands, the Bargusin Mountains and the Sayan Mountains. The climate is decidedly continental with long, cold winters but relatively warm summers with an average of 2,000 hours of sun per year. These conditions have led to an impressive variety of plant and animal life around the world's oldest lake.

CENTRAL SIKHOTE-ALIN NATURE PRESERVE

In this nature preserve between Ussuri and Amur in the west and the Sea of Japan and the Strait of Tartary in the east is the scene of a unique confluence of temperate and subtropical zones. Species of flora and fauna that usually belong to quite opposing ecosystems are found side by side here.

Covering approximately 15,000 sq km (5,800 sq mi), the central Sikhote-Alin heritage site comprises three nature and animal reserves in the mountainous regions of far-eastern Russia. It also includes the mountain range along the coast of the Sea of Japan. It was first declared a biosphere reserve in 1979. The reserve is notable for its mixed population of Siberian, Manchurian and south-east Asian animal species. Brown bears live side by side with Asiatic black bears, endangered Amur (Siberian) tigers and Amur leop-

ards, whose population is now down to very small numbers indeed. Over 100 of the area's species are on the IUCN's Red List.

Dense forests are the predominant feature of this mountain landscape stretching from Ussuri and Amur in the west to the Sea of Japan and the Strait of Tartary in the east. Numerous endangered species including the Amur tiger live here. Nearly 4 m (13 ft) long and weighing up to 350 kg (770 lb), it is the largest of the world's big cats.

NATURAL SYSTEM OF WRANGEL ISLAND RESERVE

The mountains of Wrangel Island lie in the north-eastern corner of Russia, but despite their northern latitude, the diversity of life found here is extraordinary.

Wrangel Island is north of the Arctic Circle on the western side of the Chukchi Sea. Named after the Russian admiral and Siberian explorer Ferdinand von Wrangel, the island covers an area of roughly 7,500 sq km (2,900 sq mi). Thanks to its mountainous terrain, the island was never fully glaciated during the Ice Age and it is this fact that explains the survival of plants and animals here that have died out elsewhere.

In fact, there are over 400 species and subspecies of vascular plants on Wrangel – twice the number found in any other similarly sized tundra area.

The island is home to the world's largest population of Pacific walrus – up to 100,000 of them – and boasts the world's densest concentration of polar bear dens. Musk oxen graze the tundra landscape and for grey whales migrating from Mexico this is a plentiful feeding ground. Some 100 species of migratory bird breed here as well. Wrangel Island's lemmings feature behavioral patterns that differ greatly from other Arctic lemmings, and reindeer have also adjusted to life here.

Musk oxen are not native to Wrangel Island, but thrive nonetheless.

VOLCANOES OF KAMCHATKA

The Kamchatka peninsula covers 350,000 sq km (135,000 sq mi) and has twenty-eight active volcanoes, the highest of which is Klyuchevskaya Sopka at 4,750 m (15,584 feet). In 2001, the natural heritage site was expanded to include Klyuchevskoy Nature Park.

Kamchatka is 1,200 km (746 mi) long and 480 km (298 mi) wide at its broadest point. It sticks out between the Sea of Okhotsk to the west and the Pacific Ocean and Bering Sea to the east. Two parallel chains of mountains run down its length with the Kamchatka River valley taking up most of the space in between.

Reaching heights of 2,000 m (6,562 feet), the western or central chain is dominated by extinct volcanoes. The eastern chain merges with the volcanic plateaus with still active specimens. In contrast to the marshes of the west coast, the landscape of the east coast

is characterized by cliffs and deciduous forests in the lower regions. The world heritage site boasts many native plants, while Klyuchevskoy Nature Park has large populations of sea lions, sea otters and brown bears. The peninsula also has the world's largest variety of salmonoid fish.

Kamchatka (above, Karimski Volcano) was a restricted area during the Cold War due to its sensitive location. This allowed a wide range of animal life to thrive. The most spectacular inhabitant is the Kamchatka bear, a subspecies of the brown bear.

Spain

ROUTE OF SANTIAGO DE COMPOSTELA

Pilgrims have been trudging along the Way of St James to Santiago de Compostela for centuries. Its importance for the cultural exchange between people from all over the world can be seen in the numerous outstanding buildings along the route.

The beginnings of the many-branched Way of St James date back to the time shortly after the rediscovery of the grave of St James in Santiago de Compostela in the 10th century. The pilgrimages had their climax in the 11th and 12th centuries, when sites in the Holy Land were no longer accessible. The pilgrims' route consists of a network of paths through western and southern Europe. The classic Way of St James is the "Camino Francés": Two initially separate branches arrive from the Somport Pass and from Roncesvalles in the Pyrenees and then con-

Ponferrada is the last major town before arriving in Santiago de Compostela. The original Roman citadel was transformed into the Castillo de los Templarios as early as the 12th century (above).

verge near Puente la Reina. From there, the route continues via Burgos and León through the Basque Country, Cantabria and Asturias to Santiago de Compostela.

The pilgrimage route functioned as a cultural link between the relatively isolated Iberian Peninsula and the rest of Europe. Along it, Romanesque art and Gothic church architecture, for example, made its way into Spain. In total, some 1,800 secular and religious buildings, including bridges, churches, hostelries and hospitals, form the World Heritage Site.

The Puente la Reina in the town of the same name dates from the 11th century and has six wonderfully formed arches. It is located at the confluence of the Camino Francés trails that come from Roncesvalles and Somport – all pilgrims on their way to Santiago de Compostela have to cross this bridge.

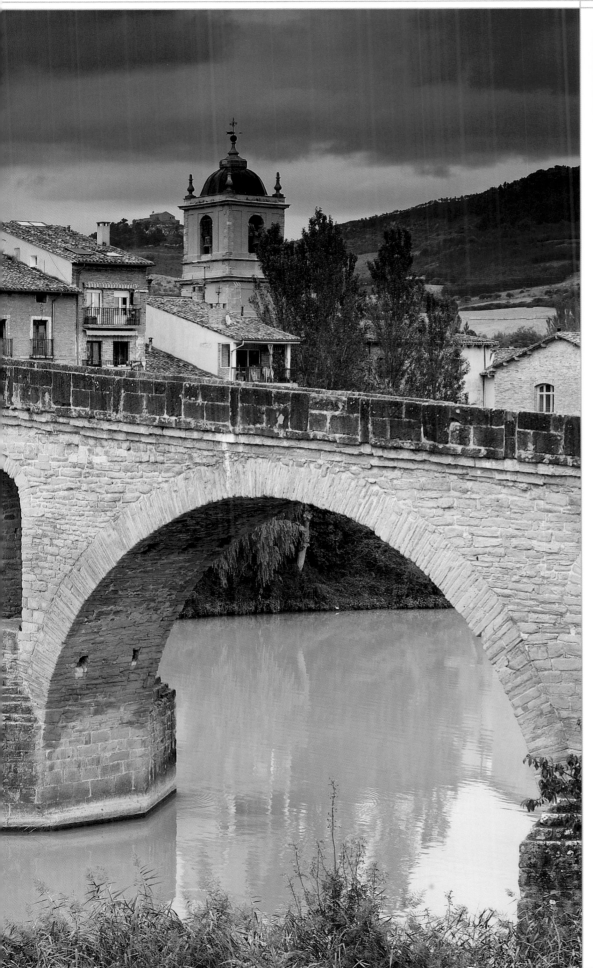

An important stopover on the Way of St James is León, once the capital of the eponymous kingdom. In the middle of the Old Town is the Gothic Cathedral of Santa María de Regla, built in the 13th and 14th centuries.

The pilgrimage Hostal San Marcos in León was designed in the plateresque style – a mixture of early-Renaissance, Gothic and Islamic Mudéjar styles.

The center of Astorga is dominated by the Cathedral of Santa María (8th century) and the Bishop's Palace (not shown), designed by Gaudí and today home to the Museo de los Caminos.

Spain

SANTIAGO DE COMPOSTELA (OLD TOWN)

The former capital of the Kingdom of Galicia is the third most important pilgrimage destination in the Catholic world. The cathedral with the tomb of St James is the focus of the Old Town, which is Romanesque in character.

The Apostle James is widely credited with having introduced Christianity to Spain, so when his alleged tomb was rediscovered in the 9th century, a Carolingian church was built in his honor above the Apostle's reliquary. In 997, the town of Compostela was rsacked by the Moors but was then rebuilt in the 11th century and given a new architectural look. As a result, the cathedral above the tomb is now predominantly Romanesque in style. The "Pórtico de la Gloria" (1188), for example, features a sculptural masterpiece by Mateo, located in the narthex behind the portal of the west façade. Enlarged and embellished many times, the church now boasts a façade in the highly elaborate Churriguerismo style and was completed in 1750.

Aside from the convents and churches such as the San Jerónimo College, outstanding buildings in the surrounding Old Town include the Gelmírez Palace (a rare example of a secular Romanesque building), the Hospital Real and the Rajoy Palace.

The cathedral in Santiago de Compostela is a hugely popular pilgrimage site.

MONUMENTS OF OVIEDO AND THE KINGDOM OF ASTURIAS

Asturias remained an outpost of Christendom even after the Moors had conquered most of the rest of Spain. Pre-Romanesque buildings from this time feature a distinctive Asturian style and have been lovingly preserved in both Oviedo itself and in outlying rural areas.

From the eighth to the 10th century, a style of architecture developed in Asturias that borrowed elements from Roman as well as Visigoth and Moorish styles. One example near Oviedo is Santa María del Naranco, a royal palace built in the middle of the ninth century and transformed into a church between 905 and 1065. Another near Oviedo is the Church of San Miguel de Lillo, which only partially survived the ages. The stone ornaments and reliefs on the portals, pillars and capitals are of note here, hinting at Oriental influences. The Church of Santa Cristina de Lena (c. 850) south of Oviedo was built on a cruciform layout before the rectangular core structure was extended. In Oviedo itself, the Church of San Julián de los Prados, built between 812 and 842, the Foncalada fountain, and the Cámara Santa, once built as a palace chapel and now the oldest part of the cathedral are all testimony to this unique style.

A jewel of Asturian architecture: the Church of Santa Cristina de Lena.

TOWER OF HERCULES

In a landscaped park at the north-western tip of Spain stands a lighthouse that once pointed the way into the natural port of La Coruña, which was already being used by the ancient Romans and Greeks.

Probably built in AD 110, the Tower of Hercules is not just the oldest lighthouse beacon still in use in the world – at a height of 41 m (135 ft) it is also one of the tallest Roman structures still standing. In 1789, Eustaquio Giannini even raised the Roman foundation using two tapering octagonal structures. The tower, which stands on a 57-m-high (187-ft) bluff, now rises to 55 m (180 ft) and is reminiscent of its ancient model: the Pharos, an iconic lighthouse in Alexandria, Egypt. Once you have managed the 242 steps to reach the beacon, an impressive panorama looking out over the churning tides of the Atlantic and the rugged coastline of Galicia unfolds before you. Off in the distance, the cityscape of La Coruña can also be made out along with a landscaped park boasting a number of sights: the foundation walls of a Roman villa, an ancient Muslim cemetery and modern sculptures that have been placed all around the park. Rock engravings in the Monte dos Bicos testify to the spiritual significance of the peninsula to its early settlers, the Phoenicians and the Celts.

According to the legend, Hercules beheaded Geryon and built this tower on top of the giant's mortal remains.

ROMAN WALLS OF LUGO

The walls of Lugo are the most important example in Europe of an ancient Roman fortification. Built during the second and third centuries, it still clearly defines the cityscape of this Spanish provincial town.

The present town of Lugo dates back to an ancient Celtic settlement. During the reign of Emperor Augustus, however, it was conquered by the Romans who subsequently named it Lucus Augusti. It was then enlarged as an important military base, the most important evidence of which is the city wall. In the centuries after its construction, the wall and the city were forced on a number of occasions to withstand attacks from hostile armies, including an ambitious effort by the Moors in 714. Thanks to enduring peace since the 10th century, the fortifications have remained more or less completely intact until today.

About 2,100 m (6,890 ft) of walls encircle the heart of Lugo. On average, they measure 11 m (36 ft) in height and nearly 5 m (16 ft) in width. Originally there were eighty-five so-called "cubos", or semicircular watchtowers, fifty of which remain. The complex has ten gates, the oldest being the Puerta Miña. The Puerta Nueva is adorned by a remarkable Roman relief. The Puerta de Santiago was not incorporated until the 18th century, but leads directly to the city's cathedral.

Visitors can walk all the way around the defensive ramparts that still encircle the Old Town of Lugo.

LAS MÉDULAS

Over centuries, the Romans mined large deposits of gold in Las Médulas, near Ponferrada in the province of León. Traces of their ancient mining activities have survived almost untouched since they were built.

In the first century AD, officials of the Roman Empire discovered and began mining the great deposits of gold buried beneath the surface of this mountainous terrain in north-western Spain. The engineers at work here employed sophisticated techniques in their extraction of the gold, based mainly on flooding the terrain that they had been previously perforated for that purpose. The ruthless exploitation of several thousand slaves also contributed to their success here, where a total of 1,000 tons of the desirable precious metal were unearthed over approximately 250 years of operations.

Countless miners fell victim to the methods, however. A Roman historian, Pliny the Elder, had already written of the dangers of flood mining, which he described as "ruina montium" (lit. to bring down the mountain). In 1992, the area containing the bizarre peaks and stone heaps created by these destructive mining methods was declared a national park due to the fact that it has remained virtually unchanged since Roman times.

In Las Médulas, gold mining operations that literally washed the rock off the mountains also changed the landscape in unexpectedly dramatic ways.

ALTAMIRA AND PALEOLITHIC CAVE ART OF NORTHERN SPAIN

The cave paintings of Altamira are seminal examples of Paleolithic culture in Europe. Together with seventeen other caves in Asturias, Cantabria and the Basque Country, they testify to the artistic sophistication of cave dwellers.

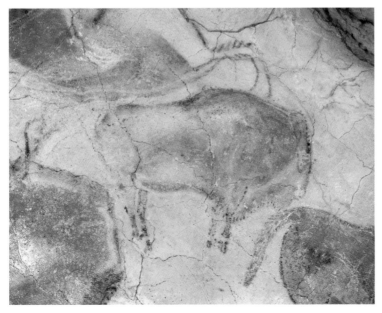

The cave paintings of Altamira were discovered in 1879 and are of a surprisingly refined artistic quality. They feature ice-age animals of the day as well as more abstract drawings. The ceiling painting in one of the auxiliary caves is particularly famous. On an area 18 by 9 m (59 by 30 ft) it depicts a life-size herd of bison. The images were drawn in ochre, black manganese and coal, and some were even engraved. Delicate shading imbues the figures with a strongly three-dimensional and realistic appearance. Northern Spain boasts stellar Paleolithic cave paintings, which led to the

decision in 2008 to enlarge the World Heritage Site of Altamira by a further seventeen caves with works from the period 35,000–10,000 BC: Chufín, Hornos de la Peña, El Pendo, Covalanas, La Garma and four caves in the Monte Castillo in Cantabria, La Peña de Candamo, Tito Bustillo, Covaciella, Llonín and El Pindal in Asturias, as well as Santimamiñe, Ekain and Altxerri in the Basque Country.

Various animals are depicted in the engravings, charcoal drawings and color paintings created in the caves of Altamira between 18,000 and 13,000 BC.

Spain

VIZCAYA BRIDGE

The 160-m-long (525-ft) Puente Vizcaya is a transport bridge that connects the two banks of the Nervión. The bridge is not only a pioneering engineering achievement but also an aesthetic enrichment of the cityscape.

The Puente Vizcaya (Vizcaya Bridge) spans the Nervión River at a height of 45 m (148 ft). Its construction came to be seen as a necessity in the 19th century as the city of Bilbao and its suburbs expanded to the other side of the river. The design by architect Alberto de Palacio y Elissague and engineer Ferdinand Arnodin consisted of a steel frame with a carriage pulled along on ropes – like a section of a gondola. It is known as a transporter bridge ("transbordador"). Ferdinand Arnodin, for his part, is regarded as the inventor of braided steel cable, which made this daring construction possible by allowing land-bound traffic to cross the river without impeding ships. The structure, also known as Puente Colgante ("hanging bridge"), was the model for similar bridges in Buenos Aires, Rio de Janeiro, Newport and Marseille, for example.
Since its inauguration in 1893, the Vizcaya Bridge has been in operation every day around the clock, except in the years between 1937 and 1941. In 1990, it was widened to include a pedestrian walkway; it moves some six million people every year.

The Puente Vizcaya has connected Portugalete and Getxo on either side of the Nervión River since 1893.

ARCHAEOLOGICAL SITE OF ATAPUERCA

The hominid fossils that have been excavated at these two sites in the Sierra de Atapuerca – Gran Dolina and Sima de los Huesos – are evidence of the earliest ancestors of present-day humans in Europe.

A wealth of fossils was unearthed in the caves near Burgos in the Sierra de Atapuerca mountains. The discoveries made it possible to conduct comparative research on an entire population from the Middle Pleistocene period.
In the Sima de los Huesos, the "Bone Pit", for example, 1,600 skeletal remains were found from at least thirty individuals dating back 120,000 to 780,000 years. The finds are of extraordinary significance in the examination of early humans in Europe. Due to its remarkable integrity, the roughly 300,000-year-old "Atapuerca 5" skull has become the focus of great attention in archaeological circles. Some features indicate the shapes of the European Neanderthal Man. In 1994, the oldest skeletal remains in Europe were unearthed in Gran Dolina cave – a 780,000-year-old cuspid. Thirty-six other items led to the postulation of a new species, the homo antecessor. It could also be assigned to an early, primitive form of Homo heidelbergensis, a precursor of Neanderthal man.

Archaeologists at work on an excavation site in the Sierra de Atapuerca.

BURGOS CATHEDRAL

Located on the pilgrimage route to Santiago de Compostela, the Cathedral of Our Lady of Burgos was built from marble-like white limestone in the 13th century and is one of the finest examples of the Spanish Gothic.

Despite a number of extensions and enlargements made during the 15th and 16th centuries, the character of this church on the banks of the Río Arlanzón remains largely intact. The design elements of the French Gothic were superbly realized here, and the architectural coherence and audacity of the building are remarkable.
The main façade is richly adorned with sculptures and flanked by two towers with large windows; it was widened in the 15th century. The northern façade and the El Sarmental entrance date back to the 13th century. The vaulted roof of the 84-m-long (276-ft) central nave is supported by two rows of six pillars each. Attached to the nave is the exceptionally deep presbytery.
The cathedral also contains another architectural jewel: the late-Gothic Capilla del Condestable (1482–1494), the dome above the tomb of Pedro Fernández de Velasco, 2nd Count of Haro and Condestable of Castile. It was designed as a star with eight rays. Similarly unusual is the Plateresque "Golden Staircase" in the northern transept, so named after its gilded wrought-iron banisters.

The main feature in Burgos Cathedral is the dome in the Capilla del Condestable, designed as an eight-armed star.

SAN MILLÁN YUSO AND SUSO MONASTERIES

In the middle of the sixth century, Saint Millán founded a community of monks in the mountains. The Romanesque abbey church of Suso and the monastic complex of Yuso, later redesigned in the baroque style, were built in his honor.

The history of this small mountain village in the province of La Rioja is closely connected with the person of Saint Millán (473–574). The church of Suso Monastery was consecrated in 974. Parts of the church nave were even hewn straight into the rock, as were some small chapels. One of the caves contained the tomb of the holy man, which became an important pilgrimage site during the Middle Ages. Yuso Monastery below Suso was begun in 1053 in the Romanesque style. Its magnificent baroque façade dates from extensive transformations in the 16th to 18th centuries. The interior of the building is richly furnished – especially worth seeing are the Royal Hall with its paintings, the cloister dating from 1572 and the sacristy from 1565 with its ornate reliquary shrines. The monastery's library holds an invaluable collection of precious manuscripts and parchment scrolls, with which it is possible to retrace the beginnings of the written form of Castilian Spanish.

Suso Monastery is the burial place of several Spanish infantas and queens.

PYRENEES: MONT PERDU

The mountain landscapes of the Pyrenees around Monte Perdido straddle the Spanish-French border and boast some of Europe's most fascinating geological formations. They are also home to some of Europe's last surviving traditional mountain cultures.

The extraordinary alpine landscapes that engulf Monte Perdido – taken from its French name, Mont Perdu – stretch across both the French and Spanish sides of the Pyrénées. They feature some impressive geological formations: On the Spanish side are the Añisclo and Ordesa canyons – two of Europe's biggest – while the French side boasts some even steeper drops as well as three of the most breathtaking glacial formations in Europe – the valleys of Troumouse, Estaubé, and Gavarniel.

But perhaps the most striking feature of this imposing mountain landscape is its unspoilt peacefulness. Focused on traditional pastoral farming, life here has remained almost unchanged for centuries, and the trappings of modern living have failed to leave any real mark on the villages, farms and fields, which are still served by seemingly ancient mountain roads. Indeed, the landscape bears testimony to a way of life in the mountains that has long since ceased to exist in most other parts of Europe.

One of the most dramatic features of Ordesa and Monte Perdido National Park: Añisclo Canyon.

CATALAN ROMANESQUE CHURCHES OF THE VALL DE BOÍ

In the 11th and 12th centuries, every village in the Catalan Boí Valley in the High Pyrenees was given its own church. Despite their isolated locations, these Romanesque structures still stand out thanks to sophisticated craftsmanship.

The churches in the Vall de Boí were most likely built on the initiative of Bishop Raimund of Roda-Barbastro, who used them to assert his claim to spiritual jurisdiction in the area. From an art history perspective, the most important churches are Santa María and Sant Climent in Taüll, which were consecrated on consecutive days in the year 1123. They display structural similarities and are both adorned with frescoes that today are kept in the Museu Nacional d'Art de Catalunya in Barcelona. The architecture too is of the highest quality. Sant Climent, the better preserved of the two, has a basilica-like cross-section, adjoined on the eastern side by one central and two side apses. The tower is built on six levels with windows and freezes in the blind arch and dentils.

The other churches in the World Heritage property are: Sant Feliú (Barruera), Sant Joan (Boí), Asunción (Coll), Santa Maria (Cardet), Natividad (Durro), Sant Quirc (Durro) and Santa Eulalia (Erill la Vall).

The Romanesque Sant Quirc de Durro at an altitude of 1,500 m (4,922 ft).

POBLET MONASTERY

The Romanesque Cistercian monastery Santa María de Poblet in Tarragona Province was for a long time an important royal residence and an important spiritual center. Cistercian monks still lived there until the 19th century.

Founded by the Duke of Barcelona in Poblet near the commune of Vimbodí, this monastery, just like the nearby Santes Creus Monastery, served for centuries as a refuge for the rulers of Aragón. The complex is enclosed by three concentric walls with some impressive gates. The Puerta Daurada, the "Golden Gate", dates from the 15th century and marks the transition from the first to the second ring.

The Puerta Real, which is quite a good example of military architecture in the 14th century, provides direct access to the actual monastic portion of the complex. Like the monastery with its Romanesque and early-Gothic cloister, the attached Santa Catalina Church also dates from the 12th century. Originally Romanesque in style, the buildings were enlarged in the 13th and 14th centuries in the Gothic style.

The monastery church was given a baroque façade around the year 1670. The two large 14th-century sarcophagi that dominate the interior of the church contain the bones of the kings of Aragón. These stone coffins are adorned with rich ornamentation and were restored in the 19th century.

The highlight of the Santa María de Poblet Monastery is its cloister.

ARCHAEOLOGICAL ENSEMBLE OF TÁRRACO

The remains of the ancient Roman provincial town of Tárraco, present-day Tarragona, in the south of Catalonia conjure up the picture of a lively trading town that was the entry point for Roman colonization of the Iberian peninsula.

The remains of the once 4-km-long (2.5-mi) fortifications here date back to the period of the town's founding by the Scipio brothers. To discover the gems of antiquity here, visitors can follow the "Passeig Arqueològic" along the length of the town wall, which still stretches for 1 km (0.6 mi). The division of Hispania in 197 BC triggered the rise of Tárraco as capital of the new province of Hispania Citerior. Tárraco takes much of its unique character from the cult of the emperor. For example, during Roman times the Jupiter Temple stood at the highest point in the city. It was later replaced by a mosque, which itself made room for the construction of a cathedral. The Archaeological Museum on the Plaça del Rei is next to the ancient Praetorium, seat of the Roman administrator. The Plaça Forum contains the ruins of the religious and economic center of the province. The amphitheater below the Old Town is also remarkable.

Tárraco, the capital of the Roman province of Hispania Citerior, was protected by mighty ramparts.

Spain

Antoni Gaudí

Few towns in the world have been marked by one single architect to the extent that Barcelona was by Antoni Gaudí (1852–1926). He gave the ancient Catalan capital a new look during his years there as a master builder, landscape artist, town planner and decorator – and in the process became a sort of folk hero. When he died, the entire city mourned his passing. Thousands paid their last respects and accompanied the coffin to "his" Sagrada Familia Church where he was laid to rest.

The son of a boilermaker from a rural background, Gaudí attended the architectural school in Barcelona, where the teachers were not quite

THE WORKS OF ANTONI GAUDÍ

Architect Antoni Gaudí y Cornet was one of the prominent representatives of Modernism. He designed magnificent buildings, in particular in Barcelona. His tour de force was the Sagrada Familia, a church originally designed in the neo-Catalan style in 1882. It is still not finished.

Eusebi Güell, a Barcelona industrialist and patron of the arts, commissioned Antoni Gaudí with what became an idiosyncratic city palace in the Catalan capital: the Palau Güell, completed in 1889 after four years of construction. As with other works by Gaudí, ornamentation and organic shapes dominate the overall style.

The Parque Güell was conceived as a small garden village and, although it

Thanks to its concrete and iron construction, Gaudí 's Casa Milà has no load-bearing interior walls.

was based on detailed plans between 1900 and 1914, the park looks as if it emerged organically. The Casa Milà, built from 1905 to 1911, is a multi-story residential house bizarrely manifested to blur the boundaries between architecture and sculpture. This concept also partially applies to the Casa Batlló, a grand city palace whose roof Gaudí shaped as a large dragon and adorned with mosaic chimneys reminiscent of "soldiers". For the interior of the Casa Vicens, Gaudí borrowed from Mudéjar architecture.

Still unfinished: Gaudí's stunning Sagrada Familia church, with its distinctive, spindle-shaped towers and organic shapes inspired by nature.

sure whether they were dealing with a genius or a madman. Eventually he found his allies in Barcelona's self-confident and progressively thinking upper classes – clients such as the industrialist Güell, who financed some of his daring projects.

Gaudí's style is Modernism, a Catalan variation on Art Nouveau, that high-lights organic shapes inspired by nature, skewed angles, pillars and columns that are reminiscent of trees, irregular floorplans and an almost overwhelming multitude of decorative elements that betray Moorish influ-ences. Fine examples of Gaudí's art are his fantastic tenement blocks and the Sagrada Familia.

The entrance to the Parque Güell (far page), commissioned by the industrialist Eusebi Güell and laid out by Gaudí (left: a contemporary portrait in relief), has two gatehouses featuring playful turrets and roofs. Also in the park is the archi-tect's former home. Drawings by Gaudí and furniture designed by him are displayed here.

Spain

PALAU DE LA MÚSICA CATALANA AND HOSPITAL DE SANT PAU, BARCELONA

Among the most remarkable structures in Barcelona are two masterpieces by Catalan Art Nouveau architect Lluís Domènech i Montaner.

The Catalan Palau de la Música Catalana (Palace of Catalan Music) is home to Barcelona's most important concert hall. It was built by architect Domènech i Montaner in 1908 for the "Orfeó Català" choir. The steel construction of this Art Nouveau building is clad in colorful ceramics and beautiful stained glass.

Another superb building designed in the Catalan Art Nouveau style is the Hospital de Santa Creu i Sant Pau in the Avinguda Sant Antoni Maria Claret. Construction of the hospital was commissioned by Catalan banker Pau Gil in his will. He envisaged a complex consisting of forty-eight independent pavilions surrounded by large gardens and linked by subterranean corridors.

The Palau de la Música Catalana, with its allegorical sculptures on either side of the stage (bottom) is the most unusual work of Lluís Domènech i Montaner. Despite its daring design, the Hospital de Sant Pau (right) also functioned in the manner expected of a hospital.

OLD CITY OF SALAMANCA

The heart of Salamanca is the Plaza Mayor, built between 1729 and 1755 and dominated by the baroque façade of the town hall. A numer of very well-preserved buildings from different periods are harmoniously integrated into the magnificent cityscape.

Salamanca was conquered by the Romans in the third century BC and later plundered on a number of occasions by the Moors. It achieved great significance after the Reconquest by King Alfonso VI of Spain in 1085. The university founded by Alfonso IX in 1218 is, together with Oxford, Paris and Bologna, one of the four most important universities in the Western world. Its façade is a masterpiece of the Plateresque style.

Salamanca is also equally rich in Romanesque and Gothic buildings. The 12th-century Old Cathedral, for example, is one of very few structures with Romanesque-Byzantine influences. The church was incorporated into the architectural complex of the New Cathedral, begun in 1513, which features both late-Gothic and baroque elements.

Plaza Mayor was laid out in baroque style according to plans by Alberto Churriguera. The square is rectangular in plan and framed by arcades. The buildings are four stories high and feature balustrades. On its eastern side (not shown here, and known as the "Royal Pavilion"), visitors can admire medallions of Spanish kings.

OLD TOWN OF ÁVILA WITH ITS EXTRA-MUROS CHURCHES

Ávila is located at an altitude of 1,114 m (3,655 ft) in the northern foothills of the Sistema Central dividing range. It is perhaps the most beautiful example of a medieval Spanish town. The city's Gothic cathedral rises gloriously above the battlements of the lovingly preserved town wall, which measures a total of 2,557 m (8,390 ft) and counts nine gates and eighty-eight towers.

The ramparts, which were begun in about 1090, were given their present appearance in the 12th century and are arranged on a square layout. The mightiest of its towers, the "Ciborro", serves simultaneously as the apse of the cathedral. The church is integrated into the fortifications like a bastion. One of the oldest cathedrals in Spain, its interior is home to masterly sculptures. Beyond the city gates there are some remarkable churches dating from the Middle Ages. Of these, San Vicente, built in the 12th century, is probably the most interesting. It boasts a wonderful collection of sculptures from the Romanesque period. Other buildings of art-historical importance in this episcopal city include San Pedro, dating from the 12th to 13th centuries, and Santo Tomás from 1482.

The most remarkable feature of the impressive city walls of Ávila is the fact that the cathedral and its apse are built directly into the walls.

OLD TOWN OF SEGOVIA AND ITS AQUEDUCT

The medieval old town of Segovia is perched on a ridge and features a rich architectural legacy of more than twenty Romanesque churches. An aqueduct built by the Romans is the city's main architectural feature.

In order to transport fresh water from the Río Frío some 18 km (11 mi) to Segovia, the Romans built an impressive aqueduct stretching a total length of 730 m (2,395 ft). The bridge was built in the second century AD and is supported by 118 arches. It was constructed from granite blocks without the use of mortar. It was restored at the end of the 15th century.

The many Romanesque churches in the city are remarkable thanks to their characteristic ambulatories, conceived as meeting points for the guilds and fraternities. Work on the late-Gothic cathedral of Segovia began in 1525, on the site of an earlier Romanesque church that had been destroyed by fire. Its slim tower rises 88 m (289 ft) high above the town; a 67-m-high (220-ft) crossing vault spans the church. The Alcázar of Segovia, a fortress situated on a rock high above the city, was given its Gothic appearance in the 13th century. It was also the location of Isabella of Castile's coronation in 1474.

The emblem of Segovia is the Roman aqueduct that traverses the Old Town.

MONASTERY AND SITE OF THE ESCURIAL, MADRID

The San Lorenzo de El Escorial Monastery is the center of the small town that served as a summer residence for the Spanish kings. Philip II planned the building as a combination of monastery, church, palace and mausoleum.

As an expression of his claim to power, and strengthened by his military victories against the French, Philip II commissioned the mighty Escurial in 1561, about 60 km (37 mi) north-west of Madrid. The lead architect was Juan Bautista de Toledo but after his untimely death, Juan de Herrera took over supervision of the project in 1567. Work was essentially completed by 1584. The complex covers a vast area of more than 30,000 sq m (322,800 sq ft) and has sixteen courtyards and nine towers. Its layout was inspired by the perfect symmetry of the Temple of Solomon in Jerusalem and for a long time it was used as a model for numerous grand complexes in Europe. Since the reign of Philip II, the bones of the Spanish monarchs have been kept in the magnificently appointed royal mausoleum. Aside from the countless private and state-rooms of the royal family, the monastic library with its valuable tomes is particularly impressive.

The library on the second floor contains frescoes by Italian artist Pellegrino Tibaldi and holds some 40,000 books.

Spain

UNIVERSITY OF ALCALÁ DE HENARES

In the 16th and 17th centuries, the University of Alcalá de Henares was one of the main centers of learning in Europe. Numerous churches and the bishop's palace still bear witness to the influence of this see.

Alcalá de Henares, known in Roman times as "Complutum", was laid to waste by the Moors in about 1000 and rebuilt in 1038 as al-Qal'ah an-Nahr. In 1088, Alfonso VI reconquered the town, handing it and the surrounding region to the archbishop of Toledo. In 1498, Cardinal Jiménez de Cisneros began expanding the city as a center of scholarship with the aim of reforming intellectual life within the Church. The Colegio de San Ildefonso opened in 1508, and at the same time construction on the Chapel and the brick Hall of Ceremonies with its magnifi-cent ceiling began. Other colleges followed soon after. The college of Rodrigo Gil was erected between 1541 and 1553, and features court-yards that are considered master-pieces of the early Renaissance. The church of the Bernardas Monastery was completed in 1626 on a rectan-gular layout with oval chapels coming off a central domed hall. Alcalá de Henares became a model for Spanish missionary settlements.

The university's Patio Trilingüe, an attractive inner courtyard.

MUDÉJAR ARCHITECTURE OF ARAGÓN

Teruel, located in the autonomous region of Aragón, remained settled by the Moors even after the Reconquest of Spain. It is thanks to their influence that the Mudéjar style developed, combining both Gothic and Islamic elements.

Teruel is located at the confluence of the Río Guadalaviar and the Río Alfambra, in the autonomous region of Aragón. In 1171, Alfonso II recon-quered Teruel from the Moors, but many of the Muslim inhabitants stayed in the now Christian town. Slowly, the different traditions began to merge, and from the 13th to the 15th centuries, a distinctive architec-tural and decorative style emerged that is still present in many towns in the region. Each of the many towers and churches of Teruel is unique in its own way as well.

The World Heritage property consists of the three brick towers of the El Salvador, San Martín and San Pedro churches and the bell tower and Artesonado ceiling of the cathedral from the 13th century. The Torre de San Salvador (around 1277) is a par-ticularly successful example of the Mudéjar style. Like the tower of San Martín (14th century), it is richly adorned with tiles.

The Cathedral of San Martín features interior furnishings with both Christian and Islamic elements.

ARANJUEZ CULTURAL LANDSCAPE

The charm of the cultural landscape of Aranjuez, located about 50 km (31 mi) south of Madrid on the rivers Tagus and Jarama, lies in the complex yet harmo-nious interplay between nature and human creation.

Aranjuez has been a summer resi-dence of the Spanish monarchs since the reign of Philip II (1527–1598), which explains not only the artful arrangement of palaces and chateaux but also the irrigation systems that bring water to the French-style ba-roque gardens, fruit orchards and veg-etable gardens. The many canals, or "acequias" and "caceras", form a charming contrast to the meandering course of the River Tagus, the lifeblood of Aranjuez. Indeed, a variety of flora and fauna flourishes along the banks of the Tagus.

The royal palace consists of a three-story main tract and two two-story wings with arcaded galleries. The vast park contains the Casita del Labrador, a maison de plaisance commissioned by Charles IV in 1803. Five years later, in 1808, the Spanish uprising against the predominance of Napoleon Bona-parte began in Aranjuez.

A simple country mansion for recreation-al purposes is what Philip II asked Juan Bautista de Toledo to build in 1560. He later asked Juan de Herrera to expand it as a vast royal palace.

HISTORIC CITY OF TOLEDO

Toledo, south-west of Madrid on the River Tagus, is one of the oldest towns in Spain. It was the location of the Visigoth councils, seat of the Moorish emirs and the residence of Castilian kings.

In more than 2,000 years of history, Christians, Muslims and Jews have lived in Toledo. Even an aqueduct and the remains of an amphitheater have been preserved from the days of the Romans. The impressive fortifications date from the seventh century – they were enlarged several times. The Emirate of Córdoba also left its mark on Toledo: Arab baths and a mosque still stand. Jews – who were tolerated by the Arabs – had two synagogues, El Tránsito and Santa María La Blanca, dating from the 12th and 14th centuries respectively. They boast magnificent sculptures. The Mudéjar style was as widely spread in Toledo as in Teruel. The Gothic Cathedral of Santa María in the center of town is a collaborative work by Flemish and French master builders from the late 15th century. It is located on a former mosque, which is itself on the foundations of a former Christian church. Its stained-glass windows are unique. Another important building is the Alcázar, sitting enthroned high above the city. The artist El Greco also lived and died in Toledo.

Toledo's Old Town sprawls over a promontory that is encircled by deep gorges of the Río Tagus on three sides.

OLD TOWN OF CÁCERES

Cáceres in the northern province of Estremadura boasts seminal monuments from various periods including churches, convents and palaces as well as preserved sections of its ancient city walls.

Only a modest section of the former ramparts remains of Colonia Norbensis Caesarina, founded by the Romans. The Almohads, who ruled here in the 12th and 13th centuries, extended the present fortifications and equipped them with numerous towers. At an impressive height of 30 m (98 ft), the Los Pozos Tower still rises above the circular walls today. Within the town itself, however, there is little left to mark the period of Moorish rule. Arab influences can now mostly be discerned in the layout of the streets and courtyards.

In addition to numerous convents and Gothic churches built in the 14th century, palaces were also constructed for the aristocracy, including El Mono and the turreted Las Cigüeñas. However, starting in the 15th century, the Catholic monarchs had many of these buildings demolished and converted, and allowed the city ramparts to fall to ruin.

The Church of Santa María and the Gothic San Mateo Cathedral, which dominates the cityscape, were also built in the 15th century.

The Gothic church and co-cathedral Santa María with its beautiful interior furnishings stands on Santa María Square.

ROYAL MONASTERY OF SANTA MARÍA DE GUADALUPE

Our Lady of Guadalupe was the patron saint of the Spanish conquerors in South America. A former Hieronymite monastery, Real Monasterio de Nuestra Señora de Guadalupe is still a major ecclesiastical center today.

According to the legend, a shepherd in the 13th century named Gil Cordero found an image of the Madonna buried in the soil – it had allegedly been created by Saint Lucas. A hermitage was built at the site of his discovery, and Alfonso XI had a larger monastic complex built on the site in 1340, to give thanks for his victory in the Battle of the Salado Creek.

Generous royal support ensured that the monastery flourished. Columbus named the first Native American he encountered "Guadalupe"; he also insisted that the first Native Americans to convert to Christianity should be baptized in this monastery. Thus, Our Lady of Guadalupe soon became known all over the Hispanic world, and her image is still kept in the Gothic church. The church's interior contains many important works of art. The precious furnishings of the Santa Ana Chapel, with its splendid bronze portal, also testify to the former glory of this monastery.

The monastery complex has four parts: a basilica, an auditorium, a cloister in the Mudéjar style and a Gothic cloister.

Spain

ARCHAEOLOGICAL ENSEMBLE OF MÉRIDA

Close to the town of Mérida are Spain's best-preserved remains from the Romans and the early Middle Ages. Augusta Emerita was founded here by the Romans as a colony for veterans who spent their retirement in the area.

The semicircular Roman theater in Mérida was donated by Emperor Agrippa and accommodated some 6,000 spectators. Its marble stage ensemble has been beautifully preserved. The amphitheater nearby was inaugurated in the year 8 BC. It accommodated 14,000 spectators who came to watch animal and gladiator fights. A complicated system of pipes allowed the hosts to flood the arena, making it possible to put on aquatic events as well.
The Circus Maximus was probably built at the beginning of the first cen-

tury. With its massive proportions, the circus offered seating for 30,000 spectators in three ranks, depending on social standing.
The tavernas and guesthouses for visitors can also still be seen today. A townhouse with floor mosaics and wall frescoes is well preserved, giving a good impression of the life of Roman soldiers in retirement.

The Los Milagros Aqueduct from the first century AD owes its colorful appearance to the materials used for its construction: granite and brick.

ROCK ART OF THE MEDITERRANEAN BASIN ON THE IBERIAN PENINSULA

These fascinating rock paintings provide unique insight into the culture and lifestyles of prehistoric humans along the Spanish Mediterranean coast.

In seemingly stark contrast to the more famous rock art in central and northern Spain, the artistic depictions on the Mediterranean coast are not found in deep and inaccessible caves. Instead, they adorn shallow rock niches, overhanging rocks and other generally well-protected but easily accessible places.
This indicates to us that these images no longer served just a select group of spiritual leaders for ritual and cultic purposes. The subject matter in fact reflects the areas of life that were

of vital concern for humans at the time. The common theme of hunting occurs particularly often as a result. The experience of the hunt is told as a virtually continuous story using series of partially modified repetitions of the motif.

The rock drawings of the Mediterranean coast of eastern Spain (right: the rock paintings of El Cogul) were created between 6,000 BC and the early Bronze Age between 4,000 and 2,000 BC.

HISTORIC WALLED TOWN OF CUENCA

The picturesque fortified town of Cuenca, between Madrid and Valencia, is perched on a rocky promontory above the rivers Huécar and Júcar. It boasts numerous well-preserved buildings from the Gothic to the baroque periods.

The Arabs founded Cuenca as a fortress in the heart of the Caliphate of Córdoba and placed it strategically upon a rocky promontory. The well-preserved walls and ramparts that still embrace the Old Town are from that time. After the Spanish Reconquest in the 12th century, Cuenca became a bishops' see. Among the numerous ecclesiastical and secular buildings that were erected in the years that followed is the first Norman Gothic cathedral in Spain, built in the 12th and 13th centuries on the site of an earlier mosque.

A peculiarity of Cuenca are the casas colgadas, or "hanging houses", which can be seen from afar. Built into the rocky slopes above the Huécar River, they seem to be floating above the abyss. On of them houses the Museo de Arte Abstracto Español, one of the largest collections of modern Spanish abstract art. The Museo Arqueológico nearby exhibits valuable discoveries from the region.

The Old Town of Cuenca, framed by two rivers, was built on a vertical rockface. It is famous for its "hanging houses".

LA LONJA DE LA SEDA IN VALENCIA

This impressive civic building in the port city of Valencia stands as a symbol for the enormous wealth of this medieval trading center.

A long period of peace began for Valencia during the reign of Isabella of Castile and Ferdinand II. Due to its strategic location and the stability that these powerful rulers brought, the port city flourished as an important trading center. One building among the secular structures of this period is particularly important: La Lonja de la Seda, the Silk Exchange.

The entire complex, which covers an area of approximately 2,000 sq m (21,520 sq ft), stands opposite the Church of Santos Juanes and the central market. Construction began in 1483 and was led by architect Pere Comte. The buildings consist of four sections: the tower crowned by battlements, the Consulado del Mar Hall, the orange tree courtyard and the pit, whose star vaulting is supported by twenty-four spiral columns. The hall was conceived as a trading temple, with the columns symbolizing trees and the domes the firmament.

One of the most beautiful secular Gothic buildings is the Lonja de la Seda. During the annual Valencia spring festival, the "Fallas", papier-mâché figures, are exhibited in the columned hall with its 16-m-high (52-ft) cross-ribbed vaulting.

PALMERAL OF ELCHE

With more than 200,000 specimens, El Palmeral in Elche on the Costa Blanca south-west of Alicante is the largest palm tree plantation in Europe.

Even before the Christian Era, seafarers were bringing palm trees from the southern Mediterranean to the village of Elche, which benefits from an unusually mild climate. The present complex of El Palmeral, however, with its creative ornamentation and highly sophisticated irrigation system, is entirely the work of Moorish master builders.

By the middle of the 12th century, the designers had completed the ramparts, the canal fed by the nearby Río Vinalopó and traversing the middle of the town, and the first plantation of date palms. The palm grove was later cultivated, enlarged and irrigated by an extensive network of waterways that has been preserved to this day.

The plantation in Elche is much more than just a palm grove, however. It is an amalgamation of gardens, parks and green areas – a giant green lung that extends across a large part of the urban area and the environs.

Ironically, just after the Reconquest freed the town from its Moorish rulers in the 13th century, James I was quick to implement a number of regulations to protect the plantations the Moors had so lovingly built; these were then adopted by subsequent governments.

The Palmeral of Elche covers an area of 1.5 sq km (1/2 sq mi). Other plants also flourish in the shadow of the palm trees.

MONUMENTAL ENSEMBLES OF ÚBEDA AND BAEZA

The twin towns of Úbeda and Baeza are about 10 km (6 mi) from each other. They experienced a meteoric rise in the 16th century, Spain's golden age, and became models for the Renaissance art of Spain and Latin America.

The small towns of Úbeda and Baeza are 9th-century Moorish settlements that feature a fortress, the Alcázar. After the reconquista in the first half of the 13th century, the basic Arabic urban designs were only minimally changed, and remained like this until the Renaissance began to take hold. The 15th century brought about a degree of prosperity to the area, but in fact this remained confined to a small minority of aristocrats and clerics.

Still, a lot of building ensued. The wall that separated the Alcázar from the residential town was demolished, and new buildings were constructed in the style of the increasingly popular Italian Renaissance.

Úbeda is almost square in plan and surrounded by a wall. Its focal point is the Plaza Vázquez de Molina with the El Salvador Church, which boasts a remarkable wooden altar. Baeza's oval layout is also enclosed by fortifications. Its cathedral is from 1570.

The urban center of Baeza is the Plaza del Pópulo, also called Plaza de los Leones, or Square of the Lions, in reference to the Fountain of the Lions.

Spain

ALHAMBRA, GENERALIFE AND ALBAYZÍN, GRANADA

Granada boasts not just one but several worthy sights: the Old Town district of Albayzín with its narrow alleyways and many squares; the Alhambra, on a hill within the city; and the Generalife Palace. The Alhambra, residence of the Arab rulers, is one of the most important Islamic monuments in Spain.

The south of Spain remained under Moorish rule even after the end of the Caliphate of Córdoba. What was the Emirate of Granada then became an independent kingdom in 1238, and it was then that the Moors built the magnificent complex of the Alhambra. By 1492, the kingdom was the last Arab possession on the peninsula and was then taken back by Ferdinand and Isabella.

The Patio de la Acequia forms the entrance to the Generalife, the Sultan's garden of relaxation, which also served as a fruit orchard and vegetable garden.

The Alhambra citadel was left to decay starting in the 16th century before a large part was eventually restored in the 19th century. The pavilions, halls and courtyards of the complex are adorned with mosaics and tiles while the individual palaces feature shaded walkways, fountains and waterworks for refreshment. The terraced gardens and water basins of the Palacio del Generalife from 1319 are considered a particularly successful artistic effort. The cathedral, built after the end of Moorish rule, holds the tombs of the Catholic kings. The Alhambra district also includes the uncompleted palace of Charles V, which was begun in 1526 without much regard for existing Moorish styles.

The Alhambra was built in the 13th and 14th centuries above Granada (top right). The Patio de los Leones (right), the Courtyard of the Lions, has a fountain propped up by twelve lion sculptures.

HISTORIC CENTER OF CÓRDOBA

During the reign of the Umayyads, Córdoba was the capital of the Spanish Caliphate and as such was a center of cultural and technological sophistication in Europe. The most outstanding monument in the Old Town is La Mezquita Catedral, which was formerly a mosque.

When the invading Arabs had expelled the last remaining king of the Visigoths in 711, they built their mosque, the Mezquita, on the foundations of the Roman Temple of Janus and a Visigoth church. Its layout forms a rectangle 180 m (591 ft) long and 130 m (427 ft) wide and was enlarged on several occasions up until the 10th century. With its "forest of columns" it is one of the most beautiful and one of the largest Islamic buildings in the world – it is also the most significant Moorish religious structure in Spain.

Immediately adjacent to the Mezquita is the Judería, the former Jewish quarter with its flower-bedecked alleyways.

It also includes the Patio de los Naranjos, a walled courtyard planted with orange trees. After the Reconquest of Córdoba in 1236, the mosque was converted to a church. The first architectural changes were not made until 1384, however, and they did little to change the overall impression of the building.
The Judería with its narrow and winding alleyways still has a Moorish feel to it. This is also where the last synagogue of Córdoba is preserved.

Córdoba had already been an important political and cultural center during the Roman Empire. In fact, the 16-arched Puente Romana over the Guadalquivir River (top left) once formed a part of the Via Augusta. The Mezquita of Córdoba seems modest from the outside, but its interior features a veritable forest of 860 columns made of jasper, onyx, marble and granite arranged in double arcades and supporting two-tone horseshoe-shaped arches (left).

Spain

Christopher Columbus

Christopher Columbus (1451–1506) is justifiably considered one of the most famous explorers in the history of the world. He crossed the Atlantic, dared to advance into entirely unknown realms, and happened to discover the New World – a fact that had not yet been proven for certain by the time he died. The grand achievement of this daredevil sailor was actually an error. In the process of looking for the most favorable sea route westward to the legendary treasures of India, he initially presumed, quite rightly, that the Earth was a sphere. He gravely miscalculated the size of the sphere, however. He believed the westerly route across the Atlantic to

SEVILLE

Three buildings in the heart of Seville constitute the city's World Heritage Site: the Alcázar's Admiralty Hall, where overseas expeditions were prepared; the Cathedral, where Columbus is buried; and the Archivo General de Indias, with important documents from colonial history.

When Moorish rulers conquered this town, they built the Grand Mosque of Seville, which was subsequently destroyed during the Reconquest in 1248. Only the Giralda remained, a minaret built in 1184 to 1196 and a masterpiece of Almohad architecture. It was converted to the bell tower of the newly built cathedral. For its part, the cathedral is the largest Gothic structure of its kind in the world. Its chapels possess superb paintings by Murillo, Velazquez and Zurbarán.

Only La Giralda, the minaret, remains of the mosque in Seville. After its extension, it is now 97 m (318 ft) tall.

The impressive palace fortifications, the Alcázar, also date back to the Moors; the decoration of the courtyards makes this apparent. In the 13th century, the palace became the royal residence and was later expanded in the Mudéjar style. The Casa de la Lonja, built between 1583 and 1598, was a commodity exchange and a hub for the trade with the colonies. In 1785, it was transformed into the Archivo General de Indias.

The Archivo General de Indias (right in the image) contains valuable documents on the history of Latin America and is next to the Gothic cathedral.

the Far East to be shorter than the easterly route around Africa, which was already being explored by the Portuguese. With that in mind, the Genoese navigator set off for the first time in 1492, in the service of the Spanish crown. He landed in the Caribbean, since known as the West Indies. After the shipwreck of the

"Santa Maria", he founded a settlement on Hispaniola (now Haïti and the Dominican Republic), laying the foundation for the Spanish and Portuguese empires in the Americas. In 1502, his final attempt led him to the Central American coast and into the mouth of the Orinoco River in hopes of reaching East Asia.

Christopher Columbus's sarcophagus in the cathedral of Seville (left) dates from 1900. Far left is a portrait from 1519 by Sebastiano del Piombo. Because Columbus wished never to be interred in Spanish soil, the sarcophagus rests on the shoulders of four messengers symbolizing the four kingdoms of León, Castile, Navarra and Aragón.

Seville Cathedral is one of the grandest Gothic church buildings in the world. Outside and inside it demonstrates a great diversity of styles from each individual construction phase: Mudéjar, Gothic, Renaissance and baroque.

The Alcázar is a jewel of Mudéjar architecture. Above is the Throne Room (Sala de Embajadores) with its gilded stuccowork and the vaulted ceiling made from larch wood. Charles V married Isabella of Portugal here.

The Indian Archive (Archivo General de Indias) holds important documents that give insight into the relationship between Spain and its colonies.

Spain

DOÑANA NATIONAL PARK IN ANDALUSIA

Doñana in Andalusia is Spain's biggest national park. Once a royal hunting ground, these extensive wetlands at the delta of the Guadalquivir river are now a safe haven for numerous rare species and a stopover for many migratory birds.

It is the diversity of its landscape that makes Doñana so special. Alongside large expanses of marshland complete with lagoons and boggy areas, the park also features dry areas whose character is more akin to a heath or savannah featuring dense forests of cork oak trees. The wetlands, meanwhile, provide a nesting place for numerous species of often rare birds. The area's large flamingo population is of particular interest. The system of lagoons within the protected area even attract wild boar and red deer while the bushy Mediterranean veg-etation includes rare plants like white thyme and offers grey herons, storks, and cranes a comfortable place to nest. Other animals found in the na-tional park include the Iberian lynx and the all-but-extinct imperial eagle. Among the very rare animals are the Montpellier snake, the white spoon-bill, the ichneumon (a type of mon-goose), and the monk vulture. Pine forests dominate the southern reaches of the park.

Great sand dunes strecht out along the Atlantic coast of Doñana.

THE BIODIVERSITY AND CULTURE OF IBIZA

This Balearic island is a World Natural Heritage and a World Cultural Heritage Site. Its claim to natural heritage status is based on posidonia, a grassy marine weed that plays a vital role in the diverse ecosystem sea around it. Its architec-ture and archaeological sites, meanwhile, speak for its cultural importance.

Ibiza's long history can be traced back to the 2nd millennium BC, and signifi-cant evidence of island life at this time has been well preserved. Two archae-ological excavation sites in particular – the Phoenician Sa Caleta settlement (700 BC) in the south-west of the is-land and the Punic necropolis Puig des Molins (5th century BC) – underline Ibiza's significance during the Phoeni-cian-Carthaginian era.

It was the Phoenicians who, some 2,600 years ago, founded the fortified upper town ("Dalt Vila") of Ibiza Old Town, and it has been occupied with-out interruption ever since.

Posidonia is a bit like a sea grass and is only found in the Mediterranean, but even here it is increasingly under threat. It provides shelter for a wide variety of marine life and produces twenty-one tons of organic biomass every year – almost as much as a trop-ical rainforest of the same size.

It took forty years to build the protective walls around the "Dalt Vila", the oldest section of Ibiza City.

SAN CRISTÓBAL DE LA LAGUNA ON TENERIFE

San Cristóbal de La Laguna is the oldest civilian settlement on Tenerife. Over the centuries, a unique Old Town has developed with magnificent buildings, a university and a number of religious monuments.

Founded in 1496 by Spanish conquis-tador Alonso Fernández de Lugo on the high green plains of Aguere, San Cristóbal (the addition of "La Laguna" refers to a lagoon that was later drained) received its original municipal charter as early as 1510. In 1701, Pope Clement XI ordered the establishment of a university, and in 1818 the town became an episcopal see.

In the same year, the Church of Santa María de los Remedios was declared a cathedral (Catedral de los Remedios). Its greatest treasure is the gilded altar screens from 1715 in the Capilla de la Virgen de los Remedios, to the right of the main altar. The oldest church in town is the Church of Nuestra Señora de la Concepción, with a lava-black bell tower built between 1502 and 1505 in the Gothic style.

The first university of the city, built in 1744 inside the Augustine Monastery of the Holy Spirit, is also dominated by a bell and clock tower that is reminis-cent of a church steeple.

San Miguel (1506) pilgrimage church, dedicated to Archangel Michael, is one of the town's most beautiful churches.

TEIDE NATIONAL PARK, TENERIFE

This Natural Heritage Site takes in the fascinating volcanic landscape of the 3,718-m (12,198-foot) Pico del Teide – Spain's highest mountain – as well as the area's characteristic flora and fauna.

Most of this national park is an inhospitable, volcanic landscape, dominated by the Pico and its caldera, whose diameter measures 17 km (11 mi). The ever-changing climate and frequent mists lend the scenery a very special atmosphere. The Teide is too barren an environment to support much vertebrate life, but it is home to three native species. One of them, the blue-throated lizard (Gallotia galloti), has come to symbolize the park. The Teide blue chaffinch, which lives in pine forests, is also found in the park. The Teide's wealth of insect life, meanwhile, encompasses 700 different species, most of them native to the Canaries. There are 168 different flowering plants in the park, fifty-eight of which are native, but the most striking plant, and the park's most common, is the Teide broom (Spartocytisus supranubius), whose white or pink flowers produce a very special honey.

Alexander von Humboldt ascended the Teide in 1799 to study climate conditions. He referred to the "Garden of the Teide" in the surrounding Orotava Valley as a world wonder.

GARAJONAY NATIONAL PARK

The mountains of Gomera, one of the Canary Islands, are volcanic in origin and reach altitudes of up to 1,487 m (4,879 feet). The trees that cover them form Europe's last remaining subtropical primeval forest.

Occupying an area of almost 40 sq km (15 sq mi), Garajonay National Park covers roughly one-tenth of the island of Gomera and crosses all six of its administrative regions. Dense forests cover the slopes of the Alto de Garajonay, the island's highest mountain. They are the last remaining subtropical primeval forest in what is considered southern Europe, and contain the world's only remaining closed laurel forest dating back to the Tertiary period. Millions of years old, this forest's location in the middle of the ocean has enabled it to survive the deteriorating climatic conditions that developed during the ice age. In terms of flora and fauna, many of the park's plants and animals are only found here. The animals that live on the Canary Islands include of course the canary pigeon and the laurel pigeon, but there are also 960 invertebrate species including 100 native animals that can be found within the national park.

This ancient ecosystem allows visitors to get a good idea of how forests might have looked some 65 million years ago.

MADRIU-PERAFITA-CLAROR VALLEY

In the Vall del Madriu-Perafita-Claror it is still possible to imagine today how humans may have once lived in the high Pyrenees and made use of the resources available to them.

Andorra is framed in by the main ridge of the Pyrenees in the north, tucked between peaks that reach an impressive 3,000 m (9,843 ft). The Madriu-Perafita-Claror Valley covers an area of more than 4 ha (10 acres), some nine per cent of the principality's territory, and is a stellar testimony to the lifestyles, economies, cultural traditions and climatic changes of the high Pyrenees over the course of the last thousand years. The landscape is characterized by glacial valleys, lakes and cirques that create a dramatic natural ensemble for any visitor.

The World Heritage Site features homes, enclosures, shepherds' summer cabins, dry-stone walls, terraced fields, mountain tracks and even the remains of an iron smelting furnace on the banks of the Madriu River at an elevation of 1,900 m (6,234 ft). It is the only such furnace of Catalan origin in existence and dates back to the 13th century.

The geography of the Madriu-Perafita-Claror Valley is very demanding on the people who live there. They still do not have pavved roads.

Portugal

HISTORIC CENTER OF GUIMARÃES

Guimarães is considered the cradle of Portugal because, in the 12th century, it was the first capital of the newly founded kingdom. It was here, too, that the Portuguese language developed.

As early as Celtic times a settlement existed here in the foothills of the Serra de Santa Catarina, to the northeast of Oporto in northern Portugal. In 1139, Guimarães became Portugal's first capital, and Alfonso I, a native of the city, proclaimed himself the first king of the country. In the Middle Ages and the early modern era, distinctive construction techniques and styles developed in Guimarães that became models for Portugal's entire colonial empire. Buildings that were typical of the period between the 16th and the 19th centuries can be seen in the city center. The Castelo on the hill, dating back as far as the 12th century, is one of the best-preserved Romanesque castles in the country. The Paço Ducal belonged to the dukes of Bragança. Also worth seeing is the town hall dating from the 16th and 17th centuries. The churches of São Miguel do Castelo, Nossa Senhora da Oliveira, Santos Passos and the Santa Clara Monastery are all exemplary as well.

Today, the Portuguese architectural style that arose in the Middle Ages still characterizes the center of Guimarães.

HISTORIC CENTER OF OPORTO

Oporto, known already in ancient times under the name Portus Cale, is famous for its superbly preserved Old Town and its many baroque churches. The cityscape is defined by houses clinging to the steep terraced slopes.

Strategically located on the estuary of the River Douro on the Atlantic coast, the Moors took notice of Oporto early and reigned here for nearly three hundred years, from 716 to 997. In the 11th century, Oporto became the capital of the county of Portucalia, which was to be the cradle of the future kingdom of Portugal.

Part of the protected ensemble in the Old Town is the Romanesque Oporto Cathedral. Its Gothic cloister makes a particularly strong impression thanks to its beautiful tile cladding. Attractive woodcarvings from the Renaissance and the Baroque embellish the interior. The Church of Santa Clara from the early 15th century forms part of the monastery of the same name, and boasts artfully gilded woodcarvings as well as rich tile decoration in the choir area. One of the most interesting civic buildings is the stock exchange, built in 1842.

The Dom Luís I Iron Bridge leads over the Douro on two levels (below, with traditional boats in the foreground) into the Old Town of Oporto, tucked between the river and the cathedral.

ALTO DOURO WINE REGION

Wine has been cultivated in the Alto Douro Region for almost 2,000 years, and the tradition has created an exceptionally charming cultural landscape whose most famous product is the port wine – a dark red or white fortified liqueur wine. The area that has been declared a World Heritage Site covers some 2,250 sq km (868 sq mi).

Port is mostly made from a blend of five grape varieties grown on the steep rocky banks of the Upper Douro River. However, it is said that since these wines did not hold up well during the crossing from Portugal to Great Britain, where it had gained widespread popularity, brandy or eau-de-vie was added to the grapes to stop the fermentation process, thus creating in the 17th century what is now port wine.

Wine has been cultivated in the Upper Douro since Roman times, and both the landscape's steep terraced slopes and the churches and "quintas", or wine-growing estates, along the way have been marked by two thousand years of the tradition. One thing hasn't changed, though: the port wines of the Alto Douro Region still mature in oak barrels near Oporto.

Only the grapes from a clearly demarcated area in the Alto Douro wine region (above) may be used in the production of port wine. Port is stored for half a year in the wine cellars of the Douro Valley and then matures in the port wineries of Vila Nova de Gaia, opposite Oporto.

PREHISTORIC ROCK-ART SITES IN THE CÔA VALLEY

Altogether, sixteen excavation sites line a 17-km (11-mi) stretch of the lower Côa Valley in north-eastern Portugal.

Where the Ribeira de Piscos and the Côa rivers converge, they have cut deep canyons and gorges into the rock to reach the mighty Douro. During the Ice Age, locals here even immortalized themselves in the rocks above the rivers with their artworks. When the rock art was discovered in the Côa Valley during preliminary investigations for the construction of a reservoir dam at the beginning of the 1990s, the news actually came out that in 1983 another major site had been destroyed by the Pocinho Dam in the nearby Vale da Casa. A storm of outrage ensued, and in response the Portuguese government turned the area into a unique archeological park. The rock engravings represent aurochs and wild goats as well as anthropomorphic figures and some hunters. The oldest are estimated to be about 22,000 years old. The prehistoric sites in the lower Côa Valley have not yet been completely explored.

In a side valley of the Douro near Foz Côa, countless images that have often been engraved into bizarre rock formations (top) form a sort of open-air gallery of Paleolithic art that is at times abstract, zoomorphic and naturalistic.

MONASTERY OF BATALHA

Together with Tomar and Alcobaça, Batalha is one of the three great royal monasteries in Portugal. The Mosteiro de Santa Maria da Vitória Cathedral is a masterpiece of the Portuguese High Gothic; the workers who erected the monastery also built the village.

On August 14, 1385, the day of the Battle of Aljubarrota against the neighboring Spanish, King João I promised to donate a Dominican monastery to the Virgin Mary. The Portuguese forces won, he kept his promise, and so the Santa Maria da Vitória Monastery was built based on plans by master builder Alfonso Domingues and transferred to the Dominican order. It was largely completed by 1402.

The monumental main façade of the abbey church is divided into three parts. With its dazzling sculptures it is considered one of the most stunning examples of the Portuguese High

The designs for the "Royal Cloister" were made by the abbey's first master builder, Alfonso Domingues.

Gothic. The choir of the abbey church features remarkable stained-glass windows while the chapter house and its star-vaulted ceiling are illuminated by 16th-century colored glass portals. The "Royal Cloister" impresses with its slender columns and delicate ornamentation that are visibly based on Moorish influences.

The Founder's Chapel (Capela do Fundador) from the 15th century adjoins the right-side nave and contains the remains of King John I and his wife. The "capelas imperfeitas", the "incomplete chapels" were designated as burial places for Dom Duarte and his wife Doña Leonor von Aragón. They reveal two different construction phases: the 14th century and the Manueline period (16th century).

In its delicate, open sandstone arcades, the monastery's "Royal Cloister" reveals obvious Moorish influences (top left). Left: The northern portal of the grand monastery church, bedecked with numerous sculptures.

Portugal

CONVENT OF CHRIST IN TOMAR

Portugal's largest monastic complex – the Convento da Ordem de Cristo – is situated on top of a hill above the town of Tomar. It was initially a fortress of the Knights Templar, then of the Military Order of Christ, and finally became the Convent of Christ. The World Heritage Site comprises the entire complex, which was built between the 12th and the 17th centuries.

The present convent dates back to a castle given by King Alphonzo I the Founder to the Order of the Knights Templar in 1159. It had been founded some forty years earlier, originally as a refuge for the pilgrims making the trek to the Holy Land. After 200 years, however, the wealth and power of the Knights was seen as a threat by Pope Clement V, who accused them in 1312 of heresy and secret teachings, thereby dissolving the order. Six years later, in 1318, Portuguese King Denis established the Military Order of Christ and transferred all possessions and rights

of the former Templars to the new order, which was then based in Tomar. The convent church of Santa Maria do Olival is said to have been modeled on the Church of the Holy Sepulcher in Jerusalem. In 1580, the Spanish King Philip II was crowned king of Portugal in the Renaissance cloister – one of seven cloisters in Tomar.

Superb frescoes adorn the fortress-like, 16-sided rotunda – the oldest part of the Convent of Christ in Tomar – in the small town of the same name on the River Nabão.

MONASTERY OF ALCOBAÇA

Alcobaça is about 100 km (62 mi) north of Lisbon in the valleys of the river Alcoa and Baça and boasts one of the most important Cistercian buildings in all of Europe.

This monastery, donated in thanks for the victory over the Moors near Santarém, was one of the most powerful Cistercian monasteries in Europe. It originates from 1153, the year when the founder of the order, Bernard of Clairvaux, died. Over centuries, the complex has been expanded several times as well as rebuilt and restored after being destroyed, for example, during the Napoleonic wars.
Some elements in the convent church still testify to the austere architectural style of the Cistercian Gothic, which mirrored the lifestyle of the order. The Gothic portal and the rose are good examples. The three-aisled church was

enlarged by nine chapels that are also among the most beautiful examples of the Cistercian Gothic. One cloister and the Gothic sarcophagi of Pedro I (the Cruel) and Inês de Castro are also from the Middle Ages.
Other than that, Portugal's largest church today sports a mainly baroque appearance. Its façade and choir ambulatory feature elaborate sculptures, columns and capitals.

The Alcobaça monastery church is home to the magnificent sarcophagi of King Pedro I and his lover Inês de Castro. The two were executed by Pedro's father, Alfonso IV, for high treason.

CULTURAL LANDSCAPE OF SINTRA

In the 19th century, the small town of Sintra became the summer residence of the Portuguese kings. Among the many structures they built set in expansive gardens are two palaces that are of particular significance.

Situated on top of a hill, the old castle dominates the town of Sintra. Its construction began as early as the eighth century and was in Moorish hands until the 12th century. Paço Real de Sintra, the royal palace in the town center, dates back in part to the 14th century, but was enlarged in subsequent centuries and underwent significant architectural changes. Its most noticeable features are the strangely shaped chimneys, which betray Islamic influences. The Coat of Arms Room, Swan Room and chapel all date back to the 14th century.

In the mid-19th century, German architect Baron von Eschwege built the Palácio da Pena as a residence for Prince Consort Ferdinand von Sachsen-Coburg-Gotha, integrating a 16th-century monastery in the process. The romantic castle combines features from various periods and the exotic gardens are among the most attractive in Europe.

The Palácio da Pena with its battlements and a miniature cloister was built on a hilltop near Sintra for Ferdinand von Sachsen-Coburg-Gotha.

MONASTERY OF THE HIER- ONYMITES AND TOWER OF BELÉM

The façades of the Hieronymite Monastery of Belém (Mosteiro dos Jerónimos de Belém), a neighborhood of Lisbon, are examples of the Manueline style. The White Tower of Belém was the setting for many historic events.

Manuel I "the Fortunate" (1469–1521), King of Portugal, was a great patron of the explorers, especially Vasco da Gama and Pedro Cabral, who were to a great degree responsible for discovering and conquering the New World and establishing the colonies. During his reign the arts and sciences flourished, and the decorative late-Gothic architectural style of Portugal was named after him. Manueline combines the Flamboyant, Mudéjar and Plateresque styles with maritime and exotic elements.

Originally, the Tower of Belém was built as a lighthouse on the Tegus estuary. As the river silted up over the centuries, the tower "moved" to the riverbank.

Starting in 1502, Manuel I had the enormous Hieronymite Monastery built in honor of Vasco da Gama, on the very site where Henry the Navigator had already erected a chapel. It holds the tomb of Vasco da Gama, whose discovery of the sea route to India secured the funding for the monastery's lovely furnishings.

The idiosyncratic Torre de Belém, a watchtower at the mouth of the River Tegus, from which the Portuguese sailors began their many legendary journeys of exploration, was built between 1515 and 1521. The massive multistory structure, which in later days also served as a state prison, shows Moorish, Gothic and Moroccan influences.

The interior of Santa Maria Cathedral impresses with its late-Gothic vaulting, stunning stained-glass windows and richly ornamented pillars.

Portugal

HISTORIC CENTER OF ÉVORA

Évora is one of the oldest trading centers on the Iberian Peninsula. The cityscape of the Old Town features magnificent architectural monuments with Roman, Moorish and other influences.

Standing at the heart of the Roman foundation of Évora are sixteen Corinthian columns – all that is left of a former temple. The preserved sections of an aqueduct and a Castellum (fortress) indicate Évora's former importance as a trading town in the Roman Empire. There are also remains of city walls and baths built by the Romans. The layout of the town itself has Oriental features as well due to a long period of Moorish rule that lasted from 715 until 1165.
The Romanesque-Gothic cathedral in Évora was begun in 1186. The mighty building resembles a fortress with its two monumental bell towers. A clois-

ter was added in the 14th century, based on the one at Alcobaça Monastery. Inside, the marble decoration of the choir room is the only embellishment; it was renewed in the 18th century. The royal palace, built in its present form under Emanuel I, is the most attractive building in town. The Jesuit university is now home to a college and a valuable collection of ancient manuscripts.

Relics from Roman days in Évora include the Corinthian columns of the Temple of Diana (above). The triple-aisled cathedral (right) is 70 m (230 ft) long and was begun in 1186.

LANDSCAPE OF THE PICO ISLAND VINEYARD CULTURE

Starting in the 15th century, inhabitants Pico Island in the Azores began growing grapes in small fields hemmed in by dry-stone walls to protect them from the strong winds and the sea spray.

Pico is the second-largest island in the Azores archipelago, named after the 2,351-m-high (7,714-ft) volcano Ponta do Pico – the highest mountain in Portugal. The soil on the island is rich in minerals and benefits from a mild ocean climate – dry summers and wet winters with stormy winds. The main source of income here is agriculture. From the moment the first Portuguese settlers arrived they began cultivating vines on Pico. Due to the strong winds and sea spray carried with them, the vines and their fruits had to be protected, which led to the

development of the "currais", a small-scale patchwork of rectangular wall boundaries that are especially common on the north-west coast. The fields often hold no more than six vines. The Verdelho grape, which yields one of the best wines on Madeira, is now only of local importance on Pico. The wine is fortified, like the one on Madeira (16 to 18 per cent alcohol).

A painstaking process: dry-stone walls snake through the vineyards on Pico Island.

CENTRAL ZONE OF THE TOWN OF ANGRA DO HEROISMO IN THE AZORES

Angra do Heroísmo sits in the shadow of a mighty volcanic crater on Terceira Island in the Azores. A number of fine historic architectural monuments have survived in the Old Town.

Angra do Heroísmo, the capital of Terceira, had already become an important port by the 15th century. The town was laid out on a grid plan and still boasts a large number of houses from its early days.

The spiritual focus of the city is the triple-aisled cathedral built between 1570 and 1618 – it is also the largest church in the Azores archipelago. The Church of São Gonçalo is adorned with very valuable tiles (azulejos), which had been introduced by the Moors and are found everywhere around the entire Iberian Peninsula. The parish church of São Sebastião is one of few churches on the Azores that was built in a purely Gothic style. It contains the remains of medieval frescoes. The former Jesuit monastery, now the Palácio dos Capitães-Generais, has been restored and serves as an administrative building.

Angra do Heroísmo (below) was given its municipal charter in 1534, making it the oldest town in the Azores. Its churches contain valuable works of art (left).

LAURISILVA LAUREL FOREST OF MADEIRA

Madeira was once covered in dense forests, but they have long since been decimated by logging. Still, today's laurel forest is largely primary forest.

The laurel forests of Madeira lie between 600 and 1,300 m (1,970 and 4,270 ft) above sea level. Along with the forests of the Garajonay National Park on Gomera, Canary Islands, they are all that is left of the laurel forests once found throughout the Mediterranean. Decimation of the laurel woodlands began in the 15th century as a result of slash-and-burn agriculture and deforestation, a widespread method of collecting firewood while creating new arable land. The result, however, is that the forests on the steep north coast of Madeira are about all that remains of the original laurel forests. Here, the dense growth of trees plays an important part in the island's water supply. The tree leaves "collect" water from the clouds, which is then retained in the undergrowth before finally being stored in the rocks. The laurel forests also help to reduce soil erosion significantly. The protection of Madeira's laurel forests has also preserved the habitat of some unique plants and animals, in particular birds and insects.

Madeira's laurel forests are home to that species of tree and cover roughly 150 sq km (58 sq mi) of the island.

RHAETIAN RAILWAY IN THE ALBULA / BERNINA LANDSCAPES

This transnational World Heritage Site covering parts of Italy and Switzerland includes two historic lines, the Albula Railway and the Bernina Railway, as well as the landscapes through which they run.

At the time of their construction more than 100 years ago, these railway lines were indeed a great feat of technical engineering that helped to develop the alpine region. The Albula line runs for 63 km (39 mi) and began operation in 1904. It leads from Thusis, in the canton of Grisons, to St Moritz, and climbs roughly 1,000 m (3,281 ft). The trains travel along one of the world's most sophisticated narrow-gauge railways with fifty-five bridges and thirty-nine tunnels.

The 61-km (39-mi) Bernina Railway was completed in 1910 and connects St Moritz with the Italian border town of Tirano. The railway line reaches 2,253 m (7,392 ft) above sea level during its steep climb over the Bernina Pass. The track passes through thirteen tunnels and galleries and over fifty-two viaducts and bridges.

The Bernina Express and the Bernina Railway operate on the St Moritz-Poschiavo-Tirano line (below: Tirano).

SANTA MARIA DELLE GRAZIE WITH "THE LAST SUPPER" BY LEONARDO DA VINCI

The church of Santa Maria delle Grazie is the work of Italian architect Donato Bramante. The refectory of the former Dominican convent houses some of Leonardo da Vinci's world-famous murals.

The church of Santa Maria delle Grazie was originally built between 1465 and 1482 by Guiniforte Solari in High Gothic style; it was the minster of a Dominican convent. In 1492, Ludovico Sforza, the Duke of Milan, decided to have the church rebuilt as the burial place for himself and his wife, Beatrice d'Este. Only a small portion of his plans was actually implemented, however.
Among the renovations that were completed was the central block with

semicircular apses, added by Renaissance builder Donato Bramante to the eastern section. Leonardo da Vinci's 4.20- by 9.10-m (14- by 30-ft) mural "The Last Supper" in the abbey refectory, which he painted between 1494 and 1498, depicts the moment when Jesus spoke the words: "One of you will betray me."

"The Last Supper" in the refectory of the Santa Maria delle Grazie Church is one of the most famous murals in art history.

SACRI MONTI OF PIEDMONT AND LOMBARDY

These pilgrimage sites perched on hills in the Italian countryside are known as the "Sacri Monti" ("Holy Mountains"). They comprise several chapels that pilgrims pass on their way to the top.

In the Middle Ages, a journey to Jerusalem was the most important pilgrimage one could make. It was where Jesus had lived, suffered, died and been resurrected. However, over the centuries, it became increasingly difficult to travel to the Holy Land, which is why people in Europe came up with the idea of replicating the stations of the cross and other places where Jesus was active (also known as the "calvary"). This initially inspired the creation of the Sacro Monte of Varallo, also known as "Nuova Gerusalemme" ("New Jerusalem"), in the

first half of the 16th century. Artist Gaudenzio Ferrari (1471 to 1546) painted forty detailed figures for this that were made to stand out from his landscapes and cityscapes in the chapels. There are around two dozen of such Sacri Monti in northern Italy. Nine have been listed as World Heritage Sites: Varallo, Orta, Varese, Oropa, Belmonte, Crea, Domodossola, Ghiffa and Ossuccio.

Episodes from the life of St Francis are dramatically depicted in twenty chapels on the Sacro Monte above Lake Orta.

RESIDENCES OF THE ROYAL HOUSE OF SAVOY

When Emanuel Philibert (1528–1580) relocated the capital of his duchy from Chambéry to Turin in 1563, residences demonstrating the absolutist splendor of the House of Savoy were built there and in the surrounding area.

Duke Emanuel Philibert and his successor commissioned the prominent builders and artists of their time to design magnificent castles and other elegant buildings in Turin. The most impressive of these is the royal palace – official residence of the House of Savoy until 1865, located at Piazza Castello in the center of Turin, built between the 16th and the 18th centuries. Along with this Palazzo Reale, the World Heritage Site in Turin also comprises the Chiablese, Madama and Carignano palaces as well as the royal armory (Armeria Reale), the Villa

della Regina and the Castello del Valentino. In addition to these are the residences in Agliè, Bra, Govone, Pollenzo, Rivoli, Stupinigi and Venaria outside of town. The final building projects carried out by the dukes of Savoy included Moncalieri Castle near Turin, severely damaged by a fire in April 2008, which once served as the residence of the most famous Savoy, King Victor Emanuel II.

The interior of the Palazzo Reale was opulent, as might be expected (above: the ballroom with coffered ceiling).

ROCK DRAWINGS IN VALCAMONICA

The Oglio River Valley is an archaeological site featuring rock drawings from the Paleolithic and Neolithic ages as well as the Bronze Age and early Iron Age. The variety of themes addressed by the artists is remarkable.

Europe's largest archaeological site for prehistoric rock carvings is located near Capo di Ponte in the sweeping Valcamonica valley in Brescia province. More than 200,000 individual carvings from prehistoric times have been preserved on some 2,000 stone slabs, the oldest illustrations dating back to the time around 6000 BC.

The vast compositions mainly depict themes from everyday life such as warriors, farmers and their equipment, wild game and domesticated animals, and of course weapons. The geometric patterns and abstract shapes that fill the spaces between the individual carvings must have made sense in some sort of ritualistic context.

The obviously "unknown artists" were likely the Camuni, an alpine people whose settlement there traces back well into the fourth millennium BC. Some finds can be viewed in the archaeological Parco Nazionale delle Incisioni Rupestri di Naquane near Capo di Ponte.

This early "graffiti" in the famous Valcamonica depicts mazes with dancing warriors and numerous animals.

CRESPI D'ADDA – COMPANY TOWN

This "company town" in Bergamo province is considered an early example of social commitment on the part of early industrialists. It was built by textile manufacturer Crespi for workers and families at his cotton spinning mill.

Crespi d'Adda is in Capriate San Gervasio in the province of Bergamo of Lombardy. The town is typical of the workers' villages built by enlightened industrialists in the late 19th and early 20th centuries who felt it appropriate to look after the needs of their employees. The Crespi family had this factory and the necessary civic infrastructure built in 1878 on a green meadow not far from the Adda River, where sufficient water would be available. The settlement is divided by a straight avenue: on the right was the factory (where more than 3,000 people earned their living in the 1920s), and on the left were the residential streets with cookie-cutter single-family homes and apartment blocks surrounded by gardens. The village of course included a school, an infirmary, a washhouse and a church. The town, which is still inhabited, has remained more or less preserved in its original state.

Brick decorations in the Lombard Gothic style adorn the factory halls. The main entrance, with the administrative buildings (below), is the factory's finest structure.

CITY OF VICENZA AND THE PALLADIAN VILLAS OF THE VENETO

The city center of Vicenza is characterized by twenty-three buildings by Palladio and around twenty villas designed by the architect in the Veneto region have been raised to the status of World Heritage Sites.

Apart from his own study of the humanities, it was the trips to Rome's ancient sites that proved crucial for Padua-born architect Andrea Palladio (1508–1580), who began his career in 1524 as a bricklayer and stonemason in Vicenza. His later buildings, which inspired a style that found widespread acceptance across Europe, harmoniously combined classical and ancient elements – "Palladian" architecture. One of his prominent early works is Vicenza's town hall, the Palazzo della Ragione, also known as the "Basilica Palladina". Opposite that is his Loggia del Capitaniato, seat of the city's military commander with arcades of high, semi-circular arches.

The year he died he also designed the Teatro Olimpico, the first free-standing covered theater building with an amphitheater-shaped auditorium. His most famous buildings outside Vicenza include the Villa Rotonda, a perfect example of architectural symmetry.

Behind the Roman "scaena frons" in the form of a palace façade with sculptures, wooden backdrops in the Teatro Olimpico create the illusion of an ancient "city".

CITY OF VERONA

The Romans founded a settlement here in 89 BC that soon developed into a major city. The grid layout on an island in the Adige River continues to make up the Old Town with its famous Arena di Verona.

Imposing monuments such as the vast amphitheater (Arena di Verona), built in the first century, or the Porta dei Borsari, built during the same period, attest to Verona's ancient origins. The High Middle Ages also left their mark on the city in the form of grandiose edifices like the Romanesque Basilica of San Zeno with its famous porch sculptures.

Verona was given its final expansion and design in the 13th and 14th centuries under the rule of the Scaligers, whose power and pomp are demonstrated by the elaborate Gothic mausoleums and the Castelvecchio with its crenellated bridge. The Gothic era brought with it the vast structure of the Church of St Anastasia as well as a modification on the cathedral. After it was annexed by Venice, Verona experienced another boom that culminated in extensive construction work by native Renaissance architect Michele Sanmicheli (1484–1559). Verona's city gates, including the Porta Nuova, and the trendsetting palazzi (Bevilacqua, Pompei), can also be attributed to him.

The edge of the Arena di Verona – the scene of impressive opera festivals held every summer – provides a view over the city's rooftops.

Italy

THE DOLOMITES

The Dolomites, situated in the north-eastern Italian Alps, have eighteen peaks higher than 3,000 m (9,840 ft) and are among the most beautiful mountains in the world. They comprise the Val Gardena, Val di Fassa, Ampezzo and Sexten Dolomites, the eastern edge of which is referred to as the Cadore region. The Dolomites are distinguished by their geological, botanical and scenic singularity, which includes a fascinating range of flora with over 2,400 types of plants.

The Dolomites cover a total area of about 1,420 sq km (548 sq mi). The Marmolada is the highest peak at 3343 m (10,968 ft), but the precipitous charms of the Three Peaks of Lavaredo and the Rosengarten ("Rose Garden") are also world-famous. The highest peak in that region is the Catinaccio di Antermoia / Kesselkogel at 3,004 m (10,900 ft).

Part of the Limestone Alps, this Dolomite range is a region of stark contrasts: lush Alpine meadows alter-

The Marmolada was first climbed in 1864 by Paul Grohmann, co-founder of the Austrian Alpine Club. It is a west-facing extension of the ridge with the only large glacier (Marmolada Glacier) in the Dolomites on its northern side. It was named after the stone that makes up its core and recalls the characteristics of marble.

nate with jagged peaks and hollows filled with moraine rubble. This contrast is explained by differences in orogeny across the various areas, which reveal recumbent folds of fossilized coral reef and rocks of volcanic origin. The Dolomites also have glaciated areas as well as karst formations typical of limestone regions; combined with the fossil record, this makes the landscape an excellent and easily referenced tectonic history. That is not the end of the story however – the floods, tremors, rock slides, and avalanches that continually reshape the earth's surface play their part here too.

The "Rose Garden" range in full alpenglow at sunset.

The Pala Group – the southernmost section of the Dolomites – is home to some of the most famous climbing in the region (here: Monte Agnér).

The Sexten Dolomites feature the most famous triad of peaks in the Alps, the Three Peaks of Lavaredo, with the largest in the middle at 2,999 m (10,000 ft).

The Dolomites were a massive coral reef in the primeval ocean of Tethys about 250 million years ago. The Brenta Group contains traces of this history (above, the Guglia di Brenta needle).

Five peaks – Neuner (9), Zehner (10), Elfer (11), Zwölfer (12) and the Einser (1) – form the "Sextener Sundial" (above, the Zwölfer at 3,094 m / 11,000 ft).

Italy

VENICE AND ITS LAGOON

This unique city stretches across the water in a lagoon north of the Po Delta. Its magnificent churches and palaces stand on millions of wooden stakes and instead of roads there are more than 150 canals spanned by over 400 bridges.

In the 15th century, Venice had its own Mediterranean fleet and was Italy's richest and largest city. When seafarers finally managed to establish a route to India around the Cape of Good Hope in the 16th century, however, the city's political importance declined. Still, it continued to thrive as a center of business and culture.

The city's most important waterway in Venice is the Grand Canal, off which many side canals branch and which itself culminates in Venice's most recognizable building: the Basilica of St Mark. Adorned with gilded mosaics, the cathedral's got its present look in the 11th century while the adjacent

San Giorgio Maggiore is one of more than 100 islands in Venice. The church of the same name was designed by Andrea Palladio in 1565.

Doge's Palace was erected in the 12th century over an existing building from 825. Venice with its islands and canals can almost be seen as an urban work of art. Hardly any other city has such a concentration of churches, monasteries, palaces, museums and theaters with so many treasures by the likes of Titian, Veronese, Tintoretto, Tiepolo, Canaletto and other artists.

St Mark's Basilica has five porch recesses and is adorned with masterly mosaics. It forms the eastern end of St Mark's Square (Piazza San Marco), which served as the cathedral's forecourt in the ninth century. The building was given its current appearance over centuries, during which it was the scene of festivities, processions and public events of La Serenissima. Napoleon called St Mark's Square "the finest drawing room in Europe".

The Piazza San Marco is surrounded by the arcaded Procuratie, formerly administrative buildings.

The condemned were once taken to prison over the Bridge of Sighs at the rear end of the Doge's Palace.

Venice at sunrise with the Piazzetta and the Doge's Palace, a triple-mast ship and San Giorgio Maggiore in the background.

The Basilica of St Mark is a cross-in-square church divided into three naves with stunning mosaic decorations.

Italy

The Gothic Franciscan Church of Santa Maria Gloriosa dei Frari is one of Venice's prominent religious buildings.

The immense baroque Basilica di Santa Maria della Salute at the entrance to the Grand Canal is a sight to behold.

Tintoretto created a grand series of pictures for the Scuola Grande di San Rocco (above, the main hall).

The Land and Water Gate of the Arsenale, the shipyard of the Republic of Venice.

The Rialto Bridge, built from Istrian limestone in the 16th century, spans the Grand Canal in a vast arc. Until 1854, it was the only means of crossing the canal on foot.

BOTANICAL GARDEN (ORTO BOTANICO), PADUA

Europe's oldest botanical garden is located in the university town of Padua, on the northern edge of the Po Plain. It is home to a number of plants that are several hundred years old and is still used as a research facility.

This botanical garden was established by Paduan botany professor Francesco Bonafede in 1545. Architect Andrea Moroni was responsible for the overall design and construction. Its layout, which consists of a large circle around which several concentric paths are arranged and into which four squares are inscribed, is meant to symbolize the structure of the universe.

A ring of irrigation canals surrounds the garden, and a high exterior wall helps protects it against theft. Over the centuries, numerous architectural decorations as well as more practical features such as irrigation fittings and greenhouses have been added.

Some of the Mediterranean and more exotic plants on the site have even managed to spread from here all across Europe. They include a few particularly old specimens such as a chaste tree dating back to 1550 and a mighty gingko tree planted here as early as 1750.

This view of the Padua Botanical Garden, created in 1854, shows the complex with squares inscribed into a circular flower-bed with the domed towers in back.

ARCHAEOLOGICAL AREA AND THE PATRIARCHAL BASILICA OF AQUILEIA

In Roman times, Aquileia in the province of Udine was a prominent port city. It also played an important role in the early Middle Ages.

The Roman colony here was founded in 181 BC. It became one of the largest cities on the Apennine Peninsula during imperial times. After being destroyed by Attila in 452, it became the seat of a patriarch who relocated to Grado in the wake of the Lombard invasion of 568. The patriarchate initially played a pivotal role in the Christianization of Central Europe and later in the emperors' policies concerning Italy, but lost its secular dominance in 1445 before being dissolved by Pope Benedict XIV in 1751.

The Roman archaeological finds here include the forum columns and the cypress-lined Via Sacra along the quay of the Roman port. They serve as splendid reminders of the ancient city's former greatness. The 11th-century cathedral was built over two early Christian basilicas from which the oldest known floor mosaics in Upper Italy have been saved.

The interior of Aquileia's basilica impresses with floor mosaics dating back to the fourth century.

MANTUA AND SABBIONETA

During the Renaissance, the city of Mantua developed under the Gonzagas into one of Italy's most important city residences while nearby Sabbioneta was used by Vespasiano Gonzaga as a ducal residence.

Both Mantua and Sabbioneta are both situated on the Po Plain in northern Italy. Mantua was founded by the Etruscans and controlled by the Gonzagas from the 14th century onwards. After the latter were elevated to the status of dukes in 1530, the city developed into a center of Renaissance fine art attracting prestigious artists such as Andrea Mantegna (1431–506), whose frescoes adorn the Palazzo Ducale, Leon Battista Alberti (1404–1472), responsible for designing San Lorenzo Church, and Giulio Romano (1499–1546), who created the Palazzo del Te, pleasure palace of the Gonzagas.

Sabbioneta was transformed into a ducal residence by Vespasiano Gonzaga (1531–1591), descendant of a branch of the House of Gonzaga who between 1554 and 1571 oversaw the emergence of a complex able to accommodate 300 inhabitants. One district was used by the military; one served as a residence; and one-third was for reception purposes and public life. Sabbioneta is still considered a fine example of an "ideal Renaissance city".

The Piazza Sordello in Mantua features the Palazzo Ducale with its arcades and the cathedral with its baroque façade.

FERRARA, CITY OF THE RENAISSANCE, AND ITS PO DELTA

Ferrara's historic center was given the title "City of the Renaissance". In 1999, this World Heritage Site was expanded to include the cultural landscape of the Po Delta, the Parco Regionale del Delta del Po and Este country seat.

The Este, one of the oldest families of Italian nobility, ruled Ferrara from the 13th to the 16th centuries. Under their tutelage it became the domain of prominent artists such as Antonio Pisanello, Andrea Mantegna, Jacopo Bellini and Piero della Francesca while poets such as Torquato Tasso and Ariosto also contributed to the city's intellectual atmosphere.

Saint George's Basilica was built in Romanesque style from 1135 to 1485. It features a splendid marble façade and ornate sculptures on its central porch. A gallery connects the 13th-century Palazzo Comunale to Castello Estense, whose interior is adorned with prized frescoes. Other buildings worth seeing are the Palazzo dell'Università (with Ariosto's tomb), the Palazzina Marfisa d'Este, the Palazzo Ludovico il Moro, Palazzo dei Diamanti, Palazzo Massari, the San Cristoforo, San Francesco and Santa Maria churches in Vado, the Abbazia di Pomposa and Castello della Mesola, an Este country estate in the Po Delta.

Castello Estense was the residence of the Estes family for two centuries.

EARLY CHRISTIAN MONUMENTS OF RAVENNA

Ravenna was once the capital of the Western Roman Empire, later the residence of the Goths, and then the center of the Byzantine portion of Italy until it was conquered by the Lombards in 751. This World Heritage Site comprises eight nearly pristine buildings with exquisite mosaics that are among the most important relics of early Christianity.

Ravenna's oldest mosaics can be found in Empress Galla Placidia's mausoleum in the church of San Vitale, consecrated in 547, whose chancel alcove is adorned with particularly elaborate mosaics. King Theodoric the Great had the Arian Baptistery erected in the early sixth century with a number of stunning dome mosaics. Sant'Apollinare Nuovo

In Sant'Apollinare Nuovo, large mosaics depict scenes from the life of Jesus. Above: Maria on the throne with Baby Jesus and angels.

was also built under Theodoric's rule as the palace church, and was first dedicated to St Martin. The king's tomb, erected around 520, is topped with a marble dome. The Orthodox Baptistery next to the cathedral features mosaics and bas-reliefs. The Oratorio di Sant'Andrea in the bishop's palace was commissioned and adorned with mosaics under Archbishop Peter II in the early sixth century. Sant'Apollinare Church, which was erected above the tomb of the first Bishop of Ravenna in 534, is outside the city in Classe. The mosaics depict the transfiguration of Christ.

The church of San Vitale was modelled on the Hagia Sophia in what is now Istanbul. It was built between 525 and 547 (top left). Twenty-four Greek marble columns connected by arcades separate the main nave (left) from each of the side naves in the Sant'Apollinare Basilica in Classe, outside Ravenna.

CATHEDRAL, TORRE CIVICA AND PIAZZA GRANDE, MODENA

The Cathedral of Saint Gimignano – one of the Italy's finest Romanesque structures – the Torre Civica, and the Piazza Grande were included in the list of World Heritage Sites as an outstanding ensemble of urban development.

The Cathedral of Saint Gimignano stands proudly on the Piazza Grande in Modena's city center. After an existing building storing relics of the saint since the eighth century collapsed in around 1000, construction of a church began under the direction of Lombard master builder Lanfranco in 1099. The church was consecrated in 1184.

The splendid sculptures in the porches and interior are works by the master Wiligelmo and his pupils, the Maestri Campionesi, stonemasons from Campione who blended Roman, Byzantine and contemporary Lombard styles.

The gabled façade, adorned with marble and blind arcades, is distinguished by its main porch with column-bearing lions and the rose window. The free-standing Campanile Ghirlandina next to the cathedral was originally Romanesque in style, but was raised to its current height in 1319 with the addition of a Gothic pinnacle. The interior contains masterful sculptures and paintings from the Late Middle Ages.

The back of Modena Cathedral is characterized by three ornate apses furnished with blind arcades.

GENOA: "LE STRADE NUOVE" AND THE SYSTEM OF THE "PALAZZI DEI ROLLI"

In the heyday of the Republic of Genoa in the early 17th century, splendid representational palaces sprang up along the wide Strade Nuove.

The first fixed layout and zoning of a European town was implemented in Genoa as early as the 16th century. It provided for the creation of the Strada Nuova ("New Street"), which was almost 7 m (23 ft) wide and thus almost double the width of an average Old Town street at the time.

The present-day Via Garibaldi is lined with grand villas and palaces where the aristocratic class and political elite established their residences. Other "new streets" were then added in the early 17th century including the Via

Baldi, the Via Cairoli, the Via Lomellini and the Via San Luca. The palaces not only served as residences, but were also used for public events. A decree in 1576 stipulated that the owners were to receive official guests of the state. Special lists ("Rolli") contained the names of the families selected for such receptions – this also explains the names of the palazzi.

Palazzi Spinola, once the residence of the Grimaldi family, provides good insight into the lifestyle of Genoese nobility.

PORTOVENERE, CINQUE TERRE AND THE ISLANDS (PALMARIA, TINO AND TINETTO)

The region north of Portovenere, with the "five lands" ("Cinque Terre") of Monterosso, Vernazza, Corniglia, Manarola and Riomaggiore, as well as the islands of Palmaria, Tino and Tinetto, is one of the most delightful coastal stretches in Italy.

The Cinque Terre cling precariously to the steep Ligurian coast between Levanto and Portovenere. There is still no direct coastal road between them, but the rough terrain can still be negotiated via footpaths and stairs. Sights here include the originally Romanesque Collegiate Church of Saint Lawrence, high above Portovenere, and the small Church of Saint Peter, a Genoese Gothic structure erected in 1277 on the site of a sixth-century building and charmingly perched on a

headland. The castle, dating back to a Roman fort complex, served to defend nearby Genoa and underwent large-scale expansion in the 17th century. The small islands are not scenic but Tino, for example, is home to the ruins of a Romanesque abbey from the 11th century while the remains of an early-Christian monastery complex have been discovered on Tinetto.

Riomaggiore is the easternmost town of the Cinque Terre.

PIAZZA DEL DUOMO, PISA

With its leaning tower, cathedral, baptistery and the famous Camposanto, the Campo dei Miracoli really is a "Field of Miracles".

In 1063, plans were drawn up by the architect Buscheto and used to begin construction on the cathedral outside what was at the time Pisa's city wall. The building's magnificent, 35-m-long (115-ft) façade was designed by Buscheto's successor, Rainaldo, and the bronze doors of the Porta di San Ranieri were crafted by Bonanno Pisano in 1180. The richly decorated coffered ceiling in the vault of the central nave is from the 16th century. The freestanding Campanile, a cylindrical structure, was begun by Bonano in 1174, but already started to lean during its construction; today it is known as the "Leaning Tower". It was long feared that it would collapse, but the tower has now been secured with a new foundation.

View of the "Campo dei Miracoli" with the circular building of the baptistery, the cathedral and the "Leaning Tower".

Due to its long construction time (1152–1358), the baptistery's design demonstrates the transition from Pisa Romanesque to Gothic. The freestanding pulpit created in 1260 is one of the highlights and features sculptures by Nicola Pisano. The chapels and cloister walls of the Camposanto – the cemetery enclosed by arcades – display murals dating back to the 14th and 15th centuries. The buildings on the Piazza del Duomo were designed as a stylistically uniform ensemble through consistent use of white Carrara marble and architectural elements such as rows of arcades and colonnades. Unlike other cities where the cathedral squares have been built up, the vastness of the overall complex here has been preserved.

The mosaic of Christ flanked by Mary and John the Baptist was created in the apse by Francesco di Simone and Cimabue. It is the main visual focus of the cathedral's central nave.

The House of Medici

The Medici family shaped the history of Florence for generations. Their rise to prominence began with Giovanni (1360–1429), who built a fortune through some clever banking deals with the Pope. His son, Cosimo "the Old" (1389–1464), then successfully managed to rule the city without even holding an official position. He was a

HISTORIC CENTER OF FLORENCE

Some 600 years ago, the capital of Tuscany became the birthplace of the Renaissance and humanism. It has played an extremely important role in European art history ever since.

The Piazzale Michelangelo provides a spectacular view over this stunning city on the Arno, with much of the attention focusing on the red dome of the Basilica di Santa Maria del Fiore, built by Filippo Brunelleschi in 1420. The freestanding Campanile, roughly 85 m (279 ft) in height and clad in colorful marble, was designed in 1334 by Giotto, who had also taken over construction of the cathedral that same year. The "Gates of Paradise" were fashioned by Lorenzo Ghiberti between 1425 and 1452 at the eastern end of the adjacent baptistery and are another world-famous sight. Michelangelo's "Pietà Palestrina" sculpture is also on display in the cathedral museum. Another church with significant works of art, and similarly revised by Brunelleschi, is the Basilica di San Lorenzo with its Medici Chapel. It was the first central-plan domed building of the Renaissance.
On the Piazza della Signoria is the Loggia dei Lanzi, adorned with prized sculptures, and the Palazzo Vecchio, the governmental palace of the Medicis. The Uffizi houses one of the world's most famous collections of paintings with works by Botticelli, Leonardo da Vinci, Michelangelo, Caravaggio, Titian, Rubens, Dürer and Rembrandt. The Palazzo Pitti, erected between 1457 and 1819, combines several styles due to its gradual construction and the adjacent Boboli Gardens from 1590 are a jewel of Italian landscape gardening. The most famous bridge in the city is the Ponte Vecchio, where previously only goldsmiths were allowed to have shops.

The Piazzale Michelangelo offers a stunning view of the Florence skyline dominated by the giant dome of the cathedral and the Palazzo Vecchio, both with their campaniles.

brilliant diplomat whom the city of Florence posthumously honored with the title "Father of the Fatherland". He is said to have spent 600,000 gold guilders as a patron of art and science. After his death his son Piero took over for five years but was then succeeded by Cosimo's 20-year-old grandson, Lorenzo (1449–1492), also

known as "il Magnifico" ("the Magnificent"). Lorenzo also eagerly supported promising artists including the young Michelangelo. He proved to be a brilliant statesman and even a talented poet. A failed conspiracy plot by his rival allowed him to govern de facto as an autocrat. In 1498, a Dominican priest named Savonarola

attempted unsuccessfully to establish a theocratic state in Florence but the Medicis returned in 1512 and Florence became a hereditary duchy in 1531. Cosimo I, who had conquered Siena in 1555, became the Grand Duke of Toscana in 1569. In 1560, he had commissioned Giorgio Vasari to build the Uffizi complex, which was first used

as administrative buildings and later became a museum with world-famous artworks. The decline of the Medicis began soon thereafter. The family died out in 1737, and the Grand Duchy of Tuscany fell to the Habsburgs.

Far left: Lorenzo de'Medici, "il Magnifico" and Grand Duke Cosimo I.

The Ponte Vecchio was given its current look in 1345, when buildings for merchants and traders were added to it.

The dome by Filippo Brunelleschi in 1434 is the main feature of the cathedral (above, the baptistery and campanile).

Legend has it that St Francis of Assisi himself laid the foundation stone for the construction of Santa Croce.

The Piazza della Signoria is graced with Bandinelli's Fountain of Neptune – completed by Bartolomeo Ammanati in 1575.

Italy

HISTORIC CENTER OF SAN GIMIGNANO

Wealth and prosperity in San Gimignano were once expressed by the construction of towers. They still characterize the skyline of this little town perched high above the Elsa Valley.

The towers in San Gimignano were erected by the city's aristocratic families who had grown rich from trade in the region's agricultural bounty. The seventy-two original structures were not only used for residential purposes and to protect their owners, but also to convey prestige. Fifteen of these towers are still standing.

The Piazza della Cisterna in the city center is surrounded by palaces and towers and makes for an impressive scene. The twin towers of the Ardinghelli still attest to the power, wealth and influence of these families. The Collegiata di Santa Maria Assunta on the cathedral square was originally a Romanesque basilica built in 1239, but it was expanded to include a transept with six chapels in the 15th century. Countless frescoes – which are outstanding examples of medieval murals and interior design – have also been preserved in the church of Sant'-Agostino and the Palazzo del Popolo, the city's council building.

From a distance, the skyline of San Gimignano looks almost like a medieval Manhattan in the evening light.

HISTORIC CENTER OF SIENA

Siena embodies the purest form of Italian Gothic. The shell-shaped Piazza del Campo is the focal point and most recognizable part of the city.

Siena's medieval road network with its fountains and gates has remained almost completely intact to the present day. The Piazza del Campo is the heart of the city and is home to the town hall, the Palazzo Pubblico. The 88-m (289-ft) Torre del Mangia tower was added to the town hall between 1325 and 1344. At the higher end of the square is the Fonte Gaia with its marble panels by Jacopo della Quercia (a replica has been installed for the original, which has been located in the Ospedale di Santa Maria della Scala since 1858).

The Santa Maria Cathedral, one of Italy's most magnificent Gothic structures, was erected in the 13th century at the highest point of the city. Its façade was designed by a series of architects including Giovanni Pisano. Among the famous art treasures it houses, the marble floor crafted by more than forty artists between 1369 and 1546 is particularly impressive. Every summer the Piazza del Campo plays host to the "Palio" – a horse race in a splendid medieval setting in which the city's various districts compete against each other.

The Piazza del Campo (right), with the Palazzo Pubblico and Torre del Mangia tower, is the heart of the city whose dominant feature is its cathedral (above).

VAL D'ORCIA

The man-made Renaissance landscape of Val d'Orcia is located some 25 km (16 mi) south-east of Siena. Paintings of this area had a significant influence on the artistic conception of an ideal landscape.

The Val d'Orcia, which once belonged to Siena, possesses an aesthetically appealing layout and design that was intended to represent the model of a good government. Indeed, this artistic archetype of the ideal Renaissance landscape can be found in a series of frescoes by Ambrogio Lorenzetti that is housed in Siena's town hall. The Val d'Orcia also inspired some Sienese painters such as Giovanni di Paolo and Sani di Pietro to create aestheticized landscape paintings where people still lived in harmony with nature.

Apart from the agricultural areas and farmhouses in the valley, the World Heritage Site also includes cities such as Pienza, Radicofani, Montalcino, Castiglione d'Orcia, Castiglione del Bosco and Castelnuovo dell'Abate. A section of the Via Francigena pilgrim route is part of it as well, along with some abbeys such as Sant'Antimo, guesthouses, chapels and a few bridges. It is identical to the Parco Artistico, Naturale e Cultura le della Val d'Orcia, which comprises the flat limestone plains and conical hills upon which some fortified settlements were built.

The aesthetic ideal of Val d'Orcia has inspired landscape painters and photographers for centuries.

HISTORIC CENTER OF THE CITY OF PIENZA

Pope Pius II commissioned Bernardo Rossellino to design Pienza as an "ideal city" of the Renaissance based on humanist criteria.

Corsignano is in the Val d'Orcia between Montepulciano and Montalcino. It was the hometown of Pius II (Pope 1458–1464), who wanted to make it the summer residence of the Curia. He even named it after this and arranged in 1459 for a makeover based on Bernardo Rossellino's plans to erect four solid structures around the new main square. The most prominent of these structures is the Santa Maria Assunta Cathedral, a triple-naved hall church built partly in Gothic style but with a Renaissance façade. This is flanked on both sides by the two-story papal residence, the Palazzo Piccolomini (Pius II's family name for civic matters). The house's rooftop gardens provide a beautiful view over the Val d'Orcia as well as the Palazzo Vescovile, the residence of Cardinal Rodrigo Borgia – later Pope Alexander VI. The Palazzo Civico, or town hall, was built in 1463 and impresses visitors with a columned loggia overlooking the Piazza. At the southern end, a garden complex joins up with Monte Amiata. The death of Pope Pius II in 1464 also marked the end of any further development plans.

Piazza Pio II with the cathedral seen from the Palazzo Civico.

SAN MARINO HISTORIC CENTER AND MOUNT TITANO

Old buildings and fort complexes attest to the continuity of this mini-state ever since the 13th century.

The tiny republic of San Marino takes up only 61 sq km (24 sq mi) near the town of Rimini in central Italy, somewhat inland from the Adriatic coast. It was founded in the fourth century by persecuted Dalmatian Christians and named after their leader, Marinus. The 756-m-high (2,480-ft) limestone Mount Titano in the south-west is part of the Apennine Range and falls steeply away to the east. Perched atop the three peaks of the massif are the medieval defense towers of Guaita, Cesta and Montale, which date back to the 10th, 13th and 14 centuries, respectively. At the base of the towers on the ridge is the capital, San Marino, with a well-preserved historic center. Apart from the fortifications, the World Heritage Site also includes historic city walls, gates and bastions.

The San Francesco (1361) and Santa Chiara (1565–1609) monasteries are also worth seeing, as is the neoclassical basilica (1835-1838).

The Palazzo Pubblico is the "government headquarters" of this small state.

HISTORIC CENTER OF URBINO

Urbino, perched atop two hills in the Marche, experienced its heyday in the 15th century when prominent Renaissance artists and scholars made it the cultural and scientific center of Italy.

Under the guidance of the Montefeltro dynasty, Italy's most famous contemporary artists created a uniquely homogenous architectural ensemble of Renaissance buildings in Urbino. The city's prominent structure is the Palazzo Ducale, which was converted from an old fort into a Renaissance palace in various shapes and forms starting in 1444. Today the castle is home to the National Gallery of the Marche, with works by painters such as Titian, Raphael and Botticelli.

Also worth seeing are the Gothic monastery and church of San Domenico with its beautiful Renaissance porch, the San Bernardino Church used as a mausoleum for the dukes of Urbino until 1482, and the church of San Giovanni Battista adorned with artistic frescoes. Urbino's development stagnated in the 16th century, allowing the town's early Renaissance gems to be largely preserved.

Urbino's backdrop is dominated by the 15th-century labyrinthine Palazzo Ducale and the giant dome of the cathedral, originally erected in 1534 and rebuilt in 1789 after an earthquake.

ASSISI, THE BASILICA OF SAN FRANCESCO AND OTHER FRANCISCAN SITES

The little town of Assisi in Umbria is inextricably linked with the life and work of St Francis, its native son and founder of the Franciscan Order.

In the 13th century, Francis of Assisi (1181/82–1226) and the Franciscan Order inspired an era in which the town of Assisi would become one of Italy's most important centers of art. The year of Francis' canonization, 1228, was also the founding year of the Basilica di San Francesco, where the remains of St Francis were transferred in 1230. The abbey church was consecrated in 1253 as a burial and pilgrimage site adorned with magnificent frescoes by Cimabue, Giotto, Simone Martini and the Lorenzetti brothers. It is considered the largest frescoed church in Italy. Other churches like San Rufino, Santa Chiara (burial site of St Clare), Santa Maria sopra Minerva and the San Pietro Abbey underscore the town's religious character. Outside Assisi, the World Heritage Site includes the church of Santa Maria degli Angeli with Porziuncola, the San Damiano and Le Carceri convents, and the Rivotorto sanctuary.

Assisi is perched on a ridge on Monte Subasio (above). Giotto's "Francis preaching before the Pope", (right) is on display in the Upper Church.

ETRUSCAN NECROPOLISES OF CERVETERI AND TARQUINIA

The necropolises of Cerveteri and Tarquinia date from the ninth to the first century BC and are among the most famous archaeological sites from the Etruscan era.

Cerveteri and Tarquinia, located in the present-day provinces of Rome and Viterbo, are two necropolises whose tombs not only attest to the very different burial rites of these very early civilizations in the northern Mediterranean, but also provide insight into their everyday culture. Cerveteri, also known as Banditaccia, is known first and foremost for its architectural monuments. A number of different types of tombs can be distinguished here: burial chambers called tumuli, hewn from tuff with large mounds of earth or tuff above them, chambered

Lid of an Etruscan sarcophagus depicting a couple from Cerveteri.

tombs, purely underground tombs, and rock tombs. The one thing they all have in common, however, is the human quest to furnish them like a residential home. Stonemasons have recovered columns, tables, beds and benches from the tuff while decorations included reliefs and on rare occasions even paintings. The sprawling complexes are like underground cities with lanes and courtyards. Iron ore was exported from there during the Etruscan heyday and ties with Greece were particularly close.

The frescoes, most of which can still be seen in the necropolis of Tarquinia, also demonstrate Greek influences. Around 200 painted tombs have so far been found with frescoes depicting the often carefree life of the Etruscan upper classes: banquets, dances and hunting scenes.

The frescoes in the "Priests' tomb" from around 530 BC are among the most impressive relics in the Etruscan necropolis of Tarquinia.

Italy / Vatican City

The Roman Empire

When the last Etruscan king of Rome, Tarquinius Superbus, was banished from Rome in 509 BC it marked the beginning of the Roman Republic. In 264 BC the Roman army was sent to war outside of Italy for the first time: to Sicily, the first of the Mediterranean nations to fall to Rome over the next 100 years. The era of the Republic

ended with internal unrest and civil wars, after which dictators such as Sulla, Pompeius and Julius Caesar came to power. After Caesar's assassination, Octavian opposed Mark Antony and was named Augustus by the Roman Senate in 27 BC. The Republic was thus replaced by the Principate. At that time, more than

HISTORIC CENTER OF ROME

This World Heritage Site was initially to include the historic center within the Aurelian Wall, with the most important monuments from antiquity. After an expansion in 1990, the transnational site now bears the full title of "Historic Center of Rome, the Properties of the Holy See in that City Enjoying Extraterritorial Rights and San Paolo Fuori le Mura".

The "Eternal City", with buildings from antiquity, the Renaissance, the baroque and the classicist periods, is a unique open-air museum not found

The Castel Sant'Angelo, a mausoleum built by Emperor Hadrian for his own burial, was made into a fort by successive popes.

anywhere else in the world. Ancient structures such as the Roman Forum, the imperial fora and Palatine Hill, the Colosseum and the Pantheon all attest to the heyday of the Roman Empire. After the Empire's collapse, Rome became the center of Christianity and the popes began redesigning large parts of the city. The protected sites of the Holy See include the Lateran complex, the patriarchal basilicas of Santa Maria Maggiore and San Paolo fuori le Mura as well as the Palazzo di Propaganda Fide, the Palazzo Maffei and the Palazzo del Sant'Uffizio.

The Roman Forum was the center of ancient Rome. Today, ruins of imperial monuments there attest to the transience of earthly power: the Triumphal Arch of Septimius Severus, the Temple of Vespasian and the Temple of Saturn (pictured from left to right).

one million people were already living in the Eternal City.

The Romans were also engineering pioneers whose roads, bridges and aqueducts were still being used in the Middle Ages. Late Antiquity began with Diocletian (r. 284–305), who implementetd extensive reforms to the administration, economy and army.

Emperor Constantine made Christianity the realm's new religion in 313, and shifted the imperial residence east to what is now Istanbul. The decline of the empire began in the fourth century and was completed by 476 when the last emperor, Romulus Augustus, was deposed by Odoacer, a Germanic general.

The legend of Rome's founding is hewn into the stone at the Capitoline Museums. The story goes that the twins Romulus and Remus, who were suckled by a she-wolf, founded the city in 753 BC (left). The museums are also home to the original equestrian statue of the famous philosopher-emperor, Marcus Aurelius (far left).

The victorious Emperor Constantine I dedicated this mighty triumphal arch to himself in 312.

Up to 50,000 spectators could attend gladiator fights and animal baiting in the Colosseum, erected under Emperor Vespasian from AD 72 to 81.

The Piazza della Rotonda with the Pantheon – a sanctuary dedicated to the gods of ancient Rome – is one of the city's finest squares.

A complex with four forums named after their builders was begun in 54 BC as an extension to the Roman Forum.

Italy / Vatican City

HISTORIC CENTER OF ROME

The Spanish Steps connect the Piazza di Spagna with the church of Santa Trinità dei Monti.

Rome's most famous fountain is the Fontana di Trevi, erected by Nicolò Salvi in 1732 and dedicated to the god of the sea.

The Fontana del Moro in front of the church of Sant'Agnese in Agone on the Piazza Navona is an elongated oval.

The Piazza Mattei with the Fontana delle Tartarughe.

Bernini's fascinating allegory of the Ganges adorns the Fountain of the Four Rivers (Fontana dei Quattro Fiumi), built in the center of the Piazza Navona in 1651.

Vatican City

Michelangelo

Along with Leonardo da Vinci, Michelangelo Buonarroti (1475 to 1564) is probably one of the most famous artists of the Italian High Renaissance. Much of the artist's work is focused on the human figure and though he was a student of Domenico Ghirlandaio, where he learned to paint frescoes, Michelangelo, who was also an architect, saw himself primarily as a sculptor; in particular a student of the sculptures of antiquity. To obtain the same perfection in his sculptural representations of the human body, he even drew models and secretly dissected cadavers.

In 1505, Pope Julius II called Michelangelo to Rome to build a tomb for

VATICAN CITY

Vatican City is the center of Christianity with St Peter's Basilica, St Peter's Square and the Vatican Palace. It is also a unique center of religious art and has therefore been included on the World Heritage List as an ensemble in and of itself.

In 1377, Rome officially declared the papal residence for itself (in the Vatican) and initiated what later became known by some as the Western Schism with a defiant Avignon. The bishops of Rome had previously lived in the Lateran; starting in the 15th century, the complex underwent massive expansions. St Peter's Basilica, the Vatican Museum and the Papal Palace are home to myriad art treasures.

St Peter's Basilica stands on the remains of the basilica erected over the alleged tomb of Peter the Apostle, consecrated in 325. Its construction began in 1506 based on Bramante's designs but it was opulently modified by the likes of Raphael, Michelangelo and other artists of the High Renaissance. The interior comprises a variety of altars, mosaics and sculptures and the dome, with a peak height of 119 m (390 ft) and a diameter of 42 m (138 ft) was designed by Michelangelo – creator of the famous frescoes in the Sistine Chapel. The artist also painted the private papal chapel, which Pope Sixtus IV built from 1473 to 1483 and where the conclave (papal election) was held, with scenes from Genesis and images of prophets and sibyls (1508–1512); its altar wall depicts the Last Judgment (1536–1541).

St Peter's Square with its elliptical complex designed by Bernini was built from 1656 to 1667 and sprawls out in front of St Peter's Basilica. It measures 240 m (787 ft) in length and is lined with a 17-m-wide (56-ft) colonnade made up of 284 individual columns on which the statues of 140 saints stand. Two 14-m-high (46-ft) fountains soar up on both sides – near the two foci of the ellipse.

View from the colonnades of St Peter's Square, in the center of which is a 26-m (84-ft) Egyptian obelisk that Emperor Caligula had transported from Heliopolis to Rome in the year 37.

him. However, both this assignment and his plans for the new St Peter's Basilica were rejected, forcing the artist to return frustrated to Florence. A new challenge led him back to Rome, however. The ceiling of the Sistine Chapel in the Vatican was to be painted and, having received the commission this time, Michelangelo spent four years in complete seclusion painting the gigantic and physically demanding frescoes. In 1547, he took over supervision of the construction of St Peter's Basilica, whose immense dome is considered his greatest architectural feat. His main works as a sculptor include the exquisite Pietà in St Peter's Basilica, and the statue of David in front of the Palazzo Vecchio in Florence (the original today stands in the Galleria dell'Accademia).

In 1498/99, Michelangelo created one of the finest artworks in St Peter's Basilica: the Pietà (far left). His portrait (left) was painted by one of his pupils around 1510.

St Peter's Basilica is a longitudinal building in the shape of a Latin cross with a central dome above the intersection, through which the light shines in.

Raphael's fresco "The School of Athens" is a homage to the ancient philosophers and was created in the pontifical chambers of the Vatican in 1510/1511.

The Sistine Chapel owes its fame to the stunning paintings by Botticelli, Perugino, Signorelli and of course Michelangelo.

VILLA D'ESTE, TIVOLI

With more than 500 springs, water features and fountains the Villa d'Este near Rome is an outstanding work of Renaissance landscape gardening that became the archetype for water gardens throughout Europe.

In 1550, Cardinal Ippolito d'Este, a descendant of the dynasty of rulers from Ferrara and the son of Lucrezia Borgia, chose a former Benedictine monastery in Tivoli to be his new residence. Some of the villa's halls have been decorated with beautiful frescoes by ambassadors of Roman Mannerism such as Livio Agresti and Federico Zuccari. On the slope beneath the villa, Ippolito d'Este commissioned Pirro Ligorio and Alberto Galvani to create a park with water features and a vast system of springs: the "Garden of Miracles". The countless fountains disperse into thousands of streams, cascades and waterfalls.

The park was redesigned starting in 1605 under his successor, Cardinal Alessandro d'Este, and Bernini was later involved with the work; the Fontana del Bicchierone fountain is attributed to him. The Organo Idraulico, or Water Organ, is a masterpiece by Frenchman Claude Venard. After a period during which it fell into disrepair, Villa d'Este was renovated under Cardinal Gustav von Hohenlohe in 1851 and became a social meeting place where Franz Liszt also liked to spend time and compose music.

Hundreds of gargoyled water spouts give the park complex a unique charm.

VILLA ADRIANA (TIVOLI)

This rural private residence of Roman Emperor Hadrian is located just under 6 km (4 mi) south-west of Tivoli and is a splendid example of the opulence and elegance of Roman architectural verve.

The artistic Emperor Hadrian enjoyed studying the people and cultures of his empire when he traveled, particularly in Greece and Egypt. As a result, the residence he built outside Rome between 118 and 134 – which is more of an imperial garden city than a traditional country estate – primarily features copies of Greek archetypes. The various elements of the complex are loosely connected and conform beautifully to the natural terrain. Italian master builders of the baroque period even modeled their work on the harmonious manner in which the buildings here are incorporated into the landscape. The palace's sanctuar-

ies were once lavishly furnished with marble. The Teatro Marittimo features a large columned hall around a pool with an island in the middle. Apart from the various thermal baths (Heliocaminus) and Canopus, named after an ancient Egyptian coastal city of the same name, the Villa Adriana complex also includes a stadium, a Greek and Latin library, an arena and an odeon, or Greek theater.

Copies of Greek and Egyptian statues line the Canopus, a 119-m-long (390-ft) lake reminiscent of the sanctuary of Serapis near Alexandria, which is surrounded by a portico of columns.

HISTORIC CENTER OF NAPLES

Naples dates back to the Greek settlement of Parthenope, whose Old Town was expanded to include a New Town ("Neapolis"). A number of Mediterranean civilizations have left their mark here.

The remains of a market from ancient Neapolis were found under the Church of San Lorenzo Maggiore. Next to the Chapel of St Januarius, the sixth-century Santa Restituta Basilica attests to the early spread of Christianity throughout this region. It forms part of San Gennaro Cathedral along with the fourth-century baptistery. The reign of the House of Anjou from the 13th century onwards saw the emergence of magnificent Gothic, Mannerist and neoclassical churches and palaces. Santa Chiara was completed in 1340, and the Castel Nuovo

was erected in the 13th century. The Palazzo Reale was built from 1600 to 1602 based on plans by Domenico Fontana. The "Spanish Quarter" was originally a garrison of the Spanish viceroys who ruled Naples from 1503 to 1734. The church of Gesù Nuovo (16th century) is an imposing example of Neapolitan baroque, while the Santa Chiara Monastery with its impressive cloister is a jewel of rococo architecture.

Castel Nuovo was once a fort and residence of the kings of Naples.

ARCHAEOLOG-ICAL AREAS OF POMPEII, HERCULANEUM AND TORRE ANNUNZIATA

These archaeological relics were buried by the eruption of Mt Vesuvius in AD 79, but impressively illustrate life and culture in Roman times.

Excavations at the foot of Vesuvius have been underway since the 18th century, unearthing the remains of settlements beneath lava up to 7 m (23 ft) thick. Only two-thirds of the area has so far been uncovered, but visitors to Pompeii can now walk across the forum surrounded by temples and through thermal baths, theaters, guesthouses and residential homes where the murals and sgraffiti are particularly impressive. Famous buildings include the "House of the

Excavations in Pompei began in 1748. Entire streets with buildings are still being unearthed even today.

Faun", depicting the Battle of Alexander at Issus, and the "House of the Vettii", both well-preserved examples of wealthy Roman homes. But even latrines, shops, bakeries and objects from everyday life like bread, crockery and writing utensils have also been found here. The fast-cooling stone has even left behind perfect "moulds" of entombed people. In Herculaneum, vast thermal bath complexes as well as rows of multi-story dwellings have also been preserved. It was not until 1967 that Villa Oplontis, probably the residence of Emperor Nero's wife from the first century, was unearthed in Torre Annunziata. Many frescoes, mosaics and marble are indicative of the Villa's former splendor.

Beneath the ash are well-preserved ancient works of art such as the „Neptune and Amphitrite" wall mosaic from Herculaneum (top left) and the fresco with the portrait of Terentius Neo and his wife from Pompeii (bottom left).

COSTIERA AMALFITANA

The region around Amalfi with its breathtaking cliffs is one of Italy's greatest natural treasures. The World Heritage Site includes the coast between Positano and Vietri sul Mare, with the mountain villages of Scala, Tramonti and Ravello.

This section of coast is accessed by a winding panoramic road that offers stunning views over the Gulf of Salerno. Positano, at one end of the route, is one of Italy's oldest settlements, and enchants visitors with its small whitewashed houses and magnificent "palazzi", which cling to the steep cliffs. The "Grotta di Smeraldo", with its bizarre dripstone formations, was discovered by accident in 1932 halfway between Amalfi and Positano.

In the ninth century, Amalfi was one of the mightiest maritime republics in the Mediterranean, and attained untold wealth through trade with the Orient. A famous native son, Flavio Gioia, is said to have invented the compass. The "Tavole Amalfitane", to this day still housed in the town hall, contains the first volumes of written maritime law.

Ravello lies somewhat tucked away in the mountains and its San Pantaleone Cathedral from 1086 is well worth seeing. The Oriental-style garden of Villa Rufolo is said to have inspired Richard Wagner to compose his opera "Parsifal".

An impressive flight of steps (right) leads up to the ninth-century cathedral in Amalfi. The view over the coast near Ravello (below) is particularly spectacular.

ROYAL PALACE AT CASERTA

In the 18th century, a palace complex whose size and opulence could rival that of Versailles was built for King Charles III in Caserta. The World Heritage Site also includes the park, an aqueduct and the adjacent San Leucio.

The official name of this site is the Palace of Caserta with the Park, the Aqueduct of Vanvitelli and the San Leucio Complex. The palace, built between 1752 and 1775, was designed to demonstrate the power of the Bourbons, who ruled Naples from 1734 to 1860. Though it was rarely used after its completion, the scale of the complex is overwhelming. The floor plan of the palace is 253 by 202 m (830 by 663 ft) with 1,217 rooms on an area of 45,000 sq m (484,200 sq ft) on five levels. The main attractions are the staircase, the chapel and the theater of the royal court with the park. The palace grounds cover 80 ha (198 acres) and are impressive for their waterworks. Complex naval battles were staged on the lake along the 3-km-long (2-mi) central axis while the canals and cascades were supplied with water via the Acquedotto Carolino, designed by Vanvitelli. The Silk Factory of San Leucio encompasses production plants and a workers' village. A plan to develop it into the Ideal City of Ferdinandopolis was abandoned following the French occupation.

"Versailles of the South": the Palazzo Reale in Caserta. The staircase gives an indication of its vast dimensions.

CILENTO AND VALLO DI DIANO NATIONAL PARK

The National Park of Cilento and Vallo di Diano is situated on what was once an important ancient Mediterranean trade route. The World Heritage Site also includes the ancient ruins of Paestum and Velia as well as the medieval charterhouse of Padula.

This national park south of Salerno features a mountainous region with largely untouched mixed forests, evergreen woods, bush regions and grasslands. In ancient times the area was a vital gateway between Greek, Etruscan and Lucan cultures. The temples of Paestum, founded around 650 BC, are in fact the most impressive examples of Greek culture on the Apennine Peninsula. The Phoenician colony of Velia was once home to the "Eleatic School" of the Greek philosopher, Xenophanes (ca. 565 to 470 BC), and the foundations of several temples, baths, houses and altars have also been preserved there.

The charterhouse of Padula, dedicated to St Lawrence and founded in 1306 by Tommaso Sanseverino, has been repeatedly rebuilt and modified over a period of more than 450 years. The baroque monastery has one of the world's largest cloisters.

The Temple of Ceres in Paestum is also sometimes referred to as the Temple of Athena.

CASTEL DEL MONTE

This octagonal castle is shrouded in the mystery of numerology. Owned by German Emperor Frederick II, who ruled over southern Italy as the King of Sicily, the castle combines various elements from antiquity, Islamic architecture and the Gothic era.

The castle of Emperor Frederick II of Hohenstaufen was erected in around 1250 not far from Andria in Apulia's Terra di Bari. It features an octagonal floor plan with eight equal octagonal towers and an octagonal courtyard. The crimson-colored main entrance portal beneath an ancient gable is adorned with Arabian ornaments while the alabaster and marble columns inside are indicative of a more opulent interior that has now disappeared. A few precious floor mosaics have however been preserved. Interestingly, there is a noticeable lack of Christian themes and motifs. It is not clear whether the emperor lived here or what it was used for. It may have served as a hunting lodge, but the unusual shape of the building has prompted much speculation over the centuries, many of them involving numerology. In ancient Arabic culture, the number eight possesses unusual powers. Frederick may have been inspired by Islamic scholars, but it is also possible that he modeled it on the interior of Aachen Cathedral.

The "Crown of Apulia" may symbolize the power of the number eight: each corner of the octagon has an octagonal tower.

THE SASSI AND THE PARK OF THE RUPESTRIAN CHURCHES OF MATERA

Over thousands of years, new caves and dwellings were hewn into the tuff in two funnel-shaped gorges near Matera; they include 150 rock churches.

The cave labyrinths of Matera in the Basilicata region were still inhabited until well into the 1950s. They formed one of Italy's largest slum areas where residents lived without electricity or water. The appalling conditions, however, forced the authorities to resettle the residents, after which the cave city fell into ruin until the Italian government introduced a program to save it in the mid 1980s.

The Sassi contain elements of virtually every era of human evolution. The original inhabitants created the first primitive cave dwellings. In the eighth century, monks left Asia Minor and fled to Matera, where they erected rock churches such as San Pietro in Principibus, Madonna della Croce, San Nicola dei Greci, Santa Maria de Idris, Santa Barbara and Santa Maria della Valle. Their frescoes are among the most impressive examples of Byzantine painting.

Matera Cathedral was constructed between 1230 and 1270. It soars above the highest point of the Old Town.

Italy

THE TRULLI OF ALBEROBELLO

The round buildings of Alberobello in the Alulia region are known as "trulli" and feel as if they must be very ancient indeed. Ironically, the origins of the style are unknown, but entire rows of houses were constructed in this style.

The trulli in Alberobello, about 60 km (37 mi) south-east of Bari near the Adriatic coast in southern Italy, are white cylindrical dwellings with a domed or conical stone roof and one single room. The walls are made from stones stacked without using mortar. For the roof, flat stone slabs are placed on top of one another in increasingly narrow circles so that each stone is half covered by the one above it and is kept in place by the latter's weight. Lime slurry is used to paint symbols on the roofs to protect against evil forces.

The origins of this form of architecture are unknown. One possible explanation is that, in the 17th century, taxes were calculated by the liege lord based on the number of brick settlements. The trulli could save taxes by being dismantled easily or converted into cairns if necessary. The style may also be reminiscent of a Stone Age culture in Apulia.

Simple round buildings with conical roofs made from stacked stone slabs were widespread in the Mediterranean back in ancient times. In Alberobello this tradition lives on in the form of "trulli". Depending on the space available, several trulli can be connected to one another (right and below).

AEOLIAN ISLANDS

Some 40 km (25 mi) off the north coast of Sicily, the Aeolian Islands owe their inclusion as a World Heritage Site to their volcanic activity. The geology and geophysics of the islands are of great interest to volcanologists.

The Aeolian Islands, also known as the Lipari Islands, comprise Vulcano, Lipari, Alicudi, Filicudi, Salina, Panarea and Stromboli. The subsidence of the Tyrrhenian Sea during the Pliocene era is what originally formed the archipelago, but new studies have shown that volcanic activity on the islands only began in the Pleistocene era, and the seven islands were then created over three distinct periods. Today only Stromboli and the Grande Fossa volcano on Vulcano are still active, although there are fumaroles and solfatara on Lipari.

The most spectacular of the islands is Stromboli. It consists solely of the volcano of the same name, which rises to an altitude of almost 1,000 m (3,300 ft) above sea level. There has been volcanic activity here for forty thousand years now, and pieces of lava and incandescent cinders still emerge from the openings in the crater – accompanied by quite significant explosions. In fact, Stromboli is one of the most active volcanoes in the world that can be observed from such a close distance.

Filicudi comprises three volcanic cones that are no longer active. Enthusiast love the island as an ideal destination for hiking and its botanical diversity.

ARCHAEOLOGICAL AREA OF AGRIGENTO

Located near the present-day city of Agrigento on the southern coast of Sicily is the Valle dei Templi, with the imposing remains of Akragas, one of the most prominent Greek colonies and trading towns in the Mediterranean.

Today, the archaeological "Valley of the Temples" stretches along the still partly visible ancient city walls of Akragas, which the Greek poet Pindar called "the most beautiful city of the mortals". Among the particularly striking Doric "peripteros" here – rows of columns strung along the rolling hills – is the Concordia Temple (ca. 430 BC). It is even considered one of the best-preserved Greek temples anywhere in the world. The Temple of Juno was built here in around 450 BC. The Temple of Heracles (ca. the end of the sixth century BC) is the youngest of Agrigento's monumental temple buildings. The largest temple was originally the Temple of Olympian Zeus, whose solid foundations and 20-m-high (66-ft) columns were constructed by Carthaginian prisoners of war. The Carthaginians gained their revenge by destroying the temple immediately after conquering the city in 406 BC and banishing its inhabitants.

Only a few columns and ruins remain of the Temple of Heracles.

LATE BAROQUE TOWNS OF THE VAL DI NOTO (SOUTH-EASTERN SICILY)

Sicily's Val di Noto is home to eight towns with a unique ensemble of late-baroque architecture and art.

After the earthquake of 1693, which devastated the entire region around the Val di Noto and killed almost 100,000 people, active construction began in the eight towns of the Val di Noto and the provincial capital of Catania. They included Caltagirone, Militello in Val di Catania, Modica, Noto, Palazzolo Acreide, Ragusa and Scicli. Reconstruction gave way to a rare ensemble of late-baroque buildings that went up in just a few short decades. Of particular art-historic importance is the cathedral in Catania, erected on the ruins of a Norman com- plex and whose façade was designed by Vaccaini in 1735, as well as the abbey church of the former Benedictine monastery of San Nicoló. The pictur- esque town of Ragusa is home to the San Giovanni Cathedral (1706 to 1760) with its elaborate façade by Gagliardi. Noto features the churches of San Carlo Borromeo and San Domenico as well as the Palazzo Ducezio.

Opposite Noto's cathedral is the Palazzo Ducezio, now the town hall (above). The elephant fountain (left) at the Piazza del Duomo is the symbol of Catania.

Italy

VILLA ROMANA DEL CASALE

This Roman villa from late antiquity was erected in an agricultural region of central Sicily. It primarily owes its art-historic prestige and inclusion as a World Heritage Site to the magnificent floor mosaics.

Most rural villa complexes tended to include an estate, although in the time of imperial Rome they often just became the summer residences of rich townsfolk. An interesting example of such a property can be found near Piazza Armerina in the town of Casale. The building that preceded the complex was built between the years 310 and 340 and may have belonged to Emperor Maximian.

Its fifty rooms included baths, gymnastics halls, studies, sitting rooms and sleeping quarters forming a maze-like cluster around the central courtyard. Even the latrines have been well preserved in Sicily's largest late-Roman residential complex. However, the villa, systematically excavated since the 1920s, is primarily famous for its more than forty floor mosaics made from multi-colored marble and presumably crafted by North African artisans. The illustrations cover more than 3,500 sq m (37,660 sq ft), and depict dolphins, fish, hunting scenes and everyday life as well as mythological themes. The best known are the erotic "bikini girls", revealingly dressed Roman women who add flair to one of the guestrooms.

The villa's floor mosaics tell of upper-class life in the Roman Empire.

SYRACUSE AND THE ROCKY NECROPOLIS OF PANTALICA

Syracuse was one of the largest metropolises of ancient Greece and the World Heritage Site also includes the pre-Grecian chambered rock tombs of Pantalica, located outside of the city.

Syracuse was founded in 733 BC on the former Ortygia Peninsula (now Ortigia Island) by colonists from the Greek town of Corinth. Cicero praised Syracuse as being the greatest of all Greek cities; Plato worked here; and Archimedes was born here.

A theater accommodating as many as 15,000 spectators was built during Greek times and later converted into an arena for gladiator fights by the Romans. Other ancient monuments here include an elliptical Roman amphitheatre and the colossal altar of Hieron II, of which only the solid base hewn from the rock remains. The Temple of Athena (fifth century BC) is situated inside the cathedral.

The necropolis of Pantalica near the town of Sortino includes roughly 5,000 chambered rock tombs dating back to the time between the 13th and seventh centuries BC, when Sicels lived here. These tombs were later used by the early Christians as residential dwellings and chapels.

The Piazza Archimede with the Diana Fountain is the center of the Old Town of Syracuse.

SU NURAXI DI BARUMINI

"Nuraghes" is the name given to Sardinia's beehive-like towers made of stone blocks that date back to the time of the Bonnanaro and Nuraghe cultures (1800–250 BC).

These peculiar stone buildings are something of an enigma from the prehistory of Sardinia. They are sturdy, conical structures which, much like the "trulli" of southern Italy, were made without mortar by stacking large stones on top of one another and tapering upwards into a single keystone.

The largest excavated complex among these fort- or bulwark-like clusters of towers is found near Barumini in the center of the island. The main tower was 20 m (66 ft) high and protected by a 14-m-high (46-ft) bastion reinforced with four towers. The bastion itself was then surrounded by a ring-shaped wall complex and topped with seven more towers of roughly 10 m (33 ft) in height. Near the fortress was a Bronze Age village, some of whose houses have been reconstructed.

Sprawling out to the north of Barumini is the Giara di Gesturi Plateau, which is famous for its wild horses. At the edge of plains are twenty-five more Bronze Age stone buildings as well. This site presumably once had about fifty of these structures, all of which would have been built in around 1500 BC.

The Su Nuraxi, or "nuraghe", near Barumini on Sardinia attest to a lost Bronze Age culture.

CITY OF VALLETTA

The capital of Malta largely owes its present-day appearance to the Order of St John whose Grand Master, Jean Parisot de la Valette, founded the city after withstanding a siege by the Ottomans in 1566.

Valletta is perched on a 60-m (197-ft) cliff above Malta's northern coast and is surrounded on three sides by the sea. For centuries, the Phoenicians, Greeks, Carthaginians, Romans, Byzantines and Arabs took turns ruling this island until it was handed over to the Order of St John after the Turkish siege in 1565. The Order then erected a fortified city typical of the times with a solid defensive section built by architects Francesco Laparelli and Girolamo Cassar from 1566 to 1571. Within the city walls, the Order of St John built palaces, churches and hospices in both Renaissance and baroque styles.

The Order's wealth and confidence are demonstrated by the lavish design of the Grand Master's palace and its two central courtyards. The baroque Church of Our Lady of Victory was erected in 1567 as a gesture for fending off the siege. St John's Co-Cathedral, constructed between 1573 and 1578 as a burial place for the knights of St John, was adorned with ceiling paintings and opulently furnished side chapels. The library, founded by the Order in 1555, houses some precious manuscripts.

St John's Co-Cathedral is the main church and is elaborately furnished.

MEGALITHIC TEMPLES OF MALTA

This World Heritage Site originally comprised the two temples of Gigantija on the island of Gozo but was later expanded to include similar complexes on Gozo and the main island – Hagar Qim, Mnajdra, Tarxien, Ta'Hagrat and Skorba.

Until the 20th century, these megalithic buildings were considered to be the work of the Phoenicians, but new dating methods have revealed that they make up the world's oldest stone temple. Of the seven large complexes, that of Gigantija on the island of Gozo is thought to be the oldest (ca. 6,000 years). These two walled temples comprise several horseshoe-shaped chambers measuring over 10 m (33 ft) in length grouped in a cloverleaf formation around an interior courtyard.
The temple complexes on the main island of Malta also follow this same ground plan. The façades of Hagar Qim were presumably completed around

2000 BC, and are up to 12 m (39 ft) high. Excavations here have unearthed sacred sculptures, the most famous of which is probably the "Venus of Malta". The religious site of Mnajdra displays richly decorated reliefs on the façades, which are second only to the ruins of the complex of Tarxien, discovered in 1914. Oracle cells and unearthed sacrificial offerings from distant lands indicate that the temples were once a pilgrimage destination in the Mediterranean.

Malta's stone monuments made from coralline limestone (left, Mnajdra) are older than the Egyptian pyramids.

HAL SAFLIENI HYPOGEUM

The Neolithic Hypogeum of Hal Saflieni on Malta is an underground temple complex considered to be among the world's oldest burial and ritual sites.

Construction work in 1902 in Paola, near Valletta, unearthed an immense underground cave system containing the remains of more than 7,000 people spread out over several different levels. A sanctuary above ground once marked the entrance to the Hypogeum (literally "underground"), a subterranean labyrinth of many passageways, chambers and alcoves reaching depths of more than 10 m (33 ft), and covering a total area of around 500 sq m (5,380 sq ft).
It has since been established that the oldest parts of the Hypogeum were excavated as early as around 3000 BC using surprisingly simple neolithic tools such as animal horns

and stone wedges, and were continuously expanded over a period of 1,300 years. The Hypogeum was used both as a cemetery and a ritual site. In the center of the necropolis was a sanctuary that presumably did not serve a public cult but was more likely reserved for initiation rituals – the archaeological finds are suggestive of sacrifices and oracle consultations. The most famous items that have been excavated here include the sculpture of the "Sleeping Lady", who was presumably a priestess.

The complex of Hal Saflieni was also used as a burial site.

ŠKOCJAN CAVES

The Škocjan caves are located in western Slovenia's karst mountains, not far from the Italian border. Nearly 6 km (4 mi) long, these labyrinthine caverns feature huge grottoes, wonderful dripstone formations and roaring waterfalls. They are also home to numerous rare plants and animals.

The Reka river disappears underground at Škocjan, where it flows for some 40 km (25 mi) before finally resurfacing near the Adriatic coast – a winding course that takes roughly eight days to complete. On its way, the river has created an eerily primeval subterranean karst landscape with all the typical signs of thousands of years of limestone erosion: steep crevices, gorges, shafts, sinkholes and basins, lakes, waterfalls, narrow passages and massive chambers. The Martelova dvorana is the largest chamber at 308 m (1,010 ft) in length, 123 m (404 ft) wide, and up to 146 m (479 ft) high.

When the snow melts, the water level in the 148-m-deep (486-ft) Reka underground canyon can rise dramatically within a short period of time. Even in summer the twenty-five raging cascades inside the "murmuring cave" are still a fantastic spectacle. The stalactites and stalagmites in the "silent cave", meanwhile, include both mighty and filigree formations with names like the "giant" or the "organ".

The Reka flows 45 m (148 ft) beneath the Cerkvenik Bridge (right) before finally emerging into the open near the Adriatic coast.

THE CATHEDRAL OF ST JAMES IN ŠIBENIK

Built between 1431 and 1535, during the transition from the Gothic to the Renaissance, St James' Cathedral on the Croatian Dalmatian coast is a building that merges local, northern Italian and Tuscan influences.

St James' Cathedral (Sveti Jakov) is a triple-naved basilica with apses and a central dome that is based on a standard Italian design. Dalmatian master builder and sculptor Juraj Dalmatinac began in 1441 by constructing the lower side aisles up to crown height, then moved on to the baptistery and the apses. Niccolò di Giovanni Fiorentino, who was a pupil of Donatello, completed the aisles after 1477 and closed the ceiling with a cantilevered barrel vault of stone panels that also forms the exterior: a technical feat at the time.

The architect from Florence also built the narrow dome over the short transept and the west front with its three-leafed clover outline – reminiscent of the cathedral in his home city. The final phase of construction was begun in 1505 by Bartolomeo and Giacomo del Mestre, with help from Ivan Masticeviç. One of the city wall towers served as the bell tower.

The most important building in Šibenik's Venetian-style Old Town is St James' Cathedral, consecrated in 1555, with its graceful dome.

PLITVICE LAKES NATIONAL PARK

The sixteen lakes of Plitvice Lakes National Park, not far from the border with Bosnia and Herzegovina, are connected by a number of cascades and waterfalls that form a stunnind series of natural terraces. They are testimony to the ever-changing, unspoiled natural landscape of the Croatian karst.

Spanning some 7 km (4 mi), this magnificent series of lakes is the result of a combination of limestone deposits and tectonic movements. The build-up of calc-sinter over thousands of years resulted in natural dams and barriers that capture water. The lakes' bluish-green shimmer, meanwhile, is due to algae and mosses. The most impressive of the park's falls are up to 76 m (249 ft) high and are found around the four lower lakes. The Plitvice river joins the in at the end of the chain of lakes to form the source of the river Korana.

Declared a national park in 1949, the region at the foot of the Mala Kapela range is home to a diverse range of flora and fauna. Deer, wolves, brown bears and some 120 species of bird are all found in its dense forests.

The contours of the terraces created by the flow of calcareous water through the lakes are constantly changing (left). A network of paths and bridges allow visitors to discover the park on foot while boats allow you to experience the beautiful landscape from the water.

EPISCOPAL COMPLEX OF THE EUPHRASIAN BASILICA IN THE HISTORIC CENTER OF POREČ

The religious ensemble of the Euphrasian Basilica in the historic center of Poreč on the west coast of the Istrian Peninsula is considered an outstanding example of the fusion of early-Christian and Byzantine architecture.

There were already Christians in the Istrian town of Poreč by the third century. In the fourth century they built a chapel that also housed the remains of St Maurus, their first bishop and a martyr of late-Roman persecution. Only fragments of the chapel remain.
The first large basilica here was built as early as the fifth century and was given its present-day shape and design under Bishop Euphrasius in the sixth century. With its wealth of care-

fully preserved mosaics, this Byzantine-style church is one of the loveliest buildings from the era.
The baptistery and the atrium, one of only a few of its kind still remaining from early Christian times, date from the same era.

The marble columns of the triple-aisled Euphrasius Basilica – the cathedral of the Croatian diocese of Poreč-Pula – come from the island of Prokonnesos near Istanbul (Constantinople at the time).

HISTORIC CITY OF TROGIR

Trogir is testimony to a level of urban consciousness that goes back to pre-Christian times. The Dalmatian coastal town originally developed from a Greek colony founded in 385 BC.

The grid-like road network is a relic of the original Greek colony here, Tragurion, which developed into one of most important coastal towns in antiquity. This town on an island came under Byzantine control in the sixth century (until about the year 1,000). Thereafter its rule became a matter of dispute between the Croats, Bosnians, Hungarians and Venetians alike, with the Venetian Republic emerging victorious from 1420 to 1797.
The Benedictine monastery features carvings and inscriptions from the third to the first centuries BC while the Romanesque-Gothic Cathedral of St Lawrence boasts masterpieces of

medieval painting. The west portal, built in 1240 by Radovan from Trogir, is one of the most important stone sculptures in Croatia. The city hall and loggia with its clock tower are from the 15th century. Kamerlengo Castle and St Mark's Tower are part of the Venetian fortifications from the 15th and 16th centuries. There are also a number of palatial residences and town houses from the Late Gothic, Renaissance and baroque.

The seaside promenade and historic city center are dominated by St Nicholas' Tower in the monastery and the bell tower of St Lawrence's Cathedral.

Croatia

HISTORIC SPLIT WITH THE PALACE OF DIOCLETIAN

Present-day Split began its life in the seventh century on the ruins of a monumental retirement home built for Emperor Diocletian in the third century.

Emperor Diocletian had a palace built here in ten years, in the style of a Roman castrum, as a residence for the period following his abdication in 305. His retirement home near the Roman city of Salona covered an area of about 38,000 sq m (420,000 sq ft) and was fortified by a wall with defensive towers. When the Avars and the Slavs invaded in around 615, some of the Salona population sought refuge in the ruins of the ancient Roman palace. The grounds then became a natural base for the development of present-day Split.

Diocletian's octagonal mausoleum was converted to a Christian cathedral by adding an entrance hall and a bell tower, while the burial site's valuable decoration remained unchanged. The Temple of Jupiter was converted into the baptistery.

The late-Gothic Papalić Palace, with its elegant courtyard, and the Cindro and Agubio Palaces – which are now Split's loveliest baroque edifices – all originally date from the city's era as a prosperous medieval trading center.

The Riva promenade (below) gives Split a real Mediterranean atmosphere. The peristyle, an atrium with columns, once led to the temples, staterooms, and living quarters in the imperial palace (right).

STARI GRAD PLAIN

Stari Grad Plain in the west of Hvar island still boasts remnants of an Ionian Greek settlement from the fourth century BC.

This plain owes its name to the adjacent coastal town founded in about 385 BC by Greeks from the island of Paros. The town and the plain are situated on a bay that extends 6 km (4 mi) into the island's interior and even served Stone-Age seafarers as a place of refuge during bad weather.

Stari Grad (old town) was almost completely destroyed following the conquest of Hvar by the Romans in 228 BC. The colonial remains are nevertheless among the oldest surviving evidence of ancient settlements.

The region's strategic location and mild climate led to quick development here as major agricultural area and trading center. The importance of the town and the area is indicated by the various fortifications built to protect them. Some sections of the original town wall still remain along with small stone buildings outside of town. The fertile lands of the Stari Grad Plain were divided up by the Greeks on geometric plots that were mainly used for growing wine and olives. Remains of the ancient boundary markings can even be seen here after twenty-four centuries. The plain itself is now a nature reserve.

The bell tower of the Church of St Stephen at the water's edge creates a picturesque backdrop.

OLD CITY OF DUBROVNIK

Formerly known as "Ragusa", Dubrovnik, the "Pearl of the Adriatic", became a strong maritime and trading power in the 13th century. The magnificent cityscape was reconstructed following a devastating earthquake in 1667, and the damage caused by artillery fire during the Yugoslav Wars (1991/92) was repaired with the help of international aid.

Dubrovnik, given its current name only in 1919, was one of the most important centers of trade with the eastern Mediterranean (Levante) in the Middle Ages. In the 14th century, the town known then as "Ragusa", even managed to withstand efforts by Venice and Hungary to exert power here. Formally under Turkish sovereignty starting in 1525, it determined its own fate as a free republic until Dalmatia's annexation by Napoleon in 1809. The

The fortifications that completely encircle the historic city center are one of Dubrovnik's landmarks.

mighty fortifications with walls up to 6 m (20 ft) thick and 25 m (82 ft) high still testify to its former defensive capabilities.

Ragusa was also a humanist stronghold that exerted tremendous influence on Slavic literature and painting. In fact, it was here that Croatian developed as a written language between the 15th and 17th centuries. The town was destroyed by an earthquake in 1667, but major landmarks such as the rector's palace and the monastery were restored. Many of the buildings, including some interiors, and the cathedral were restored in baroque style.

Dubrovnik boasts a breathtaking panorama: the historic waterfront and the Sveti Ivan fortress (top left); Luža square (center left) with the 31-m (102-ft) clock tower (1444) and the baroque church dedicated to Dubrovnik's patron St Blasius, built between 1706 and 1715 by Marino Gropelli; and the cloisters of the Franciscan monastery (left) built in 1360 in the western part of the city.

Bosnia and Herzegovina

OLD BRIDGE AREA OF THE OLD CITY OF MOSTAR

Mostar is an unusual example of both multicultural urban life and the unfortunate conflicts that are often associated with it. The capital of Herzegovina, and in particular the Stari Most (Old Bridge) over the Neretva River, which was rebuilt with international support between 1998 and 2004, symbolizes the coexistence of different religious, cultural and ethnic communities.

In Mostar the Croats and the Muslims initially fought together against the Serbs at the beginning of the 1990s. They ran the town together for about six months, but then began to fight amongst themselves in 1993/94.

The armed forces of the Bosnian Croats eventually attacked the town's iconic Old Bridge, which subsequently collapsed in November 1993. Many other buildings, especially in the Bosnian eastern section, were badly damaged or destroyed during the conflict.

Reconstruction work began in 1998 in the divided town, which was initially administered by the EU with tremendous international support. The renovation work, led by experts and using new building materials in places, was based on the well-documented architecture of Mostar before the war.

The Old Bridge, destroyed in 1993, was reopened on July 23, 2004, amid great celebration (below). Right: A mosque on the east bank of the Neretva River.

MEHMED PAŠA SOKOLOVIĆ BRIDGE IN VIŠEGRAD

The Mehmed Paša Sokolović Bridge in Višegrad was completed in 1571, and is considered a masterpiece of Ottoman architecture.

The Mehmed Paša Sokolović Bridge is located just beyond a sharp bend in the Drina River. There is a plain on the relatively narrow right bank that made it possible for Višegrad castle to expand while the left bank is dominated by rocky cliffs. These landscape features made it necessary to build a 120-m (394-ft) access ramp at right angles to the bridge. In 1566, Grand Vizier Mehmed Paša Sokolović (Sokollu) commissioned Sinan with the project, a master builder for the entire Ottoman Empire starting in 1538, and one of the greatest architects of the time.

On the route north of Sarajevo from the Danube to the Adriatic coast, this bridge served as a checkpoint in the central Balkans. For centuries the Drina River has been the subject of heated disputes as a boundary between the Christian Occident and the Islamic Orient. Ivo Andrić's novel "The Bridge over the Drina" (1945) paid tribute to the famous structure from the perspective of the Grand Vizier.

Sokolović Bridge is about 180 m (600 ft) long, 15 m (49 ft) at its highest point, and spans the Drina River with eleven arches (above and right).

STUDENICA MONASTERY

Founded by Serbian King Stefan Nemanja, Studenica is the largest of Serbia's orthodox monasteries. The two main churches house priceless Byzantine paintings going back to the 13th and 14th centuries.

Tucked away in the forest south-west of Kraljevo, Studenica represents one of the first highlights of medieval Raška-style Serbian architecture. Only three of what were originally ten churches have survived the centuries. Of those three, the single-nave Church of the Virgin is the largest and the oldest, built between 1183 and 1196. Its portals, windows and architectural sculptures are predominantly Romanesque in style and were built by Italian Benedictine monks.
The duodecagonal dome, on the other hand, is the work of Byzantine master builders. The magnificent frescoes, which date from after 1208/09, are

also Byzantine in origin, and further scenes were added in 1568.
Stefan Uroš II Milutin, who ruled from 1243–1276, had the King's Church built in 1313. Its interior is decorated with masterful frescoes, the loveliest of which depict the life of Mary. The smallest of the three, with only a few surviving frescoes, is St Nicholas' Church built of quarry stone in the early 13th century.

The Crucifixion of Christ is one of the most beautiful frescoes on the west wall of the Church of the Virgin.

STARI RAS AND SOPOĆANI MONASTERY

There are only a few surviving monuments from the first capital of the medieval Serbian state of Raška, which is south of present-day Novi Pazar. The nearby Sopoćani monastery, however, was built in around 1260 by King Stefan Uroš I and houses one of the largest collections of medieval paintings.

Old Ras, or Stari Ras, includes the remains of a medieval fortress as well as St Peter's Church, built around the turn of the 10th century. The World Heritage Site is situated on a hill that had already been settled by the sixth century BC. It even boasts the remains of a circular Roman building that was discovered beneath its Byzantine rotunda. The Church of St George from 1170 has the oldest Byzantine frescoes in Serbia (from the 12th/13th centuries) and used to be part of a fortified monastery.

The Sopoćani monastery west of Novi Pazar was built as the burial site for King Stefan Uroš I. The depiction of the Dormition of the Virgin is one of the most valuable among the paintings dating from between 1263 and 1268 in the Raška-style church.

The monastery's Holy Trinity Church was destroyed at the end of the 17th century and restored after World War I. The largest fresco, the "Dormition of the Virgin", depicts her soul ascending as a baby being received by Christ.

GAMZIGRAD-ROMULIANA, PALACE OF GALERIUS

This late-Roman compound with the palace, basilicas, temples, baths and an adjoining memorial complex was built by Emperor Galerius at the turn of the fourth century. It reflects the building patterns of the second tetrarchy (from the Greek, "one of four rulers").

The palace here was built by Galerius – the regent responsible for the Danube region and the Balkan Peninsula – who was appointed the title of "Caesar" by Diocletian in the year 293 prior to his successful campaign against the Persian King Narseh in 297 and 298. Later, as the highest-ranking "Augustus" (as of 305) and most powerful man in the land, Galerius had the complex extended, enlarged and redecorated.
He had two mausoleums built, for himself and his mother, on a hill to

the east of the palace. Flanking burial mounds, known as tumuli, were then used for the apotheosis, a ritual intended to exalt the deceased to the rank of a god. Following the emperor's death in 311 the complex was continuously inhabited and converted until the seventh century.

Galerius, who enjoyed a successful military career, gave his palace the character of a fortified complex encircled by a wall of defensive towers. He named it Felix Romuliana after his mother Romula.

MEDIEVAL MONUMENTS IN KOSOVO

Three more sacred buildings were added in 2006 to the earlier Dečani Monastery World Heritage site, namely the monasteries of Peç and Gračanica and the Church of the Holy Virgin of Ljeviša. The site was then renamed "Medieval Monuments in Kosovo" and added to the list of World Heritage in Danger due to the lack of a management plan for its preservation.

Medieval Serbian art and architecture, which reached its climax in the 14th century, evolved at the crossroads between two cultures: Byzantine from the east and Latin from the west. The historic Kosovo Field ("Kosovo polje") is home to many architectural monuments from this era, the largest of which is the five-nave Romanesque-Gothic Pantocrator Basilica from 1335 at the Visoki Dečani Monastery. The frescoes inside the church feature narrative cycles and over 1,000 figures of

saints – the entire palette of Byzantine iconography. Michael Astrapas and Eutychios, Stefan Uroš II Milutin's two court artists, ensured that the Palaiologic Renaissance named after the Palaiologos (the last Byzantine dynasty, 1259–1453) became a feature of Serbian painting. Their main works are in the church at Gračanica.

The monastery at Peć includes three related churches. Above: The frescoes in the Church of the Holy Apostles.

Montenegro

DURMITOR NATIONAL PARK

Formed by glaciers during the last ice age, the Durmitor mountains and their highest peak, Bobotov Kuk, at 2,522 m (8,274 ft) were declared a World Heritage Site in 1980. In 2005 the area was expanded by more than 320 sq km (124 sq mi) to include the national park.

Raging amongst the dense coniferous forests and clear mountain lakes, the Tara is one of the last untamed whitewater rivers on the Balkan peninsula. The gorges of the Dinaric karst are up to 1,300 m (4,265 ft) deep – the deepest in Europe.

With the exception of the skiers and hikers around the Žabljak plateau, most of the Durmitor mountains have been spared from human intervention. Alongside deer and chamoix, the park is also home to a number of animals that have become very rare in Europe including brown bears, wolves, wildcats, eagles, black grouse and capercaillies. About three-quarters of the mountain flora are native. The black pines make up some of Europe's last primeval forests.

Fog banks float over the Black Lake (Crno jezero), which reaches 49 m (180 ft) in depth and can be reached via a number of hiking trails. In the background is Mount Žabljak. The name Durmitor is presumably from the Celtic meaning "Mountains with many lakes".

NATURAL AND CULTURO-HISTORICAL REGION OF KOTOR

In the Middle Ages, Kotor was an important center of commerce, icon painting and stone masonry. Kotor Bay, which extends about 30 km (19 mi) inland, has seven islands and is considered one of the loveliest on the Adriatic Coast. The historic town center was rebuilt after an earthquake in 1979, and the World Heritage Site includes both the natural and cultural treasures of the region.

Founded by ancient Greek colonists, Kotor and its large natural harbor once equaled Venice as a seafaring and trading town in the 13th and 14th centuries. Today, the town is still enclosed by an imposing, 5-km-long (3-mi) wall with covered battlements that extend as far as the ruins of the Sveti Ivan fortress 250 m (820 ft) above the historic town center. The Romanesque Cathedral of St Tryphon (Sveti Tripun) was built in the 12th century but its twin-tower façade was not completed until 1681. The Church of St Lucas (1195) is an early example of a religious building in the medieval Serbian Raška style. A number of palatial residences and patrician houses date from the Renaissance and baroque era in particular.

The coastal town of Perast (right, with St Nikola Church) overlooks the Bay of Kotor. In July the island of Gospa od Škrpjela (above) is a popular pilgrimage desination out in the bay.

WOODEN CHURCHES OF MARAMUREŞ

The eight 17th- and 18th-century wooden churches making up this World Heritage Site represent the religious architecture typical of northern Romania.

The wooden churches of Maramureş each represent different stylistic eras of the independent architectural traditions in this remote area between the northern reaches of the Eastern Carpathians and the Rodna Mountains. The reason for the wooden construction was the Hungarian crown's prohibition of the building of orthodox churches out of stone in Transylvania. Oak, pine, elm and beech were thus the building materials of choice. Characteristic features include the narrow naves with double-shingle roofs and the slim bell towers on top of them. The interiors of the churches are decorated according to Orthodox tradition, with brightly painted frescoes on wooden backgrounds usually depicting scenes from the Old Testament or the lives of saints. The pillars and beams are decoratively carved. The wooden churches in Bârsana, Budeşti, Deseşti, Ieud, Plopiş, Poienile Izei, Rogoz and Şurdeşti are especially harmonious while featuring a successful combination of Byzantine and Gothic styles.

The wooden church in Ieud was built in the mid-18th century with an interior covered in decorative paintings.

VILLAGES WITH FORTIFIED CHURCHES IN TRANSYLVANIA

The villages here and their fortified churches comprise the most impressive buildings in the area settled by the Transylvanian Saxons.

The "church fortresses" erected on a hill in the middle of the village were intended to protect the villagers from attack and plunder by the Turks that invaded Transylvania. Most of them were built between the 14th and 16th centuries.

Biertan is especially impressive with its three rings of walls linked via covered crossways, a series of defensive towers and an imposing church. The interior of the town's late-Gothic church is dominated by a winged altar occupying the entire presbytery wall. Its portraits of the saints are masterpieces of what is referred to as the Transylvanian Renaissance. In addition to Biertan, the World Heritage Site also includes the fortified churches in Câlnic, Prejmer, Viscri, Dârjiu, Saschiz, and Valea Viilor.

German colonists brought in by the Hungarian kings starting in the 12th century, referred to by the authorities as the "Saxons", were given their own administration here, but their culture is now threatened by emigration.

The fortified church that dominated the town of Biertan (above) was completed in the 16th century. Left: The fortified church's Catholic tower.

Romania

DACIAN FORTRESSES OF THE ORĂŞTIE MOUNTAINS

These protective fortresses were built by the Romans in the first centuries BC and AD. They display the unusual fusion of military and religious architecture in Europe during the late Iron Age.

Following the Celtic and Germanic tribes who had settled here, the region north of the Lower Danube was ruled for two centuries by the Dacians and the Geto people, to whom they were related. Each tribe had their own economic and political center that was protected from attack by ramparts, moats, walls and palisades. These defensive compounds can now be found throughout Romania.

The six fortresses making up this World Heritage site in the Orăştie Mountains (Broos) in south-western Transylvania are evidence of a sophis-ticated Dacian culture. Fortresses, forts, watchtowers, roads, terraces, houses and sanctuaries were built on an area of 500 sq km (193 sq mi) and make use of the landscape's natural features. Having excavated roughly 3 ha (7 acres) on Dealul Grădiştea hill, archaeologists have unearthed the former capital of Sarmizegetusa Regia. The site includes circular altars with the appearance of a "sun".

The large circular altar on Dealul Grădiştea hill was originally comprised of six rows with sixty andesite pillars.

HISTORIC CENTER OF SIGHIŞOARA

This former "Saxon settlement" known as Schäßburg was a major center of commerce and has been referred to as the "Pearl of Transylvania". The historic center is considered the best preserved architectural complex in Romania.

This town was founded in the 12th century by craftsmen and merchants from Germany. It was the sixth of the seven fortresses in Transylvania.

First official mention of the town was in 1280 as "Castrum Sex", and the flourishing trading and commercial center in the Kokel Valley was given town status in 1367. The historic center comprises some 150 lovingly preserved town houses, most dating from the 16th and 17th centuries.

A wood-covered staircase with 176 steps leads up to the Church on the Hill. The Dominican monastery church became a Protestant church when the Transylvanian Saxons ultimately converted to Lutheranism.

The town's landmark is the magnificent 14th-century clock tower that forms part of the medieval fortifications around the upper section of the town. Figures representing the seven days of the week have been emerging from the inside of the clock tower on the hour since the 17th century.

The clock tower of Sighişoara was rebuilt in the baroque style after a fire in the town in 1676.

MONASTERY OF HOREZU

The monastery of Horezu in Walachia is considered a masterpiece of the "Brancovan" style – an art movement dating back to Prince Constantine Brancovan, who ruled from 1689–1714. It merges both western and eastern European influences with prominent Italian elements while also combining them with orthodox folk art.

Commissioned by Prince Constantine Brancovan and built between 1691 and 1702, the monastery at Horezu is surrounded by a white defensive wall. The expansive courtyard, with the church towering in the middle, is lined on three sides by verandas, staircases, loggias and double arcades that are decorated with elaborate stone carvings depicting flowers, leaves and fruit.

The path leading to the church passes beneath a stone canopy and crosses an atrium supported by ten beautifully ornamented columns. The magnifi-cent frescoes decorating the interior of the church are based on Byzantine originals. They are the work of Walachian and Greek artists.

The monastery with its large rectangular courtyard (right is a view of one of the side chapels) was originally intended as the final resting place for its benefactor. History took a different course, however, and Prince Constantine Brancovan was beheaded together with his four sons in the presence of the Turkish sultan in Istanbul because he had refused to convert to Islam.

CHURCHES OF MOLDAVIA

The elaborate, brightly-colored, late-Byzantine façades of the monastery churches in southern Bucovina were more than mere decoration – they were a pictorial "Bible of the Poor" and a place where the faithful could pray and partake in religious instruction. The World Heritage Site consists of seven such churches.

During the 15th and 16th centuries, Moldavian Prince Stephan III (who ruled from 1457–1504 and was also known as Stephan the Great) and his successors – particularly Petru Rareş – built some forty churches and monasteries around the capital Suceava. The outside walls of the churches were often painted to the eaves, a tradition introduced in Humor in 1530 that ended in about 1600 with the paintings in Suceviţa. The churches making up the World Heritage Site are the ones in Humor, Voroneţ, Moldoviţa, Pătrăuţi, Probota, Suceava and Arbore.

Moldoviţa monastery was built by Prince Petru Rareş.

The intention of the paintings was that any members of the congregation who failed to get a place in the church itself would be able to participate in worship outside. The effigies also communicated biblical content to the common people, the majority of whom did not understand the official Church Slavonic. The paintings depict the lives of the saints, scenes from the Bible and the hymns to the Virgin Mary. They also contain references to political events such as the siege of Constantinople by the "infidels". The paintings dating from 1541 in the church in Arbore are of particular artistic value.

Voroneţ was built by Stephan the Great in 1488 and is the oldest monastery in Moldavia. The artistic quality of the still original outdoor frescoes has earned the church its name the "Sistine Chapel of the East".

Romania / Bulgaria

THE DANUBE DELTA BIOSPHERE RESERVE

The area where the Danube flows into the Black Sea in eastern Romania is a tapestry of tributaries, channels, lakes, woodlands, bogs, reed islands, marshes and sand dunes that provides a habitat for some 300 species of bird, 45 species of fish and 1,150 varieties of plant. Growing at a rate of 40 m (130 ft) every year, it is the second-largest river delta in Europe. Part of it is in Ukraine.

Interrupted only by islands of floating reeds and the wooded dry land areas, this marshy delta landscape is one of the world's largest and most important biosphere reserves. Its wetland areas are home to rare plants and countless varieties of insects. Swans, geese, herons, pelicans, glossy ibis and spoonbills are also just some of the large birds found here.

Including the lagoon system, this World Heritage Site covers an area of some 626,000 ha (1.5 m acres) and is an important resting place for migratory birds. There are also large stocks of fish in the protected waters, including the now rare sturgeon. However, the biosphere reserve is threatened by both water pollution and the commercial exploitation of its reed beds.

These are the largest wetlands in the world that are also home to the largest reed and cane belt in the world. In spring, the delta's riparian forests are mostly flooded.

SREBARNA NATURE RESERVE

Covering an area of 9 sq km (3 sq mi), the Lake Srebarna Nature Reserve in north-eastern Bulgaria is home to a wide range of water birds – many of them endangered species. During the migration season, flocks of geese, cranes and storks take to the skies above the reserve.

This ornithological paradise is located west of Silistra, not far from the Danube. Around eighty different types of bird visit the reed-covered lake every year – some passing through, others spending the winter, and others like the great egret and the rare Dalmatian pelican even raising their young here. The total number of breeds on the reserve and the three Danube islands is currently 233. Srebarna was designated a protected nature reserve in 1948, but between 1982 and 1994 a combination of flood prevention measures and droughts caused the region to dry out. The lake was connected to the river again in 1994, and thanks to regular flooding it has been almost fully regenerated.

Lake Srebarna may only be an average of 2 m (7 ft) deep, but it still boasts examples of roughly half the plant species found in all of Bulgaria's wetland areas. Some 400 hectares (990 acres) of the lake's surface are covered by reeds. Dalmatian pelicans (below) and great egrets migrate through here.

THRACIAN TOMB OF SVESHTARI

The magnificent interior decoration of the tomb of Sveshtari has afforded it special status among the many burial sites left behind by the Thracian people.

In 1982, an almost pristine Thracian tomb from the third century BC was discovered under a mound close to the village of Sveshtari – roughly 40 km (25 mi) north-east of Razgrad in north-eastern Bulgaria. Indications tell us it was once the burial site of a ruling couple belonging to the Indo-Germanic Thracians; buried next to a man aged about sixty is a young woman in a sarcophagus.

From an anteroom there is a corridor of about 4 m (13 ft) in length that leads to a square burial chamber with 4.5-m-high (15-ft) barrel vaulting "supported" by a decorative circumferential frieze featuring ten large female figures (caryatids) each 1.2 m (4 ft) in height. The wall paintings in the lunettes above them portray scenes from the lives of the rulers buried there; one of these depicts the king mounted on a horse and a goddess crowning him with a laurel wreath. These features make Sveshtari one of the most magnificent examples of Thracian grave construction.

The female figures in robes resembling acanthus leaves and the decorated columns of the frieze only appear to support the vaulting in the Thracian tomb at Sveshtari. Their role is in fact purely decorative and they have no load-bearing function.

MADARA RIDER

This 23-m-high (75-ft) early-medieval monumental carving is the only one of its kind in Europe. It is located on a cliff face in Bulgaria.

This giant carving close to the former capital Pliska, around 80 km (50 mi) west of Varna in north-eastern Bulgaria, depicts a rider with a spear triumphing over a lion cowering beneath the horse's hooves. The horse is being followed by a dog.

Situated in direct proximity to important finds that go back to the third century BC, this monument was attributed to the ancient Thracians for a long time. Inscriptions that have subsequently been excavated, however, describe events that only took place during the period between 705 and 831. The rider is therefore thought to depict Khan Tervel, who ruled the First Bulgarian Kingdom (681–1018) from 701 to 718, prior to its Christianization and who defended it against Byzantium's claims to power. This would make the Madara Rider the oldest historical document from medieval Bulgaria.

The figure depicted in this nearly 3-m-high (10-ft) rider was a source of mystery for a long time. The oldest of three inscriptions carved into the roughly 100-m-high (328-ft) cliff face refers to the reign of the Bulgarian Khan Tervel. The National Archaeological Museum in Sofia has a copy of the monument.

ANCIENT CITY OF NESSEBAR

This former trading center on a narrow peninsula on the Black Sea coast is one of the oldest settlements in Europe. Thracian walls, the Greek town complex with an acropolis, an agora, and temples, as well as the ruins of medieval churches, testify to more than 3,000 years of history in Nessebar.

Founded by the Thracians in the sixth century BC as Mesembria, the original settlement here was later taken over and fortified by the Greeks. Protected by walls, it then developed into a flourishing center of commerce that was coveted by many ruling powers but ultimately fell under Ottoman rule in 1371.

Nessebar still features a number of 18th- and 19th-century buildings.
Top: A view of the port.
Above: The façade of the St John Aleiturgetos Church with its rows of limestone and brick.

Remains of the Greek, Roman and Byzantine fortifications can still be seen along the coast and in the port. Of the many churches crowded onto the small peninsula since the fifth century, only ten remain, and largely as ruins. The 14th-century St John Aleiturgetos Church is a good example, with a façade comprising beautiful stonework in different shades as well as ceramic and marble carvings.

The frescoes of St Stephen's Church (New Metropolitan Church) are spread across 600 sq m (6,456 sq ft).

Bulgaria

ROCK-HEWN CHURCHES OF IVANOVO

The paintings in the hermitages, cave monasteries, rock-hewn churches and chapels on both sides of the Roussenski Lom River are seen as outstanding masterpieces of medieval Bulgarian art.

The caves hewn into the soft limestone cliffs near present-day Rousse are thought to have been the work of hermits starting in the 11th century. Over centuries, the caves were connected via passageways and platforms to a residential and monastery complex. The earliest Byzantine-style paintings date from the 12th or 13th centuries, the most important of which are to be found in the central religious building, the Holy Mother of God Church, usually referred to simply as "Carkvata" ("the church"). The remarkable artistic quality of these 14th-century frescoes is indicative of links with the Tarnovo School of painting at the czarist court. The complex fell to ruin following the Ottoman conquest of the Second Bulgarian Empire at the end of the 14th century.

The only frescoes to survive are those in the Holy Mother of God Church, commissioned by Czar Assen II in around 1232. They depict scenes from the lives of Christ and John the Baptist and have been open for viewing again since 2002 after being restored with UNESCO support.

THRACIAN TOMB OF KAZANLAK

This vaulted brick tomb dating from the end of the fourth century BC was discovered in 1944. The paintings in its burial chamber illustrate the high standard of Greek-influenced Thracian art.

This amazingly well-preserved Thracian tomb was discovered by soldiers excavating a bunker in the central Bulgarian town of Kazanlak, which is situated in the Rose Valley between the Balkan Mountains and the Sredna Gora hills. Its architecture and paintings were largely undamaged even though the tomb had already been plundered in antiquity.

The relatively small complex is accessed via an atrium that leads to a passage of about 2 m (7 ft) in length. Its walls are painted with scenes of war and battle. The circular burial chamber at the end of the passage reaches a height of up to 3 m (10 ft) and is vaulted with a bell-shaped dome. A young ruling couple buried here is depicted during an apparent farewell bid at a funerary banquet. Servants stand at their side with burial objects. In the frieze above it, three charioteers appear to be engaged in an exciting race.

The main frieze of the burial dome depicts splendid horses being led by their bridles. A copy has been made for visitors in order to truly preserve this unique evidence of Thracian burial art. The original complex is now open to scientists only.

BOYANA CHURCH

The paintings by an unknown master in the Kaloyan Church in Boyana are considered a highlight of medieval religious painting in Bulgaria. They belong to the few intact artworks from the Orthodox Church from the era of the Latin Empire (1204–1261).

Situated in the Vitosha Mountains on the outskirts of Sofia, the oldest sections of Boyana church are thought to be from the 10th century. A two-story extension was added to the church in 1259.

The frescoes that extend over both floors depict stories from the Bible, particularly the life of Jesus and the lives of the various saints. There are around 240 people portrayed, including the benefactor: the governor Kaloyan and his wife Dessislava. Whoever the Boyana artist was, he managed to combine elements of Western and Latin art with the traditions of the Orthodox Church. The scenes and figures – all of the faces have individual features – demonstrate the artist's precise powers of observation and profound sense of humanity. The formalized Byzantine iconography of the biblical scenes is enriched with details from local culture and custom.

Boyana church comprises three sections built in the 10th/11th, 13th, and 19th centuries. The dome with the apse is the oldest part of the church. The fascinating frescoes here (right: Mary with Child) benefited from extensive restoration work that was completed in 2002.

RILA MONASTERY

Rila is the oldest and largest monastery in Bulgaria. The complex's 19th-century decor is a masterpiece of local religious art.

This monastery was founded in the ninth century by the hermit Ivan, who had withdrawn to the inaccessible forests of the Rila Mountains to get closer to God. It was close to his cave that the monks who followed him began building a monastery that was later to be granted a wide range of privileges by the Bulgarian czars. The complex experienced its heyday in the 14th century before falling into disrepair after the Ottoman conquest of Bulgaria and being magnificently rebuilt between 1816 and 1862.

The monastery buildings comprise several floors positioned around a 3,000 sq m (32,280 sq ft) courtyard dominated by the five-storey Hrelyu Tower (1335). The jewel of the complex is the Church of the Birth of the Virgin Mary. Its interior, like the open arcade that surrounds it, is decorated almost throughout with frescoes providing religious instruction or inviting the faithful to worship.

Pavel Ivanovich, architect of the ornate monastery church in Rila, chose to highlight key design elements such as bands of stone in different hues and the offset arrangement of the five domes (left). The frescoes feature more than 12,000 motifs (below left) and are mostly from the Samokov and Bansko schools of painting. The congregation and altar are magnificently decorated (below).

PIRIN NATIONAL PARK

Pirin National Park covers roughly 270 sq km (104 sq mi) of south-western Bulgaria. The coniferous forests that lie beneath its impressive mountain peaks contain some very rare plant species and many, like the Macedonian pine, are only found in this area.

Pirin National Park occupies the northern half of this heavily fissured mountainous terrain where forty-five of the peaks reach an elevation of more than 2,600 m (8,500 ft). Towering above them all is the 2,914-m-high (9,560-ft) Vihren, the third-highest mountain in the entire Balkans.

The Bayuvi Dupki reserve forms the heart of the park. Some seventy glacial lakes are remnants from the last ice age and – along with the park's waterfalls and caves – are typical of this limestone landscape. Among the wide variety of flora here, the black pine and silver fir are two of the park's coniferous trees, both of which are on the IUCN's Red List of Threatened Species. Some of the trees are over five hundred years old. This mostly pristine landscape is also home to numerous rare birds and mammals such as the wolf, European brown bear, golden jackal, and golden eagle. The European Nature Heritage Fund collaborates with private and volunteer environmental enthusiasts to maintain the park.

The vegetation at Pirin National Park ranges from beech woodlands to treeless alpine pastures. Its landscape is a refuge for a few dozen European brown bears.

Albania

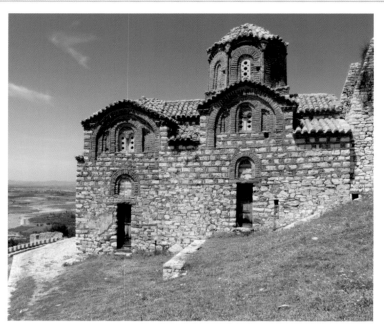

HISTORIC CENTERS OF BERAT AND GJIROKASTRA

Situated on the Drinos and Osum Rivers, respectively, the historic centers of Gjirokastra and Berat – listed by UNESCO in 2008 – are a largely authentic representation of the Ottoman cultural legacy in the Balkan region.

Having been settled since prehistoric times, Berat is characterized by its fort and its buildings erected on a sloping hillside. Several mosques and Orthodox churches here bear witness to the once peaceful cohabitation of the different communities in this part of the Balkans.

The citadel from the late 13th century forms the heart of present day Gjirokastra on the south-eastern slopes of the Mali i Gjerë Mountains, where wealthy landowners settled in the vicinity of the castle as early as the 14th century. The town had its heyday in the 17th century when the bazaar (Pazari i vjetër) developed north of the citadel. The tower-like stone buildings known as "kullë" are well-adapted to the extreme climate. They consist of a large ground floor for shops or workshops, above which are the winter living quarters with small windows that are easily heated. The floor above that contains the summer living quarters.

Berat (above left)) is also referred to as the "Town of a Thousand Windows". Above right is an Orthodox church. Right is a bazaar street in Gjirokastra.

BUTRINT

Butrint was inhabited by a number of different cultures and peoples from ancient times through to the Middle Ages. The ruined city therefore features impressive monuments and ruins from these different eras.

According to Virgil, Butrint, which is situated on a peninsula in southern Albania, was founded by a group of Trojan refugees. A more likely version of its history, however, is that the first settlers were adventurous colonists from Corfu. The town was Roman at the time of the birth of Christ. It soon become a bishopric and reached the height of its powers under Byzantine rule. Following its occupation by the Venetians it gradually began to show signs of decline starting in the 15th century.

Excavations in and around Butrint have revealed monuments that provide interesting insights into each period of the city's ever-changing history. In addition to the remains of several medieval buildings, the ruins of ancient settlements have also been discovered: two sixth-century circular walls on the slopes in what is now the area near the shore, a Greek theater, Roman baths, and a baptistery.

The baptistery (right) was excavated at this World Heritage site by Italian archaeologists at the start of the 20th century. The structure dates back to the early Christians.

NATURAL AND CULTURAL HERITAGE OF THE OHRID REGION

Ohrid in south-west Macedonia was an important hub of orthodox Christianity in the 9th and 10th centuries.

Founded by the Illyrians as Lychnidos, Ohrid's advantageous location was not lost on the Romans and in the 4th century it was made a bishopric. In the 9th century, Clement and Naum, disciples of the Slav apostles Cyril and Methodius, also founded numerous monasteries here. At the end of the 10th century, the town was both a see of the Greek Orthodox Church and, temporarily, the capital of Bulgarian Tsar Samuil's empire. The town then fell under the rule of the Serbian Dusan before being conquered by the

The church of St John at Kaneo was built in the 13th century. Its striking octagonal tower is a sign of the region's Orthodox Christian heritage.

Ottomans in 1394, under whose control it remained until 1913. The 11th-century church of St Sophia was built under archbishop Leo, but its conversion to a mosque by the Turks was at the expense of its impressive dome, bell tower, internal galleries and the church's frescoes, which dated from the 11th–14th centuries. These were finally uncovered during restoration work in the 1950s. There are more Byzantine frescoes in the Church of St Clement, which is also home to the best collection of icons anywhere in the former Yugoslavia. The Old Town of Ohrid is a conservation area that features many charming houses built in typical Macedonian style.

Before it was converted to a mosque in the 15th century, the Church of St Sophia featured a splendid iconostasis and equally impressive frescoes (top left). The interior of the church at the Monastery of St Naum, which is dedicated to the archangel Michael, also has beautiful frescoes and icons (left).

Greece

ARCHAEOLOGICAL SITE OF AIGAI (VERGINA)

It was in modern-day Vergina that the ruins of Aigai were found, the first capital of the ancient kingdom of Macedonia in what is now northern Greece. The city reached its zenith between the seventh and fourth centuries BC and tombs that are up to 3,000 years old bear witness to the area's long history of settlement.

One of the most important discoveries here is a monumental royal palace from the third century BC that is richly decorated with mosaics, frescoes and stuccowork. Equally important are the Macedonian royal tombs containing numerous burial objects and fascinating frescoes including "The Abduction of Persephone" attributed to the painter Nikomachos. One of the royal burial chambers contained the tomb of Philip II, murdered in Vergina in 336 BC and whose son Alexander went on to establish a vast empire and take on the name "the Great". Other finds from the Hellenist era include a theater, a gymnasium, the remains of the city's fortifications, two temples, a Demeter sanctuary and a stoa. One of Apollo Chresterios' oracles is also thought to have been here. Beneath the city is a cemetery with Iron Age burial mounds.

The Palace of Palatitsia from the third century BC once served the Macedonian kings as a summer residence. Only its ruins remain today.

PALEOCHRISTIAN AND BYZANTINE MONUMENTS OF THESSALONIKA

Thessalonika boasts a number of monuments dating from early-Christian and Byzantine times. They were built over a long period of time extending from the fourth to the 15th century.

Thessalonika was originally founded by Cassander, a Macedonian king. Situated on the Thermaic Gulf in the Aegean Sea, the city has endured a volatile history under Macedonian, Roman, Byzantine, Ottoman and Venetian rule; it was also home to the largest community of Sephardic Jews in Europe until their deportation in 1941.

Thessalonika was an important base from which Christianity quickly spread through Europe. Like those in the Churches of St David, the mosaics in the Church of St Demetrius built in the late fifth century are among the greatest masterpieces of early-Christian art. The dome of Hagia Sophia, built after the year 700, is supported by a windowed tambour.

In the Church of St Demetrius, one of the largest churches in Greece, the five naves are separated by four rows of Corinthian columns.

MOUNT ATHOS

A total of twenty monasteries make up this autonomous monastic state on the Khalkidiki peninsula south-east of Thessaloniki. It is one of the most important places in the Orthodox Christian world.

The first monastery on Hagion Oros – the "Holy Mountain" – was built back in 963, but this monastic republic's autonomy dates back to even earlier in the Byzantine period. Neither men under the age of twenty-one nor women are allowed to enter the monasteries, which are currently home to about 1,400 monks. Mount Athos has been a particular focus for Orthodox Christianity since 1054, and its influence has been felt even in the secular world. In the 14th century some 3,000 peasants were employed by the Athos monasteries to farm the republic's 20,000-hectare (49,500-acre) property, for example.

The style of icon painting practiced at Athos plays an important role in Orthodox Christian art history, while the influence of the characteristic architecture here can be seen as far away as Russia. Of the twenty monasteries, seventeen are Greek, one Russian, one Serbian, and one Bulgarian. Each monastery courtyard contains a domed church with three apses. The monastic cells and other buildings are positioned around the courtyard.

Hilandar Monastery (right, the main church with its splendid dome and chapels surrounding it) is dedicated to the Presentation of Mary.

METEORA

Meteora's monasteries were built on steep, rocky peaks high above the earthly world below. Many of the monasteries date back to the 14th century.

The Meteora Valley is north of the town of Kalambaka and its twenty-four monasteries – five of which are still occupied today – were built over centuries on a series of rocky peaks that tower over the valley. They are a truly breathtaking sight.

The highest monastery is Megalo-Meteoro, founded around 1360 by Athanasius, bishop of Alexandria, and granted special privileges in 1362. The Monastery of St Nicholas Anapausas, meanwhile, perches atop of one of the other high peaks and was founded in 1388. Varlaam monastery was established in 1517 and rebuilt between 1627 and 1637. It takes its name from the 14th-century hermit who first

built a church here. Between 1961 and 1963, Varlaam was converted into a museum housing the most valuable treasures from the monasteries. It can be accessed via a bridge.

The Monastery of Roussanou was recently occupied by nuns. With its octagonal church, Roussanou resembles a smaller version of Varlaam and it is accessed via a bridge that was constructed in 1868. There are 130 steps to the Holy Trinity Monastery whose church was built in 1476.

The Agia Triada Monastery is perched at 550 m (1,800 ft) on a rock plateau covering 6,000 sq m (64,600 sq ft).

OLD TOWN OF CORFU

The three forts in the town of Corfu were designed by Venetian engineers and served as defense against Ottoman aggressions for four centuries. The layout and architecture of the homogeneous Old Town are still characterized by the former occupying powers of France and Britain.

The town of Corfu – its official name being Kerkyra – is the capital of the Ionian island of the same name. Its origins as a settlement go back to the eighth century BC. Corfu later became the first Greek town to submit to the Romans in 229 BC, and the town came under Venetian rule in 1204; it was later taken by them from 1386 to 1797. Having been besieged by the Turks in 1537 and 1571, the Venetians began building fortifications with the citadel further away from the inhabited center. As a safe haven on the first of the Ionian Islands at the mouth of the Adriatic Sea, Corfu was

always of tremendous strategic importance. The system of defenses was reinforced between 1669 and 1682. Corfu became French for two years in 1797, and was British from 1814 to 1864. The Old Town extends between the old and the new forts, and its buildings are a legacy of many cultures and epochs but the neoclassical heritage still predominates.

The Old Town of Corfu is characterized by neoclassical façades of English origin in particular, with the winding staircases and arcade passageways between them adding an Italian flair.

ARCHAEOLOGICAL SITE OF DELPHI

The oracle of Apollo once spoke at Delphi, which made this sanctuary in the northern reaches of the Gulf of Corinth in central Greece an important religious center during ancient times.

Delphi enjoyed enormous political influence between 590 and 450 BC. The Greeks sought advice at Delphi and found it in the instructions of their god Apollo, who communicated the will of Zeus through his oracle. In the Temple of Apollo, the oracle Pythia would communicate the will of the gods which was then translated by her priestesses. Excavations of the ruins at the Apollo sanctuary and in the surrounding area began in 1892. The south-east of the complex marks the beginning of the holy road where the Greek city-states were represent-

ed through splendid gifts and treasuries. This ends at the large square with the Hall of the Athenians and the forecourt of the Temple of Apollo at the center of the complex. In addition to the temple and the treasuries, the most important buildings and monuments include the stadium, the theater, the Sanctuary of Athena Pronaia, the Altar of the Chians and the columns with the Naxian Sphinx.

Three of the Doric columns of the round temple in the Sanctuary of Athena Pronaia (fourth century BC) have been rebuilt.

Greece

Philosophers and poets

Greek intellectual history began with the Homeric epics, the "Iliad" and the "Odyssey". Between the eighth and third centuries BC in Athens and the other city-states, in the Greek colonies of Asia Minor and Lower Italy, and on the Mediterranean islands ideas and norms were developed that still influence Western civilization to this day.

ACROPOLIS, ATHENS

With the Parthenon, the Propylaea and the Erechtheon, the Acropolis comprises some of the most important works of classical Greek architecture.

The hill upon which the Acropolis of Athens stands shows evidence of settlement that dates back to the early Stone Age. Formerly a royal fortress, the Acropolis was converted into a religious site as early as the sixth century BC. Following its destruction by the Persians, the sanctuaries were rebuilt in the second half of the fifth century BC. The image of the Acropolis in Athens is dominated by the Parthenon, built between 447 and 422 BC as a temple dedicated to the goddess Athena, whose image was kept inside the building.

The Erechtheon, named after the legendary king of Athens, was built be-

To the south of the Erechtheon is the Porch of the Caryatids, supported by six of the robed female figures.

tween 421 and 406 BC and houses several religious sites under one roof. The Propylaea, built between 437 and 432 BC, are the monumental gates in the walls surrounding the Acropolis. The Temple of Athena Nike, dating from between 425 and 421 BC, was built by the architect Kallikrates and is one of the world's oldest surviving Ionian-style buildings.

The Parthenon was commissioned by Athenian statesman and general Pericles and designed by the sculptor Phidias. It forms the center of the Acropolis and is the main temple of the complex perched on a plateau created from the rubble of an Athena Temple.

Indeed, ancient Greece provided the foundations of our modern culture. The Greeks "invented" philosophy and theater as we know it, logic and poetry, physics and ethics, music and psychology, medicine and the documentation of history and, last but not least, the concept of democracy. Their attempts to grasp the rules of nature are still being pursued today. The same applies to the contemplation of right and wrong, or to issues of aesthetics and politics.

Although the Greeks considered theirs to be the only true culture, they explored foreign lands and studied history – sound familiar? Almost every Hollywood blockbuster follows the ancient theories of Greek drama. Even modern medicine attempts to first determine the causes and the course of a disease, as was taught by Hippocrates. The tragedies and comedies of Sophocles or Aristophanes are still performed in our theaters, and there is still no philosopher who has not read the works of Plato and Aristotle.

Opposite page: Aristotle (left, 384–322 BC) and Plato (right, 427–348/347 BC) are two of the most important Ancient Greek philosophers.

Greece

ARCHAEOLOGICAL SITES OF MYCENAE AND TIRYNS

With the exception of the Minoan civilization of Crete, Mycenae and Tiryns were the two greatest cities of the Mycenaean civilization, Greece's "Bronze Age epoch" on the mainland.

The Mycenaean civilization dominated the entire eastern Mediterranean from the 15th to the 12th centuries BC and played an important role in the development of classical Greece. Its name derives from the Bronze Age Palace of Mycenae which, according to Greek mythology, was the home of the Atreid dynasty founded by Perseus, son of Zeus. Most of the ruined buildings in Mycenae date from the 13th century BC. Excavations here began in 1874 under the direction of Heinrich Schliemann. The main gate, known as the Lion Gate, is particularly impressive and features two carved – now headless – lionesses. Directly behind that is the circle of royal graves that contained the golden death mask of Agamemnon, who led the Greeks against Troy. The Mycenaean palace of Tiryns is just a short distance from Mycenae and was also excavated by Schliemann. Having reached its zenith during the 15th century BC, it is still unclear to why the palace was destroyed in around 1200 BC.

The Lion Gate forms the entrance to the Palace of Mycenae.

SANCTUARY OF ASKLEPIOS AT EPIDAURUS

This theater is the most impressive example of classic Greek architecture in Epidaurus.

The complex at Epidaurus is situated in a narrow valley in the eastern reaches of the Peloponnese and extends over several levels. It formed the center of the cult of Asklepios, which spread throughout Ancient Greece in the fifth century BC. In Greek mythology this god of medicine was the son of Apollo, who had passed his healing powers on to him. In its day, Epidaurus was an important healing and religious site featuring baths and hospital buildings.
Beyond the Sanctuary of Asklepios, the most important monuments include the Temple of Artemis, the Tholos, the Enkoimeterion and the Propylaea. The sandstone used as the building material came from a nearby quarry. The theater dating from the beginning of the third century BC is the best-preserved building of its kind in Greece. Its sophisticated construction and in particular its excellent acoustics are especially impressive.

The semi-circular theater of Epidauros accommodates around 14,000 people. The seating is arranged around the orchestra where the choir stood in ancient drama.

ARCHAEOLOGICAL SITE OF OLYMPIA

Olympia was an important religious center in the first century BC as well as the venue for the games to which it gave its name.

Olympia has been inhabited since the third millennium BC and from the end of the second millennium it was a cult site dedicated to Pelops, the son of Tantalos. Subsequently a center for the worship of Zeus, the games staged in his name were numbered as of 776 BC when the first lists of winners were recorded.
The first excavations at Olympia began in 1875. In addition to temples and treasuries housing the consecration gifts of the individual Greek cities, the expansive cult site also features a great many sports facilities, the remains of which have now been unearthed. They includ the gymnasium to the north and the stadium with its sizable foyer.
The Temple of Zeus in the center of the complex was built in around 470 BC, but the oldest of the sanctuaries is a temple dedicated to Hera from the seventh century BC. The stadium was relocated in the fourth century BC and separated from the religious section by means of the Echo Stoa.

Olympia's athletes trained in the Palaestra, a building dating from the early third century BC and marked by semi-fluted columns.

TEMPLE OF APOLLO EPICURIUS AT BASSAE

Built out of dark limestone, the Temple of Apollo Epicurius in the Arcadian Mountains features the oldest known Corinthian capitals.

The Temple of Apollo Epicurius (the healer) was built in Bassae in around 430 BC. It was apparently designed by Iktinos, architect of the Parthenon at the Acropolis. The building was commissioned by the residents of the nearby town of Phigalia in gratitude for their having been spared from the plague thanks to a medicinal plant.
The temple in Bassae was discovered in 1765, excavated and then to a large extent rebuilt. Its precise orientation with a passageway of Doric columns on a north-south axis is unusual. The east-west direction common at other sites is acknowledged here by means of an entrance on the eastern side. At the heart of the temple, in what is known as the "cella", was a high-quality carved frieze depicting fighting Centaurs and Amazons that can now be viewed in the British Museum in London. The discovery of the oldest known Corinthian columns, which have since lost their capital, makes the temple all the more valuable.

Only thirty-nine of the columns of the Temple of Apollo Epicurius in Bassae still exist, having been raised to their original position following rediscovery of the site.

ARCHAEOLOGICAL SITE OF MYSTRAS

The mountain fortress of Mystras, north-west of Sparta, was the center of a Byzantine intellectual movement that emerged between the 13th and 15th centuries. Mystras fell into decline after 1770 and was abandoned in 1834.

Built by the Frankish prince William of Villehardouin, this fortress fell into the hands of the later Byzantine emperor Michael VIII following William's capture in 1260. Mystras was then ruled by "despots" (governors) until about 1460. From the end of the 14th to the beginning of the 15th centuries it was probably the most important city after Constantinople.

The Brontochion Monastery here features the Agioi Theodori and Aphentiko churches in the northern section of Mystras. The main Agioi Theodori church dates from the 13th century.

Built in 1311, the Aphentiko church is a three-naved basilica with colorful frescoes from the 14th century below the cross-vaulted dome. The gallery built for ceremonial purposes is also a typical feature of the style of architecture associated with Mystras. The remarkable Pantanassa Convent, built in 1428 as one of the last major construction project, is decorated with vibrantly detailed frescoes.

The Aphentiko Church (14th century) is a combination of basilica and cross-vaulted dome.

DELOS

According to Greek mythology, the island of Delos was the birthplace of Apollo. As such, it became the focus of the cult of Apollo.

As the alleged "birthplace" of the god Apollo, Delos became an important religious and pilgrimage destination during the seventh century BC. In the fifth century BC the island was the center of the first Delian League and later developed into an important commercial center that was also used by the Romans in the second century BC. The emergence of new trading centers, pirate raids, and attacks by the soldiers of Mithridates of Pontos in the first century BC ultimately led to the decline of Delos' significance.

Excavations revealed the remains of several houses whose courtyards were decorated with intricate mosaics. They include a variety of images such as dolphins, tigers, tridents and portraits of the gods. The three Temples of Apollo here are reached via the holy road and are the plainest of all of the sanctuaries dedicated to this god. To the west is the Artemision, the temple dedicated to Apollo's sister who, like him, is also said to have been born on the island. The holy site includes the seven monumental Naxos Lions – the oldest rounded animal sculptures in Greek art – and the Dionysus sanctuary.

Marble lions guard the mythical birthplace of Apollo in Delos.

MONASTERIES OF DAPHNI, HOSIOS LUKAS AND NEA MONI OF CHIOS

Although these three Byzantine monasteries are quite far from one another, they exhibit similar construction principles and design features.

The Church of Daphni near Athens is smaller than the other churches but its main appeal is the artistic brickwork and its sophisticated mosaics from the 11th century are still in good condition. The Hosios Lukas Monastery near Delphi in central Greece features two churches. The smaller and the older one, Theotokos, was built in around 1000. The Katholikon, with its cross-in-square ground plan, crypt and galleries is from the beginning of the 11th century. The elaborate interior decoration – marble floors, mosaics and wall murals – is still in near pristine condition. Nea Moni Monastery on Chios is also from the 11th century and features cisterns, a refectory (changed several times) and a square tower to the south-west. The lovely mosaics at Nea Moni are considered one of the most important testimonies to Byzantine graphic art.

The monastery of Daphni is famous for its mosaics. Its central dome features Christ as ruler of the world surrounded by the prophets.

PYTHAGOREION AND HERAION OF SAMOS

The ruins of the sanctuary of Hera and the remains of the ancient city of Pythagoreion are testimonies to the long history of the island of Samos.

The island of Samos experienced its heyday under the tyrant Polycrates who ruled in the middle of the sixth century BC. Polycrates was responsible for some ambitious architectural projects and surrounded himself with poets, musicians, and scholars including Herodotus and Aesop. The island of Samos thus developed into one of the important cultural centers of the eastern Mediterranean in the sixth and fifth centuries BC.

The fortifications of the ancient capital city of Pythagoreion were built during the classical period and later expanded and restored in the Hellenist period. In addition to the fortified wall, excavations have also revealed part of the ancient city including an aqueduct extending for about a mile. Heraion, founded in the 10th century BC, lay to the west of the city. It was continually expanded and converted over the centuries that followed, especially under Polycrates. The Temple of Hera is particularly impressive due to its size. The relics discovered here can be viewed at the archaeological museum in Vathy.

The remaining columns of the temple are 8 m (26 ft) in height.

Greece

HISTORIC CENTER OF PATMOS WITH MONASTERY AND CAVE

The Monastery of St John with its valuable library and the Cave of the Apocalypse are the most important monuments in the historic center of the island of Patmos. They commemorate St John the Theologian who is said to have been banished to the island in the years 95/96.

This monastery situated high above the "chorá" (historic center) of Patmos dates from the early 11th century, but its current incarnation is from the 17th century. In ancient times it was the site of a temple dedicated to Artemis. The present-day complex is built of dark stone and it resembles a castle more than it does a monastery. The courtyard with its well-preserved frescoes, the library and exhibits from the treasury in the monastery museum are all worth seeing. The valuable pieces even include the deed of foundation of the Monastery of St John from 1088 – it is some 2 m (7 ft) long. A place of pilgrimage until the mid-16th century when the Turks gained took over the island, the monastery's religious ceremonies have changed little since early Christian times. The cave, where St John is said to have written the Apocalypse, has been converted into a church.

The impressive paintings in the inner atrium of the monastery church date from the 16th century.

MEDIEVAL CITY OF RHODES

The architectural legacy of the Old City of Rhodes is characterized by medieval buildings dating from the occupation by the Order of St John of Jerusalem. There are also some monuments from the era of Ottoman rule.

Settled for thousands of years, the island of Rhodes became Macedonian with Alexander the Great but gained independence again before becoming part of the Byzantine Empire. The island was occupied by the Order of St John of Jerusalem in 1310 and became part of the Ottoman Empire in 1523. Rhodes remained under Turkish rule until 1912 when it was captured and occupied by Italy until 1943. The island has only belonged to Greece since 1948.

The city of Rhodes on the north end of the island owes it current appearance to the building activities of the crusaders. The Street of the Knights is a well-preserved example of a 15th-century street lined with "lodgings", the meeting houses of the knights from the different countries. The street begins close to the Byzantine cathedral and leads to the Palace of the Grand Masters of the Order of St John, rebuilt by the Italians based on old engravings. Today, the Knights' Hospital, built between 1440 and 1489, is home to an archaeological museum.

The Street of the Knights (above) takes you back to the Middle Ages. An early Christian baptismal font (right) stands in front of the Great Hospital built in around 1350.

PAPHOS

The area around Paphos in south-western Cyprus features a series of important archaeological sites providing impressive illustrations of the island's more than 3,000 years of history.

This ruined site was inhabited by the Phoenicians starting in the 13th century BC, and is situated close to the village of Kouklia, south-east of the modern-day city of Paphos. The Myceneans then built a temple of Aphrodite here in the 12th century BC. The remains of the site in old Paphos are in the shape of an oriental sanctuary built out of large limestone blocks. In the middle of the sanctuary courtyard there was a tapered rock symbolizing the goddess of love, beauty and sexual desire.

In the fourth century BC, the "new" Paphos of antiquity was founded on the site of the present-day city, where there was also a temple of Aphrodite. The ruins of numerous buildings, fortified walls and tombs as well as sophisticated mosaics all bear testimony to the importance of ancient Paphos as a trading center well into Roman times. However, the site also features important early Christian and Byzantine monuments: fortress ruins, catacombs and churches with splendid interiors.

The Roman floor mosaic in the House of Aion, discovered in 1962, depicts the end of the flute contest between Apollo and Marsyas.

PAINTED CHURCHES IN THE TROODOS REGION

Hidden away in the Troodos Mountains in Cyprus are a number of churches and chapels decorated with splendid Byzantine murals dating from the 11th and 12th centuries.

There are monasteries, chapels and churches with important works of Byzantine art to be found amidst the Troodos Mountains in the heart of Cyprus. The related World Heritage Site encompasses ten churches spread through several villages: Stavros tou Agiasmati, Panagia tou Arakou, Timios Stavros, Agios Nikolaos tis Stegis, Panagia Podithou, Panagia Phorbiotissa, Church of St John Lampadistis, Panagia tou Moutoulla, the Church of the Archangel Michael, and, as of 2001, Ayia Sotira tou Soteros. Nikolaos tis Stegis is a domed cross-in-square church from the 11th century and one of the few examples of Byzantine painting from the early Komnenos period. The wall murals inside the church at the Monastery of St John Lampadistis date from the second half of the 15th century. They demonstrate a local painting style of the late Byzantine school. The single-room Panagia Podithou painted church near Galata dates from 1502.

The frescoes in the 12th-century Panagia Phorbiotissa Church are among the most valuable from the Byzantine era.

CHOIROKOITIA

The archaeological site of Choirokoitia is one of the most important prehistoric settlements in the eastern Mediterranean.

In prehistoric times the island of Cyprus played a key role in the development of neolithic culture. Choirokoitia, situated between Larnaca and Limassol, is an unusually well-preserved archaeological site from this era of cultural development and one of the oldest remains of human settlement on Cyprus.

Choirokoitia was established on a southern slope in the Maroni River valley. The settlement originally comprised a series of two-story buildings built of solid stone on circular foundations, surrounded by a protective wall. The largest of the buildings have an outside diameter of 10 m (33 ft) and an inner diameter of 2 to 5 m (7 to 17 ft). The roughly 2,000 inhabitants who lived here during the first settlement period made very little use of ceramic objects and used tools made of stone and wood. The existence of blades and arrowheads made from obsidian is the only indication of contact and trade with other cultures.

The foundations are all that remain of the original buildings.

Turkey

Constantine the Great

Although Constantine (ca. 280–337) was not baptized until shortly before his death, he can still be considered the first Christian emperor of Rome. Influenced by his mother, St Helena, he brought religious freedom to Christians and supported the new church. His efforts heralded a new age, but he also once again picked up on the old idea of a unified empire based on his predecessor, Diocletian's, concept of a tetrarchy, in which power within the vast Roman Empire would be divided among four individuals.

The son of a high-ranking official, Constantine made his way very early on into the Roman imperial court in Nicomedia (now Izmir). After initial

HISTORIC AREAS OF ISTANBUL

Istanbul's Old Town boasts a plethora of religious sights that attest to the city's eventful history as capital of the Eastern Roman Empire, and later as the center of the Ottoman Empire. Four areas have been put under protection here: the Archaeological Park at the tip of the peninsula, the Suleymaniye Quarter, the Zeyrek Quarter and the area around the Theodosian Wall.

From 330 to 1930, what is now Istanbul bore the name Constantinople, a city that experienced centuries of prominence as the capital of the Byzantine Empire after being founded by Emperor Constantine.

Probably the most famous building in Istanbul is a monument dating back to the time of the Eastern Roman Empire: the Hagia Sophia, built by Justinian from 532 to 537 on the ruins of a basilica consecrated by Constantine in 360. It represents the highlight of Byzantine opulence.

After the Ottomans conquered the city in 1453, Hagia Sophia was converted to a mosque. The mosaics were covered with plaster, and additions were made, including four minarets. Little Hagia Sophia – the former Orthodox church of Saints Sergios and Bakchos (527–536) – is older than its larger namesake and is now a mosque.

Other churches from Byzantium have also been preserved like the Hagia Eirene, inaugurated in 532, and given its present-day appearance after the year 740. Like the Sehzade Mosque, erected in about 1550 by master builder Sinan, the Sokullu Mehmet Pasha Mosque (1572) was perfectly adapted to its site. The Sultan Ahmet Mosque (1609–1616) owes its nickname "Blue Mosque" to the interior, which is decorated in shades of blue.

The most imposing element of the Hagia Sophia, which is almost 1500 years old and serves as a museum today, is the 55-m-high (180-ft) dome. Wooden signs bearing Mohammed's name and the first four caliphs in Arabic script indicate its intermittent use as a mosque.

military successes in Britannia, his troops proclaimed the young general emperor in the year 306, but autarchy was yet to be established.

At the battle of Ponte Milvio near Rome in 312, Constantine defeated the Western Roman Emperor Maxentius, a crucial element in the creation of early-Christian legends. His ultimate

goal was achieved twelve years later, in 324, when Constantine governed the Roman world and introduced the dynastic principle of hereditary succession to the throne. He appointed Constantinople as the empire's capital. Rome and the West, now threatened by mass migration of people, immediately diminished in importance.

A 10th-century mosaic in the Hagia Sophia depicts Mary with her child (left). Justinian on her right offers Mary a church, the Hagia Sophia, while Constantine presents her with his city of Constantinople. Far left: Constantine the Great in an 11th-century fresco in the Apple Church, or Elmali Kilise, in Göreme.

The Sultan Ahmet Mosque, also known as the Blue Mosque, is the symbol and main mosque of Istanbul.

Numerous stained glass windows adorn the Blue Mosque, which is predominantly decorated with blue Iznik tiles.

No less than 336 columns in twelve rows support the 140-m-long (459-ft), 70-m-wide (230-ft) Yerebatan Saray cistern.

Inside the dome of the mausoleum at the Chora Church, an outstanding example of Byzantine church architecture.

Turkey

HISTORIC AREAS OF ISTANBUL

Sultan Suleiman relocated his residence and harem to the Topkapi Saray after a fire in the Old Palace in 1540/41.

The Suleymaniye Mosque, named after Sultan Suleiman the Magnificent, was built from 1550 to 1557.

The Grand Bazaar stretches over 32 ha (79 acres). Visitors can shop and haggle in around sixty shopping alleys.

The Egyptian Bazaar, laid out in an L-shape, is also worth seeing. Around 100 traders offer their wares here.

The Padishah's festival room was the center of the harem in the Topkapi Palace, comprising 300 rooms.

Turkey

CITY OF SAFRANBOLU

The half-timbered houses around the medieval mosque date back to the late Ottoman empire and are typical of the skyline in Safranbolu, the "saffron city", in Karabük province.

Safranbolu was built on a rocky promontory between the valleys of the Isfendiyar Mountains, around 300 km (186 mi) north-east of Istanbul and 30 km (19 mi) from the Black Sea. The city owes its name to the saffron fields that once surrounded it.
Starting in the 13th century, Safranbolu became an important stop for caravans on the main east-west trading routes between Europe and the Caucasus. It maintained its prominent status as a trading hub until modern railways were built in the early 20th century. The former trading square, the bazaar quarter known as "ersa", is worth a visit.

Safranbolu's most important edifices were built around the year 1320. These include the Old Baths, the Suleiman Pasha Mosque, and the Old Mosque, all surrounded by half-timbered houses dating back to the late-Ottoman period. Other examples of traditional Turkish architecture can also be admired in Safranbolu including a number of villas, a caravanserai and some beautiful mosques.

The old caravanserai, the residence of Suleiman Pasha, is located between the Köprülü Mehmet Pasha Mosque (1662) and the Izzet Mehmet Pasha Mosque (1796).

ARCHAEOLOGICAL SITE OF THE CITY OF TROY

Containing relics from nearly 4,000 years ago, Troy is itself one of the world's most famous archaeological discoveries.

The best-known account of the conquest of Troy is attributed to Homer, but the city of Troy was not actually re-discovered until the 19th century. In 1822, archaeologist Charles McLaren identified a 32-m-high (105 ft) hill as its location. German archaeologist Heinrich Schliemann was then able to demonstrate the accuracy of this theory between 1870 and 1890 when he performed extensive excavations that ultimately led his successors to find the remains of nine of Troy's major settlement periods.
The successive development of the civilization of Asia Minor, from the

Bronze Age to the Roman Empire, is documented in Troy's different layers of stone and deposits. The city had a strategically important location near the Dardanelles, which connect the Black Sea with the Sea of Marmara and the Aegean Sea. The layers document the time from 3000 BC onwards, when Troy acted as a fort, capital and royal residence. It was conquered by the Romans in 85 BC, and was forgotten soon after the founding of Constantinople.

Heinrich Schliemann began his excavations in Troy's lowlands in 1870.

HATTUSHA: THE HITTITE CAPITAL

The ruins of Hattusha, the former capital of the Hittite Empire, which stretched across Anatolia and the northern part of present-day Syria in the second millennium BC, are located near the village of Bogzakhale, around 150 km (93 mi) east of Ankara.

The oldest pre-Hittite settlement was limited to a natural fort that sprawled over the so-called lower town and was already enclosed by walls in the 18th century BC. The region that is present-day Anatolia was in fact the homeland of the Hittites around 1600 BC. The empire's founder was Labarna Hattusili I, who appointed Hattusha as the capital, and it was from here that the ruler drove his southward expansion of the empire.
The ruins of the former capital were re-discovered in the 19th century, and excavations began in the early 20th century. The almost 7-km-long (4-mi)

city wall was predominantly made from solid stone blocks with just the upper section made of mud bricks. The remains of five gates have been preserved with three of the entrances displaying reliefs of sphinxes, lions and a warrior.
The excavations also unearthed about 30,000 cuneiform script tablets, since deciphered, that gave good insight into the history and culture of the Hittites, an empire that faded in the 12th century BC.

The Lion Gate in the south-west was one of the entrances to the upper town.

GREAT MOSQUE AND HOSPITAL OF DIVRIĞI

Wonderful examples of medieval Seljukian architecture can be found in Divriği, an iron-ore city that had the misfortune of being destroyed repeatedly throughout its history.

The city of Divriği is located in the province of Sivas in Central Anatolia, and was already fiercely sought-after in early Islamic times. On a number of occasions it fell under Arabic rule and in the ninth century, Divriği was used by the Paulicians – a Byzantine sect that had allied itself with the Emir of Melitene – as a base for military excursions against the Eastern Roman Empire. Christophoros, brother-in-law of Macedonian Emperor Basileios I, managed to defeat the Paulicians on their own soil in 872. The city and fort were then destroyed

on the emperor's orders. After the Great Seljuk Empire claimed victory over Byzantium in 1071, Divriği was designated Emir Mengücek. The successors of the Mengücekids who established themselves here can be traced in building inscriptions. In 1228/29, Emir Ahmet Shah had the Great Mosque built. The sumptuous complex attests to the growing wealth achieved by Divriği after the main trading routes were built.

Opulent stonemasonry adorns the mosque's main doorway.

GÖREME NATIONAL PARK AND THE ROCK SITES OF CAPPADOCIA

The stunning cliffs and pyramid-like tuff formations in the Göreme valley in Cappadocia make for a truly bizarre landscape. Hundreds of chapels dating back to the Byzantine period are hewn into the rock here.

The tuff formations of Nevşehir Province (Cappadocia) are the result of volcanic activity, shaped into their current forms by the process of erosion. The Christian population of the Byzantine provinces of Asia Minor once sought refuge from Arab persecution here, building homes, monks' cells and chapels into the soft tuff. Starting in the 6th century, complete cave villages and entire underground cities were built in the Göreme valley and surrounding areas.

The World Heritage Site encompasses both the rock formations and the cave dwellings. These include numerous monasteries and churches whose construction draws on several Byzantine styles of the period. The first figurative motifs in the church paintings date from the 9th century.

After the Christianization of Anatolia by the Apostle Paul, early-Christian communities in Göreme built residential dwellings, chapels and churches into the rock.

THE ANCIENT CITY OF HIERAPOLIS-PAMUKKALE

Alongside its famous calc-sinter terraces, the World Heritage Site of Pamukkale (formerly Hierapolis) also boasts numerous baths, temples and other monuments dating back to Hellenistic and Roman times.

The area around the hot springs of Pamukkale was settled very early, becoming part of the Roman province of Asia in the second century BC. The city of Hierapolis itself was built in 190 BC by order of King Eumenes II of Pergamon. Though primarily intended as a fortification, Hierapolis also had its own baths right from the start, around which the residential buildings, temples, early-Christian chapels and other structures sprang up. The ruins of these buildings can still be seen today. The last of these ancient buildings is from the fourth century.

The area around the ruins is one of extraordinary natural beauty. Roughly 100 m (330 ft) up Mount Çökelez, the spectacular hot springs emerge from a ledge protruding out of the rock face and flow down into the valley below. Over time, deposits from the mineral-rich water (sinter) formed petrified waterfalls, forests of limestone stalactites, and terraced basins. The overall effect is otherworldly.

Calc-sinter terraces in Pamukkale, which is Turkish for "cotton fortress".

RUINS OF XANTHOS AND THE SANCTUARY OF LETOON

Lycian, Hellenic, Roman and Byzantine ruins here bear witness to the complex history of the ancient city of Xanthos.

Xanthos was the center of Lycia, which was conquered by the Persians in around 545 BC, and the region around Xanthos is rich in monumental burial sites dating back to the sixth and fifth centuries BC. Particularly worth mentioning here are the Lion Tomb, the Harpy Monument and the Nereid Monument. The city's archaeological treasures, some of which date back to the seventh century BC, also include an acropolis and a theater.
One of the most significant cultural monuments in the area is "Letoon", the sanctuary of Leto, the mother of Apollo and Artemis who, according

to the myth, is said to have come to this place after the birth of her "holy" children. Burial sites, the sanctuary and the rock inscriptions all document Lycian culture as well as the origins of the Indo-European languages, a language family that was already prevalent across Europe and large parts of South-Western Asia and the Indian subcontinent in ancient times.

The Roman amphitheater of Xanthos was built in the year 150 inside a Lycian necropolis with funerary columns that are more than 5 m (16 ft) high.

MONUMENTAL BURIAL SITES ON NEMRUT DAĞ

King Antiochos I of Commagene chose the 2,150-m (7,054-ft) plateau of the Nemryt Dağ as a gravesite and place of religious worship.

Antiochos I ruled the Commagene from 69 to 36 BC. It was a small independent empire created in the third and second century BC, at the time of the Diadochi after the collapse of the empire of Alexander the Great. Antiochos chose the top of Nemrut Dağ, near ancient Arsameia, as his final resting place, appointing the site located in the Taurus Mountains, in what is now south-eastern Turkey, as a place of religious worship and a "throne of the gods". His goal was to establish himself as a living god.
Three terraces are clustered around the tumulus of the ruler's grave

mound. The entrance to the northern terrace was guarded by sculptures of lions and eagles, the remains of which have been preserved, while the eastern and western terraces each formed a large "open-air temple". The western terrace was largely destroyed, but it certainly must have been a mirror image of the eastern terrace – even the inscriptions were worded almost identically.

The Greek and Persian roots of Commagenic art are expertly combined in the fascinating monumental stone heads on the Nemrut Dağ.

Georgia

MOUNTAIN VILLAGES OF UPPER SVANETI

The Svans – a Georgian tribe in north-western Georgia, in the historic region of Svaneti – have a unique culture with their own language and icon worship. Today, the members of this tribe live in the Greater Caucasus spread between some forty mountain villages.

A remarkable medieval culture has survived in the remote mountain villages of the Caucasus. The exact origin of the Svan people, who have lived in isolation for centuries, is unclear, and their language, which has no script, is only distantly related to present-day Georgian. The early Christianization of the Svans led to the development of an independent system into which elements of the original animistic religion were incorporated.

The township of Ushguli is home to the oldest of the traditional stone towers, up to five stories high and furnished with machicolations. They were built next to residences in the 12th and 13th centuries to protect the inhabitants from possible attacks.

Ushguli, one of the highest villages in Europe, is perched in Upper Svaneti at an elevation of more than 2,200 m (7,218 ft). The town, once impregnable, is surrounded by the 5,000-m (16,405-ft) glacier-covered peaks of the Central Caucasus. It is best accessed on horseback over mountain passes.

BAGRATI CATHEDRAL AND GELATI MONASTERY

King Bagrat III (ca. 963–1014), who ruled unified Georgia after 1008, built what was once the country's mightiest cathedral. Only its ruins remain in the West-Georgian town of Kutaissi. The Gelati Monastery, built outside the city in 1106, is home to wall mosaics and frescoes spanning more than seven centuries.

Little has been preserved of the magnificent mosaics that once adorned the interior of Bagrati Cathedral, built in 1003. Turkish invaders plundered and destroyed the Orthodox cathedral in the 17th century.

Gelati Monastery, on the other hand, which became a spiritual center in Georgia soon after its founding and attracted scholars from all over the country to teach at the newly founded academy, still contains some partial works. Remains of a hospital built around the same time were found outside the walled complex, at the center of which stands the church of St Mary, erected in the 12th century. Since Turkish attacks on Kutaissi, only ruins remain of most of the monastery buildings. Luckily, a few historical treasures were preserved.

The Church of St Mary (above) in Gelati Monastery was built under Georgian King David the Builder. The dome of Bagrati Cathedral (right) collapsed during a Turkish invasion in 1692. Many façades, porches and crosses have been preserved.

HISTORICAL MONUMENTS OF MTSKHETA

Mtskheta – the former capital of the East Georgian kingdom of Kartli – is named after Mtskhetos, the oldest son of the mythical ancestor, and lies just a few miles north of Tbilisi. It was an important political and cultural center for more than 800 years.

Since excavations began at the site in 1937, a royal residence, the ruins of an acropolis, thermal baths as well as a necropolis with cist graves and monolithic sarcophagi have been uncovered. A woman's grave with burial gifts from the second century reveals a wealth of information too. Mtskheta is of great significance to the history

The cross-in-square church (top) that forms part of the Samtavro Monastery complex is home to the burial sites of Georgia's first Christian ruler and his wife. Bottom: The Jvari Church sits majestically atop a mountain ridge.

of Georgia's Christianization. The Jvari Church (586 to 605), built around a wooden cross believed to perform miracles, is one of the country's best-preserved early-Christian structures. The name of Svetitskhoveli ("life-giving pillar") Cathedral, built from 1010 to 1029, also relates to a miracle said to have taken place in a building that existed previously on the site. Samtavro Monastery, with one of Georgia's most beautiful cross-in-square churches, similarly dates back to the 11th century.

Images of apostles and saints adorn the tomb of King Marian, who was buried in Samtavro Monastery along with his wife, Queen Nana.

Armenia

MONASTERIES OF HAGHPAT AND SANAHIN

These two monasteries – founded by Queen Khosrovanush in around 960 – are some of Armenia's most important historic buildings.

Four churches, a library, a bell tower, a refectory and several chapels were built between the 10th and the 13th centuries on the site of a previous fortified monastery in the northern Armenian province of Lori, near the present-day border with Georgia. The "gavits" – as the halls are known – are each supported by four pillars, in the center of which is a dome-like vault with apertures for light. They are typical of Armenian monastic buildings of the time.

The Holy Cross Church at Haghpat Monastery is from the 10th century and features a domed hall that was given a porch early in the 13th century. The benefactor's portrait in the gable of the eastern façade is unique. Sanahin Monastery is separated from Haghpat Monastery by a beautiful gorge. The important monastic library (12th–13th centuries) tends to be overlooked from a distance – a protective measure that proved valuable during the many regional wars.

The Holy Cross Church is the oldest part of the Haghpat Monastery complex. The quaint bell tower is set at a distance from the main buildings.

CATHEDRAL AND CHURCHES OF ECHMIATSIN AND THE ARCHAE-OLOGICAL SITE OF ZVARTNOTS

Echmiatsin has been the religious center of the Armenian church since the start of the fourth century as well as the residence of the Catholicos, its spiritual leader.

In the seventh century, Catholicos Nerses III, educated in Byzantium, built a magnificent palace in the city of Echmiatsin, west of Yerevan, with the great three-storey round church of St Gregory. Today, only ruins remain of the complex edifice.

The three main churches of Echmiatsin – the cathedral, St Hripsime Church and St Gayane Church – as well as the remains of Nerses' palace in nearby Zvartnots document the spiritual and artistic innovation that distinguished the Armenian church in its early years.

They constitute the highlight of the cross-in-square style of church building that characterized sacral architecture in the region in the seventh century. In their basic form, the cathedral and the churches of these two martyrs date back to the fifth and seventh centuries, respectively. The churches were renovated in the 17th century, and the cathedral was redecorated with Islamic influences.

A spectacular ceiling fresco adorns Echmiatsin's cathedral.

MONASTERY OF GEGHARD AND THE UPPER AZAT VALLEY

The Geghard monastery complex is at an elevation of 1,700 m (5,578 ft) on the site of an ancient spring sanctuary located at the end of gorges formed by the Azat River. A fragment of the Holy Lance made the place an important destination for pilgrims.

This monastery complex east of Yerevan owes its unique character to the cave churches and graves hewn out of the tuff. Pagan spring cults are said to have worshipped here as early as pre-Christian times and the name of the original structure, allegedly dating back to Gregory the Illuminator (ca. 240–322), suggests that: "Airi-vankh" means "cave monastery".

The present-day name of "Geghard" ("lance") refers to the legend of the Holy Lance, which the Apostle Jude is said to have brought to Armenia, and which was once supposedly hidden here as a relic. At the start of the 13th century, Geghard Monastery came under the control of the Zakharyan family, who also had the central Mother of God Church built in 1215. A few decades later, the monastery was taken over by the Proshyan family, who used it mainly as a burial site.

A large cross surrounded by rosettes, statues of saints and images of animals adorns the entrance of a church carved into the rock at the Geghard monastery.

WALLED CITY OF BAKU WITH SHIRVANSHAH'S PALACE AND MAIDEN TOWER

The walled Old Town of Baku features the Shirvanshah Palace and Maiden Tower and brings together diverse cultural influences of Western Asia.

Traces of settlement from as early as the Paleolithic Age can be found on the site of present-day Baku, the capital of Azerbaijan on the western shores of the Caspian Sea. The inner city, at the southern bay of the Absheron Peninsula, is still largely surrounded by the immense wall built between the 11th and 13th centuries. Soaring out of the wall is the Maiden Tower, which rises to 32 m (105 ft) above a foundation dating from the sixth/seventh centuries BC. The foundations from the 14th-century Gabala fortress have now been excavated.

The Shirvanshah's sprawling palace complex stretches down the western slope of the Old Town over several terraces towards the sea. The highest terrace was reserved for the ruler's residential palace. The skyline of old Baku is dominated by the Grand Mosque, the 18th-century Zoroastrian temple and the former caravanserais and bathhouses.

The Shirvanshah's Palace has five courtyards over three levels and includes the old mosque and the royal mausoleum (left). Below is the caravanserai.

GOBUSTAN ROCK ART CULTURAL LANDSCAPE

This World Heritage Site in the semi-desert region of central Azerbaijan consists of three areas with around 6,000 rock paintings. Settlements and burial sites have also been found here.

The three flat-top hills of Jinghirdag-Yazylytepe, Boyukdash and Kichikdash are situated on a plateau in the foothills of the Caucasus near the Caspian Sea. They are covered by large limestone blocks that form numerous caves and stone recesses.
Most of the rock paintings within are actually engravings. They can be classified into several groups based on their age. The ones from the Old Stone Age depict boats – the water level of the Caspian Sea was probably higher at the time, and the three hill regions were islands – wild animals, fish and

hunters. One cave shows tattooed women, while another bears only images of pregnant women. Ritual scenes, dances and sacrifices as well as early domesticated animals are typical of the Neolithic Age. Goats, carts and horsemen then appeared during the Bronze Age. The Iron Age gave rise to images of armless, human-like figures while the Middle Ages saw camel caravans, armed horsemen and Islamic symbols.

The diverse range of motifs includes anthropomorphic figures and goats.

The large stupa of Bauddhanath with its colorful prayer flags fluttering in the wind (below) is one of the most important Buddhist sanctuaries in Kathmandu Valley. Statues of Buddha such as this reclining version from the seventh/eighth centuries in the Isurumuniya Monastery (right) are all over the Sacred City of Anuradhapura in Sri Lanka.

ASIA

Syria

ANCIENT CITY OF ALEPPO

Located at the crossroads of ancient trade routes, this city in the far north-west of what is now Syria boasts the remains of numerous different civilizations. Discoveries from Citadel Hill have provided evidence that Aleppo was settled as early as 3,000 BC.

With 6,000 years of history behind it, Aleppo (Halab) is one of the oldest continuously settled places in the world. Two of the more outstanding monuments among a vast array of medieval madrassahs, palaces, caravanserais and hammams in the ancient city are the Citadel and the Great Mosque of Aleppo.

The Citadel in its present form dates from the late 13th century while the mosque was founded back in 715 by the Ayyubids and rebuilt following a fire in 1190. The mosque is also adorned with a masterpiece of medieval Syrian architecture: the elaborate, 48-m-high (157-ft) minaret from the end of the 11th century.

There was an Assyrian-Hittite temple on the citadel hill as far back as the 10th century BC. When the Seleucids rebuilt the city in the third century BC, they included the construction of fortifications high on the promontory. Also worthy of mention is the Halawiye Madrassah, built in 1124 on the ruins of the Byzantine Cathedral of St Helen, dedicated to the mother of Emperor Constantine.

An arched bridge leads to the upper gate of the Citadel, built in 1211.

CRAC DES CHEVALIERS AND QAL'AT SALAH EL-DIN

The fortress of the Hospitaller Order of St John, Crac des Chevaliers, and the Fortress of Saladin, are stone testimonies to the interaction between Christians and Muslims over more than three centuries.

The Crac des Chevaliers fortress can be seen from a great distance, towering over the plains of the Homs Gap atop the 755-m-high (2,478-ft) Jebel Khalil in the southern foothills of the Ansariye Mountains. The Emir of Homs had the first fortress built here in 1031, but it fell to the knights of the Hospitaller Order of St John in 1142 who then modernized the stronghold. During the Crusades it formed part of a communication chain comprising towns and fortresses that provided crusaders with vital information on their routes. It was only in 1271 that the Mameluk Sultan Baibar forced the fortress into surrender.

Qal'at Salah El-Din, the Fortress of Saladin east of Latakia, is located on a ridge surrounded by ravines on three sides. The first stronghold, built in the 10th century, was captured in 975 by the Byzantines under Emperor John I Tzimiskes who extended it into an imposing fortress. It was home to the crusaders in the 12th century until it fell to Sultan Saladin in 1188.

Crac des Chevaliers: a superb example of a crusader fortress in the Middle East.

SITE OF PALMYRA

These monumental ruins in the Syrian desert are testimony to the former political and economic power of the Roman colony of Palmyra, and to the empire of the legendary queen Zenobia.

Although this commercial city situated between Damascus and the Euphrates enjoyed great importance as an intermediary point between East and West even in pre-Roman times, Palmyra's zenith coincided with the increased Roman presence in the Middle East. Located at the crossroads of north-south as well as east-west caravan routes, the oasis city that is now Tadmur attained its auspicious economic position when it was awarded colony status by Emperor Caracalla.

Palmyra benefited greatly from its links with the Silk Road and rose quickly in importance. In the third century, Queen Zenobia, who ruled the Palmyran Empire from 267, transformed the city into a magnificent residence based on Roman models, thus merging the culture of the Hellenistic Orient with that of the Parthians and the Romans. Palmyra's highlights include the temple of Baal, a long colonnaded street, its theater, agora, burial mounds and its underground burial compartments in the "Valley of the Tombs" are all testimony to the sophistication of Palmyran art.

Palmyra, an ancient trading city in central Syria, features what was once a grand colonnaded street, the start of which was marked by the mighty Hadrian's Arch.

ANCIENT CITY OF DAMASCUS

Enjoying around 5,000 years of history, Damascus is one of the oldest cities in the world. This historic city is also inextricably linked with the Old Testament and the history of Islam.

The Prophet Mohammed is said to have once refused to visit the city of Damascus because he did not want to enter any other paradise before achieving heavenly paradise. Damascus today still lives up to its poetic epithet, the "Diamond of the Desert". The historic city center, with its magnificent mosques, vibrant markets and vast palace complexes is particularly impressive. Damascus has been Islamic since the eighth century. The Great Mosque here was built in 705, at the height of the Umayyad Dynasty, on the foundations of a former Christian church. It is one of the oldest Islamic places of worship and a representative not only of the Umayyad style but also of Islamic architectural sophistication in general. The city's famous markets (souks) are tightly grouped around the Umayyad Mosque, the covered Souk al-Hamidiya being the most famous. A number of other architectural highlights such as the Maristan al-Nuri, a hospital built in 1154, the Nur al-Din Madrassah, and the Saladin Shrine (1193) are also in this neighborhood.

The ancient city of Damascus is a maze of narrow alleyways (below). The Umayyad Mosque also served as a Christian church until its conversion in 705 (left).

ANCIENT CITY OF BOSRA

This powerful trading city in southern Syria is at the crossroads of the main routes to the Red Sea. It was also an important cultural center boasting magnificent palaces and a large amphitheater.

Founded by the Nabateans, Bosra was an important trading hub for nomad tribes that reached its height under the Romans, who captured the city in 106 BC. Emperor Trajan made Bosra the capital of the province of Arabia and expanded the commercial center with a number of grandiose buildings. Even after the fall of the Roman Empire, Bosra continued to play a vital role as the seat of both a bishop and a Byzantine orthodox metropolitan. Under Islamic rule it was an administrative center as well as an important place of pilgrimage on the route from Damascus to Mecca. Bosra still boasts impressive Roman, early-Christian and Islamic monuments. The ancient amphitheater, one of the best-preserved of its kind, was converted into an Arab fortress in the Middle Ages as a response to the threat from Crusaders. The remains of a magnificent early-Christian episcopal church and a basilica have also survived. The most distinctive examples of Islamic architecture are the Friday Mosque and the al Mabrak Mosque, both built in the 12th century.

The Roman theater in Bosra was converted into a citadel during the Seljuk and Ayyubid eras.

Lebanon

OUADI QADISHA AND THE FOREST OF THE CEDARS OF GOD (HORSH ARZ EL-RAB)

Ouadi Qadisha, the "Holy Valley", and its cave monasteries is one of the most important early-Christian settlements in the world. Nearby is the country's most famous forest: the majestic cedars are the symbol of Lebanon.

The Ouadi Qadisha begins 120 km (75 mi) from Lebanon's capital, Beirut. In early Christian times monks built hidden cave churches and monasteries such as the Qannubin Monastery in the solitude of this dramatic landscape. The Qadisha Grotto, on the old road from Bscharre, features impressive stalagmites and stalactites and a waterfall that flows from the cave in the spring. Nearby is a cedar forest known as Horsh Arz al-Rab, the Cedars of God. In the shadow of the country's highest peak, the 3,088-m (10,132-ft) Qurnat as-Sawda, is a forest of around 400 mighty cedars, some of which are said to be more than 1,500 years old – which dates them back to the time when King Solomon built his palace and temple of cedar wood in Jerusalem. The wood was once a cherished export commodity.

Lebanon was once covered by vast cedar forests. Qurnat as-Sawda mountain has one of the larger remaining sections.

RUINS OF ANJAR

These ruins north of Beirut are part of a palace city built by the Umayyad Caliph Walid I in the eighth century. Based on the Roman example, it represents unique evidence of the Umayyad ruler's urban planning skills.

Caliph Walid I planned his palace city of Anjar based on a Roman example of the ideal city. The strictly geometric layout of the complex is reflected in its basically square outline with sides measuring about 200 m (660 ft). The palace's four gates are reinforced with round towers used to protect the entrances to the city, which was entirely enclosed by a wall.

As was common practice with Roman cities, the grid layout was divided up at right angles by main axes as well as the Cardo and the Decumanus (main and secondary main street), which were lined with grand colonnades. A four-part arched monument at the intersection of the axes, the Tetrapylon, marked the city center. The palace of Umayyad ruler Walid I in the south-east of the city has now been partly rebuilt. Adjoining it to the north was the mosque. Further north was the small palace reserved for women, and beyond the Cardo were the residential quarters for the palace servants.

The archways and remains of the magnificent arcades that once lined the main streets of Anjar are an indisputable indicator of the fact that the buildings of this palace city were designed based on Roman examples.

RUINS OF BYBLOS

Idyllicly situated on the Mediterranean coast, Byblos is one of the oldest cities founded by the Phoenicians. It had the most important port in the Levant during the Bronze Age and later become a base for the Crusaders.

Situated on the coast north of Beirut, Byblos is today an appealing fishing port at the base of an ancient fortress built during the Crusades. Built by the Phoenicians, this coastal city was already a thriving center of trade between Mesopotamia and the Mediterranean even back in the third century BC. Known to the Akkadians as Gubla and to the Phoenicians as Gebal ("ships"), the city's current name is Jubail. Indeed, it was ships that ensured Byblos' prosperity as an important transshipment point for Lebanese cedar wood being exported to Egypt, for example. (The Pharaoh's barque, unearthed during excavations close to the Great Pyramid of Giza, was made of cedar wood that is said to still have something of the characteristic scent). Imports to Byblos included alabaster, gold and papyrus. The Greek name Byblos ("writing material") is thought to derive from the trade in papyrus – Alexander the Great conquered and Hellenized the city in 332 BC. The building of the Temple of Baalat Gebal, dedicated to the goddess of the city, began in around 2800 BC, with further temples also planned but never built.

The Obelisk Temple in Byblos dates from around 1600 BC.

RUINS OF BAALBEK

The massive columns and mostly intact ruins of the temple in Baalbek are among the most magnificent relics of Roman architecture in the Middle East.

The name "Baalbek" (meaning "Lord of the Beqaa Valley") dates back to Phoenician times and the city's founding. During the Seleucid-Hellenistic epochs in the third and second centuries BC, it was known as Heliopolis, the "City of the Sun", and rock tombs still survive from this era. The most important remains, however, are those left by the Romans, who built one of the largest temples of antiquity here.

The monumental Jupiter Temple, for example, was begun under Emperor Augustus in 14 AD, on the ruins of a Phoenician cult site; it took roughly fifty years to complete the complex. The six surviving columns, each 20 m (66 ft) high, are a Lebanese landmark

on a par with the national cedar trees. The Bacchus Temple, a masterpiece of Greco-Roman architecture and the best-preserved ancient temple complex in the Middle East, dates from the same era. The dimensions of even this, the smallest of the complex's temples, are larger than those of the Acropolis in Athens. Baalbek is also famous for the gigantic blocks of stone that form the the foundations of this mighty temple complex.

The almost completely intact Temple of Bacchus (above) is from the first half of the second century. The Venus Temple (left) was used as a church in the Byzantine era.

TYRE

Situated in what is now southern Lebanon, Tyre, now known as Sur, was one of the most important port cities on the Mediterranean during the Phoenician period. The most impressive buildings, however, are mostly from the Roman era.

The wealth of the Phoenicians was in part based on the robust trade in purple dye. For thousands of years the dye obtained from the mucous secretions of one of several predatory snails was so valuable that it was typically worth several times its weight in gold. At the time, the Phoenician city of Tyre was the exclusive production site for purple dye and therefore constantly a target of foreign powers. Babylonian King Nebuchadnezzar's troops besieged Tyre in the sixth century BC, but their efforts were in vain. Alexander the Great's soldiers later captured the port city in 332 BC, and Roman troops marched into the city of

Tyre in the first century BC. The most important monuments here are, like many sites in the region, attributed to the Romans. Two key archaeological sites here are particularly worthy of mention: the imperial city and the necropolis. The first features parts of the Phoenician city wall, colonnaded Roman avenues and hot springs, relics of the Byzantine era, and a crusader cathedral. The famous Triumphal Arch of Tyre forms part of the necropolis outside the city gates.

The columns on the beach of this former port city are partial the ruins of a palaestra, an ancient sports complex.

Israel

OLD CITY OF ACRE

Crusader Baldwin I captured the much disputed city of Acre in 1104. After the fall of Jerusalem in 1191, this city on Haifa Bay on the Mediterranean coast was the capital of the crusader kingdom for a century. In the 18th century the Ottomans converted the crusader castle into a gigantic fortress that was once placed unsuccessfully under siege by Napoleon for sixty-one days.

It was the crusaders' last stronghold in the Holy Land, but even after the fall of Acre in 1291, this former capital of the Kingdom of Jerusalem continued to experience an eventful history. It ultimately came under Mameluk, Umayyad, Bedouin and Ottoman rule over the centuries that followed the decline of the crusaders. The Ottomans secured the proud walled city in the 18th century.

The old city of Acre, a classic example of Islamic town planning, includes the Hospitaller quarter with the sizable citadel from the Crusader era, a number of places of worship such as the Jezzar Pasha Mosque – lined with palms, arcades and built in the 18th century in the Turkish rococo style on the foundations of a crusader cathedral – the Khan al-Umdan caravanserai, and buildings from the Ottoman era, some of which were built directly on top of the crusader city.

The clock tower of the Khan al-Umdan caravanserai and the Sinan Pasha Mosque dominate the old port of Acre, which was protected by mighty walls on both the sea and the land sides.

BÁHA'I HOLY PLACES IN HAIFA AND THE WESTERN GALILEE

This World Heritage site includes a total of twenty-six buildings, monuments and other sites spread over eleven locations, the majority of which are situated in an extensive garden in Haifa.

The origins of the Báha'i faith lie in Iran where, in 1844, a man with the self-proclaimed title of "Bab" (meaning "gate" in Arabic) declared himself bearer of a revelation that a second messenger of God would soon arrive and bring the things promised in the world's great religions. This messenger would be Baha'u'llah (Arabic for the "Glory of God"). The two men faced opposition from religious and secular rulers in Iran. Bab was executed and Baha'u'llah was banished to Acre. Following his death in 1892, the Báha'i began developing their World Center on Mount Carmel in Haifa and the surrounding area. The main building is the magnificent Bab Mausoleum, reached via a long staircase with nineteen terraces. There is also the neoclassical administrative building, an archive and other buildings used for spiritual and educational purposes. The most important Báha'i site is the Shrine of Baha'u'llah in Acre.

The Bab Mausoleum with its impressive dome constitutes the architectural focal point of the Hanging Gardens on Mount Carmel in Haifa.

WHITE CITY OF TEL AVIV – THE MODERN MOVEMENT

With around 4,000 buildings constructed in the Bauhaus – or Classic Modern – style, Tel Aviv has more edifices from this unique architectural movement than any other city in the world.

By any reckoning, Tel Aviv is a new city. Founded in 1909, it was conceived as a place to provide new homes for the thousands of Jewish immigrants flooding in under the British Mandate in Palestine. The "White City" is a reflection of this new beginning, its buildings being based exclusively on the ideals of modernist architecture. The master plan was drawn up by British architect Sir Patrick Geddes with an array of modernist complexes being built under his direction until 1948. The plans were provided by Bauhaus-influenced architects who had practiced their trade in Europe before emigrating here: Arie Sharon, Zeev Rechter, Richard Kauffmann, Dov Karmi and Genia Averbuch to name a few. The result was "large-scale Bauhaus", even though not all of the architects based their work on the Dessau and Weimar Bauhaus. Engel House by Zeev Rechter, for example, was originally supported on the stilts typical of Le Corbusier's buildings.

Behind the mostly white, Bauhaus-inspired façades (right, Rothschild Boulevard) were often simple apartments.

BIBLICAL TELS – MEGIDDO, HAZOR, BEER SHEBA

Although the history of these three settlements goes back to pre-Biblical times, the sophisticated irrigation systems that supplied the towns with water still inspire awe in visitors today.

The settlement mound of Megiddo, close to Mount Carmel, was the site of an important fortress that controlled much of the trade and military routes between Egypt and Mesopotamia from about 4,000 to 2,000 BC. It is primarily famous for its riding arena and impressive stables.

Hazor, the largest of the three archaeolgical excavation sites here, encompasses an area of approximately 200 ha (494 acres) including the upper town and the unwalled lower town. Situated close to the Sea of Galilee, this town already had a vibrant and sizable population of around 20,000 people in the second millennium BC.

The excavation site near Beer Sheeba in the Negev Desert still boasts the remains of walls indicative of a planned iron-age town. There was a fortified settlement here from 1100 BC with Maccabee, Roman and Byzantine troops having been stationed here as a stronghold for military operations in the region.

The ruins of Megiddo also include the remains of King Solomon's legendary stables (left).

ARCHAEOLOGICAL SITES OF MASADA

This fortress, built by Herod the Great on a rocky plateau in the Negev Desert, was rediscovered in 1838. It was here, in 73 AD, that around 1,000 Jews committed an unthinkably large-scale collective suicide in order to avoid surrendering to the Roman army besieging them. The site is considered a symbol of the Jewish fight against oppression.

Around the time of the birth of Christ, the Kingdom of Judea was ruled by Herod the Great and enjoyed independence from Rome. To solidify his position, the king had a seemingly impregnable fortress built atop a rocky plateau 441 m (1,447 ft) above the Dead Sea. It was here that around 1,000 resistance fighters barricaded themselves in during the first Jewish uprising against Rome in 73 AD – before committing mass suicide. Herod's palace within the fortress walls had a series of residential buildings and is considered an outstanding example of a luxury Roman residence. Of even greater interest, however, is the siege and warfare machinery used and abandoned by the Romans around the fortress. It includes a mighty ramp used by soldiers to storm the fortress.

The fortress complex is enclosed by a casemate wall behind which forty towers, palaces, lodgings and of course warehouses were located.

INCENSE ROUTE – DESERT CITIES IN THE NEGEV

Negev means "dry land" and the desert of the same name certainly lives up to its title. Nevertheless, trade and irrigation systems enabled prosperous towns to develop in the region.

The dromedary camel was domesticated for use as a beast of burden in the third century BC, a development that opened up entirely new possibilities for the transport of goods through these sparsely populated desert areas. As a result, a brisk trade soon developed between the Arabian Peninsula and the Mediterranean.

The Nabatean capital of Petra in what is now Jordan was one of the most important commercial centers, but in order to avoid those areas of Judea occupied by the Romans, caravans instead travelled 2,000 km (1,243 mi) across the Negev Desert. The valuable commodity the were selling: incense. The World Heritage site encompasses towns, fortresses and caravanserai along the incense route, including the Nabatean towns of Haluza, Mamshit (Kurnub), Avdat (Oboda), and Shivta (Sobata), the fortresses of Nekarot, Kasra, and Moa, the Ein Saharonim crater spring, the caravanserai at the Ramon Gate, the Makhmal ascent and the Griffon fortress.

The ruined city of Avdat (Oboda) reflects the importance of the incense trade.

Jerusalem

OLD CITY OF JERUSALEM AND ITS WALLS

It was in the City of David and of Christ that the Prophet Mohammed experienced his visionary Night Journey. This city – situated at a massive cultural crossroads – has been ruled by Babylonians, Romans, Arabs, crusaders and Turks.

There is hardly another location on the planet that possesses as diverse a history as Jerusalem. With significant monuments from Judaism, Christianity and Islam this city represents a colorful patchwork of the main epochs that have defined its character. All of them are found within the walls of the Old City: the citadel with the Tower of David, the Armenian Quarter with the St Jacob Cathedral, the Jewish Quarter with the ruins of Hurva Synagogue, the Ha'ari and Ramban synagogues, the "Burnt House" and of course the Wailing Wall.

The Wailing Wall, 48 m (53 yds) long and 18 m (59 ft) high, is the western section of the Second Temple wall and the most important sanctuary and monument in the Jewish faith.

The Temple Mount, where according to the Old Testament Abraham was to sacrifice his son Isaac and, according to Islam, Mohammed ascended to heaven, takes up nearly 20 per cent of the Old City. The Via Dolorosa, the "Way of Suffering", where Christ carried his cross in the New Testament, begins in the Muslim Quarter close to the Lion's Gate (St Stephen's Gate); the last five stations lead to the Church of the Holy Sepulcher.

The Dome of the Rock, decorated with mosaics and built in 691 by Caliph Abd al-Malik based on the original Church of the Holy Sepulcher, dominates the Temple Mount. It is here that the Prophet Mohammed is said to have ascended to heaven.

Byzantine and Arab architects participated in building the Dome of the Rock at the end of the seventh century. It is the oldest Islamic religious building.

Jews settled mainly in the district beneath the Wailing Wall even in the early Islamic era, with a Jewish community developing there starting in the middle of the 13th century.

The Chapel of St Helena belongs to the Armenian community that lives in the Armenian Quarter.

The façade of the Dome of the Rock, a marvelous octagonal construction, is clad with priceless marble tiles.

According to the Jewish faith, the Day of Judgment will come with the Messiah passing through the Kidron Valley below the Mount of Olives. This hill north-east of the Old City is therefore home to a Jewish cemetery with a memorial.

Jordan

QUSEIR AMRA

From the outside this desert castle built by the Umayyad Caliphs is quite un-assuming. Its interior, however, features highlights of early-Islamic art including magnificent mosaics and frescoes depicting a variety of figures.

It was here between 705 and 715, around 100 km (62 mi) north-east of what is now the Jordanian capital of Amman, that Umayyad ruler Walid I decided to convert his caravanserai into a desert residence with a three-nave reception hall and a hammam – a Turkish-style bath.

What is most remarkable about the construction is the extravagant interior decoration of the reception hall and of course the hammam itself. Although it is one of the oldest in the Islamic world, it was built in the Roman style. The walls are decorated with frescoes in shades of blue, brown and ochre yellow.

The paintings depict both erotic and everyday scenes as well as hunting motifs and the "six rulers" – princes from different cultures for which the Umayyad Caliph aimed to become the legitimate successor. The Quseir Amra murals come from a time, namely during the Umayyad era, when Islam still permitted the depiction of living beings. The Byzantine-style floor mosaics are also of a high quality.

The Austrian Arabian explorer Alois Musil discovered the desert castle Quseir Amra (below) in 1898. The fascinating frescoes include depictions of Dionysus with cupid (right).

UM ER-RASAS (KASTROM MEFA´A)

Most of this archaeological site east of the Dead Sea has not even been excavated yet, but what has been unearthed stems from the Roman, Byzantine and early Islamic eras.

Originally a Roman military camp, Um er-Rasas developed into a town in the fifth century, and a majority of the religious buildings also date from this era. Worthy of particular mention are the mosaics in a basilica dedicated to the martyr St Stephan. According to an inscription, they date from the year 756, by which time the Umayyads had already introduced Islam to the region. The mosaics are framed by a topographic outline of the region, including Madaba and Amman to the north. These illustrations are thought to demonstrate that this part of Jor-

dan was originally Christian territory. Two distinctive square towers are rare evidence of the Stylites, or Pillar Saints, an ascetic tradition that was widespread in Syria during the fifth century in particular. They were monks who spent their lives atop a tower or pillar as a sign of particular dedication. The remains of earlier agricultural activities can be found in the area surrounding the ruined city of Um er-Rasas.

Um er-Rasas was originally the base for a mounted Roman regiment.

PETRA – ROCK NECROPOLISES AND RUINS

Archaeologically speaking, the most important legacy of the Nabateans, a Semitic people that was eventually immersed into the Greco-Roman realm, is situated half way between the Gulf of Aqaba and the Dead Sea, hidden within the Jebel Harun Mountain. Petra, or "rock", was the name given to this necropolis by Greek historians.

In 169 BC, the Nabateans selected a location perfectly protected by nature for their capital: the rocky valley floor of the Wadi Musa, an almost inaccessible spot behind Siq Canyon that is narrow but 200 m (656 ft) deep. Petra's most impressive constructions are its gigantic tombs hewn into the rock. They have elaborate façades with mighty pillars, cornices and gables that reveal an intriguing interplay between traditional Arabian construction and

Beneath the Obelisk Tomb – so named for the four pyramid-shaped obelisks decorating its façade – is a Triclinium, a formal dining room where the funeral feast was held after the burial.

Hellenistic architecture. The heavily decorated tombs with melodic names such as the "Pharaoh's Treasury" indicate that the Nabateans believed in life after death.

Petra was occupied by the Romans in the year 106, and became a Roman Municipium in the third century. By the fourth century it was made into a diocesan town as capital of the province of Palaestina Tertia. As a result, the old city center still features a paved Roman road and a triumphal arch. With the relocation of the trade routes under the Sassanids, Petra fell into obscurity and was only rediscovered in 1812 by Swiss orientalist and traveller Johann Ludwig Burckhardt.

Petra's most impressive monument is the Hellenistic-style "Pharaoh's Treasury" (Khazne al-Firaun). Contrary to what its name indicates, however, it was actually used as a tomb.

Yemen

OLD CITY OF SANA'A

The tall clay residential towers with elaborately ornamented façades are what characterize the Old City of Sana'a, capital of Yemen and once one of the loveliest locations along the Incense Route.

This World Heritage city dates back to a Sabaean fortress and began its rise to prosperity in 520 under Himyarite rule. Yemen converted to Islam in 628 – and the Prophet Mohammed is said to have personally commissioned the construction of the first mosque in Sana'a.

While the Great Mosque from the seventh century is indeed impressive, the Old City is undisputedly of even greater historical significance. It features a cluster of high-rise buildings that are up to 1,000 years old, some of them with up to eight floors. The lower floors are built using traditional stone construction, while the upper floors are of unbaked mud brick. These towered buildings have unique façades that are often decorated with elaborate ornamental elements. These are in turn highlighted with white paint and adorned with horizontal stucco friezes extending for the height of the upper floors.

The most common form of building decoration in the Old City of Sana'a consists of semi-circular skylights with floral or geometric stucco borders and filled with glass of different hues.

The Old City of Sana'a in Yemen boasts a unique form of architecture.

OLD WALLED CITY OF SHIBAM

The impressive tower buildings in the almost untouched historic center of the desert city of Shibam in the Hadramaut region are built from air-dried bricks and rammed clay.

The age of this city on its raised rocky plateau is a matter of dispute among experts in the field. A settlement was founded in the third century here by the residents of the city of Shabwa – around 150 km (93 mi) east of Shibam, it was at one point the ancient capital of Hadramaut before being plundered and destroyed by foreigners and never rebuilt.

The 500 ancient townhouses in Shibam's Old City, some of them several hundred years old, reach heights of almost 30 m (98 ft). The Old City is enclosed by a high wall forming a large rectangle measuring 400 by 500 m (438 by 470 yds). The upper façade section of the closely clustered clay brick buildings features traditional white paintwork that requires regular attention. Binding agents such as powdered alabaster are mixed with paint to prevent deterioration but the clay brick upper floors still need to be renovated every ten years.

Shibam in the Wadi Hadramaut is often called the "Chicago of the Desert". Its traditional towered buildings can reach up to nine floors.

HISTORIC TOWN OF ZABID

Zabid, the capital of Yemen in the Middle Ages, lies in the Tihama, one of the hottest desert areas on earth. For centuries the historic town of Zabid was the intellectual hub of the Arab and Muslim world.

A unique style of desert architecture developed over centuries in the lowlands of Yemen along the Red Sea coast. The style can be seen at just about every turn in the historic Old Town of Zabid, which was once protected by a mighty wall and a citadel. The houses consist of a rectangular room known as a murabba, which opens out onto an inner courtyard, but the so-called Tihama style is most evident here in the form of richly ornamented, brightly painted stucco elements adorning the façades and the doorframes like a precious wall hanging. Zabid's intellectual hub is the Medina with numerous Koran schools grouped around the Iskandariyah Mosque. The town's other important religious buildings are the Asair and the Great Mosques.

The architecture with its simple, clear lines is also a reference to the Shafi'i teaching, the most important Islamic religious law in the Tihama.

With nearly 100 mosques, the Bab al-Nasr citadel (above) and its numerous richly-decorated buildings, Zabid was the perfect backdrop for the filming of Pier Paolo Pasolini's film classic "Arabian Nights" in 1974.

SOCOTRA ARCHIPELAGO

The 250-km (155-mi) long Socotra Archipelago lies just off the Horn of Africa and has four main islands: Socotra, Abd al-Kuri, Samha and Darsa. The islands' importance lies in their great biodiversity.

The abundance of ingredients essential for making incense such as myrrh and aloe, combined with its strategic location at the mouth of the Gulf of Aden, has made Socotra a destination for seafarers since the time of the Egyptian pharaohs. Still, the islands remained largely unknown to Europeans into the late 19th century, and scientific study on Socotra only began when Yemen opened up politically in the 1990s.

Socotra, the main island in the archipelago, covers an area of 3,626 sq km (1,400 sq mi) and rises to 1,503 m (4,931 ft) above sea level. Geologically, it is a continuation of the Horn of Africa, but since there has been no land connection for about fifteen million years, its isolated location has made it possible for unique plant and animal life to develop. There are no mammals here at all, and 90 per cent of the reptiles are native. The vegetation is also varied, and the world beneath the waves is also extremely diverse.

Dracaena cinnabari (above), the dragon tree, is native to Socotra and exudes a natural resin once known as "dragon's blood". It was used as an ingredient in incense, natural remedies, embalming mixtures and varnishes.

ARCHAEOLOGICAL SITES OF BAT, AL-KHUTM AND AL-AYN

Together with the Al-Khutm archaeological site and the Al-Ayn necropolis, the fortress of Bat is the most impressive testimony in Oman of a Bronze-Age settlement and the Neolithic cult of the dead.

The historic site of Bat lies in the interior of the Sultanate of Oman close to the oasis of the same name. What survive are the remains of four towers and an ancient settlement. At the foot of the steep cliffs of the western Hajar Mountains are honeycomb-like tombs of layered stone walls. This type of burial architecture was widespread during the Hafit period (3500–2700 BC). These so-called "honeycomb graves" can also be found in Wadi Al-Ayn at the foot of the Jebel Misht and in the eastern Hadar Mountains. The number of buildings and tombs indicates that this region was already densely populated in the third millennium BC, with links to the copper trade routes with Mesopotamia. Bat and the surrounding settlements were abandoned towards the end of the third millennium BC, however, for reasons that remain unknown to this day.

The "honeycomb graves" of this World Heritage Site are around 4 m (13 ft) high and have a diameter of about 8 m (26 ft). They are made of brown limestone that breaks into brick-like blocks when hammered.

AFLAJ IRRIGATION SYSTEMS OF OMAN

This World Heritage Site comprises five canals that are remnants of an expansive irrigation system built thousands of years ago. It even features underground portions and is still in use today.

The Aflaj irrigation system comprises a single "falaj", or "distributor": they distribute the precious water required for humans to live year-round in the region's desert towns. It is used as drinking water as well as for agriculture and livestock breeding.
The Falaj oases feed off groundwater stored in the beds of the stone that fill vast areas north and south of the Oman Mountains. The groundwater, which lies relatively close to the surface at the foot of the mountains, is then brought to the surface by means of long tunnels. In the oasis the water reaches the distribution channels – its location secured by a round, brick watchtower – and is directed further from here above ground. The person responsible for the water supply opens and closes the channels according to the specific applications. Irrigation is carried out in a seven- or ten-day rhythm.

The Aflaj irrigation system in the Sultanate of Oman is thought to be more than 2,500 years old. There are some 3,000 channels still in use today.

BAHLA FORT

This massive fort about 200 km (124 mi) south of Oman's capital, Muscat, is considered a classic example of Oman's clay architecture. The huge complex comprises no less than fifteen gates and 132 defensive towers.

Bahla oasis lies surrounded by a fortified clay brick wall that is 12 km (7 mi) long and 5 m (16 ft) high. The settlement sits at the foot of the mighty Jebel Achdar mountain, which rises to 3,100 m (10,171 ft). With its high towers built of unbaked brick and straw, the fortress oasis of Hisn Tamah is considered a masterpiece of clay architecture. Its commanding position above the Wadi has meant that the location has always been of strategic importance.
Bahla hill had been fortified even in pre-Islamic times, but the present fort dates back to the 17th century and is said to have been built by the Nabhani people who had already made Bahla the capital of Oman back in the 15th century. The clay fort had been put on the red list of World Heritage Sites in Danger between 1988 and 2004 because it was feared that the construction's original character could be compromised by unprofessional restoration methods. Ultimately, it was an international team of specialists that managed to complete the professional renovation of the fort.

The fort has been almost completely renovated at this point. Traditional techniques have been used rather than modern methods.

LAND OF FRANKINCENSE

The frankincense trees of Wadi Dawkah, Shisr oasis and the ports of Khor Rori and Al-Balid in the province of Dhofar in southern Oman were the site of the flourishing frankincense trade from ancient times through to the early Middle Ages.

Incense was one of the most expensive commodities in antiquity and, up until the first century BC, the exclusive product was transported to the Mediterranean and Mesopotamia via caravans. The trade route was lined with prosperous towns, some of which have since disappeared.
It was only at the beginning of the 1990s that satellite images enabled the discovery of the ruins of an ancient city on the edge of the Rub' al-Khali desert, also known as the "Empty Quarter". The remains of buildings very close to the present-day oasis town of Shisr were also discovered, providing evidence of the fact that this had once been a commercial centre. When the incense trade shifted to the seas in the second century, the Yemeni Hadhramaut Kingdom established the important port of Samaramm on the Khor Rori lagoon close to Taqah. In the Middle Ages, however, this incense port was surpassed by the city of Al-Balid as the commercial hub. The ruined city of Al-Balid is thought to be the port of Zhafar described by those journeying to Arabia.

Frankincense is the dried resin of the frankincense tree (Boswellia serrata).

QAL'AT AL-BAHRAIN – ANCIENT HARBOUR AND CAPITAL OF DILMUN

The origins of what is now Bahrain are still a mystery but we do know that the northern tip of the island was continuously inhabited between 2300 BC and the 16th century AD. Over time, the sedimentary layers around these settlements have reached depths of nearly 12 m (39 ft).

The oldest remains here, one quarter of which has been excavated, was a center of the Dilmun civilization. "Dilmun" is the Sumerian word for "paradise" and is used to refer to a Bronze Age empire that included Bahrain and parts of the Arabian mainland. In fact, ancient Qal'at al-Bahrain was the most important trading hub between Mesopotamia and the Indus Valley. The remains of houses near the sea are from this era, as is the wall that was expanded in around 1450 BC using surprisingly durable mortar, which explains the settlement's good state of preservation. The wall seems to have fallen into disuse by around 500 BC with some of the houses having been built on its remains.

Bahrain was a flourishing trading town for millennia. The imposing fortress built by the Portuguese was placed on the ruins of earlier settlements.

AL-HIJR ARCHAEOLOGICAL SITE (MADÂIN SÂLIH)

The stone city of Al-Hijr (Madâin Sâlih) is Saudi Arabia's first World Heritage Site. Along with Petra in Jordan, the city previously known as Hegra is one of the best-preserved legacies of the Nabatean civilization.

The Nabateans, originally a nomadic trading people, are thought to have settled in the north-western part of the Arabian Peninsula back in the fourth century BC. In the year 106 AD the kingdom became the Roman province of Arabia Petraea and Madâin Sâlih (in Arabic: Al-Hijr), a former trading post around 350 km (217 mi) north of Medina, developed into a magnificent city during the first century. Unlike those in Petra, many of the monumental tombs in Madâin Sâlih bear inscriptions that are important testimonies to the everyday life and civiliza- tion of a people about whom very little is actually known. The sanctuary of Jabal Ithlib north of the city has also survived: a bizarre rock formation, the walls of which are decorated with drawings and inscriptions. There are also reservoirs that showcase Nabatean hydro-engineering prowess – they had developed irrigation systems to enable farming in the desert.

The monumental stone tombs in the hot desert of Saudi Arabia attest to sophistication of the Nabatean civili- zation (right and above).

HATRA – RUINS OF A PARTHIAN CITY

This well-fortified city dating from the Parthian Empire is around 100 km (62 mi) south-west of Mosul in present-day Iraq. Despite many an effort, it was even able to fend off Roman attempts at conquest.

Founded in the fifth century BC on an important Mesopotamian caravan route, it was only in the third century AD under the Parthians that Hatra managed to attain a recognizable level of prosperity as a trading city and religious center. The Parthians, for their part, intentionally preserved the cultural legacy of the great empires in the Middle East and even initiated a renaissance of Persian culture.

This revival of Persian tradition can be seen in architectural forms such as the iwan, a vaulted niche form that features in the Great Temple of Hatra,

for example. Excavations within the ring-shaped city walls have also un-earthed numerous Parthian-style carv-ings and statues. They depict religious themes, deities, rulers and dignitaries and testify to the sophisticated skills of Parthian stonemasons. The city of Hatra was conquered and destroyed in around 240 by the Sassanids, also Persians, probably under the rule of King Ardashir I.

The Great Temple of Hatra was home to a number of fine statues.

ASHUR (QAL'AT SHERQAT)

Founded in the third millennium BC in northern present-day Iraq, Ashur was once the capital of the mighty Assyrian Empire. The city's development can be traced in the remains of the buildings that have survived from that time.

Situated on the right bank of the Tigris River, Ashur was long overshadowed by the Assyrian cities of Nimrud and Nineveh, where excavations in the 19th century unearthed sensational monumental works of art. It was only between 1903 and 1914 that German archaeologist Walter Andrae began excavating the city of Ashur on the ruins of Qal'at Sherqat. There are still thousands of smaller finds and texts from these initial excavations await-ing expert attention.

It is possible that Ashur was founded by the Ancient Sumerians in around 2,700 BC. Roughly one thousand years later, trade brought prosperity

to the city along with national impor-tance. In 614 BC, however, it was laid waste by the Medes and Babylonians. The city was then resettled in the first century BC as a Parthian administra-tive center. During this time an agora with public buildings was built in the north, while a palace and a sanctuary dedicated to the god Ashur were built in the south. This renewed prosperity under the Parthians lasted less than two centuries, however, as Ashur was destroyed once again by Sassanid ruler Schapur I (r. 241–272).

This cuneiform monument dates from the ninth century BC.

SAMARRA ARCHAEOLOGICAL CITY

The provinces of the Abbasid Empire that extended from Tunisia to Central Asia were ruled from the city of Samarra in the ninth century. Around eighty percent of the city has yet to be excavated.

The city of Samarra was founded north of Baghdad by the Abbasid caliph Al-Mu'tasim Billah some time after 834 AD. The imperial city built of baked brick and mud brick had no fortifying walls because it was pro-tected on all sides by either the Tigris River or by canals.

The largest mosque from this era, however, was built here in the ninth century with fortified walls and semi-circular towers set at regular intervals. The 52-m-high (177-ft) minaret still stands and is often referred to as "malwiya", or snail, due to its spiral

staircase that can be ascended with a donkey. A short staircase at the very top once led to a wooden pavilion. The minaret was modeled on ancient architectural designs including the ziggurat. The Abu Dulaf Mosque is situated in the north of the city and the caliph's palace on the main street above the Tigris River is the only sur-viving palace from this era.

The 52-m (171-ft) spiral minaret was built using clay bricks. Caliph Al-Mutawakkil built the unusual spiral tower between 849 and 851.

Iran

ARMENIAN MONASTIC ENSEMBLES OF IRAN

Of the impressive complexes in the former Armenian province of Vaspurakan, three important monasteries survive on Iranian soil: St Thaddeus near Maku, St Stepanos, and the Chapel of Dzordzor. They are among the oldest Christian monasteries in the world.

Christianity became the official state religion in Armenia after the baptism of King Tiridates III in 301, hence the country's claim to being the first Christian nation in the world. As testimony to this commitment, there are three monasteries in Iranian Azerbaijan close to the borders with Turkey and Armenia.

The oldest one, St Thaddeus, dates from the seventh century. Construction of St Stepanos monastery on the banks of the Araxes River began in the ninth century. It is unclear when the Chapel of Dzordzor, not far from St Thaddeus, was built, but it was destroyed in the 17th century and under threat by a dam construction project in 1988. The Armenian church and the Iranian historical monuments authority managed to obtain a last-minute postponement, however, enabling the church to be relocated and rebuilt 600 meters away, complete with its characteristic pleated roof.

The St Thaddeus monastery is one of the oldest legacies of Armenian culture.

TAKHT-E SOLEYMAN

This World Heritage Site lies to the south-west of Lake Urmia in north-western Iran. It includes a Zoroastrian sanctuary from the Sassanids and an Islamic-era hunting palace.

Takht-e Soleyman, or the "Throne of Solomon", lies in a mountain volcanic region in the Iranian province of West Azerbaijan, a valley with natural hot springs that are rich in minerals. The site also includes a small lake that reaches depths of up to 120 m (394 ft) and which was formed by an artesian well.

The Sassanids built a Zoroastrian sanctuary on the northern shore of the lake in the sixth and seventh centuries that include a temple complex, courtyards, columned halls, archive rooms, treasuries and a number of options for accommodation. Zoroastrianism, an ancient oriental monotheistic religion, teaches the ongoing battle between the principles of good and evil, light and darkness.

South of the sanctuary are the as yet unexcavated remains of a hunting palace from the Mongolian dynasty of the Ilkhanids dating back to the 13th and 14th centuries.

The fortified wall of quarried stone around the Sassanid Zoroastrian sanctuary originally featured two gates and towered bastions.

SOLTANIYEH

Soltaniyeh, around 250 km (155 mi) north of Teheran, was the capital of the Mongolian Ilkhanid khanate in the 13th and 14th centuries. The grand mausoleum of the Ilkhanid ruler Öljeitü is one of the key architectural works of the Mongolian period.

The tenets of Islam actually forbid the construction of extravagant burial sites, but the Mongolian period in Iran saw the development of a certain type of building that would become a model for later burial monuments. The style was later reflected in India's Taj Mahal, built by Persian architects.

Legend has it that the Mongolian ruler Öljeitü originally had the mausoleum built to house the remains of Caliph Ali and his son Hussein, both of whom he wanted to bring to Soltaniyeh from Baghdad. His plan never came to fruition, however, and the subordinate khan, who was subject to the khanate of China at the time, transformed the construction into his own tomb.

The octagonal foundation of the mausoleum, built from 1302 to 1312, supports one of the oldest double-shelled domes in the Islamic world with a diameter of about 25 m (83 ft). The exterior is decorated with bright ceramic tiles while the dome has no stays at all and is an impressive 50 m (164 ft) high. It is surrounded by eight slender minarets.

The 50 m-high (164-ft), double-shelled dome of the mausoleum features stucco decoration and elaborate ornamentation.

BISOTUN

Persian King Darius I created an impressive monument to himself in the sixth century BC: the monumental bas-relief of Bisotun, carved directly into a rock face on the trading route between the Iranian high plateau and Mesopotamia, in the present-day province of Kermanshah.

This stunning bas-relief depicts King Darius I (550–486 BC) looking to the right, an image commissioned by the king himself after ascending to the Persian throne in 521 BC. He is wearing traditional Persian garb, a bracelet and a ruler's diadem. In his left hand he is holding a bow as a sign of the sovereignty of his kingdom. With his left foot he is treading on the chest of a figure lying at his feet.

Legend has it that this figure is Gaumata, the Median Magus and pretender to the throne whose murder created the opening for Darius's meteoric rise to power. To the right is a group of rebels with their hands bound and ropes around their necks.

An inscription on the wall tells the sequence of Darius' victorious battles between 521 and 520 BC, the most decisive of which took place in Bisotun itself. The decryption of the writing, which was done in Elamite, New Babylonian and Ancient Persian languages, is one of the most important historical endeavors undertaken by Iranian scholars.

The bas-relief of Bisotun was carved into the vast rock face at a height of about 100 m (328 ft).

MEIDAN EMAM, ESFAHAN

Isfahan is about 350 km (217 mi) south of Teheran on the edge of the Zagros Mountains. It developed into an ensemble of Islamic architecture and a center of scholarship in the 16th and 17th centuries under the Safavid Shah Abbas I. The outstanding architectural ensemble here includes the former royal square and is lined with a series of impressive buildings.

Shah Abbas I (r. 1587–1629) was a ruler who was very much focused on construction projects and who had his residence redesigned on a relatively regular basis. As a result of his enthusiasm for architecture and the arts, Isfahan developed into one of the most important cities of culture in what is now the Middle East and South Asia.

His most important building project was the gigantic Naqsch-e Jahan (Plan

The four 27 m-(89 ft)-high entrance portals to the Imam Mosque are magnificent in appearance.

of the World) square, later renamed the Meidan-e Shah (King's Square) and known as Meidan-e Imam since the Iranian Revolution in 1979. Surrounded by two-story arcades, each side around 500 m (547 yds) long, it is one of the world's largest and most impressive plazas. It is framed by four imposing building complexes: in the south the former Royal Mosque now known as the Imam Mosque; in the east the Sheykh Lotfollah Mosque; in the west the royal Ali Kapu Palace ("High Gates"), and in the north the magnificent Portico of Qaysariyyeh. The most important building is the Imam Mosque with its traditional Iranian four-iwan design.

The Ali Kapu Palace (1598) forms the entrance to the royal residence (top left). The Lotfollah Mosque on the royal square was the royal family's private mosque, which is why the minarets and the courtyard are absent (left).

RUINS OF TCHOGHA ZANBIL

The massive 13th-century step pyramid in the south-west Iranian province of Chuzestan was once the center of a holy site and is considered one of the most magnificent buildings of Elam religious architecture.

The Tchogha Zanbil step tower dates from what is considered the golden age of the Elamite Empire, which took place during the rule of King Untash-Napirisha from 1275 to 1240 BC. The king had his own residential complex built close to the capital Susa, the focal point of which was a magnificent ziggurat (a Babylonian term for the stepped temple towers of Mesopotamian and Elam architecture that form the basis of the Biblical tale of the Tower of Babylon).

This particular ziggurat is surrounded by three concentric walls and has five levels built of unbaked clay bricks. It was originally 52 m (171 ft) in height but has been reduced to 25 m (82 ft) by time and history. It is thought to have initially been clad with glazed bricks while the upper levels featured studded bricks (clay studs).

The tower's platform, which could be ascended during ceremonies, presumably, once featured a sanctuary that was dedicated to the primary Elamite gods. Surrounding the giant ziggurat was a holy site with temples. The city itself was actually outside of the wall surrounding the holy site.

A circular altar stands in front of the south-west entrance to the ziggurat.

SHUSHTAR HISTORICAL HYDRAULIC SYSTEM

The hydraulic engineering systems of the city of Shushtar in the south-west of present-day Iran are thousands of years old and were considered a wonder of the world even at the height of Persian influence.

The origins of the Shushtar hydro-engineering systems in the province of Khuzestan date from the fifth century BC. The project, executed during the reign of the Sassanids, involved diverting the Karun River into canals around Shushtar, effectively surrounding the city with waterways. A subterranean network of canals then supplied the population and the fields with water. Numerous mills were also built and in the centuries that followed, the water management trend, which also served the purposes of land reclamation, was expanded by means of carefully planned bridges, artificial waterfalls and dams.

The historic hydraulic system naturally contributed to Shushtar's development into a prosperous agricultural center, despite its arid location. The city's irrigation system is also an important testimony to diverse historic influences left behind by the Romans, the Elamites, Mesopotamians and the Safavids.

Parts of the hydraulic system have been in continuous use since before the birth of Christ and are still fully intact to this day.

PERSEPOLIS

The construction of this royal residence on an artificial terrace in what is now south-western Iran was commissioned by the Achaemenid King Darius I. It features gatehouses, palaces, treasuries, a throne room and a reception hall.

King Darius I, the most important of the Achaemenid rulers, laid the foundation stone for this magnificent residence in 520 BC. Although he already had two capital cities at the time, Pasargadae and Susa, he still felt compelled to present the world with a palace reflecting the magnitude of his impressive empire. The most outstanding work of Persian-Achaemenid art was thus built here on an artificial terrace covering roughly 125,000 sq m (1,345,000 sq ft). The construction of the complex took almost sixty years. Darius I only lived to see the completion of the palace, the treasury, and the reception hall and the Apadana, which features thirty-six pillars nearly 20 m (66 ft) high as well as wonderful carvings. Darius' son Xerxes continued with his father's ambitious plans but he himself did not live to see the completion of the monumental Hall of One Hundred Columns. This was completed by the grandson, Artaxerxes.

"Darius's Dream" was ultimately reduced to ashes by Alexander the Great in 330 BC. The last Shah of Iran, Reza Pahlavi, then had parts of the city rebuilt in 1971.

Built by Xerxes I, the main entrance to the royal residence of Persepolis was known as the "Gate of all Nations".

PASARGADAE

Pasargadae, north-east of Shiraz in the present-day province of Pars, was the first royal capital of the Achaemenid Empire.

Cyrus the Great, founder of the ancient Persian Empire under the Achaemenid dynasty, and his successor King Cambyses II had Pasargadae built between 559 and 525 BC as the empire's first capital. The glamorous royal city was built on the Morghab Plain, the place where Cyrus defeated the Mede King Astyages in a decisive battle in 550 BC.

The ruined city of Pasargadae with its monumental gates, palaces, gardens and Cyrus II's mausoleum is generally considered one of the most remarkable examples of Achaemenid art and architecture. The holy area contains the remains of the fire temple with its altars as well as the king's tomb, a quadratic construction with a gabled roof all resting on a base of six steps. The palace complex features the oldest example of a Persian "paradeisos", or paradise garden. The walled area used to contain artificial watercourses, lakes and other small palaces. The glorious era of Pasargadae was cut short, however, when Darius moved the capital of his empire to Persepolis in 520 BC.

King Cyrus himself commissioned the building of his tomb (left), but it was only completed under his son Cambyses. Only the columns from the southern section of the magnificent reception hall have survived (below).

BAM AND ITS CULTURAL LANDSCAPE

The city of Bam was founded during the Achaemenid era between the sixth and fourth centuries BC around an oasis on the edge of the Lut Desert. Arab peoples then occupied it in 642 and built the Hazrat-e-Rasul Mosque in 650. The mighty, and reputedly impregnable citadel, was built in the 10th century.

Bam benefited from its fortuitous location at the crossroads of trans-Asian trade routes. Even cotton was grown in this semi-arid region, and the textiles produced here were of renowned quality. The walled heart of the city, including the citadel, is the area now referred to as Old Bam, in Persian Arg-e Bam. Due to foreign invasions, the area has been completely abandoned on several occasions throughout its history.

The World Heritage Site encompasses the historic city with the citadel, which covers 500 sq m (5,380 sq ft) and towers 200 m (656 ft) above the city. Four mighty gates originally provided access through the thick walls to the interior of the fort, which once had bazaars, mosques, a caravanserai, palatial living quarters and administrative offices. Located in an oasis, Bam was once surrounded by date palms and fruit trees.

Old Bam was reduced to rubble by an earthquake in 2003 (photo before the quake). The historic part is being rebuilt.

Kazakhstan

SARYARKA: STEPPE AND LAKES OF NORTHERN KAZAKHSTAN

This World Heritage Site includes the nature reserves of Naurzum and Korgalzhyn as well as a large area of Central Asia steppe. The wetlands in the reserves are of great significance for many migratory birds while the steppe is home to many rare species of bird as well as the endangered saiga antelope.

The Kazakh Uplands (Saryarka) are in eastern and central Kazakhstan, mostly at elevations of 300 to 500 m (990 to 1,640 ft), although the land can rise to about 1,000 m (3,280 ft) in the east. The landscape to the north is characterized by a grassy steppe while rocky, semi-arid desert is typical of the south.

The wetlands of Naurzum and Korgalzhyn are important stopovers for migratory birds traveling from Africa, Europe and South Asia to their breeding grounds in Western and Eastern Siberia. Many of these birds are endangered or at least very rare. The seasonal hydrological, chemical, and biological processes in the wetlands, brought about when conditions alternate between wet and dry, are of great interest to scientists as well. The steppe areas of the World Heritage Site are home to more than half of the country's native plants as well as the rare saiga antelope.

Blooming flowers create a colorful landscape on the Saryarka steppe.

MAUSOLEUM OF KHOJA AHMED YASAWI

The Mausoleum of Khoja Ahmed Yasawi in Turkestan, Kazakhstan, was built under the rule of the Mongolian Emir Timur (Tamerlane). The mausoleum is one of the best-preserved buildings from this era.

Khoja Ahmed Yasawi was an influential Sufi teacher in the 12th century. As a Muslim mystic he naturally also integrated pre-Islamic shamanist notions into his teachings. These would later form the basis of the religion practiced by the Turkish dervishes (of whirling dervish fame). Yasawi spent the greater part of his life in the town of Turkestan, known as Yasi at that time; hence the teacher's epithet Yasawi, meaning "he from Yasi". He died in the mid-12th century and a small tomb built in his honor soon became popular with pilgrims.

More than 150 years later, however, Timur ordered the building of a much larger mausoleum. Famous Persian master builders then came to experiment with new architectural forms later used in Samarkand, the capital of the Timurid empire. Yasawi's mausoleum is about 60 m (196 ft) in length and 50 m (170 ft) wide. It features the largest intact, historic dome in Central Asia.

The entrance to the mausoleum is decorated with colorful mosaics with wonderful geometric patterns.

PETROGLYPHS WITHIN THE ARCHAEOLOGICAL LANDSCAPE OF TAMGALY

There are several thousand rock carvings as well as the remains of related human settlements and burial sites near Tamgaly, Kazakhstan.

More than 5,000 rock carvings, also known as petroglyphs, were found near Tamgaly on the banks of the Ili River in the northern Tien Shan Mountains. The majority of the petroglyphs are prehistoric, the oldest thought to date from the second half of the second millennium BC.

The carvings are spread out across forty-eight complexes that include settlements and burial sites. They bear witness to the domestication of animals, social organization and rituals of these prehistoric pastoral peoples.

Many of the carvings depict deer and hunters but also include images of a god, though it is unclear whether this is Buddha or Shiva. The motif extends back at least as far as the eighth century when Chinese influence in Central Asia began its decline. The remains of settlements in this region comprise several layers and also show signs of foreign occupation.

The petroglyphs are found on rocks and stones within a radius of around 10 km (6 mi) of Tamgaly.

ITCHAN KALA

With its alleyways, mausoleums, mosques, minarets and madrassahs, the well-preserved Itchan Kala Old Town of Khiva in Uzbekistan feels like the setting for the Arabian Nights.

The Old Town of Khiva, known as Itchan Kala, in the province of Khorezm in western Uzbekistan near the border with Turkmenistan, was once the last caravan stop before the desert crossing that led to Iran. It is a classic example of the Islamic architecture of Central Asia.

Generally characterized by a pale, sandy shade of ochre, the Old Town is interspersed with brightly decorated ceramic domes and minarets. The incomplete Kalta Minor minaret in front of the Amin Khan Madrassah looks stunted at 28 m (92 ft), having originally been planned as a 70-m (230-ft) structure, but it features extravagant

decoration, as does the minaret of the Islam Hodsha Madrasa. The Old Town section, 400 m (1,300 ft) wide and 720 m (2,375 ft) long, feels like an open-air museum and is enclosed by a clay wall featuring bastions and imposing gates.

Adjoining the wall is the fort from the 17th century and the former ruler's residence Kunja Ark. Alla-Kuli Khan had a new palace, the Tash Hauli, built at the other end of the town at the beginning of the 19th century.

Decorated with attractive tiles, the Kalta Minor minaret in front of the Amin Khan Madrassah is still unfinished.

HISTORIC CENTER OF SHAKHRISYABZ

Along with Samarkand, Mongolian ruler Timur (Tamerlane in English) was also responsible for the rise of Shakhrisyabz, one of the oldest cities in Central Asia and his former royal seat.

This city around 80 km (50 mi) south of Samarkand at the foot of the Zarafshan Mountains owes its Persian name Shakhrisyabz ("green city") to its lush gardens. Its long history goes back to the time of Alexander the Great, but Shakhrisyabz reached the height of its fame in the 14th and 15th centuries as the royal seat of the ruler Timur, who was born here. Its glory ultimately faded with the decline of the Timurid Empire in the late 15th century.

Extensive complexes were built in Shakhrisyabz until the rule of Timur's

scholarly grandson and astronomer Ulugh Beg. The royal residence was protected by a wall 4 km (2.5 mi) long while two axial roads defined the town's uniform layout. Timur's expansive Ak-Sarai, or "White Palace", survives as a ruin only. To the east of it is the mausoleum for Timur's son Jahangir, which is quite well preserved. The Kok Gumbaz Mosque was built under the rule of Ulugh Beg, as was the Gumbad-i Sayyidan Mausoleum.

The Kok Gumbaz Mosque with its restored portal was built in 1436.

HISTORIC CENTER OF BUKHARA

Situated at a large oasis in the Kisilkum Desert, Bukhara was once an important center on the Silk Route.

Bukhara enjoyed wealth and prosperity during the last centuries before the Christian Era due to its importance as a trading center along the Silk Route between China, India and Europe. In fact, the city experienced two golden ages: from the ninth to the 10th century under the Samanids, and in the 16th century when, in addition to many madrassahs and mosques, the characteristic domed market buildings were built.

The Ark, or citadel, towers at the edge of the historic Shakristan town center. This symbol of secular power has its religious counterpart on the west side of town: the Bala Haus Mosque. The mausoleum of Ismael Samani from the

10th century — a square building of baked clay with inlaid decorations — is one of the few constructions in Central Asia to survive Mongolian conquest. Bukhara's landmark is the 46-m (151-ft) Kalan minaret from the 12th century, from which criminals were once thrown do their deaths.

The Mir-i Arab Madrassah was finished in 1536. The Sheik is said to have financed the construction of this scholarly institution by selling members of the Shiite faith into slavery.

Uzbekistan

Timur (Tamerlane)

Timur (1336–1405) was preceded by his reputation for ferocity. Once he had captured a city, he did everything in his power to live up to that reputation as well. Following the conquest of Baghdad, for example, he is said to have had 90,000 decapitated heads stacked into a giant pyramid. Known as "Tamerlane" in Europe and

SAMARKAND – CROSSROADS OF CULTURES

The oasis city of Samarkand on the Silk Route is resplendent with masterpieces of Islamic art and culture.

First written mention of Samarkand dates back to the year 329 BC when Alexander the Great captured the city formerly known as Marakanda. Even at that time this oasis city in the Zarafshan River valley was a prosperous center of trade, handicrafts and culture. Once the Silk Route linked China with the Mediterranean, in the first century BC, Samarkand quickly became a cultural crossroads. The wealthy trading city was captured by the Chinese, Arabs, Samanids and Seljuks before finally being destroyed by Genghis Khan's troops in 1220.

The Tilla-Kari Madrassah, meaning "gold-decorated", was built in the 17th century. It served as a Koranic university and as the main mosque in Samarkand. Restoration of the prayer room was begun in 1970 and today the iwans, arches and dome are again resplendent.

In 1369, Mongolian ruler Timur made Samarkand his imperial capital. He commissioned the best artists, architects and scholars of the day with the construction of a magnificent city. His grandson Ulugh Beg, a skilled astronomer and ruler of the Timurid dynasty after 1447, continued Timur's work. The Registan, surrounded by three madrassahs, is one of the most splendid squares in Central Asia.

Registan square in Samarkand is surrounded by the magnificent Ulugh Beg, Tilla-Kari and Sher-Dor madrassahs (from left to right in the image).

in English, Timur conquered vast areas of Asia with his army mounted warriors – from Mongolia all the way to the Mediterranean. He came from a Turkic-Mongolian tribe and saw himself as the rightful successor to Genghis Khan, but he lacked the latter's political skill and enforced his Islamic faith with a more violent approach. In Syria, the Christians were either "converted" or killed. In India, he fought the existing Muslim rulers whom he felt to be too tolerant of other faiths.

Timur, whose epithet "the lame" referred to a physical disability, was born in Shakhrisyabz in present-day Uzbekistan. His capital was in the same area, Samarkand, an ancient trading center on the Silk Route. He and his successors hired the best master builders to construct unique edifices such as the Bibi-Khanum Mosque or the Gur Emir Mausoleum, which houses Timur's sarcophagus as well as the remains of his son, grandson, teachers and several ministers.

Timur ruled over what was at times a mighty empire extending from the Ganges to the Mediterranean. The image next to his portrait shows the palace-like Gur Emir Mausoleum with its melon-shaped, 34-m-high (112-ft) ribbed dome. Timur is buried in the building's crypt.

Turkmenistan

KUNYA URGENCH

The ruins of this city in northern Turkmenistan, close to the border with Uzbekistan, bear the signatures of Arab, Seljuk, Mongolian and Timurid cultures.

Kunya-Urgench was already an important trading center by the first century AD. Captured by the Arabs in 712, it then became the capital of the Khwarezmian Empire in 995, an empire that had achieved prosperity on the basis of sophisticated irrigation technologies. The Seljuks, a Muslim dynasty that was a target in the first crusade, come to conquer the empire in 1043. It was only after its liberation in 1194, however, that Khwarezm achieved its greatest expansion from the Caspian Sea to the Persian Gulf. The Mongolians under Genghis Khan destroyed the city in 1220 but Kunya-Urgench rose to become a major city again within just a few years.

The loveliest of the buildings that survived from this era include the Sufi dynasty's burial mosque, also known as the Turabek Khanum Mausoleum. It was built by one of the Uzbekistani khan's governors for his preferred wife. Timur conquered the Khwarezmian Empire over the course of five campaigns at the end of the 14th century, but Kunya-Urgench was destroyed again in the process and finally abandoned in the 17th century.

The eight-sided Turabek Khanum Mausoleum is the largest tomb in Kunya-Urgench. Its 20-m-high (66-ft) dome is decorated with unusually sophisticated geometric patterns.

STATE HISTORICAL AND CULTURAL PARK "ANCIENT MERV"

The oasis city of Merv in the Karakum Desert is Turkmenistan's most important cultural possession and once served as the capital of several empires. The city's ruins bear testimony to more than 4,000 years of history.

Merv, referred to in Ancient Persian texts as "Mouru" or "Margu", was the seat of the governor of the ancient Persian-Achaemenid Empire that rose to power in the fourth century BC on the territory previously ruled by Alexander the Great. Under Arab rule this trading city on the Silk Route was rebuilt as the capital of the Khorasan Empire in the seventh century and later went on to become the base for Islamic expansion into Central Asia and China. Under the Abbasid Caliphate (750–1258) Merv became an important center of learning and attracted philosophers from throughout the Islamic world.

The city then reached its height in the 12th century under the Seljuk Sultan Sanjar and his successors, who expanded Merv into a magnificent royal seat with fortifications. The rise was short-lived, however, as the Mongols captured and destroyed the city in 1221. The most remarkable building to survive the centuries is Sanjar's Mausoleum from the 12th century.

Only a few of the walls from the former Virgin Fortress Kis Kale are stall standing.

PARTHIAN FORTRESSES OF NISA

Between the third century BC and the third century AD, the Parthian kings ruled over an extensive realm that stretched from the Euphrates to the Indus. The excavations in Nisa, close to Ashgabat, bear testimony to this era.

Arsaces I (prior to 250 BC – 217 BC), ruler of the Parthian people, rebelled against the Seleucid governors in around 250 BC and gradually took control of the Persian Empire. His dynasty, the Arsacids, soon referred to themselves as Parthians. They adopted Persian traditions and merged with the Iranian people.

The fortresses of Nisa comprise Old Nisa, with the royal fortress, and New Nisa, where the majority of the population lived. Old Nisa covers a 14-ha (35-acre) area of ruins on top of a hill. It is surrounded by a fortified wall with more than forty towers and the central complex features five important buildings.

New Nisa also has a continuous wall reaching up to 9 m (29 ft) in height. There is evidence of several settlement phases here, and life in the forts continued after the fall of the Parthian Empire until such time as the Mongolians destroyed the city in 224.

Nisa, the former Parthian capital, is now a ruin on a hill that features the remains of a wall and buildings that were only discovered in the 1930s.

SULAIMAN-TOO SACRED MOUNTAIN

Sulaiman-Too is a series of peaks in the Central Asian highlands close to the Kyrgyzstan town of Osh, at the crossroads of important trading routes on the Silk Route. It has been considered holy by both Islamic and the pre-Islamic faiths. Kyrgyzstan's first World Heritage site, it features discoveries from the Stone and Bronze Ages as well as rock paintings, religious sites, historic roads and mosques.

This mountain on the Silk Route has been a pilgrimage site for more than 1,500 years. A visit to the "Throne of Solomon" (Sulaiman-Too) is said to help against infertility and pain as well as grant long life.

Archaeologists have found more than 100 prehistoric rock paintings here depicting people, animals and geometric figures. They are evidence that the mountain, known as Bara-Kuch (or "lovely mountain") until the 16th century, has been worshipped for thou-sands of years. The individual religious sites, seventeen of which are still in use, are linked via footpaths. The mountain is thought to have become a largely Muslim sanctuary during the 16th century when two mosques were built on Sulaiman-Too. Solomon, the King of the Israelites, is worshipped as a prophet by the Muslims.

A museum forming part of the World Heritage site displays religious artifacts found on the holy mountain.

MINARET AND ARCHAEO-LOGICAL REMAINS OF JAM

The Minaret of Jam in Ghur Province in western Afghanistan is an especially impressive example of the style of architecture and ornamentation typical of medieval Islam.

The narrow Hari Rud valley, west of Chaghcharan in the isolated mountain landscape of the Hindu Kush, is home to the second-highest minaret in the world: the 65-m (213-ft) Minaret of Jam. Built in 1194, it is a brick construction and elaborately decorated with ceramic tiles. It symbolizes the era of the Ghurids, who ruled the region in the 12th and 13th centuries and whose sphere of influence extended as far as the Indian subcontinent. The Minaret of Jam actually became the model for the renowned Qutb Minar in Delhi.

Jam was long forgotten after the decline of the Ghurid dynasty, before it was rediscovered by an archaeological expedition in 1957. The remains of a fortress, a palace, a Jewish cemetery, a bazaar and a protective wall in the area surrounding the minaret are of historical interest.

The exterior of the minaret is decorated with geometric patterns and inscriptions from the text of the 19th sura of the Koran, which tells the Islamic version of the birth of Jesus Christ.

CULTURAL LANDSCAPE AND ARCHAEOLOGICAL REMAINS OF THE BAMIYAN VALLEY

The Bamiyan Valley, around 200 km (124 mi) north-west of the Afghan capital of Kabul, owes its fame to a location on important trading routes.

Bamiyan, at the crossroads of trading and pilgrimage routes between China and the Mediterranean as well as between India and Central Asia, was where the Hellenistic civilization first encountered Buddhism, which had begun its development in India in the sixth and fifth centuries BC. When Kanishka, the king of the Kushans who ruled Bamiyan in the first century BC, converted to Buddhism he laid the foundation stone for Bamiyan to become a Buddhist center that would attract scholars and pilgrims.

Under his tutelage, some 900 caves were dug into the rocky cliffs of the Bamiyan Valley and decorated with religious frescoes and stuccowork. Two monumental statues of the Buddha were later carved here but their fate was a sad one. When the region came under the Islamic rule of the Taliban, it was decided in March 2001 that the statues would be completely destroyed using explosives.

The large empty space (left) once contained a giant statue of Buddha.

Pakistan

BUDDHIST RUINS OF TAKHT-I-BAHI AND NEIGHBORING CITY REMAINS AT SAHR-I-BAHLOL

Takht-i-Bahi was a prominent monastery in the Gandhara era that experienced its heyday from the first to the fourth century AD. The World Heritage Site also includes the ruins of Sahr-i-Bahlol, a smaller fort nearby.

One of the most important trading routes, on which the teachings of the Buddha also spread to the East, led through the Swat Valley in what is now northern Pakistan. The Takht-i-Bahi Monastery is perched on a mountaintop along this route, some 15 km (9 mi) north-west of Mardan. The center of these monasteries is the „vihara", a square or circular atrium. The hemispherical part of the stupa soars up from the middle, around which the monks lived in small cells.

Previous findings have shown that a settlement existed here in the first century BC, but its heyday began in the first century AD, when the region experienced a golden age of Buddhist influence. The oldest buildings date back to the seventh century and the complex was rediscovered in 1836 by the French General Court, which was serving a maharajah.

The monastery ruins provide a spectacular view over the Swat Valley.

ROHTAS FORT

Sher Shah Suri, also known as Sher Khan, the Lion King, had this fort built after his victory over the Mughal ruler, Humayun. The result is in one of the most impressive examples of early-Islamic military architecture.

Sher Shah Suri (ca. 1486–1545) was a powerful Pashtun ruler who founded the Suri Dynasty, which briefly interrupted Mughal domination in India. Though his empire only lasted eleven years after his death, the modernization programs that he introduced greatly influenced the northern part of the Indian subcontinent for many years to come.
Rohtas Fort was built as a military base between 1541 and 1547 at a strategically favorable location in the Punjab, in a region that is now northern Pakistan. The immense walls are more than 4 km (2.5 mi) long, and are topped with towers and bastions.

Of the twelve monumental gates, the Sohail Gate on the south-western side of the fort is particularly impressive in its design and dimensions. The external ramparts protect the palace complex as well as buildings used for military and civil purposes. The fort was never attacked, but Mughal rulers quickly took it over, resulting in the preservation of one of South Asia's most imposing military structures.

The walls and bastions of Rohtas Fort have been preserved virtually unchanged. The Sohail Gate (right) and the Kabul Gate are particularly striking elements of this defense complex.

TAXILA RUINS

The most famous archaeological site in what is now northern Pakistan covers several complexes dating back to the time between the fifth century BC and the second century AD. The most important among the ruins are Bhir Mound, Saraikala, Sirkap and Sirsukh.

Taxila, the former capital of the Gandhara Empire, was strategically positioned on an old military road that led from the west over the Khyber Pass to Calcutta. Ashoka the Great of the Mauryan dynasty began as the governor of Taxila before becoming ruler of the largest empire in ancient India in the year 268 BC. He is said to have converted to Buddhism at Bhir Mound, a move that ultimately resulted in the large-scale proselytization of India.
Sirkap dates back to the Greco-Bactrians, and Sirsukh was established by Kushan ruler Kadphises, a promi-

nent patron of Buddhism. The forms typical of Gandhara art emerged as a result of contact with Greek and northern Indian culture.

The Jaulian Buddhist monastery was built on a hill near Sirsukh. Though the main stupa has suffered over the centuries, the votive stupas surrounding it (right) impressively demonstrate the stylistic elements of the Gandhara culture, shaped by both Greek and Indian influences. Lotus blossoms alternate with ancient columns, and the drapery of the Buddha figures is reminiscent of ancient Greek statues.

FORT AND SHALAMAR GARDENS IN LAHORE

The metropolis of Lahore in north-eastern Pakistan is right on the border with India. It is home to two masterpieces of Mughal architecture.

According to common legend, Lahore was founded by Loh, a son of the mythical hero, Rama. The city first made history around the year 1000, when the Ghaznavid Sultan Mahmud built his capital here. After being attacked and destroyed by the great conqueror Timur (Tamerlane) in 1397, the Mughal emperors laid the foundations for Lahore's second heyday in the 16th century. Under Akbar the Great (r. 1556–1605), Lahore became one of Asia's most beautiful cities and the Mughal emperor transformed the existing fort into an extremely impressive symbol of imperial power.

The Shalamar Gardens are a superb example of horticulture during the Mughal era and date back to Shah Jahan (r. 1628-1658), who had them built in 1641. Home to grand cypress trees and poplars, the gardens stretch over three terraces and cover an area of 16 ha (39 acres).
They were placed on the UNESCO Red List in 2000 a road construction project led to the partial destruction of the nearly 400-year-old irrigation system and the surrounding walls.

Mughal Emperor Jahangir had the Alamgiri Gate built in 1618.

ARCHAEOLOGICAL RUINS AT MOENJODARO

Moenjodaro, south-west of Sukkur on the lower reaches of the Indus River, was once the center of the Indus culture. The archaeological ruins attest to one of the world's oldest advanced civilizations.

The Indus, or Harappa, culture was rediscovered only very late – in 1922 – but its links with the advanced civilizations of the Nile in Egypt and the Tigris-Euphrates Valley in Mesopotamia were immediately obvious. Trade with these cultures to the west had been active between the third and the second millennium BC, a fact proven by objects such as stamp seals, the likes of which were only found in Mesopotamia.
The excavations at Moenjodaro show that the Indus culture was very likely more egalitarian than aristocratic or

imperial. It is not dominated by grand palaces or monumental buildings dedicated to a ruler, but rather by residential homes of brick. Important public buildings such as the "Great Bath" or the "Granary" were built on an acropolis or citadel, and always in the western "lower town". Moenjodaro was a large settlement with an estimated 35,000 people and the excavated site covers an area of roughly 2.5 sq km (1 sq mi).

The ruins here provide an indication of the scope of the Indus civilization.

HISTORIC MONUMENTS AT MAKLI, THATTA

Along with Lahore, Thatta is Pakistan's most architecturally significant city. Some of the mausoleums here are highlights of Islamic stonemasonry.

The most magnificent mausoleums of the 15-sq-km (58-sq-mi) necropolis at Thatta, which was the capital of three dynasties in its time, were built under the Samma sultans and Tarkhan rulers. During their reigns, the region of the present-day Sindh province was of great political and economic importance in its own right until being forced to accept the rule of the Mughal emperors towards the end of the 16th century.
The Great Mosque was commissioned by Mughal Emperor Shah Jahan in 1644, for example, while the Samma mausoleums lie on the northern part

of the hill. Nizamuddin was one of the most prominent Samma sultans at the end of the 15th century. His tomb with decorative details is a jewel of Sindh architecture.
The Tarkhan gravesites were Islamic in style as well. The magnificent tomb of Mirza Jan Baba, who died in 1570, is a structure of yellow limestone with walls that are completely decorated with arabesques and vine motifs.

Inside the Great Mosque, small mosaics made of turquoise-colored tiles alternate with the clear lines of reddish bricks and white grouting.

India

NANDA DEVI AND VALLEY OF FLOWERS NATIONAL PARKS

The region around the 7,816-m (25,643-ft) Nanda Devi peak on the border of Nepal and China is an important sanctuary for endangered plants and animals.

These days virtually no part of the world is beyond the reach of mass tourism and, despite being almost inaccessible to humans, the environment around Nanda Devi, deep in the Himalayas, needs protection against the relentless encroachment of civilization. Established in 1980, this national park around India's second-highest peak is home to not only the seriously endangered snow leopard, wanted for its rare winter pelt, but also musk deer, and large herds of blue sheep (bharal) and goat antelope (goral).

The adjacent Valley of Flowers National Park is famous for its meadows and native species of wild flower, notably the Himalayan maple, the blue poppy and a type of saussurea. The multifaceted landscape here is also home to several rare animals such as the Asiatic black bear. Nature plays a role in Hindu mythology as well: Nanda Devi means "Goddess of Joy".

Nanda Devi National Park provides a haven for blue sheep (right) as well as the beautiful and rare snow leopard.

RED FORT COMPLEX

The Red Fort in Delhi, known by locals as "Lal Qil'ah", represents the zenith of the Mughal Empire's grand style of architecture.

Shah Jahan, the fifth Great Mughal of India, ruled from 1628 to 1658 and was a very enthusiastic commissioner of grandiose buildings. Between 1639 and 1648, he had a fortified palace built in Shahjahanabad, an area north of the earliest settlements of Delhi. It is located right next to the older Islamic Salimgarh Fort, built by the son of the great Pashtun ruler Sher Suri, Islam Shah Suri, in 1546. The buildings are collectively known as the Red Fort Complex.

The structure owes its name to the immense external walls made from red sandstone, which light up spectacularly at sunset. Inside, the complex houses magnificent palaces, large

halls for receiving audiences and hosting festivities, and the Pearl Mosque. For all its remaining splendor, however, only a vivid imagination can really do justice to the opulence this complex once possessed. Many precious stones, copper and jewels that once covered the walls have unfortunately gone missing over the centuries. The Fort was particularly badly plundered on two occasions: in 1739 by Persian troops, and in 1857 by British troops.

Vast halls with intricately decorated arches, columns and windows are typical of the buildings at the Red Fort.

HUMAYUN'S TOMB, DELHI

The emphasis on the central axis, the high arching dome and the Persian arches make Humayun's Tomb the first building of its kind in India. It quickly became a model for numerous Mughal edifices.

Nasir ud-din Muhammad Humayun (1508–1556), the second ruler of India's Great Mughal Empire and son of the dynasty's founder, Babur, was a trendsetter when it came to architecture and building projects. But his control over the empire (1530–1540, and 1555–56) was interrupted by the unexpected arrival of Sher Suri, a Pashtun (Afghan) conqueror who outmaneuvered Humayun while he was away on expedition. The young and very adventurous regent was forced to spend the next fifteen years in exile in Persia, but it was from there that he returned not only with an army of soldiers but also of master builders

and craftsmen who would ultimately change the course of Indian art and architectural history. The new inspiration they brought can be seen in the dome of Humayun's Tomb, which sits atop a high tambour, and the arches were replaced by architraves and corbels of Persian design. The façade of white marble and red sandstone also dates back to old Persian building traditions.

Humayun's Tomb was his wife's idea, Haji Begum. It was not until 1570 that the Great Mughal, who had died fourteen years earlier, reached his final resting place in the burial chamber.

QUTB MINAR AND ITS MONUMENTS, DELHI

The first Islamic building in Indian territory is a superb example of the fusion of Hindu and Islamic architectural styles.

Toward the end of the 12th century, Muslim invaders under Qutb-ud-Din Aibak conquered northern India and the Rajput fort of Lal Kot, the settlement that preceded Delhi. They then looked to local builders and traditions to construct their first mosque, which is why the Quwwat-ul-Islam ("Power of Islam") Mosque was built as a hall of pillars with the reddish-yellow sandstone typical of Delhi, and with a layout that is more characteristic of Jain sanctuaries. Only the décor and elaborate calligraphic scrolls adorning the walls and façades are traditionally Islamic. Soaring out of the mosque's ruins is the 72-m-high (236-ft) Qutb Minar with a base diameter of around 15 m (49 ft) that tapers to just under 3 m (10 ft) at its apex. The clearly defined grooves made of red sandstone distinguish the minaret from other similar structures – it was the first time they were used as stylistic elements in Indian architecture and they cover three of the five levels. The top two were destroyed by lightning in the 14th century and later reconstructed in marble.

The Qutb Minar can no longer be climbed due to its fragile state.

FATEHPUR SIKRI

No other place in India displays a purer Mughal style than the royal capital south-west of Agra, in the present-day state of Uttar Pradesh.

Mughal emperor Jalaluddin Muhammad Akbar, also known as Akbar the Great, fulfilled a solemn promise by building the residence of Fatehpur Sikri ("City of Victory"). He also left the city with a palace of pure Mughal splendor. The promise was made to Sufi holy man Salim Chishti, one of the ruler's advisors who lived not far from Agra. After Salim's prophecy of the Great Mughal having three sons came true, Akbar vowed to build a residence close to the wise man's home.

The foundation stone for this was laid in 1569, and the Great Mosque, with the mausoleum for Sheik Salim, was completed just three years later. More than ten years in total were spent on building the residence. In the end, a fabulous capital city with various levels, palaces and terraces emerged in this hilly landscape, but the royal suite had to abandon the city in 1585 because of a water shortage. Nine gates are recessed into the 6-km-long (4-mi) walls, and the buildings are made almost exclusively of red sandstone. The palace and mosque form the center of the complex.

The Great Mosque is home to the mausoleum of Sufi holy man Salim Chishti, to whom Akbar had promised to build Fatehpur Sikri. Sufi followers still come to pray within its walls.

AGRA FORT

Construction on the Red Fort of Agra, in the present-day state of Uttar Pradesh, was started by Akbar the Great in 1565. The building was then expanded into a sprawling palace by his grandson, Shah Jahan. The complex clearly displays the different aesthetic preferences of both rulers.

Like its namesake in Delhi, this fort owes its name to the red sandstone from which it was built. It was designed by Akbar the Great to protect the future capital of the Mughal Empire but after the fortress walls and gates had been erected he stopped construction because he was building a luxurious new residence in Fatehpur Sikri. He abandoned that location after just ten years, however, (see above) and went to rule in Lahore, only returning to Agra just before his death. His successor, Jahangir, did not do much for the city, and Agra was given no new architectural highlights until Shah Jahan, the "King of the World", came to reside here from 1632 to 1637.

The artistic regent had many of Akbar's buildings demolished and replaced by magical palaces and mosques made of white marble and embedded with semi-precious stones. The most impressive of his architectural endeavors are the Public Audience Hall and the Pearl Mosque.

The Amar Singh Gate is typical of the imperial style employed by the Mughal Akbar the Great, but it differed greatly from the splendid architecture of his artistically minded successor.

India

Shah Jahan

His tears filled a lake, and still reflected in it today is the silhouette of one of the world's most beautiful tombs, the Taj Mahal – a gleaming white monument to the perpetual sadness of its sponsor, Shah Jahan, built in memory of his favorite wife, Mumtaz Mahal, the "Jewel of the Palace", who died in 1631.

Shah Jahan was born in Lahore in 1592 and came to the throne in 1628. As a prince he focused less on the glory of war and was instead much more interested in the arts and other sublime pleasures, but these tendencies did not stop him from violently asserting his claim to the throne when the time came.

TAJ MAHAL IN AGRA

The tomb that the great Shah Jahan built for his wife, who died in 1631, in the northern city of Agra, is one of the finest examples of Indo-Islamic architecture.

The name of this World Heritage Site and architectural gem built of white marble is based on a sobriquet of Arjumand Banu Begum (Mumtaz Mahal), who is buried here. She was the favorite wife of Shah Jahan and it means "Jewel of the Palace". The building represents the zenith of the architectural style developed in Humayun's Tomb.

The symmetrically designed mausoleum is positioned on a square foundation at the end of a long parterre decorated with fountains. The central dome sitting atop a high tambour is

One of the central architectural elements of the Taj Mahal is its iwan, a vaulted space with a gateway-like opening that dates back to the Persian Sassanids.

accompanied by domed gazebos and the façades face the four points of the compass. Four minarets accentuate the corners of the white marble terrace. The heavy Persian influence likely dates back to the first master builder, Isa Afandi, who was brought by Shah Jahan from the Iranian city of Shiraz. Artists and craftsmen from the region between Uzbekistan and Turkey helped with the construction while the marble marquetry was created by Italian artisans.

The Taj Mahal complex, with its white marble tomb, large garden, mosque and guesthouse was built on the banks of the Yamuna River.

Shah Jahan was lucky to reap the rewards of his predecessors' work, particularly his grandfather Akbar the Great, and displayed unprecedented opulence in his court. He also ordered the construction of buildings that became masterpieces of Indo-Islamic architecture: the three-domed Pearl Mosque at Agra Fort, a new palace for

his temporary residence, public audience halls and of course the Taj Mahal. Shah Jahan died in 1666, and he was laid to rest beside his beloved wife in her glorious white tomb. By then, however, his third son Aurangzeb had already deposed him and placed him under house arrest in 1658.

The ivory miniatures to the left show Shah Jahan (right) and his wife, Mumtaz Mahal (left), whose empty cenotaphs (far left) lie in the main room of the Taj Mahal. The actual tombs are located in a crypt beneath.

India

KEOLADEO NATIONAL PARK

Set in the marshes of Rajasthan, Keoladeo is an ornithological paradise where the bird population is at its highest after the monsoons, a time when local waterfowl are joined by large numbers of often rare migratory birds.

This national park's wetland area was actually man-made as a hunting ground for the maharajas of Bharatpur, and the marshy natural depression provided plentiful bounty for their recreational pursuits. One day's hunting frequently yielded several thousand birds.

In the 19th century, the maharajas expanded the abundant marshland by constructing artificial canals and dams. In the middle of an otherwise extremely dry terrain, their creation would later become a popular breeding ground for birds of all kinds. Today the protected area is a permanent home to some roughly 120 species including one of the world's largest heron colonies. In winter, around 240 different species of migratory bird also settle here, among them the rare Siberian crane (or snow crane) and the falcated duck. The Siberian crane has always been one of the park's biggest attractions. Back in 1976, more than one hundred of them spent the winter here, but the bird is now feared to have become extinct.

The artificial wetlands of Keoladeo National Park cover an area of less than 30 sq km (12 sq mi). Despite its small size, however, the park is a sanctuary for many endangered animals.

MANAS WILDLIFE SANCTUARY

This wildlife sanctuary lies at the base of the Himalayas in Assam, not far from the border with Bhutan, and is most famous for its numerous tigers and elephants. It takes its name from the fast-flowing Manas River.

The Manas Wildlife Sanctuary borders on Bhutan's Royal Manas National Park. The grasslands constitute about 60 percent of the sanctuary's terrain and are home to – among other animals – wild buffalo and pygmy hogs. Until it was spotted in Manas, the latter was thought to have become extinct. The grassy savannahs, woodlands and rivers that characterize the Manas landscape are also home to numerous species of bird.

The core of the reserve, which was declared a wildlife sanctuary in 1928, was unfortunately badly decimated in the 1992 civil war. That same year, UNESCO placed the park and its ecosystem on the seriously endangered list due to damage. In 1992–93 thirty-three rhinoceroses were killed and of the 2,000 elephants only a few dozen were left, but thanks to rehabilitation efforts their numbers were back up to 700 by 2006. The Bengal tiger population had also risen to around sixty.

The Manas Sanctuary boasts a growing population of Indian elephants. Two bulls are posturing here.

KAZIRANGA NATIONAL PARK

Covering 430 sq km (166 sq mi) in the heart of Assam, Kaziranga National Park is one of the region's last territories untouched by human intervention. Rare animals found here include the world's largest population of the endangered one-horned rhinoceros.

Conditions in Kaziranga National Park are closely linked to the heady fluctuations of the Brahmaputra river. During the monsoon season in July and August, for example, two thirds of the park is regularly under water, forcing the animals to retreat to higher ground both inside and outside the park.

Local conservationists here have traditionally focused their attention on the fate of the one-horned rhino. At the beginning of the 20th century, its population was already so depleted that hunting licenses were banned. The region was declared a nature reserve in 1908, became a wildlife sanctuary in 1950, and then a national park in 1974. Today the number of one-horned rhinos is estimated at around 1,500 and some of the park's animals were recently moved to the nearby Manas Wildlife Sanctuary in a bid to boost the rhino population there as well.

Rhinos are not the only animals in Kaziranga, which boasts plentiful elephant, buffalo and several deer populations. There are also gibbons, tigers, wild boar, and rare birds including bearded bustards and grey pelicans.

One-horned rhinos prefer the high-grass swamps and open marshes.

SUNDARBANS NATIONAL PARK

The Sundarbans are the largest mangrove forests in the world. More than half of the area is in the Indian section of the Bay of Bengal and the rest is in Bangladesh. The forests are a refuge for the severely endangered Bengal tiger. The national park covers roughly 1,300 sq km (500 sq mi) and was created in 1973 order to protect the unique flora and fauna that exists here.

The Sundarbans are a highly complex system of rivers, channels and marshlands in the mighty delta of the Ganges, Brahmaputra and Meghna rivers. The diversity of this wetlands ecosystem is a result of its position in the transitional zone between freshwater and saltwater. Animals such as dolphins, otters, pythons, turtles, water monitors, crocodiles, storks, herons, cormorants and curlews are all found here, not to mention chital and Barasingha deer, the rare rhesus macaque, wild boar, and of course Bengal tigers. There are roughly 250 of these regal cats living within the park and they can reach 2.5 m (8 ft) in length (without tail) and weigh up to 280 kilos (615 lbs). It was the hunting zeal of the maharajahs and British officers, an innate human fear of this man-eating "night predator", and the encroachment by human civilization in the 20th century that brought this majestic animal to near extinction.

Mangroves are salt-tolerant green plants that thrive in tropical, coastal marshes and anchor themselves with stilted roots in soft muddy soil.

CHHATRAPATI SHIVAJI TERMINUS (FORMERLY VICTORIA TERMINUS)

This train station in Mumbai (Bombay) – formerly known as Victoria Terminus – beautifully merges European and Indian stylistic elements.

The largest British monument is not actually in the UK, but in Mumbai, India. At its inauguration in 1887, this splendid train station was named Victoria Terminus and only later called Chhatrapati Shivaji Terminus after a Marathi warlord who fought for the Hindu identity against the Islamic Mughals. The building was designed in the "neo-Gothic" revival style by British architect Frederick William Stevens and based on the St Pancras Station in London. Construction began in 1878.

With its domes, turrets, columns, minarets and pointed arches, the train station also displays numerous elements of Indian palace architecture. Under British direction, many Indian craftsmen and artists worked on the construction, incorporating their rich building skills and knowledge. The station became a symbol of Mumbai and contributed toward its image as a "Gothic City".

The train station combines British Gothic Revival and Indian palace architecture.

ELEPHANTA CAVES

This rock sanctuary dedicated to the Hindu god Shiva is located on an island in the Mumbai Harbor. It is famous for its stonemasonry depicting the popular deity in its many manifestations.

Before this island was renamed "Elephanta" in the 16th century, it is said to have originally been called "Gharapuri" ("City of Ghara priests"), a name that originates from a group of Portuguese who regained their bearings using a stone elephant they had found in the harbor – and which can still be seen in Mumbai's Victoria Gardens. The sculptures found in the rock caves date back to the seventh century and represent a zenith of early Hindu art. The 6-m-high (20 ft) portrait of Shiva Mahadeva, for example, depicts the god with three faces and a grand headdress. It is of monumental proportions.

Shiva, along with Brahma and Vishnu, two other very important deities in the Hindu pantheon, is considered to be a god of creativity and is worshipped in the form of a phallus (or lingam) or an ecstatic dancer, as Shiva Nataraja. The god often appears with an entourage of half-divine, half-demonic beings. Like Shiva, these legions of deities have also been displayed in Elephanta.

The Hindu god Shiva, with his three faces – the creator, the preserver and the destroyer – is depicted in the rock caves of Elephanta Island.

MAHABODHI TEMPLE COMPLEX AT BODH GAYA

Mahabodhi Temple Complex, located about 100 km (62 mi) from Patna in the northern Indian state of Bihar, is closely related to the life of Buddha and the religious history of the Indian subcontinent.

The first great empire to emerge on the Indian subcontinent was founded by King Ashoka (r. 273–232 BC), who converted to Buddhism and built a temple on the site where Buddha purportedly attained enlightenment under the Maha Bodhi tree. The building that replaced the original structure – the roughly 50-m-high (164-ft) Mahabodhi Temple – was erected during the Gupta Dynasty (320–540), which further promoted Buddhism as the national religion.

The structure plays an important role in Indian architectural history as one

of South Asia's oldest brick temple towers. The stone reliefs and sculptural decorations on the balustrades are particularly impressive. The temple became a popular pilgrimage site even in its early days, but when Hinduism increasingly began to squeeze Buddhism out of the region, it gradually fell into disrepair. The first restorations took place in the 19th century and a systematic, scientifically-supervised restoration began in 2002.

The Mahabodhi Temple is one of the four tallest Buddhist sanctuaries in the world.

KHAJURAHO GROUP OF MONUMENTS

These twenty preserved temples from the heyday of the Chandella Dynasty are distinguished by an extremely successful combination of architecture and sculpture. They are predominantly characterized by Hindu elements.

Khajuraho is located in the state of Madhya Pradesh and became famous for the erotic motifs on the external walls of its temples, which are divided into several groups. In the village are the Brahma, Vamana and Javari temples. East of these are the Jain sites, today still part of a living cult. The ensemble of the Lakshmana, Kandariya, Vishvanath and Chitragupta temples is proof that Khajuraho was the center of the Chandella Dynasty in the 10th and 11th centuries.

All the temples follow a similar principle, oriented from east to west. The

entrance hall is situated in the west, followed by a foyer, a main hall, a vestibule and a cella. The tower-like roofs above the building sections grow taller towards the cella. The roof of the cella – referred to as the "sikhara" – is the characteristic architectural element of Khajuraho, symbolizing Mount Meru, the center of divinity. The cella is home to the east-facing cult image.

The sexual unions depicted as reliefs on the exterior walls symbolize fertility and the re-creation of the world.

India

BUDDHIST MONUMENTS AT SANCHI

India's oldest Buddhist sanctuary is north-east of Bhopal in Madhya Pradesh and was an important religious center until well into the 12th century.

The pilgrimage site of Sanchi is home to one of India's oldest Buddhist religious buildings. According to the tradition here, King Ashoka, the first great patron of Buddhism, is said to have founded the complex. Though it is not fully proven, at least a portion of the buildings were certainly commissioned by him.

The splendid stonemasonry around the larger stupa 1, allegedly built over Buddha's mortal remains in the middle of the third century BC, is a highlight of craftsmanship and artistry. The hemispherical sanctuary is in turn encircled by a palisade through which

four immense stone gates grant visitors entry – each one facing a point of the compass. The gates were built in the first century BC and decorated with artistic reliefs illustrating scenes from Buddha's life in a very realistic manner. Apart from two more recent stupas, the remains of several monastery buildings and other temple complexes have also been preserved.

Impressive reliefs adorn the stone gates, also called toranas, of the Sanchi stupas. Most of the motifs depict scenes from Buddha's life.

ROCK SHELTERS OF BHIMBETKA

This archaeological site on the edge of the Vindhya Range in the state of Madhya Pradesh includes around 500 caves and overhanging rocks that feature myriad engravings and rock paintings. They were created between the Middle Stone Age and the Middle Ages.

The rock art of Bhimbetka gives us an indication of how people lived on the Indian subcontinent several thousand years ago. The paintings are mostly done in red and white, but there are also other colors on display. Many animals are depicted, including buffaloes, tigers, lions, wild boars, elephants, horses, antelopes and even crocodiles. People can be seen dancing and playing music, waging war against each other and riding horses and elephants. Religious symbols can often also be made out, as can later illustrations of Hindu deities. Even emotions such as fear, joy and happi-

ness can be made out in the skillfully rendered stick figures. The paintings were not discovered until 1958.

One of South Asia's most elaborate Stone-Age archaeological sites can also be found near Bhimbetka, in Barkhera, where thousands of Acheulean stone tools are scattered over fields and in the forest here.

Images of elephants and horses can also be seen in the rock caves.

CHAMPANER-PAVAGADH ARCHAEOLOGICAL PARK

Along with prehistoric sites from the Copper Age, this partly excavated and restored archaeological site in Gujarat also includes an old Hindu city perched high on a hill and an Islamic city out on the plain.

This archaeological park is home to the ruins of the city of Champaner, located at the base of the roughly 800-m-high (2,625-ft) fortified mountain of Pavagadh, which rises directly out of the plain. On the way up to the summit there are numerous ruins of an ancient Hindu city including the impressive outer walls with gates and even a summerhouse. At the peak is a temple on which an Islamic sanctuary was established to mark the religion's "victory" over Hinduism.

Champaner was the capital of Gujarat in the 15th century, and is the only

place in this region to have been preserved unchanged from the Islamic era that predated the Mughal rulers. It is home to lovely palaces, minarets, fountains, mosques, ponds and tombs. Champaner is an excellent example of the coexistence and symbiosis of Hindu and Islamic architecture in the Sultanate of Gujarat. The style is the most elaborate of all the 15th- and 16th-century provincial trends.

The Jama Masjid (Friday Mosque), with its minarets, is one of the archaeological park's architectural gems.

AJANTA CAVES

These rock temples situated about 100 km (62 mi) north of Aurangabad, in the state of Maharashtra, originate from different centuries and contain wall paintings of surprisingly high artistic quality. They were forgotten for centuries before being rediscovered by British officers in 1819.

This Buddhist monastery complex is cleverly hidden in a gorge-like bend of the Waghora River where monks carved twenty-nine caves from the nearly vertical walls of the canyon in two construction phases. The first phase covers the period from the second century BC to the second century AD while the second occurred during the Gupta Era in the fifth to sixth centuries.

Wall paintings, which are extraordinary in terms of their artistic design and narrative quality, have been lovingly preserved in eight of the twenty-nine Ajanta caves. They depict scenes from Buddha's life as well as the so-called jatakas – legends about his previous incarnations. The predominantly red and brown Gandhara-style figures in the caves date back to pre-Christian times and are primarily characterized by clear contour drawings.

Padmapani, the lotus holder, is one of the large Mahayana Buddhism Bodhisattvas symbolizing compassion and sympathy. It is depicted in cave 1.

Almost without exception, they face the direction in which the narration progresses. On the other hand, the figures in the cave temples from the fifth century, which vividly illustrate court life and everyday life, are extremely realistic, particularly in their depiction of facial expressions. The images in the Ajanta wall paintings often also display erotic themes.

The interiors of these caves are surprisingly large. The colonnades are particularly impressive with their monuments while the halls have sculptures in their recesses that are hardly inferior to any other "top-side" temples in terms of their magnificence.

India

ELLORA CAVES

The thirty-four temple and monastery buildings in Ellora are famous for their elaborate decorative sculptures chiseled out of the natural bedrock about 30 km (19 mi) north-west of Aurangabad.

The Maharashtra Plateau is riddled with canyons carved deep into the basalt rock, a material that proved particularly suitable, from a geological perspective, for building monolithic rock temples. Indeed, the main thing that all of these Ellora sanctuaries have in common is that they were not built into the rock, but rather carved out of it. The main supporting elements are all made from the base rock itself, as is most of the ornamentation and many of the decorative sculptures.

Of the temples and monasteries carved out of a steep face that stretches over 2 km (1.3 mi), seventeen are Hindu, twelve are Buddhist and five are Jain.

All of the temples have a similar design comprising an entrance hall, a foyer, a main hall and a cella, or inner chamber. The latter contains the cult image, which is why its roof is also the highest, and symbolizes Mount Meru. At the architecturally striking Kailasa Temple – the largest rock sanctuary at Ellora, and one that mimics an open-air brick building – the roof of the cella appropriately represents holy Mt Kailash, home of the Hindu god Shiva.

The 30-m- (98-ft-) high Kailasa Temple was chiseled out of the rock as a monolith.

GROUP OF MONUMENTS AT PATTADAKAL

The royal capital of the Chalukya rulers in the seventh and eighth centuries combines the architectural styles of northern and southern India.

Two things led to Pattadakal becoming a melting pot of architectural styles: its location on the border of northern and southern India, in the interior of the present-day state of Karnataka, and the tolerance of the Chalukya rulers, who rose to great power in the mid-sixth century. A good example of northern Indian styles is the small Kashi Vishvanath Temple, which is characterized by the structural unit of a sikhara tower and cella (sikhara), preceded by an entrance hall. Visitors can only walk around the cella's main cult image on the outside of the building.

Southern Indian styles, promoted more energetically by the Pallava rulers in the seventh century, are represented by the procession route that was built around the cella. The temple room with its shrine and the spacious entrance hall virtually open out onto one another. The best example of this is the Virupaksha Temple. Pattadakal's largest complex dedicated to the Hindu god Shiva is decorated with elaborate stonemasonry.

The Virupaksha Temple is the largest sanctuary in Pattadakal.

CHURCHES AND CONVENTS OF GOA

This former Portuguese territory on the Indian Ocean was an important stronghold of the Catholic Church in South Asia during colonial times and is a unique site for colonial Renaissance and baroque architecture.

Goa was the most important Portuguese trading base in India and one of its most important in Asia. The Portuguese had managed to capture the coastal strip in 1506, and Alfonso de Albuquerque (1453–1515) founded a Catholic enclave there four years later. Old Goa (Velha Goa) is some 10 km (6 mi) inland, and was abandoned in the early 19th century because of rampant malaria. A new city was therefore built downstream, but the old churches and convents were not surrendered. Today they stand proudly virtually in their original splendor.

St Francis' Church dates back to the year 1521. The Sé Catedral, at that time Asia's largest church, came a bit later, in 1562. The most important mission site, the Bom Jesus Cathedral, which is also home to the tomb of St Francis Xavier (1506–1552), was erected in 1594. This famous Jesuit was responsible for bringing Christianity to both India and Japan.

The Convent of St Francis of Assisi was a mosque in pre-Portuguese times. Together with the Sé Catedral, it forms an immense complex of buildings.

GROUP OF MONUMENTS AT HAMPI

The ruins of the former Vijayanagar, the last capital of India's eponymous Hindu empire before Islam reached the region, can be found in a small town in the state of Karnataka. The site gleams with opulently decorated buildings, superb examples of the Dravidian style of southern India.

The ruins of Hampi, former capital of the last great Hindu empire of Vijayanagar (1336–1565), resemble a grand open-air museum of southern Indian architecture. They are encircled by a wall and feature the palaces and temples of Dravidian princes. The Vittala Temple, for example, was begun in the first half of the 16th century but never completed. It impresses visitors with sculptured pillars as well as an 8-m-high (26-ft) temple chariot cut from a single block of stone. In addition to its opulent decorative figures, the highlight of Virupaksha Temple is the gate tower (gopura), which is more than 50 m (164 ft) high. The temple is dedicated to Shiva. A previous sanctuary was located here as early as the ninth century. While the temples are mostly in the northern part of the city, the palace buildings are clustered in the south. Wall reliefs here depict great epic tales such as the Ramayana.

Above: A chariot carved from a single block of stone in the Hampi temple district.

SUN TEMPLE, KONÂRAK

This sun temple is dedicated to the Hindu god Surya and features some elaborate stonemasonry. It is one of the most important Brahman sanctuaries of ancient India.

As early as Vedic times, the Hindu sun god Surya formed a type of trinity with the god of fire, Agni, and the god of thunder, Indra. The deity had always been worshiped by the Hindus as a giver of life. Konârak is in the federal state of Orissa near the Bay of Bengal.

The sun temple at Konârak, with its 75-m-high (246-ft) pyramidal sikhara and the cella beneath features an image of the chariot in which the god rides over the firmament every day. The twelve wheels on the base wall thus symbolize the sun in two ways: the roundness of the wheel embodies its shape while the number of wheels symbolizes the twelve months the earth needs to orbit our central star. While the temple's walls were adorned with figures, the surfaces of the high base and the wheels are completely covered with detailed reliefs and stone carvings right down to the center of the spokes. The temple at Konârak was completed in the 13th century but the complex was abandoned shortly thereafter for reasons still unknown.

The immense and ornate sun wheels are some of the most recognizable images in the sun temple at Konârak.

GROUP OF MONUMENTS AT MAHABALIPURAM

About 50 km (31 mi) south of Chennai (Madras) is one of the most imposing archaeological sites in South India. It features some of the finest examples of Dravidian architecture in the country.

After the Pallavan prince Narasimhavarman I, who ruled between 625 and 645, had conquered the neighboring settlements and became familiar with the breathtaking architecture of the Chalukya rulers, he ordered the beautification and enhancement of his own city of Mahabalipuram. The facelift included the construction of some of India's finest Dravidian architecture, buildings whose shapes would become synonymous with the southern portion of the subcontinent. To test out the various styles of cult hall architecture, Narasimhavarman commissioned five rathas. They were not actual temples, but monumental sculptures carved out of the bedrock. Ratha no. 5 quickly became the prototype for a number of later Dravidian temples. Even Narasimhavarman's successor modelled his coastal temple in Mahabalipuram on ratha no. 5.

In the crevice of the gigantic bas-relief "Descent of the Ganges", Shiva is depicted as allowing the river to flow through his hair in the presence of a number of other creatures and animals.

MOUNTAIN RAILWAYS OF INDIA

A total of three of India's spectacular narrow-gauge mountain railways have been declared World Heritage Sites: the Darjeeling-Himalaya Railway, the Nilgiri Mountain Railway and the Kalka-Shimla Railway.

The Darjeeling-Himalaya Railway in West Bengal, which reduced travel times between Calcutta and Darjeeling from six days to less than twenty-four hours, was the first Indian railway built exclusively with Indian finances. Constructed by the British company Gillanders Arbuthnot & Co. between 1879 and 1881, it reaches an altitude of 2,175 m (7,136 ft) above sea level at Ghum.

The Nilgiri Mountain Railway reaches nearly 2,000 m (6,562 ft) between Mettupalaiyam and Udagamandalam in Tamil Nadu. The indigenous Todas people lived in the Blue Mountains (Nilgiris) far removed from the outside world until well into the 19th century, when the British took an interest in the region and had the railway built. The track passes 1,330 m (4,364 ft) over a 20 km (12.5 mi) stretch between Kallar and Coonoor.

Starting in 1903, the almost 100-km-long (62-mi) Kalka-Shimla Railway connected the town of Kalka, at 625 m (2,051 ft), with Shimla, the "summer capital of British India" over 2,000 m (6,562 ft) above sea level in Himachal Pradesh, in the far north of India.

Passengers on the Nilgri Mountain Railway wait for the departure signal.

GREAT LIVING CHOLA TEMPLES

This World Heritage Site includes three ornately decorated temple complexes from the Chola dynasty that once ruled the southern portion of the Indian subcontinent. They are located in Thanjavur (Tanjore), Gangaikondacholisvaram and Darasuram.

Southern India was ruled by the Chola dynasty from the ninth to the 12th centuries. Thanjavur, about 350 km (218 mi) south of Chennai in the state of Madras, was its royal residence from 907 to the early 11th century, a capital built by the Chola kings in southern Indian style following the trend of the Pallava princes in Mahabalipuram. The Brihadishvara Temple of Thanjavur, commissioned by King Rajaraja and completed in 1010, is one of the most formidable constructions of the time. The temple tower (sikhara) above the cella, built over thirteen floors, is a terraced granite pyramid topped with a large keystone and measures 60 m (197 ft) in height. The tower had a gilded copper roof at one point. The large number of phallus symbols, countless Shiva images and many depictions of the bull, Nandi, Shiva's mount, indicate that the complex is dedicated to the god of creation and destruction, Shiva.

Imposing sculptures welcome visitors to the Brihadishvara Temple in Thanjavur.

Bangladesh

THE SUNDARBANS MANGROVE FORESTS

Located in the delta of the Ganges, Brahmaputra and Meghna rivers, in the Bay of Bengal, the Sundarbans are the world's largest mangrove forests. The unique wetland ecosystem is shared by India and Bangladesh.

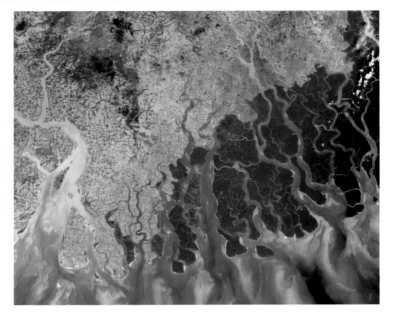

Three massive rivers converge here at the largest mangrove forest in the world: the Ganges, Brahmaputra and Meghna. A large variety of animals enjoy the transitional habitat between freshwater and saltwater. The Bengali section of the Sundarbans is defined by the ebb and flow of a coastal environment and covers an area of about 10,000 sq km (3,800 sq mi).
The core areas of the protected area in Bangladesh are directly adjacent to the Indian area and cover about 1,400 sq km (540 sq mi). The Sundarbans are unique in that they protect the interior of the country from increasingly frequent tropical storms, but the mangrove forests themselves are in danger. Climate change, rising sea levels, increased salt content in the freshwater, oil contamination, poaching and illegal logging are rapidly jeopardizing this delicate ecosystem.

In this satellite image you can see the mangrove forests in dark green while the arms of the rivers are displayed in lighter blue stretching out through the marshy areas of the Gulf of Bengal.

HISTORIC MOSQUE CITY OF BAGERHAT

The architectural wealth of this historic mosque city attests to the power of the once independent Bengali sultans of the Middle Ages.

Present-day Bangladesh was conquered by Muslims around the year 1200, and became part of the vast Mughal Empire starting in 1576. The city formerly known as "Khalifatabad", located in what is now southern Bangladesh, was founded by General Ulugh Khan Jahan during the reign of Sultan Nasiruddin Mahmud Shah in the 15th century. In just a few years, Khan Jahan had many mosques, mausoleums, palaces and administrative buildings erected, roads laid and bridges constructed that connected his city on the edge of the vast Sundarbans mangrove forests with the important cities of the Sultanate of Bengal. The prominent structures of the some fifty preserved buildings, mostly built of bricks, are the monumental Shait Gumbad Mosque, the Bibi Begni Mosque, the Chunakhola Mosque and Khan Jahan's mausoleum, which all date back to the 15th century. Khan Jahan is worshiped as a saint; his mausoleum is a Muslim pilgrimage site.

One of the largest and oldest mosques in Bangladesh is the Shait Gumbad Mosque, built under Khan Jahan and featuring seventy-seven domes.

RUINS OF THE BUDDHIST VIHARA AT PAHARPUR

The brick ruins of this once very influential monastic city in South Asia are some of the most important cultural monuments of the Bengali Middle Ages. It is also the largest Buddhist monastery complex on the Indian subcontinent.

The "Great Monastery" of Mahayana Buddhism – Somapura Mahavira – was also a prominent religious center outside of the Bengal region during the Pala dynasty. Its influence reached as far as Cambodia, and was not just limited to spirituality. The architectural complex of the monastic city also helped shape the style of architecture for Buddhist monasteries in distant South-East Asia.
This vast monastery complex, whose 177 monk cells are grouped around a central stupa, was built on a multi-level terrace in the eighth century. It was commissioned by Dharmapala, the second ruler of the Buddhist Pala family. Around 300 years later, when the Hindu Sena family came to power after defeating the Palas, the monastery lost its importance and was completely forgotten about by the 12th century. The monastery complex and sixty effigies on the site were not rediscovered until the 19th century.

The monastery complex at Paharpur was an important religious and spiritual center for Buddhists, Hindus and Jains.

ANCIENT CITY OF SIGIRIYA

The kings of Anuradhapura were responsible for building the mountain fort and capital city on "Lion's Rock". The complex at the center of the island was completed towards the end of the fifth century and is monumental proof of the standard of art and engineering in the early days of Sri Lankan history.

The fort perched on top of the 200-m-high (656-ft) "Lion's Rock", or Sinhagiri, soars majestically out of the surrounding tropical vegetation. It was not only built for defense purposes, but also as a royal pleasure palace, a fact evident from the magical and often very well preserved tempera paintings on the path leading up the steep pathway. They depict celestial nymphs – elegant, erotically dressed, bejeweled female figures with fashionably styled hair.

The path to the summit once started at the Lion's Gate, of which only the paws remain. The citadel itself is also nothing more than ruins now, but the remains of the halls, baths, bridges, gardens and fountains of the complex

The fort is on top of a heavily eroded volcano about 200 m (656 ft) high. The path leads over ledges and narrow steps.

designed by King Dhatusena in the fifth century are still clearly distinguishable. The king's son, Kassapa, who was able to occupy the royal throne following his father's death (which he arranged himself) and by expelling his half-brother, Moggallana, resided in Sigiriya for eighteen years before Moggallana returned, prompting a decisive battle during which Kassapa lost his life.

Countless illustrations of elegantly dressed women once adorned the walls of the pathway that leads up to the island fort. The so-called "apsaras", heavenly nymphs, can be seen scattering flowers from the clouds to greet the arriving king.

Sri Lanka

SACRED CITY OF ANURADHAPURA

The first capital of the Singhalese kingdoms is home to many Buddhist monuments including giant stupas, Buddha figures and a holy tree.

The founding of the sacred city of Anuradhapura is related to a holy tree. In 244 BC, the story goes, a Buddhist nun named Sanghamitta brought to Sri Lanka a branch of the tree under which the meditating Buddha is said to have attained enlightenment. The 2,200-year-old tree is now not only the oldest known Mahabodhi tree in the world, but also the spiritual and geographical center of the city.

The Isurumuniya shrine from the third century BC also goes back to the Mahabodhi branch. It was founded by laymen who consecrated themselves monks after being awed by the won- ders that occurred after planting the branch. One of the country's most beautiful reliefs is here too. The imposing Ruvanveli Dagoba, whose dome is 110 m (361 ft) high, was built in the second century BC. The Abhayagiri Monastery dates back to the first century BC, while the Jetavana-Dagoba, once just under 130 m (427 ft) tall and the world's largest stupa, dates back to the fourth century. The statue of the Samadhi Buddha was also created at around the same time.

The Ruvanveli Dagoba, with its mighty dome, is 110 m (361 ft) tall.

GOLDEN TEMPLE OF DAMBULLA

The five cave temples of Dambulla are right in the center of Sri Lanka and feature seemingly countless statues and wall paintings. They date back to the dawn of Sri Lankan Buddhism.

There are three traceable periods in the emergence of the "Black Rock" as a spiritual center. The first began in the early first century BC under King Vattagamani Abhaya, who had fled Anuradhapura before the second major wave of Tamils and found shelter here among the granite rocks during fourteen years of exile. The sanctuary was then forgotten and not rediscovered until the 12th century – the second period. The third period came during the reign of King Kirti Sri Rajasinha (1747 to 1782). In the "Temple of the Divine King" (Devaraja Vihara), the first cave, is a fascinating, 14-m-long (46-ft) statue of the reclining Buddha. The largest and most impressive cave is the "Temple of the Great King" (Maharaja Vihara). The "Great New Temple" (Maha Alut Vihara), the third cave, was commissioned by King Kirti Sri Rajasinha. The fourth cave dates back to the oldest period from the first century BC, and commemorates the heroic Queen Somavathi. Finally, the fifth cave temple demonstrates the tastes and styles of 1820, the year of its renovation.

No less than 154 Buddha statues have been counted in the richly decorated cave temples of Dambulla.

ANCIENT CITY OF POLONNARUWA

This medieval royal residence in north-central Sri Lanka includes important structures and outstanding examples of Singhalese statuary. The monumental statues of the Buddha are particularly breathtaking.

Polonnaruwa first became a seat of government in the eighth century, but after Anuradhapura was destroyed in 1017, it became the capital, ruled by both Indian and Singhalese kings. The most notable among the latter was Parakrama Bahu I (r. 1153–1186), whose era is considered one of cultural and economic prosperity that saw the creation of temples, schools, hospitals, irrigation systems and a magnificent palace. Polonnaruwa was abandoned in the 13th century, but the major works from the heyday of Parakrama Bahu I have been rediscov- ered: the palace district with council chamber and bath, the "Round Reliquary" with its moonstone, a crescent-shaped flagstone, the "House of Eight Relics", the 55-m (180-ft) Ruvanveli Dagoba and the Thuparama Dagoba. Four large Buddha figures carved into the granite have been preserved from the Gal Vihara cave temple and a 14-m (46-ft) reclining Buddha is a masterpiece of stonemasonry.

Reclining, standing and meditating Buddhas can be admired in the Gal Vihara Temple.

SACRED CITY OF KANDY

Sri Lanka's most sacred relic, one of Buddha's teeth, is found in the "Temple of the Tooth" in Kandy. A colorful procession with tens of thousands of participants is held every year to honor the lone body part.

This religious city was founded by King Vikrama Bahu III (r. 1357–1374), but a majority of the buildings date back to King Vikrama Rajasinha (r. 1798–1815), the most famous ruler in Kandy's history. He commissioned the wooden public audience hall in the old palace and Kandy Lake in the city center, a body of water that was apparently created because the king wanted to be able to access the southern Malwatte Temple from his palace on dry ground, which required that a dam be built through the rice fields. A pond quickly formed behind the dam, which made the king so happy that he had it expanded into a stately lake with a circumference of around 4 km (2.5 mi).

The "Temple of the Tooth" (Dalada Maligawa) is the most important pilgrimage site for Sri Lankan Buddhists. The precious relics are kept in a valuable shrine on the second floor of the two-story building. The "Temple of the Flower Garden" (Malwatte Vihara) is today one of two main temples of the Siyam Nikaya Order native to Sri Lanka.

The "Temple of the Tooth" is home to a precious Buddha relic – a tooth – and is therefore carefully guarded.

SINHARAJA FOREST RESERVE

At an altitude of 500–1,100 m (1,600–3,600 feet), this hilly reserve is dominated by tropical rainforest. The area is rich in orchids and native species.

Located in south-west Sri Lanka, the Sinharaja Reserve is the island's last remaining area of primeval rainforest. Its name means "Realm of the Lion". The area between Ratnapura and Matara covers 85 sq km (33 sq mi) and was declared a biosphere reserve in a bid to protect it from excessive and illegal logging – an activity that had already damaged many of Sri Lanka's other forests. Not surprisingly, humans have long exploited these tropical rainforests for economic gain. They provided building materials for houses and were a source of all manner of medicines and exotic spices. The rapid growth of the local population, however, means that this complicated ecosystem cannot survive any continued large-scale human intervention. New laws have therefore been introduced to forbid all types of exploitation other than the collection of kittul fibers from the leaf sheath of the fishtail palm tree (Caryota urens). Nonetheless, illegal slash-and-burn activities and gem mining continue to cause serious damage.

The very first nature reserve in Sri Lanka in fact dates back to 1875, when the area was under British colonial rule.

OLD TOWN OF GALLE AND ITS FORTIFICATIONS

The history of this port city is primarily one of colonization, in which the Portuguese, Dutch and British all left their architectural marks.

Galle was a trading town even during what we would call biblical times when it was still known as "Tarshish". King Solomon apparently acquired his precious stones from here. Caliph Harun al-Rashid also used the port to exchange goods with the Chinese Empire, but the town was unknown to Europeans until 1505, when it was captured by the Portuguese. They were then displaced by the Dutch in 1640, who in turn had to make room for the British in 1796.

The former fort and the Old Town, which are protected by solid walls dating back to the year 1663, are the main attraction. The 21st century still appears to be light years away in the alleyways and houses of the burghers, the name given to the present-day descendants of the Dutch colonials who resided here. Virtually nothing remains of the Portuguese era since the Dutch built over nearly everything. Mighty bastions, city gates, baroque churches and the Government House are reminders of their heyday.

The old fort of Galle juts far out to sea. The tsunami of Christmas 2004 hit the port town hard: almost 4,000 locals lost their lives in the tidal wave.

Mongolia

UVS NUUR BASIN

The name of this basin comes from the Uvs Nuur salt lake in northern Mongolia. It is part of a transnational heritage site that shares territory in both Mongolia and Russia.

The Uvs Nuur region extends all the way to the autonomous Republic of Tuva in Russia. It is 600 km (375 mi) across and about 160 km (100 mi) from end to end. The region is notable for its wide range of ecosystems, which represent all of central Asia's landscape and vegetation zones from marshlands, deserts and steppes to different types of forests, rivers, freshwater lakes, alpine areas and permanent snowfields. Mountains, cliffs and granite rocks in strange, often pillow-like shapes complete the national park's unique landscape. For thousands of years nomads have roamed the grasslands here living in yurts.

Today, the stability of the region's ecology makes the Uvs Nuur basin a good place to measure global warming. Its various ecosystems are home to a wide variety of native plants and invertebrates. Both the saline Uvs Nuur lake and the freshwater Tere Khol lake are home to numerous seabirds and seals, and in summer the two lakes provide a resting place for migratory birds. The entire Uvs Nuur Basin has been a UNESCO Biosphere Reserve since 1997.

Nomads and their animals still roam the Uvs Nuur Basin and live in yurts.

ORKHON VALLEY CULTURAL LANDSCAPE

The cultural landscape of the Orkhon Valley in the Khangai Mountains covers vast areas of pastureland where many Mongolians still live as nomads. It also includes archaeological sites in the outlying areas of Kharkhorin.

The Orkhon Valley is located in the Khangai Mountains, the cradle of the Mongolian nation. In the 13th and 14th centuries, Kharkhorin (Karakorum) was the capital of the Mongolian Khans who succeeded Genghis Khan (1155–1227). It was from here that their entire empire was governed. But the Orkhon Valley was settled long before that. A political center for large parts of Central Asia had been established here since as early as the sixth century. The World Heritage Site comprises vast pasturelands on both sides of the Orkhon, and many excavation sites.

The Mongolian form of Lamaism (Tibetan Buddhism) also has its roots in the Orkhon Valley, which is home to the Erdene Zuu Monastery, begun in 1586 under Abtai Sain Khan. In its heyday, 10,000 monks called the monastery home. Unfortunately, it was completely destroyed in 1937 before re-opening in 1990.

The Orkhon (top left) is Mongolia's lifeline. During excavations in the area, archaeologists found pieces of gold jewelry and various seals (above right). Right is one of the Buddha figures in the Erdene Zuu Monastery near Karakorum.

CAPITAL CITIES AND TOMBS OF THE ANCIENT KOGURYO KINGDOM

This World Heritage Site covers three cities – only partially excavated – and forty tombs from the time of the Koguryo Kingdom, which ruled over present-day Korea and parts of northern China during the first centuries AD.

Koguryo is the name of one of three kingdoms that existed in ancient Korea. It was created through the merger of five tribes in the border area between Korea and Manchuria. After its founding in the second century BC it began expanding northward, particularly in the fourth century AD. Its growth resulted in conflicts with the Chinese and in 427 the capital was moved to Pyongyang. The empire reached its zenith in the fifth century before being destroyed in the seventh century. Archaeological sites in China include three cities – Wunu Mountain City, Wandu Mountain City and Guonei City – in the present-day city of Ji'an. There are also forty tombs, fourteen of which are from royal families. The wall paintings in the underground burial chambers are particularly striking.

The tomb complexes marked out by cairns or mounds are impressive evidence of the Koguryo era.

THE GREAT WALL

This colossal border construction from ancient China was the largest building project in pre-modern history. It took nearly 2,000 years to finish, but the wall could still never really protect the kingdom from invasions.

The first evidence of the construction of a "long wall" on China's northern border dates back to the year 214 BC. China's first emperor, Qin Shi Huang-di, had unified the country shortly before that, and these ramparts were meant to keep out unwelcome neighbors from the north. Protecting the country's agriculture bounty from the people of the steppe proved a difficult task, however, and for the next 1,900 years the bulwark went through a number of phases of disrepair and reconstruction.

During the Ming dynasty in the 15th and 16th centuries, the wall was not only rebuilt but also enlarged and reinforced beyond any previous versions. It was in that era that the present-day wall of more than 6,000 km (3,728 mi) was built, in particular the 2,000-km (1,243-mi) section from the Bohai Sea to the Yellow River, which is on average 7–8 m (23–26 ft) high and 6 m (20 ft) wide. The watchtowers were used as lodging for soldiers and enabled messages to be sent using beacons. The best preserved/restored section of the wall is at Badaling north-west of Beijing.

At over 6,000 km (3,728 mi) long, the Great Wall is the largest construction on earth, but not all parts of it are in as good a condition as those shown here (left at Mutianyu, above at Badaling).

MOUNTAIN RESORT AND ITS OUTLYING TEMPLES, CHENGDE

The summer residence of the Manchu emperors combines southern Chinese garden art with the steppe and forest landscape of northern China. The monasteries built in the area give insight into the diplomatic customs of the empire.

In Chengde – on the way to the imperial hunting grounds – the Manchu emperors found the ideal place to flee Beijing's summer heat. Plentiful water allowed for landscape gardens in southern-Chinese style with dams, bridges and gazebos while the actual palace buildings were much simpler and more intimately designed than in Beijing. Magnificent Buddhist monasteries and temples were built outside the roughly 5-sq-km (2-sq-mi) walled area in an attempt to clearly display to the messengers from Mongolia and Tibet – which had been annexed to the Manchurian Empire – the might of their new political homeland.

The most impressive temple in the imperial summer palace (below) at Chengde is the Temple of Sumeru, Happiness and Longevity. The central hall of the "Temple of Universal Peace" is home to a 22-m (72-ft) statue with forty two arms depicting Guanyin, the goddess of mercy and compassion (right).

PEKING MAN SITE AT ZHOUKOUDIAN

When the bones of a prehistoric man were discovered in cave deposits that were up to 50 m (164 ft) deep, it provided scientists with some significant information on the history of human evolution.

There is a treasure chamber of evolutionary history located not far from Beijing. It is a cave that was apparently inhabited for some 230,000 years, and in which ash deposits as well as human and animal remains reached right up to the ceiling. In 1928 the bones of a prehistoric man including a skull were found in there. This Sinanthropus pekinensis, the so-called Peking Man of the homo erectus species, was around 150 cm (59 in) tall and had a brain one-third smaller than that of Homo sapiens. There have recently been disputes regarding the extent to which the cave's inhabitants already could control or use fire, or were even able to hunt. The tools only comprised simple hand axes. Nearby another discovery was made, this time of 11,000- to 18,000-year-old bones of Homo sapiens. These findings at Zhoukoudian have thus made the evolutionary process more comprehensible than at any other place on earth.

The excavations at the cave in Zhoukoudian and the surrounding area are still underway.

IMPERIAL PALACES OF THE MING AND QING DYNASTIES

This World Heritage Site includes the imperial palace from the Ming dynasty in Beijing and the palace of the Manchurian Qing dynasty in Shenyang. The complex in Beijing has also been referred to historically as the "Forbidden City", since mere mortals were refused entry.

As "sons of heaven", the emperors of China were subject to the concept of global harmony and as such acted as intermediaries between heaven and earth. The third Ming emperor, who appointed Beijing as his residence, designed his new palace with this in mind. The massive square complex faces all four points of the compass and symbolism is omnipresent. The triad of main halls and the three-leveled terrace on which

The Shenyang imperial palace covers an area of 60,000 sq m (645,600 sq ft) and the imperial throne is in the "Hall of Great Government" (above).

they were erected, for example, embody the emperor's male yang. The cloud dragons that adorn the beams, thrones and the emperor's garments represent his beneficent powers. The yellow glaze on the roofs was solely reserved for imperial buildings.

The imperial palace in Shenyang features 144 buildings and was constructed between 1625 and 1783. It attests to Manchu cultural traditions. In fact, the Qing dynasty originated from the Manchurian capital once known as "Mukden" (1625 to 1644) before moving to Beijing.

The Forbidden City is now a museum with magnificent halls and art treasures. The emperor would sit on the Dragon Throne (center) in the richly decorated "Hall of Highest Harmony" (top). Beijing's imperial palace was protected by walls and a moat (bottom).

China

TEMPLE OF HEAVEN: AN IMPERIAL SACRIFICIAL ALTAR IN BEIJING

The Altar of Heaven is the most important sacred site from ancient China. It is where the emperor would offer sacrifices to the heavens every year.

The white marble altar terrace in the south forms the center of a complex whose area is even larger than the imperial palace. On the longest night of the year, the winter solstice, the emperor would offer up silk and sacrificial victims here surrounded by participants of the ritual. The "soul tablets" of the heavens and heavenly manifestations (sun, moon, planets, lightning and thunder) as well as the imperial ancestors would be set up on the terrace. These tablets are still stored in the halls of the imperial Vault of Heaven and its smaller auxiliary halls. However, the showpiece of the complex is the circular Hall of Prayer for Good Harvests, distinguished by the three-tiered blue roof. The structure, probably the most harmonious in China, embodies the circular flow of time. The four main pillars represent the seasons, the twelve inner columns the months, and the twelve external columns the hours of a day (in a 12-hour cycle). If time followed its proper course, rain and sun would come at the right time so the people could enjoy a successful harvest. The emperor would pray for this in the temple hall.

The Hall of Prayer for Good Harvests is on a circular plaza with three terraces.

SUMMER PALACE, AN IMPERIAL GARDEN IN BEIJING

The last of the great palace building projects of imperial China is a grandiose fusion of architecture and landscaping.

Originally built in 1750, destroyed in 1860 during the Opium War and then rebuilt once more starting in 1885, the Summer Palace is more a rural park than a building of rulership. It owes its present-day appearance to Empress Dowager Cixi, who had it refurbished for herself as an old-age residence at the end of the 19th century. To do so she used resources intended for a war fleet; while her anti-reform policy brought about the kingdom's collapse her lovely summer palace maintained the illusion of Manchurian China as a great empire and cultural universe.

The complex is home to an intimate southern-Chinese landscape garden with small pavilions and a lotus pond as well as a Tibetan monastery. The 728-m (2,389-ft) colonnade on the northern banks of Kunming Lake has been depicted in Chinese landscapes, theatre pieces and novels. The symbols of longevity are ever-present as well: pines, bamboo, "mushrooms of immortality" and other symbols, sometimes in nature, and sometimes in the ornamentation.

The Zhichun Pavilion at the Summer Palace is on an island in Kunming Lake.

IMPERIAL TOMBS OF THE MING AND QING DYNASTIES

The tombs of members of the royal family were carefully selected based on geomantic considerations (Feng Shui tradition).

The imperial tombs of the Ming (1368 to 1644) and Qing dynasties (1644 to 1911) embody a philosophy that was embraced for more than five hundred years and a concept of power that created and maintained feudal China. The impressive Xianling Mausoleum in Hubei province is the largest individual Ming tomb in the country. It contains both an old and a new burial chamber. Emperor Jiajing (r. 1521–1567) had his father's tomb converted into a colossal imperial burial site comprising a total of thirty buildings. The imposing burial sites of the Qing dynasty are located in two places, each roughly 100 km (62 mi) outside of Beijing. The eastern Qing dynasty tomb site, consecrated in 1663 near Zunhua, includes a total of fifteen tombs. The tombs in the western portion were built in Baoding, south-west of Beijing, in 1723.

China's most concentrated cluster of tombs from the Ming dynasty is located in a valley of the Tianshou Mountains near Beijing. Visitors enter through the Gate of Honor (top).

YUNGANG GROTTOES

The 252 Yungang grottoes are the largest artificial caves in the world. They were carved into the sandstone between the years 460 and 525 starting with the Buddhist Emperor Wen Chengi.

Being devout followers, the emperors of the Wei dynasty had raised Buddhism to the status of national religion. Emperor Tai Wudi, however, suddenly banned Buddhism in 446 and died unexpectedly soon after. His grandson, Wen Chengdi, saw this as being a sign from the heavens. To atone for his grandfather's sacrilege, he had the Yungang or "Cloud Ridge" grottoes hewn into the Wuzhou mountains. The monk Tan Yao managed to recruit more than 10,000 people to work on the gigantic construction, which began in the year 460. Five years later, the first five grottoes honoring the five Wei rulers were completed. The other grottoes were created over the following thirty to forty years until the Wei capital was moved to Longmen.

The Buddha sculptures in the Yungang grottoes range from 2 cm (8 in) to 17 m (56 ft) in height. The ear of the largest seated Buddha measures 3 m (10 ft) and his feet are 4.5 m (15 ft). In one grotto are 12,000 smaller Buddha sculptures on which eighty-three artists spent six long years working.

Some of the Buddha figures hewn into the stone at the Yungang grottoes bear the features of the Wei emperors.

MOUNT WUTAI

Mount Wutai (Wutai Shan), a mountain range in north-eastern Shanxi province, is one of the four sacred mountains of Buddhism along with the Emei Shan, Putuo Shan and Jiuhua Shan.

The first Buddhist monks came to Mount Wutai to seek enlightenment more than 2,000 years ago. More than 100 monasteries once adorned its high, green valleys with colorful prayer flags. Even Ming dynasty emperors traveled to this range with its five distinctive peaks to seek advice from the monks.

Today visitors to the mountain can admire the variety of Chinese Buddhist temple architecture: The Foguang Temple, for example, was built around the year 900 and is one of China's oldest and tallest wooden buildings. The Nanchan Monastery is famous for its large, ornate Buddha Hall, and the Shuxiang Temple features twelve colorful statues telling stories of Manjusri, one of Buddha's pupils today who is considered to be the Bodhisattva (enlightened one) and whose abode is on Mount Wutai. He is the protector of scholars and, as a celestial builder, helps earthly architects construct sacred sites.

Chinese, Tibetans, Mongolians and Manchus all consider Mount Wutai (also known as the "Five Finger Mountain" because of its five peaks) the residence of an enlightened being in whose honor Buddhists built fifty-three monasteries and temples.

MOGAO CAVES

Buddhism was brought to China via the Silk Road. Along that route near Dunhuang, in Gansu province, 492 grottoes decorated with wall paintings and sculptures display the world's largest series of Buddhist illustrations.

For more than one thousand years merchants, generals, wealthy widows and simple monks would try to add emphasis to their various pleas, prayers and hopes for salvation here at the Dunhuang oasis. They dug grottoes into the stone in honor of the gods on a nearby rock face and adorned them with scenes from the life of the Gautama Buddha, images from paradise and scenes from the material world along with all manner of ornamentation. In 1900, a Taoist monk discovered a bricked-up library with more than 50,000 texts from the fourth to the 10th centuries in cave number 17.

The rows of grottoes, which once totaled more than 1,000 before more than half of them fell into disrepair, cover 1,600 m (2,581 yds) over multiple levels along a long cliff face. Around 45,000 sq m (484,200 sq ft) of murals and 2,400 colored clay figures ranging in size from 10 cm (4 in) to 33 m (108 ft) have been preserved. The images show Indian, Chinese and even Hellenic influences and attest to the Silk Road's importance in the cultural exchange across Asia.

Valuable wall paintings in the Mogao Caves illustrate Buddha's life.

ANCIENT CITY OF PING YAO

Ping Yao was founded as early as pre-Christian times and was expanded in the 14th century. It is a perfect example of Chinese architecture during the Ming and Qing eras, and the urban development of the last few centuries can clearly be seen here.

The historic center of Ping Yao was reinforced with an imposing 12-m-high (39-ft) and, on average, 5-m-wide (16-ft) city wall in 1370 under the rule of Ming Emperor Hong Wu. It forms a square with a total length of more than 6 km (4 mi). Under its protection is a carefully planned network of residential streets with a number of well-preserved merchants' homes and banking houses that provide an insight into everyday living and business operations in ancient China. Ping Yao owes its wealth primarily to banking and the work of local merchants. When the trading routes changed at the end of the 19th century, the city lost importance as a trading center.

Ping Yao also lost its rank as a prominent financial center following the rise of the Chinese coastal cities, particularly Hong Kong and Shanghai, towards the end of the 19th century and early 20th century. The development actually protected the ancient city of Ping Yao from being destroyed as a result of modernization.

Black brick houses characterize the Old Town of Ping Yao, which was once an important financial center for China.

YIN XU

Yin Xu was the capital of the later Shang dynasty around 1300 to 1066 BC. Jade workshops, bronze foundries, palaces, tombs and countless marked bones were found here.

The Bronze Age in China began with the Shang dynasty (ca. 16th–11th century BC) whose origins can be traced back to a tribe from the lower reaches of the Yellow River (Huang He). The empire's capital was moved several times in its early years but Emperor Pan Geng then appointed Yin as his capital. This move gave the dynasty a boost, but the collapse of the Shang dynasty also saw the capital, Yin, fall rapidly into disrepair before becoming Yin Xu, the ruined city of Yin. Yin Xu's area spans a total of around 30 sq km (12 sq mi) and includes regions both north and south of the Yellow River. A district of palaces and ancestral temples is situated on the southern banks where the most important discovery was the tomb of Fu Hao – the only tomb fully preserved from the Shang Dynasty. The second district is situated on the northern banks of the Yellow River and comprises princes' graves as well as the tombs of some 2,000 servants or slaves who were probably sacrificed for the dynasty's ancestors.

In 1976, archaeologists discovered the tomb of Fu Hao, the wife of Shang king, Wu Ding. It contained a wealth of burial objects.

China

M O U N T   T A I S H A N

The sacred mountain of Taishan is north of the city of Tai'an in the province of Shandong. In Chinese mythology, the 1,545-m (5,069-ft) peak is associated with heavenly powers, and the tradition of Chinese emperors making sacrifices to the mountain goes back to the 2nd century BC.

The Taishan massif is the highest alpine region for 1,000 km (600 mi) in any direction, and its streams and sheer faces are truly magnificent. Because it faces the sunrise, the range was believed to preside over both life and death. The first Chinese emperor, Qin Shi Huangdi, ascended the mountain as part of his first tour of the newly unified empire. Before him, Confucius had pronounced Taishan a place that allowed man to see how small the world really was. Many more famous figures followed Confucius up Taishan, where more than one thousand stone inscriptions testify

Taishan is one of the five sacred mountains of Taoism.

to their journeys. Nearly 100 temples once lined the path to the summit, twenty-two of which have survived. Nature worship dates back more than 2,500 years in China, and it was here that this tradition was most splendidly expressed. In fact, the ritual performed here is so elaborate and politically significant that it has only occurred four times since the beginning of the common era. The penultimate occasion was in 725, when Emperor Xuanzong made the ascent, commemorated by a 13-m (43-ft) gilded inscription in the rock.

The famous inscription left by Tang emperor Li Longji (top right) provides a backdrop for a monk's tai chi exercises. A fresco in the Temple of the Mountain God at the base of the Taishan (right) shows that the emperor was obliged to take part in a pilgrimage procession in order to ascend the mountain. Before the ascent he spent the night in the temple.

TEMPLE AND CEMETERY OF CONFUCIUS AND THE KONG FAMILY MANSION IN QUFU

The place where Confucius (551–479 BC) was born and died is the center of a cult that is prominent all over East Asia. It is not only where the wise man was buried but is also home to the largest Confucius temple on earth. The World Heritage Site includes the cemetery with the scholar's tomb as well as the residence of the Kong Family from which Confucius was descended.

In 195 BC, the founder of the Han dynasty came to Qufu, south of Jinan in Shandong province to offer the first sacrifice to Confucius. It was the earliest confirmed date connected to the cult of China's great teacher. Once his

Confucius' gravesite is in the Kong Family Forest, a 200-ha (494-acre) area 2 km (1 mi) north of Qufu.

teachings had been made official state philosophy, Confucius' heirs were entrusted with organizing ritual sacrifices until well into the 20th century, for which they received vast imperial fiefdoms. Their residence is still next to the temple. With a length of 685 m (2,247 ft) and a width of 150 m (492 ft), the sanctuary here is significantly larger than any other Confucius temple in East Asia. The roof of the main hall was glazed yellow as a sign of an imperial privilege dating back to the year 1730.

Confucius, his relatives, and all local descendants were buried at a nearby cemetery, the so-called Kong Family Forest. It is China's largest and oldest cemetery still used today.

The Kong family residence includes an altar and some valuable furnishings.

LONGMEN GROTTOES

The Longmen ("Dragon Gate") grottoes are among the largest cave temple complexes in China. They are situated on an cliff roughly 1,000 m (3,281 ft) long on the Yi River just a few miles south of Luoyang in Henan province.

Over 2,000 grottoes and recesses line the steep slopes of Dragon Mountain above the Yi River. Measuring around 1 km (0.6 mi) in length, Longmen is the largest man-made cave formation in China. The grottoes, which were a sacred site, feature priceless inscriptions and are home to more than 100,000 stone Buddhist statues as well as richly detailed ceiling and wall decorations. The grotto sanctuaries were first developed by the rulers of the Northern Wei dynasty as early as 494 after they had moved their capital to the ancient city of Luoyang, a famous center of Buddhism. The Guyang caves from the early years of

495 to 499 as well as the Binyang caves from the years 500 to 532 have also been lovingly preserved. The cave complex was further expanded in the following centuries, a period known as the Golden Age of Buddhism, under the rulers of the Sui and Tang dynasties. From the fifth to the ninth centuries, the so-called Longmen style then inspired the emergence of a Buddhist form of sculpture typical of northern China that was distinguished by an extremely high degree of artistic creativity.

The 17-m (56-ft) Buddha statue of Vairochana is the centerpiece of the Fengxian Temple.

MAUSOLEUM OF THE FIRST QIN EMPEROR

Qin Emperor Shi Huangdi was buried here more than 2,000 years ago surrounded by thousands of individually crafted terracotta figures depicting the organization of the military and imperial court.

Just after China's first emperor Qin Shi Huangdi had unified the territories, he began building a burial site befitting of his rank about 30 km (19 mi) northeast of Xi'an. The fact that the site contained more than just an impressive burial mound only became clear when farmers drilling wells in 1974 discovered broken fragments of large warrior statues. The warriors turned out to be part of an army of about 7,600 soldiers that is still not completely excavated – all of them unique. Lined up in battle formation in underground chambers, the army was there

to protect the deceased's tomb and, in turn, his empire against evil powers from the netherworld. It also documented the high rank of the tomb's owner. Many of the larger-than-life figures that would originally have been painted have now been restored and moved back to their original position. Other valuable burial objects include two life-size bronze teams of horses. Only one quarter of the gravesite has so far been excavated.

The terracotta army is lined up in battle formation and spread over three caverns.

ANCIENT BUILDING COMPLEX IN THE WUDANG MOUNTAINS

This once remote highland is China's most important center of the Taoist religion. In the 15th century, impressive temples and monasteries were built here on the emperor's orders.

Taoist hermits have been retreating to this remote mountain region in north-western Hubei province since at least the era of the Eastern Han dynasty (AD 25–220). According to legends spread during the Tang era (618–907), the area was once home to the heavenly emperor of the north. As a result of these tales, monasteries were established and the Wudang Mountains were transformed into a series of pilgrimage sites. Driven by political motives, the third emperor of the Ming dynasty, Yongle, ultimately had new, palatial monasteries

built here from 1412. Around 300,000 workers were employed for the projects. A total of 129 of the religious sites have been preserved, but most visitors and pilgrims want to see the Golden Hall, a 14-sq-m (151-sq-ft) building made entirely of bronze constructed in 1416 that is perched at the summit of the 1,612-m (5,289-ft) Tianzhu peak, the tallest mountain in the region.

The "Monastery of Highest Harmony" is among the many temples, monasteries, shrines, caves and hermitages here.

LUSHAN NATIONAL PARK

The name "Lushan" refers to a specific mountain as well as a mountain range north of the Yangtze River in Jiangxi province. Amidst this magical landscape the beauties of nature form a rare ensemble of temples, monasteries and mementos dedicated to historic personages.

Few mountains have been sung about as often as the Lushan. It was not just virtually every major Chinese poet who honored it with a visit and left behind inscriptions, but also prominent philosophers, painters, monks and even politicians. The "Mountain of the Supernatural Being" was a favorite pilgrimage site of both Taoists and Buddhists, and its lakes, waterfalls, forests and cliffs predestined it as a summer getaway. The mountain, often shrouded in mist, greatly influenced the development of Chinese landscape painting and in a way was only rivaled by the Huangshan.

Zhu Xi (1130–1200), a master of neo-Confucian philosophy, taught at the Bailudong Academy on Lushan in the 12th century. The numerous temple monasteries at the foot of the 1,400-m (4,593-ft-) high mountain also include Donglin Monastery, the center the of the Buddhist Jingtu school founded by the monk Huiyan in 384.

The breathtaking Lushan Mountains, with their temples and pagodas high above the Yangtze, not only inspired poets but also became a destination for Chinese landscape painters.

CLASSICAL GARDENS OF SUZHOU

The many residential gardens in Suzhou were built by merchants, writers and civil servants for their own recreation and are today pleasant inner-city refuges.

Suzhou, located just to the west of Shanghai, owes its wealth to the Imperial Canal. The many canals spanned by stone bridges were and still are important inner-city traffic routes. However, the city is primarily famous for the residential gardens which, with their ponds, artistically arranged rocks and sparse, symbolic plants have preserved an element of the city's former atmosphere.

The "Blue Wave Garden" at the Canglang Canal, for example, dates back to the year 1044, its name a literary allusion to the corruption prevalent during the period. The "Humble Administrator's Garden", created in 1509, is considered the most characteristic of the Ming-era gardens and stretches over some 4 ha (10 acres). The "Lion Grove" (from around 1342) owes its name to the bizarre rock formations found here. Measuring just 0.5 ha (1 acre) in size, the "Lingering Garden", created in 1522 and remodeled in around 1770, is one of the smallest yet most popular gardens in Suzhou.

Suzhou is also called the Venice of the East because of its many canals and bridges.

MOUNT HUANGSHAN

Huangshan is a city in southern China whose administrative area includes the famous Huangshan mountains, where rocks appear to float in a sea of clouds as if nature had conjured up a fantasy landscape.

"There is no mountain as beautiful as Huangshan", is how the famous Ming-dynasty geographer Xu Xiake (1587–1641) allegedly described this place. He was famous for his travel writing, and it is not difficult to see what he was talking about here. Although it covers only around 150 sq km (59 sq mi) of Anhui province, there are no fewer than seventy-seven peaks between 1,000 m (3,300 ft) and 1,850 m (6,000 ft) all tightly packed into the region around Huangshan, or "Yellow Mountain". On around 250 days of the year mist drifts through the deep valleys in such thick patches that, seen from above, the landscape looks like a sea on which the mountaintops are floating. Over the centuries a number of pavilions have been built from which people can gaze down over the fabulous scenery that so resembles the Chinese artistic ideals of a perfect landscape. The beauty of Huangshan, which had great influence on China's classical academic culture, is perfected by the ancient pine trees that grow out of the craggy rock faces here.

The Huangshan mountains are one of the most famous mountainous regions in China. With its strangely shaped rocks and gnarled pines (below) it corresponds to the Chinese landscape ideal.

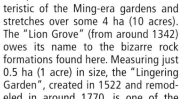

ANCIENT VILLAGES IN SOUTHERN ANHUI – XIDI AND HONGCUN

These two traditional towns provide an authentic picture of the social order and morals of Chinese feudal society.

The complex of the Hongcun and Xidi settlements in the south-eastern corner of Anhui province (in the Yixian district) is defined by the pattern of a medieval road network that was a result of houses being built to face southward. Many of the two-story brick homes date back to the time between the late 15th century and the 17th century and are evidence of the continuous adherence to an architectural style that hardly changed in two thousand years of imperial rule. The rich decoration proves that the houses were built for wealthy, high-ranking families who were part of the newly created class of merchant princes who settled in South Anhui. One of the special features is the water supply system that was created as early as the 14th century during the economic revival of rural regions.

Pitched roofs and diverse styles of lattice windows and small porthole-like openings are typical of the buildings in Xidi and Hongcun. Fine lines and muted colors recall Chinese ink-and-wash paintings.

MOUNT WUYI

The subtropical forest in the Mount Wuyi region is not only rich in flora and fauna and a paradise for some rare species; its steep rocks and crystal-clear rivers also give it a unique beauty.

At the highest point of the Wuyi Mountains in far north-western Fujian province is a subtropical forest habitat that has survived intact for millions of years. Almost 2,500 higher plant species and around 5,000 types of insects as well as 475 kinds of vertebrates have been found here so far. Because the average altitude in the Wuyishan is only 350 m (1,100 ft) above sea level, temperatures are relatively mild here even in winter. The nature reserve is of biological importance, of course, but the highly impressive landscape also has a charm of its own. This is due in particular to the thirty-six rocky peaks towering into the sky on both sides of the Jiuquxi, or Nine Bend river, which rises in the west of the region. This stretch of landscape can be explored by boat and has some curious features such as the high, shell-shaped grotto with spring water flowing out of the top of it. In another place there is a vertical crack in the rock at the end of a tunnel-shaped cave that is only half a meter (1.5 ft) wide and around 100 m (330 ft) long revealing a strip of gossamer sky.

Literary figures and scholars enjoyed the remote region around Wuyi as a retreat.

WULINGYUAN SCENIC AND HISTORIC INTEREST AREA

More than 3,000 overgrown quartz-sandstone towers dot the landscape of both of these national parks. It is also home to the highest natural bridge on earth.

The peaks in Wulingyuan are spread across the two areas of Zhangjiajie and Tianzishan and along the banks of the Jinbianxi. They were formed by erosion from a layer of sediment 500 m (1,600 ft) thick. The valleys between the peaks are so narrow that it is impossible to farm there, which is why this region in Hunan province in south-eastern China still remains uninhabited. Almost all the distinctive rocks have colorful names and the whole area is densely overgrown with water courses.

Special attractions here include two natural bridges, one of which is 26 m

(85 ft) long and spans a 100-m (330-ft) chasm. The other is a spectacular 40 m (130 ft) long and 350 m (1,150 ft) above the valley floor. There are also numerous subterranean wonders including the stalagmite forest in a 12,000-sq-m (129,000-sq-ft) cavern in nearby Huanglong Dong, Yellow Dragon Cave.

The rock labyrinth in Wulingyuan was still below sea level 100 million years ago.

DAZU ROCK CARVINGS

More than 1,000 years ago, about 10,000 sculptures were hewn from the living rock roughly 100 km (60 mi) from present-day Chongqing.

A kaleidoscope of 1,000-year-old Buddhist sculpture adorns the rock faces of Dazu, which are between 7 and 30 m (23 and 98 ft) high and up to 500 m (1,640 ft) wide. Unlike in the large rock temple complexes of northern China, which were predominantly built in artificial grottoes, the colored sculptures and reliefs in Dazu are mostly out in the open.

Figures of the Buddha, identified by their simple monk's attire, are featured particularly often here, as are the bodhisattvas, who refuse to enter Nirvana in order to instead help the people and rescue them from earthly misery. Images of the Buddhist version of paradise illustrate the bliss that

awaits pious believers. But guardian deities, scenes from hell and even secular themes are also addressed here. The latter provide an insight into everyday life at the time the carvings were created.

The roughly 10,000 sculptures on the Treasured Summit Hill were made by just one single monk. Dazu is also famous for its 31-m-long (102-ft) reclining Buddha depicted entering Nirvana as well as a gilded thousand-armed Guanyin.

The stone reliefs in Dazu include thousands of representations of Buddha.

JIUZHAIGOU VALLEY SCENIC AREA

Three alpine valleys of north-western Sichuan province feature a unique abundance of natural wonders with brightly hued lakes, torrential cataracts, rare animals and generally lush vegetation.

These three densely forested valleys start at 2,000 m (6,500 ft) and rise to form a Y-shaped ensemble towered over by snow-covered peaks that reach heights of 4,700 m (15,500 ft). The karstic subsoil here enriches the trickling rivers with calcium salt, which re-emerges in the form of large sinter terraces. Cataracts then gush over tree-covered tufa embankments, the largest waterfall of which plunges down an impressive 80 m (260 ft). Several lakes gleam in a variety of hues, from yellow and bright green to blue and turquoise.

With secluded valleys tucked away in its breathtaking mountains, Juzhaigou is also a refuge for rare plant and animal species including giant pandas and golden hair monkeys as well as a number of species of birds.

The name Jiuzhaigou means "Valley of Nine Villages", a reference to the nine Tibetan villages in the 60 sq km (23 sq mi) area. The fascinating landscape features waterfalls and snow-capped mountains as well as about 120 lakes that shimmer in different hues depending on the time of year.

HUANGLONG SCENIC AREA

In addition to an impressive alpine and glacier landscape, visitors here will also experience a succession of sinter terraces almost 4 km (2.5 mi) long that winds its way through a forested valley.

This glacial valley is in the autonomous region of Ngawa in Sichuan province, and rises from around 3,000 m (9,800 ft) above sea level to the high snow-capped mountain of Xuebaoding at 5,588 m (18,300 ft). It is also known as a refuge for the giant panda. Over time, yellow sinter terraces formed here at the bottom of a densely forested valley where the water shimmers in varied hues due to the algae and bacteria living in it. Adjoining basins thus possess very different tones which, combined with the reflections of the foliage, sky and clouds results in a fascinating play of light and color. There are also trees growing in some of the pools. The main attraction of the reserve is a steep travertine area around 2.5 km (1.5 mi) long and 100 m (33 ft) wide covered by a runnel just centimeters deep. The phenomenon is associated with a yellow dragon (Huanglong in Chinese), which explains how the World Heritage Site gets its name.

The terrace-like pools in Huanglong valley formed during the ice age when the whole region still lay under a glacier.

MOUNT QINGCHENG AND THE DUJIANGYAN IRRIGATION SYSTEM

Mount Qingcheng and the irrigation system in Dujiangyan are in the western part of the city of Chengdu, which has always been characterized by economic and spiritual independence.

The pristine nature and particularly the flora and fauna of this mountain situated on the eastern edge of the Tibetan Plateau have for centuries inspired hikers to express their feelings and engrave messages into the rock. Halfway up the mountain is the Cave of the Heavenly Master, Tianshi Dong, which is worshipped by Taoists as a sacred site. The hermit Zhang Daoling lived here in the second century before founding the Taoist "Five Pecks of Rice" movement.

The Dujiangyan hydraulic engineering project to regulate the mighty Min River was established east of the mountain on the edge of the Red Basin during the third century BC. An artificially raised island separates the bodies of water and channels them into canals.

Mount Qingcheng is the fifth of the famous Taoist mountains in China. Many temples from the third to the eighth centuries line the path up to the summit.

THE SICHUAN GIANT PANDA SANCTUARIES

Around 900 of these animals live in the Sichuan panda reserves, including thirty percent of the world's remaining wild giant pandas. The area also has some of the most diverse plantlife outside of the tropics.

The Sichuan Giant Panda Sanctuary in south-central China is situated in the Qionglai and Jiajin mountains. In addition to seven nature reserves, it comprises nine "scenic parks" that are also open to visitors. The nature reserve is home to almost one-third of all wild giant pandas and is thus the most important conservation and breeding area for this endangered species. Among the other species is the red panda, previously thought to be related the larger bear, the snow leopard and the clouded leopard. The area is also a veritable treasure trove for the medicinal plants used in traditional Chinese medicine. One reason for the abundance of plants is the enormous diversity in the landscape – the difference in altitude between the lowest and highest point is around 5,700 m (18,700 ft).

Bamboo is typical of southern China and forms the basic diet of the giant panda. When large areas of bamboo plants died off in 1975, around 140 bears starved to death as a result. Since then the number of pandas living in the wild has risen again but their habitat is still in danger.

China

MOUNT EMEI AND LESHAN GIANT BUDDHA SCENIC AREA

Among the four sacred mountains of Chinese Buddhism, the status of the highest one goes back to the 2nd century. The largest Buddha in the world in nearby Leshan is also part of this World Heritage Site.

Craggy rocks, deep crevices, mountain streams, waterfalls, towering peaks and dense forests with trees over 1,000 years old await visitors to sacred Mount Emei ("Towering Eyebrow Mountain"), which is an impressive 3,000 m (9,800 ft) high. Located on the south-western edge of the Red Basin in Sichuan, it has been a sanctuary for hermits since the Eastern Han period (AD 25–220) with the first Buddhist temples and monasteries built here not long after that. Legend has it that Samantabhadra,

The name of this mountain means roughly "Towering Eyebrow Mountain".

the bodhisattva of the law and patron saint of Emeishan, is said to have taught here. There is a statue over 8 m (26 ft) high in remembrance of him in a mountain temple.

There are now more than 200 monasteries and hermitages in the area and the stream of pilgrims has continued to grow. Some sacred buildings go back as far as the Sui period (AD 581–618), but most are from the 17th century. Attractions for pilgrims in the region include the 71-m (233-ft) sitting Buddha statue in Leshan, 35 km (22 mi) away at the confluence of the Minjiang, Dadu and Qingyi rivers. It was sculpted from a single rock face in the 8th century by Buddhist monks.

Qingyin-Ge, the Pavilion of Clear Sound (top right), is at 710 m (2,330 ft) above sea level on the path to the summit of Mount Emei. A giant Buddha has watched over the confluence of the Dadu and the Minjiang rivers for more than 1,200 years.

THREE PARALLEL RIVERS OF YUNNAN PROTECTED AREAS

In north-western Yunnan, three rivers – the Yangtze, Mekong and Salween – run more or less parallel to each other for around 170 km (105 mi). Almost all northern hemisphere landscapes and ecosystems can be found in this area along with an astounding range of biodiversity.

Geologically speaking, the Sanjiang Bingliu region is exceptionally diverse. It features magnetic rocks, limestone with karst phenomena, weather-beaten granite and sandstone formations. In some places the three rivers form dramatically steep gorges up to 3,000 m (9,850 ft) deep. In total, the area boasts 118 mountains over 5,000 m (16,400 ft) high, the highest of which is Kawagebo at 6,740 m (2,211 ft).

Three Parallel Rivers National Park is in the biogeographical convergence zone between the Palearctic and Oriental regions and thus features both temperate and tropical zones. During the ice age the area was a corridor for many types of flora and fauna moving south before the imminent glaciation.

The Yangtze (left) has carved a spectacular gorge 15 km (9 mi) long through the Yunnan mountains.

OLD TOWN OF LIJIANG

Lijiang, in the strategic transition zone between Central and South Asia, was once a distant outpost of the Chinese Empire. The historic center of the city blends harmoniously into its surrounding mountain landscape.

Unlike most settlements from the era, the Old Town of Lijiang never required a city wall because of its strategically sheltered location in the mountains, tucked deep into a valley on the western edge of Yunnan province, not far from the Myanmar border. The still lively marketplace here is located at the center of the narrow maze of alleyways lined with historic buildings of differing architectural styles. Due to its location, Lijiang not only features buildings that combine elements of various cultures; it is also a very multicultural city with over a dozen ethnic groups.

For centuries, Lijiang has boasted a unique irrigation system supplied by three canals. This result of this complex network of canals, nearly every house in the town has its own "babbling brook" flowing around it. The numerous parks and glistening streets also make Lijiang a jewel among Chinese cities. Although many buildings were damaged in an earthquake in 1997, most have now been restored with the help of international aid.

The Old Town of Lijiang (left) is considered one of the best preserved in China. Black Pool Park (above with the Shuocui Bridge) is located at the foot of Mt Xianshan north of Lijiang and provides a spectacular view of the Jade Dragon Snow Mountain.

China

Dalai Lama

In the Tibetan form of Buddhism known as Lamaism, the Dalai Lama ("Ocean of Knowledge") is considered the reincarnation of "Chenresi", Tibet's protector deity. The Dalai Lama has resided in the mighty Potala Temple Palace in Lhasa since 1642 as the spiritual and earthly leader of all Tibetans. Born the son of a farmer in 1935, Lhamo Dhondup was just two years old when a delegation of Tibetan high priests sought out his humble family home, where a prophecy is said to have shown them the way. It is reported that the young boy recognized objects that once belonged to the earlier incarnations of the Dalai Lama, thereby confirming the prophecy. Since then, he is

HISTORIC ENSEMBLE OF THE POTALA PALACE, LHASA

The Dalai Lama's residence is both a monastery and a fort where Tibet's religion and politics merge into an impressive architectural ensemble. Following expansions in 2000 and 2001, the World Heritage Site now also includes not only the Potala Palace itself but also the Jokhang Temple and Norbulingka Palace.

A unique politico-religious culture manifests itself in this grandiose construction soaring 110 m (361 ft) above the Lhasa Valley. Its main section, the White Palace, is over 320 m (1,050 ft)

The courtyard of the Red Palace is home to richly decorated and colorfully painted wooden balconies.

long and was built under the fifth Dalai Lama, the first high priest of Tibetan Buddhism, who exercised political power. The central Red Palace, which was later crowned with golden roofs and is home to the complex's most important treasures, was built after he died. The complex has a total of around 1,000 rooms and covers an area of almost 130,000 sq m (1,398,800 sq ft). Its lavish splendor attests to a degree of religious devotion that equals the unfortunate levels of deprivation in Tibetan life.

The Potala Palace was the residence of the 14th Dalai Lama and the seat of the Tibetan government until he fled to India in 1959.

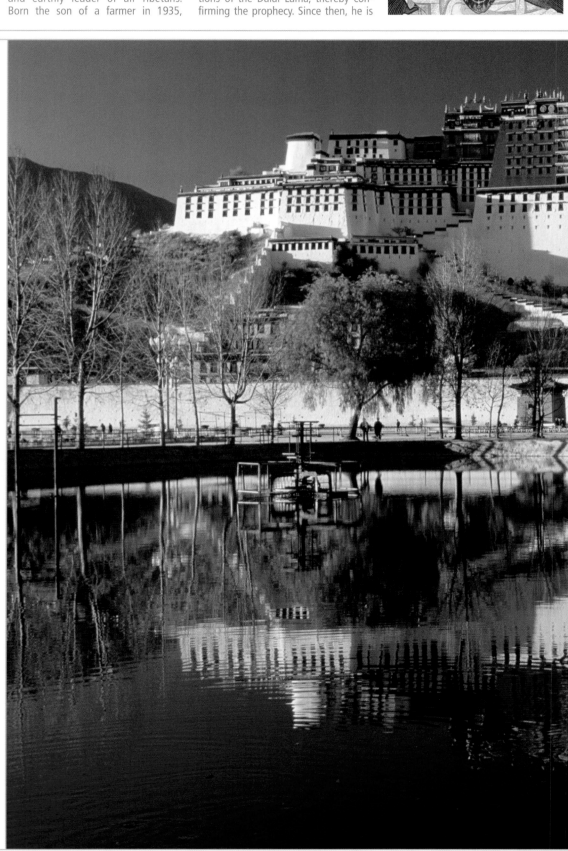

considered by the Tibetans to be the 14th reincarnation of their divine king. He ascended the Lion Throne at four under the monk's name "Tenzin Gyatso", but in 1950 the Chinese seized the country and brutally suppressed its ancient traditions; the Dalai Lama no longer ruled Tibet. After much bloodshed – tens of thousands of Tibetans

have been killed and 6,000 monasteries and temples destroyed since then – and unsuccessful uprisings the Dalai Lama fled to India in 1959. He established a democratic government-in-exile for his occupied country near Dharamsala. In 1989 he received the Nobel Peace Prize as a charismatic figurehead for peaceful relations between peoples.

A mural (far left) in the Potala Palace depicts the fifth Dalai Lama, Ngawang Lobsang Gyatso (1617–1682). The sitting room of the 14th Dalai Lama (left) has been preserved in its original state. He fled to India on November 17, 1959, nine years after Chinese troops invaded Tibet and took over the country.

China

SOUTH CHINA KARST

The region around Guilin features bizarre limestone formations that have become icons of the southern Chinese landscape. They exist in an area covering 500,000 sq km (310,000 sq mi), of which the World Heritage Site includes a series of 1,000 sq km (386 sq mi) areals with particularly striking formations in Shilin near Kunming, Libo near Guiyang and Wulong near Chongqing.

In tropical southern China, distinctive limestone formations known as karsts have developed through millions of years of carbonic acid reactions. The erosion results in strange and wonderful shapes such as cone, tower and stone forest karsts. The Shilin karst in Yunnan, for example, is made up of stone forests with deep, sharp channels. The Libo karst in Guizhou on the other hand illustrates the transition from cone to tower karst. Dolines (sinkholes) with gorges, caves and bridge-like structures dominate the Wulong karst in Chongqing. Caves in particular show how carbonic acid reactions can also deposit dissolved limestone and form stalactites, stalagmites and sinter terraces.

Two hundred and seventy million years ago, a karst mountain range – the Shilin karst ("stone forest") – developed from a shallow sea close to present-day Kunming. The rock formations often resemble animals or people and have names such as "Birds feeding their young" or "A phoenix grooming". The area can be viewed from an observation pagoda as well (right).

MOUNT SANQINGSHAN NATIONAL PARK

Characterized by lush forests, countless waterfalls and fantastically shaped rock formations, Mount Sanqingshan National Park in south-eastern China is a breathtaking landscape of extraordinary beauty.

Mount Sanqingshan National Park in the province of Jiangxi is at the western end of the Huyaiyu range. The protected area is 230 sq km (89 sq mi) at elevations mostly ranging from 1,000 to 1,800 m (3,300 to 5,940 ft), with the highest peak, Huyaiyu, at 1817 m (5,961 ft). These differences in elevation mean the national park features both subtropical and maritime climates with rainforests as well as evergreen regions. The unique granite formations of the Huyaiyu chain are also among the attractions here, with many of the forty-eight peaks and eighty-nine pillars resembling human figures or animals. Banks of fog and mist increase the effect by creating a shifting landscape of unusual and fascinating light effects such as the so-called "white rainbow". The age of this mountain chain – up to 1.6 billion years – has also made research of the area of great interest to geologists.

Mountains with trees growing horizontally out of rock formations and clinging to jagged cliffs (right) give the landscape of Mount Sanqingshan National Park an almost unreal appearance.

FUJIAN TULOU

The "earthen" houses here were built as fortified residential complexes between the 12th and 20th centuries. These environmentally-conscious constructions, combined with the idea of communal living, are interesting from an architectural perspective.

The Hakka settlements in the mountainous region of south-western Fujian province are tucked in among rice paddies, tobacco fields and tea plantations near the border of Guandong province. The size and construction of these "earthen" houses, called "tulou", show how the people of the area adapted their lifestyle and even their architecture to the conditions of the region, which was frequently under threat of attack during the time of the Ming and Qing dynasties.

The two- to five-story houses with walls made of raw earth and tiled roofs generally form a ring around a lively inner courtyard. Only open to the outside world through a few windows and one single entrance, the tulou of Fujian also function as virtually impenetrable fortresses due to their construction and dimensions. The earthen buildings are inhabited by family clans, and can house between 100 and 800 people depending on the size.

Viewed from above, these round earthen houses in Fujian look like modern football stadiums.

KAIPING DIAOLOU AND VILLAGES

This World Heritage Site features the bizarre residential towers of the southern Chinese city of Kaiping as well as the surrounding villages.

"Diaolou" means "fortress tower", and the construction of such multi-storied fortified housing blocks was particularly common in the southern Chinese province of Guangdong as a response to banditry during the Ming era and it has continued to the present day. A surge of emigration from Kaiping to America began in 1839, but many expatriate Chinese started migrating back to their ancestral home at the end of the century, prompting further bandit activities. Of the 1,833 Diaolou towers still standing today, a total of 1,648 were built by returned expatriate Chinese

between 1900 and 1931. The World Heritage Site covers a representative section of these fortress towers in the townships of Sanmenli, Zili, Majianlong and Jinjiangli. Most of them have a terrace with balustrades at the bottom and a balcony with arcades at the top; this balcony area also houses the ancestral shrine.

Returning expatriates combined local traditions with elements of European, American and other architectural styles from their adopted countries when building the residential towers in Kaiping and its surrounding areas.

HISTORIC CENTER OF MACAO

The monuments in the former Portuguese colony of Macao are proof in solid stone of the centuries of exchange between China and the West.

Fishermen have lived by the sheltered bay of the Yu-Jiang Delta since long before the Portuguese came to what they referred to as Macao. Seafarers navigating the Chinese coast would often stop here due to its convenient location. The Portuguese began settling this area in the 16th century, making Macao the oldest city in East Asia to have been continuously inhabited by Europeans. These colonialists first erected a number of Catholic churches as well as simple houses made using wattle and daub masonry. They then fortified their city in the early 17th century to protect it from attacks, but Chinese authorities prevented the city from experiencing any

kind of boom until Macao became an independent port city in 1848. It belonged to Portugal after 1849 and, towards the end of the 19th century, developed into an enclave of the elite and wealthy. After 1949, Macao became a sanctuary for anyone fleeing the mainland, and in 1999 the city with the oldest Western-style university in China was returned to the People's Republic in a "one-country, two-systems" arrangement.

With its fountains, mosaic pedestrian zones and beautiful façades, the central square of Macao, the Largo do Senado, is reminiscent of the cities founded by the former colonial power.

Nepal

KATHMANDU VALLEY

The capital of the Kingdom of Nepal, including its surrounding towns, is a treasure trove of medieval Himalayan art and culture.

It is not just the pagoda-like roofs of the palaces, temples and residential buildings or the wealth of exquisite carvings that account for the almost indescribable charm of the Kathmandu Valley. Nor is it the opulence of the golden temple treasures that make this place so breathtaking. It is indeed the whole atmosphere which fascinates, and it is the people who fashioned this atmosphere long before the first capital city was even founded back in 723. This valley's inhabitants have always demonstrated their religious fervor in the form of splendid buildings. The holiest Buddhist site is Swayambhunath Temple, whose oldest pagoda was built in the fourth century BC, while Hindus go to the temples of Pashupatinath to worship.

Six Buddha statues with their right hands appearing to touch the earth sit at the entrance to the Swayambhunath Temple.

The valley is littered with small venerated temples and shrines, indicating the importance of religion in everyday life in Nepal.

The oldest of the secular buildings here date back to the 17th century and are located in the royal residence cities of Kathmandu, Patan and Bhadgaon. Historically these three towns were the capitals of individual sub-empires that have now been merged to form one metropolis. As in the other cities, Kathmandu's main square is the Durbar Square. Adjoining it are the royal palace and a number of temples. Bhadgaon is more like an open-air museum, exuding the Nepalese atmosphere characterized by the architecture of the Malla rulers.

The Garuda column defines Durbar Square in Patan (top right). The Golden Temple of Patan (right) was founded in the 11th century.

LUMBINI, THE BIRTHPLACE OF THE LORD BUDDHA

According to the story, Queen Maya gave birth to Siddhartha Gautama, the founder of Buddhism, in a grove near Lumbini in the year 623 BC. A temple was erected here in her honor.

The story of the Buddha starts with Queen Maya, who had a dream in which a white elephant with nine tusks descended from heaven and entered her body. As her pregnancy progressed she decided to travel to her parents' home. En route, she gave birth to a son out of the side of her body while standing in a grove near the city of Lumbini. Straight after his birth, this son took seven steps in the direction of each of the four points of the compass and a lotus flower bloomed in each of his steps. This miraculous birth scene is depicted in the Maha Maya Temple. One of the most important patrons of Buddhism, the Indian King Ashoka, had a stele erected here that attests to the fact that this grove near Lumbini – the birthplace of Siddharta Gautama – has been an important pilgrimage site for a long time indeed, even before written sources told of the place. A pilgrimage site was officially created here in 1978.

A stone relief illustrates the scene of the Buddha's birth while his mother, Maya, holds onto a tree branch.

SAGARMATHA NATIONAL PARK

The mountains around Everest are not only a popular destination for trekkers, but also a showcase of the fascinating flora and fauna of the eastern Himalayas.

The popularity of trekking has created real environmental problems for the Himalayas, and it was in an effort to protect the delicate ecological balance of Nepal – and above all the area around Mount Everest – that the site was declared a national park in 1976. The Nepalese call the world's highest mountain Sagarmatha, or "Head of the sky", while the Tibetan name, Chomolungma, means "Goddess mother of the world". The Cho Oyu and Lhotse peaks also exceed 8,000 m (26,250 ft) – like Everest – and with other peaks reaching altitudes of 7,000 m (23,000 ft), this is by far the highest mountain region in the world.

Mount Nuptse, on the other hand, is known not for its towering 7,879-m (25,850-ft) summit but for its 3,000-m (9,850-ft) south face, while Ngozumpa glacier is the longest in Nepal at 20 km (12 mi). For a short period in summer the snow on the southern slopes melts away to reveal an amazing array of flowers and around thirty different mammal species live within the park – but still no yetis.

Mount Everest was created roughly fifty million years ago when the Indian subcontinent collided with the European plate. Because these tectonic movements have not yet ceased, the mountain grows about 3 cm (1.5 in) a year.

CHITWAN NATIONAL PARK

Nepal's oldest national park is dominated by sal forests and extensive areas of elephant grass. It is also home to one-horned rhinoceroses and a number of other endangered animals.

The origins of this park in southern Nepal go back to land that was designated as a protected area by King Mahendra in 1962 in order to help save the one-horned rhino. The reserve was then made into a national park in 1973. Today, roughly 400 of these prehistoric creatures live here along with about 200 snow leopards and eighty tigers. All three species are strictly protected.

Some of the most common wildlife in the park includes sambar and chital deer, four-horned antelopes, wild boar, sloth bears, wild bison (gaur), rhesus macaques and langur monkeys that swing through the treetops. At dusk, mongoose and honey badgers go out hunting, and at night the howl of the golden jackal rings through the darkness. Mugger crocodiles and gharials – famous for their striking, elongated jaws – doze away the days in the park's rivers. They can measure up to 7 m (23 ft) but present no real threat to humans. The Bengal monitor, another of the park's resident species, is found in the more open areas. Chitwan National Park is also an idyllic home for over 400 species of bird.

There are still several hundred one-horned rhinoceroses living within the boundaries of Chitwan National Park.

COMPLEX OF KOGURYO TOMBS

The Koguryo tombs in Pyongyang and the surrounding area are some of the most important legacies of the Koguryo Empire, which ruled over north-eastern China and the northern part of the Korean Peninsula from the first century BC to the seventh century AD.

Founded by King Tongmyong, who is still venerated today, the Koguryo Empire existed for some 700 years (37 BC–AD 668) and was one of the mightiest empires in East Asia in the years after Christ's birth. It is thought of as the birth of Korean culture. In ancient times, burial mounds with beautiful frescoes were built for the kings, their families and members of the aristocracy.

From the more than 10,000 Koguryo tombs discovered in Korea and China (Manchuria), around seventy are part of the World Heritage Site and thirty are located on North Korean soil. Their murals provide unique insight into a culture characterized by Confucianism and Buddhism as well as everyday life in the northernmost of the three early Korean empires.

The Koguryo Empire expanded in the fourth century, which led to the capital being moved from the Yalu River to Pyongyang in 427. In the seventh century, the Koguryo Empire succumbed to the southern Silla Kingdom, which was supported by troops from the Chinese Tang dynasty.

A hunting scene is is depicted in the Yaksuri tomb near the port of Nampho.

JONGMYO SHRINE

Ancestral worship plays a major role in Confucian rites and it is for this reason that Korea's last royal dynasty, which oriented its culture on its vast neighbor, China, made Neo-Confucianism the official national and moral philosophy of the country. It also created a central area for worshiping its royal ancestors.

The famous Jongmyo shrine, which means "Shrine of the royal ancestors", was built by Yi Song-gye (1335–1408), founder of the Yi or Joseon dynasty. The building was given its present-day appearance in around 1600, after most of Korea's public buildings had been savagely burnt down during an invasion by the Japanese under Toyotomi Hideyoshi in 1592. The interior contains the ancestral tablets of the nineteen most important Yi dynasty kings. The traditional ceremonies featuring instruments, songs and dancing have been practiced here virtually unchanged since the 15th century.

The complex in the South Korean capital, Seoul, has been well preserved and is actually still used on a regular basis. The ancestral worship rites are only held once a year these days – on the first Sunday in May – and this is the only time the public is permitted to enter.

The ancestral tablets of the Joseon dynasty were stored in the main hall of the Jongmyo Shrine (right: a long columned corridor).

CHANGDEOKGUNG PALACE COMPLEX

King Taejong had a "secondary residence" built near the Jongmyo Shrine in Seoul between 1405 and 1412.

The vast Changdeokgung ("Palace of prospering virtue") is one of five royal palaces from the Joseon dynasty in Seoul that is not just still standing but has been lovingly preserved. Since it lies to the east of the previous Gyeongbokgung ("Palace greatly blessed by heaven"), it was also called Dongwol ("Eastern Palace"). The complex includes a U-shaped "Secret Garden" that was previously reserved only for the emperor with a lake in the middle and around 300 trees. The various administrative, reception and residential buildings were burnt down several times, but were always rebuilt. The palace was the seat of government from 1611 to 1872 when Korea sealed itself off from the outside world. The prominent buildings include the magnificent throne or public audience hall, whose present-day form dates back to 1804.

Changdeokgung's throne or audience hall (right), also known as the "Hall of Beneficent Government", is made of blue tiles, which were solely reserved for royal palaces. The vast complex features a number of interior courtyards, pavilions and gardens, and was finished in just eight years.

HWASEONG FORTRESS

Towards the end of the 18th century, the 22nd king of the Joseon dynasty, Jeongjo (1752–1800), had a new residence built approximately 50 km (31 mi) from the capital, Seoul. It is a remarkable example of contemporary military architecture combining advanced levels of Eastern and Western expertise.

King Jeongjo, who reigned from 1776 until his death in 1800, had the entire city of Suwon relocated to build the fortress of Hwaseong. The whole complex was finished in just thirty-three months. Meeting the latest standards of military engineering, the wall is more than 5 km (3 mi) long and 4–6 m (13–20 ft) high, with four main gates – Changanmun, Paldalmun, Changnyongmun and Hwasomun, the largest of which is on the west side – and two floodgates. Watchtowers and canon towers were also placed on the crest of the wall at regular intervals and bastions were positioned in front of the fortress. Hwaseong fortress fell into disrepair starting in the early 19th century and the complex suffered serious damage in World War II and in the Korean War between 1950 and 1953, but it was rebuilt and restored in the 1970s.

Hwaseong Fortress, designed wholly for defensive purposes, has four entrance gates (left: Changanmun), two floodgates and five secret gates. The four corner towers each have five watchtowers and canon towers, five observation towers and one signal platform (below).

ROYAL TOMBS OF THE JOSEON DYNASTY

This World Heritage Site covers forty (out of 119) royal tombs spread across eighteen locations that were built over more than five centuries from 1408 to 1966. They reflect the significance of ancestral worship in South Korea.

The first centralized Korean state emerged in the year 668 following the unification of the three kingdoms of Koguryo, Paekche and Silla, the latter of which had Chinese support and asserted itself over the other two in the battle for supremacy. After a phase of territorial fragmentation in the ninth century, the Koryo Empire (from which the European name of "Korea" is derived) was founded in North Korea by Wang Kon in 918 and brought all of Korea under its rule. Mongols first appeared in Korea in 1231 and ruled the country until the mid-14th century. Thereafter, General Yi Song-gye founded the Yi dynasty (1392–1910), under which Korea was given the name of Joseon ("Land of the morning calm"), which is why it is usually referred to as the "Joseon dynasty". It experienced a cultural heyday in the 15th century.

The rulers of the Joseon dynasty were buried according to the principles of Pungsu, the Korean version of feng-shui in which wind and water play an important role. Their backs faced a hill and they faced toward the south.

Republic of Korea

HAEINSA TEMPLE AND THE DEPOSITORIES FOR THE "TRIPITAKA KOREANA" WOODBLOCKS

Haeinsa monastery on Mt Kaya in South Gyeongsang province is home to the Janggyeong Panjeon depository, specially built to store one of the Buddhist world's most venerated artifacts: the Tripitaka Koreana, the most extensive collection of Buddhist texts on wooden printing blocks.

Exactly 81,258 wooden master copies are stored in the Tripitaka, the "Three Baskets Teachings" of Mahayana Buddhism, which covers 1,496 titles, but since they are carved on both sides, there is actually a total of 162,516 "pages". Every page has twenty-two lines, each with fourteen Chinese characters – Chinese because Koreans did not have their own alphabet at the time. It took 200 monks twelve years to complete the collection in 1248. The pre-treatment of the wood was also a masterstroke. To prepare it

Haeinsa is Korea's third-largest monastery complex and originally dates back to 802. Approximately fifty of the buildings here were constructed between the 15th and 18th centuries.

for eternity, a new and unusual process was used. It was stored in seawater, freshwater, in the ground and then in fresh air each for three years at a time. Then the wood was carved. The woodblocks, which are now more than 760 years old, can still be used for printing.

The climate inside Janggyeong Panjeon, built in 1488, is perfectly adapted to suit the priceless items it contains: 81,258 wooden printing blocks. They have even withstood fires and wars. The Tripitaka Koreana did have a predecessor, but this fell victim to the pillaging Mongols in 1232. The second version was blessed with a much longer life.

SEOKGURAM GROTTO AND BULGUKSA TEMPLE

Bulguksa south-east of Gyeongju is South Korea's most visited temple. Along with the neighboring Seokguram Grotto, it is also a masterpiece of Buddhist art from the time of the Korean Silla Kingdom (668–935).

Bulguksa ("Temple of the Buddha land") and the Seokguram Grotto were dedicated in the eighth century by a high-ranking official as a way of worshiping his ancestors. Seokguram Grotto was built as an artificial cave temple using granite blocks. It contains one of the most important Buddhist sculptures in the world: the 3.5-m (11.5-ft) white granite Buddha, Siddharta Gautama, designed in the style of the Chinese Tang dynasty and sitting in the lotus position, one of the classic Buddhist sitting postures. The trea-sures at Bulguksa, located around 13 km (8 mi) south-east of the former Silla capital of Gyeongju, include the stone steps fitted together with solid cubic blocks that lead to Buddha's "heavenly" kingdom, and the most famous pair of pagodas in Korea: the simple Shakyamuni Pagoda representing Buddha's peace and tranquillity, and the richly decorated Treasure Pagoda symbolizing the believer's rich "inner world".

This gilded bronze Buddha is also worshipped in Bulguksa temple.

GYEONGJU HISTORIC AREAS

As the "Golden City" (or Kumsong) of the Silla Kingdom, Gyeongju was the center of the first centralized Korean state from the seventh to the 10th century. Today, this town in south-eastern South Korea is at the center of a national park.

Starting in the first century, when rulers of the Silla Empire died they were laid to rest beneath what ultimately resulted in 200 burial mounds in Gyeongju and the surrounding areas. The grid-like road network and the ruins of old buildings and palace complexes attest to the capital's expansion after the regional kingdoms were unified in the seventh century. A second residence, Pyolgung, with its Anapchi Pond, was built in the seventh century not far from Banwolsong Palace, founded in the first century. The 9.2-m-high (30-ft), flask-shaped observatory, Cheomseongdae, was erected in around 640 and the "Terrace for Contemplating the Stars" is the oldest observatory in East Asia. Nearby are the lower levels of the brick pagoda at Punhwang Temple, the oldest preserved pagoda ruins in Korea. There are also remains of the most prominent temple of the Silla period, Hwangjong (seventh century).

The historic district of Gyeongju also includes the area around Mt Namsan with its monumental Buddha reliefs. This is said to have been the birthplace of Hyokkose, the founder (in 57 BC) and first ruler of the Silla Kingdom.

GOCHANG, HWASUN AND GANGHWA DOLMEN SITES

The Korean Peninsula is home to the world's largest cluster of prehistoric megalith cultures. Tens of thousands of dolmens are still standing here, a few hundred of which are in Gochang, Hwasun and on Ganghwa Island.

Ancestral worship played a major role in the prehistoric megalith cultures of Asia. In East Asia, megalith structures have been discovered in western China and on the Yellow Sea coast; they first appeared in Korea during the Bronze Age. The dolmen sites of Gochang in south-western Chollabuk province, Hwasun in Chollanam province and on Ganghwa Island resemble large stone tables with two tall, vertical stone slabs supporting an oblong capstone. The top is over 1 m (3 ft) thick and can weigh up to 300 tonnes (330 tons); the buildings are at least 2 m (7 ft) high. Apart from dolmens, the other megalith buildings on the Korean Peninsula also include stone "houses" made from four vertical stone slabs erected over tombs.

The dolmens on Ganghwa Island were built over tombs or on hills and are probably some of the oldest megalith buildings in Korea. They were either originally covered with soil, or the deceased were "laid to rest" here before the family members entombed the bones in family graves.

JEJU VOLCANIC ISLAND AND LAVA TUBES

Three sites and natural landscapes on the South Korean island of Jeju make up this World Heritage Site, which contains important phenomena concerning the geological development of the island and the region.

The island of Jeju, off the south coast of Korea, is an undersea shield volcano on a continental plate. It was formed over a hot spot – a "weak point" – in the earth's crust that was dissolved from the interior of the earth and pushed outward by rising magma. The conservation area around Mount Hallasan, the highest mountain in South Korea at 1,950 m (6,400 ft), makes up the largest part of the Natural Heritage Site; the surrounding region ranges in elevation from 800 m (2,600 ft) to 1,300 m (4,200 ft) and includes a crater with a 1.6 hectare (4 acre) lake, a trachyte dome, waterfalls and basalt columns. The geomunoreum, part of the World Heritage Site, comprises five lava tunnels formed when the top layer of lava cooled and solidified to create a roof over an area through which liquid lava continued to flow. When the lava stopped, a hollow tube was left. The 182-m (597-ft) high tuff cone Songsan Ilchulbong in eastern Jeju was formed by a volcanic eruption on the shallow seabed.

Hallasan, the highest summit on Jeju, is an extinct volcano.

Japan

SHIRETOKO

Due to the distinctive climatic features, the ecosystems on the Shiretoko peninsula and in the surrounding sea are exceptionally rich in nutrients and contain a great many species.

Cold winds blowing in from Siberia cause the sea to freeze off the coast of Shiretoko in north-eastern Hokkaido, the lowest latitude in the northern hemisphere to experience seasonal ocean ice. Large quantities of phytoplankton, which represent the start of the marine food chain, thrive beneath this ice. They are the staple diet of krill and other tiny aquatic animals that nourish crustaceans and small fish, which in turn are consumed by larger fish, marine mammals and sea eagles. Large numbers of salmon and trout also swim upstream here to spawn. They of course provide food for Hokkaido brown bears as well as for the endangered Blakiston's fish owl and Steller's sea eagle.

One of the reasons for the enormous productivity of the marine ecosystem is the different salt content in the layers of water, which scarcely ever mix because no large rivers flow into the Sea of Okhotsk. A total of 223 types of fish, including ten types of salmon, and twenty-eight sea mammals have been documented off the coast of Shiretoko. The Steller's sea lion, almost hairless apart from its mane, needs special protection.

Waterfalls gush over the steep cliffs of Shiretoko into the sea.

SHIRAKAMI-SANCHI BEECH FOREST

One of the last ancient Siebold's beech forests in East Asia is symbolic of the preservation of natural habitats despite the dense human population in Japan. The World Heritage Site comprises around 170 sq km (105 sq mi).

Ancient forests once covered almost all of Japan, with Siebold's beech leading the way. Though most forests were severely decimated by logging, protracted discussions in the 1980s led to an agreement to protect the trees that had been spared in northern Honshu. The largest primeval beech forest in East Asia is now an important sanctuary for the most northerly monkey population in the world as well as Asiatic black bears, the Japanese serow, a member of the goat family, and eighty-seven types of bird including the black woodpecker, which is on the IUCN's Red List of Threatened Species. Over 500 types of flora also grow in the Shirakami-Sanchi forest including some rare orchids. The mountains here reach elevations of 1,240 m (4,000 ft) and are the source of fifteen rivers. The lack of established trails has led the odd herb gatherers astray here on at least one occasion but the part of the ancient forest that is a World Heritage Site is virtually untouched by human activity.

Some of the beeches in northern Honshu are more than 200 years old.

HISTORIC VILLAGES OF SHIRAKAWA-GO AND GOKAYAMA

A centuries-old style of folk architecture has been nurtured in three historic mountains villages of Honshu. The villages are characterized by large multi-story houses with steep thatched roofs.

The unusual half-timbered houses in the villages of Shirakawa-go and Gokayama in northern Honshu (in Gifu and Toyama prefectures) all have steep, thatched roofs based on the Gassho style. The design allows them to withstand heavy loads – 2 to 4 m (7 to 13 ft) of snow fall during the long harsh winters here. Silkworm rearing is another reason for this lasting architectural tradition. The process requires a certain amount of covered space, which is provided by the high roofs that usually have two to four – sometimes five – intermediate floors.

The houses also have room for forty to fifty people. The villages of Shirakawa-go and Gokayama have preserved their traditions in a manner unheard of in other parts of Japan. Elsewhere in the country, economic advancements and social change have largely caused the ancient architecture to disappear, instead of adapting it to modern needs.

Almost every one of the thatched, half-timbered houses in the village of Shirakawa-go is surrounded by gardens and fields.

SHRINES AND TEMPLES OF NIKKO

Tokugawa Ieyasu, founder of the Tokugawa shogunate, chose this Buddhist sanctuary as his burial site. Nature and architecture form a harmonious ensemble here.

Nikko is around 150 km (93 mi) north of Tokyo and lies at the entrance to the national park of the same name. The charming landscape here includes groomed lanes with centuries-old Japanese cedars leading to the temples outside the city. Rinno-ji Temple, for example, dates back to the eighth century. Its "Hall of the Three Buddhas" (Sambutsudo) was built in 848 and houses two Kannon figures as well as an 8-m-high (26-ft) statue of the Amida Buddha. Tokugawa Ieyasu (1543–1616), whose shogunate began his family's 268-year rule over Japan, is buried in the Toshogu Shrine, which displays obvious Chinese influences.

The three wise monkeys – see no evil, hear no evil and speak no evil – are symbols of Japanese restraint.

The mausoleum, which allegedly required the efforts of 15,000 craftsmen and artists, was built in just two years (1634–1636) by Ieyasu's grandson, Iemitsu, based on Ieyasu's plans. The difference could not have been greater between this structure and the elegantly simple buildings of the powerless emperors in distant Kyoto.
Three splendid gates – Niomon, Karamon and Yomeimon – delineate the shrine district. The red-painted buildings here were furnished by Japan's prominent artists and the district boasts three courtyards that combine elements of Japan's two main belief systems, Buddhism and Shintoism. The five-story red-and-gold-painted pagoda as well as the Drum Tower and the 12-m (39-ft) bell tower dominate the district.

The road to Nikko's shrine district passes the Shinkyo Bridge (top left). The largest building in the complex is the Sambutsudo Hall of the Rinno-ji Temple (left).

Japan

Zen

Zen is a method of discovering the world's "eternal truths" through meditation and concentration. It was founded by Indian monk and scholar, Bodhidharma, in the sixth century, and was brought to Japan in the 13th century by Eisai and Dogen, two founders of the Zen sect. Zen found a particularly warm welcome among

HISTORIC MONUMENTS OF ANCIENT KYOTO (KYOTO, UJI AND OTSU CITIES)

The former imperial city was the center of classic Japanese aristocratic culture for more than 1,000 years. Exquisite temples, shrines, palaces and gardens attest to its erstwhile power.

The World Heritage Site includes seventeen sites in Kyoto, Uji and Otsu: three Shinto shrines, thirteen Buddhist monasteries – some of which were founded as palaces and therefore also have gardens – and Nijo-jo castle. The latter was built in 1601 to represent the shogunate and it was here that

Japanese landscaping seeks to outdo nature in terms of beauty and perfection, while the architecture and arrangements at Enryaku-ji Temple symbolize nature.

the Tokugawa shoguns stayed during visits to Kyoto. The castle is the antithesis of the gardens and tea pavilions that convey the more humble spirit of Zen Buddhism such as the moss gardens of the Saiho-ji or Koke-dera temple (1340), or the dry garden of Ryoan-ji temple. In the latter, fifteen boulders are scattered around a rock garden of 300 sq m (3,228 sq ft). The thatched Shinto shrines are also simple in their construction. At the Byodo-in temple (11th century) in Uji, a statue of Buddha in the main hall overlooks a lake and inspires hope that paradise is accessible.

The Golden Pavilion in the imperial city of Kyoto was built in 1394.

the Samurai warrior caste, which was required to exercise a certain amount of discipline and asceticism to distance itself from the more extravagant life at court.

Zen pupils were expected to gather their insights intuitively, guided by a master. The Soto sect believed that hours of meditation in a lotus position (Zazen) combined with deep breathing freed the mind of distracting deliberations. The Rinzai sect uses physical blows or shouts as "aids to enlightenment". The Zen master can also ask paradoxical questions (Koan) to challenge purely rational thinking, and even mundane activities such as making tea can become meditative through deliberate movement. Other aspects of cultural life also reflect metaphysical depth: Noh theater, the art of flower arrangement (Ikebana), calligraphy, Haiku (a three-line, seventeen-syllable poem) literature, landscape painting, garden landscaping, and military skills such as archery and fencing.

In Kyoto's most famous Zen garden (far left) – the "dry garden" (Karesansui) of the Ryoan-ji Temple – stones of various shapes and sizes are set in fine white gravel that is raked into wave patterns. The stones symbolize islands in a sea on which boats sail. The garden, built around 1450, is only 25 by 10 m (82 by 33 ft) in size.

This pavilion, which is part of the Daigo-ji Temple complex, blends harmoniously into its natural surroundings.

A giant gilded Buddha statue is housed in the main hall of the Byodo-in Temple, known as the "Phoenix Hall".

"The Sea of Silver Sand" in the garden of the Silver Pavilion is designed to project moonlight onto the building.

The partitions and sliding doors of the shogun residence at Nijo-jo were painted between 1601 and 1603 in Kano style (after the Kano family) with landscape themes on a gold background.

Japan

HISTORIC MONUMENTS OF ANCIENT NARA

The temples and shrines of Japan's first permanent imperial residence mark the start of the aristocratic age and the first heyday of Buddhist art in the country.

Like its Chinese role model, the Tang metropolis of Chang'an, the new Japanese capital of Nara was laid out in a grid-like design – and completed in just four years. In the north stood a mighty imperial palace where seven emperors resided until the end of the Nara Period (710–784). From there, a wide thoroughfare heading south divided the city into two equal rectangles. The various schools of Buddhism, which had only just been introduced to Japan, also erected temple complexes and monasteries here. The Kofuku Temple district, for example, was established in 710 and continuously developed until the 11th century. Its three-tiered pagoda (1143) of the Kofuku-ji is one of the finest in Japan due to its harmonious proportions. The Todai-ji district (728) is the center of the influential Kego sect and is home to one of the world's largest wooden buildings: the Hall of the Great Buddha (Daibutsu) is colossal at 58 m (190 ft) long, 51 m (167 ft) wide, and 49 m (161 ft) high.

The Daibutsu – a colossal statue of Buddha made from gilt bronze in the Todai-ji temple complex – is one of Nara's highlights.

SACRED SITES AND PILGRIMAGE ROUTES IN THE KII MOUNTAIN RANGE

The Kii Mountains are home to three sacred sites: Yoshina and Omine, Kumanosanzan, and Koyasan. The Kii Peninsula on Honshu Island has been a pilgrimage site for 1,200 years and it is here that the religious tradition of Japanese Shintoism, based on the worshiping of divine natural forces, was mixed with Buddhism.

These sacred sites are connected to one another and to the imperial cities of Nara and Kyoto to form a single unit with the pine forests, brooks, rivers and waterfalls. Temples and monastery buildings are placed based on the natural flow of the landscape. In darker areas of dense cedar forests formidable guardian figures in the temples keep evil spirits and demons away from the sites.

The temple city of Koyasan dates back to Kukai, a priest who in 816 retreated to this remote mountain region and discovered a synthesis between local Shintoism and the Buddhism that had come from Korea and China in the sixth century. The Shingon ("true word") sect was born.

A monk sweeps the entrance to the Kumano Hongu Shrine.

HIMEJI-JO

The largest and best preserved Japanese castle from the dawn of the Tokugawa shogunate fulfils the purposes of function, design and aesthetics.

After a century of civil wars, Japan experienced a boom in castle building. They were designed simultaneously as forts and castle complexes that would express the new political order established in the name of the Tokugawa shogunate, which began in 1600. The builder of Himeji Castle just 50 km (31 mi) west of Kobe was a vassal to the Tokugawa Ieyasu. The center and architectural showpiece of the 22-ha (54 acre) complex surrounded by a moat and a curtain wall is the tower, which is six stories high on the outside and seven on the inside. The interior is crafted entirely of wood and the walls above the solid stone base were plastered to protect against fire attacks. Defensive as well as representational purposes are equally weighted here, a fact that is demonstrated by toy-like embrasures with alternating circular, triangular and square shapes. These provided effective flank protection for the access routes leading up to the castle gates. The gates' decorative iron mountings perfectly combine aesthetics with protective function.

From 1601 to 1609 Terumasa Ikeda had a new castle complex ("White Heron Castle") constructed with 83 buildings on the ruins of an old fortress. The largest of these buildings is the mighty main tower (right), with its interwoven eaves.

ITSUKUSHIMA SHINTO SHRINE

This shrine complex is located in one of Japan's most beautiful coastal landscapes off Miyajima Island in the Seto Inland Sea, not far from Hiroshima. Appearing to float on the water, it perfectly embodies the Shinto concept of worshipping nature.

According to the legend, this shrine was dedicated to the three daughters of the storm deity and is said to have been built in the year 593. It is probably true, for Miyajima – better known as Itsukushima – Island had been a sacred district since very early times, and, until the 11th century, could only be entered by priests. Even today there is no cemetery there in order to preserve the sacred site's purity.

Even though the main buildings date back to between 1556 and 1571, the entire complex with its bright ornamental paintings more effectively

The red camphorwood Torii off Miyajima island – pictured here gleaming in the sunset – was modeled on an older gate. It is only surrounded by water at high tide.

maintains the style of the Heian era (from the eighth to the 12th centuries), when it was originally built with a similar design. Eight larger and several smaller buildings were erected on stilts here in the shallow waters and connected to one another via galleries while other structures on land formed the "Outer Shrine". The 16-m (52-ft) Torii, the "entry gate" to the holy district, was added in 1875. This eighth gate at the Itsukushima Shrine stands in the middle of the sea 175 m (282 yds) off the coast and completes the harmonious scene. It is not surprising that this particular Torii is considered to be one of Japan's most famous structures.

Left: The Shinto shrine illuminated at night by stone lanterns includes the main hall and the hall of purification. Visitors must wash their hands and mouth before entering the sanctuary.

Japan

BUDDHIST MONUMENTS IN THE HORYU-JI AREA

This temple complex includes the world's oldest preserved wooden buildings as well as a number of very precious sculptures that are over 1,000 years old.

Horyu-ji is about 10 km (33 mi) southwest of the old imperial city of Nara and dates back to the dawn of Japanese Buddhism, which was raised to the status of the national religion in the early seventh century. Construction began here in 607 at the behest of Prince Regent Shotoku (573–621), but the original temple complex, modeled on a Chinese version, almost completely burned down in 670. The buildings that are now considered the oldest wooden structures in the world – the main hall ("Golden Hall"), the five-story pagoda, the middle gate, and the adjacent gallery – were begun before 710, the start of the Nara Period. Six figures in the main hall likely originate from the predecessor building that was burned down. This would make them the oldest preserved sculptures of their kind in Japan. Horyu-ji was expanded as early as the eighth century and the World Heritage Site comprises a total of forty-eight buildings, eleven of which are more than 1,100 years old.

Horyu-ji's treasures include gilded wooden sculptures depicting Buddha (right) and guardian spirits.

HIROSHIMA PEACE MEMORIAL (GENBAKU DOME)

The "Atomic Bomb Dome" is a reminder of the first time a nuclear weapon was used for military purposes. It symbolizes a new dimension of destruction and a memorial for peace.

August 6, 1945, changed the world. In order to force the Japanese Empire into unconditional surrender in the last days of World War II, the USA decided to use a newly developed weapon. The first atomic bomb, oddly named "Little Boy", was dropped by the B29 bomber Enola Gay and detonated 570 m (1,870) above the center of the port city of Hiroshima. Everything within a 4-km (2.5-mi) radius was destroyed. Between 90,000 and 200,000 civilians were killed including thousands of Korean forced laborers. The second atomic bomb was dropped on Japan three days later in Nagasaki, on August 9. Between 25,000 and 75,000 people died there. The agony of the survivors (Hibakusha) struck by the radiation was of previously unfathomable proportions. People are still dying from the long-term consequences of this nuclear attack.

Hiroshima's former chamber of commerce and industry with its burnt-out dome now symbolizes the horror of modern war, which reached new levels of terror with the unleashing of nuclear energy.

YAKUSHIMA CEDAR FOREST

Three-thousand-year-old Japanese cedars are the most precious botanical specimens in the primeval evergreen forest on Yakushima island.

This island of granite lies 60 km (37 mi) off the southern tip of Kyushu Island and rises to 1,935 m (6,350 ft) above sea level. Annual rainfall of up to 1,000 cm (390 in) combined with a range of different climatic zones from the subtropical coastal region to the alpine mountain regions have enabled about 1,900 plant species to flourish here. The central, more temperate zone is home to a unique primeval forest with ancient Japanese cedars and sickle pines (Cryptomeria japonica). This pine, distantly related to the Lebanese cedar, is a member of the cypress family and can grow to 40 m (130 ft) in height. Its timber was preferred in Japanese construction and the timber trade played an important part in the Yakushima economy until the 1960s, at which point, one-third of the island was declared a national park due to the large number of giant ancient trees still standing. The most famous is the Jomon Cedar, discovered in 1966. Its trunk has a diameter of 16 m (52 ft) and it is reckoned to be about three thousand years old.

The park's chief attraction is Jomonsugi, an almost untouched forest with mosses, lichens and sacred Japanese cedars.

GUSUKU SITES AND RELATED PROPERTIES OF THE KINGDOM OF RYUKYU

From the 12th to the 17th century these islands were an independent kingdom that grew wealthy through trade with Japan, China, Korea and South-East Asia.

Castles on the Okinawa Peninsula known as "Gusuku" were a visible sign of wealth. The first of these mighty structures was erected between 1237 and 1248 in the southern part of the island on a hill named "Shuri", near the present-day city of Naha. Shuri was the first center of the now politically unified group of islands and this was where the king resided. The castle was the role model for a series of other castles that the Ryukyu princes had built in the early 14th century: Nakijin, Ozato, Katsuren and the largest, Nakagusuku. Today mostly just ruins, the former Gusuku attest to the mastery of the local architecture and stonemasonry. The Kingdom of Ryukyu lost its independence when a Japanese army captured the group of islands in 1609.

In the early 14th century the kingdom was split for 100 years into three sub-kingdoms whose rulers built their own castles, including Nakijin (below). Shuri Castle (left), the royal residence until 1879, was rebuilt between 1958 and 1992.

IWAMI GINZAN SILVER MINE AND ITS CULTURAL LANDSCAPE

The Iwami Ginzan Silver Mine is in a craggy mountainous region on the coast of Honshu. Along with the ruins of the silver mine, the World Heritage Site includes the surrounding cultural landscape with mining settlements and silver smelters from the 16th to the 20th century plus two transport routes on which the ore was sent to the coast to be shipped to Korea and China.

Japanese merchant Kamiya Jutei was the first to exploit the silver deposits in south-western Honshu in around 1530. He enjoyed protection from the Ouchi family, which controlled the Iwami region at the time, and earned its money through trade with Korea and China. Silver exports flourished for two centuries. In the 17th century, annual production peaked at 1,000 to 2,000 kg (2,205 to 4,410 lb) of pure silver. Yields gradually declined thereafter. In the mid-19th century annual extraction was just 100 kg (220 lb) and the mine was closed in 1923. The World Heritage Site comprises fourteen sites including the ruins of mines, shafts, smelting furnaces, settlements fortress complexes, transportation routes, shrines, temples, burial monuments and three port cities..

The mine's success was due to plentiful deposits, advanced extraction and conveyance methods (tunnels), plentiful labor and favorable trade relations.

Thailand

HISTORIC TOWN OF SUKHOTHAI AND ASSOCIATED HISTORIC TOWNS

The first capital of the independent Thai Empire is now a ruin west of modern-day Sukhothai in northern Thailand. It is proof of the country's trendsetting Buddhist art and architecture. The World Heritage Site also includes the historic parks of Si Satchanalai and Kamphaeng Phet, founded by the Sukhothai rulers.

The Thai kings shook off Cambodian Khmer domination in the 13th century. After the Khmer were banished in 1238, the Kingdom of Sukhothai was created under the legendary King Sri Indraditya from a principality in the southern portion of the Thai area. His son, Ramkhamhaeng, (r. 1280–1300)

Sukhothai Historical Park covers several dozen temples inside and outside the walls of Old Sukhothai. Colossal Buddha statues watch over the Wat Sra Sri.

later expanded the dominion as far as Luang Prabang in the north (Laos) and the Malay Peninsula in the south. Sukhothai Historical Park attests to the size of the first Siamese capital. Earlier buildings such as the San Ta Pha Daeng and Wat Si Sawai temples still demonstrate considerable Khmer influence but Sukhothai soon developed its own style, as seen at the Wat Mahathat, the central complex. Once a vast monastery with numerous halls and depositories for relics and urns (chedis), it is still impressive as ruins. The seated colossal Buddha at Wat Si Chum is a good representation of the soft and elegant Sukhothai style with its slender Buddha statues.

The Wat Mahathat has some 200 chedis including the central Khmer-style chedi. It was the religious center of Old Sukhothai. The name means "Temple of the Great Relic" and refers to the Buddha relics stored in the temples bearing this name.

Si Satchanalai Historical Park is about 50 km (31 mi) from Sukhothai and was the second residence of the Sukhothai Kingdom. The Wat Chang Lom Temple, with its bell-shaped chedi dome is surrounded by stone elephants.

Every image of the "Enlightened One" (above, a 15-m (49-ft) statue at Wat Si Chum) should have "thirty-two features of beauty" in order to reveal the full effect of the belief – for example, long earlobes or draped, flame-like hair.

About 80 km (50 mi) from Sukhothai is Kamphaeng Phet, one of the former capitals of the Sukhothai Kingdom. It is home to the Wat Phra Kaeo ("Temple of the Emerald Buddha"), which also includes these Buddha statues.

BAN CHIANG
ARCHAEOLOGICAL SITE

Ban Chiang is the most important prehistoric archaeological site in all of South-East Asia. The excavations here have provided information on the highly developed culture here where rice was grown, ceramics crafted and metal (bronze and iron) manufactured.

In the mid-1960s, an American student discovered painted shards of earthenware that were over 3,000 years old in Ban Chiang, a village on the Khorat Plateau in north-eastern Thailand. Systematic excavations starting in 1972 then unearthed extraordinarily highly developed ceramics artefacts that had originated from 3600 BC until the settlement was apparently surrendered in about 400 AD – a time span that has now been divided into three periods. However, the age of bronze items found in 1974 was long disputed. Initial tests have demonstrated that bronze crafting was possible around the year 4500 BC, so it can be assumed that these date back to no earlier than 2000 BC. The excavations also showed that rice growing on irrigated paddies as well as pig and chicken breeding constituted the livelihood of the people here. Domesticated water buffalo were already being used at the time for rice growing.

Wat Pho Sri Nai temple in Ban Chiang contains ceramics and human bones from prehistoric times.

THUNG YAI AND
HUAI KHA KHAENG
WILDLIFE SANCTUARIES

Taken together, the Thung Yai and Huai Kha Khaeng forest sanctuaries in western Thailand cover an area of 6,100 sq km (2,350 sq mi) and constitute one of South-East Asia's largest wildlife reserves.

In the mountainous country along the Burmese border, rivers and streams rush down slopes varying in height from 250 m (820 ft) to 1,800 m (5,900 ft) and savanna-type highlands (Thung Yai) alternate with dense forests of bamboo and tropical trees like teak. These two protected areas were deliberately not registered as national parks since this would have required opening them to the public, like the parks south and east of the Sri Nakharin dam. Special permission is needed to visit Thung Yai and Huai Kha Khaeng. As a result, large animals such as tigers, leopards, clouded leopards, elephants, bears and tapirs live almost undisturbed by humans. It is, however, permitted to log tropical timber within a prescribed area.

A wide variety of animal species can be found in these grasslands and evergreen forests such as gaur (or wild ox, right), the hog deer and the northern pig-tailed macaque.

HISTORIC CITY OF AYUTTHAYA

The capital of the second Thai Empire was founded in around 1350. It is now an open-air museum of sophisticated Buddhist culture with temples, monasteries, palaces and monumental sculptures that still attest to the former splendor of Ayutthaya, situated on a river island.

"The Invincible One" (a translation of the name "Ayuttahaya") was a sizable metropolis boasting 375 monasteries and temples, roughly 100 city gates and twenty-nine fortresses in its heyday. But the much-lauded city turned out not to be totally invincible after all, succumbing to a Burmese attack in 1767 when the invaders destroyed the city and killed or enslaved its population. As the residence of thirty-three kings, for more than 400 years Ayutthaya was the political and cultural center of an empire which, as the successor of the Angkor Empire, spanned the entire South-East Asian mainland.

The most important monuments include the temple complexes of Wat Phra Si Sanphet, Wat Mahathat and Wat Rajaburana in the historic center of the ruined city.

Countless statues of the Buddha are worshipped at Ayutthaya. Four classic postures are distinguished among them: standing, striding, sitting and reclining. The Buddha statues in Ayutthaya are mostly seated and wrapped in colored cowls. Along with corncob-like prangs and bell-shaped chedis, dozens of Buddha statues also characterize the temple ruins (below: Wat Chai Wattanaram).

DONG PHAYAYEN–KHAO YAI FOREST COMPLEX

The tropical forest of Dong Phayayen–Khao Yai covers over 6,000 sq km (2,300 sq mi) and is a valuable refuge for endangered animals of all kinds.

This forest area lies in a rough hill and mountain landscape that rises 100 to 1,350 m (330 to 4,430 ft) above sea level and extends from the southern part of the Khorat plateau to the Cambodian border. It comprises the four national parks Khao Yai, Thap Lan, Pang Sida, and Ta Phraya and the Dong Yai Wildlife Reserve. There are several vegetation zones here ranging from rainforest to bush and grassland, in which 800 animal species flourish. In the Dong Phayayen-Khao Yai region there are almost 400 types of birds including endangered species such as copper doves, maroon orioles, green peafowl and the masked finfoot. Among the most endangered mammals are the Indian elephant – Khao Yai has the largest herd with 200 – and various cat species including Bengal cats, clouded leopards, tigers and marbled cats (which, although related to tigers, are no bigger than domestic cats) and Asiatic gold cats, the latter being practically extinct everywhere else due to the destruction of the rainforest.

Khao Yai is the most accessible of the four national parks that make up the Dong Yai Wildlife Reserve World Heritage Site.

Laos

TOWN OF LUANG PRABANG

In Luang Prabang, Buddhist tradition and Laotian architecture combine with the European colonial style of the 19th and 20th century to form a unique mosaic.

Luang Prabang embodies traditional Laos more than any other city. Even though the political power of the country has been based in Vientiane (Wiang Chang) since French colonial times, Luang Prabang still prospers as the country's cultural center. Situated at the point where the Nam Khan River opens out into the upper reaches of the Mekong, the city was named at the end of the 15th century after the almost 1-m (3-ft) tall Buddha statue, Pha Bang, from the 14th-century; a temple was erected specially to house the figure. At that time, Luang Prabang had already been the center of one of three Lao kingdoms, the Lan Chang ("Land of a million elephants"), for one and a half centuries as the city of Muong Swa. The old royal capital today still has a number of Buddhist temples and monasteries housing many great artistic treasures. The most magnificent complex is the 16th-century royal temple, Wat Xieng Thong. While the temples were built from stone, the secular buildings were made of wood.

The garden of the former royal palace is home to the Wat Sala Pha Bang temple (right). Inside the Wat Xieng Thong temple, named after a Bodhi tree, or thong, monks pause devoutly in front of a giant Buddha statue (below).

VAT PHOU AND ASSOCIATED ANCIENT SETTLEMENTS WITHIN THE CHAMPASAK CULTURAL LANDSCAPE

The Wat Phu temple district is a fine example of Khmer culture and blends harmoniously into the old cultural landscape of Champasak.

Between the 10th and 13th centuries, Champasak belonged to the Khmer Empire of Angkor, which expanded its rule up the Mekong as far as Wiang Chan (now Vientiane). At the time, the region between the holy mountain of Phu Kao and the lowlands was systematically groomed for rice growing; irrigation systems, temples and two cities on the banks of the Mekong were built. It was intended to reflect the Hindu view of the world based on a principle of unity between the universe, nature and humans. The World Heritage Site includes the temple district of Vat Phou, 8 km (5 mi) from the Champasak (also known as Bassac), at the foot of the Phu Kao, which was built as a Shiva sanctuary in the 10th century under Angkor ruler, Jayavarman IV. Only ruins remain today.

A path leads up ninety steep steps from the temple ruins at the foot of Phu Kao to the former Shiva sanctuary (right: the main temple) on the mountain.

TEMPLE OF PREAH VIHEAR

This fascinating Hindu temple complex on the Cambodian-Thai border owes its World Heritage Site status to an unparalleled location in the Dongrek Mountains, unique architecture that blends seamlessly into the landscape, and extremely artistic stonemasonry.

This temple's history dates back to the ninth century when a hermitage existed here. In the 11th century, the hermitage was followed by a temple complex dedicated to Shiva, one of the three main Hindu gods, and it was coninuously developed until well into the 12th century. The final expansion work was performed under Khmer King Suryavarman II (r. 1113–1145). The ensemble is perched atop a 525-m (1,722-ft) cliff and provides a spectacular view over the Cambodian lowlands. The 800-m-long (2,625-ft) complex is built on the hillside in such a way that, at the end of their

Pilgrims climb steep steps up to the Temple of Preah Vihear.

climb over stairs and streets, pilgrims enter the main sanctuary through five gate towers, so-called gopurams. Many buildings have collapsed over time, but the preserved sections are still in good condition. Triangular gables display scenes from the Hindu Mahabharata epic, which includes the stories of Vishnu and Krishna.

The temple's territorial affiliation is still disputed between Thailand and Cambodia but the International Court of Justice in The Hague awarded it to Cambodia in 1962. However, it is often the subject of armed conflicts between the two states. The area was the scene of the Khmer Rouge's surrender in 1998.

The various reliefs and sculptures of the temple complex illustrate scenes from Hindu mythology.

Cambodia

Apsaras

Dancing is divine, and there is a lot of dancing in the Hindu pantheon. Shiva himself is the god of dance; indeed, it is through dance that he destroys the old cosmos in order to create a new one. So it is no surprise that dancing for us came from worshipping our gods. In South-East Asia temple dances are still sacred.

In the ancient Indian epics, Brahma, the creator of the world among the supreme trio of Hindu gods, is the one who brought apsaras, or "heavenly female dancers", into being. They live at the side of gandharvas, or "heavenly musicians", on the sacred Mount Meru in the palace of Indra, a "secondary" god who is responsible

ANGKOR

South-East Asia's largest cultural monument covers an area of approximately 400 sq km (154 sq mi), a grandiose product of the Khmer Empire.

The founder of the Khmer Empire was Jayavarman II, who ascended the throne in 802. As a divine king of with absolute spiritual and secular power he acted as the intermediary between heaven and earth; as a human he lived in a palace and was worshipped in the temple as a god. By the 13th century, Angkor's rulers had converted to Hin-

A stone embankment several hundred feet in length leads from the main entrance to the ensemble with the striking temple towers (prangs).

duism and were worshipped in the form of the Linga (phallus of the destructor of the world, Shiva). Later they were worshipped as the incarnation of Buddhist bodhisattvas. The Bayon Temple in Angkor Thom displays evidence of this shift. Jayavarman VII (r. 1181–1218) had fifty-four towers erected, each of which had four 1-m-high (3-ft) faces of the Bodhisattva, Avalokiteshvara, looking in the four directions of the compass.
Since a temple always became the divine king's tomb after his death, every Khmer king built a new sanctuary for himself, which explains the vast number of sanctuaries around Angkor. The largest is Angkor Wat, the temple of Suryavarman II (r. 1113–1150), under whom the Khmers had their heyday.

Angkor Wat is the largest temple complex in Angkor, the old Khmer capital.

for war and rain, among other things. The task of the apsaras is to keep the gods (devas) and goddesses (devatas) entertained. A selection of particularly beautiful apsaras is constantly sent to earth by Indra in order to seduce the people, but more importantly to dissuade them from striving to be "like the gods".

Apsaras played an important role in the art of the Khmer Empire. In the temple reliefs of Angkor, they dance individually or in groups for thousands of people. They are featured in the frequently depicted scenes from epics such as the Ramayana and Mahabharata, and since the divine kings of Angkor received their kingdom from the hands of Indra, dance was very important in the royal court.

Some 2,000 apsaras and devatas adorn the walls of Angkor Wat's galleries. Apsaras (far left) are usually depicted dancing on lotus blossoms with bent knees, while devatas (left) are generally standing up and often in recesses.

The Prasat Kravan temple east of Angkor Wat was built in about 920. The sanctuary is one of Angkor's last brick temples.

The artistic reliefs on the Banteay Srei temple, built by a Brahmin in 967, illustrate scenes from the divine epics of India.

The exteriors of these towers are adorned with faces of the Bodhisattva, Avalokiteshvara, which distinguish the Bayon temple from others.

The Ta Prohm temple district demonstrates the power of the tropical jungle, which had completely overgrown Angkor before it was "rediscovered".

Vietnam

HA LONG BAY

Situated in the Gulf of Tonkin in North Vietnam, this island landscape with its bizarre shapes contains about 2,000 limestone islets and cliffs. Wind, weather, and time have conspired to create this dramatic natural artwork.

Ha Long Bay contains dense clusters of limestone karsts that rise out of the water to impressive heights of 100 m (330 ft), and are reminiscent of Chinese landscape paintings. The cliffs and mountains present an extraordinary variety of shapes: the range extends from broad-based pyramids to high overarching "elephant backs" and slim needles. The inhabitants regard this island landscape as the result of mythical events rather than as a natural phenomenon. A dragon ("Ha Long", hence the name) is supposed to have fallen from the mountains, or out of the sky, and to have created this natural wonder when he destroyed an invading army with great blows from his mighty tail – or maybe he was simply giving vent to his rage at being disturbed? The channels and gorges thus created were flooded with water when the dragon dived into the sea. The geological facts are rather less dramatic: after the last ice age, the thick limestone layer along this part of the coast sank and was covered with water. These bizarre forms are the result of erosion.

Ha Long Bay is home to a brisk boat traffic (large image). Almost every one of these innumerable islets has its own name (right).

PHONG NHA–KE BANG NATIONAL PARK

The central feature of this national park is its tropical karst region, which exhibits varied geological features and is the oldest such region in Asia. It also contains a multitude of caves and underground rivers.

Phong Nha Cave is where this nature reserve in the Minh Hoa province of north-central Vietnam gets its name. It is, after all, the country's largest and most beautiful cave and its name means "Cave of the Teeth", which refers to the numerous stalactite and stalagmite formations inside it. The Cham people who ruled central Vietnam in the first century erected Buddhist shrines in some of these caves, and remnants of them can still be seen. Geomorphologically speaking, the caverns reveal more than 400 million years of the earth's history. The latest research has established that there are fourteen indigenous species of flora in the national park and nearly 400 animal species. Among the 113 different kinds of mammals are many threatened species, especially monkeys, and it wasn't until the 1990s that the Vu Quang ox or saola (Pseudoryx nghetinhensis) and the giant muntjac (Megamuntiacus vuquangensis) were discovered.

The first photograph of a Vu Quang ox (right) was taken in 1996 – it can weigh up to 100 kg (220 lb).

COMPLEX OF HUÉ MONUMENTS

Hué is located in the center of the country not far from the South China Sea and was the residence of the Nguyen dynasty starting in 1687. After that it was the capital of Vietnam from 1802 until 1945. The splendid architecture here is closely related to traditional Chinese buildings and the World Heritage Site includes palace, temple and tomb complexes.

Nguyen Anh, who reunited a divided Vietnam in 1802 and who ascended the throne as Emperor Gia Long, had a grand fortified residence built in the center of Hué and based it on the styles often used for Chinese palace complexes. The imperial city (Dai Noi) in the southern part of the citadel was home to the royal suite and servants and the "Forbidden City" at its center was solely reserved for the ruler and his family. However, unlike the imperial palace in Beijing (China), the complex in Hué was not built in the traditional North-South direction, but rather diagonally offset. The residence's most elaborate construction is the southern "Midday Gate" (Ngo Mon). Seven Nguyen emperors also had gravesites built for themselves outside of Hué.

This opulently decorated gate is the entrance to the main Thien-Mu temple, or "Pagoda of the Heavenly Lady", with the seven-story Phuoc Duyen tower.

HOI AN ANCIENT TOWN

This port city was an important trading center from the 15th to the 19th centuries. The balanced mixture of Asian and European influences is evident in the city's layout, houses and temples.

In 1516 the first Portuguese ships dropped anchor off the Vietnam coast, accompanied as they were by Jesuit missionaries. In 1535, Hoi An was established as the first Portuguese trading post in the region and quickly developed into a pulsating city. Chinese and Japanese then came to settle in what was also known as "Phai Fu" and began trading as well. The Portuguese were of course followed by more Europeans while porcelain, varnish, spices and mother of pearl were bought and sold. Each nation had its own district. Even when the Vietnamese Empire, which had been split after fifty years of civil war, lost interest in trading with Europe at the end of the 17th century, Hoi An continued to be an important "Gateway to the West". In the 18th century, large parts of the city were destroyed during the Tay Son uprising. The increasing aggradation of the Thu Bon River ultimately led to Hoi An losing its status as Vietnam's most important port city; Da Nang rose in the 19th century to take that position. French colonial buildings in the Old Town add to Ho An's special charm, many dating back to the late 19th century.

The Japanese bridge in the ancient town of Hoi An connected the districts of the Chinese and Japanese who settled here.

MY SON SANCTUARY

This religious and cultural center of the Cham people is home to the oldest and largest preserved relics of an empire that ruled central Vietnam for almost 1,000 years until their demise in the 15th century.

The empire of the Cham, a Malay-Indonesian people, dates back to the year 192 when the collapse of the Han dynasty in China led to the local Han governor founding his own kingdom in the region around the present-day city of Hué. An empire of initially four, then later two, states began developing in around 400 and took a variety of influences from Indian culture. The rise was accompanied by constant battles between the local tribes and the Chinese colonies.
A first wooden temple was built in My Son during the reign of King Bhadravarman, but this was burned down just 200 years later. One of Bhadravarman's successors then built the first brick temples in the seventh century, a move that started an architectural tradition that would last until the 13th century. After their capital in Vijaya was captured by Confucianist Vietnamese in 1471, the Hindu Cham people disappeared from history. In present-day Vietnam, they are now just a small minority.

The Cham people primarily worshipped the god Shiva beneath the "Beautiful Mountain" (My Son). The temple towers stand on a square base and taper upwards. Pilasters, friezes and statues of gods divide the exteriors.

Philippines

HISTORIC TOWN OF VIGAN

The historic town of Vigan is the best example in Asia of a preserved Spanish colonial style city.

In 1574, Spanish conquistador Juan de Salcedo founded a city in north-western Luzón Island in the Philippines that quickly became a trading center second only to Manila. Fortunately, the almost completely intatct colonial architectural fabric was protected from the urban redevelopments of later generations as well as from the bombings of World War II. The Spanish merchants in Vigan were not alone, however, and many Chinese traders settled here as well, allowing Asian architects to also leave their own mark on the city. The manor houses with their solid brick walls, tiled courtyards, balustrades, and dark polished hardwood internal flooring are typical of the architecture here. Some of the city's prominent buildings are grouped around the Plaza Salcedo and include the neo-classical Provincial Capitol Building, the 18th-century residence of the archbishop and St Paul's Cathedral built between 1790 and 1800. The triple-naved church is watched over by stone lions, traditional Chinese guardian figures, at each of the main wings' two gates. The finest and best-preserved colonial houses are located in the former mestizo quarter and also display many Chinese elements.

Calle Crisologo is situated in the center of the former mestizo quarter.

RICE TERRACES OF THE PHILIPPINE CORDILLERAS

The Ifugao, an Igorot ethnic group, have been growing rice on the emerald-green terraces in mountainous northern Luzón for over 2,000 years.

Wet rice cultivation is one of the most important cultural achievements in Asia's long history. Among the most skillful cultivators of this staple food are the Ifugao, an indigenous mountain folk from a province of the same name in the Philippine Cordilleras. The World Heritage Site here covers five main areas on Luzón: two in Banaue (Battad and Bangaan) and one in each of the municipalities Mayoyao, Kiangan (Nacadan) and Huangduan. They are all located in the Banaue Valley, a region about 20 km (12 mi) long whose steep slopes are covered with rice terraces created through strenuous manual labor. The terraces are an average of 3 m (10 ft) wide and are separated from one another by 10- to 15-m-high (33- to 49-ft) stone walls of stacked rubble that are built to fit the natural contours of the terrain. An elaborate system of bamboo pipes, canals and small sluice gates serve as the irrigation scheme and enable every single area from the highest terrace all the way down into the valley to be filled with water.

The rice terraces in the Philippine Cordilleras are also known as the "Eighth Wonder of the World".

BAROQUE CHURCHES OF THE PHILIPPINES

The Spanish colonial churches in the Philippines are considered unique because they form a successful synthesis of European baroque with local arts and craft traditions.

Spanish colonial architecture in Asia is best observed the region's only Catholic country. In a predominantly Buddhist or Islamic environment, the Catholic priests had to use their church buildings to demonstrate the power, grandeur and stability of their Church. For this reason, the places of worship from this time were elaborate bastions of the faith. Four of them have been listed as World Heritage Sites: the Church of San Agustín in Manila's Intramuros Old Town quarter (founded in 1571), the Church of La Nuestra Señora de la Asunción in Santa María on Luzón (1765), the Church of Santo Tomás de Villanueva in Miagao on the island of Panay (1797) and the Church of San Agustín in Paoay on Luzón (1710). San Agustín in Manila is the oldest stone church the country and even withstood World War II while nearly the entire Old Town was laid to waste; la Nuestra Señora is like a fortress; Santo Tomás has a richly decorated exterior; and San Agustín in Paoay has a separate bell tower.

San Agustín in Manila is also known as the "Mother of all Philippine churches".

PUERTO PRINCESA SUBTERRANEAN RIVER NATIONAL PARK

The main attractions of this national park are the tropical karst landscape and the longest navigable subterranean river in the world.

This national park is about 80 km (50 mi) north-west of Puerto Princesa, the capital of the island of Palawan. Its most impressive features are the limestone formations in the St Paul range, a chain of rounded limestone mountains that runs from north to south and whose highest peak is Mount St Paul at 1,027 m (3,369 ft). For geology enthusiasts the main attraction here is an underground river that flows for about 8 km (5 mi) — more than 4 km (2.5 mi) of which are navigable. Over time it has hollowed out a series of enormous caves that can reach heights of 60 m (200 ft) and are filled with huge, strangely shaped stalagmites and stalactites that also feature in the smaller caves. This cave system terminates in a large grotto where daylight shines in.

This park has stunning limestone and karst formations with an underground river below it that rises just south-west of Mount St Paul. It re-emerges in St Paul's Bay after having followed an almost entirely subterranean route.

TUBBATAHA REEFS NATURAL PARK

This maritime national park in the middle of the Sulu Sea consists of two ring-shaped atolls that are famous for their extensive coral reefs and fascinating underwater world. In 2009 the Tubbataha Reef Marine Park, which was declared a Natural Heritage Site in 1993, was enlarged to include the surrounding protected area, a move that effectively tripled the park's size.

About 180 km (110 mi) off the south coast of Palawan are two small atolls that represent the focus of this marine park. The atolls are very hard to reach and have an elevation of only 1 m (3 ft), but it is an almost undisturbed habitat for a great variety of animals such as the now rare hawksbill and green turtles, all kinds of swallows and boobies, and numerous corals — there are more than 40 kinds including branching and cabbage corals. The larger northern reef is also known as "Bird Island" and forms an oval about 16 km (10 mi) long and 4.5 km (2.8 mi) wide around a lagoon of coral sand, thus providing an ideal nesting site for birds. The southern atoll is smaller and separated by 8 km (5 mi) of sea. With about 380 species of fish belonging to at least forty genera this part of the park contains an even more diverse underwater world.

The underwater world includes ribbon eels (left) and giant squirrel fish (above).

Malaysia

MELAKA AND GEORGE TOWN – HISTORIC CITIES OF THE STRAITS OF MALACCA

With their traditional buildings these two historic cities reflect Malaysia's varied colonial history.

Melaka on the south-west coast of Malaysia was founded at the end of the 14th century and very quickly developed into a lively trading and maritime city. Various colonial powers including the Portuguese, Dutch and British have definitively left their mark on the architectural landscape, the most recognizable building being the Stadthuys (town hall) from 1660. This was where the Dutch governor held court and it is still the oldest preserved Dutch building in Asia. It is used as a museum today.

The atmosphere in George Town is very multicultural. Located about 450 km (280 mi) further north on the island of Penang, its population includes Malays, Chinese, Indians, Burmese and numerous other minorities. British colonial-style buildings are reminders that the city was founded as a British trading post in 1786.

The Stadthuys represents Melaka's Dutch heritage (right side of image). On the left is the Tan Beng Swee Clock Tower and the Christ Church.

KINABALU PARK

Kinabalu Park is in the Malaysian province of Sabah, at the northern end of the island of Borneo. It is particularly famous for its very ancient flora and its mountain, which is the highest in south-east Asia.

Mount Kinabalu, after which the park is named, forms an impressive focal point for the site – at 4,095 m (13,435 ft) it is the highest mountain between the Himalayas and New Guinea. Founded in 1964 as one of the first national parks in Malaysia, Kinabalu is primarily known for its ancient and diverse vegetation. Kinabalu Park alone has almost as great a variety of flora as can be found in Europe, for example, spread out over distinctive zones from tropical lowland to alpine plateaus.

In the lowest area the tropical rainforest contains more than 1,200 wild orchid species and many rhododendrons. The flowers vary in color from the deepest red to pale pinks and whites. Further up in the highlands the mountain forests feature forty different types of oak draped in green mosses and ferns before making way for pine forests. Closest to the summit is an alpine region of meadows and shrubs along with other forms of dwarf vegetation.

The jagged peak of Mount Kinabalu in Borneo towers above Kinabalu Park and offers a fascinating panorama of the surrounding mountains and low-lying areas with their varied habitats.

GUNUNG MULU NATIONAL PARK

The world's largest complex of caves can be found in the spectacular mountains of Gunung Mulu National Park in the Malaysian province of Sarawak on Borneo. The system of caverns provide insight into the geological development of our planet as well as the history of cave animals. In addition, the national park is an important refuge for a broad range of plant and animal life both above and below ground.

Geological periods of time are unimaginably long for humans to comprehend. This cavernous landscape emerged some thirty million years ago when a layer of volcanic rock that had been ground into sand and sediment was covered by the sea. Over millions of years, corals and other marine creatures began forming limestone deposits on top of it. Changes in sea level then forced the land to warp so that mountains such as Gunung Api at 1,750 m (5,741 feet), which consists of pure limestone, rose up next to the

sandstone. The highest peak, Gunung Mulu at 2,377 m (7,799 ft), conceals a huge system of caves carved out by underground rivers and inhabited by numerous bats and insect species.

Gunung Mulu National Park forms part of a spectacular tropical karst landscape, with its jagged limestone formations (right) and the huge complex of caverns.

TROPICAL RAINFOREST OF SUMATRA

Three national parks have been combined here to form one World Natural Heritage Site. Together they protect one of the world's last major continuous expanses of rainforest.

This World Natural Heritage Site includes Gunung Leuser National Park in the north, Kerinci Seblat in the central portion, and Bukit Barisan Selatan which is further toward the south of Sumatra. Around 10,000 plant species flourish in this vast area including seventeen unique native plant types. In fact, more than fifty percent of the plant types present in Sumatra can be found beneath the park's flowering canopy. Among the most famous of them are the largest flowers in the world (Rafflesia arnoldii) as well as the flowers with the largest unbranched inflorescence, the Titan arum (Amorphophallus titanum).

Gunung Kerinci in the national park of the same name is an active volcano and Sumatra's highest peak.

The variety of fauna is just as great, and only part of it has been classified. To date, 580 bird species have been identified, twenty-one of which are endemic. The most spectacular animals here are orangutans, tigers, rhinoceroses, elephants, serows, tapirs and cloud leopard. This level of biodiversity equals the wide range of geological formations and habitats here. Beyond the tropical rainforest there are majestic mountains, forests, lakes, volcanoes, fumaroles, waterfalls, caves and wetlands.

The rainforest in Gunung Leuser National Park (top left) is a refuge for threatened animal species including orangutans (left). In the communities of these "forest people" (orang means person, utan means forest), the young are raised solely by the females. Captive animals are taught how to survive in the wild in the Orang Utan Rehabilitation Center.

Indonesia

UJUNG KULON NATIONAL PARK

Ujung Kulon was Indonesia's first national park. Its importance rests above all on these last remnants of lowland rainforest and the small population of very rare Javan rhinoceroses.

Java is the smallest but most important of the Greater Sunda Islands in the Malay archipelago. Ujung Kulon national park comprises the peninsula of the same name in south-western Java and the islands of Krakatau, Panaitan, and Peucang in the Sunda Strait. It includes Javan lowland rainforest, coastal coral reefs and the plants and animals on the volcanic island of Anak Krakatau. The most endangered species in this rainforest is the Javan rhinoceros which, at one point, had been reduced by poaching to a population of twenty-five. This now seems to have risen back to sixty specimens. Still, together with the Indian rhino this one-horned beast is the most endangered large mammal on the planet. The timid Javan banteng is more numerous in the national park along with deer, apes, leopards, saltwater crocodiles, and hornbills.

Three of the world's five species of rhinoceros are native to Asia: the Javan (right), the Sumatran, and the Indian rhinoceros.

BOROBUDUR TEMPLE COMPOUNDS

This temple complex on Indonesia's main island of Java is the most important Buddhist sanctuary outside India.

The temple complex of Borobudur was built in the eighth century and symbolizes the cosmological concept of Mt Meru, the "navel of the world", with its different levels: the "World of Desire", the "World of Forms" and the "World of Formlessness".
Five "earthly" galleries are built on a strictly square floor plan. This is where various reliefs tell of Buddha's life, while others also depict the old Jataka legend. Three "heavenly" circular terraces then rise up on the platform above the galleries. They hold a total of seventy-two stupas, each of which once surrounded a Buddha statue and which are oriented towards the main stupa on the top terrace. The complex was allegedly abandoned with the decline of Buddhism and the rise of Islam on Java in the 14th century.

According to legend, Buddha himself is said to have designed the stupa by folding his beggar's garb into a hill, placing his beggar's bowl on the top and crowning it all with a stick. As a whole, Borobudur embodies "a monument of the divine, in which the universe converges and which stands before the universe as a sanctuary" – as art historian Karl With once said.

PRAMBANAN TEMPLE COMPOUNDS

Once the most important sacred Hindu site on Java, Prambanan was dedicated to the gods Brahma, Vishnu and Shiva.

Visible from great distances, the towers dominate this temple complex where construction probably began as early as the eighth century. Evidence suggests that the main temple, Lara Jonggrang, was not completed until around the year 915, however. It was dedicated to Shiva, the Indian god of procreation who is considered the "Mahadeva", or mightiest deity. That is the reason his symbol, the phallus (Lingam), appears everywhere. Brahma and Vishnu each have their own temples, albeit smaller, to the north and south of the central main tower. The complex as a whole is thus dedicated to the "Trimurti" – the trinity of supreme Hindu deities. The complex was largely destroyed by an earthquake in 1549 and the remaining debris was long used as a quarry. It was not until 1937 that reconstruction of the complex began; it was essentially completed in 1953. It was again damaged by another severe earthquake on May 27, 2006, but has now been re-opened to the public.

The World Heritage Site includes Prambanan (right) as well as four other complexes in the immediate vicinity: Lumbung, Burah, Asu and Sewu.

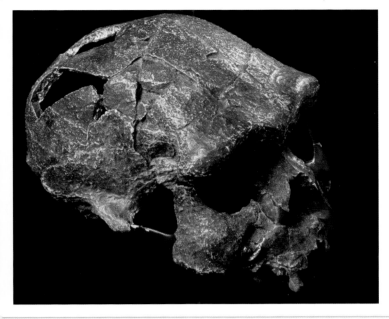

SANGIRAN EARLY MAN SITE

The archaeological site of the "upright ape-man", Pithecanthropus erectus, provided valuable insight into the history of human evolution.

After anthropologist and geologist Eugène Dubois discovered the cranium of the "Java Man", Indonesia was considered one of the earliest sites of human development. Dubois named his discovery Pithecanthropus erectus" after the Greek word "Pithecanthropus" for "ape-man".

During his excavations between 1936 and 1941, anthropologist Gustav Heinrich Ralph von Koenigswald discovered further fossilized remains of bones bearing human features. These ones were estimated to be around 1.5 million years old. Sangiran in Central Java is now unquestionably one of the world's most important archaeological sites for early human remains. Com-parisons between the "Java Man" and "Peking Man" showed that both groups were part of the Homo erectus species, which already largely displayed the physical features of present-day humans. There are also remains of the animals that these early humans hunted in this area.

The approximately sixty hominid fossils that have been discovered so far in Sangiran all belong to the Homo erectus species (left, a skull of a "Java Man" found in Sangiran).

KOMODO NATIONAL PARK

The Komodo dragon is found in the wild only in this national park, where it enjoys ideal conditions for hunting wild pigs and deer in the rainforest and savannah of its protected area.

This national park is not limited to the island of Komodo, which is only about 35 km by 25 km (22 by 15 mi) and part of the Lesser Sunda Islands. The park's area also encompasses the smaller neighboring islands of Padar, Rinca and Gili Montang as well as the west coast of Flores.

The abundant vegetation is divided between tropical monsoon rainforest, grassland and savannah and in a number of places there are even mangrove forests. The featured attraction of course is the Komodo dragon (Varanus komodoensis), the world's largest species of lizard. This diurnal ground-dweller lives on mammals like wild pigs, deer, larger birds, vipers and even tortoises. The park authorities estimate the total population of these roughly 3-m-long (9-ft) "dragons" at around 6,000; on the island itself there seem to be at most 3,000 specimens, possibly far fewer. These wondrous creatures can be viewed by tourists in the presence of park wardens, but their aggressiveness should not be underestimated.

The Komodo dragon uses its long, deeply forked tongue to waft the faintest of scents onto an olfactory organ seated in its palate. It can detect carrion at a distance of 5 km (3 mi).

LORENTZ NATIONAL PARK

South-East Asia's largest nature reserve is in Irian Jaya, the Indonesian part of the island of New Guinea. It combines diverse scenery with a vast variety of flora and fauna over an area of 25,000 sq. km (9,700 sq mi).

This unique national park boasts a complex geological structure and an unmatched variety of species. The area is roughly divided into swampy lowlands and a higher mountainous regions. The central mountainous region emerged from two converging continental plates, a process that is still not complete. The glaciated summits of the range reach elevations of 5,000 m (16,400 ft). The lowlands are a swampy plain with largely undisturbed forests and countless watercourses where the vegetation consists of simple plant cultures on the beach and rather more complex ecosystems in the inland evergreen forests. The most varied flora in New Guinea can be found still further inland at an altitude of 600–1,500 m (2,000–4,300 ft): some 1,200 tree species grow here alone. Many of the bird of paradise species here are native as well, and there are loads of amphibians and reptiles that remain largely unresearched.

The Papuan soft-shelled turtle lives in rivers and feeds on small fish and crustaceans.

The saltwater crocodile (below, Australia's Kakadu National Park) grows to lengths of up to 6 m (20 ft) and is the largest living reptile on earth. With its steep, partly wooded rock faces, many people believe Milford Sound on New Zealand's South Island is "the most beautiful end of the earth". The sound opens out into the Tasman Sea.

AUSTRALIA OCEANIA

Australia

Dream Paths

When the earth was still barren and empty, the ancestors of Australia's Aborigines roamed the land and dreamt of the following day's adventures. By putting their dreams into practice, they were able to make all aspects of life an expression of the original creative force. "Dreamtime" is an expression still used today.

The Aborigines see in certain places representations of their ancestors' existence, and therefore made them into sacred sites. Only through them can the legends of Dreamtime be witnessed and thus become real.
The Aborigines' fight for their land must also be viewed with this in mind: It is not just a question of economic

KAKADU NATIONAL PARK

Kakadu National Park boasts not only diverse scenery but also impressive Aboriginal rock paintings.

Kakadu National Park, which was expanded to cover 20,000 sq km (7,700 sq mi), is 250 km (155 mi) east of Darwin and encloses five distinct kinds of landscape. In the tidal river estuaries, mangroves have established root systems in the silt, protecting the hinterland from the effects of wave action. In the rainy season, the coastal areas transform into a bright carpet of lotus flowers, water lilies, and floating ferns. Rare waterfowl such as the brolga, the Jesus bird, the

"The Wet" is what Australians call the rainy season between November and April, when the expansive marshlands are covered in water lillies.

white-faced heron, the great Indian stork, and the snake bird are native to the area, as is the saltwater crocodile, the largest living reptile on earth. The adjoining hills with rich tropical forest, savannah and grassy plains vegetation form the greater part of the park and offer refuge to endangered species like dingoes and wallabies.
The park gained international acclaim in the middle of the 20th century when excavations uncovered stone-age tools that were at least 3,000 years old. Numerous rock paintings reveal details of the hunting habits, myths and customs of the Aboriginal tribes who lived here.

The South Alligator River and its filigree tributaries (left) flow through Kakadu National Park.

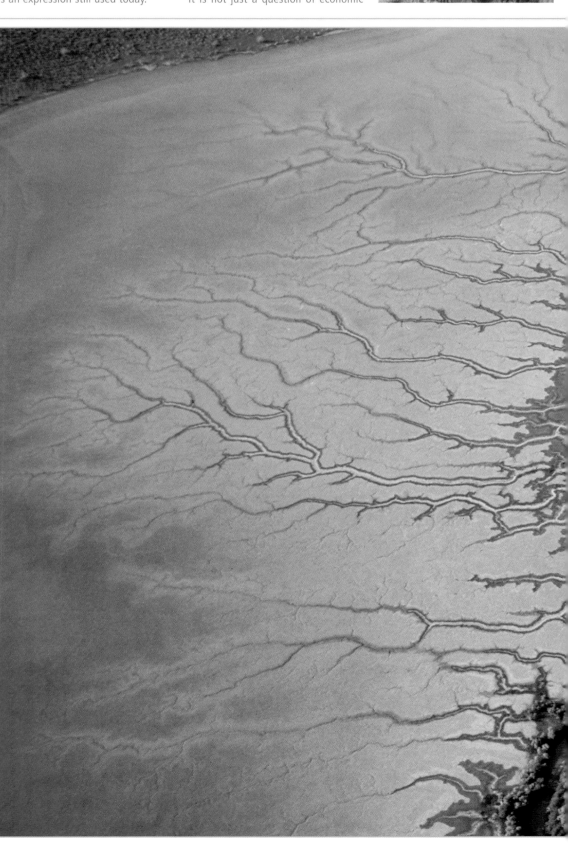

resources, but also the spiritual justification of their existence. The mythical ancestors of the Aborigines left behind visible signs of their wanderings in the form of hills, cliffs, caves and waterholes. These mythical paths of the creators – also known as Dream Paths – cover the entire country in a vast network. Each centimeter of soil

over which their ancestors wandered is honored by the Aborigines, and its original purity and power must not be touched. The Aborigines demonstrate their spiritual connection with a place by painting it with pictograms, marking it out with stones or placing wooden sculptures and boxes for totem objects on it.

Aboriginal body painting (far left) often relates to the mythical origins of a group. Over 5,000 Aboriginal rock drawings were discovered in Kakadu National Park. One particular style is the "X-ray style" (left, on the Nourlangie Rock in Kakadu National Park), in which even parts of the skeleton and organs are depicted.

Australia

PURNULULU NATIONAL PARK

Purnululu National Park near Hall's creek in the northern part of Western Australia is distinguished by extraordinary dome-shaped sandstone formations molded by erosion. "Purnululu" means "sandstone" in the language of the indigenous Kija Aborigines.

In the heart of Purnululu National Park is the stunning Bungle Bungle mountain range, which rises a relatively modest 578 m (1,896 ft) above sea level. More impressive than their height is that the mountains are composed of Devonian quartz sandstone and are approximately 370 million years old.

Over the last 20 million years, horizontally striped, beehive-shaped rock formations have been created by the effects of erosion from weather and water. The stripes are characteristic of softer, porous rock, where cyanobacteria are able to grow and ultimately

The unconventional scenery of the Purnululu National Park is composed of hundreds of sandstone domes, cupolas, and pyramids, towering like beehives up to 300 m (990 feet) above the surrounding grassland.

darken the surface. The harder, interposed strata are orange, betraying the presence of iron and manganese. The tones change depending on the seasons and are especially striking after rain. Between the domed rocks there are gullies with streams and pools fringed with large Australian fan palms (Livistona australis). Aborigines have inhabited the Purnululu area for millennia, leaving behind numerous rock paintings and burial sites.

There are about 130 bird species here, including the European bee-eater and bright budgerigars, the most striking creatures in the park.

This extraordinary region with its rock formations and paintings was "re-discovered" by a film team only in 1982, after which it became so popular that a national park was established to protect it all.

SHARK BAY

The distinguishing features of this protected area are the varied species of seagrass meadows, stromatolite colonies and the world's largest population of dugongs.

The Shark Bay Marine Park, a coastal area of dramatic cliffs, lagoons and sand dunes about 800 km (500 mi) from Perth is home to a large number of endangered aquatic and land animals. The nearly 5,000 sq km (1,900 sq mi) of seagrass meadow is among the richest in species variety in the world. They serve above all as a refuge for small fish, crustaceans and larger crabs. They also foster the formation of stromatolites (layered algal accretionary structures). In the shallow, brackish waters these tiny organisms, in existence for 3.5 million years, form cabbage-shaped clumps that poke out of the water at low tide.

In summer in Shark Bay you can see humpback whales mating, marine turtles laying eggs and dugongs raising their young. These sea mammals, once thought to be extinct, number about 10,000 here, one of the world's largest populations.

The islands and cliffs are home to several rare seabirds. Australasian gannets, fish and sea eagles, and pied cormorants hunt for fish in the abundant waters. The most popular animals are the bottlenose dolphins.

Viewed from above:, the varied seagrass meadows in the shallow waters of Denham Sound look like dark clumps.

ULURU–KATA TJUTA NATIONAL PARK

The spectacular geological formations of Uluru and Kata Tjuta rise like mountainous islands right in the middle of this vast continent.

In the middle of a sprawling savannah south-east of Alice Springs is the "Red Heart of Australia": Uluru–Kata Tjuta National Park. The immense monolith, Uluru (or "shady place", formerly called Ayers Rock), and the thirty-six summits of Kata Tjuta (or "many heads", once called The Olgas), are the best-known natural wonders of Australia.

Their formation began 570 million years ago and is closely linked with that of the formation of continental Australia. Unlike the surrounding rock formations, the hard stone of these monoliths weathered only slowly. They tower today over the plain as

mighty, petrified testaments to earth's prehistory. Uluru is a mystical place for Aborigines, with rock paintings and sacred sites. It was a meeting place for the ancestors when they created the land and its creatures during their wanderings in Dreamtime. There are also rock paintings at Kata Tjuta. Despite the inhospitable climate, the Anangu Aborigines have lived here for thousands of years.

Uluru (left) rises like an island out of the plains and has a circumference of about 10 km (6 mi). The area's designation as a World Heritage Site is also related to the mythological importance of the rock.

WET TROPICS OF QUEENSLAND

This coastal region between Townsville and Cooktown in Queensland is about 450 km (280 mi) long and one of the most extensive and diverse rainforest areas in the state. The World Heritage Site covers 9,000 sq km (3,400 sq mi) and includes about twenty national parks and protected areas.

Tropical rainforest once covered the entire Australian continent. Today it only covers parts of the Great Dividing Range, the depressions of the Great Escarpment and a section of the Queensland coast where, unlike other areas of Australia, the tropical climate has remained stable for millions of years now.

The result is a diverse animal and plant biotope with more than 800 species of tree that create a "layered" forest. Beneath the almost impenetrable canopy of the giants reaching 50 m (164 ft) are more than 350 species of higher plants, in particular ferns, orchids, moss, and lichen.

The animal kingdom is also abundant. Wet Tropics National Park boasts the greatest variety of fauna on the continent. Roughly one-third of Australia's marsupials and reptiles and two-thirds of all bat and butterfly species are indigenous to this area – only a tiny fraction of the whole continent.

Tree ferns (right) grow to 20 m (66 ft) tall in the rainforests of Wet Tropics.

GONDWANA RAINFORESTS OF AUSTRALIA

The World Heritage Site once known as "Rainforests of the East Coast" was renamed "Gondwana Rainforest of Australia" in 2007 and encloses fifteen national parks and conservation areas in Queensland and New South Wales.

The new name here refers to the former southern hemisphere supercontinent, Gondwana, which split up into the continents we currently have at the end of the Mesozoic period. All of the UNESCO-protected regions under this name can be found in the transitional zone between a damp, tropical climate and a warm, temperate zone, the result being that a huge variety of vegetation has been able to develop within a relatively small area. The World Heritage Site includes the Border Ranges, Mount Warning, Nightcap, Washpool, Gibraltar Range, New England, Dorrigo, Werrikimbe, Barrington Tops, Springbrook, Lamington, Mount Chinghee, Mount Barney (partially), Main Range and Mount Mistake (partially) national parks.

Barrington Tops and Border Ranges are famous for their enormous variety of bird species. Satin bowerbirds, rainbow lorikeets, king parrots, and kookaburras can all be seen here relatively frequently.

A cascading river splashes over rocks in Dandahra Canyon in the Gibraltar Range National Park.

GREATER BLUE MOUNTAINS

Not far from Sydney there is an expanse of pristine landscape that to this day has only been partly explored. The Blue Mountains emerged about a million years ago during the Pliocene era and are part of the Great Dividing Range.

The magnificent landscape of the Blue Mountains is also a living laboratory of jagged sandstone formations, caves and complex ecosystems. Though they are not very high – between 600 and 1,000 m (1,970 and 3,280 ft) – these mountains are very steep, with many valleys and canyons that still remain untouched by humans.

There is an unprecedented variety of eucalyptus species here, along with plentiful rare and endangered plants. Around 150 indigenous plants and trees flourish in these dense forests, including the Wollemi pine, which was first first discovered in 1994. It is actually regarded as a living fossil, with roots going back 90 million years. Cave paintings and rock drawings also attest to early Aboriginal settlement.

The Blue Mountains are a globally unique example of dynamic interaction between extreme climate conditions, adapted eucalyptus species, nutrient-poor soil and fire. The name is derived from an optical illusion – the eucalyptus appear blue in the haze of oils exuded by the trees.

The Greater Blue Mountains fascinate with canyons, waterfalls and dramatic rock formations. The most famous is the "Three Sisters" (right), which rises some 300 m (990 ft) above Jamieson Valley.

SYDNEY OPERA HOUSE

Sydney Opera House is one of the greatest constructions of the 20th century, and also an iconic symbol of Australia.

It was a little-known Danish architect, Jørn Utzon, who surprised the world when he won the architecture competition for the Sydney Opera House project in 1955. But his extremely bold design was so difficult to implement that the government initially delayed construction. When work finally began in 1959, it was still not clear whether Utzon's "shell" roofs would actually be feasible. The original plan had been to cast them in concrete, but this proved to be too expensive, so Utzon proposed assembling the shells from pre-cast concrete ribs.

The exterior of the shell-like roofs is covered in ceramic tiles, which turned out to be very problematic to fit. The tiles were first laid into a mold with the enameled side down, and then poured out with liquid concrete. These elements were then fastened to the roof with bolts. The open ends are glazed with a total of 2,000 panes of varying sizes. In 1966, the architect fell out with the government, and an Australian team took over construction management.

Surrounded by water on three sides, it is not just the silhouette – which looks like upright seashells or ballooning sails, depending on the angle – but also the location of the Sydney Opera House that make this a unique monument in the history of architectural design.

FRASER ISLAND

Fraser Island in Queensland is the world's largest sand island. it is still partially covered with primeval lowland rainforest and provides a habitat for rare birds and frogs.

Despite being 120 km (75 mi) in length, the surface of Fraser Island at the southern end of the Great Barrier Reef has actually been shifting for 140,000 years. The crescent dunes, which can reach heights of 250 m (820 ft), migrate up to 3 m (10 ft) to the north-east every year, driven by the constant south-westerly winds.

No sooner had the island been discovered in 1836 than the settlers began exploiting its diverse tropical rainforest. The Queensland kauri, the bunya-bunya tree, the tallow and blackbutt eucalyptus, and the 70-m (230-ft) high satinay tree were the most common victims.

Today, only small areas of the island's interior are covered in rainforest. The remaining landscape is diverse and offers a refuge for over 240 species of bird. The mangrove honey-eater lives in the mangroves on the coast, while the ground parrot is found on coastal heaths. The red-green king parrot seeks nectar in tropical forests, and the stubble quail is indigenous exclusively to the damp moor areas.

With the exception of a few volcanic rock formations, Fraser Island is composed almost entirely of sand. The crescent-shaped dunes (left) can rise to 250 m (820 ft) in height.

Australia

THE GREAT BARRIER REEF

The Great Barrier Reef follows the north-eastern coast of Australia from the 10th to the 24th parallel south. Coral polyps, in their singular underwater world, have been building this largest of natural "construction projects" for 8,000 years.

This barrier reef, which is composed of about 2,500 individual reefs and 500 coral islands, follows 2,000 km (1,250 mi) of the eastern coastline of continental Australia at a distance of 15 to 200 km (9 to 124 mi). It was formed by coral polyps working symbiotically with cyanobacteria. Able to swim from birth, the polyp larvae hatch in the spring and settle on the reef near the water's surface. They then develop a skeletal structure and form a colony with others of their kind. When they die off, their coral skeletons are ground to a fine sand. The algae then "bake" the sand into

The oldest living coral reef in the world reaches from the Tropic of Capricorn to the estuary of the Fly River (New Guinea). The creator of this singular world is the humble coral polyp (above).

an additional layer of the reef, upon which new polyp larvae can settle. The result of thousands of years of this cycle are reefs and islands.
Among the 1,500 species of fish that thrive in the waters surrounding the reefs are the brilliant and exotic coral trout, the golden damselfish, the parrotfish and the stingray. Hundreds and thousands of varieties of birds, corals and molluscs also live here. Bird species include pelicans, frigate birds, noddies and a number of terns including sooty, roseate and crested.

One of the most beautiful sections of the reef is near the Whitsunday islands. The vast variety of marine species include all manner of fish, coral and starfish that fill the crystal-clear waters and delight divers and tourists throughout the year. The reef is the habitat of colorful flora and fauna in which a great number of sharks also lurk.

WILLANDRA LAKES REGION

Traces of 40,000-year-old settlements along with fossilized human remains can be found on the banks of the Willandra Lakes Region in south-western New South Wales. The area dried out very rapidly about 15,000 years ago.

In 1968, exciting prehistoric remains were found in a lunette dune known as the "Wall of China", situated on what 24,000 years ago had been the shores of Lake Mungo in the Willandra Lakes Region. Next to 18,000-year-old tools were human skeletons approximately 35,000 to 45,000 years old – the oldest traces of Homo sapiens sapiens, or modern humans, ever found in Australia.

A further scientific sensation came to light during the examination of a 30,000-year-old camp fire. Proof was found in the remains that, in the course of 2,500 years, the earth's magnetic field had shifted by 120 degrees to the south-east.

Rare animals like the emu, Australia's largest bird at up to 1.75 m (6 ft) tall, have made the grassland of the Willandra Lakes Region their home along with thousands of parrots and budgerigars. Prehistoric-looking monitors – among the largest lizards in the world – warm themselves in the midday sun.

Mungo National Park (below) makes up part of the Willandra Lakes Region's 2,400 sq km (950 sq mi).

AUSTRALIAN FOSSIL MAMMAL SITES AT RIVERSLEIGH / NARACOORTE

Riversleigh in north-western Queensland and Naracoorte in south-eastern South Australia are among the most spectacular and important fossil sites on earth.

Painstaking work in a karst cave in Naracoorte, Victoria, has led to the excavation, collection and reconstruction of lungfish, reptile, monotreme, marsupial and other mammal skeletons. Among them are echidnas and platypuses, so-called 'missing links' in the development of reptiles into mammals. The reconstruction of skeletons from extinct species like the marsupial lion, with its prehensile paws, or the 3-m-tall (10-ft), short-faced kangaroo has answered many questions about mammal development.

Discoveries at Riversleigh's fossil sites, located in Boodjamulla (Lawn Hill) National Park, have contributed greatly to our understanding of continental drift, which began about 45 to 50 million years ago. Bones have been found from a time when Australia was part of the Gondwana supercontinent, along with proof of south-east Asian species who arrived via landbridges.

Victoria Cave (Naracoorte) is a treasure trove of prehistory. Below: The reconstruction of a marsupial lion skeleton.

ROYAL EXHIBITION BUILDING AND CARLTON GARDENS IN MELBOURNE

Built for the world exhibitions in 1880 and 1888, this ensemble is one of Australia's most important historic complexes.

Starting in 1851, so-called 'World Exhibitions' were held at somewhat irregular intervals in alternating cities. The common goal of the events was to present the public with information on new accomplishments in science and technology around the world. More than fifty such events were ultimately held between 1851 and 1915. Buildings exercising a great influence over the architecture of their time were often erected for these exhibitions. In Melbourne, Joseph Reed designed the Royal Exhibition Building and the associated gardens. It is constructed of bricks, timber, steel and slate. Reed's design was based on Byzantine, Romanesque and Renaissance styles.

Carlton Gardens have remained more or less intact since 1880, and are laid out in a style typical of the 19th century: wide streets, carriageways, footpaths, trees and clusters of trees, two small lakes and three fountains.

The dome of the Royal Exhibition Building is around 60 m (197 ft) high.

LORD HOWE ISLAND GROUP

Situated 600 km (370 mi) from Port Macquarie, this island group owes its World Heritage status to the spectacular topography and its flora and fauna, much of which is unique to this group.

About seven million years ago a 2,000-m-high (6,600-ft) shield volcano erupted in the Tasman Sea off the east coast of continental Australia. As a result of erosive rain, wind, and wave action, however, the only remains of this colossus are now the twenty-eight islands that form the Lord Howe island group.

Because of its isolated geographical location, a quite distinct biotope has developed here. Home to some 220 species of plants, of which roughly one-third are unique to the area, the dense cloud forests have become the habitat of many endangered bird species including the wedge-tailed shearwater, the Kermadec petrel (nesting on the steep cliffs), the colorful white-bellied storm petrel and the flightless Lord Howe woodhen.

To the south-west coast of the group, stone coral and calcified red algae form a fantastic reef that is home to diverse species of exotic fish such as the coral trout, the parrotfish and the sablefish.

Lord Howe Island (above, a view of Mount Lidgebird) is the largest of the group.

Australia

TASMANIAN WILDERNESS

The national parks of Western Tasmania are home to temperate rainforests and unique animal life. They are considered one of the world's last untouched ecosystems.

This World Heritage Site between Cradle Mountain and Tasmania's south-western cape is composed of five national parks – Lake St Clair, Franklin–Lower Gordon Wild Rivers, South-West, Walls of Jerusalem and Hartz Mountains – as well as several other conservation areas.

Deep canyons, jagged peaks, eroded plains, raging waterfalls and trough-like lakes are typical of this glaciated landscape. At greater altitudes, there are expanses of moor and heath. Closer to sea-level there are stretches of bogland. Although the temperate rainforest has been heavily logged, there are still traces of primeval mixed forests with numerous subantarctic and Australian tree species.

Having died out in mainland Australia centuries ago, the Tasmanian Devil is now unique to Tasmania.

An exceptional range of animals roams this diverse landscape, including many unique local species. The endangered orange-bellied parrot, the Tasmanian wedge-tailed eagle, the Tasmanian devil and the Pedra Branca lizard, for example, occur only in Tasmania. Archaeological finds such as rock paintings, stone tools and the remnants of canoes attest to the first human settlement of the island over 30,000 years ago.

Cradle Mountain–Lake St Clair National Park is one of the most impressive places in Tasmania, a massive island separated from the mainland by the Bass Strait. Part of the World Heritage area, Cradle Mountain rises to a dramatic 1,545 m (5,070 ft). Among the creatures in the park are Bennett's wallaby and the tiger quoll. Stately red cypresses stand at the Artists' Pool below the mountain (right).

MACQUARIE ISLAND

This small subantarctic island is home to an interesting spectrum of wildlife as well as being the highest point in the Macquarie Ridge, which formed underwater as a result of the convergence of the Indo-Australian and Pacific plates.

Macquarie Island is a mere 35 km (22 mi) in length and just 5 km (3 mi) wide. It is situated roughly 1,500 km (930 mi) south-east of Tasmania and 1,300 km (800 mi) north of Antarctica. It is a paradise for elephant seals and fur seals as well as numerous bird species.

King and emperor penguins congregate in sprawling colonies in the winter and spring along with stormbirds and some species of albatross who nest here. The only sign of human habitation is a research station. The island's location in a subduction zone makes it of great geological interest – it is the only place on earth that features exposed formations from the earth's crust that would otherwise lie deep beneath the surface. The island was named after Lachlan Macquarie, British governor of New South Wales from 1810 to 1821, after a surprise discovery in 1810 by Australian seal hunter Frederick Hasselborough. Initially the island was under the jurisdiction of New South Wales but was later given over to Tasmania.

Elephant seals (females, left) and various species of penguin, such as the Gentoo penguin, the royal penguin and the king penguin are ubiquitous on Macquarie Island in the South Pacific.

HEARD AND McDONALD ISLANDS

These are the only subantarctic islands that still experience volcanic activity. As such, they provide great insight into the dynamic processes of the earth's core. Their ecosystems remain largely unaffected by outside influences.

These two islands lie some 4,000 km (2,500 mi) south-east of Perth and about 1,500 km (930 mi) north of Antarctica. At 2,745 m (9,000 ft), Mawson Peak (aka "Big Ben") on Heard Island, is the highest mountain in Australia – higher than 2,228-m (7,350-ft) Mount Kosciuszko in the Snowy Mountains of New South Wales – and an active volcano.

Since 1992, McDonald has also experienced volcanic eruptions. Glaciers and ice sheets cover about eighty percent of the island's surface while the inhospitable climate permits only sparse vegetation, grasses and algae. To date, forty-two varieties of moss have been recorded but many of the lower plants, algae and mosses have yet to be classified. The islands have been spared unwelcome "settlers" like cats, rats and hares, so the penguins, sea mammals and seabirds live undisturbed.

These islands give us an important look at geohistory as well as the undisturbed evolution of certain flora and fauna. Macaroni penguins (left), Antarctic fur seals, elephant seals (above) and the king penguin (background) all live here.

KUK EARLY AGRICULTURAL SITE

The Kuk swamp region lies at an altitude of around 1,500 m (4,922 ft) in the southern highlands of the Pacific island of New Guinea. Archaeological excavations show that the soil here had been cultivated by humans at least 7,000 years ago – long before any known South-East Asian influence on the island.

This area covering just over a square kilometer (300 acres) provides us with unique evidence of the early development of agricultural techniques. The earliest proof of plant cultivation in Kuk, as opposed to merely collecting plant products, is believed to date back some 10,000 years.

Well-preserved remains show that the people inhabiting this swampy region actually began creating arable hills and terraces around 7,000 years ago. They also used wooden tools to dig irrigation and drainage ditches, thus ensuring better usability of the areas they intended to cultivate. Kuk is indeed proof that the various forms of farming around the world emerged not only independently from one another – but more often than had previously been thought. Until now, only the Fertile Crescent in the Middle East, parts of China, Central and South America and the eastern United States were considered to be centers of such human innovation.

In the rural regions of Papua New Guinea (below), the "taro" (right) is one of the oldest agricultural crops to be grown.

CHIEF ROI MATA'S DOMAIN ON VANUATU

This World Heritage Site actually covers several sites dating back to the early 17th century. It is located on three islands of the South Pacific island state of Vanuatu – Efate, Lelepa and Artok – and is associated with Chief Roi Mata, who was famous for his legacy of social progress and peace.

According to the tradition, Chief Roi Mata is said to have been the first ruler to unify the warring tribes of this South Pacific archipelago before dying of poisoning around 1600. Realizing that he was about to die, the chief bid farewell to his followers on the island of Efate, then retreated to a cave on the island of Lelepa to await his passing. He was finally buried on the island of Artok.

In 1967, archaeologists in the northwest of Artok discovered the tomb some 100 m (130 yd) from the coast and subsequently provided the first scientifically supported proof of the actual existence and former power of this chief, whose place of residence, death and burial has now been classified as a World Heritage Site.

The island of Efate, which is part of the South Pacific island state of Vanuatu, was once ruled by the famous Chief Roi Mata, whose moral ideals continue to be passed on even today. He also established social and political structures that still exist on the island.

Solomon Islands

EAST RENNELL ISLAND

Rennell Island is the southernmost in the Solomon Islands chain and the world's largest dry coral atoll. The southern third of the island is a World Heritage Site that includes Lake Tegano. At 150 sq km (60 sq mi), this saltwater lake, with jagged limestone islands of its own, is the largest in the Pacific islands.

Because of its geographical seclusion, a unique array of flora and fauna has managed to evolve on East Rennell without significant interference from humans or "non-native" species such as rats or snakes. For its size, therefore, this atoll – 85 km (53 mi) long and 15 km (9 mi) wide – has the densest concentration of indigenous species in the world.

Its pristine forests offer a rich habitat for many rare plants including a variety of orchids and screw pine trees.

The first European to discover the Solomon Islands, to which Rennell Island belongs, was the Spaniard Álvaro de Mendaña de Neyra in 1568 (above: Kanggave Bay).

The Rennell flying fox, for example, is one of the eleven species of bat found here and is unique to the island. Approximately forty species of bird nest on the island, including four native species and nine native subspecies.

There are also two varieties of sea snake, one of which, the Laticauda crockeri, is also found in freshwater areas (as is Hydrophis semperi). The other is the striped sea snake, Laticauda colubrina, which can grow to a length of 1.8 meters (6 ft) and weigh 1.3 kg (3 lb). A further five gecko, four skink and three land snake species have been recorded, along with twenty-seven varieties of snail and over 700 different insects.

A glimpse underwater reveals a wealth of exotic sea lif including anemone fish (top left), reef sharks (middle left) shrimp, clown triggerfish (left), prawns and red lionfish.

New Zealand

The birds of New Zealand

New Zealand emerged roughly 100 million years ago on a tectonic fold thrown up at the unstable border of two continental plates. This geological development then provided the spawning grounds for an impressive selection of indigenous species. In fact, most of the insects and one quarter of all the bird species are found nowhere else on earth.

Because New Zealand was separated from other land masses so early, there were no land mammals for a long time. With no natural predators, many species of bird eventually lost their ability to fly. Colonists then brought rats, dogs, martens and foxes with them, thereby transforming – and endangering – the natural woodland habitat of many flightless birds.

TONGARIRO NATIONAL PARK

New Zealand's oldest national park (established in 1887), in the middle of North Island, can be traced back to a gift from the Maori to the New Zealand government. Its 750 sq. km (300 sq. miles) enclose three active volcano systems.

The history of this volcanic landscape began about two million years ago, when the Indo-Australian and Pacific continental plates converged. Due to the resistance provided by the plates, a large amount of frictional energy was released which then melted the surrounding rocks. Hot magma result-

A showcase of primordial strength: 2,797-m (9,000-ft) Mount Ruapehu.

ed, and strong volcanic activity began above the friction points. The eruptions of the three active volcanoes, Tongariro, Ngauruhoe and Ruapehu, are evidence of this ongoing process – which led to the creation of the largest lava plateau in the world.
The national park was initially established in 1990 in recognition of the landscape's geological importance. In 1993, it was expanded, becoming the first World Heritage Site to be designated both a natural and cultural treasure. The distinction of the mountain at the heart of the park was prompted by UNESCO's recognition of its cultural and spiritual importance to the Maori people.

Tongariro's main attraction are the volcanic cones (large image: Ngauruhoe, with Tongariro in the background).

The kiwi is a nocturnal flightless bird of the Apterygidae family with a total population estimated at about 5,000. The Takahe (Porphyrio mantelli), a member of the rail family (Rallidae), is much less common. In fact, it was considered extinct until being re-discovered in 1945 by a walker in Fjordland National Park. A good example of acute endangerment – despite in-

tensive conservation attempts – is the kakapo. This timid creature was also thought to be extinct, until 1974, when a few specimens were discovered on Stewart Island. By 2005 their number had risen to eighty-six. The moa (Dinornis maximus), a giant flightless bird, has long disappeared, having been hunted to extinction by the Maori.

The kiwi, New Zealand's national bird, is a nocturnal animal, hiding in burrows hidden by thickets during the day (far left). Kea, takahe and kakapo (left) are three other species native to New Zealand.

For the Maori, New Zealand's volcanoes are holy places shrouded in myth, or "tapu". Above: Ngauruhoe.

Snowcapped all year: Mount Ruapehu and its crater lake.

The Taranaki Falls contribute to the park's fascinating effect on visitors along with…

… Mahuia Rapids Cascades. The impressive landscape in Tongariro was formed by millions of years of lava flows.

New Zealand

TE WAHI-POUNAMU – SOUTH-WEST NEW ZEALAND

Four national parks on the south-western end of the South Island offer impressive mountainscapes as well as ancient species of animals and plants.

At about 26,000 sq km (4,100 sq mi), Te Wahipounamu (in Maori: "place of jade") is one of the largest conservation areas in the world. It includes Westland, Mount Aspiring, Mount Cook and Fjordland National Parks. Spread over large parts of the south-western coast of the South Island, Fjordland is the largest of the four conservation areas and owes its name to its coastal fjords. Its submerged valleys can be 400 m (1,320 ft) deep. Up to 10,000 mm (394 in) of precipitation fall annually on this glaciated landscape, ideal conditions for subtropical rainforest. There are many species of plants and animals still in existence here that were indigenous to Gondwana millions of years ago – the southern hemisphere's former supercontinent.

Trees here are often overgrown with carpets of lichen and creepers; countless varieties of fern flourish in the undergrowth; and unique birds live in seemingly impenetrable foliage. Sea lions and dolphins swim alongside indigenous Fjordland penguins in the crystal-clear waters of the coast.

At 3,754 m (12,310 ft), Mount Cook is the highest mountain in New Zealand. It rises from the Southern Alps like Mount Tasman at 3,498 m (11,470 ft) and is also dominated by glaciers. The two picturesque lakes at the foot of Mount Cook, Tekapo and Pukaki, teem with fish, and in early spring the lakeshore comes alive with blossoms. Mount Aspiring and Westland National Parks are equally dramatic glacial landscapes. The Fox and Franz-Josef glaciers in Westland stretch down through steep valleys almost to the coast.

The dying rays of a long summer day on the peaks of Mount Cook and Mount Tasman (top right) with their snow-capped summits reflected in Lake Matheson. Fox Glacier in the south and the Franz-Josef Glacier in the north of the park should both be enjoyed from atop the ice itself (middle right). Challenging trails await visitors in Mount Aspiring National Park. Right: The magnificent Routeburn Track.

NEW ZEALAND'S SUBANTARCTIC ISLANDS

These five island chains in the South Pacific possess a lively ecosystem. The diverse – and often unique – biotope has developed Antarctic Ocean and subtropical ocean currents come together.

The uninhabited Auckland, Campbell, Antipodes, Snares and Bounty island groups are both south and east of New Zealand and, with the exception of the low cliffs of the Bounty Islands, they are carpeted with lush moorland. The deep fjords of Campbell and Auckland islands show signs of a prolonged period of glaciation while, with the exception of the Bounty islands, the groups possess the richest

Royal albatrosses (top, on the Campbell islands) only pass through to nest. Otherwise they usually remain on the water or in the air, unlike the southern giant petrel (above, on the Auckland Islands).

variety of flora of all the subantarctic islands. Of more than 250 species, thirty-five are native and thirty are very rare. The world's southernmost forests are on the Auckland Islands and feature countless tree ferns. Among 120 recorded varieties of bird, forty are seabirds, of which five nest only here. Of twenty-four species of albatross, ten are unique to the islands, including the southern royal albatross. Two of four penguin species are also unique here, and the rare New Zealand sea lion calls it home.

The Snares Islands are home to the Snares penguin, native only here.

Four colossal figures guard the entrance to the great rock temples of Abu Simbel. They represent King Ramesses II, who had the 20-m-high (66-ft) seated effigies carved into the rock in the 13th century BC (below). A bizarre world of sand and rock characterizes the border area between the nature reserves of Aïr and Ténéré in Niger (right).

Morocco

MEDINA OF TÉTOUAN (FORMERLY KNOWN AS TITAWIN)

Tétouan owes its strategic status between Morocco and Moorish Spain to the many Muslim refugees who came here and left their mark on life in the medina after the fleeing the Catholic Reconquista.

Tétouan is in the foothills of the Rif mountains less than 50 km (31 mi) south-east of Tangiers. It is known as the "white dove" due to the white-washed houses within the mighty walls of the medina where numerous mosques and souks have survived seemingly untouched. In front of the Bab er-Rouah ("Gate of the Winds"), one of the entrances to the medina on Hassan II Square, is the Royal Palace, Dar el-Makhzen, built in the 17th century during the reign of Moulay Ismail. In the medina itself, traditional souks with workshops and shops make for a lively oriental bazaar atmosphere in a maze of narrow alleyways. The streets open out onto squares with tiled fountains. Mosques and minarets dot the cityscape while madrasas and mausoleums in Moorish style mix in with fondouks (hostels) and former caravanserais. At the north-western edge of the medina is the 17th-century kasbah where the earliest buildings actually date from the late 13th century.

Hassan II Square is at the crossroads between the Old Town and New Town. It forms the focal point of Tétouan.

MEDINA OF FEZ

Although not the capital, Fez in northern central Morocco is the intellectual and spiritual heart of the country. The World Heritage Site comprises the Old Towns of Fez el-Bali and Fez el-Jedid, where the architecture reflects distinctive periods under different rulers.

Fez was founded by the Idrisid dynasty as a twin town on a major trade route through the Sahara to the Mediterranean. The oldest part of town, Fez al-Bali, is surrounded by a city wall with twelve gates and was settled by Andalusian refugees from the Moorish part of Spain and by families from Kairouan in present-day Tunisia. Their Kairaouine Mosque can accommodate more than 20,000 worshippers and is the center of the university which, founded in 959, enjoys great standing in the Muslim world today. The Andalusia Mosque also dates back to the early days of the town.

Fez experienced a heyday during the Merenid dynasty in the 14th century. The Royal Palace, the Great Mosque and the Mellah (Jewish quarter) are from that period. Qur'anic schools, mosques and the Merenid tombs show the importance of the Fez al-Jedid quarter, mainly a district of artisans and traders. After taking over in 1911, the French kept the historic towns and built a modern city.

Gates like the Bab Bou Jeloud define the cityscape in Fez (right). One of the oldest Qur'anic schools in Fez is the Sahrij Madrasa, built in 1323 (above).

ARCHAEOLOGICAL SITE OF VOLUBILIS

Excavations here testify to the prosperity of this settlement, which was once the most important town of the Roman province of Mauretania Tingitana.

Volubilis, north of Meknès, was the most important Roman settlement in what is now modern Morocco. Established at the time of Carthaginian rule, the town was incorporated into the Roman Empire in AD 44. During the period that followed, magnificent secular and religious buildings were constructed, and these have been systematically excavated since 1887. A particularly active era of building occurred during the reign of Emperor Septimius Severus (r. 193–211), a man to whom northern Africa owes many of its architectural treasures. The central avenue, the Decumanus Maximus, extends some 900 m (2,953 ft) across the town which in its heyday counted more than 10,000 inhabitants. The originally five-aisled basilica from the second century served as a courthouse and assembly building. Meanwhile, residential homes such as the enormous Gordian Palace and villas like the House of the Followers of Venus featured richly worked mosaic floors and illustrate the everyday life of Roman governors und citizens.

The splendid Triumphal Arch of Caracalla was built in 217 to honor the eldest son of Emperor Septimius Severus.

HISTORIC CITY OF MEKNÈS

Meknès is one of the four former imperial cities of Morocco and is worth visiting for its superb medina and many mosques, but the ruins of the giant palace district of Sultan Moulay Ismaïl is an absolute must-see.

Meknès developed around an ancient Berber fortress and was conquered and destroyed several times by rulers of the Almoravid, Almohad and Merenid dynasties before experiencing its own period of prosperity during the reign of the Alawite Sultan Moulay Ismaïl (1672–1727). Ismaïl made Meknès the capital and impressed even his European contemporaries with his "Versailles of Morocco". The despot's architectural achievements have indeed entered the annals of history as his subjugation of rebellious tribes all over Morocco provided an army of slaves to build his "ville impériale", which comprised palaces, housing, stables, grain silos, water stores and workshops. Only ruins remain of the complex today, but not far away is the mausoleum of the sultan himself. Among the city's mighty gates, the Bab el-Mansour from the 18th century is particularly impressive. The medina boasts one of the largest souks in Morocco, several mosques – including the grand mosque – and the Bou Inania Madrasa, a Qur'anic school with a beautiful courtyard and roof terrace.

The mausoleum of Sultan Moulay Ismaïl comprises several rooms and courtyards all tiled with mosaics.

PORTUGUESE CITY OF MAZAGAN (EL JADIDA)

The origins of El Jadida go back to the 16th-century Portuguese fortress of Mazagan, the walls and four bastions of which are completely preserved. In the Old Town visitors will encounter many traces of a Portuguese past.

The story of El Jadida commences in around 1500 when the Portuguese built a fortress here on the Atlantic coast not even 100 km (62 mi) south of what is now modern Casablanca. Over the centuries, the fort was continuously enlarged as a bulwark against attacks and sieges. That strategy worked well until the Moroccans finally succeeded in taking and pillaging the fortress of Mazagan at the end of the 18th century. Conquest by Arab ethnic groups and a Jewish community then followed, but despite the town's turbulent history, El Jadida ("the new one") continued to grow. Anyone entering the Old Town through one of its three gates will be reminded of Europe. Especially interesting are the Church of the Assumption of Mary, built in Manueline style, and the Portuguese cistern. Mosques synagogues and churches as well as the mansions of European merchants from the 19th century bear witness to the cosmopolitan history of the city.

Within the fortifications of Mazagan is the ancient Portuguese cistern, whose columns are reflected in the rainwater.

Morocco

MEDINA OF MARRAKESH

The emblem of this southermost former imperial city of Morocco is the Minaret of the Koutoubia Mosque. This oasis was once an important center for trans-Saharan trade and for several dynasties it served as the capital and seat of government.

Of the structures built in the early days of the medina, the roughly 10-km (6-mi) city walls have been lovingly preserved along with their twenty gates and 200 towers, some of which were added later. The Almohad sultans also bequeathed upon Marrakesh the Koutoubia Mosque with its minaret from 1153; it is one of the most beautiful buildings in the city. Together with the Giralda of Seville and the Hassan Tower in Rabat, the nearly 80-m (262-ft) masterpiece of Spanish- and Moorish-influenced architecture set the style for many minarets all over Morocco. Behind the mosque is the tomb of Yusuf ibn Tashfin, who founded the city.

The Menara gardens date back to the Almohad dynasty in the 12th century. The pavilion on the edge of the pond dates from the 19th century.

The 12th-century Bab Agnaou is the most attractive city gate in Marrakesh and leads to the kasbah, an ancient fortified town of the Almohads. Another treasure is the Ben Youssef Madrasa from the 14th century. It was built by the "Black Sultan", a Merenid ruler. The 16th century under the Saadi dynasty was also a busy period of building. Dating from this time are the well-preserved Saadian Tombs where the interior rooms of the necropolis feature magnificent decorations in cedar, stucco and mosaics. Aside from several palaces (Royal Palace, Bahia Palace, ruins of the El Badi Palace), the souks and market squares in Marrakesh are fantastic. The World Heritage Site here also inclues the Agdal and Menara gardens, which are just outside the city walls.

Hustle and bustle define life on Djemaa el-Fna, the central market place with its artists and entertainers (top). The "Hall of the twelve columns" is the most luxuriant room in the Saadian mausoleum (right).

MEDINA OF ESSAOUIRA (FORMERLY MOGADOR)

The Old Town of Essaouira is completely surrounded by fortifications and reflects the influence of European military architecture in the region. Its origins go back to the Portuguese fortress of Mogador.

This village on the central Atlantic coast of modern Morocco was already being utilized as a trading station by the ancient Phoenicians. They were followed in the first century BC by the Romans who established a major center for the production of purple dye here. Later, the Portuguese built a military port, then a port for the trade in sugar, salt and ostrich feathers. In the middle of the 18th century, Mogador was rebuilt under Sultan Sidi Mohammed ben Abdallah. He commissioned architect Théodore Cornut with the task, who modeled the town on the French city of Saint Malo, which explains the European ambience and grid-like layout featuring arcades and whitewashed houses with blue doors and shuttered windows. The Old Town contains the kasbah, the original fortress, the Mellah (Jewish quarter), the Medina and the souks. When Morocco gained independence in 1956 the town was renamed Essaouira.

The Porte de la Marine (left) was built during the reign of Sidi Mohammed ben Abdallah. The fortifications appear defiant with battlements atop the wall (below).

KSAR OF AÏT-BEN-HADDOU

The Ksar Aït-Ben-Haddou in south-eastern Morocco makes a breathtaking impression. This Ksar, meaning "fortified city" in Arabic, is probably the most beautiful and best-preserved of its kind in the country.

Located on the banks of the Asif Mellah, on the once strategically important route from Marrakesh to Ouarzazate, Aït-Ben-Haddou perches proudly on its hill like a castle. It comprises altogether six nested kasbahs – fortified homes surrounded by earth walls and towers. The ground floor of these houses was utilized to process agricultural goods, whereas the upper floors served as living quarters. The reddish earth and clay brick structures of the ensemble are dominated by the granary towers. The former significance of the settlement can be seen in the partially well-preserved and artistically decorated buildings as well as the agadir, or granary, which has since become derelict. Named after a Berber tribe that once lived here, the complex is a representative example of the architectural style of the northern Sahara, which probably emerged from an early pre-Islamic construction style. Because of its unified appearance, the ksar has often been a setting for historic films such as "Gladiator" and "Lawrence of Arabia".

The clay was worked immediately while still wet in order to create the heavily adorned upper floors and corner towers of the ksar. Mud bricks were used as an alternative.

Algeria

KASBAH OF ALGIERS

Above the Bay of Algiers lies the picturesque kasbah of Algeria's capital. This Old Town with its citadel, mosques and the Moorish palaces conveys a vivid image of Muslim culture and lifestyle.

Originally founded by the Phoenicians, this settlement only developed fully as an important trading center after the Arab conquest. In the 16th century the town fell under Spanish rule, after which the inhabitants asked the pirate Hayreddin Barbarossa for help. After conquering Algiers he then pledged his allegiance to the Ottoman sultan and for centuries Algiers remained a pirating stronghold that the various European states fought over.

The French were next to occupy the metropolis, and did so from 1830 until 1962; during that time it did not grow beyond the walls that encircled the Kasbah and the citadel until the end of the 19th century. Most of the buildings in the kasbah date from the Ottoman period – only the Jemaa el-Kebir, or Grand Mosque, with its eleven naves is older. It was built in the Almoravid style, on the site of an earlier Christian basilica. Its elaborate minbar (pulpit) from 1017 features rich carvings and the minaret dates from 1323. Also noteworthy is the El Jedid, or New Mosque, built in 1660 in the Byzantine style.

Countless staircases and alleyways wind their way through the Old Town of Algiers.

AL QAL'A OF BENI HAMMAD

The once magnificent capital of the Berber Zirid dynasty located at the foot of the Hodna Mountains has been a field of ruins since its destruction in the 12th century. It is considered an important crossroads between Eastern and Western Islamic art and culture.

The residence of the Zirid rulers, built in the early 11th century by the ambitious founder of the dynasty, Hammad ben Bologhine, bears witness to the glorious history of the Maghreb. The most important North African artistic styles of the period found expression here in the form of palaces, gardens and water features. The sophisticated combination of architectural and decorative elements also marks Beni Hammad as the birthplace of basic Moorish styles. For example, the eight-celled muqarna (corbel) was developed here – a decorative device consisting of several pointed niches – as well as the seven-celled stalactite vault. The palace of the Hammadid emirs comprised three complexes separated from each other by gardens, pavilions and water basins. One of the most stunning and largest of the palaces was the Dar el-Bahar, or "Castle at the Sea", built around a giant pool. The 25-m-high (82-ft) minaret of the great mosque, which features a 13-aisled prayer hall, is today preserved only in part.

The ruins still reveal the solid masonry of the fortress, which failed to withstand the Almohad onslaught in 1152.

TIPASA

This ancient site combines the unique architectural styles of the Phoenician, Roman, early Christian and Byzantine periods and provides valuable insight into the life of its former occupants.

On the Mediterranean coast about 70 km (43 mi) west of Algiers is the archaeological site of Tipasa. Originally a Phoenician trading port, the settlement developed into a major Punic town, which then became a Roman colony in the first century and eventually evolved into one of the most important strategic centers for the Roman conquest of Mauritania. In 430 the Vandals seized the city and as a consequence the Christians who had lived there fled to Spain or were persecuted by the heretics. After the Byzantine ascent to power in the sixth century, Tipasa declined in importance and gradually fell into ruin. Remains of a forum, the amphitheater, some villas, baths and a kitchen where a spicy fish sauce was produced have been preserved from the Roman period. Right down by the sea is the early-Christian Grand Basilica, which features nine naves and beautiful mosaic floors, and the remains of the Kbor er Roumia, the royal mausoleum of Mauritania.

The remains of wall sections, columns and arches all form a unified whole to reveal the former structure of this trading post with its long Decumanus, or boulevard.

DJÉMILA

This small village 900 m (2,953 ft) above sea level between Wadi Guergour and Wadi Betame contains the ruins of the Roman military colony of Cuicul. The buildings here were cleverly adapted to the hilly terrain.

One of the best-preserved Roman city ruins in Algeria, Cuicul was founded in the years 96 to 98 during the reign of the Roman Emperor Nerva on the site of an earlier Berber settlement. Established as a garrison town and veterans' settlement, its population already numbered more than 10,000 inhabitants in the second century. Cuicul had its heyday in the third century when it grew beyond the confines of its original ramparts, and a new forum was laid out surrounded by magnificent buildings. With the rise of Christianity in the fourth century, construction in the city boomed again. From the fifth century, however, Cuicul began to decline. The well-preserved religious and public buildings, some of which still feature their original mosaics, were excavated starting in 1909. The appearance of Cuicul was defined by two forums, the market of Cosinus, the Temple of the Severan Family, the triumphal Arch of Caracalla, the theater, and the Grand Baths. A Christian district sprang up in the south, of which the baptistery from the fourth century has been nicely preserved.

A main road leads into the town where a triumphal arch was built in honor of Emperor Caracalla.

TIMGAD

This settlement of veterans was built during the reign of Emperor Trajan in the Aurès Massif. Excavations began in 1880. A superb example of Roman town planning, Timgad was one of Numidia's most important cities in the third century.

This military colony was laid out in AD 100 according to the latest technological developments of the day and to serve retired Roman legionaries once they were released from their twenty-five years of service in the army. The town was planned on a grid-like military layout with two main avenues – the cardo running north-south and the decumanus on an east-west axis. Most of the buildings date from the second century, for example the 4,000-seat theater (161–169), the Arch of Trajan, the Capitol, several large baths, the public library, the forum and the market of Sertius. In the fourth and fifth centuries, Thamugadi, as the Romans referred to the town, became the main seat of the Donatists. At the end of the fifth century, Vandals and Berbers came and destroyed the place before the Byzantines eventually rebuilt it. However, during the Arab invasion in the seventh century it was sacked again and abandoned for good. Despite all of this, the town still conveys a vivid image of everyday life in antiquity.

Imposing structures, most of all the well-preserved Triumphal Arch of Trajan from the end of the second century, speak of the significance and prosperity of ancient Thamugadi.

M'ZAB VALLEY

This oasis region looks back on thousands of years of human habitation. The towns founded at the beginning of the 11th century here are an example of settlements and a lifestyle ideally suited to their surroundings.

The Mozabites, a Berber ethnic group from the Ibadite Muslim community, built five fortified hamlets, or ksours, in the valley of the Oued M'zab, which carries water only once a year. The towns were: El-Atteuf, Bou Noura, the holy city of Beni Isguen, Melika and Ghardaïa. The last and largest was Ghardaïa. Like the other settlements, it was laid out on a clifftop around a mosque and encircled by ramparts. The mosque's minaret also served as a watchtower while the mosque itself was conceived as an independent fortress with a granary and a weapons arsenal. Despite a simple design, the cube-shaped homes here were well thought out. The earth-colored buildings, which often had as a source of light only a single opening in the roof, are well adapted to the desert climate and their architecture reflects the traditional family structure. Palm groves and gardens were placed outside the fortifications and kept alive with the aid of an ingenious irrigation system. In summer, inhabitants would move to these oases with their fortified homes and watchtowers.

Ghardaïa seems like a mirage in the desert sand, with the minaret of the central mosque towering high above the houses of the desert settlement.

Algeria

TASSILI N'AJJER

Many prehistoric rock paintings have been preserved in the jagged terrain of the Hoggar mountains – invaluable documents of the earliest period of human development. This desert region, characterized by numerous ravines and bizarre rock formations, is home to rare animals and plants.

The Tassili N'Ajjer mountain plateau ("Plateau of the Rivers") covers an area roughly the size of England in one of the least hospitable areas of the Sahara – near the border of Libya and Niger. In 1933, a number of cave paintings were discovered in this magnificent rocky landscape. So far, more than 15,000 drawings and engravings have been documented, with images that date back to various periods, the earliest being 6000 BC. They document decisive stages in human cultural development from a time when today's desert still enjoyed

This mountain range resembles a moonscape. Its appearance is the result of erosion, with rocks jutting straight out of the sand like giant stalagmites.

a damp, even tropical climate. The rock paintings, protected from the ravages of the elements in remote ravines and caves, depict hunters and herds of elephants, giraffes and buffaloes. Domestication also seems to have been practiced, as herdsmen are shown grazing their animals out on the savannah. The indigenous Saharan cypress and the Saharan myrtle are typical of the vegetation depicted, and among the indigenous animals are the endangered Barbary sheep, the dorcas gazelle, the caracal lynx and the sand cat.

Certain styles and phases can be distinguished in the hunting and ritual scenes of Tassili N'Ajjer. The earliest motifs are abstract and very schematic but in later periods vitality, movement and elegance predominate (right and below). People are often even shown with clothing and body decoration.

People observed their surroundings and carefully captured them in detailed images. One example is their depiction of a herd of giraffes where the body shapes, coats and proportions were all painstakingly reproduced by the artists.

The subjects in the images ranged from fish and hippopotamuses to bovines and camels and were executed using a variety of different techniques.

The oldest depictions show little realism and represent their subjects mainly in outline. Here a hunter with his hunting tools.

Tunisia

DOUGGA/THUGGA

The 70-ha (173-acre) Dougga excavation site some 100 km (62 miles) south-west of Tunis reveals the ruins of a Roman settlement. Impressive monuments from pre-Roman times are also preserved.

Ancient sources first mention Thugga (modern: Dougga) in connection with an expedition by Agathocles at the end of the fourth century BC. Built on a hill in the middle of fertile country-side, the settlement was an important base in the Punic Empire before it fell to the Romans. Among the pre-Roman remains, the three-level Mausoleum of Ataban dating from the second century BC stands out; it was built as the tomb for a Punic prince and is crowned by a pyramid.

The city experienced a veritable boom in construction from the first half of the second century AD until the third century. During the reign of Septimius

Severus, Thugga became a prosperous Roman provincial town, with about 20,000 inhabitants. Many finds and ruins date from this period. Numerous ancient structures have since been ex-cavated, including the forum framed by temples, the aqueduct that fed the baths, a theater as well as villas and houses used for a variety of purposes.

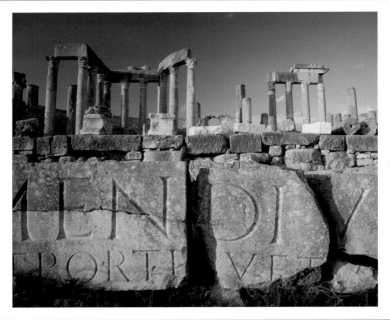

One of the most impressive monuments in the settlement of Thugga, excavated between 1903 and 1938, is the theater.

ICHKEUL NATIONAL PARK

This national park includes both Lake Ichkeul (100 sq km / 39 sq mi) and its tributaries as well as the 511-m-high (1,680-ft) Djebel Ichkeul massif. The park is home to one of North Africa's most important wetland areas.

Ichkeul National Park is roughly 25 km (16 mi) south-west of Bizerta and connected to the Bizerta Lagoon by Oued Tinja. The region immediately surrounding sizable Ichkeul Lake, which teems with aquatic life, is fed by streams from the Mogod mountains, but the lake in fact has both fresh and salt water; the salt content increases in the dry summer months and decreases with the heavy winter rainfall.

Various species of rushes, irises, swamp lilies, reeds and water lilies grow in this fertile wetland region. The conservation area is also a refuge for Tunisia's largest mammal,

the water buffalo, which can weigh up to 1,200 kg (2,900 lb), and almost 200 species of bird, of which the majority are waterfowl such as ducks and coots. In the winter, it is home to hundreds of thousands of migratory birds from Europe. Nowhere else in north Africa are there so many gray geese, for example. Fossil deposits of hominids, primates, and extinct giant mammals have also been found in the area.

The dense vegetation around Lake Ichkeul teems with life. Among the inhabitants are the widgeon and the ferruginous duck (right).

ARCHAEOLOGICAL SITE OF CARTHAGE

On a peninsula in the Bay of Tunis lies what was probably the most famous town in North Africa: the Phoenician town of Qart Hadasht, also known as Carthage. Only sparse remains are left now of the once powerful city.

According to archaeological finds, Car-thage was founded by Phoenician settlers in about the eighth century BC. A defensive wall more than 40 km (25 mi) long protected this Punic town, home to a people that came to dom-inate Mediterranean trade during the Magonid dynasty (Hamilcar, Hasdru-bal, Hannibal). With the Roman victory in the Third Punic War in 146 BC, how-ever, Carthage was laid to waste. The Romans then built upon the ruins and Carthage experienced a renewed hey-day as the capital of the province of Africa. After a period of Byzantine rule,

the Arabs took their turn destroying the metropolis. Excavations have re-vealed ruins near the port, on top of the Byrsa castle hill (now dominated by the Cathedral of Saint Louis), and in the Tophet, a sacred precinct where human sacrifices were made. From the Roman period there are remains of the Thermae of Antonius Pius as well as villas with mosaics built on top of the Punic necropolis, an amphitheater, and a circus and cisterns.

Ruins are the silent witnesses of Carthage's rich history.

MEDINA
OF TUNIS

In the medina of Tunis is the largest preserved historic town center in the Maghreb region. Some 700 structural monuments bear witness to the heyday of this Mediterranean metropolis, particularly from the period between the 12th and 16th centuries.

Ancient Tunis, originally settled by the Numidians and one of the oldest towns in the Mediterranean region with a natural port, underwent swift development only after the seventh century, when it was conquered by the Arabs. In its heyday, during the reign of the Hafsid dynasty, more than 100,000 people lived here. In the 16th century, the Ottomans conquered the much-coveted city. In the early 17th century, around 80,000 Spanish Moors brought a new economic upswing. In 1881, the Turkish

The minarets rise into the blue sky above the narrow alleyways of the medina with its whitewashed houses.

Husseinites were forced to yield to the French. The most important building in the medina of Tunis is Ez Zitouna, the "Olive tree mosque", which dates from the eighth century and whose 184 columns were made with stones plundered from the monuments in ancient Carthage. The Sidi Youssef Mosque in one of the many souks was built by the Turks in the 17th century. With its octagonal minaret and green tiles it quickly became a model for other Turkish mosques. Further architectural highlights here are the monumental Bab el-Bhar Sea Gate and Tourbet el-Bey, the magnificent 18th-century mausoleum of the Husseinites.

If you're lucky, you can get great views of the minaret of the Ez Zitouna Mosque (19th century) from the superb mosaic terrace of one of the neighboring houses (top left). Everything the heart desires: each lane in the souk is typically dedicated to a particular trade (left).

Tunisia

MEDINA OF SOUSSE

Ancient Hadrumet was a major Phoenician settlement founded in the 11th century BC. It came under the rule of various cultures until being taken over by the Arabs in the seventh century, after Rome had fallen for good. It wasn't long before the town flourished again under the Aghlabid dynasty (800–909).

The ninth-century medina, which has hardly changed over the centuries and is still surrounded by its original ramparts, is one of the world's most important examples of Arab architecture. Shortly after the Aghlabids revived the city in the wake of the Roman Empire, the grand mosque was built in the style of a kasbah with walls and towers. Next to the mosque, and not far from the entrance to the medina, is the tower of the ribat. It belonged to a fortification along the coast that was built in around 800 and consisted of a chain of defensive monasteries called ribats. Warrior monks lived here and, in addition to warring, they offered the local population shelter from attack. Another fine monument from the Aghlabid era is the Bou Fatata Mosque, built in about 840. Located in the south-western corner of the Old Town is the kasbah, home to the Archaeological Museum with relics from Punic, Roman and early Christian days. The Khalef el Fatah Tower is still a lighthouse.

An aerial shot of the grand mosque with its battlement walls and domed corner towers reveal the defensive nature of the structure.

KAIROUAN

Located some 150 km (93 mi) south of Tunis, this town was founded by the Umayyad descendant Uqba ibn Nafi in around 670 as an advance post of the conquering Arab army. It flourished under the Aghlabids around the turn of the 10th century.

The grand medina in Kairouan is still encircled by its original city walls. The quarter grew up around the grand mosque, which was begun at the time of Kairouan's foundation in 670. The most important and the oldest Islamic structure in North Africa, this mosque became the model for the all Moorish religious architecture in subsequent years. The prayer hall looks like a forest of marble columns. The minbar, or pulpit, decorated with lovely inlay work, was created in 862, making it the oldest intact Islamic pulpit anywhere. The water basins built by the Aghlabids as early as the ninth century were fed by an aqueduct and are still intact. Aside from its grand mosque, Kairouan boasts other outstanding Islamic structures: the Barber's Mosque (Zaouia Sidi Sahab), a mausoleum and madrasa complex from the 17th century; the Sidi Abid el-Ghariani Mosque and the Mosque of the Three Doors. Kairouan is still one of the world's most important Islamic centers.

Kairouan is marked by contrasts. Via the gate of the grand mosque you enter an arcaded courtyard (above). Behind it are the narrow lanes of the medina (right).

PUNIC TOWN OF KERKUANE AND ITS NECROPOLIS

This former Punic town probably had its origins in the sixth century BC. During the First Punic War it was destroyed by the Romans, but the original structure of the settlement can be made out from the well-preserved ruins.

This town at the tip of Cape Bon in the north-eastern corner of Tunisia was probably a Phoenician harbor even before Carthage existed. Its importance as an archaeological site lies in the fact that this is the only Punic town that is still more or less intact. Laid out like a horseshoe, the settlement covers an area of about 10 ha (25 acres) and is bordered by the sea on its eastern side. Excavations have revealed a double wall that protected the town, the foundation walls of houses, which were built around an inner courtyard with fountain, and an ancient road network. Almost every house had its own bath and a highly sophisticated irrigation system. Architectural details indicate influences from other regions and Mediterranean cultures, indicating robust cultural exchange. Purple, a Phoenician monopoly at the time, was produced here. The World Heritage Site also includes the Arg el Ghazouani Necropolis with roughly 200 rock graves and burial chambers.

The remains of the settlement of Kerkuane reveal sophisticated town planning.

AMPHITHEATER OF EL JEM

The Roman Amphitheater of El Jem in Central Tunisia was built in about AD 230 and is now a testimony to the former prosperity of one of the main olive cultivation centers in the Maghreb.

This ancient Punic settlement gained in importance during the time of Julius Caesar, who founded the town of Thysdrus here in 46 BC. It lay on a major traffic route in the heart of a vast olive-growing region that would eventually satisfy most of Rome's demand for the precious oil. After completion of the amphitheater, however, the town fell victim to a destructive rebellion of large landowners protesting the introduction of an olive oil tax. After the Roman withdrawal, the arena was converted into a fortress and during the seventh century it even served as a refuge for Dihya Kahina, the female leader of the Berbers, in her battle against the Arab conquerors. The amphitheater is one of the largest in the Roman Empire with an oval structure measuring 148 by 122 m (486 by 400 ft) and over 40 m (131 ft) high; it accommodated more than 30,000 spectators who came to watch sports contests, bloody gladiator spectacles and animal baiting. Pageants and plays were also performed in the adjacent theater that has not yet been excavated.

Though the amphitheater was misused as a quarry and partially dynamited in the 17th century, it is still in much better condition than the Roman Coliseum.

Libya

ARCHAEOLOGICAL SITE OF LEPTIS MAGNA

Together with Sabratha and Oe, Leptis Magna is one of the ancient Tripoli, or "three cities", founded here by the Phoenicians. It served mainly as the trading hub and a port for the export of grains and olives.

Leptis Magna, situated in the Wadi Lebda estuary some 100 km (62 mi) east of Tripoli, was controlled by Carthage and became a Roman colony in the first century BC. Despite repeated attacks by desert tribes, the post flourished, increasing its number of inhabitants from 15,000 during the time of the Third Punic War to 80,000 during the Roman era. Excavations began in the 1920s and have exposed numerous ancient buildings. Under the reign of its most famous native son, Emperor Septimius Severus, born here in 146, the city experienced its greatest construction phase. The port was enlarged and linked with the hot springs district by a columned boulevard. A new imperial forum was built, the largest in the southern Mediterranean. Near the harbor is the ancient center with the "Old Forum", the Temple of the Liber Pater and the Roma and Augustus Temple. West of there is a market, an Augustine theater, the Chalcidicum trading yard, and Hadrian's Baths. Only the necropolises from the original Phoenician city have been discovered.

The ruins of the market buildings testify to the former grandeur of Leptis Magna.

ARCHAEOLOGICAL SITE OF SABRATHA

Originally a Phoenician trading settlement, this town was both the start and end of the trans-Saharan trade route. It later became one of the "three cities" of Sabratha, Leptis Magna and Oea in ancient Tripoli.

After the sack of Carthage and a brief spell under the reign of the Numidian King Massinissa, Tripolitania came under Roman rule and developed into a prosperous city. In the third century, Sabratha became an Episcopal see but in the middle of the fifth century it fell to the Vandals; in the sixth century, the Byzantines conquered the city only to lose it in the seventh century to the Arabs who were then followed by the Ottomans in the 16th century. Many well-preserved Roman remains exist in Sabratha just 70 km (43 mi) west of modern-day Tripoli (ancient Oea), including the theater built in about 200, the columned forum, the Temple of Antonius, the Jupiter Temple and the basilica dating from the first century, the public baths, fountains, latrines and other buildings. During the early Christian era a church was built into the Roman courthouse basilica. On the coast is the Justinian Basilica whose mosaic floor can now be seen in the museum of Sabratha.

The most impressive monument in Sabratha is probably the theater with its colossal backdrop, the frons scenae.

ARCHAEOLOGICAL SITE OF CYRENE

By the fourth century the ancient Greek colony of Cyrenaica had grown into one of the largest cities in Africa.

Originally, Cyrene was inhabited by settlers from the Greek Aegean island of Thera, now Santorini. After Alexander the Great died, the colony referred to as Cyrenaica fell to the Ptolemaic dynasty and in 74 BC to the Romans. The town flourished during the reign of Augustus while Trajan had to subdue rebellions in 117. After a renewed boom under Hadrian, Cyrene began to decline, and in the fourth century the once flourishing city was abandoned. Remnants from the Greek period include a Temple of Zeus dating from the fifth century BC, the Temple of Apollo from the fourth century, and the Temple of Artemis from the sixth century BC. The Greek theater was converted to an amphitheater under Hadrian and next to the agora is the Sanctuary of Demeter. The Odeon was converted by Hadrian and the Gymnasium became a forum as early as the first century. Near the south gate is the Roman theater and a basilica that features precious mosaics dating back to the early Christian period. Outside the city limits is a vast necropolis as well.

A round temple with statues of Demeter and Kore is situated on the agora.

OLD TOWN OF GHADAMÈS

The small oasis town of Ghadamès in the border triangle of Libya, Tunisia and Algeria is characterized by its typical Saharan architecture. In its heyday Ghadamès was a major staging post for caravans.

The ancient city of Cydamus was founded as a garrison town by the Romans. It became an Episcopal see under the Byzantines and was finally Islamized by Arab invaders under the leadership of Uqba ibn Nafi during their expedition through Tunisia in the eighth century. The ancient caravan hub maintained trading connections with Timbuktu and the coast of Morocco while caravans brought slaves, gold, leather and ivory from the south in exchange for cotton, sugar and other European goods. When the slave trade ended, the Berber town began to decline. Now most of its inhabitants live in the new town but maintain their homes in the ancient mud city, where many live during the hot summer months. Traditionally it is the preserve of women before their wedding to decorate the whitewashed rooms inside the house with red adornments. Light comes through a central opening in the roof and the mudbrick houses are closely huddled together, separated by alleyways that are partially roofed with mats where the semi-darkness keeps things relatively cool.

The walls of the rooms are artfully decorated inside the house (left). A lane protected by walls (below).

ROCK-ART SITES OF TADRART ACACUS

The oldest rock images in Tadrart Acacus, which were not discovered until the 1960s, are about 14,000 years old. Their subject matter allows us to draw conclusions about the fauna and climate of that time in the Fezzan region.

Tadrart Acacus in south-western Libya on the border with Algeria has the oldest rock and cave paintings in the region where hunters and gatherers 14,000 years ago immortalized antelopes, elephants, rhinoceroses and other animals. They indicate that a more humid climate once prevailed in this now arid region. The youngest images of this "herdsman's art" are estimated at about 6,000 years old and depict spotted domestic cattle and sheep and their shepherds. Illustrations of a religious nature from a more recent time seem influenced by Pharaonic Egypt. The images of horses date from a later period (1500 BC), when a semi-arid climate already prevailed in the region. The newest depictions are images from the "Camel Phase", around 100 BC, when the environs of the Tassili N'Ajjer mountain range became a desert and the dromedary appeared on the scene. The animal quickly became one of the main subjects.

The rock illustrations and engravings indicate times when the living conditions here were more hospitable.

Egypt

WADI AL-HITAN

Fossilized precursors of modern whales, the Archaeoceti, have been found in Egypt's Wadi Al-Hitan ("Valley of the Whales").

Wadi Al-Hitan is 250 km (155 mi) west of Cairo in an extraordinary landscape of sand dunes and cushion-shaped rock formations molded by desert winds. The main attractions in this dry valley, however, are 380 preserved whale fossils from sixty million years ago, when the earliest ancestors of whales lived on land but close to the shore. The Mesonychids are most closely related to modern ungulates, but were carnivorous and resembled the common otter. The animals whose remains were found in the valley developed from them.

Zeuglodon isis lived 45–38 million years ago, was more than 20 m (66 ft) long, hunted in the water and likely only came on land to reproduce. At that stage its back legs had atrophied and instead of forelimbs it had five-digit fins. The fossils of the whales are preserved in sandstone, slate, marl and limestone, rock strata from the bottom of the prehistoric Tethys Ocean that once stretched south beyond the current Mediterranean coast. The oldest strata in the valley are about forty million years old and contain a number of whale and manatee skeletons as well as shark's teeth, turtles and crocodiles. Fossilized whales were also found in some younger strata.

Numerous whale fossils lie embedded in the desert sand

ABU MENA – RUINS OF AN EARLY CHRISTIAN HOLY CITY

The churches in this key early Christian pilgrimage destination were built in the Coptic style. The faithful from many different countries came here to the tomb of Saint Menas of Alexandria.

The reason why the tomb of Saint Menas is located roughly 40 km (25 mi) west of Alexandria of all places, is explained by a popular legend: The camel that was meant to bring home the body of the legionnary, who had incidentally been born in Egypt and suffered a martyr's death in Asia Minor in 296, suddenly refused to keep continue walking. Soon after that, reports of miraculous healings and of blessings emanating from a spring beside the martyr's grave began spreading along the caravan route.

However, when the spring dried up by the 12th century, the pilgrimage site fell into disrepair. The basilicas uncovered during excavations in Abu Mena feature the style elements typical of Coptic architecture including triple-aisled floor plans, mighty walls built of mud bricks, extra-high central naves, columns, ceiling vaulting and three-part apses.

The pilgrimage site of Abu Mena comprises churches and the Grand Basilica (above) as well as pilgrim accommodation and cisterns (right).

HISTORIC CAIRO

This metropolis developed out of several smaller constituent towns to the north-east of the original capital of Fustat. Encircled by walls, Cairo boasts more than 600 noteworthy buildings from all the different Islamic architectural styles.

In 969, the Fatimid military leader Gawhar al-Siqilli laid the foundation stone for a new caliphate that would be called Al-Kahira ("the Victorious"). All of the major religious and secular buildings in Cairo were built after that date. Construction began in 970 on the Al-Azhar Mosque, the third mosque in Egypt, and it is still being built, expanded and renovated today. Since 989 it has housed the University for Islamic Shia Law and the Arab Language. The director of this world center of Sunni tradition simultaneously represents the highest spiritual authority in Egypt. The Khan el-Khalili bazaar has been next to the mosque

There is a multitude of historic buildings in Old Cairo and minarets rise high above the cityscape to point the way.

since 1382. Construction on the city's most recognizable icon, the Citadel, began in 1176 during the reign of Sultan Saladin; it was completed in 1207. The fortress was the mightiest in the Islamic world until 1825, when a large part of it was destroyed by a gunpowder explosion. In its place, the Mosque of Mohammed Ali, the governor, was built in 1830 – the so-called Alabaster Mosque. One of the oldest houses of worship is the Ibn Tulun Mosque, built in 876 based on the Great Mosque of Samarra in Mesopotamia. It is captivating in its size and simplicity. Another jewel is the Sultan Hassan Mosque from the 14th century with its two minarets. Old Cairo is also home to the first mosque in the country, commissioned by the Arab conqueror Amr ibn al-As in 641.

The Ibn Tulun Mosque with its domed fountain in the courtyard dates from the ninth century (top left). The large prayer hall of the Al-Azhar Mosque (left).

Egypt

MEMPHIS AND ITS NECROPOLIS – THE PYRAMID FIELDS FROM GIZA TO DAHSHUR

The relics of Memphis along with the necropolises and pyramids of Saqqara, Giza, Abusir and Dahshur are among the colossal examples of ancient Egyptian high culture.

Memphis is the former capital and royal residence of the Old Kingdom of Egypt. Aside from some temple ruins, the only remains here include the colossal limestone figure of Ramesses II, the massive alabaster sphinx from the 15th century BC, and

The pyramids of Khufu, Khafre and Menkaure are architectural masterpieces.

the roughly 50-ton sacrificial tables on which the Apis bulls were embalmed. The oldest preserved monumental stone structure built by humankind is in the giant necropolis of Saqqara to the west: the tomb of the Pharaoh Djoser, shaped as a stepped pyramid. Extending for about 7 km (4 mi), the necropolis contains the burial places of twenty kings from almost all periods of ancient Egypt. Excavations in nearby Abusir uncovered four pyramids and a tomb from the Fifth Dynasty. Farther south near Dahshur, two pyramids of the Pharaoh Snefru and three pyramids from the Twelfth Dynasty still stand tall. The most impressive burial site is near Giza with nine pyramids, more temples and the tombs of important officials.

The most important monument, however, is the Great Pyramid of Khufu (Cheops), built in about 2560 BC. It is flanked by the Pyramid of Menkaure and the Pyramid of Khafre, who also ordered the Great Sphinx to be built not far from the mortuary temple. The 85-m-long (279-ft) and 20-m-high (66-ft) stone creature sporting a lion's body and a human head was carved from a single block of limestone.

The Great Sphinx and the Pyramids of Giza are among the most impressive monuments ever created by humans.

The enormous statues of Memphis are fascinating, especially the limestone figure of Ramesses II.

The 60-m-high (197-ft) stepped pyramid of Pharaoh Djoser (c. 2609–2590 BC) towers above the necropolis of Saqqara.

A major find in the necropolis of Abusir was the shaft tomb of Iufaa, which contains a sarcophagus made of basalt.

The Serapeum, where Apis bulls were venerated and buried, holds a magnificent sarcophagus with inscriptions.

Egypt

Ramesses II

Born the son of Seti I in around 1298 BC, Ramesses grew up in an environment in which he was introduced to and forced to face the duties of a ruler from an early age. Seti I took Ramesses along on his expeditions when he was still quite young, and soon made him a co-regent. When Seti died in about 1279 BC, Ramesses became the new pharaoh. The first years of his reign brought the legendary Battle of Kadesh (c. 1274 BC), which he later had depicted in colossal reliefs, presenting himself as a great general – though the battle brought no clear victory to either the Egyptians or the Hittites. In fact, a definitive peace treaty was not signed until about fif-

ANCIENT THEBES WITH ITS NECROPOLIS

Magnificent temple complexes and tombs bear witness to the former splendor of Thebes, the city of the god Amun and the capital of Egypt during the Middle Kingdom.

The first temples, palaces and residential districts at Thebes were built on the east banks of the Nile from the end of the third millennium BC. Starting with the 11th Dynasty (2119 BC) Thebes grew in importance as a temporary capital as well as a royal burial site and place of worship for Amun-Re, the god of the Egyptian Empire. During the 18th and following dynasties (from 1532 BC), numerous monumental structures were erected here. The metropolis comprised the giant palace and temple complexes of Luxor and al-Karnak on the east banks of the Nile and the necropolises and mortuary temples on the west bank. Among the complexes, the Temple of Amun in Karnak assumed a key role as the largest and most important in ancient Egypt. The Great Hypostyle Hall was built during the reign of Seti I and Ramesses II. It features 134 columns arranged in sixteen rows richly decorated with hieroglyphics that visitors are unlikely to forget.

On the opposite bank of the Nile, west of Thebes, is the Deir el-Bahari Necropolis. Theses rock graves, especially in the Valley of the Kings and the Valley of the Queens, hold the burial sites of numerous kings, queens and highly placed officials. The site also includes the terraced temple of the female Pharaoh Hatshepsut, the funerary temples of Ramesses II and Ramesses III, the Colossi of Memnon, the guardian figures of the former mortuary temple of Amenhotep III and Deir el-Medina and the village of the necropolis workers.

The vast temple at Luxor began during the reign of Amenhotep III. Under Ramesses II it was enlarged. The courtyard lined by columns and statues was entered through a pylon towering next to an obelisk.

teen years later. However, Ramesses the Great did manage to establish political stability both within his realm as well as outside of Egypt and led the country to economic prosperity. His reputation is reflected in the countless monumental structures that he had built for his own glorification. After about sixty-six years in power

he died at the grand age of nearly eighty-five and was buried in the Valley of the Kings. This was not to be his final resting place, however. When the mummy was rediscovered in 1881 in the necropolis of Deir el-Bahari north of Thebes, it lay hidden in the so-called Royal Cache, together with other mummies. Why? After the

death of Ramesses XI, unrest broke out in the country and as a consequence the mummies were reburied elsewhere.

A colossal statue of Ramesses II was salvaged in Memphis. It is among the finest of its kind (left). A figure of the Pharaoh in the Temple of Luxor (far left).

The main sanctuary in the temple at Karnak is the temple complex dedicated to the Egyptian empire god Amun-Re.

Murals decorate the mortuary temple of Ramesses III in Medinet Habu; among them a depiction of the god Khnum.

The mortuary temple of Hatshepsut in the valley of Deir el-Bahari has several levels that are linked with each other.

The virtually undamaged royal tomb of Tutankhamen in the Valley of the Kings (view of the sarcophagus chamber).

Egypt

NUBIAN MONUMENTS FROM ABU SIMBEL TO PHILAE

Among the most famous structures in the region are the two rock temples in Abu Simbel built by Ramesses II and the Temple of Isis in the Sanctuary of Philae. Between 1960 and 1964, they were saved from the floods of the Aswan Dam.

Without the aid of UNESCO a number of irreplaceable monuments would have been submerged beneath Lake Nasser, at that time the largest man-made reservoir in the world. Instead, the structures were measured, cut into pieces and reassembled 65 m (213 ft) above their original position. Two rock temples built by Pharaoh Ramesses II are breathtaking even in their new location. The Grand Temple was dedicated to the gods Amun-Re, Re-Harakhte, Ptah and the deification of the pharaoh himself. The entrance is guarded by four 20-m-tall (66-ft) fig-

ures while the interior has rooms that stretch up to 63 m (207 ft) into the rock and are adorned with hieroglyphs and reliefs. The Small Temple was dedicated to Ramesses' wife Nefertiti and the goddess Hathor. Six colossal statues adorn the façade here. The temples of Amada, Derr, Wadi es Sebua and Dakka were also salvaged between Abu Simbel and Philae.

Giant statues of Ramesses II line the hall of the Grand Temple of Abu Simbel (right). Ptolemy's Temple of Isis is on the Nile island of Agilkia (below)

SAINT CATHERINE AREA

Saint Catherine's Monastery, situated in the desert landscape below Mount Sinai, or Jebel Musa (Mountain of Moses), is one of the oldest testimonies of Christian monasticism in the Middle East. It contains valuable art treasures and written documents.

The Greek Orthodox monastery dedicated to Saint Catherine was founded in about 550, making it the oldest Christian monastery in the world that has been preserved continuously in its original function. Its isolated location in the heart of the southern Sinai Peninsula made it ideally suited for the ascetic tradition, not just standard Christian monasticism. Indeed, hermit monks had been living on Mount Sinai (Mount Horeb in the Old Testament), where Moses was allegedly given the Ten Commandments, since the fourth century. In the sixth century, Byzantine Emperor Justinian had

fortifications built around the intricate, labyrinthine monastic district, which for more than 1,000 years has also housed a mosque. The basilica is also from the sixth century and a superb example of Byzantine architecture. Aside from a large number of valuable icons it also houses the Mosaic of the Transfiguration, its greatest treasure and one of the finest works of early Christian art.

Standing on rugged terrain, the monastery with the "Chapel of the Burning Bush" has survived the centuries without any significant damage.

GEBEL BARKAL AND THE SITES OF THE NAPATAN REGION

Gebel Barkal is the holy mountain of the Kushites – the name given by the ancient Egyptians to the Nubians, who lived in the central Nile Valley below Aswan. Five archaeological sites contain the remnants of homes, palaces, pyramids and tombs.

In the 14th century BC, Tutankhamen wore sandals with soles depicting black-skinned Nubians. His message was to symbolically trample this folk from the "miserable Kush" with every single step to took. The hostility lasted thousands of years. The story was that one of Tutankhamen's predecessors, Thutmose III, had advanced to Gebel Barkal as early as about 1450 BC and built the Napata stela (an inscribed column). At the foot of the distinctive mountain he built the large Temple of Amun. This Egyptian supremacy lasted for centuries until the tide turned in the eighth century BC: the Kushites conquered Egypt and entered the history books of the Pharaonic Empire as its 25th dynasty. But their reign lasted barely 100 years. In 660 BC they were driven from the throne by the Assyrians and retreated to their land of origin. In the sixth century BC the capital was moved from Napata to Meroe, downstream on the Nile, but Napata remained the spiritual center of the Kingdom of Kush, even after the Romans had plundered and devastated the town in about 23 BC.

The turbulent history of assimilation and exchange here is reflected in the archaeological finds of Napata that have been preserved at Gebel Barkal, in El-Kurru, Nuri, Sanam and Zuma. Their architecture and religion as well as the script and the administrative structures were clearly influenced by Egyptian culture; the Egyptian god Amun was venerated as chief god in Napata. Inscriptions on the walls of the vast temple complex at Gebel Barkal contain reports of the accession to the throne, sacrifices to the gods and accounts of military campaigns. Egyptian influence is also apparent in the pyramid tombs that the kings of Kush and influential private people had built for themselves in Napata.

Though much smaller, Nubian pyramids – built over subterranean burial chambers – reveal the Egyptian inspiration (top and center). Left: Bright frescoes decorate the burial chamber of King Tanutamun, who ruled in the seventh century BC.

Mauritania

BANC D'ARGUIN NATIONAL PARK

This bird sanctuary covers a total area of around 12,000 sq km (4,700 sq mi), half of which is directly on Mauritania's Atlantic coast. It is one of the largest ornithological breeding grounds in west Africa and many migratory birds from Europe and Asia spend the winter here.

Located halfway between Nouakchott and Nouadhibou in the transition zone between the Atlantic Ocean and the Sahara Desert, this national park features long stretches of coastline frequented mainly by seabirds. They populate mangrove swamps, coastal sand dunes, open water and the small, sandy islands grouped off the coast around the main island of Tidra. About 100 species regularly breed and winter here. The number of pairs that mate here fluctuates between 25,000 and 40,000.

Among the other residents of the shores and coastal waters, which also teem with fish, are flamingos, pelicans, herons, spoonbills and cormorants as well as assorted species of sea turtle and dolphin.

Situated where the Sahara and the Atlantic converge, Banc d'Arguin National Park represents a unique transition zone between sand dunes, sandbanks, silt and mudflats, reefs, peninsulas and islands – an ideal habitat for seals and pelicans.

ANCIENT KSOUR OF OUADANE, CHINGUETTI, TICHITT AND OUALATA

Testimony to a grandiose past, these four fortified cities – known as ksour in North Africa – are located along the ancient caravan routes of the Sahara. For the most part they are preserved only as ruins.

Oualata, in the south-eastern Mauritanian Sahel, was an important trading town in 11th and 12th centuries and with its famous Qur'anic school and library it was also a bulwark of Islamic scholarship. The single- and two-story residential stone houses built closely together are rendered with red-brown clay and, following ancient traditions, the façades, doorframes and window recesses are painted with red-brown ornaments on a white background. The cities of

Tichitt and Ouadane were built in the mid-12th century and possess an equally charming architectural style. Chinguetti, founded in the 13th century, is the most famous desert settlement of the country's interior. It was once an assembly point for pilgrims on their way to Mecca and is one of the seven holy cities of Islam.

The ruins and towers of Ouadane (above) and the houses and the walled courtyards of Chinguetti (right) have a unique charm.

TIMBUKTU

During its heyday in the 15th century, this legendary town on the River Niger was the most important transshipment hub for the trans-Saharan trade and a center of Islamic scholarship.

Timbuktu is located in what is northern present-day Mali on the southern edge of the Sahara. It became one of the key trading and cultural metropolises in West Africa during the heyday of the Mali Empire. which began in roughly 1330. After 1468 it belonged to the empire of the Songhai. By 1591 the Moroccans had conquered it and before the arrival of the French in 1894 it had been ruled by the Tuareg.

The World Heritage Site here includes three mosques as well as sixteen mausoleums and cemeteries. Djinguereber Mosque is the oldest and was built almost entirely from clay. It is one of the most impressive testimonies to the history of the city. Sidi Yahya Mosque was built in about 1440 and is the smallest religious building here. The focal point in the northern districts is the medieval university and Sankoré Mosque with its pyramid-shaped minaret constructed from clay and wood. It quickly became a model for Islamic buildings in Sub-Saharan Africa. Otherwise, the townscape is defined by block-shaped mud brick structures in which the lower floors contain shops and common rooms while the roof terraces serve as sleeping quarters.

A masterpiece of mud-brick building: Sankoré Mosque from the 15th century.

TOMB OF ASKIA

This pyramid-shaped royal tomb in Gao was built from unburned mud bricks and is a relic from the era of the Songhai Empire that dominated the trans-Saharan trade in the 15th and 16th centuries.

The city of Gao in north-eastern Mali was for a long time the residence of the Songhai kings, whose mighty empire lasted – with few interruptions – from the seventh to the 16th centuries. The dominion attained its greatest power during its final decades and its borders roughly coincide with those of present-day Mali. The Songhai rulers became very wealthy through their trade with Morocco, Arabia, India and China, the most important goods on the market being salt and gold. Modern Gao is now largely a new town and the only location to have survived from the era of the Songhai Kingdom is the tomb of Askia Mohammed, who founded the last Songhai dynasty. Originally he was a general under the powerful King Sunni Ali, who ruled from 1464 to 1492, but when his son, Sunni Baru, ascended the throne he was usurped from power by Askia Mohammed in 1493. The latter expanded the empire and secured the borders. Upon his returned from a pilgrimage to Mecca he introduced Islam as the state religion and this tomb was built for him.

The pyramid-shaped clay structure in Gao is the burial place of the last Songhai king, Askia Mohammed. It is 500 years old and measures 17 by 15 m (56 by 49 ft).

OLD TOWNS OF DJENNÉ

The imposing mud structures of Djenné illustrate the glory of the Mali and Songhai empires. As the main hub of trade on the inland delta region of the Niger River, this city once handled all of the cotton fabric, gold and slave trade heading to North Africa.

Djenné is located on a floodplain between the Niger River and one of its major tributaries, the Bani. For many centuries the town maintained close trade links with Timbuktu, which could be reached by water. In fact, the city's economic and intellectual rise continued even after its incorporation into the Songhai Empire in the 15th century. To protect its immensely valuable trading interests, a 2.5-km-long (1.5-mi) clay wall was built with multi-story battlements and magnificent portals along with palaces and the famous Great Mosque. The latter was demolished in the 19th century but rebuilt between 1907 and 1909 in the traditional Sudanese Sahel mud brick style. The older city districts contain the houses of the traders and artisans from the 16th to 19th centuries. The Djenné style, which was employed in many of the multistory buildings features not only flat roofs and magnificent façades but also style elements imported from North Africa.

The Great Mosque of Djenné with its tapering minarets and the battlement-equipped walls is one of the most beautiful mud brick structures in the world.

Mali

Masks and dances of the Dogon

The Dogon are a farming people known in particular for the impressive locations they have chosen for their villages: the Bandiagara Escarpment. Their box-shaped houses made of clay and their domed granaries seem to be glued to the steep rock faces. Another spectacular sight are their rituals and dances, at the heart of which

CLIFF OF BANDIAGARA (LAND OF THE DOGON)

This escarpment is a striking 150 km (93 mi) long and lies east of the city of Mopti. It is the home territory of the Dogon, a culture famed for its mud huts and masks.

This World Heritage Site includes not only the scarp and dip slopes of the Bandiagara escarpment and the plain that spreads out below, but also the 250 Dogon villages and the Songo community that occupies the surrounding region. In the world view of the Dogon, all elements of the universe are closely interlinked in an intimate chain of symbolic relationships. This view of life has a direct influence on the architecture of their dwellings, temples and communal buildings which are designed based on religious and mythological considerations.

The façade of a house, a village, a garden, a field or a shroud can all display similar patterns. The village is laid out in an anthropomorphic shape passed down to them by their mythical ancestors, and the architecture of the mud huts reflects the duality of man and woman. The most spectacular Dogon villages are situated on steep cliffs with square-shaped mud huts and clay granaries with conical roofs piled up in several layers. Men and women each have separate granaries in which millet, their staple crop, is stored along with other items such as jewelry. Among these are the temple-like round towers of the Binu shrines and the Toguna with its roof of millet stalks, the meeting place for older adult males.

Dogon mask-making, which plays a central role in their culture, is also closely connected to mythology. There are around 100 different kinds of masks that are donned for special festivals and rituals.

The mud huts of the Dogon cling to the cliffs of the Bandiagara escarpment like bird's nests. Many can only be reached by ladder. Even graveyards are built here.

is a distinctive and mysterious system of masks. We owe much of what we know about it to the work of ethnologist Marcel Griaule, who stayed with the Dogon on several occasions in the 1930s to research the material and spiritual aspects of their culture. The religious explanation of the mask rituals is a creation myth that yielded a complex cult of ancestors and the dead. The most important ceremony in this context is the Sigui ceremony, which takes place only about every sixty years. It serves to renew relations with the ancestors and also as an initiation rite for new members of the masked society. The Great Mask or "Imina na" is carved specially for the event and consists of a box-like mask and a plank several meters high painted with zigzag and rhomboid patterns and symbolizing a mythical serpent. Dozens of different types of mask can be distinguished and they are moved during the ceremonies in specific dance moves according to rhythms of the music and drums.

The masks of the Dogon are a product of sophisticated carving traditions (left). Apart from during the Sigui ceremony, the masks are worn mainly during rituals to honor the dead, whose souls are therewith delivered to their final destinations. The exact meaning of the masks is only known to members of the secret mask societies.

The Dogon did not move into the Hombori Mountains until a few hundred years ago, but they still call it home.

These rock paintings come from a cave near Songo, where the Dogon conduct circumcision ceremonies three times a year. The images depict ancestral figures, animals and historic events.

For the image of this mask, red, white and black pigments were applied by hand onto the rock.

AÏR AND TÉNÉRÉ NATURAL RESERVES

The Aïr massif and Ténéré desert provide a fantastic backdrop for the flora and fauna of the Sahara and Sahel and are home to unique prehistoric rock art.

Africa's largest nature reserve covers some 80,000 sq km (31,000 sq mi) and includes the Aïr massif in north-western Niger, which runs for 400 km (250 mi). It is a crystalline peneplain of volcanic origin that rises 700 m (2,300 ft) at its center with a series of steep peaks separated by sandy valleys (koris) that culminate in Mt Gréboun at 2,310 m (7,580 ft). The Ténéré desert to the east gradually changes from gravel plains and sand into a sea of dunes at its center. Rain may not fall here for years at a time and there are vast fluctuations in temperature. On the moister south-west-

ern slopes of the Aïr are grass prairies. Palms and acacia shrubs thrive on groundwater beneath the koris while olive trees and cypresses take hold in the mountains. Aïr mouflon, wild ases and desert foxes also live here. Prehistoric humans created rock art in the northern part of the range as well. The oldest paintings and engravings, from the neolithic period, indicate domestication of animals between 7000 and 3000 BC as well as a damper savannah climate.

Rock and desert converge in the transition zone between Aïr and Ténéré.

"W" NATIONAL PARK

This transnational nature reserve is the largest in West Africa and takes its name from a meandering section of the Niger river at its northern edge that forms a W shape.

The entrance to this colossal national park and nature reserve, which covers over 10,000 sq km (3,900 sq mi), is about 150 km (93 mi) south of Niamey in the borderlands between Niger, Burkina Faso and Benin. One section of approximately 2,200 sq km (845 sq mi) in Niger is recognized as a World Heritage Site.

The park is on the right bank of the river Niger in a transition zone that consists of both Sudanese savannah and wooded areas with gallery forests in the Sudan-Guinea zone. On the eastern border of the park, near the Niger, the Mékrou river has cut a deep ravine into the sandstone and in the

rainy season the river is transformed into raging rapids. In the dry season, water lilies grow in the rock pools that remain.

Green monkeys and baboons live in the lush vegetation on the banks of the Mékrou and other tributaries of the Niger while hippos, Cape buffaloes and large herds of elephants inhabit the dry savannah and gallery forest beside the rivers and streams. Roughly seventy mammal and 450 bird species call the park home.

Primates like the olive baboon and the green monkey (right) live in "W" National Park.

CIDADE VELHA, HISTORIC CENTER OF RIBEIRA GRANDE

The present-day fishing village of Cidade Velha on the Cape Verde Islands tells of the rise and fall of the first Portuguese colonial station in the tropics.

Cidade Velha was founded in the year 1462 on the Cape Verdean island of Santiago, initially known as Ribeira Grande. The island's isolated island location and simultaneous proximity to the west coast of Africa made it an ideal staging post for the trans-Atlantic slave trade, which had its heyday here in the 17th century and brought immense riches to the town as slaves were shipped from here to the New World. The mélange of people from Africa, Europe and Asia also made Ribeira Grande a cultural melting pot and as such the cradle of a new and autonomous Creole culture.

Some buildings still testify to the city's former prosperity. The Church of Nossa Senhora do Rosário, for instance, has an alabaster façade and was the first colonial church in the world. Pirate attacks at the end of the 16th century led to the construction of the Real de São Felipe Fortress, but it was not able to protect Ribeira Grande from its fate in 1712. Its inhabitants fled to the new capital Praia, and Ribeira Grande became Cidade Velha, the Old Town.

View from the ancient Portuguese fortress toward Cidade Velha, the first European colonial city in the tropics.

DJOUDJ BIRD SANCTUARY

In the former delta area of the Senegal River, between the Gorom tributary and the main river, is a bird colony that is unparalleled elsewhere in West Africa.

Situated about 60 km (38 mi) north-east of St Louis on the Mauritanian border, this bird sanctuary is one of the largest in the world covering an area of 160 sq km (60 sq mi). It is home not only to many resident birds but also to countless migratory species from Europe and Asia, depending on the time of year. After an exhausting flight over the Sahara, up to three million of these birds then nest up for the winter near these richly stocked waters.

When the backwaters of the delta evaporate away in the dry season, the birds make their way to the few remaining water sources – the Gorom, which never dries out, and the bays of Lake Djoudj. Around 1.5 million waterfowl and waders then populate the expanses of this unique paradise for birds, including flamingoes, cormorants, cranes, spoonbills, herons, storks, black-tailed godwits, white-faced whistling ducks, spotted redshanks, Arabian bustards, aquatic warblers and other rare species. The conservation area isn't just home to feathered inhabitants, however. Turtles, crocodiles, warthogs, jackals, and gazelles can also be found here.

West Africa's largest pelican colony has a population of over 10,000 and is a particular attraction for visitors and ornothology enthusiasts.

ISLAND OF SAINT-LOUIS

Saint-Louis, founded in 1659, was one of the first French trading posts in West Africa and for a while the capital of Senegal.

The center of Saint-Louis is located on an island in the estuary of the Senegal River. Multiple bridges connect it with the mainland and an elongated spit of land. The first French settlement in Africa, Saint-Louis initially consisted of trading posts that were constructed on a grid-like layout. The first colonial buildings with their characteristic wooden balconies date from the 18th century. With the growing importance of the trans-Atlantic slave trade, the transshipment village of Saint-Louis grew to about 10,000 inhabitants at its peak.

The town was given its present appearance after the abolition of slavery in 1848, when a multiethnic society of French, Moorish and African peoples such as the Wolof and the Tukulor began defining the cultural makeup of the place. The city flourished after 1854, during the rule of the liberal Governor General Louis Faidherbe, but the heyday came to an end in 1897 with the construction of a steel bridge. The most important buildings are clustered around the Place Faidherbe, including the cathedral and the Governor's Palace, both dating from the 19th century.

Bridges connect the Island of Saint-Louis with the Senegalese mainland and with the Langue de Barbarie Peninsula, which protects it from the open seas.

NIOKOLO-KOBA NATIONAL PARK

One of the largest nature reserves in West Africa, this region offers a last refuge for savannah animals such as lions and antelopes, whose habitats once stretched as far as the coast.

A large portion of this national park's 10,000 sq km (3,900 sq mi) area of south-eastern Senegal is in the transition zone between dry savannah and Guinea's wetland forest. It is bordered to the south by the upper reaches of the Gambia River and territory belonging to Guinea, and to the north it runs out into dry savannah in eastern Senegal. The three great rivers of the Gambia basin – the Gambia itself, the Koulountou in the west and the Niololo-Koba in the east – meander for miles through this wetland area. During the rainy season, wide expanses of the park turn into marsh and mud, and along the rivers and streams, wooded savannah turns into luxuriant vegetation of gallery forest with about 200 species of trees and shrubs. This biosphere is also home to numerous animals: around eighty mammal species live here including hippopotamuses, a tiny population of elephants, giraffes, Cape buffaloes, gazelles, giant elands, leopards, cheetahs, jackals and hyenas.

African wild dogs live in packs of seven to eight adults and a few young.

Senegal

ISLAND OF GORÉE

This island off the Senegalese coast near Dakar has been occupied by several European colonial powers in its time. It is both a symbol of and a memorial to the suffering of the trans-Atlantic slave trade.

From the 15th to the 19th centuries, the Island of Gorée, which is only about 35 ha (86 acres) in size, was occupied by all of the major European colonial powers including Portugal, Holland, Great Britain and France. Trading companies from these lands fortified the island and shipped tens of thousands of African slaves from here to ports all over the Americas. As if slavery were not insult enough, for each African that reached his destination alive, there were probably four or five who died on the way.

The population of this small volcanic island had a strong ethnic mix from the beginning and it is from these "métis" (mixed blood) families that the population of local slave traders

This historic painting gives insight into the everyday life of the troops occupying the fort, in this case the Dutch troops.

grew in the 18th century. Traders and their wives, so-called "signares", commissioned mansions for themselves where they lived on the upper floors while their human freight awaited shipment in the cellars. Today the island is a memorial site and three museums and a preserved slave house document the history of this grim trade. The Governor's Palace and a fortress built by the French give an impression of life during colonial times.

Before they were sent on away, slaves were imprisoned in the cellars of the Maison des Esclaves (slave house) with its distinctive double staircase. The traders lived on the top floor.

The colorful houses and colonial buildings of Gorée reveal the European background of this former slave island.

In about 1850, Fort d'Estrées was built at the northern tip of Gorée. Today it houses the historical museum of the island.

Decaying neoclassical villas once housed slave traders on the upper floors and cattle and slaves on the ground floor. Today they are the homes of the island's poorer inhabitants.

The signares, the female offspring of European men and African women, enjoyed special status and also owned slaves themselves.

STONE CIRCLES OF SENEGAMBIA

More than 1,000 stone circles and other megalith monuments dot a wide swathe along the Gambia River in Senegal and Gambia. They were set up between the 16th and the third centuries BC.

The megalith stone circles of Senegal and Gambia are in a territory that was once known as Senegambia. The ones that comprise this World Heritage Site include four large groups: Sine Ngayène, Wanar, Wassu and Kerbatch. Altogether, they number ninety-three stone circles and a number of tumuli, or burial mounds. Some have now been excavated, but the seemingly close connection between the tumuli and the megaliths has yet to be deciphered – all of the stone circles are located near such burial mounds. The building material used was laterite, a reddish-brown stone containing large amounts of aluminum. It was worked with stone tools and shaped into almost identical cylindrical or polygonal stone columns, mostly measuring 2 m (7 ft) in height. Eight to fourteen columns were typically arranged in a stone circle with a diameter of 4 to 8 m (13 to 26 ft). The finds indicate that this expansive ritual landscape was laid out over the course of more than 1,500 years and that its builders belonged to an extremely productive and creative culture.

These stone columns stand tall in Wassu, on the middle section of the Gambia River in the country of the same name.

JAMES ISLAND AND RELATED SITES

James Island, along with another six sites in Gambia, are places of national remembrance related to the relationship between Europeans and Africans within the context of colonial rule and the trans-Atlantic slave trade.

"…in the village of Juffure, four days upriver from the coast of The Gambia, West Africa, a manchild was born to Omoro and Binta Kinte." Thus begins the novel "Roots" by Alex Haley. The young Kunta Kinte was then kidnapped by slave traders and ultimately shipped from James Island to America. James Island is located near Juffure, 30 km (19 mi) upstream from the vast estuary in Gambia. In 1651, the Dutch built a fortress here. Ten years later, it was taken over by the British. The fortress served as a staging post for the trade in gold and ivory, and then the less glamorous business of slave trading. Up to twenty prisoners were often locked up in a tiny dungeon here only to wait there for months before being sent away forever. A chapel and a warehouse in Albreda, the house of the brothers Maurel in Juffure (formerly the Portuguese settlement of San Domingo), and the canons on St Mary Island and Fort Bullen are also part of the site.

Ruins remind us today of the former military significance of Fort James as a control post on the Gambia River.

MOUNT NIMBA STRICT NATURE RESERVE

This reserve where Liberia, Guinea and Côte d'Ivoire come together is a trans-national World Heritage Site shared between the latter two countries.

Straddling the border of the Ivory Coast and Guinea, Mount Richard-Molard in the Nimba massif is the highest peak in both countries at 1,752 m (5,748 ft). It is also the focal point of this conservation area of 180 sq km (70 sq mi) featuring an almost uninterrupted forest canopy where deciduous trees predominate the lower slopes, a montane forest thrives above 1,000 m (3,300 ft), and at the summit a mountain savannah reigns supreme. Around forty plant and 200 animal species are indigenous to the reserve, among them elephants, buffaloes, antelopes, lions, hyenas, guenons and chimpanzees. Pygmy hippos and dwarf crocodiles also live in the wetlands while vultures, snakes and rare amphibians such as the Mount Nimba viviparous toad (Nectophrynoides occidentalis) make their way around. The site is threatened due to iron ore mining and poaching by refugees from the Côte d'Ivoire. It has thus been inscribed on the UNESCO Red List since 1992.

Reptile, primate and big-game species populate the Nimba mountains like this dwarf crocodile (right), the Diana monkey, and the African buffalo.

COMOÉ NATIONAL PARK

Comoé is the largest and most diverse game reserve in the Côte d'Ivoire. Situated in the north-east of the country it comprises of a variety of habitats in the transition zone between savannah and rainforest.

This national park owes its name to the Comoé, a massive river between 100 and 200 m (350 and 700 ft) wide that flows from north to south for approximately 230 km (148 mi) through the park's 11,500 sq km (4,500 sq mi). Due to its proximity to the river, this park features vegetation that typically only occurs much further south including bush savannah, dense rainforest regions and gallery forests that all provide the rich animal life here with plenty of habitat diversity. The Comoé itself is shrouded in dense gallery forest and continues to flow even in the dry season, making it a happy home to hippopotamuses, croc-odiles and numerous bird species that live on its lush banks. The savannah, meanwhile, is home to Cape buffaloes, warthogs and eleven species of ape and antelopes. The forests in the southern part of the park are the preserve of elephants and while predators such as lions, leopards and hyenas also patrol the area, their numbers are few. This World Heritage Site is unfortunately also threatened by poaching and overgrazing.

The riparian savannah landscape along the upper Comoé is ideal for a variety of fauna including the leopard.

TAÏ NATIONAL PARK

This nature reserve includes the greater part of Africa's remaining tropical rainforest, which once stretched across Ghana, the Côte d'Ivoire, Liberia and Sierra Leone.

The dense tropical vegetation of this reserve in south-western Côte d'Ivoire, which covers an area of 3,300 sq km (1,320 sq mi), is characterized by a number of indigenous species as well as a primeval forest whose canopy of foliage and liana trees up to 50 m (164 ft) in height barely allows light to penetrate. Two kinds of forest are distinguished here according to their undergrowth and the composition of the forest floor. In the north and south-east, poorly nourished Diospyros manii forest predominates while in the south-west the damper soil of Diospyros-spp. forest is most common.

Taï National Park's luxuriant primary forest boasts 1,300 plant species and it is not uncommon for giant felled trees to lie across wild streams. It also features mangroves with stilt and buttress roots as well as tree ferns. Elephants, pygmy hippopota-muses, leopards, antelopes and buf-faloes also live here along with many varieties of birds and ten species of apes including chimpanzees.

The tropical rainforest is also home to a number of reptiles such as the flap-neck chameleon and the green bush viper (left).

RUINS OF LOROPÉNI

The historic settlements of Loropéni are immensely important testimonies to centuries of trans-Saharan gold trade in the present-day territory of Lobi in southern Burkina Faso.

This cultural site in what is now Bur-kina Faso features the remains of a former fortress that protected the precious gold trade. In those days, gold was transported across the Sahara and into Europe and Asia via numerous intermediate traders. The ruins here are in the commune of Loropéni in the southern part of the country near the border with Ghana, Togo and the Côte d'Ivoire. The imposing stone walls reach 6 m (20 ft) in places and make up the best-preserved part of a group of altogether ten fortification com-plexes in the region. Recent research indicates the structures are at least 1,000 years old and the settlement was probably built by the Kulango or the Loron, who controlled the extrac-tion and processing of gold during the heyday of the trans-Saharan trade from the 14th to the 17th centuries. The buildings were likely abandoned at the beginning of the 19th century, but our knowledge of the historic com-plexes is still limited because a large part of the structures has not yet been excavated. The ruins of Loropéni con-stitute the first listing for Burkina Faso in the list of World Heritage Sites.

The mighty stone walls indicate the importance of the gold trade in the countries of the Sahara.

Ghana

ASANTE TRADITIONAL BUILDINGS

The Asante once had a highly complex political system at the center of which was the cult of the Golden Stool. Their capital was Kumasi, where a number of traditional buildings now form a World Heritage Site.

The Asante were a warrior people of the Akan Group that lived in the territory of present-day Ghana. After gradually defeating all of the neighboring tribes starting in 1700 they then rose to become a regional superpower with the gold and slave trades bringing them previously unthinkable riches. The Golden Stool, which is sacrosanct for every Asante and allegedly still in existence today, became a symbol of the empire's unity.

The Asante put up bitter resistance against British colonial forces and were only finally subjugated around 1900, after a total of seven wars. In the process, the capital Kumasi was largely destroyed. Many historic records were lost, unfortunately, and palaces, ritual sites and residential areas were annihilated. Only a few traditional houses built of earth, clay, bamboo, wood and iron remain today on the northern and north-eastern outskirts of the city of Kumasi – witnesses of the great Asante civilization. Since the buildings were mostly constructed using natural, non-durable materials they are laborious and expensive to maintain and conserve.

Only a few Asante fetish houses such as Darkwa-Gyakye near Kumasi, are still preserved today.

FORTS AND CASTLES OF GHANA

The fortresses built along the 500-km (311-mi) stretch of Ghanaian coast are witnesses of the region's colonial past, when several European nations fought for supremacy in West Africa.

The staging posts here were originally built to secure the brisk trade in gold, pepper and ivory. São Jorge da Mina (Elmina) was the first fortress in 1482, used by the Portuguese in an attempt to keep their European rivals away from their markets, but the lucrative slave trade with the Americas, which began in 1505, soon attracted merchants of other European nations to the "Gold Coast", as Ghana was called then. In the 17th century, the Dutch conquered the Portuguese fortresses, but in the years that followed, the British, French, Dutch, Germans, Swedes and Danes all competed to wrest control from each other. Along the coast of modern Ghana dozens of forts and trading posts were built from the 16th to the 18th centuries. The best-preserved of them, which served the slave trade almost exclusively after 1630, are São Jorge and Cape Coast Castle. Further fortresses can be found in the Western, Central, Volta and Greater Accra regions.

São Jago da Mina (above) and Cape Coast Castle (right) served as transshipment posts for the trans-Atlantic slave trade.

KOUTAMMAKOU, THE LAND OF THE BATAMMARIBA

This roughly 500-sq-km (193-sq-mi) cultural landscape of agricultural plains, forests and villages owes its distinction as a World Heritage Site to the Takienta tower-houses of its residents, the Batammariba.

Koutammakou – a stretch of land in north-eastern Togo that extends into neighboring Benin – is home to one of the main attractions of the country: the Tata, fortified mud-brick houses of the Batammariba (Tamberma), and the Takienta (mud tower-houses) that have become a symbol of the country. Families normally live in a circular compound ("Tata") consisting of round single-room buildings that are connected with each other by a wall. The compounds were up to two floors high and served different purposes, either as residential quarters or as granaries. At the top they were covered by either flat or conical thatched roofs which, combined with the use of clay as the building material, gave them a charming appearance. The tower-houses and their arrangement in the villages reflect the social structure of the Batammariba. The villages have ceremonial squares, places for the initiation rituals and assembly places.

Tata mud-brick houses and their Takienta mud tower-houses and grain silos look like small-scale fortresses.

ROYAL PALACES OF ABOMEY

The former capital of the Fon kingdom of Dahomey is home to the palace complexes of the 18th- and 19th-century feudal ruler. They are richly adorned with mythological subjects and sculptures.

The Kingdom of Dahomey, which emerged in the 17th century in what is the present-day city of Abomey in southern Benin, was able to expand its sphere of influence continuously even after the reign of King Agadja (r. 1708–1732) who took over the commercial settlements of the various colonial powers that had conducted the slave trade from here during the 16th century. In the 19th century, the borders of the empire were pushed further north and, in order to acquire slaves, they fought several wars against the Yoruba of modern Nigeria. Rituals serving the sacred cult of the king demanded human and animal sacrifices, and they were not banned until the reign of King Ghezo. The World Heritage Site in Abomey comprises Akaba Palace as well as the royal district containing the residences and tombs of twelve Dahomey kings. Each palace is surrounded by walls and possesses several courtyards. The main construction material is clay. Bas-reliefs and statues adorn the walls and illustrate the everyday life and lifestyle of the Fon.

Guézo Jalalahennou – the Palace of King Ghezo (top left) – is embellished with reliefs (above and left) depicting episodes from history and mythology.

Nigeria / Cameroon / Central African Republic

OSUN-OSOGBO SACRED GROVE

This sacred grove near the city of Oshogbo is located in one of the last few remaining virgin forests in southern Nigeria. For the Yoruba people this area is the seat of Osun, the goddess of fertility and of the "water of life".

The Osun River flows through this sacred grove and its embodiment, the goddess Osun, resides here. The faithful can reach the forty different shrines and nine squares dedicated to Osun and other Yoruba deities via walking trails and every year in August, the inhabitants of the village of Oshogbo make a pilgrimage to the holy sites. Since many communities in Nigeria no longer possess a sacred grove of their own for the purposes of worship, this event also attracts the inhabitants of other Yoruba cities. By about 1950, almost all of the sacred groves had been desecrated or deforested to make room for teak-wood plantations. The Sacred Grove of Osun-Osogbo, however, was saved thanks to the involvement of Susanne Wenger, an Austrian artist (1915–2009) who had been initiated into the religion of the Yoruba. Through the "New Sacred Art" movement she founded, a new form of religious art emerged at the cult site as well. The Grove thus became a place of encounter and exchange between Western and African art.

In an area of about 75 ha (185 acres) Yoruba deities are venerated with shrines, works of art and sculptures.

SUKUR CULTURAL LANDSCAPE

This landscape in north-eastern Nigeria is characterized by terraced fields and iron processing, but the ruins of the Palace of the Hidi, the former chief of the Sukur, are an architectural highlight.

The Sukur cultural landscape stretches out over a plateau near the Mandara Mountains on the border with Cameroon. The associated World Heritage Site is dedicated to the region and its landscape and reflects in many ways the cultural legacy of its inhabitants – the shape of the terraced fields, the conical fountains and the iron-smelting furnaces as well as the unmistakable architecture of its villages and the Palace of the Hidi.

Sukur first made a name for itself through its iron-smelting activities, which date back to the 17th century. At the top of the plateau, above the terraced fieds, is the Palace of the Hidi. German explorer Heinrich Barth had already mentioned the legendary wealth of the chief of the Sukur back in 1857. The ruins of his circular ritual building, the grain silos and the terraces cover an area of 120 by 100 m (394 by 328 ft), all of which is surrounded by a mighty stone wall with gates and niches.

The Sukur Plateau is a landscape rich in contrasts, with rocky hills, terraced fields, walls and homesteads.

DJA FAUNAL RESERVE

The Dja Faunal Reserve is almost entirely within the domain of the Dja River in south-eastern Cameroon and is distinguished by an exceptionally diverse animal population, including many primates.

The Dja Faunal Reserve's 5,000 sq km (1,900 sq mi) are situated nicely in a natural bend in the upper reaches of the Dja River. The region is not readily accessible to the public, which has been instrumental in making it one of the world's largest continuous areas of preserved rainforest, including the biodiversity that comes along with that distinction. The forest, which is composed of about fifty different tree species, provides a habitat for an immense variety of animals, including more than 100 mammals. Sitatungas (marsh buck), bongos (a forest antelope species) and the extremely rare African forest elephant all call the reserve home, for instance, but it is especially prized for its population of great apes (gorillas and chimpanzees), largely undisturbed rainforest and a panoply of primates, including pottos, moustached monkeys, lowland gorillas, and lesser white-nosed monkeys. However, the area, which is inhabited only by a few pygmies, is threatened by bush fires as well as poachers who still insist on keeping many of the animals in their sights.

The Dja River (above), which joins the Sangha and then flows into the Congo, gives its name to this Cameroonian conservation area.

MANOVO-GOUNDA ST. FLORIS NATIONAL PARK

The importance of this reserve in the Central African Republic is based on its wealth of plants and animals, in particular its waterfowl and megafauna.

A portion of this area in northern Central African Republic was declared a national park as early as 1933, and it can be divided into three zones of vegetation: the grassy plains of the north, which flood in the rainy season, the gentle hills of the savannah in the transition zone, and the jagged sandstone mountains to the south. On the northern plain, various species of waterfowl including marabou storks and white pelicans share about 2,000 sq km (770 sq mi) of the park with lions, leopards, cheetahs, wild dogs, buffalo, red-fronted gazelles, giraffe, hippos and numerous primate species, among other creatures. The forest elephant and the almost extinct black rhinoceros are in particular need of protection here. These rare species still fall victim to unscrupulous poachers and in the 1990s illegal hunters reduced the wildlife population by eighty percent (as well as murdering several park rangers). A further danger is the continued misuse of the reserve as pasture for domesticated animals.

The Gounda is one of five rivers in the park (above). Many waterfowl and hippos live on its banks.

ECOSYSTEM AND RELICT LANDSCAPE OF LOPÉ-OKANDA

Lopé-Okanda in Gabon is one of the most unusual interfaces of dense tropical rainforest and dry extinct savannah. West African peoples migrated through this territory to northern Congo over thousands of years and major archaeological sites from the Neolithic and Iron ages testify to their movements.

Just below the Equator in the northern reaches of the Central African rainforests is the middle section of the Ogooué River, where open savannah and riparian forests alternate over an area of roughly 1,000 sq km (386 sq mi). The open countryside is the result of human intervention that began in the Stone Age and has continued ever since, especially through bush fires, which permitted humans to advance into the interior of the country. The Bantu people and other tribal cultures from the area south of the Sahara all took this route. The river valley and the surrounding hills are an important archaeological guide

Neolithic rock art proves the presence of humans here as early as 4,000 years ago.

documenting the fact that the area has been settled for about 400,000 years. Drawings have been found on round rocks here depicting humans with iron tools such as throwing knives, but the most frequently found images are of single or multiple concentric circles and other geometric shapes. Less than one-tenth of the pictures represents smaller mammals or reptiles, but the close proximity of different forest and savannah ecosystems has nonetheless had a favorable effect on biodiversity here. So far some 1,550 species of flowering plant have been cataloged here.

The landscape of Lopé-Okanda boasts an exceptionally large number of mammal species, including the sun-tailed monkey.

Democratic Republic of the Congo

GARAMBA NATIONAL PARK

Garamba National Park on the Sudanese border in the north-eastern corner of the Democratic Republic of Congo is home to several large mammal species including the rare northern white rhinoceros.

From broad savannah and grassland to forest and marshy lowlands, Garamba National Park on the river of the same name provides an extraordinarily diverse range of animal habitats. This 5,000-sq-km (1,900-sq-mi) area was declared a national park back in 1938 and more than forty species of mammals live in the barely accessible conservation area, among them elephants and hippos. The park was in fact specifically established to protect giraffes and the northern subspecies of square-lipped rhinoceros, commonly known as the white rhino. Due to strict regulation in the park, the population of fifteen in 1984

was expanded to around forty by 2003, but the last specimens living in the wild are found only in this park. Sadly, the already tiny population has declined in recent years as a result of war and poaching, and it is feared that this species will die out in the wild. The park, which is covered in grass the height of a human, can also be explored by elephant. The docile giants are trained for this task in Garamba's unique elephant school.

The white rhinoceros owes its puzzling name to a mistake in translation – the English "white" was derived from the Boer "wijde", meaning broad.

OKAPI WILDLIFE RESERVE

This reserve in north-eastern Congo is famed for the okapi, after which it is named. This striking ungulate with zebra-striped legs is only found in the wild here in the rainforests of the Congo and has only been known to science for a little more than a century.

The Okapi Wildlife Reserve covers 14,000 sq km (5,400 sq mi) and was officially declared a conservation area in 1992. It covers about one-fifth of the Ituri rainforest in the Congo basin, one of the largest runoff basins in Africa. The reserve has charming scenery including the impressive waterfalls on the Ituri and Epulu rivers, but was initially established to protect the okapi, which was first recorded by Sir Henry Morton Stanley in 1890. He had never seen the animal and knew it only from descriptions by the local Batwa tribe, picturing it as vaguely similar to an ass. On evidence

of skeletal remains, British Governor Sir Harry Johnston (responsible for the species' scientific name, Okapia johnstoni) categorized the animal, which had initially been considered a member of the Equus (horse) family, among the giraffes. Living specimens were not spotted by Europeans until the early 20th century. About 30,000 of them are thought to still live in the wild, of which some 5,000 are in the Okapi Wildlife Reserve.

In contrast to its long-necked cousin, the okapi lives exclusively in the rainforest feeding on twigs, leaves and tree shoots.

SALONGA NATIONAL PARK

This national park flanking the Salonga, an eastern tributary of the Congo river in the middle of the Democratic Republic of the Congo, contains one of the largest continuous areas of rainforest in central Africa.

Salonga was declared a national park in 1970. Covering 36,000 sq km (13,900 sq mi) it is the second-largest national rainforest park in the world. Together with Maiko National Park the Salongo area, which consists of two equal sections separated by a corridor of human settlement 50 km (31 mi) wide, was placed under protection to preserve large ecologically vital portions of the Central African rainforest that had already either fallen victim to forest fires or been consumed by ever-expanding agriculturalization. The national park is only accessible by water and is thus a refuge for many species including

okapi, bongo antelopes, aquatic genets, Congo peafowl and the African slender-snouted crocodile. The forest elephant of the Central African rainforest can also be found here. Probably the best-known inhabitant of the Salonga, however, is the pygmy chimpanzee, known as the bonobo (Pan paniscus), a great ape and a close relative of the chimpanzee found only in the wild in conservation areas in southern Congo.

Bonobos (above) are probably the most famous animal inhabitants of the Salonga National Park in the central Congo basin.

KAHUZI-BIEGA NATIONAL PARK

One of the last few remaining groups of eastern lowland gorillas, which are close relatives of the mountain gorilla, live in the forests of this conservation area in eastern Congo.

Like Virunga, Kahuzi–Biega National Park about 100 km (62 mi) west of Lake Kivu was also established for the specific goal of protecting gorillas, in this case eastern lowland gorillas (Gorilla beringei graueri) rather than mountain gorillas (Gorilla beringei beringei). These impressive great apes live in small troops at an altitude of between 2,100 and 4,000 m (6,900 and 13,200 ft).
The vegetarian "gentle giants" can live for up to 40 years and older males have silver-gray markings on their backs. They intimidate rivals by rearing up with a roar and beating their chests. These gorillas, which are diur-

nal, forage for their diet of leaves until sundown and then sleep at night in improvised nests made of branches and leaves. This conservation area in the shadow of two extinct volcanoes, Kahuzi and Biega, shelters two further primate species as well, one of which is the common chimpanzee, our closest relative. Their natural enemy, the leopard, also lives here along with elephants, buffaloes and numerous other species.

The total world population of eastern lowland gorillas has declined to only a few thousand, the majority of which live in Kahuzi–Biega National Park.

VIRUNGA NATIONAL PARK

In the Western public consciousness, Virunga National Park is virtually synonymous with its most famous inhabitants, mountain gorillas, but its varied scenery provides a habitat for many other species as well.

Virunga National Park covers some 8,000 sq km (3,000 sq mi) of the Great Rift Valley north and south of Lake Edward – also known as Lake Rutanzige – in north-eastern Congo on the Ugandan and Rwandan borders. It is part of an area established in 1925 as Albert National Park, the first African national park. Over time, the greater part of the park has been agriculturalized but Virunga still offers unparalleled biodiversity: swamps, steppes, savannah, lava plains, rainforest, snowfields on the Rwenzori mountains – highest peak is at 5,109 m (16,760 ft) – and volcanoes, both extinct and active.

The western side of the Rwenzori mountains gets roughly 3,000 mm (118 in) of rain annually.

The fauna is equally varied. Around 200 mammal species populate the national park including elephants, hippos, lions, leopards, okapis and a number of antelope and primate species. Migratory birds from Siberia and Europe even spend the winters here.
The mountain gorilla, which is threatened with extinction, has found one of its last refuges here in the Virunga mountains. American zoologist Dian Fossey began her extended study here in 1967, initially on the Congolese and then on the Rwandan side of the border. Of today's estimated population of 700 specimens about half of these great apes live in Virunga, and the Democratic Republic of Congo, Uganda and Rwanda conduct special patrols to save these close relatives of humans from extinction.

Since "Gorillas in the Mist", the rare mountain gorillas (top left) have been the most famous inhabitants of Virunga National Park.

Ethiopia

SIMIEN NATIONAL PARK

This park is located 100 km (62 mi) north of Gondar in northern Ethiopia and includes a region of mountain plateaus characterized by dramatic precipices and raging rivers.

In the Simien massif, millions of years of constant erosion have created some of the world's most striking scenery, with mountain peaks rising up to 4,500 m (14,800 ft) high above basalt valleys, roaring rivers banked by jagged rocks and cliffs, and ravines that plunge to depths of up to 1,500 m (5,000 ft). Standing over all of this is Ras Dashen which, at an impressive 4,620 m (15,160 ft), is the fourth-highest mountain in Africa and was first climbed by Europeans in 1841.

The national park, named after the mountain plateau, provides a habitat for several extremely rare species, among them the gelada baboon, the Simien red fox, and the Walia ibex. In 1996, when the population of foxes and ibexes fell beneath the critical level of twenty and 250 specimens respectively, the park was inscribed in the UNESCO Red List. The most critical aspect threatening the site is the increased settlement in within the national park.

Simien National Park impresses with its high mountain plateaus (right). The rare Ethiopian wolf also lives in the park (below), traveling in small packs and feeding mainly on mice and rats.

AKSUM

The capital of the Aksumite Empire in the northern section of the country was the political and cultural center of ancient Ethiopia. The giant stelae are particularly impressive monuments from among the ruins of the rulers' palaces.

The Kingdom of Aksum was the dominant power in the heart of ancient Ethiopia until the beginning of the 10th century, and historic sources testify to its existence since the first century. It converted to Christianity as early as the fourth century under King Ezana. The ruins of the capital, Aksum, are silent witnesses to the splendor of this former trading town and are dominated by about 130 giant stelae, obelisk-like monoliths made from trachyte. By the time it was found, one 33-m (108-ft) stele had fallen to the ground and broken into several pieces. The second-largest stele was taken to Rome by Mussolini's troops

in 1937, but in 2008 the 24-m (79-ft) monument was once again erected in Aksum. These monolith pillars are thought to be copies of the multistory "ghost houses" of the Hadhramaut region, the origin of immigrants who came to northern Ethiopia in the seventh century. The Cathedral St Mary of Zion was the royal coronation church. According to legend, the Ark of the Covenant from the Temple in Jerusalem is kept here.

The stelae of Aksum are thought by some to be multi-level tomb stelae, by others to be altars at the foot of which animals were sacrificed.

Ethiopia

FASIL GHEBBI, GONDAR REGION

Fasil Ghebbi, the fortified town and Royal Enclosure of the Ethiopian Emperor Fasilides and his successors, is home to several impressive structures that reveal both Asiatic and European influences.

The fortified town of Fasil Ghebbi is located at an elevation of 2,300 m (7,546 ft) above sea level at the foot of the Simien Mountains on the northern shores of Lake Tana in the Gondar Region. It was built in the 16th and 17th centuries as the residence of Emperor Fasilides and his successors. Within its 900-m-long (2,953-ft) city walls are a number of public and private buildings including five palaces just in the Royal Enclosure of Gemp as well as churches and monasteries that were initially introduced by Jesuit missionaries.

Major buildings in the palace district are the castle of Emperor Fasilides (r. 1632–1667), the oldest preserved structure; the magnificent palace of his grandson Iyasu the Great

The area of Fasilides Castle covers just under 8 ha (20 acre) and also includes the library, which is rendered in yellow. It was built under Emperor Yohannes I.

(r. 1682–1706); the library of Emperor Yohannes I (r. 1667–1682); and the castle of the Empress Mentewab (r. 1730–1755). Similarly magnificent was the "Palace of the Son of the Empress", whose rooms were said to have been furnished in ivory and featured mirrors. At the end of the 19th century, Fasil Ghebbi was badly damaged during the Mahdi rebellion against Anglo-Egyptian rule.

Fasilides Castle (top left) was built in about 1635. The "Singers' Hall", of which only ruins remain (left), was part of the palace commissioned by Dawit III, a son of Emperor Iyasu.

Ethiopia

ROCK-HEWN CHURCHES, LALIBELA

In the heart of the Ethiopian uplands, eleven medieval churches can be seen that were hewn from the rock. Today they are still a popular destination for pilgrimages.

The famous rock churches of Lalibela, located some 2,600 m (8,531 ft) above sea level, were built at the end of the 12th century during the reign of Gabre Maskal Lalibela, the most important king of the Zagwe Dynasty. Formerly known as Roha, the capital was renamed in his honor. Architecturally speaking the eleven churches are among the most important religious buildings in Sub-Saharan Africa. Each of them was hewn from the surrounding volcanic tuff over the course of several decades; they are linked with each other by a labyrinth of tracks and tunnels dug out of the rock. The most popular destination for pilgrims, who still make their way to Lalibela in large numbers, is Bet Maryam, St Mary's Church. Bet Medhane Alem, which boasts five

Unlike the monolithic rock churches of Lalibela, the Church of Bet Abba Libano from the 13th century was built into an existing cave.

aisles, is the largest monolithic church in the world, but the best known is probably Bet Giyorgis, which is laid out in the shape of a Greek cross. Priests guard the treasures inside the churches of Lalibela, which contain manuscripts, crucifixes and frescoes. Like every other Ethiopian church, they also have so-called "tabots", copies of the tablets of stone that Moses received on Mount Sinai. On festival days they are wrapped in silk fabrics and carried outside the church.

Ingenious architects cut the monolithic rock churches of Lalibela, including Bet Giyorgis (top and right), from the soft volcanic tuff.

LOWER VALLEY OF THE AWASH

Major paleontological finds have been unearthed in the Awash Valley in north-eastern Ethiopia, around 100 km (62 mi) west of the border with Djibouti. They shed light on a key phase in the development of humankind.

The Lower Valley of the Awash became famous when skeletons of the hominid species Australopithecus afarensis were discovered during excavations here. From the remains that were found in 1974, anthropologists have been able to reconstruct a skeleton, complete in a broad outline, of a prehistoric human who had walked upright at that time. This hominid had lived here as early as three million years ago or more, when the valley was still a savannah covered in trees with primeval horses, prehistoric rhinoceroses and saber-tooth tigers

roaming the area. Shaped by their environment, these ancestors of modern humans began to walk upright. The skeleton, forty percent complete and around 3.2 million years old, belonged to a 1.10-m-tall (3 ft, 7-in) tall female later named "Lucy" after the Beatles song. Most recently researchers found the skeleton of a three-year-old girl who had died here some 3.3 million years ago.

On the banks of the Awash River, anthropologist Donald Johanson found the semi-intact skeleton of "Lucy".

LOWER VALLEY OF THE OMO

The area of the national park on the lower course of the Omo River in Ethiopia is not only a habitat for many wild animals but, since the 1930s, has also been a major site of discovery for fossilized hominid skeletons and stone tools.

The Omo River flows for roughly 800 km (497 mi) before emptying into Lake Turkana on the southern border of Ethiopia. The lower course of the river, where sedimentary layers are up to four million years old, has become famous for excavations featuring prehistoric objects including animal and hominid fossils from the Pliocene and Pleistocene eras. The skeletal remains, some of which date from more than three million years ago, probably belonged to an Australopithecine.

Some 2.5-million-year-old stone tools that were used by Homo habilis were also unearthed. More recent hominid remains were found near the Omo in-

cluding parts of a Homo erectus and an early Homo sapiens. Research indicates that Homo sapiens lived in East Africa 200,000 years ago: Two skulls and skeletal remnants found in the valley in 1967 have now been dated.

Significant hominid fossils were found in the Omo Valley (above) and the most recent fossils of Australopithecus afarensis and of Homo habilis were discovered in the Lake Turkana Basin (left).

Ethiopia

TIYA

At the archaeological excavation site of Tiya about 100 km (62 mi) from the Ethiopian capital of Addis Ababa, elaborately decorated stone stelae attest to a little-known pre-Christian culture.

There are 160 archaeological sites in the Soddo Region south of the Ethiopian capital, Addis Ababa, of which Tiya is the most important. Thirty-six elaborately adorned stone stelae, each measuring 1 to 2 m (3 to 6 ft) in height, were found there. They are remnants of an ancient Ethiopian culture. Of these stelae, thirty-three are still standing along a 45-m (148-ft) long axis; three more are a little farther away. These obelisk-like monoliths are either semi-spherical, conical or humanoid in shape and richly adorned with symbols carved into the stone. But the meaning of the carvings has so far been hard to deci-

pher. Three key repeating motifs have been identified at this stage: circles, leaves and swords – symbols that probably had a specific meaning during burial ceremonies. The most recent excavations reveal that the field of stelae marks the mass graves of men and women aged between eighteen and thirty who were interred here in an embryonic kneeling position. It has not yet been possible to establish the exact age of this vanished pre-Christian culture.

It is assumed that the stelae were erected before the beginning of the Christian era.

HARAR JUGOL, THE FORTIFIED HISTORIC TOWN

The town of Harar Jugol, often known simply as Harar, is surrounded by ramparts. With its many mosques, traditional town houses and buildings constructed in Indian and Muslim styles it exerts a special charm.

Ethiopia is known primarily as a Christian country, but about half its inhabitants are Muslims. Harar, their holy town, is located in the eastern region of the country on a 1,885-m (6,185-ft) plateau surrounded by savannah and desert. The Old Town is encircled by ramparts, known as "jugol", dating from the 13th to 16th centuries. Five historic gates provide access to the city and a sixth gate was opened by the Italians in 1936 when they occupied the city.

The most common style of town house ("gegar") features three rooms on the

ground floor and a courtyard. In 1887, Indian traders came to Harar and introduced a new style of house: simple rectangular buildings, often two floors high, with a veranda overlooking either the road or the courtyard. Harar was given its present appearance as an Islamic city in the 16th century and features a maze of narrow alleyways and façades that are closed to the outside.

The Shewa Gate (above), narrow lanes, colorful houses and eighty-two mosques (right) define the Harar cityscape.

BWINDI IMPENETRABLE NATIONAL PARK

Bwindi is in extreme south-western Uganda and is known both for the diversity of its trees and ferns as well as its rare species of butterflies and birds. The montane forest is also one of the last refuges of the rare mountain gorilla.

The barely accessible Bwindi National Park (Bwindi means "impenetrable") lies in a transition zone between the steppes and the mountains, and is distinguished by its unique variety of flora and fauna. There are more than 100 indigenous varieties of fern, and the national park's montane forest is composed of no fewer than 160 tree species. The forests here are among the oldest in Africa. Woodland birds make up about two-thirds of the 300 avian species so far recorded, and there are about 200 varieties of butterfly.

Having said that, the reserve is really most famous for its mountain gorillas. On its upper slopes around 300 specimens still live in docile family groups led by a "silverback" and make up about half the total world population of this endangered species. They can be observed from a distance on tours organized by the park.

Bwindi National Park is located on the edge of the Western Rift Valley in south-west Uganda. It covers 330 sq km (130 sq mi) and incorporates both mountain and lowland rainforest.

RWENZORI MOUNTAINS NATIONAL PARK

The montane forest and marshlands of the Rwenzori area are a habitat for many endangered species including plants of extraordinary size.

The Rwenzori mountains are located on the border between Uganda and the Democratic Republic of the Congo. Formed by tectonic activity, the range is 120 km (74 mi) long and 50 km (31 mi) wide, and its highest elevation it rises to 5,109 m (16,760 ft) on top of Mount Stanley. The park itself covers an area of 1,000 sq km (390 sq mi) in south-western Uganda. The upper reaches of the park feature glaciers, lakes and waterfalls and have a bewildering variety of plants including lobelias, which normally grow to 30 cm (12 in) in height but can reach 6 m (20 ft) here.

Some fern species grow unhindered to heights of 10 m (33 ft), and some types of heather can grow as big as trees. This immense biodiversity is mainly attributable to a combination of mineral-rich soils, stable temperatures, high humidity and the fact that the frequently thick cloud cover greatly reduces the amounts of strong ultraviolet light that enter.

In the tropical montane forests of the Rwenzori mountains, oversized alpine plants grow at an elevation of 4,000 m (14,000 ft).

TOMBS OF THE BUGANDA KINGS AT KASUBI

The tombs of the Buganda kings are of great importance as a spiritual center to the Baganda, the main ethnic group in Uganda. Their palace architecture dates from the culture of the Ganda in the pre-colonial Kingdom of Buganda.

The Kabaka Tombs are located on Kasubi Hill, close to the Ugandan capital of Kampala. They are an excellent example of the enduring traditions and skills of the Baganda people. In the Muzibu Azaala Mpanga, a straw-covered domed building, the female descendants of the Kabaka – as the Bugandian rulers are known – commemorate the last four kings of their empire: Mute-sa I, Mwanga II, David Chwa II and Edward Mutesa II. The latter was forced to abdicate in 1966 by Milton Obote, who then became the President of Uganda.

The kings' descendants are also buried here. The roof of the circular tomb, which has a diameter of about 30 m (98 ft), is supported by mighty pillars that are wrapped in bark. The structure was built as a palace as early as 1882 and converted into a burial site in 1884.

The tomb of the kings at Kasubi is an impressive straw-covered wooden structure that is over 7 m (23 ft) tall at its highest point.

Kenya

SACRED MIJIKENDA KAYA FORESTS

Eleven separate kaya forests were declared a World Heritage Site in Kenya as an example of how myths and spiritual traditions, on the one hand, and the natural environment on the other have always been and still remain interdependent for the Mijikenda people.

According to their myths, the nine ethnic groups of the Mijikenda people were expelled from their original homeland in Somalia and in about the 16th century founded a number of fortified villages in the dense forests along the Kenyan coast. The villages, known as "kaya", were built in forest clearings and could only be reached via specified tracks. The kaya forests were closely linked with the spiritual world of the Mijikenda – they buried their dead here and venerated the shrines of their ancestors.

The forests have enjoyed special protection for hundreds of years because of their spiritual significance. Religious taboos forbade not just the felling of the trees but any human intervention in the surrounding flora and fauna. The forests cover between 30 and 300 ha (74 and 741 acres) and have developed into unique biospheres of their own where many of Kenya's native plant species flourish.

Dancing girls from the Giriama, one of nine Mijikenda ethnic groups.

LAMU OLD TOWN

Lamu, located on the island of the same name in the Indian Ocean, is one of the oldest and best-preserved Swahili towns in East Africa. Its inhabitants traded far and wide, creating a very distinctive culture here.

The island archipelago of Lamu off the northern Kenya coast was settled as early as the 12th century. The subsequent encounter between the local Bantu population and the Arab traders quickly made Lamu a focal point for the Islamic-influenced Swahili culture of East Africa.

In about 1500, the island was brought into the Portuguese sphere of influence and in the early 19th century it was occupied by the rulers of Oman. Indeed, influences from Europe, the Arab world, Persia and even India have intermingled with Bantu traditions on Lamu, which is particularly evident in the Old Town. The white-washed stone houses, which are several stories high, and the narrow alleyways built in the Arab style date back to before 1830. Built from coral stocks and mangrove wood, the houses feature impressive courtyards, verandas and beautifully carved front doors. The Swahili artisans here are best known for their woodcarving and basket weaving products. Lamu is an important center of both Islam and of the traditional Swahili culture in East Africa.

Seen from above, the roofs in the Arab old town of Lamu look like a patchwork blanket.

LAKE TURKANA NATIONAL PARKS

This World Heritage Site is composed of three national parks. From north to south they include Sibiloi, Central Island and South Island.

In the desert-like steppe of far north-western Kenya near the border with Sudan and Ethiopia is Lake Turkana, an endorheic lake with a high salt content. Sibiloi National Park on its eastern shore covers 1,500 sq km (580 sq mi) and is a habitat for lions, zebras, antelopes and gazelles, but it is much better known as a breeding ground and stopover for wading birds, flamingos, pelicans, seagulls and other migratory birds.

In the middle of the lake is a bare volcanic rock that makes up Central Island, which is 5 sq km (2 sq mi) in size and is home to the nests of numerous waterfowl species. It also provides a refuge for quite a large colony of Nile crocodiles.

South Island, abou 100 km (62 mi) further to the south from Central Island, has very similar fauna as well as a population of hippos. Significant paleontological finds including Australopithecus, Homo habilis, Homo erectus and Homo sapiens have been made in Koobi Fora, a promontory of the national park that juts out into the lake.

Large colonies of flamingoes live on the shores of Lake Turkana.

MOUNT KENYA NATIONAL PARK

The slopes of Mount Kenya are characterized by a succession of highly diverse vegetation and forest zones.

At 5,199 m (17,057 ft), the impressive massif and twin summits of Mount Kenya are the highest peaks in the country. Their slopes are covered in meadow and forest up to an elevation of about 2,000 m (6,600 ft), at which point the moist deciduous forest is replaced by evergreen cloud forest. Beyond this that is a zone of dense bamboo growth after roughly 2,500 m (8,200 ft). Above 3,500 m (11,500 ft) is open grassland that then merges into moorland on the higher slopes. Predominately ericaceous berries and and a variety of shrubs grow in this area of heathland; of particular note is the tree heath, which can grow to a height of around 10 m (33 ft). Giant lobelias and various species of

Groundsel thrives on Mount Kenya despite harsh conditions at elevations of over 3,500 m (11,599 ft).

groundsel, which can reach a height of 5 m (17 ft), grow in the alpine zone where the actual boundaries of the national park begin. Although these two plants display many similarities in form, they are not related. Above this zone lies the Afro-alpine zone covering the summits, with several cirque glaciers in the extinct volcano. Animal life in Africa's most diverse national park is usually found in the more nutrition-rich regions of bamboo groves and green forest. Species include elephants, rhinos, cape buffaloes along with a few rare animals such as bush and rock hyrax. Around 150 varieties of birds are scattered throughout the various vegetation zones as well.

Although waterfalls cascade over rock formations and giant heath bushes still grow here on Mount Kenya, above 4,300 m (14,200 ft) only glaciers, lakes, rocks and snowfields await visitors.

Tanzania

Maasai

Maasai herdsmen and warriors still pursue their largely traditional semi-nomadic way of life in the vast expanses of the Serengeti in northern Tanzania and southern Kenya. They live from and with their livestock, whose needs also determine the rhythm and the routes of their wanderings. The Maasai once owned more than enough land for their purposes, but during the colonial period they lost all their best grazing grounds. In recent decades the establishment of national parks has further restricted their pastures. Overgrazing and a lack of water were the consequences, a problem that was further exacerbated by an expansion of grain cultivation,

SERENGETI NATIONAL PARK

The Serengeti is a giant area of savannah east of Lake Victoria that stretches from north-west Tanzania into neighboring Kenya. Covering roughly 15,000 sq km (5,800 sq mi) of Tanzanian territory, the vast herd migrations here are now the main feature in the national park.

Throughout the year, mighty herds of more than two million Boehm's zebras, white-bearded wildebeests and Thomson's gazelles roam the grassland and savannah of the Serengeti in search of food and water, often covering distances of up to 1,500 km (930 mi). Overcoming great hardship, these animals have always followed the same routes, which are dictated more or less by the alternation of the dry and rainy seasons. Meanwhile, their natural enemies are hot on the trail: lions, leopards, cheetahs and hyenas. Hardly anything else on earth portrays the struggle for life – eat or be eaten – on such an imposing scale as this mass animal migration in the Serengeti.

This area, which is among the world's richest in terms of animal life, is also home to giraffes, Cape buffaloes, topi and kongoni antelopes, elands, hippos, rhinos, hyenas, African wild dogs, patas monkeys, aardwolfs, crocodiles, emus and elephants. The latter are not indigenous, but were introduced in 1957. Over thousands of years, a biosphere for very diverse species has developed here.

All this changed, however, at the end of the 19th century with the arrival of Europeans when big game hunters dealt the animal kingdom a blow from which it may never fully recover. The Serengeti was placed under partial protection as early as 1921 and under full protection in 1929. The national park was inscribed in 1951.

"Kopjes" – Dutch for "little heads" – jut out of the grassland everywhere on the Serengeti. These rock formations of gneiss and quartzite once lay under the earth's surface and have been exposed after thousands of years of erosion.

urban sprawl and climate change. For the Maasai, keeping cattle is much more than an economic activity. The larger the herd, the higher the social status of its owner. According to their tribal mythology, the Maasai also regard themselves as the rightful owners of all cattle. Stealing cattle, like hunting lions, is one of the tests

set for young warriors but both lead to a conflict with the law these days. The patriarchal Maasai society is divided into different age sets of warriors, junior elders and senior elders. The young warriors live in their own separate kraal villages; it is their main task to defend the settlement and the livestock. The elders make all

the decisions concerning affairs of the common good.

The Maasai work as herdsmen from an early age. They wear bright garments made of sheets that are loosely wrapped around the body with lavish bead decorations on their head, neck and arms.

The great migrations are also followed by the herds of elephant that live in family units in the Serengeti.

On their search for water and fresh greenery, giraffes journey across the savannah from north-east to south-east.

Within a herd it is hard to make out the outlines of a single zebra. This puts predators at a disadvantage.

For predators like lions, the great animal migrations mean plentiful food and carefree days.

Tanzania

NGORONGORO CONSERVATION AREA

This stunning conservation area covers 8,000 sq km (3,000 sq mi) of the floor of the Ngorongoro crater in northern Tanzania. It is a popular grazing area for massive herds of wild animals.

For a long time the Ngorongoro crater area was part of Serengeti National Park. It only became an independent conservation area in 1974. The newly established park then included Empakaai crater with its freshwater lake, as well as the active volcano, Oldonyo, the Olduvai Gorge and the Laetoli site, where fossilized remains of early ancestors of Homo habilis (early ancestors of Homo sapiens sapiens) have been found. Between the savannah and steppes of the crater is an area of marsh and acacia forests while the crater floor, largely covered in grass-

land, serves as pasture for the Maasai's herds. Unfortunately, it has suffered severely from overgrazing due to the extent of their pastoralism. The indigenous wildlife of the Ngorongoro area consists principally of wildebeest, gazelles, eland, waterbucks and zebras. Elephants, hippos, black rhinos, lions, hyenas and leopards round out this cross-section of Africa's diverse wildlife.

Thousands of wildebeest and zebras graze on the expansive grassy plains of the Ngorongoro crater.

KILIMANJARO NATIONAL PARK

In northern Tanzania, on the Kenyan border, the savannah is interrupted by the volcanic massif of Kilimanjaro. Approximately 750 sq km (295 sq mi) here were designated as a national park to protect its unique montane forest.

Kilimanjaro is composed of three main volcanic cones and numerous smaller summits of volcanic origin. To the west is the 4,000-m-high (13,200-ft) Shira; in the middle is Kibo, at 5,895 m (19,340 ft), the highest point in Africa; and to the east is Mawenzi, the smallest at 5,270 m (17,290 ft). The other ridges form a chain running south-east to north-west. Although not far from the equator, Kilimanjaro's peaks are always covered in snow. This massif in the middle of the savannah boasts extremely diverse climatic areas and vegetation zones. Above

the savannah there is a region of cultivated land once covered in a forest savannah that now only exists on the northern slopes. This zone merges into a deciduous montane forest that rises to 3,000 m (9,900 ft) followed by expansive grassy uplands which in turn are replaced by the cold desert of the summit region. The national park is home to many endangered animal species.

Sulphurous fumaroles within Kibo's snow-covered crater are indicative of volcanic activity.

SELOUS GAME RESERVE

Africa's largest game reserve in south-eastern Tanzania is home to about one million animals including, among many others, the "big five": elephants, rhinos, buffaloes, lions and leopards.

The Rufiji river is one of the largest in east Africa and its numerous tributaries flow through the Selous Game Reserve, whose area of 50,000 sq km (19,400 sq mi) were declared a conservation area at the beginning of the 20th century. Approximately 200 km (124 mi) from the capital, Dar es Salaam, the area is largely avoided by humans because of the presence of tsetse flies, and thus provides a largely undisturbed habitat for a variety of wildlife.
More than 150,000 wildebeests, 100,000 elephants, 150,000 buffaloes, 50,000 antelopes and zebras each, and about 20,000 hippos have been

documented. The world's largest crocodile population also lives here, and the various vegetation zones on the reserve are host to a considerable number of giraffes and big cats including cheetahs, leopards and lions. These zones encompass steppe, savannah, lightly forested grassland, and the thick undergrowth of the gallery forest on the banks of the Rufiji and its sources, the Luwegu and the Kilombero. Miombo forest dominates the landscape.

Roughly 100,000 elephants have found a home in the Miombo forest.

RUINS OF KILWA KISIWANI AND RUINS OF SONGO MNARA

On two small islands off the Tanzanian coast stand the ruins of two former port towns that were once of great importance in the trade with Asia.

Persians from Shiraz are typically regarded as the founders of this former city-state on the island of Kilwa Kisiwani, 30 km (186 mi) south of Tanzania's capital, Dar es Salam. Starting in about AD 1000, much of the trade with the countries of the Indian Ocean was conducted through Kilwa. Among the traded goods were precious items such as gold, silver and pearls as well as porcelain from China, stoneware from Persia and pottery from Arabia. The town's decline began at the end of the 14th century, a process that was completed with the arrival of Portuguese in 1505.

Of the remaining monuments, the ruins of the Sultan's Palace of Husuni Kubwa, built between 1310 and 1333, are worth seeing. Other historic buildings include the former Portuguese Gereza Fort, the small domed mosque and the great mosque from the 12th to the 15th century – the largest in East Africa. The World Heritage Site also includes remains of buildings on the island of Songo Mnara, in particular the main mosque, which was built from coral limestone.

The 16 domes of the mosque in Kilwa Kisiwani are supported by 30 columns.

STONE TOWN OF ZANZIBAR

Stone Town, the heart of Zanzibar City, is a fine example of a successful Swahili trading town with Omani roots.

Numerous finds on the east coast of Africa document the early existence of a trading network that spanned the entire Indian Ocean to East Asia. The Islamization of East Africa had already begun before the year 1000 through the proliferation of Arab Omani trading posts in African communities, but an original Afro-Arabic coastal culture only developed with the arrival of the Shiraz Persians. The Portuguese controlled the area starting in the 16th century before the Omanis regained influence. In 1840, Zanzibar became the capital of the rulers of Oman. It was the beginning of the final phase of the Arabization of Swahili culture.

Under Omani rule, the trade in ivory, gold, spices and slaves flourished. Today the cathedral from 1873 is on the site of the former slave market. Remnants of Omani rule include the former sultan's palace ("People's Palace") with the "House of Wonders", the National Museum building, Beit al-Amani and the Arab Fort.
Also worth seeing are the Old Dispensary, a four-story former pharmacy, Livingstone's House and the decorated front doors of homes built using coral limestone.

The wealthy Arabic-Indian upper classes of Zanzibar once lived in the magnificent houses of Stone Town.

KONDOA ROCK-ART SITES

About 100 km (62 mi) north of Dodoma is a collection of prehistoric and more recent images created partly by hunter-gatherers and farmers of the region.

Tectonic activity in the nearby Great East African Rift Valley caused slab-like fragments of sedimentary rock to form in Kondoa. The vertical faces of these rocks have been used for artistic depictions for at least 2,000 years. According to estimates there are between 150 and 450 such sites in Tanzania, which probably also served as refuges for the people living in this wild region. Most are located on slopes exposed facing east, on the edge of the Maasai veldt. Even until recently, families living on the plains sought shelter under such overhanging rocks during the rainy season.
The oldest rock-art works are realistic depictions of animals such as ante-

lopes, giraffes and elephants as well as stylized images of humans and geometric shapes – all in red. The age of the most northerly examples of this southern African hunter-gatherer rock-art is still debated among scientists. At any rate, such works were still produced in relatively recent times, and some sites still serve as ceremonial sites for the indigenous people, a remarkable example of a tradition that is probably thousands of years old. The World Heritage Site also includes three archaeological excavation sites.

The subjects of the Kondoa rock drawings are mostly animals such as antelopes.

Zambia / Zimbabwe

VICTORIA FALLS (MOSI-OA-TUNYA)

Victoria Falls is one of the most amazing spectacles of nature in the world. The waters of the Zambezi River plummet here over a series of basalt cliffs into a chasm over 100 m (330 ft) deep.

The first intimation of just how much of a presence Victoria Falls has comes into view at a distance of about 20 km (13 mi) in the form of a cloud of mist rising 300 m (990 ft) into the air. Then comes the deafening thunder of the Zambezi River – the natural and political border between Zambia and Zimbabwe – as it plummets 100 m (330 ft) into the depths and makes this a truly international World Heritage Site.

This natural spectacle is echoed in the indigenous name for the five falls: Mosi-oa-tunya, meaning "Smoke that thunders". At high water in March and April the falls become a continuous curtain of water almost 2 km (1.5 mi) wide depositing roughly

The deep gorge into which the Zambezi drops at the Victoria Falls was cut by the river itself during the course of millions of years.

10,000 cu m (353,000 cu ft) of water per second into the gorge. During the rest of the year's dry season the curtain divides up into smaller individual falls, among which Rainbow Falls are the highest. The area around the falls is home to some thirty mammal, sixty-five reptile, and twenty-one amphibian species.

David Livingstone, a Scottish scientist and missionary, was the first European to discover Victoria Falls in 1855. He named them after the reigning queen of England.

Even today the water continues to erode the stone – Victoria Falls are still "moving".

MANA POOLS NATIONAL PARK

Situated on the southern banks of the Zambezi river, this national park and its associated safari areas of Sapi and Chewori is a wildlife paradise.

Mana Pools was established as a national park in 1963 and a year later the neighboring safari ranges of Sapi and Chewore were also placed under protection. Situated at the point where the Zimbabwe, Zambia and Mozambique borders meet, these three areas together cover an area of about 7,000 sq km (2,600 sq mi), with Chewore making up about half of that. The Zambezi River forms the park's natural border to the north and regularly floods the grasslands and forests of the conservation area. "Mana Pools" refers to the four permanent pools created by this process.

This fertile landscape is home to many animals: about 400 bird species, thousands of elephants roaming the plains, and herds of buffalo and zebra that provide plenty of fodder to predators such as leopards and cheetahs. The Chewori Safari Area is now home to one of the largest populations of giant white rhinoceros while hippos and a large number of the otherwise endangered Nile crocodile roam the peaceful courses of the Zambezi.

This hippopotamus is barely visible among the water hyacinths in a pool in Mana Pools Park.

KHAMI RUINS NATIONAL MONUMENT

The ruins of Khami are of great significance in the history of Zimbabwe. The town was once an important trading center but it was abandoned in the 16th century.

The second-largest town of ruins in Zimbabwe is located only a few miles west of Bulawayo and was named after the river on whose banks it was built. The complex was created in the 15th century after Great Zimbabwe had been abandoned and for about 200 years Khami was the capital of the Torwa state. When the Rozwi came to power they moved their seat of government to Danangombe about 80 km (50 mi) away. The remains of the buildings including a palace complex, terraces and walls are spread over more than 40 ha (99 acres) and

the stone walls were all built without mortar. Archaeological excavations have also unearthed Chinese porcelain from the era of Emperor Wanli. The objects from Asia and Europe attest to the fact that Khami was once a major trading town. It is thus possible that Portuguese merchants were among the visitors to the town. A giant crucifix formed of granite blocks lets us assume that missionaries also found their way to Khami.

The walls of Khami also served as fencing for cattles grazing in the meadows.

MATOBO HILLS

The majestic rocky landscape of the Matobo Hills in south-western Zimbabwe – some 30 km (19 mi) south of Bulawayo – features polished granite blocks with rock drawings that date back to the Stone Age.

The Ndebele have lived in the Matobo Hills since the 19th century. They call the bare granite boulders that lie stacked on top of each other like toys "bald heads" – "amatobo" in the Sindebele language – which explains the name of the present-day World Heritage Site. The granite blocks were shaped by the elements and polished by the wind.
In the Silozwane Cave there are a good number of rock drawings to admire including the occasional 2-m (5-ft) giraffe. It is still possible to identify exactly which animals are depicted. Even the structure of termite wings was painstakingly reproduced.

Some of these drawings are believed to have been created around 20,000 years ago by hunter-gatherers who are most closely related to the present-day San (bushmen) and thousands of these sites are thought to exist.
The Shona Mwari religion that is practiced here today can be traced back to the Iron Age, making it one of the oldest orally transmitted traditions in southern Africa. The prehistoric caves with their rock art are still sacred places for the people who live there.

The prehistoric rock-art in the Matobo Hills depicts animals and hunting scenes.

GREAT ZIMBABWE NATIONAL MONUMENT

The ruins of "Africa's Acropolis" in south-eastern Zimbabwe is a rather unusual stone structure for Africa but the complex is an important testimony of the Shona culture.

Portuguese historian João de Barros described the ruins of Great Zimbabwe as "impressive" as early as 1552. An Arab legend even gives them Biblical status. However, archaeological finds have proven that the walls are the remains of an important trading center of the Shona culture. This ethnic group, which belongs to the Bantu language group, settled the region between the 11th and the 15th centuries.
The town, which had more than 10,000 inhabitants, was encircled by elliptical walls with a length of 250 m (820 ft) and a height of more than 10

m (32 ft), making them one of the largest structures in pre-colonial Sub-Saharan Africa. The wall was built from granite blocks that were tightly stacked on top of each other without mortar. Within this ring is a parallel wall that probably encircled the houses of the ruler. Excavations confirm that gold, copper and iron were already being worked in Zimbabwe. After its heyday, the town was finally abandoned in about 1450.

The elliptical fortification wall at the Great Zimbabwe complex (above).

Malawi

LAKE MALAWI NATIONAL PARK

Located at the southern end of the third-largest lake in Africa, this is the first national park devoted exclusively to the conservation of fish; it is home to several hundred species of tilapia, many of which are native.

In 1616, Portuguese explorer Gaspar Boccaro reported on the existence of a great body of water in south-eastern Africa. In 1859, Scottish scientist and missionary David Livingstone reached the shores of what he called Lake Nyasa, now known as Lake Malawi. The lake is fed by fourteen tributary rivers, the Ruhuhu being the largest, and only has one effluent river, the Shire, which feeds the Zambezi. Three countries – Tanzania, Mozambique, and Malawi – border the lake, which is 500 km (310 mi) long and 50 km (31 mi) wide. This unique park was established in 1980 at the southern end of the lake, on Malawian territory.

Its 100 sq km (39 sq mi) area include Cape Maclear, three sections of shoreline, twelve islands and part of the lake nearest the shore. Its clear waters reach depths of 700 m (2,240 ft) and are home to more than 200 species of fish, eighty percent of which are native here. For this reason, the lake is as important for the study of evolution as the Galapagos Islands.

Mumbo Island is off Cape Maclear and is covered by the Miombo forest of fig and baobab trees. The people who live on Lake Malawi have always lived off fishing, which they do in their dugout canoes (right).

CHONGONI ROCK-ART AREA

The highlands of Central Malawi is an area where the plentiful rock-art is still used in ritual ceremonies. Over thousands of years the BaTwa hunter-gatherers as well as the Chewa people have all left their marks here.

The Chongoni Mountains consist of a flat, grass-covered plateau with steep slopes, smaller granite hills and some expansive valleys with large rock formations. Natural Brachystegia forests crawl up the hillsides. An astounding 127 sites in the area feature rock drawings that are often located on overhanging granite boulders.

The earliest – red-colored – drawings date back to the BaTwa, a pygmy people who began settling here in the late Stone Age. They left behind schematic drawings of animals and humans as well as geometric patterns of circles, lines and wavy shapes. The white drawings, on the other hand,

were created from the late Iron Age and continued until well into the 20th century. They were the work of the Chewa, a local farming people. They mostly represent animal figures, but many are also connected with female initiation rites and were probably in fact drawn by women. More recent figures refer to the nyau secret society. These masked dancers conduct burial rites and are regarded as spirits; their masks are also depicted in the rock art.

The white drawings of the Chewa were often added immediately on top of the red BaTwa Stone Age drawings.

ISLAND OF MOZAMBIQUE

The city of Mozambique is on the island of the same name, which in turn provided the name of the country. For 500 years this island was an outpost of the Portuguese trading empire, and it is a fine example of the Portuguese colonial baroque style in East Africa.

The island city of Mozambique in the Indian Ocean is linked with the mainland via a 5-km-long (3-mi) bridge and was already the site of an Arab trading settlement as early as the 10th century. In 1498, on his search for a faster sea route to India, Vasco da Gama landed on the island, and it quickly became one of the main ports and transshipment locations for the Portuguese colonial powers in Africa and Asia.

Until 1975 it still served as an administrative seat, capital and trading post for the colony of Portuguese East Africa, which would ultimately become Mozambique. Between 1558 and 1620, the Portuguese built the São Sebastião fortress, a fine example of the local baroque style that has remained largely unchanged since the 16th century. Persistent use of this style is what made the island a unified architectural ensemble including fortifications and churches. Local tradtions in the city mingle with Portuguese, Arabic and Indian influences.

Probably the oldest European building south of the Equator is the Capela de Nossa Senhora do Baluarte (Chapel of Our Lady of the Bulwarks) from 1521.

TSODILO

In the Tsodilo Hills, in the middle of the Kalahari Desert in north-western Botswana, there are roughly 4,500 rock drawings by the San people, some of which date back thousands of years. Archaeological finds confirm that the region has been settled since the Paleolithic era.

For the San, who still live in this region, the Tsodilo Hills are a holy place that is filled with the spirits of ancestors. There is a strict no-hunting law that has been in force for probably thousands of years – in the middle of the barren Kalahari Desert – where springs still bubble and trees provide shade despite the most severe droughts. Rhinoceroses, giraffes, antelopes, longhorn cattle, lions, hippopotamuses and a variety of fish that were all painted on the rocks here by the San attest to the species diversity in the region, where a lake must have existed in earlier times. But the images also depict everyday items such as baskets of the style still woven by the San today, and of humans. Some of the rock art is difficult to access and has been done so high up on the rocks that the artists must have used some sort of scaffold to complete them. Many of the roughly 4,500 rock images date from the years 800 to 1300. For historians, they provide a chronology of human life and of the changing environment in this part of the world.

The San regard the Tsodilo Hills as the cradle of humankind.

TWYFELFONTEIN OR /UI-//AES

Twyfelfontein, an area that is known as /Ui-//aes in the Khoekhoe "click" language of the indigenous people here, contains one of the largest collections of petroglyphs in Africa.

Thirty-five decorated surfaces with about 2,075 identifiable depictions have been discovered so far in the Damara highlands of Namibia. Two techniques have been distinguished up to now: pecking, that is, chiseling out the rock with a hard object, and stone engraving, where the surface is roughened. One of these rock drawings is the "Dancing Kudu", a fabled being in a dancing pose. Among the rock art are also depictions of human figures as well as human and animal footprints. Scientists are certain that the rock images were created by the San hunter-gatherers, who lived in this area for 2,000 years before they were displaced by the Damara pastoralists in about 1000. Some archaeological finds, also from Twyfelfontein, date from the Neolithic Age while the rock-art and objects show continuous habitation of this area by hunter-gatherers. The drawings express the interplay between lifestyle, belief and ritual practices in these cultures.

Antelopes, lions, zebras, rhinoceroses and giraffes can be recognized in many of the rock engravings in Twyfelfontein.

MAPUNGUBWE CULTURAL LANDSCAPE

From 950 to 1300, Mapungubwe was the seat of the largest kingdom in southern Africa. Archaeologists have found burial places here with valuable jewelry as well as the remains of a settlement where more than 5,000 people must have once lived.

Mapungubwe is now an extensive open savannah landscape at the confluence of the Limpopo and Shashe rivers, on the South African side of the tri-border region of Zimbabwe, Botswana and South Africa. Starting in AD 900, the center of a powerful kingdom was established here whose subjects belonged to a highly sophisticated culture. Merchants from Mapungubwe exchanged gold, ivory and ore with Arab traders for glass beads and fabrics from India as well as porcelain from China. These relationships are documented in Arabic chronicles from as far back as the 10th century. Mapungubwe's prosperity was based on agriculture and cotton cultivation, but climate change led to the decline of the kingdom in the 14th century. Among the most significant archaeological finds are the ruins of the city centers with their palaces, tombs and artistically worked gold jewelry – including a golden rhinoceros.

Excavations of the royal tombs and ruins of the city of Mapungubwe began in 1933.

FOSSIL HOMINID SITES OF STERKFONTEIN, SWARTKRANS, KROMDRAAI AND ENVIRONS

The caves of Sterkfontein, Swartkrans, Kromdraai and environs are among the greatest paleo-anthropological sites on Earth. Excavations have provided invaluable insights into the development of humankind.

Australopithecus africanus was the first human ancestor to walk upright. For more than three million years these hominids, of which more types exist besides Australopithecus africanus, populated southern Africa and the East African Rift Valley. Australopithecus was 1.5 m (5 ft) tall, weighed between 35 and 60 kg (77 and 132 lbs) and lived an average twenty-two years. The first preserved skull of the species was discovered in 1924 by South African researcher Raymond Dart and became known around the world as "Taung Child". The discovery is still considered proof of Darwin's theory that the developmental leap from ape to human occurred in Africa. Further finds in caves of the Makapan Valley confirm the origin and development of humankind over a time span of three million years, up to the use of fire some 1.8 million years ago.

These caves are an archaeological treasure trove for scientists.

VREDEFORT DOME

The Vredefort meteorite crater about 120 km (75 mi) south-west of Johannesburg is now considered the largest and oldest of its kind. It is thought to be a little over two billion years old and has a diameter of 190 km (118 mi).

The greatest natural disasters in history have been caused by asteroids. Scientists believe they even influenced evolution, and it is possible that the dinosaurs died out due to the effects of a meteorite strike. The exact composition of the mass of rock that thundered down in southern Africa is difficult to determine today, but it was possibly an asteroid with a diameter of about 12 km (7.5 mi) traveling at a speed of about 20 km (13 mi) per second; or perhaps a smaller comet core moving at a still higher speed. When a meteorite hits the earth, its energy is converted into heat with such speed it leads to a powerful explosion and a crater. Material blasted out by the impact falls to form the crater wall. Proving this cause of this type of crater can be difficult because storms and weather can level the surface after the presumed incident. However, the Vredefort crater features certain properties that speak in favor of a meteorite: horn stone on the surface, a stone that only occurs in deep underground strata, breccia, baked stones, and other changes to the subsurface caused by the impact.

The semi-circular structure of the Vredefort meteorite crater can be clearly seen from the air.

UKHAHLAMBA / DRAKENSBERG PARK

The rock art of the San is several thousand years old and can be found amidst the spectacular natural scenery of Drakensberg Park in eastern South Africa. It is right on the border with Lesotho.

The silent majesty of the mountainous Drakensberg region is home to both the eland and the now-rare bearded and Cape Griffon vultures. Unique cultural treasures can be found here, where erosion has split the softer sandstone strata under the weight of blocks of basalt. Unique evidence of San (Bushman) rock art has been discovered in caves and under rocky overhangs. Many of these images date back only 300 years, but have been painted over 4,000-year-old layers of pigment. Groups of San lived as hunters and gatherers in this area into the first half of the 19th century. The often multicolored paintings were located in places that were probably used at particular times of the year for ritual purposes. The addition of antelope blood to the paints as a fixative suggests a spiritual element to many of the depictions: it is assumed that the eland, too, held some mythological importance. Several of the paintings show dancing figures with nosebleeds, representative of ritual trances perhaps.

Around 35,000 rock paintings were created here by the San.

ISIMANGALISO WETLAND PARK

This reserve on the north-eastern coast of South Africa is among the largest national parks in the world and has a striking diversity of habitats.

The 2,500 sq km (950 sq mi) of iSimangaliso Wetland Park are stretch over large parts of Maputaland in north-eastern South Africa and up to the Mozambican border. The conservation area includes radically differing ecosystems that provide the unique wildlife of Africa with protected habitats. Lake St Lucia, covering an area of 350 sq km (130 sq mi), is the heart of the national park. It is part of the marsh system created by the Hluhluwe River on its way to the Indian Ocean. The area is home to Africa's largest crocodile population, a large population of hippos and more than 400 bird varieties including pelicans, spoonbills and fish eagles.

Rare somango monkeys and other tree-dwellers live in the densely forested dunes, and the remote sandy beaches around Cape Vidal provide a habitat for several species of sea turtle. Off the cape are extensive coral reefs – among the southernmost on earth. The expansive grassland of the interior is a habitat for nearly all of Africa's big game species including both the white and black rhinoceroses.

Fossils have revealed the secrets of the ages on the shores of Lake St Lucia (above). Africa's largest population of crocodiles find a welcome home here in this vast swamp area.

RICHTERSVELD CULTURAL AND BOTANICAL LANDSCAPE

Richtersveld in far north-western South Africa is a spectacular mountain desert landscape with unusual succulent flora. The semi-nomadic herdsmen of the Nama have lived there for two thousand years.

The Nama are considered the last remaining branch of the Khoikhoi who, together with the San, were the original inhabitants of southern Africa. In the beginning the Khoikhoi – pejoratively labeled as "Hottentots" by the Europeans – lived on the Oranje River and on the south-west African coast. However, they were systematically decimated and forced into more inhospitable areas by colonialists. Still, the Nama have been able to survive despite the isolation of Richtersveld. Here they are also able to pursue their semi-nomadic lifestyle, which includes migration to pastoral areas that change with the seasons – a tradition that has continued for 2000 years already. Their portable domed houses, known as "haru oms", consist of overlapping wooden hoops that are covered with woven rush mats. The houses have only one room, which serves for both cooking and sleeping. The Nama are known for their strong oral tradition.

The quiver tree can reach heights of up to 9 m (30 ft) and flourishes in the mountain deserts of Richtersveld.

ROBBEN ISLAND

This island north of Cape Town has been used as both a hospital and a prison over the last 400 years. Its most famous inmate was Nelson Mandela.

Portuguese navigators are said to have interned their first prisoners on Robben Island as early as around 1525. Located just 11 km (7 mi) north of Cape Town, the island's guests were then followed by slaves, the chiefs of many South African peoples, prisoners of war and finally political "dissidents" who were banned to the island by the Dutch or British colonial masters, and during the 20th century by the Apartheid regime.

In the period from 1846 to 1931, Robben Island was converted into a massive hospital and in 1936 the army took over the island, during which time it functioned as an army training ground all the way up until the 1950s. In 1961 the Apartheid regime reconverted the area into a prison, this time with a high-security wing for political prisoners. The last remaining prisoners left Robben Island in 1996. On September 14 of the same year the South African parliament declared the island and its buildings a national monument. The best-known of the structures is the high-security wing with the infamous "Section B", where Nelson Mandela was imprisoned until 1982.

Robben Island is in Table Bay on the Atlantic coast. It is home to the former prison where Nelson Mandela was kept for more than 18 years.

THE CAPE FLORAL REGION

Relative to its area, the southern tip of Africa has the greatest number of plant species of any region on earth, more than even any tropical rainforest. Eight conservation areas in the Cape region are World Heritage Sites.

Botanists divide the earth into various floral kingdoms. Each of them is determined by a relatively uniform grouping of plant species distinguished by the species endemic to the region or subregion. The smallest, most peculiar and also the most diverse region is the Cape Floral Region on the southern tip of Africa, where 6,000 flowering plants, a high percentage of which are endemic, grow in the closest proximity to one another. The Cape Floral region and its 5,530 sq km (2,135 sq mi) of space make up 0.02 percent of Africa's total area but are home to twenty percent of its plant varieties. Foremost among them are 450 species of proteaceae and ericaceae, and the unique fynbos vegetation, a shrub that has adapted perfectly to the region's periodic bushfires. There are various refined strategies that promote seed dissemination and pollination by insects here, which continues to inspire the evolution of further species. The theory of adaptive radiation, whereby one species diversifies into several within a short period and adapts to fill specific ecological niches, has also provided insights into flowering plant evolution.

A sea of yellow daisies is typical of the southern tip of Africa.

RAINFORESTS OF THE ATSINANANA

Six separate national parks in eastern Madagascar have been grouped together under the heading "Rainforests of the Atsinanana", and they play an important part in the preservation of the island's biological diversity.

Madagascar has been separated from continental Africa for sixty million years. This extended period of isolation is responsible for both the evolution of new plant and animal species as well as the preservation of many ancient species. Madagascar and its associated island group is thus home to around 12,000 endemic plant species. The best-known animals are the lemurs – of the family once known as prosimians and now called strepsirrhines. Only Australia, thirteen times the size, has more indigenous species than Madagascar. Forests, especially rainforests, are the cradle of species diversity; unfortunately, only 8.5 percent of the former rainforest area of Madagascar now remains. The six areas of this World Heritage Site cover an area of about 5,000 sq km (1,900 sq mi) and include: Marojejy, Masoala, Zahamena, Ranomafana, Andringitra and Andohahela national parks. They are separate, but some of the parks are still connected by stretches of unprotected forest.

The Andringitra mountains are considered holy by the island's inhabitants.

TSINGY DE BEMARAHA STRICT NATURE RESERVE

Bizarre rock faces, undisturbed forests, majestic lakes and mangrove swamps are all components of this unique natural paradise, which is also home to many rare varieties of animals and plants.

The imposing karst landscape of the Bemaraha Plateau on the west coast of Madagascar lies at roughly the same latitude as the capital, Antananarivo. Its spectacular highlights include the Manambolo River Canyon and the bizarre Tsingy, a "forest" created by limestone formations. The undisturbed rainforests, lakes and mangrove swamps within the conservation area meanwhile provide a habitat for numerous orchid species. The Bemaraha Strict Nature Reserve's 1,500 sq km (580 sq mi) are particularly important as the habitat of the lemur, which occur in the wild almost exclusively on Madagascar. This prosimian species reached the island more than forty million years ago and discovered ideal living conditions. In fact, Madagascar's extremely remote location has led to the evolution of around forty different species of lemur, and the region is also home to numerous birds, bats, amphibians, and reptiles including geckos and chameleons.

The Tsingy limestone "forest" is home to many lemurs.

ROYAL HILL OF AMBOHIMANGA

The holy site of Ambohimanga, not far from the present capital of Antananarivo, is the cradle of the state of Madagascar and the heart of the Merina Kingdom.

Madagascar was settled early on by sailors from South-East Asia, Africa and Arabia. Starting in the 16th century, the Portuguese and the French quarreled over supremacy on the island before it became a French colony in 1896. Still, from the 16th to the 18th centuries, Madagascar was subdivided into several regional kingdoms until the Merina kings united the island at the end of the 18th century. The kings' residence is situated atop Ambohimanga Hill, meaning "Blue Hill". It is one of twelve sacred places in the vicinity. Among the historic sights in Ambohimanga are the royal swimming pool, the royal tombs, the Rova (royal palace) and the palace's citadel, which was built from rosewood. It is still used today for the ritual worship of ancestors and other traditional ceremonies. For the cultural identity of the Madagascans, the royal town of Ambohimanga is of an inestimable importance.

From the balustrade of the queens' summer palace in Ambohimanga visitors can enjoy superb views of the majestic surrounding region.

Mauritius

AAPRAVASI GHAT

The historic Aapravasi Ghat camp attests to the fate of more than half a million Indian contract laborers hired by the British Empire between 1834 and 1920 to work the sugar plantations on Mauritius.

The abolition of slavery in the colonies of Europe's states forced plantation owners around the world to look for newer sources of cheap labor. In 1834, the British government began what they called a "great experiment": They hired contract workers from India to replace the African slaves that had been working throughout the entire empire. This triggered one of the largest migrations in history, for which the island of Mauritius served as a staging post – on the one hand due to its proximity to India and on the other hand because of the emergence of its own plantation economy. The colonial authorities recruited workers who were forced to commit to several years and were in return given wages, housing and subsistence. Around seventy per cent of the 1.2 million inhabitants of Mauritius today are of Indian origin. The stone structures of Aapravasi Ghat in the capital, Port Louis, served as a transitional camp for the newly arrived workers and dates from the 1860s. The system of hiring contract labor marks the early beginnings of work-related migration and the globalization of the labor market.

Aapravasi Ghat was a camp for workers from the impoverished states of India.

LE MORNE CULTURAL LANDSCAPE

Le Morne Mountain rises to a dramatic 500 m (1,640 ft) directly above the Indian Ocean in the south-western corner of Mauritius. It is covered with tropical vegetation. The mountain is now a slavery memorial site and a symbol of the escaped slaves' struggle for freedom.

Under Dutch rule between 1721 and 1735, slaves were brought to Mauritius for the first time from Africa, Madagascar and Asia to work in the sugar cane plantations. Up until the abolition of slavery in 1835, many slaves managed to escape, and so entire communities of so-called maroons developed, escaped Africans and Asians. They hid on the barely accessible peaks of the Le Morne, establishing small settlements in the caves and rocky cliffs of the mountain. Mauritius, an important staging post for the eastern slave trade, thus gained the epithet of the "Maroon Republic", an island of escaped slaves. The history of the maroons was passed down orally and forms part of the cultural heritage of the population. Le Morne is a memorial to slavery as well as a symbol of the Creole identity of the island's people.

"Sega" is celebrated at the foot of Le Morne, a dance that stems from the days of slavery and is considered the quintessence of the national culture of Mauritius.

ALDABRA ATOLL

Inaccessible to the general public, these four islands form the world's largest coral atoll. Over 150,000 giant tortoises are the chief attraction on the western-most island chain of the Seychelles in the Indian Ocean.

Scattered amidst the turquoise-blue Indian Ocean, the Seychelles islands conform to most fantasies of a tropical paradise The four islands of the Aldabra Atoll include: Picard, Polymnia, Malabar and Grande Terre. Together they encircle a shallow lagoon and are themselves in turn surrounded by a coral reef. Due to its remote location, a completely natural environment has been allowed to develop here virtually untouched by human intervention.

The Aldabra Atoll, inscribed as a conservation area in 1976, is home to a diversity of flora and fauna that is astonishing for an oceanic island. It is a natural nesting place for numerous seabirds, but the atoll is best known for the population of Aldabra giant tortoises (Dipsochelys dussumieri), a species of Seychelles tortoise. These reptiles can reach weights of 250 kg (550 lb) and ages of 100 years. Green and hawksbill turtles can also be found here.

Arab seafarers named the remote atoll of the Seychelles al chadra, the "green islands", when they discovered them many centuries ago (below). The giant sea turtles that call this island chain home can be distinguished by their comparatively small heads.

VALLÉE DE MAI NATURE RESERVE

The home of the Seychelles palm is a high valley at the heart of the island of Praslin. This tree has the largest seed in the plant kingdom and lives for several hundred years.

Just north of the main island of Mahé is Praslin, the second-largest island in the Seychelles group. In 1966 the Vallée de Mai Nature Reserve was established within Praslin National Park, right at the heart of this granite island. This conservation area of only 20 hectares (49 acres) ensures the preservation of the Seychelles palm (Lodoicea maldivica), a living remnant of prehistoric vegetation.

Many prehistoric plant species have been saved here due to the long evolutionary isolation of the island group, but for a long time all that was known of these were the seeds of a plant known as coco de mer, which could weigh up to 18 kg (40 lb) and which the Portuguese navigator Ferdinand Magellan presumed to be the fruit of a tree growing in the depths of the sea.

The Vallée de Mai is also the habitat for a wealth of animal life. Various species of chameleon and gecko and many birds live here, including the endemic lesser Vasa parrot, the Seychelles cave swiftlet, the Seychelles black bulbul and hummingbirds.

The prehistoric forest and idyllic waterfalls of the Vallée de Mai were untouched until 1930, which ensured the preservation of this ancient biosphere.

This sculpture below depicts the wind god with a rattle and comes from Copán in Honduras. Copán was an important settlement and spiritual center of the Mayans that experienced its heyday in about 700. Right: The distinctive peak of Mount Assiniboine in the Canadian Rocky Mountains rises to 3,618 m (11,871 ft). It is also known as Canada's Matterhorn.

THE AMERICAS

KLUANE / WRANGELL-ST. ELIAS / GLACIER BAY / TATSHENSHINI-ALSEK

These transnational parks offer visitors a fascinating plethora of flora and fauna.

The first binational UNESCO World Heritage Site is made up of Kluane (in the Yukon Territory), Tatshenshini-Alsek (in British Columbia) and Wrangell-St Elias and Glacier Bay national parks (both in Alaska). It constitutes the largest inland nature reserve in the world and features massive ice fields, mighty glaciers, towering mountains, rushing waterfalls, roaring rivers, serene lakes and vast expanses of tundra and forest. Despite a climate typified by long winters, the local flora is astonishingly varied. Forested areas at elevations of 1,100 m (3,600 ft) boast betula, berry bushes, and deciduous and evergreen tree species including the impressive Sitka spruce, which reaches heights of up to 90 m (300 ft). Varieties of willow and mountain meadow grasses can be found at subalpine elevations of 1,100

Mount Huxley (3,828 m, 12,600 ft) is reflected in a small lake.

to 1,600 m (3,600 to 5,200 ft) while heather, wildflowers, lichen, bushes and cripple birch are characteristic of the alpine tundra between 1,600 and 2,000 m (5,200 and 6,600 ft). The diversity of the animal life is also impressive, with black, brown and grizzly bears patroling rivers teeming with fish while rare Dall sheep and mountain goats share the upper slopes. The national parks are home to 170 species of bird as well as red deer, wolves, red foxes, lynxes, muskrats, Arctic hares, gophers and chipmunks.

Two hundred years ago Glacier Bay was under a thick sheet of ice that has since retreated. Now a colorful array of flowers blossom here in springtime.

Kayak and canoe routes lead from the campground on Lake Kathleen into the interior of Kluane National Park.

Among the severely endangered and protected animals in the park is the mountain goat (Oreamnos americanus).

Walruses (Odobenus rosmarus) are the largest eared seals. They protect themselves from the frigid temperatures of Glacier Bay with a thick layer of blubber.

The two rivers Tatshenshini and Alsek (shown here at their confluence) give the national park its name.

Canada

NAHANNI NATIONAL PARK

The South Nahanni river – one of the world's wildest and most beautiful – gave this barely accessible national park its name.

The source of the 540-km-long (335-mi) South Nahanni river is 1,600 m (5,240 ft) above sea level on Mount Christie in the Mackenzie mountains of Canada's Northwest Territories. The national park area extends along both sides of the river as a narrow strip 320 km (200 mi) long that begins just south of Mount Wilson. The hot mineral springs in the area, including Rabbitkettle Hotsprings among others, ensure a mild zone that is home to vegetation that would otherwise be unusual for such northerly latitudes. A variety of ferns, wild mint, rosebushes, parsnips, goldenrod, asters and a number of orchids can be found here. The river itself meanders for 120 km (75 mi) through tundra overgrown

The mineral-rich water bubbling out of Rabbitkettle Hotsprings has formed bizarre sinter columns and terraces.

with grasses, lichen and dwarf shrubs that provide food for caribou, large North American reindeer with shovel-like antlers. Its course descends through numerous rapid sections that present considerable challenges to the many whitewater rafters.

With a drop of 90 m (295 ft), Virginia Falls is among the most impressive of the waterfalls here, and the three main canyons are similarly breathtaking with sheer walls rising to heights of 1,300 m (4,250 ft). Bizarre rock formations and caves are typical for this landscape as well. The South Nahanni river also flows past several imposing peaks that reach elevations of 2,700 m (8,300 ft) before it finally disperses into a number of distributaries not far from the southern end of the national park.

Caribous (top) and grizzly bears (right) are some of the spectacular animals that roam this stunning park along with the graceful moose.

WOOD BUFFALO NATIONAL PARK

Canada's largest nature reserve was established in 1922 to protect the last herds of wood buffalo.

The current bison population, including both wood bison and the equally endangered prairie bison, which has in many cases joined the greater herds, amounts to some 6,000 specimens, the world's largest group in the wild. The conservation area is divided into three habitats: a prairie upland cleared by forest fires; plateaus with meandering rivers, oxbow lakes, salt flats, marshes and bog areas; and the Peace and Athabasca river delta, an enchanting world of reed meadows, marshland and shallow lakes.
The park is also home to a number of other animals including moose, caribou, black bears, gray wolves, muskrats, beavers, minks, foxes, lynx, stoats and red squirrels. In addition, the delta is an ideal habitat for 227 species of birds. Over a million wild geese, swans and ducks inhabit the area including the acutely endangered whooping crane. The indigenous Cree, Chipewyan and Beaver peoples have adapted seamlessly with this ecosystem and their descendants still live here today.

Symbol of the prairie – the mighty bison grows to lengths of 3 m (10 ft) and can weigh up to 1 metric ton (2,200 lb).

SGANG GWAAY

The thirty-two totem poles and ten cedar long houses of Ninstints village on SGang Gwaay Island (Anthony Island), south of the Queen Charlotte Islands (Haida Gwaii) in British Columbia, attest to the ancient culture of the Haida Nation.

The Haida culture had already existed for thousands of years by the time the last inhabitants of Ninstints (the English version of the village named after its chief in the 19th century) abandoned the small island of SGang Gwaay in about 1880. At the time, diseases brought by the Europeans had seriously decimated this tribe, an indigenous people of the Pacific North-Western Coast of North America. Today only an estimated 2,000 Haida remain.
Beautifully carved and painted totem poles here display wonderful designs and often measure several meters in height. They tell of the history of this small but proud nation, which did not come into contact with Europeans until the end of the 18th century. Artisans created these poles to honor prominent tribe members. They depict scenes from everyday life, fabled animals and mythical figures. An opening was carved into the totem poles for the ashes of the deceased, and the tops of the poles feature the emblem of the respective clans.

Wind and weather have caused the originally bright paint of the totem poles to fade almost completely.

Canada

The Haida

Before white trappers "discovered" the Queen Charlotte Islands, around 8,000 Haida lived on the archipelago they called Haida Gwaii. They were organized in two clans. The Raven Clan was subdivided into twenty-two families while the Eagle Clan had twenty-three. Each family consisted of about forty members.

CANADIAN ROCKY MOUNTAINS

The four national parks of Banff, Jasper, Yoho and Kootenay were established to preserve the unique landscape of the Canadian Rocky Mountains along with its largely undisturbed biotope. This World Heritage Site has been expanded over the years to include the provincial parks of Mount Robson, Mount Assiniboine and Hamber.

The Canadian Rockies are a 2,200-km (1,400-mi) long section of what is known as the American Cordillera, which runs from north to south along the western "spine" of the Americas, from Alaska to Tierra del Fuego. The largest of the four national parks, Jasper, is also the most northerly and boasts a number of peaks over 3,000 m (9,900 ft), mighty Maligne Lake, which stretches over 20 km (13 mi), hot sulphur springs, and the largest continuous glacier field in the Rocky Mountains.

Banff National Park, which is traversed by the roughly 625-km-long (400-mi) Bow River, adjoins the park in the south and was founded back in 1855. Picturesque Lake Louise lies at the foot of the imposing 3,364-m (11,040-ft) high Mount Victoria glacier. To the west are Kootenay and Yoho National Parks where the waterfalls on the Yoho River are among the world's highest.

Mount Robson and Mount Assiniboine Provincial Parks owe their respective names to these two imposing peaks, each of which is nearly 4,000 m (13,200 ft) high. The Rocky Mountain parks, set amid impressive glaciers, primary forests, and raging torrents are an undisturbed habitat for many species that have become quite rare including grizzly bears, moose, mountain goats, lynxes, wolves, beavers and golden eagles.

Mount Robson, in the national park of the same name, rises to 3,954 m (12,970 ft), the highest mountain in the Canadian Rocky Mountains. The Native Americans call it Yuh-hai-has-hun, "the mountain of the spiral path".

Hunting and fishing grounds as well as the villages were passed down within a clan, as were certain legends and songs along with names and tattoo styles – Haida tattoos were the most lavish in North America. According to Haida beliefs, humankind was created by the raven, a cunning bird that picked the first humans from cockleshells he had found on the beach. He then flew into the realm of the god of the heavens and stole from him the sun, the moon and the stars. Raven is also said to have taught humans how to build houses, which he had gleaned from the beavers.

The Haida lived in solid wooden structures made of cedar wood, with a totem pole in front of each house. Summer was dedicated to hunting as well as whaling and fishing. They followed whales in giant canoes made from a single cedar trunk and in the forest they hunted game. The Haida were fearsome warriors who engaged their enemies in sea battles where their solid canoes were typically superior. They wore leather armor and helmets, built palisades and fortifications, and after the arrival of the white man they even equipped their canoes with sails.

The Haida were advanced in the art of mask making (left).

The Ramparts with their imposing rock faces in Banff National Park are a popular destination for climbers.

One of the highlights of Yoho National Park is the scenery along Kicking Horse River.

The summits of the Canadian Rocky Mountains reflect beautifully on the surface of Lake Herbert.

The numerous oligotrophic lakes in Kootenay National Park are part of the endangered ecosystem here.

Canada

HEAD-SMASHED-IN BUFFALO JUMP

In the Porcupine Hills of Alberta, a sandstone wall over 10 m (32 ft) tall recalls an unusual method of the bison hunt that was common with Native Americans.

Among the gently undulating hills of the prairie, entire herds of wild bison were driven toward the abyss by hunters brandishing spears. At great speed, the animals could not react to the danger in time and the momentum of the stampede pushed them over the cliff to their deaths. The bison were then carved up and whatever meat was not intended for immediate consumption was dried to preserve it. The skins were worked into garments and tents while the bones provided raw materials for weapons and everyday tools. So-called "buffalo jumps" also existed in other parts of North America but this was the largest and oldest of its kind. The method actually remained common until the introduction of rifles; allegedly the last jump took place here in 1850.

Local finds have provided valuable insights for archaeologists into the life of Native Americans since 3600 BC. They include traces of marked trails, a Native American camp and a burial mound with large numbers of bison skeletons.

The rock cliff over which Native American hunters once drove herds of bison is near Fort Macleod in south-western Alberta.

DINOSAUR PROVINCIAL PARK

Seventy-five million years ago giant reptiles roamed the area that is now Dinosaur Provincial Park, a bizarre landscape on the Red Deer river in Alberta.

During the Cretaceous period, roughly seventy-five million years ago, a variety of dinosaur species inhabited North America. Some of the particularly well-developed Triceratops specimens actually reached heights of around 15 m (50 ft), although they died out along with the other dinosaur species at the end of the Mesozoic period. No other region on earth possesses greater deposits of these giant reptilian creatures.

The numerous fossils here include those of turtles, fish, various mammals and other amphibians and afford scientists fascinating insight into the animal world of 200 million years ago. The exciting finds can be viewed in the park museum. The area itself also has its scenic charms including the Badlands, a barren erosion zone where the power of wind and weather has transformed the sandstone into an otherworldly landscape. The river banks feature dense vegetation despite the desert-like climate, and this provides an optimal habitat not just for a few species of red deer but also for a variety of birds including curlews, Canada geese and nighthawks.

The loamy soil of the Canadian Badlands in south-eastern Alberta led to a barren, eroded landscape formed by wind and weathering. Seventy-five-million-year-old dinosaur fossils have been found here.

L'ANSE AUX MEADOWS NATIONAL HISTORIC SITE

A Viking village on the island of Newfoundland is some 1,000 years old and was the first settlement founded by Europeans in North America – long before Columbus arrived.

In the lore of the far north there has always been talk about the legendary journeys of the Norse adventurer Leif Eriksson. His explorations to the myth-enshrouded "Vinland" were finally verified in 1960 when scientific proof was found for the early Atlantic crossings by Scandinavian seafarers. Near L'Anse aux Meadows on Newfoundland Island, archaeologists Helge and Anne Stine Ingstad discovered remains of a Viking settlement established and occupied as early as the beginning of the 11th century. In fact, the site looks similar to Viking villages in Iceland and Greenland. Three of eight excavated houses have now been reconstructed. Together with some tools that were found they conjure up an image of the hard life led by the first Europeans here, who probably left after only a few years. The inhospitable climate and the hostile attitude of the native population drove them from their hoped-for paradise in Newfoundland.

Vast dwellings – now overgrown with grass – attest to the presence of the first Vikings in North America.

GROS MORNE NATIONAL PARK

Over 4,500 years ago the Dorset Eskimos settled in the diverse landscape along the west coast of Newfoundland. It would later become the site of Gros Morne National Park – long before the Vikings became the first Europeans to land here.

This national park takes its name from the 806-m (2,650-ft) high Gros Morne headland; adjoining this "great hill" is also a 600-m (1,970-ft) high limestone plateau that sets the tone for the area with meandering streams, moor lakes and moraines. The subarctic climate has given rise to tundra vegetation that is not found this far south anywhere else in the world. Caribou, grouse, Arctic hares, Arctic foxes and lynxes can all be found here.

The Long Range mountains, whose rock formations have yielded valuable geological discoveries, are of particular interest to scientists. Gros Morne National Park's picturesque fjords

Moose live on water lilies and other water plants in the park.

were formed during the last ice age and Western Brook Pond, an enclosed fjord lake surrounded by walls up to 600 m (1,970 ft) high is an incredible natural spectacle. The coastal region is characterized by steep cliffs, shifting dunes and a great variety of wild birds who derive as much benefit from the teeming waters as the seals.

Archaeological finds have shown that there were settlements on the site of the modern park as early as 2500 BC. The Dorset Eskimos were followed in around AD 800 by the Beothuk Native Americans, who were given the name "redskins" by Europeans because of the red-ochre body paint, which they also used to paint their houses and possessions. There is much to suggest that this culture had contact with the Vikings, including some suspicion that so-called "blond Indians" were the result of intermarriage.

Gros Morne National Park is characterized by deep fjords, stony coastlines and deserted beaches.

Canada

MIGUASHA NATIONAL PARK

Miguasha National Park is home to the most significant Devonian fossils in the world including the lobe-finned fish, predecessor to the first four-legged vertebrates.

Located on the south coast of the Gaspésie Peninsula in south-eastern Québec Province, this area was first studied in 1842 by German-Canadian doctor, physicist and geologist Abraham Gesner (1797–1864). It is named for the color of its rock formations which, in the language of the Native American Mic-Mac tribe, are referred to as "miguasha", or reddish.

In 1985, Miguasha and the steep cliffs of the 350- to 375-million-year-old Escuminac rock formation were declared a conservation park, and since then some 5,000 fossils have been identified, conserved and recorded on computer including vertebrates,

invertebrates, plants and spores from the Devonian period. One of the best-known finds is the "Prince of Miguasha", a fossilized Eusthenopteron, an extinct lobe-finned fish species that lived during the Upper Devonian, about 370 million years ago. The creature's gills, rudimentary lungs and a strong endoskeleton likely allowed it to leave the water for short periods. Precursors of the humerus, ulna and radius of later land vertebrates can be seen in the fore-fins.

Fossilized remains of five of six fish classes that lived during the Upper Devonian have been found here (right).

HISTORIC DISTRICT OF OLD QUÉBEC

The first French town to be founded in the "New World" has retained the feel of an 18th-century European city until today.

The capital of Québec Province is the heart of Francophone Canada: more than ninety per cent of its inhabitants are French speakers. The settlement, founded in 1608 on the shores of the Saint Lawrence River, developed rapidly into a major transshipment hub for trade between the New World and the French motherland.

After the houses below Cap Diamant had suffered from fires on too many occasions, the citizens withdrew to the knoll and built the "Haute-Ville", or Upper Town. The Place Royale and the Rue Notre-Dame form the heart of the Lower Town with its lovingly restored houses from the founding

period. Churches, military buildings, monasteries and schools were then concentrated in the fortified Upper Town. During the French and Indian war, the town came under possession from both sides several times until ultimately the British prevailed. In the period that followed, defenses were built to prevent possible attack by the US army. The fortifications are unique in North America.

A gem in the Lower Town is the Place Royale (above), which has been faithfully restored. Québec's emblem is the Château Frontenac from 1892 (right), named after a French governor.

RIDEAU CANAL

The Rideau Canal between Ottawa and Kingston on Lake Ontario is the only artificial waterway in North America from the 19th century that is still in use today; most of its original structures are intact as well.

The British Royal Engineers Corps began construction on this impressive canal in 1828 and finished it within just four years. The main reason for its rapid completion was that instead of digging the entire canal they built dams that backed up the water of the Rideau and Cataraqui rivers. In doing so, a chain of dammed sections were formed and then linked with one another by a series of fifty locks. In between were a series of lakes that served as reservoirs.

At vulnerable points in the waterway, defensive installations were erected, so-called blockhouses. Fort Henry, for example, guards the east side of the

port of Kingston. After rebellions in the British colony, fortified guardhouses also had to be built for the lock keepers.

The roughly 200-km-long (124-mi) canal initially served military purposes that helped control the northern part of North America. As early as the mid-1800s it had lost its strategic importance, however, and became a major transport route for tapping the virtually untouched interior.

About fifty locks, some of which are operated manually, overcome the elevation differences on the canal. Left: A lock below Capital Hill.

JOGGINS FOSSIL CLIFFS

Joggins Fossil Cliffs in the Canadian province of Nova Scotia are famous for their wealth of prehistoric finds. The cliffs and their roughly 300 million-year-old fossils are the most significant source of remains from the Carboniferous period.

In 1851, Canadian geologist Sir William Dawson discovered the first fossilized specimens of Hylonomus here, an extinct reptile species that measured about 20 cm (8 in) in length and was one of the first creatures to adapt fully to life on land. English naturalist Charles Darwin, founder of the modern theory of evolution, even used finds from Joggins to develop his revolutionary scientific principles.

The area of particular paleontological interest covers about 7 sq km (2 sq mi) along the coast of the Bay of Fundy in Nova Scotia where fossilized rain forest tree stumps, reptile fossils and specimens of the earliest amniotes

(egg-laying vertebrates) have been found from the Carboniferous period – 354 to 290 million years ago. No site in the world yields such evidence of life on land for that period. The 15 km (9 mi) of cliffs, rocky plateaus and beaches contain fossilized traces of three ecosystems: an estuary, a floodplain covered in rain forest, and a marshy plain with freshwater pools.

Thanks to erosion caused by one of the most dramatic tidal ranges in the world – up to 15 m (50 ft) – fossilized tree stumps and reptiles (left) were discovered on Joggins Fossil Cliffs.

OLD TOWN LUNENBURG

The superbly preserved Old Town of Lunenburg is a great example of a the colonial settlements built under British rule in North America.

The German name of this town is no accident. Founded in 1753 on the south coast of Nova Scotia, the village named after the German town of Lüneburg was originally established by 1,453 mainly German-speaking settlers who found the conditions here ideal. The densely forested peninsula provided a plentiful supply of timber, the sea ensured rich fishing yields and the fertile soil was ideally suited for agriculture. The geometric layout of the settlement, as if designed on a drawing board, conformed with British colonial regulations stipulating straight roads and rectangular plazas. At least twenty-one North American villages complied with this model, but

nowhere can the old structure be seen as clearly as in Lunenburg. Of the 400 or so historic buildings in the Old Town, seventy per cent date from the 18th and 19th centuries. More than ninety-five per cent of these were wooden and many were painted in bright colors. Although the settlers worked mainly as farmers in their native lands, they soon proved themselves successful fishermen and shipbuilders. As a result, the town quickly flourished as a center of trade.

Wooden houses from the colonial period still give Lunenburg its characteristic feel. Among them is the Zion Evangelical Lutheran Church of 1891 (left).

WATERTON-GLACIER INTERNATIONAL PEACE PARK

Glacier National Park in the United States and Waterton Lakes National Park in Canada were merged in 1932 to form the first "International Peace Park" in the world.

Waterton-Glacier International Peace Park was a joint undertaking of the Rotary Clubs of Alberta (Canada) and Montana (USA). It was established on 30 June 1932 as a "sign of peace and goodwill between Canada, the USA and a confederation of Blackfoot Indians". The Peace Park is situated on the Alberta–Montana border and features remote mountain valleys, windswept peaks and stunning fairy-tale scenery with some 650 lakes and a wealth of flora and fauna. More than 1,200 varieties of plants and sixty mammal, 240 bird, and twenty fish species inhabit the alpine meadows, prairies and taiga forests here. Over 200 archaeological excavation sites have also yielded information

The Prince of Wales Hotel's location affords a wonderful view of the magnificent mountain panorama.

about the living conditions of the park's primeval inhabitants, who were already present as far back as 8,000 years ago – obviously long before the first European fur trappers turned up in the area at the beginning of the 18th century. Over the course of the 19th century, prospectors, adventurers and settlers forced the Native Americans out onto reservations created by the government to exert control over their populations.

The majestic peaks of the Rockies reflect beautifully on the surface of calm lakes in Glacier National Park. Right: The pyramid-shape of Mount Grinnell on the shore of Swiftcurrent Lake.

Double Falls is an unusual natural phenomenon with two opposing waterfalls just yards apart from each other.

The remote valleys of the Peace Park, Waterton Lakes National Park (founded in 1895) and Glacier National Park (founded in 1910), are home to a variety of animals including bighorn sheep, which are ubiquitous in the Rockies, wolves, gophers, cougars and lynxes.

After a period of near extermination in the park, timberwolves have managed to fight back and create at least small packs in this remote region.

United States of America

OLYMPIC NATIONAL PARK

The most striking aspect of this national park situated in north-west Washington State is the temperate rain forest full of moss-covered trees.

Olympic National Park, which covers much of the Olympic Peninsula west of Seattle, is hemmed in by the Pacific Ocean to the west, the Strait of Juan de Fuca to the north and Puget Sound to the east. Its geographic location has created a unique biosphere with coniferous trees (firs, spruce and cedar) growing in the damp primeval forest. Their trunks often have circumferences of 7 m (22 ft) while some specimens can be much larger still; "Sitka Spruce" has a girth of nearly 30 m (66 ft) and is the record holder here. Thirteen plant species, mostly wild flowers, are also endemic to the region, which is divided into three ecological zones. Douglas, hemlock and giant fir, Sitka spruce, bigleaf maple and western red cedar make up a rain forest that is home to elks, pumas, black bears and beavers. The almost circular cluster of the Olympic mountains in the park's interior forms a glaciated landscape of exquisite beauty. Eleven river systems rise here and create an ideal biotope for salt and freshwater fish. The roughly 100 km (330 mi) of Pacific coast is a habitat for mussels, crabs, sea urchins and many seabirds. Gray whales also pass by on their annual migrations.

The moss-covered trees and branches of the temperate rain forest in Olympic National Park have an enchanting effect.

YELLOWSTONE NATIONAL PARK

The world's oldest national park is a majestic landscape of mountains, rivers and lakes as well as more than 3,000 geysers. Approximately ninety-six percent of its total area (around 9,000 sq. km, 3,500 sq mi) is in Wyoming, three percent in Montana and one percent in Idaho.

The heart of this national park is the 2,000-m-high (6,600-ft) Yellowstone plateau, a formation surrounded by mountains that rise up to 4,000 m (13,200 ft). The volcanic origin of this landscape is still visible and petrified forests bear witness to the streams of lava and ash rain that flowed through this region some 60,000 years ago. Indeed, the earth has not yet come to rest here, as is evident in the many hot springs, fumaroles and geysers. Of these, Old Faithful is the most famous, firing a stream of water 60 m (200 ft) high into the air roughly every hour. Spring pools with multi-colored boiling water, bursting mud bubbles, and hot steam shooting from rock fissures attest to the forces that are still at work beneath the earth's surface.

This World Heritage Site, which was founded in 1872 and named after the yellow rock forming the banks of the Yellowstone river, is home to a variety of animals as well, with the grizzly bear reigning supreme but also featuring wolves, bison and elk, a North American stag with great antlers.

The waterfalls (above, Upper Falls) and geysers of Yellowstone display the natural forces at work here. The Grand Prismatic spring (right) gets its bright coloration from microorganisms.

REDWOOD NATIONAL PARK

The largest plants in the world are sequoias, or redwood trees, after which this World Heritage Site on the north coast of California is named.

The coastal redwood (Sequoia sempervirens) is an evergreen conifer that was once widespread throughout North America. Today there are only a few patches of these primeval giants remaining on the American West Coast. These majestic trees can reach 100 m (330 ft) in height and are now protected in a number of state parks, three of which – Jedediah Smith, Del Norte Coast Redwoods and Prairie Creek Redwoods – were combined in 1968 to form Redwood National Park in northern California. About one-third of the park's area (446 sq km, 160 sq mi) consists of sequoia forest. The Tall Trees Grove near Orick has the largest specimens, the star of these being the "Nugget Tree", the tallest in the world with a height of 111 m (365 ft). The imposing trees regularly reach 500 to 700 years of age and some have been around for 2,000 years. Other giants grow at the higher elevations including Sitka spruce, Douglas and hemlock fir, bigleaf maple and Californian laurel. Seals, sea lions and a variety of seabirds also live on the Pacific coast with pumas, skunks, Roosevelt elks, white-tailed deer, gray foxes, black bears, otters and beavers.

The last remaining redwoods on the Pacific coast were saved from logging in 1968 with the declaration of a national park (below). Rare birds such as the Virginia Owl (left) also find refuge here.

YOSEMITE NATIONAL PARK

The mountainous scenery of this World Heritage Site in eastern California encompasses vast coniferous forests and crystal-clear glacial lakes. It is one of the most impressive creations of the Ice Age.

Yosemite National Park in the Sierra Nevada Mountains is among the most celebrated granite plateaus in the world. This landscape of stunning valleys, dramatic peaks, glacial lakes and waterfalls was carved out by ice-age glaciers. Imposing monoliths jut out from the Merced River valley with Half Dome, the park's iconic peak, a particularly impressive example at 2,700 m (8,900 ft). There is a concentration of waterfalls here that is rare in the world as well. At 740 m (2,440 ft), Yosemite Falls are the second-highest in America, but there is a plethora of equally imposing natural spectacles of this kind here.

There is a wide variety of vegetation as well. As many as thirty-seven tree species have been recorded, including some 3,000-year-old giant sequoias, and the mountain meadows possess a great number of herbs and wildflowers. Although grizzly bears and wolves have not managed to survive here, there are still black bears, pumas, chipmunks, squirrels, fisher martens, black-tailed deer, pikas, wolverines and many species of bird in the park.

The 2,700-m-high (8,900-ft) Half Dome at the eastern end of the valley represents a challenge for climbers.

United States of America

GRAND CANYON NATIONAL PARK

This bewilderingly colossal formation cut into the stone by the Colorado river over the course of millions of years affords visitors an impressive glimpse into the earth's history. The Grand Canyon in north-western Arizona is certainly one of the most spectacular chasms in the world.

Although Garcia López de Cárdenas of Spain was the first European to lay eyes on the magnificent spectacle of the Grand Canyon in 1540, the area was not properly mapped until the middle of the 19th century. The Grand Canyon's geohistory is still scientifically disputed, however. Some conjecture that the river began seeking a path about six million years ago across the rocky plateau, which over time was transformed into this unique chasm that naturalist John Muir called the "greatest of God's earthly places". Wind and weather also contributed to the bizarre formations on the rocky walls where the sequence of strata is easily discernible and clearly documents the different periods of geological history. Fossils found here afford insight into life in prehistoric times.

Only the hardiest of plants and animals are able to survive the temperatures of up to 50° C in the canyon. They include various cactuses, thornbushes, rattlesnakes, black widows and scorpions. Because of the extreme conditions, the river is a habitat for very few species of fish, but iguanas, toads and frogs live on the banks of the river. In some locations even beavers and otters survive. Only the forests on the northern and southern edges offer a viable habitat for a large variety of flora and fauna.

Numerous finds here attest to a history of human settlement in the Grand Canyon going back some 4,000 years. The most impressive are the cliff dwellings of the Anasazi, which are thousands of years old. Among the Native Americans still living here are the Hulapai, who are responsible for the Grand Canyon's latest attraction, the "Grand Canyon Skywalk", which offers visitors the chance to "hover" over the canyon floor at a height of 1,200 m (3,900 ft) while standing on a horseshoe-shaped steel bridge with a glass floor and walls.

The Colorado river winds for 450 km (280 mi) through this gorge, which is up to 1,500 m (4,900 ft) deep and varies in width between 5.5 km (4 mi) and 30 km (19 mi). At Horseshoe Bend the river curves in a shape that gave it its name.

CHACO CULTURE

This World Heritage Site is located in north-western New Mexico and consists of the Chaco Culture National Historical Park combined with Chaco Canyon, Aztec Ruins National Monument and some smaller excavation sites.

The term "Chaco Culture" refers to the heyday of a people often referred to as the Anasazi but whose descendants prefer to be called the Ancient Pueblo Peoples. They were a culture of simple farmers that lived mostly in multi-level housing complexes known as pueblos. Between 850 and 1250, their spiritual and cultural center was located in Chaco Canyon, where they established monumental dwellings connected with each other by small streets. Characteristic for this type of settlement are the so-called "cliff dwellings" – houses built into the natural overhanging rocks. In Chaco Canyon there are twelve large pueblos and numerous smaller settlements that altogether provided housing for a total of 6,000 to 10,000 people. "Pithouses" are round and oval buildings that are half-sunk into the ground; "kivas" are the round ceremonial structures with a diameter of up to 22 m (72 ft). The best-known settlement is Pueblo Bonito, which features thirty-six kivas and 800 rooms on four levels. The Golden Age of this culture ended mysteriously in about 1300 – likely due to drought.

In Pueblo Arroyo, kivas can be admired, the circular cult sites of the prehistoric Ancient Pueblo Peoples.

MESA VERDE NATIONAL PARK

These rock dwellings in south-western Colorado were created between the sixth and the 12th centuries and are unique in terms of their number and condition.

The oldest and best-preserved ruins of the Ancient Pueblo Peoples are found on the elongated Mesa Verde ("Green Table") at an elevation of 2,600 m (8,531 ft). The area was declared a national park back in 1906. Archaeologists have discovered and restored entire villages in the canyons and rock recesses. Many houses were built straight into the rock, some in quite extreme positions, which likely indicates a protective stance against enemy tribes in the area.

Of the 4,600 or so ruin sites in the national park, many have been kept in excellent condition. The best-known is the four-level Cliff Palace whose 220 rooms and twenty-three "kivas", or ceremonial structures, accommodated more than 200 residents; the Long House in Rock Canyon with its 181 rooms and fifteen kivas; and Spruce Tree House, which was built for about 110 occupants and featured 114 rooms and eight kivas. The complex was first discovered by white people in the winter of 1888, when two cowboys happened upon the walls of the Cliff Palace during their search for stray cattle.

These rock houses are visible evidence of the skills developed by the Ancient Puebloans in building solid dwellings in an inhospitable environment. Their culture disappeared mysteriously.

PUEBLO DE TAOS

Pueblo de Taos is a settlement situated on a tributary of the Rio Grande that has been inhabited exclusively by the Tiwa people for more than 700 years. The well-preserved adobe dwellings are impressive testimony to the persistence of pueblo culture.

The oldest structure in Taos Pueblo in northern New Mexico dates back to the founding days of the village at the end of the 13th century. The preferred building material of the pueblo people has always been air-dried mud bricks known more commonly as adobe. The ceilings were made with wooden beams combined with wattle and daub. Three kivas are constructed for each main building and traditional ceremonies are still performed here today (despite many Puebloans having converted to Catholicism). Originally, the block-shaped living units of the two multi-level, maze-like central buildings in the pueblo could be accessed from outside only by rope ladders or roof hatches. Other Ancient Pueblo Peoples from the surrounding areas also used to gather here in order to exchange meat and furs for foodstuffs and textiles from the bustling pueblo.

The Pueblo People bake their bread in cleverly domed adobe ovens (above). The fortress-like complex of Pueblo de Taos reveals that the encounters between different groups of Pueblo Peoples was not always amicable.

CARLSBAD CAVERNS NATIONAL PARK

Near the small town of Carlsbad in south-eastern New Mexico there is a complicated labyrinth of bizarre limestone caves that fascinates scientists and tourists alike.

At first glance, the desert and forest scenery around the Guadalupe mountains might be less than exhilirating, but the actual charms of Carlsbad Caverns National Park's 200 sq km (75 sq mi) are hidden below the surface in an extensive cave system. Millions of years ago, the effects of water and sulphides began hollowing out a subterranean reef dating back to the Permian era and ultimately creating giant cracks, fissures and chambers – the modern-day Carlsbad Caverns. More than eighty caves have been discovered so far, of which the Lechuguilla Cave is both the deepest at 477 m (1,600 ft) and the longest at 133 km (83 mi). Hundreds and thousands of bats sleep in the Bat Cave, and rock art from the time before Columbus has also been found. The New Cave features a fascinating array of stalagmites and stalactites, but there are many natural wonders still to be discovered in this fantastic fairy-tale cave world.

Over millions of years, deposits of lime have created impressive stalagmites and stalactites in the Carlsbad Caverns.

United States of America

STATUE OF LIBERTY

For more than 120 years, Lady Liberty has greeted those arriving by ship at the entrance to the harbor of New York City. For millions of immigrants she has represented the symbol of hope for a new life of opportunity.

At a dinner party in Paris in 1865, political activist Édouard René Lefebvre de Laboulaye and sculptor Frédéric-Auguste Bartholdi fulminated against the rule of Napoleon III. In an effort to annoy the self-important despot they came up with the idea of giving a statue to the Americans. The Colossus of Rhodes ultimately became the model for the lady, who was then dismantled and shipped to America in several boxes. On October 28, 1886, the Statue of Liberty was unveiled in New York Harbor, much to the delight of President Grover Cleveland, who delivered the festive inauguration speech. The dimensions of the statue in New York are far from those of the original model, however: 46 m (152 ft) high; circumference of the head (from ear to ear) 3 m (10 ft); length of index finger 2.44 m (8 ft); and length of the nose 1.4 m (4.5 ft). A steel frame by Gustave Eiffel is concealed under her robes and the concrete foundation weighs 27,000 tons. She stands on the broken chains of slavery holding a tableau with the date of the American Declaration of Independence (July 4, 1776) in her left hand.

The Statue of Liberty greets visitors to New York on Liberty Island, south-west of the southern tip of Manhattan.

INDEPENDENCE HALL

Both the Declaration of Independence and the Constitution of the United States were signed in this red-brick building in Philadelphia – birth certificates of the new land and indispensable foundations of freedom and democracy.

"We hold these truths to be self-evident, that all men are created equal, that they are endowed by their Creator with certain inalienable Rights, that among these are Life, Liberty and the pursuit of Happiness." With this Declaration of Independence of the United States of America, formulated by Thomas Jefferson, world history was written in a two-story building on Chestnut Street in Philadelphia on July 4, 1776. With its signing, the thirteen colonies officially ceded from the British empire. In 1787, the "Founding Fathers" then adopted the Constitution here in Independence Hall.

The struggle for independence had actually begun with the convention of the First Continental Congress in Carpenters' Hall in 1774. The most popular symbol of this struggle for freedom is the Liberty Bell, which hangs today in the Liberty Bell Center on Market Street in Philadelphia. Philadelphia was only the capital of the young association of states until 1790.

Built in the Georgian style in 1753 as Pennsylvania State House, Independence Hall became the birthplace of the United States in 1776.

CAHOKIA MOUNDS STATE HISTORIC SITE

The earthen mounds of Cahokia in south-western Illinois are impressive testimonies to a sophisticated culture that was all but forgotten by history.

North-east of St Louis, archaeologists found traces of the largest ancient indigenous settlement north of Mexico. In its heyday, roughly between 1050 and 1150, some 10,000 to 20,000 people might have lived here. The 120 artificial earth mounds served either as burial places or were built as terraced foundations for residential structures. A fortification wall even protected them from any outside threats while the center of the settlement was additionally fortified with palisades. Around the complex were numerous villages and satellite towns. The largest of the rises, Monk's Mound, covers about 5 ha (12 acres) and is more than 30 m (98 ft) high – the largest indigenous structure north of Mexico. We can only speculate about the everyday life of this culture, but their society was evidently highly developed and hierarchically structured. They were engaged in productive agriculture and at the top was a paramount chief who called himself the "Great Sun".

The vast extent of Monk's Mound can be seen from the air. It was presumably used as a ceremonial site and served as the center of a settlement.

MONTICELLO AND THE UNIVERSITY OF VIRGINIA IN CHARLOTTESVILLE

Thomas Jefferson was not only the architect of the Declaration of Independence but also an active master-builder in the literal sense.

Apparently, Jefferson's wide-ranging political activities included governor of Virginia, ambassador to France, foreign minister, vice-president and president, but that apparently was not enough to satisfy this multi-talented character, so he tried his hand successfully at designing his own estate: Monticello. Built to his own plans, the plantation home near Charlottesville in Virginia was inspired by the Villa Capra in Vicenza, Italy, built by Andrea Palladio in the 16th century. Roman neoclassicism had finally made its way even to Virginia. The path to the mansion with its octagonal dome leads through a park and the interior furnishings are very functional. The seat of the University of Virginia was also designed by Jefferson. The main building is a rotunda modeled on the Roman Pantheon around which the academic and residential buildings of the campus are grouped.

With its neo-Palladian style, the Monticello country estate represents a piece of the Old World within the New.

MAMMOTH CAVE NATIONAL PARK

Mammoth Cave is the world's largest and most convoluted cave system. Its tunnels are a habitat for more than 200 species.

The karst scenery on the banks of the Green River in Kentucky is not spectacular at first glance. Its charm lies beneath the ground, where a network of tunnels that would take days to discover leads visitors through a bizarre world of limestone formations created over millions of years by dripping water. These giant chambers, with their impressive stalagmites and stalactites, were formed from crystallized layers of calcium carbonate over 300 million years, starting in the Carboniferous period. Water slowly penetrated the porous stratum of sandstone to reach the layer of limestone beneath, after which chemical processes created hollow spaces that dried out as the water table dropped. Water with high mineral content then dripped through the cave forming columns of calcite deposits. The enormous caves are a habitat for extraordinary creatures such as the blind cave fish, the Kentucky cave crab and the cave cricket. Various salamander and frog species also live here, and the caves are an important refuge for several endangered species of bat.

A spotlight reveals the dimensions of the underground scenery.

GREAT SMOKY MOUNTAINS NATIONAL PARK

The establishment of this breathtakingly beautiful national park in the southern Appalachians of North Carolina and Tennessee saved a primeval forest landscape with an incomparably varied biotope.

This national park is best known for the gentle mists that frequently shroud the mountains; it looks like smoke, hence the park's name. This high level of humidity is a result of lush vegetation and high precipitation. The enormous area, which was inscribed as a national park as early as 1934, has sixteen peaks that are higher than 1,800 m (5,950 ft), a plethora of beautiful mountain streams and rivers with a total length of 3,000 km (1,850 mi), and numerous waterfalls. Roughly 130 species of deciduous and coniferous trees can be found in the primeval forest that makes up one-third of the total area along with a wealth of shrubs, lichens, mosses and fungi. The animal life is similarly diverse and includes black bears and white-tailed deer as well as many species of birds and reptiles.

This national park contains some of the most beautiful deciduous forests in the Americas.

United States of America

EVERGLADES NATIONAL PARK

In southern Florida, mangrove forests and marshlands overgrown with seagrass form a unique ecosystem in which a fascinating variety of plants and animals thrive.

Everglades National Park was established in 1947 and is the only subtropical conservation area in North America. Covering an area of roughly 6,100 sq km (2,355 sq mi), this park includes the southern portion of the Everglades, a diluvian swamp landscape where a fascinating biotope has evolved due to the constant shift between rainy and dry seasons: brackish water zones; keys (small islands); the coastal zones with yuccas, agaves and cactuses; mixed zones of salt and freshwater with the famous mangrove swamps; cypress swamps with the true Everglades (vast expanses of sedge); hammocks (limestone islands

The Everglades are a paradise for birds like this great blue heron.

with trees on them); and pine groves. Amidst this diversity it is no wonder that the animals living here represent such a large variety of species. Among them are the Florida panther, various dophins, sea cows (manatees), sea turtles, snakes, aligators, crocodiles, pelicans and cormorants. Along the coast, the dense mangroves are home to countless microorganisms, amphibians, snails and fish. Overall, the Everglades boast over 1,000 plant and 700 animal species. Unfortunately, however, this biodiversity is under immense pressure due to increased demand for drinking water in nearby cities, growing agriculture areas and expanding fishing grounds.

Swamp cypresses (above) grow vertically out of the water but form horizontal roots to take in oxygen. The Everglades' marshland and waters provide ideal living conditions for otherwise endangered animals such as the snowy egret (middle) or the Mississippi alligator (below).

LA FORTALEZA AND SAN JUAN NATIONAL HISTORIC SITE IN PUERTO RICO

San Juan is the capital of Puerto Rico, an unincorporated island territory of the United States in the Caribbean. This picturesque town is surrounded by massive ramparts and was considered impenetrable for hundreds of years.

The powerful fortifications betray the importance that Spain placed on the port and city of San Juan. Visible from a distance, they jut out into the sea from the tip of the island and dominate the harbor entrance with their 40-m-high (131-ft) walls. The impressive complex consists of four parts. The first, La Fortaleza or "Palacio de Santa Catalina", has been the seat of the Governor of Puerto Rico since 1822. Fort San Felipe del Morro (1539) was built at the harbor entrance and is the most conspicuous part of the entire complex. San Juan de la Cruz (1606) was strategically placed before Fort San Felipe del Morro. The fourth, San Cristóbal (1634), defended the citadel from attacks from the interior. Despite these efforts, however, Puerto Rico passed without a struggle to the United States in 1898, at the end of the Spanish-American War.

Fort San Felipe del Morro guards the entrance to the harbor of San Juan (left).

HAWAII VOLCANOES NATIONAL PARK

Nowhere else on earth can volcanic activity be better observed than on Hawaii's "Big Island". Two of the most active volcanoes on earth are part of Hawaii Volcanoes National Park, and to this day lava is still forcing its way to the surface from the depths of the earth.

The landscape of the main island's south-eastern coast is in constant upheaval due to the eruptions of the Mauna Loa (4,170 m, 13,680 ft) and Kilauea (1,250 m, 4,100 ft) volcanoes. At relatively short intervals these two active giants release measurable quantities of red-hot lava that then flow down to the sea where it cools in clouds of steam. This process has increased the area of the island by 81 hectares (200 acres) in just the last thirty years. Local religion explains the eruptions as manifestations of the moods of the goddess of fire, Pele. For geologists, the eruptions are not just an impressive natural spectacle, but also the object of intensive study. Mauna Loa, for example, has been created by layer upon layer of cooled lava. The slopes of the more active Kilauea meanwhile provide insight into the various forms taken by volcanic vegetation.

Kilauea spilling lava into the ocean (left). Local lore says that when lava flows, Pele, the goddess of fire, is angry.

Mexico

ARCHAEOLOGICAL ZONE OF PAQUIMÉ, CASAS GRANDES

The pre-Hispanic ruins in the federal state of Chihuahua in northern Mexico are something of an enigma to archaeologists. Having reached its zenith in the 14th and 15th centuries, the settlement was suddenly abandoned just prior to the arrival of the Spanish conquistadors.

These ruins cover 60 ha (148 acres) along the west bank of the Casas Grandes River. Their former inhabitants belonged to an Oasisamerican culture ("Oasisamérica") that also once lived in the present-day states of New Mexico and Arizona. Ceramic finds indicate that there must have been intimate links with the Mogollon culture of northern Mexico and the south-western United States. The buildings there and in Paquimé had several stories and were made from air-dried clay bricks (adobe).

As one of the most important interfaces between northern and southern Mesoamerican cultures, Paquimé's late period architecture was clearly influenced by Toltec constructions. By the time the Spanish conquistadors had overrun Mexico in the 16th century the settlement had already been abandoned, but the reasons for the culture's demise are still unclear.

The cuboid constructions are easily discernible in the archaeological site of Paquimé in Casas Grandes.

EL VIZCAÍNO WHALE SANCTUARY

Every year the coastal waters of this marine sanctuary play host to pods of whales both mating and giving birth to their calves. Blue whales and humpbacks as well as seals, sea lions and elephant seals all make appearances in these warm and safe environs.

Along with a series of other bays and inlets, the lagoons of Ojo de Liebre and San Ignacio form a unique marine habitat that begins about halfway down the Baja California peninsula in Mexico and stretches all the way down the Pacific coast. Between December and March, these comparatively warm waters teem with gray whales who come here to mate as well as give birth and raise their young after working their way across 8,000 km (5,000 mi) of ocean from their summer home in the cold

Bering Sea. In fact, almost half of the world's population of gray whales is born in the waters of Baja California. What's more, five of the world's seven species of sea turtle are found here, and the coastal areas are an important wintering place for thousands of migratory bird species such as the Pacific Brent goose.

El Vizcaíno's coastal sanctuary is host not only to gray whales but also to humpback whales (right). The latter has been a protected species since 1966.

ROCK PAINTINGS OF THE SIERRA DE SAN FRANCISCO

Not far from the Whale Sanctuary of El Vizcaíno, impressive rock paintings cover the walls of the almost inaccessible caves of the Sierra de San Francisco. They bear witness to the existence of an important pre-Hispanic culture on the Baja California peninsula.

The center of the Baja California peninsula is an inhospitable, sparsely settled desert region. In the pre-Columbian period, however, it was home to a thriving culture that has since all but disappeared. Indeed, little is known about the former inhabitants of this barren region, but the detailed rock paintings from between 100 BC and AD 1300 tell at least of their existence. They mainly feature a surprising diversity of human and animal figures. Even whales can be found on the walls

and roofs of the Cueva del Palmarito or in the Cañon de Santa Teresa. There are also abstract motifs inserted between the more tangible figures. The out-sized images in vibrant hues reflect highly sophisticated techniques in which ground volcanic rock was used for the different colors while outline sketches and shading produced vivid representations.

The motifs were painted in deep-red and brown tones like the ones here on the walls of the Cueva la Pintada.

ISLANDS AND PROTECTED AREAS OF THE GULF OF CALIFORNIA

This World Heritage Site includes no less than 244 islands, rocky isles and exceptional sections of coast. With its incredible variety of flora and fauna, the gulf and its islands are considered a "natural laboratory" of evolution.

The Gulf of California is 1,100 km (680 mi) long and between 90 and 230 km (55–140 mi) wide. It adjoins the Pacific Ocean and is sandwiched between the west coast of Mexico and the Baja California peninsula. Nine regions here have been placed under protection, with a total surface area of approximately 18,000 sq km (7,000 sq mi); three-quarters of that is marine area. From north to south, these biosphere reserves, conservation areas and national parks include: Upper Gulf of California and Colorado River Delta Biosphere Reserve; Islands and Protected Areas of the Gulf of California; the Island of San Pedro Mártir; El Vizcaíno; Bahía de Loreto; Cabo Pulmo; Cabo San Lucas; the Marías Islands and Isabel Island. Over 200 bird species from some twenty orders are found here along with thirty species of mammal and five of the world's seven species of turtle. Of the 891 species of fish in the marine conservation area, ninety are endemic.

The spectacular scenery of the islands includes dramatic cliffs, sandy beaches and lapis lazuli-colored ocean.

HISTORIC CENTER OF ZACATECAS

This town in the valley of the Río de la Plata in Central Mexico is one of the loveliest testimonies to Spanish colonial architecture in the New World. It owes its existence to rich silver reserves.

When Spanish conquistadors arrived at the 2,700-m-high (8,859-ft) Cerro de la Bufa on their search for precious metals in 1546 they decided to found a town. The abundant silver reserves turned the settlement into a prosperous trading hub in the 16th and 17th centuries, after which it was made a base for missionary efforts by a number of religious orders. In addition to lovely civic buildings, the churches and monasteries here were built in the Churriguerist style, an ornate version of Latin American baroque. The most outstanding religious building is the cathedral, whose ostentatious façade exhibits a mixture of Christian and Indian ornamentation. The Church of Santo Domingo as well as several monastery complexes (San Agustín, San Francisco and San Juan de Dios) are significant from an art-history perspective while other 18th- and 19th-century buildings such as the Palacio de la Mala Noche, the Teatro Calderón, the Palacio de Gobierno, the large aqueduct and the iron construction of the Mercado González Ortega bear witness to the town's former wealth.

From an aerial perspective, the cathedral from 1760 is the dominant building in Zacatecas.

AGAVE LANDSCAPE AND ANCIENT INDUSTRIAL FACILITIES OF TEQUILA

The town of Tequila, after which the popular spirit is named, is the heart of a cultural landscape characterized by the blue agave plant. The active ingredient in tequila, Mescal, is obtained from the pineapple-like agave plant.

This World Heritage site comprises an expansive landscape stretching from the foothills of the extinct Tequila Volcano to the Río Grande, an area dominated by the cultivation of the blue agave plant (Agave tequilana). The site includes the settlements of Tequila, Arenal and Amatitán with their large distilleries – some of which are still in operation – and numerous haciendas, some of them dating back to the 18th century. The distilleries are built of baked and dried bricks and adorned with plaster of an ochre hue, decorative windows and neoclassical or baroque ornamentation. There are still some "tabernas" here – as illegal distilleries were called during the Spanish era. The area also has archaeological sites of the Teuchitlán culture, which influenced the region from the third to the 10th centuries BC.

The name Tequila may only be used for the spirit obtained from the juice of the blue agave.

Mexico

HISTORIC TOWN OF GUANAJUATO AND ADJACENT MINES

Guanajuato is about 400 km (249 mi) north-west of Mexico City and is one of the silver mining towns in Central Mexico that features magnificent colonial baroque edifices reflecting the fabulous wealth it once enjoyed.

Situated at an elevation of 2,084 m (6,838 ft), Guanajuato's rise to prosperity began in 1548 when the Spanish discovered sizable silver deposits here. The town's subsequent development is inextricably linked to its architectural history. The wealth of the mine operators is reflected in magnificent villas such as the Casa Rul y Valenciana. Grandiose churches were also built including the neoclassical Nuestra Señora Basilica or the late baroque Franciscan Church of San Diego. The La Compañía and La Valenciana churches are gems of the Churriguerist style, a Mexican version of baroque. In contrast to what was common practice elsewhere in the area, the town does not have a grid layout but is instead a labyrinth of narrow alleyways. The World Heritage Site also comprises the historic mines and their infrastructure, including the Boca del Infierno, a shaft dropping down to a depth of 600 m (1,969 ft).

There are two buildings that rise above the town's skyline: the Nuestra Señora de Guanajuato Basilica from the late 17th century and, behind it, the university.

PROTECTIVE TOWN OF SAN MIGUEL AND THE SANCTUARY OF JESÚS NAZARENO DE ATOTONILCO

The fortified town of San Miguel de Allende and the pilgrimage church of Jesús Nazareno de Atotonilco in the central highlands are an outstanding example of architecture in Mexico between the 16th and 19th centuries.

Franciscan monk Juan de San Miguel founded this town in about 1542 and named it after himself. It was an important trading post and stop along El Camino Real, the former royal route and silver route to the territory's interior. San Miguel also played a key role in Mexico's fight for independence, after which it was renamed San Miguel de Allende in 1826 in commemoration of the national hero. Its cultural significance rose towards the end of the 16th century and lasted well into the 18th century. Its baroque and neoclassical buildings and churches bear witness to that. The 18th-century Jesuit pilgrimage church of Jesús Nazareno in Atotonilco 15 km (9 mi) outside of town is seen as one of "New Spain's" most outstanding baroque buildings. Its interior is decorated with paintings and murals by Rodríguez Juárez and Miguel Antonio Martínez de Pocasangre.

The pilgrimage church of Jesús Nazareno in Atotonilco boasts magnificent murals.

HISTORIC MONUMENTS ZONE OF QUERÉTARO

Querétaro's layout reflects both indigenous and Spanish settlement patterns and influences. The protected World Heritage Site includes no less than 200 street blocks with around 1,400 monuments.

Querétaro is divided into two sections along a north-south axis: one with a Spanish grid-like road network, and one characterized by the indigenous Otomí, Tarascans and Chichimeca with a more irregular layout. The historic center of Querétaro, around 250 km (155 mi) north-west of Mexico City, features numerous colonial buildings and plazas from the 17th to the 19th centuries. The Church of San Francisco in the Jardín Obregón was founded in the 17th century as a Franciscan monastery and now houses the town museum. The Convento de la Cruz church recalls the Spanish conquest of the town while the convents of Santa Rosa and Santa Clara are outstanding baroque ensembles. The Plaza de Armas and the Jardín de la Corregidora are surrounded by magnificent palatial buildings in the baroque style and the aqueduct outside of town is an impressive construction that stretches for half a mile.

Querétaro's churches and former monasteries like the Templo de la Cruz bear testimony to the influence the Catholic Church and its religious orders.

FRANCISCAN MISSIONS IN THE SIERRA GORDA OF QUERÉTARO

The five Franciscan missions 250 km (155 mi) north of Mexico City were built in the second half of the 18th century. The church façades are of particular interest as an example of joint creative efforts involving the Indios as well.

Franciscan Father Junípero Serra made his way through to the rocky, subtropical Sierra Gorda in the eastern part of the state of Querétaro in around 1750 in order to bring the Gospel to the Indios. At the time, every mission was required to build a church, convert the local population, and then settle them around the church. It was only then that the actual Christianization could take place. The Franciscans were particularly successful, building five mission stations within just a few years: Santiago de Jalpan, Santa María del Agua de Landa, San Francisco del Valle de Tilaco, Nuestra Señora de la Luz de Tancoyol and San Miguel Conca. The façades of the mission churches feature great detail since people often gathered in the front of the buildings. The design of the angels, fanciful ornamentation and plant patterns bears witness to the fusion of European and Indio culture in the last phase of Christianization.

Motifs from both the Bible and local traditions bedeck the church façades such as this one in Tancoyol.

HOSPICIO CABAÑAS, GUADALAJARA

This hospice was originally founded to take care of people in need – a unique facility at that time. Its chapel houses important murals from the 20th century by Mexican muralist José Clemente Orozco.

The hospice building in the capital of the federal state of Jalisco in the western Mexican highlands was designed by Manuel Tolsá (1757–1816) at the beginning of the 19th century. Upon completion the complex proved to be a masterpiece of neoclassical architecture. Behind the façade are twenty-three patios lined with delightful arcade passages and seemingly endless corridors. The design and implementation also takes into consideration the needs of handicapped and sick people by dispensing with an upper floor, for instance. The building design also allows for plenty of space and light. The focal point of this large complex, which covers about 2.4 sq km (1 sq mi), is formed by the chapel with its impressively large-scale murals by José Clemente Orozco (1883–1949). He created a series of images here between 1938 and 1939 retelling Mexico's turbulent history using powerful colors.

The dome of the chapel of the Hospicio Cabañas houses the "El Hombre del Fuego". completed by José Clemente Orozco in 1939.

EL TAJÍN, PRE-HISPANIC CITY

The ruins attributed to the pre-Hispanic culture of the Totonac people is situated in the jungle of Veracruz about 150 km (93 mi) north-east of Puebla. Their main attractions are the "Pyramid of the Niches" along with several ball courts.

According to the latest research, Tajín dates back to the second century. Archaeological finds from the ruins also indicate that a strong relationship between Teotihuacán and Tajín reached the height of its powers after the fall of the Teotihuacán Empire in around 800. The city was subsequently destroyed and abandoned in around 1200 when the region fell under the influence of Mexico's powerful Tenochtitlan culture.

The ruins can be divided into three major areas: Tajín, Tajín Chico and the Hall of Columns. They each have a right-angled or trapezium-shaped square as their focal point with edges lined by pyramids. The best known of these is the Pyramid of the Niches, which features six platforms and is dedicated to the gods of wind and rain. It originally comprised 365 richly decorated niches that seem to indicate calculations associated with astronomy and a calendar. The largest building is the Hall of Columns. It is about 45 m (148 ft) in height and decorated with carvings. Tajín is thought to have once been the center of the Totonacs' religious ball games.

The area covered by the ruined city of El Tajín is lined with a number of beautifully preserved step pyramids.

HISTORIC CENTER OF MORELIA

Once known as Valladolid, this town's historic center is one the loveliest and oldest surviving colonial urban ensembles in the Americas. The uniform pink tones of many of the old buildings give the town a unique character.

Situated about 250 km (155 mi) west of Mexico City, the capital of Michoacán enjoyed a rapid rise after it was founded in 1541 by the Viceroy of New Spain. The first church, Iglesia de San Francisco, was consecrated in 1546. The Renaissance-style structure was attached to a monastery that now houses an arts and crafts museum. Another twenty churches were then built. In addition to the baroque Santa Rosa de Lima with its Churrigueriststyle altar screens, the cathedral built between 1660 and 1744 on the east side of the Zócalo is also worthy of mention for its baroque twin-tower façade and blue and white dome that dominate the town's skyline. There are over 200 historical buildings in the Old Town center as well as several colleges that bear witness to Morelia's importance as an intellectual center. The town also played an important role in the fight for independence. Miguel Hidalgo, for example, was active here and the town is named after the local freedom fighter José María Morelos. There are two museums documenting the battle of the intellectuals against the Spanish.

The Santuario de Guadalupe church is an impressive baroque building. Its interior decor dates from 1915, however.

THE MONARCH BUTTERFLY BIOSPHERE RESERVE

The Mariposa Monarca Biosphere Reserve is about 100 km (62 mi) north-west of Mexico City. Every winter it plays host to millions of monarch butterflies that seek out the moderate climate of the Mexican uplands.

This biosphere reserve covers 56 ha (139,000 acres) of montane forest at an elevation of 3,000 m (9,900 ft) above sea level. It is named after the migratory monarch butterfly, which in the fall travels south for some 4,000 km (2,500 mi) from the USA and Canada to Mexico. Every year, the bare rocks of the Mexican plain are the scene of a fascinating natural spectacle as several hundred million of these butterflies arrive on the reserve and turn the whole landscape orange. Their migration is quite an astounding phenomenon: hatching in North America, the creatures come to Mexico, spending the winter in a kind of suspended animation. In the spring they then return north, but only the fourth generation will return to Mexico. The biosphere reserve was established in the 1980s and is home to several sanctuarios, or protected zones, intended to preserve the butterfly's habitat from increasing human settlement and unregulated logging.

The wings of the monarch butterfly (Danaus plexippus) are orange in color with black and white markings.

Mexico

PRE-HISPANIC CITY OF TEO-TIHUACÁN

Situated about 50 km (31 mi) north-east of Mexico City, Teotihuacán is one of the most important ruined cities in Mesoamerica. The monumental dimensions of the complex are especially impressive.

When the Aztecs discovered this massive city complex in the 14th century it had already been abandoned for more than 700 years. The main buildings of the complex still survive along the central north-south axis and were built in around 200 BC. The Quetzalcoatl Temple and the large pyramids were built roughly 200 to 300 years later. Teotihuacán was in fact the largest city in the Americas in the year 350, boasting an estimated 150,000 inhabitants. Its prosperity was largely based on the processing of obsidian, a type of volcanic rock used to produce implements.

The view from the Pyramid of the Moon looks out over the Street of the Dead towards the Pyramid of the Sun over an area of 5 ha (12 acres).

The city began its decline in the seventh century and was finally abandoned in around 750. In addition to the Street of the Dead, which is more than 2 km (1.2 mi) long and 40 m (130 ft) wide, the most important constructions here include the 65-m-high (213-ft) Pyramid of the Sun, the somewhat smaller Pyramid of the Moon and the Quetzalcoatl Temple. Other outstanding structures include the carefully restored Palacio de Quetzalpapalotl with its lovely murals and carvings, as well as the Yayahuala, Zacuala and Tepantitla palaces.

The walls of many of the buildings in Teotihuacán are decorated with murals illustrating the religion of the former inhabitants. They portray mythical animals as well as human figures such as this priest with his magnificent feather headdress.

Teotihuacán culture also produced remarkable works of sculptural art. The front of the Quetzalcoatl Temple, for example, features a number of works of the feathered serpent – the image of the god Quetzalcoatl.

Painted stone masks like this one are thought to represent the dead and played an important role in ancestor worship. The sealed mouth – a symbol of death – and the large earrings are especially conspicuous.

The Quetzal bird (Pharomachrus mocinno) was venerated in ancient Mexico as the holy bird of the god Quetzalcoatl and therefore not killed.

Mexico

LUIS BARRAGÁN HOUSE AND STUDIO

Luis Barragán is one of the most outstanding architects of the 20th century. One of his best creations is his house and studio in Tacubaya, a suburb of Mexico City.

Luis Barragán was born in 1902 in the town of Guadalajara in Mexico. He initially studied to be an engineer but ultimately decided to teach himself architecture. He lived in Paris for a time, where he attended lectures by Le Corbusier. Barragán based his work on the architecture of North Africa, Mexican folk tradition and American minimalism. He finally settled in Mexico City in 1936 where he began developing his own personal style that featured basic geometric shapes but incorporated natural elements as well. He referred to himself as a landscape architect and received the Pritzker Prize in 1988 – the highest accolade for an architect. The Casa Barragán, which was its owner's home and place of work until his death in 1988, was built in 1948. The three-story concrete building features a surprising interior of bright shades, sophisticated effects of light and shadow, and a highly unusual layout of rooms.

The photographs by René Burri capture the characteristic elements of Barragán's unusual house.

HISTORIC CENTER OF MEXICO CITY AND XOCHIMILCO

Aztec heritage in Mexico City is inextricably linked with Spanish colonial legacy. This World Heritage Site comprises two separate areas and pays tribute to the building achievements of both cultures.

The Aztecs founded their capital of Tenochtitlán in around 1370. The center of the city constitutes a religious site in and of itself, with giant pyramids and temple complexes. When the conquistadors arrived in 1521 they leveled the settlement and built Mexico City on its ruins. Some of the most important historical buildings are grouped around the main square, Zócalo. The ruins of the Templo Mayor, for example, are the most important relics of the Aztec era. The National Palace now serves as the president's official residence and houses some of the most important wall paintings by Diego Rivera (1886–1957), many of which illustrate important periods in Mexican history.

The cathedral embodies a mixture of styles from Renaissance to neoclassicism and is one of the largest churches in Latin America. The floating gardens of Xochimilco south of Mexico City are the remains of an Aztec lagoon town.

The Cathedral (above) is on the north side of the Zócalo (formally known as Constitution Square), while Aztec cultural remnants can be found on the reed islands and lakes of Xochimilco (right).

CENTRAL UNIVERSITY CITY CAMPUS OF THE UNIVERSIDAD NACIONAL AUTÓNOMA DE MÉXICO (UNAM)

The ensemble of buildings, sports facilities, open spaces and pathways here is an outstanding example of modernist architecture in Latin America.

Before becoming autonomous in 1929, the first university in Latin America, founded in 1551, consisted of a number of buildings scattered around the city center. Plans to bring the faculties together were made in the 1930s, but not actually completed until 1949–52. The Pedregal de San Ángel site, which was still outside of the city at the time, was selected as the location and the master plan for the layout was drawn up by architects Mario Pani and Enrique del Moral, who made consistent reference to the principles of contemporary architecture – always incorporating local traditions and building materials. More than sixty architects and graphic artists were ultimately involved in the project. All of the buildings are surrounded by open spaces – esplanades, courtyards or gardens. The successful integration of sculptural and pictorial works into the architecture is especially remarkable.

The Juan O'Gorman library features a fusion of art and architecture.

ARCHAEOLOGICAL MONUMENTS ZONE OF XOCHICALCO

Xochicalco, now a complex of pre-Columbian ruins about 100 km (62 mi) south of Mexico City, near Cuernavaca, reached its height in the Epiclassic Period (650–900) after the decline of Teotihuacán.

At one time this fortified city complex was one of the most important political and cultural centers of what is now southern-central Mexico. The styles here clearly reflect influences from the area's different cultures as well. Three levels are distinguished at the archaeological site. The uppermost features the central square situated on an artificial mound and accessed via two porticos. In the middle of the square are two pyramids that served religious purposes. One of these, the Temple of the Feathered Serpent, owes its name to the giant, carved serpent winding its way around the building. The seated human figures and the three steles indicate Mayan influences. The complex also includes a number of ball courts. There are twenty round altars relating to a calendar system and a square altar that represents the ceremonial year. To date, Xochicalco has not been attributed to one particular culture, but the city was abandoned in the 10th century and subsequently fell into ruin.

Human figures surrounded by serpents adorn the base of the "Temple of the Feathered Serpent" (left). Above: A view of the archaeological site.

Mexico

HISTORIC CENTER OF PUEBLA

The fourth-largest city in Mexico, Puebla, is characterized by magnificent religious and civic buildings in the colonial baroque style. The vibrant tile and stucco ornamentation on many of the buildings is unique here.

Although not part of the World Heritage Site, Cholula was once one of the most important religious sites in the Aztec realm. Located between four volcanoes – Popocatépetl, Ixtaccíhuatl, La Malinche and Citlaltépetl – 100 km (62 mi) south-east of Mexico City, Spanish conquerors put an end to Aztec rule here in 1519, destroying the settlement in the process. In demonstration of their power they built their churches atop the mighty pyramids of the town. Shortly thereafter and not far away, the Spanish founded the town of Puebla, which soon developed into a thriving commercial center where agricultural products were traded and the popular Talavera pottery was produced. Colorful ceramic tiles (azulejos) are still omnipresent in the town's historic center. The majority of the World Heritage Site comprises buildings from the 19th century, when Puebla experienced a period of rapid growth. The most outstanding of the roughly seventy religious buildings are the Renaissance cathedral with its tiled dome and the San Francisco Church with its lovely tiled façade.

Buildings like the Santa Rosa Convent with its historic kitchen predestined Puebla as a World Heritage Site. Its colorful tiles give it a unique charm.

EARLIEST 16TH-CENTURY MONASTERIES ON THE SLOPES OF POPOCATÉPETL

Franciscans, Dominicans and Augustinians were heavily involved in the wholesale Christianization of Mesoamerica. Their monasteries on the slopes of Popocatépetl south of Mexico City still bear testimony to their efforts.

The first monasteries founded at the foot of Popocatépetl in the early 16th century marked the start of a building spree for mission stations throughout the region. The consecration of the first Franciscan base in Cuernavaca in 1525 was followed by the building of about 300 more monasteries that were also founded by Dominicans and Augustinians. The World Heritage Site comprises a total of fourteen monasteries including Atlatlahuacán, Tetela del Volcán, Cuernavaca, Tepoztlán, Zacualpan de Amilpas, Hueyapan, Yecapixtla, Tlayacapan, Yautepec, Totolapan, Ocoituco, Tochimilco, Huejotzingo and Calpan. The basic construction features are the same for all of them: The ground floor atrium is surrounded by a wall incorporating chapels at each of its four corners. The main churches, typically with a single nave, were intended to impress the Indios with their size.

Above: Wall paintings depicting martyrs in the Cathedral of Cuernavaca. Right: The atrium in Tepoztlán.

HISTORIC CENTER OF OAXACA AND ARCHAEOLOGICAL SITE OF MONTE ALBÁN

By the time the Spanish had built their baroque city of Oaxaca in the 16th century, the nearby settlement of Monte Albán had already existed for more than 2,000 years. Both sites now enjoy World Heritage Site status.

The Olmecs were the first to build a city overlooking a valley in the high Sierra Madre del Sur in southern Mexico; they did so in the eighth century BC. Their complex was later occupied by the Zapotecs who built a ceremonial complex with monumental buildings on an artificial plateau. Between 300 and 700 the city boasted some 50,000 residents but it began to decline in about 800. The site was then used by the Mixtecs, but only as a burial site. In addition to pyramids and temples, Monte Albán has remarkable carved slabs with "Danzantes" (depicting the torture of prisoners of war, not dancing). Establishedd in 1529, Oaxaca boasts historic markets and an arcade-lined plaza. Among the city's religious buildings, two elaborate baroque churches stand out: the cathedral (1544–1740) and the Church of Santo Domingo (1666).

Santo Domingo (left) is considered the loveliest church in Oaxaca. The pyramids and buildings of Monte Albán (below) extend over a grand plateau.

HISTORIC MONUMENTS ZONE OF TLACOTALPAN

With its arcade-lined alleyways and many green squares, this river port on the Gulf of Mexico boasts a unique and vibrant combination of Spanish and Caribbean culture.

Tlacotalpan is situated at the mouth of the Papaloapan River and had already enjoyed a long history by the time Juan de Grijalva became the first European to sail along the coast of Veracruz in 1518. The Totonacs ruled the area between 900 and 1200, and were followed by the Olmecs until Montezuma took over the region in 1471. The stretch of land was conquered by the Spanish in the mid-16th century, who undertook a systematic expansion of the town. Following repeated destruction by fire, however, the town's present-day appearance largely dates from the 19th century. The magnificent town hall as well as numerous civic and private buildings, were built in around 1850. The latter are stand out due to their idiosyncratic architecture and bright hues. The arcades and porticos of the buildings line the historic streets with their green squares and patios adding to the quaint atmosphere.

Arcaded façades and porticos line the streets of Tlacotalpan. Pastel shades, low buildings and a great many green areas create a small-town atmosphere.

Mexico

PRE-HISPANIC CITY AND NATIONAL PARK OF PALENQUE

The ruins of one of the most impressive Mayan cities rise proudly out of the jungle of Chiapas in southern Mexico. Although discovered in 1784, systematic excavation of the site only took place in the 20th century.

The Mayan city of Palenque was built between the third and fifth centuries and reached its zenith between the sixth and eighth centuries. Its most important buildings also date from this period. The hieroglyphics in the "Temple of the Inscriptions", a step pyramid with a summit temple, have been deciphered and are the most important written records left by the Maya. The intact burial chamber of Mayan Prince Pacal, complete with burial objects, was discovered inside the pyramid in 1951. In addition to other buildings such as the Temples of the Cross group, the "palace" is of particular interest. It comprises several buildings grouped around four courtyards. The tower is 15 m (49 ft) in height and thought to have been used as an astronomical observatory while a table on the upper floor served as an altar. Almost all of the buildings in the center of Palenque are decorated with carvings and stucco ornamentation.

The so-called "palace", with a tower that was most likely used as an observatory, is one of the most important buildings in Palenque.

HISTORIC FORTIFIED TOWN OF CAMPECHE

Encircled by a fortified wall, the historic center of Campeche is not only one of the loveliest examples of a baroque colonial town in Central America; it is also a good example of military architecture from the 17th and 18th centuries.

Founded in 1540, Campeche initially served as the base for the conquest of the Yucatán Peninsula in the name of the Spanish Crown, but the important port soon became a lucrative target for notable pirates like Henry Morgan and William Parker who saw fit to plunder it on a repeated basis. The impressive town wall is 2,500 m (8,250 ft) in length and was built in a hexagonal shape between 1668 and 1704. The overall defensive complex with its four bastions ("baluartes") is now one of the best preserved in the Americas. The bastions and the two forts now house museums, galleries and botanical gardens. Export of the red textile dye "Palo de Tinte" brought a second era of prosperity to Campeche in the 19th century and many magnificent buildings survive from this period including palatial townhouses, the Teatro Toro and a number of churches such as the Catedral de la Concepción, San Francisquito and San Román, built between 1540 and 1705.

The alleyways of the historic center boast churches, colorful buildings and original cobblestones.

PRE-HISPANIC TOWN OF UXMAL

The ruins in Uxmal and the buildings in nearby Kabáh, Labná and Sayil about 80 km (50 mi) south of Mérida represent the impressive zenith of classic Mayan architecture.

Much like its neighboring sites, Uxmal was an important urban center from the eighth to the 10th centuries. The central building here is the nearly 40-m-high (131-ft) "Pyramid of the Soothsayer". This imposing structure, which was dedicated to Chaac, the god of rain, is in fact the fourth building to have been built on the site of earlier temples.

The expansive Governor's Palace, which is decorated with an impressive stone mosaic frieze, stands on a platform 15 m (49 ft) in height. Mosaics can also be found on other buildings in Uxmal. The ornamented columns of the large Palace of Sayil, for exam-ple, are even more spectacular than the frieze on the façade.

The triumphal arches in Labná and Kabáh, which once stood over paved streets, are some of the last of these rare Mayan architectural gems. The "Palace of the Masks" in Kabáh owes it name to the 250 stone masks of the god Chaac on the front. Like many Mayan towns, Uxmal was mysteri-ously abandoned in around 1200.

Masterpieces of Mayan architecture: the so-called "Governor's Palace" and the "Pyramid of the Soothsayer".

PRE-HISPANIC CITY OF CHICHÉN ITZÁ

These impressive ruins extend over an area of 300 ha (741 acres) in the northern Yucatán and are in fact the legacy of two pre-Hispanic civilizations, the Maya and the Toltecs.

The Chumayel manuscript, a Mayan chronicle from the start of the Spanish Conquest, says that Chichén Itzá is thought to have been founded by the Maya in around 450. It features distinctive buildings in the architectural style typical of the Maya, such as the "House of the Nuns" or the "Church". In the 10th century, Toltec groups took over the town, which had actually been abandoned by the Maya, and initiated a second era of prosperity that lasted about 200 years. This resulted in Toltec-style sculptures and carvings with depictions of warriors and picto-rial maps. The observatory ("Caracol") and the step pyramid ("Castillo") – with a summit temple dedicated to the Mayan deity Kukulkán – are representative of this epoch. Other buildings like the "Warriors' Temple" and the "Temple of the Jaguar" as well as nine ball courts adorn the town center while the "Cenote Sagrado" fountain on the outskirts may have been a sacrificial site for Chaac, the rain god.

The façades of the stone buildings, such as the "House of the Nuns" (left), is typical of the Mayan Puuc style.

SIAN KA'AN BIOSPHERE RESERVE

This nature reserve on the Caribbean coast of Mexico features a range of biotopes that provide ideal living conditions for over 100 species of mammals, rare amphibians, some 350 species of bird and other tropical flora.

Covering a total area of over 5,000 sq km (1,900 sq mi) on the eastern Yucatán peninsula, Mexico's largest nature reserve – referred to in the Mayan language as Sian Ka'an, meaning "a gift from heaven" – offers sublime living conditions for a variety of unique flora and fauna. One distinct advantage in this area is that only around 2,000 humans live here, mostly in the towns of Punta Allen and Boca Paila. No less than seventeen different zones of vegetation exist here, all in close proximity to one another, including evergreen, decidu-ous, coniferous and rain forest; mangrove swamps, savannah and flood plain; and 100 km (62 mi) of coral reef and lagoons. These are a habitat for rare predators such as jaguars as well as monkeys, crocodiles and sea turtles. A quarter of the area of the park is taken up by ocean. Sian Ka'an also has twenty-three archaeological sites with cultural relics as old as 2,300 years.

The brown pelicans who have made the Sian Ka'an coastline their home are among the world's endangered species.

ANCIENT MAYA CITY OF CALAKMUL, CAMPECHE

The Mayan city of Calakmul is situated amidst the tropical rainforests of the Yucatán and boasts a long history of settlement. The large number of carved steles is a typical feature of this site.

In about 300, the Maya began building stone monuments with hieroglyphics that recorded important events or achievements by their kings. These steles, which included precise dates, are not only an important historical reference for this major Central American civilization, but also works of art with intrinsic aesthetic value. Some 120 steles have been discovered to date in Calakmul on the southern Yucatán near the border with Guatemala and Belize. Pyramid-shaped temples – such as the 50-m (164-ft) step pyramid – can also be found here along with tombs. A total of more than 5,000 stone buildings joined by a network of streets are testimony to a highly developed settlement. Calakmul's stature characterized the classic Maya period but eventually went into decline in the 10th century after about 1,200 years of continuous habitation. It was forgotten for nearly a thousand years but today the ruined city is of tremendous importance for research into Mexico's pre-Columbian cultures.

The pyramids and the carved steles are Calakmul's main attraction.

BELIZE BARRIER REEF

The longest barrier reef in the northern hemisphere lies on the edge of the continental shelf off the Belize coast. This unique and fascinating underwater paradise is a refuge for many endangered species.

The Atlantic Ocean's largest series of coral reefs naturally forms a highly complex ecosystem. It is composed of over 250 km (155 mi) of barrier reef, three large atolls that are further offshore, and hundreds of scattered islands known as "Cays" on which roughly 170 plant species thrive. Its dense mangroves, sandy beaches and charming lagoons offer ideal living conditions for birds of all kinds including some endangered species such as the red-footed booby, the magnificent frigate bird and the lesser noddy. The World Heritage Site itself covers about 1,000 sq km (390 sq mi) and consists of seven conservation areas and national parks. It includes various types of reef made up of sixty-five different varieties of coral. These bizarrely shaped growths and columns are a habitat for innumerable species including 250 different water plants and 350 molluscs, sponges and crustaceans, and some 500 species of fish ranging from eagle rays to groupers. Highly endangered marine animals such as manatees as well as loggerhead and hawksbill turtles also live in the conservation areas.

The reef system is home to about 500 species of fish and countless schools of the colorfully shimmering creatures.

TIK'AL NATIONAL PARK

Tik'al in north-eastern Guatemala is among the most important ruins left by the Mayan culture. This gigantic complex features temples and palaces that were built here in the 3rd century AD.

Tik'al is different from the other Mayan sites in that it is located in the middle of a national park. The park's 600 sq km (230 sq mi) of primeval forest are in turn home to howler monkeys, birds, tree frogs and many other animals. At the height of Tik'al's expansion (ca. AD 550–900), as many as 90,000 people lived in this temple city and more than 3,000 structures and buildings have so far been excavated in the 15 sq km (6 sq mi) of the heart of the city. They include great palaces, simple houses and fields for games. The most spectacular are the five colossal step pyramid temples, one of which is 65 m (215 ft) tall and therefore the largest known existing Mayan structure. In around AD 800, this cultural complex boasted twelve temples all constructed on a grand platform. Near here, archaeologists have uncovered numerous tools and religious objects as well as a series of valuable grave accessories. No significant building work was attempted in Tik'al after the 9th century, and the city was finally deserted during the 10th century. It is a spectacluar site.

The contours of a monumental pyramid temple can be seen through the mists of the Petén rainforest in Guatemala.

ARCHAEOLOGICAL PARK AND RUINS OF QUIRIGUÁ

Monumental steles and intricate calendars are among the highlights of the Quiriguá archaeological park eastern Guatemala close to the border with Honduras. This Mayan city was at its height during the eighth and ninth centuries.

The first settlers arrived here in about 200 AD but Quiriguá only reached the height of its powers between the seventh and 10th centuries before being abandoned for centuries. An important turning point in the history of the city came in 738 under the rule of Cauac Sky, who had the powerful ruler in Copán (in present-day Honduras) beheaded. Quiriguá had previously been politically dependent on Copán but the tables had now turned. The city, whose wealth was based on the trade in jade and obsidian, for example, consequently rose to become a center of political power. The majority of the steles date from this era of prosperity in the eighth century. The finely worked sculptures on these sandstone monoliths are sculptural masterpieces and tell of political and military events – including the aforementioned execution. The giant Stele E weighs 60 tonnes (66 tons) and is more than 10 m (33 ft) high.

Stele I depicts Jade-Sky, the last ruler of Quiriguá. The combination of bas- and high-relief carvings as well as frontal portrayals are distinctive style elements.

ANTIGUA, GUATEMALA

Although Antigua, Guatemala was destroyed by an earthquake in 1773, the ruins retain their baroque grandeur to this day. The city is a fascinating testimony to early Spanish colonial architecture.

In 1543, Spanish conquerors successfully "refounded" the "noble" and "royal" city of Antigua. Located in the highlands of Guatemala at the foot of three volcanoes, the earlier settlement had been destroyed by a mudslide. Perched at an elevation of 1,500 m (4,923 ft), this capital of the Spanish colonial empire in Mesoamerica developed into a major city with up to 70,000 residents in the decades that followed. The first papal university in Central America, San Carlos de Borromeo, was even founded here in 1675. The building, with its courtyard and elaborately decorated arcades, has been made into a museum.

Antigua, with its chessboard layout and Italian Renaissance style, flourished for two centuries before being destroyed by an earthquake in 1773. Today, its impressive ruins together with rebuilt cathedrals, monasteries, palaces and townhouses bear testimony to the city's former economic, cultural and clerical importance. The grandiose baroque colonial buildings still make it plain to see why Antigua was once considered the loveliest capital in the New World.

Close to La Merced Church, the Arco de Santa Catalina spans one of Antigua's carefully restored streets.

RÍO PLÁTANO BIOSPHERE RESERVE

This biosphere reserve in the Río Plátano contains a considerable portion of the world's second-largest continuous area of rainforest. Due to its varied ecosystems, it is also home to a fantastic wealth of animal and plant life.

This biosphere reserve covers about 8,300 sq km (3,200 sq mi) of the Río Plátano, from the north coast on up to an elevation of 1,300 m (4,250 ft) in the interior of Honduras. Beyond untouched beaches lie lagoons and mangrove forests, coastal savannah with beak-sedge and other marsh plants, and palms and umbrella pines. Further into the interior are tropical and subtropical rainforests and all the diversity that these bring. Over 2,000 vascular plant species grow here alongside numerous trees including Spanish cedar, mahogany, balsa and

sandalwood. The reserve also provides many animal species with a life undisturbed by civilization. Just a few thousand people live here – indigenous Miskito, Pech and Tawahka, the Garifuna (a group with Caribbean and African roots), and mestizos who continue to live by their age-old traditions. There are also archaeological sites on the reserve that contain remnants of both Mayan and other pre-Columbian culture.

The white-nosed coati is one of the many rare species that call this reserve home.

MAYA SITE OF COPÁN

These ruins cover around 30 ha (74 acres) in north-western Honduras near the border with Guatemala. At its zenith in about 700, Copán was one of the most important city-states in the Mayan realm.

Mention of Copán had already been made by Diego García de Palacio in 1570, but excavation of the site only began in earnest in the 19th century. In fact, hundreds of ruins are still thought to be buried beneath mounds of earth in the Copán Valley. The center of the city that has been unearthed to date comprises the "Acropolis", a complex of interconnected buildings in the shape of pyramids, temples, and terraces. Altar Q, which bears the carved names of sixteen Copán rulers, is particularly remarkable, but the "Hieroglyphic Staircase" is considered Copán's most important monument. The sixty-three steps are covered with

nearly 2,500 glyphs – the longest Mayan text discovered to date – recording the dynasty's achievements from its founding through to the consecration of the staircase in 755. Also remarkable is the ball court with its three marker stones. It is the only court of this type anywhere. So far, fourteen altars and twenty steles from between 618 and 738 have been restored. The base of Stele H contained two fragments of a gold figure.

The ruins of the Mayan city of Copán feature detailed steles from the eighth century depicting rulers and their deeds (pictured is Stele B).

JOYA DE CERÉN ARCHAEOLOGICAL SITE

El Salvador's most important Mayan site was buried for centuries under a layer of ash and provides unique insights into everyday life 1,400 years ago in this major civilization.

The Mayan settlement in western-central El Salvador was buried under thick layers of ash after a volcanic eruption in around 600. Untouched until its rediscovery in 1976, excavations that begun in 1978 have revealed spectacular finds from the well-preserved site. The several hundred residents of Joya de Cerén were farmers who lived in thatched, clay-brick houses that included living quarters, storage facilities and kitchen buildings. The village also featured a sweat lodge and a large community hall as well as two other buildings that may have been used by healers, shamans or other specialists. Ceramics as well as implements made of stone, wood and bone have been extracted in near pristine states. Maize, beans and chili were staple crops but there were also herb gardens, fruit and cocoa trees as well as an agave garden. In 2007 the oldest manioc field to date was discovered, proof that the Maya cultivated the plant 1,400 years ago – it caused a sensation in the scientific world.

Joya de Cerén is the first site to reveal aspects of everyday life in a Mayan city.

RUINS OF LEÓN VIEJO

The ruins of León Viejo, which was abandoned at the beginning of the 17th century, provide an authentic impression of a Spanish colonial settlement in Latin America from the time of the early Spanish conquest.

"Old León" is around 30 km (19 mi) from present-day León in western Nicaragua. The former capital of the province of Nicaragua was founded in 1524 by Francisco Hernández de Córdoba in the territory of the Chorotega Indians and served as an effective base for further conquests in the Pacific region. But León, which became a diocesan town in 1531, was a smaller settlement even at its zenith in around 1545 – its Spanish population numbered only about 200 people. Many residents fled the town following the eruption of the Momotombo Volcano in 1578, and the town was completely abandoned after an earth-quake in 1610. With its grid-like layout the settlement on Lake Xolotlán was initially fortified and largely comprised of simple buildings built of wood, bamboo and clay. It included a residence for the governor, a royal foundry, a cathedral, and the La Merced Monastery. The foundations are all that remain of many of the buildings today. Archaeological excavations have been ongoing since 1968.

Brick floors and stone foundations – as in the case of the royal foundry – and coins are all that remain of this former colonial settlement.

GUANACASTE CONSERVATION AREA

This extensive conservation area in north-western Costa Rica allows visitors to observe fascinating and vital ecological processes on land and in the coastal waters. The area is a habitat for many rare species.

This area of 1,000 sq km (386 sq mi) in north-western Costa Rica consists of three national parks and several smaller conservation areas. It extends from the Pacific coast across the 2,000-m-high (6,600-ft) mountains of the interior all the way to the lowlands on the Caribbean side. Guanacaste encompasses coastal waters, islands, sandy beaches and rocky coastland as well as mountainous and volcanic landscape of the interior – including the still active composite volcano, Rincón de la Vieja. No less than thirty-seven wetlands can be found here, along with mangroves and a tropical rainforest as well as tropical dry forests where the trees shed their leaves in the hot season. This last bastion of intact tropical dry forest in Central America measures roughly 600 sq km (232 sq mi), which makes it one of the largest protected forest areas in the world. In total, some 230,000 species flourish in the various ecosystems here, an impressive diversity that is a result of Guanacaste's location in a biogeographical area with both neotropic and neoarctic life from South and North America.

Tropical dry forest (below) is characteristic of several sections of the Guanacaste National Park. The area is also a refuge for acutely endangered species such as the Green sea turtle (left).

COCOS ISLAND NATIONAL PARK

Cocos is the only island in the eastern Pacific to be covered in tropical rainforest. Due to its distance from the mainland, it is home to flora and fauna that exists nowhere else in the world.

Legend has it that some notorious pirates buried treasure on Cocos Island in the 17th and 18th centuries. No trace of their bounty has ever been found, but the treasure that this island does have to offer lies in its tropical rainforest. Located a long 550 km (340 mi) to the south-west off the Pacific coast of Costa Rica, this 24-sq-km (9.6 sq mi) island offers a diverse landscape of dramatic cliffs dropping off into the sea, rushing waterfalls and peaks covered in primeval forests. Due to its remote location, a number of native species have evolved here such as the huriki tree and a native palm.

In addition, three bird, two reptile and more than sixty insect species are found only on Cocos Island. Some 100 sq km (40 sq mi) of coastal waters around the island also belong to the national park and these contain large fringing reefs with thirty-two species of coral and a wealth of marine life. Dolphins, sharks, manta rays and roughly 300 other species of fish also live in the waters surrounding Cocos Island.

The colorful reef system around Cocos Island offers animals such as the bluespotted cornetfish (left) an ideal habitat for continued survival.

Costa Rica / Panama

TALAMANCA RANGE AND LA AMISTAD NATIONAL PARK

This transnational conservation area shared between Costa Rica and Panama is home to a great diversity of plant and animal life.

This unique conservation area covers 8,000 sq km (3,100 sq mi) of the central Cordillera de Talamanca range. Stretching from southern Costa Rica into western Panama, it is home to a tremendous variety of scenery and wildlife at elevations varying from sea level up to 3,800 m (12,600 ft). The greater part of the reserve is covered in tropical rainforest that has been growing here for 25,000 years. At elevations above the expansive lowland plains there are cloud forests and areas of Páramo with bushes and grasses as well as sections of evergreen oaks, moorland and lakes. Due to its topographic and climatic variation – and not least due to its geo-

The largest undisturbed rainforest zone in Central America is in this transnational conservation area.

graphical location at the intersection of North and South America – the park boasts a spectacular diversity of animal and plant life.

Archaeological finds within the park also suggest the possibility of human habitation here dating back thousands of years, but this research is still in its infancy. Today about 10,000 members of the indigenous Teribe, Guaymi, Bribri and Cabecar peoples live in reservations inside the park where they still follow their ancient traditions and way of life.

The park's forests and streams (top) are home to reptiles and amphibians like the tree frog (middle) as well as 200 mammal species including the jaguar (right).

COIBA NATIONAL PARK AND SPECIAL ZONE OF MARINE PROTECTION

This conservation area consists of Pacific islands that were spared from El Niño storms and temperature fluctuations. As a result the area has retained a great variety of species.

Declaring 4,000 sq km (1,550 sq mi) of the south-western coast of Panama as a national park has protected not only the rainforests on the island of Coiba, but also on thirty-eight smaller islands in the Gulf of Chiriquí and the surrounding ocean. These islands, which have been separated from the mainland for millennia, are of great interest to naturalists because of the unique species and subspecies living here. Among these endemic creatures are rodents like the Coiban agouti as well as several subspecies of howler monkey, opossum and white-tailed deer. Coiba is also a refuge for endangered species like the crested eagle and the scarlet macaw that have died out in other areas of Panama. The marine areas of the park are especially rich in animal life; the reef here is the second-largest in the Central East Pacific.

Along with imposing manta rays, the protected waters of the Gulf of Chiriquí are home to a number of shark species.

FORTIFICATIONS ON THE CARIBBEAN SIDE OF PANAMA: PORTOBELO-SAN LORENZO

The mighty fortifications on Panama's Caribbean coast once protected the "treasure chests" of the Spanish empire from unrelenting attacks by pirates.

When Columbus dropped anchor in 1502 on the Caribbean side of the Isthmus of Panama he named the bay "Puerto Bello". The town founded here in 1597 was then called San Felipe de Portobelo after King Philip II. Located at the northern end of the Camino Real facing Panama City and the Caribbean coast, Portobelo developed quickly into the main hub for goods moving between Spain and Latin America. At the same time, 30 km (19 mi) further up the mouth of the Río Chagres, San Lorenzo developed into the second gateway to the mainland. From the start, the two settlements were attacked and destroyed repeatedly by the likes of Francis Drake and Henry Morgan, only to be rebuilt and more heavily fortified. The imposing fortifications along the bay and in San Lorenzo at the mouth of the Chagres are now unique examples of Spanish military architecture from the period between the 16th and 18th centuries.

The Portobelo fort protected the vital trading port on the Caribbean coast.

ARCHAEOLOGICAL SITE OF PANAMÁ VIEJO AND HISTORIC DISTRICT OF PANAMA

The historic heart of Panama City is an impressive testimony to Central American architecture and history from the 16th century.

Founded on the Pacific coast in 1519, the settlement of Panamá rapidly became an important center for the trade in precious metals from the Andes. First it was an administrative center and then a diocesan town with up to 10,000 residents. Following its destruction by Welsh privateer Henry Morgan in 1671, a more heavily fortified settlement was built almost 8 km (5 mi) west of the ruins of the "old" town. What is now the historic district then reached new heights in the mid-19th century on the back of the California Gold Rush. Both towns have a European-style layout with straight roads and numerous plazas. Together they possess a fascinating range of Spanish, French and American architectural styles from the 16th to the 19th centuries. The important buildings include the cathedral with its five naves as well as the La Merced and San Francisco monasteries.

Elegant façades along Avenida Central in historic Panama City bear witness to the prestige of days gone by.

DARIÉN NATIONAL PARK

Until recently, the extent of the biodiversity in this enormous tropical wilderness could only be speculated. Scientists believe that thousands of species still remain to be documented in Darién.

This national biosphere reserve in eastern Panama covers more than 6,000 sq km (2,300 sq mi) and stretches from the Pacific coast to the 1,800-m-high (5,950-ft) mountains along the Caribbean coast. The vast area encompasses an incredibly diverse range of habitats, from sandy and rocky beaches to mangrove intertidal flats and various types of rainforest. Indeed, its ecosystems are considered the most diverse in the American tropics. Extremely rare orchids as well as forty kinds of native plants call this area home. This wealth of habitats ensures fantastic biodiversity, as does the park's location at the most extreme meeting point of both South and North American species. Among the 450 bird species living in Darién, five are only found here. The park also provides refuge for a number of acutely endangered species such as the harpyie, tapir, jaguar and the puma. Some areas of the park are still inhabited by members of the indigenous Kuna, Emberá and Wounaan peoples as well.

Cuipo trees (above) are found all over these rainforests, which stretch far into the beautiful mountains.

Cuba

OLD HAVANA AND ITS FOR-TIFICATIONS

During Spanish rule, Havana was one of the most important cities in the New World. Many of the baroque and neoclassical buildings in the Old Town (La Habana Vieja) date from this period.

Between the 16th and 18th centuries, the Spanish built a number of imposing fortifications in Havana including the Castillo de la Real Fuerza, the Castillo de los Tres Reyes del Morro, the Fortaleza de San Carlos de la Cabaña and the Castillo de la Puntan. All of them were designed to protect this vital trading port from attack by privateers and navies interested in the lucratvie gold and silver passing through here on its way to Spain.

The historic center of Havana, whose skyline is dominated by the Capitol dome, has its own special appeal inspired by the romantic charm of its pastel-colored colonial-era buildings.

The Old Town streets are interspersed with pleasant squares. The main square, Plaza de Armas, has particularly impressive colonial-era buildings such as the Palacio del Segundo Cabo. The Palacio de los Capitanes Generales is one of the city's loveliest baroque buildings while the baroque and neoclassical aristocratic residences with wrought-iron balconies are beautiful to see. The cathedral, completed in 1704, stands out from the many churches with its distinctive curved coral limestone façade and two asymmetrical towers. The former presidential palace now houses the Museum of the Cuban Revolution.

The fort of San Carlos de la Cabaña, the Palacio de los Capitanes Generales, and the 18th-century cathedral referred to by the Cuban author Alejo Carpentier as "stone interpreted as music", are all part of Old Havana's impressive array of historic buildings.

VIÑALES VALLEY

Against the backdrop of dramatic rocky outcrops in the Viñales Valley in south-western Cuba, farming culture still thrives in the form tobacco plantations and traditional agriculture.

The entire village of Viñales is a protected monument. Its charming main street is lined with small wooden houses. Locally made cigars are smoked on nearly every corner – Viñales lies at the center of Cuba's economically vital tobacco-growing region. The valley itself covers an area of roughly 132 sq km (51 sq mi) in the Sierra de los Organos and features the bizarrely-shaped "mogotes", rocky outcrops that rise out of the valley floor and were formed 150 million years ago. They were part of an extensive cave system that eventually collapsed and left behind these gigantic formations.

Tobacco is planted here towards the end of the rainy season and harvested between January and March. During the summer the fields are planted with malanga, bananas, maize and sweet potatoes. Traditional farming methods have hardly changed over the centuries and the rural architecture reflects the multi-ethnic society that has become established here. It is a society that is proud of its culture and that maintains an important historical social legacy for country.

The rocky outcrops in Viñales Valley are the remnants of a collapsed system of caves.

URBAN HISTORIC CENTER OF CIENFUEGOS

Cienfuegos on the southern-central coast of Cuba was founded in 1815 and developed into port in about 1830. Its name commemorates the Spanish general and governor José Cienfuegos.

The first residents of this coastal town were Spanish, who were followed by French immigrants largely from Bordeaux, New Orleans and Florida. As the town grew in importance based on the export of sugar, it was redesigned in the neoclassical style with a grid-like layout. Its planners wanted to implement new ideas of healthy urban living. The straight streets were intended to ensure air circulation – in the 19th century bad air was thought to be a common cause of disease – and the buildings in Cienfuegos often have just two floors, allowing light to

reach all of the homes and rooms. The layout of the squares reflects the importance of public life. The building styles were mixed in later periods but the town's overall appearance makes a harmonious impression. In addition to the residential buildings, the governor's palace, the San Lorenzo School, the cathedral, the Teatro Tomás Terry and the Palacio de Ferrer (Casa de la Cultura) are wothy of note here.

The Government Palace of Cienfuegos, built between 1928 and 1950, is on the south side of Plaza Martí.

TRINIDAD AND THE VALLEY DE LOS INGENIOS

Founded in 1514 on the southern-central coast, Trinidad is one of Cuba's most charming cities. Many of its buildings date from the 18th and 19th centuries when Trinidad prospered from the trade in sugar and slaves.

The lovingly restored buildings on Plaza Mayor give the square an almost unchanged historic appearance. Palacio Brunet and Palacio Cantero are magnificent examples of Spanish Mudejar architecture while other impressive 19th-century buildings can be found on Plaza Serrano as well. A number of former townhouses here are now home to museums. Several churches such as the La Popa monastery chapel with its rather plain baroque façade are also well preserved in Trinidad. The many houses comprising just one floor with veran-

das and balconies mean that the city has a small-village feel while bright and contrasting hues emphasize a distinct Caribbean lightheartedness. The World Heritage Site also includes the sugar cane plantations together with the historic sugar mills in the nearby Valle de los Ingenios (Valley of the Sugar Mills). For the best view of the valley go up the Manaca Iznaga tower.

The Plaza Mayor is Trinidad's "living room" and it is here that the loveliest colonial-era buildings are found.

Cuba

HISTORIC CENTER OF CAMAGÜEY

Camagüey is one of the first seven Cuban villages founded in the name of the Spanish crown. It reflects European medieval influences and its layout is a testimony to colonial-era planners.

Founded in 1514 on the Bay of Nuevitas, the town of Camagüey was actually relocated twice before being built in its current location farther inland in 1528. Its original coastal setting had made it an easy target for attack by pirates. The settlement was named after the Indian tribal area in which it was founded: Camagüebax. For the most part, Camagüey was economically independent due to its local sugar and tobacco plantations. As a result, the town also developed its own architectural style. Unlike other towns in Cuba, for exam-ple, Camagüey does not have a symmetrical layout and the town's structure follows more of an irregular pattern. Narrow alleyways enclose blocks of differing sizes and are more reminiscent of medieval layouts in Europe than New World grids. The historic center reflects numerous periods including neoclassical, baroque and even art nouveau, all of which give Camagüey its unique charm.

Arcades and façades with stucco ornamentation bear testimony to Camagüey's former wealth.

SAN PEDRO DE LA ROCA CASTLE, SANTIAGO DE CUBA

Repeatedly damaged by earthquakes and hostile attacks, San Pedro de la Roca Castle has been restored and expanded on many occasions throughout history. Today the building is one of the best-preserved examples of Spanish-American military architecture.

Santiago de Cuba in the south-east of the island was founded by explorer Diego Velázquez in 1514. Its strategic location meant that the settlement soon developed into an important economic and political center. In the 17th century the Spanish reacted to increasing threats to Santiago by rival colonial powers and pirates with the construction of San Pedro de la Roca Castle, known as "El Morro". Begun in 1638 in the style of the Italian Renaissance, this imposing fortress on a rocky outcrop overlooking the narrow entrance to the Bay of Santiago features towers, bastions and powder stores. It was designed by renowned military architect Juan Bautista Antonelli, who was also responsible for the fortress of the same name in Havana. The building extends up the rocky cliff on platforms linked via a series of staircases.

The "El Morro" fortress was built high above the port entrance of Santiago de Cuba to protect against pirates and rival colonial powers.

ARCHAEOLOGICAL LANDSCAPE OF THE FIRST COFFEE PLANTATIONS IN SOUTH-EASTERN CUBA

The remains of former coffee plantations at the foot of the Sierra Maestra range are an impressive testimony to the agricultural conditions in the Caribbean during the era of slavery.

French refugees from Haiti brought coffee to south-eastern Cuba at the end of the 18th century and the dry climate proved ideal for growing the lucrative bean. Its cultivation required cheap labor, however, which is why this profitable trade with its plantation system extended well into the 19th century and was inextricably linked with slavery. As a result, over one million Africans were shipped just to Cuba for this purpose, and an independent infrastructure with roads and irrigation systems was built to serve the plantations. With an area covering more than 80,000 ha (197,600 acres) between Santiago and Guantánamo, the World Heritage Site here includes the remains of 171 historic coffee plantations. A plantation is made up of the manor house, the slave quarters, terraces for drying the beans, and machinery and workshops.

"Secaderos" was the name given to the terraces where coffee beans were dried.

DESEMBARCO DEL GRANMA NATIONAL PARK

These unique limestone formations are arranged like terraces at the edge of the Sierra Maestra and provide a vital habitat for rare land and marine species.

This national park was named after the yacht on which Fidel Castro, Che Guevara and eighty-one companions made landfall at Las Coloradas in Cuba to overthrow the Batista dictatorship in 1956 (a reconstruction of the boat can be seen there today). This unique marine landscape of karst caves and canyons surrounding Cabo Cruz is one of the best-preserved of its kind in the world. It consists of limestone terraces rising up to 360 m (1,180 ft) out of the sea and reaching depths of 180 m (590 ft) beneath the surface. The total protected area (with buffer zone) covers 400 sq km (155 sq mi) and lies at the still active convergence of the Caribbean and North American continental plates. The exact number of plant varieties in the national park has not yet been established, but more than 500 have been recorded so far; roughly sixty percent of those are endemic. The animal world is equally diverse. A series of caves used for ritual purposes by the pre-Columbian Taino culture is also of interest.

The rare West Indian manatee, a variety of sea cow, lives in the waters off the coast of this national park.

ALEJANDRO DE HUMBOLDT NATIONAL PARK

The relatively undeveloped eastern end of Cuba still retains fantastic natural landscapes. These – such as in the Alejandro de Humboldt National Park – represent probably the last refuge for many of the island's unique species.

This national park north-west of the town of the same name in the Alturas de Baracoa mountains is largely dedicated for use as a biosphere reserve. It covers a total of about 700 sq km (270 sq mi), 20 sq km (8 sq mi) of which are marine and boast a particularly rich diversity of ecosystems: a coastal region of coral reefs and mangroves with a relatively large population of otherwise endangered manatees; wetland forests; and a mountainous region around the 1,168-m (3,830-ft) high El Toldo, with its considerable groves of endemic Cuban pines. More than 400 species of plant and animal are found exclusively here, the "Noah's Ark of the Caribbean", a statistic that tops even "centers of endemism" such as the Galápagos Islands by several orders of magnitude. The national park was named after the famous German explorer and natural scientist Alexander von Humboldt, who spent four and a half months in Cuba between 1801 and 1804, mainly in Havana.

The Cuban solenodon is a very rare creature native to these parts.

COLONIAL CITY OF SANTO DOMINGO

The layout of the first town founded by Europeans in the New World roughly corresponded to Renaissance ideals and became the model for all the new towns subsequently founded in the Spanish colonial empire.

Santo Domingo was officially founded by Christopher Columbus' brother Bartolomeo in 1498, but after being destroyed by a hurricane it was relocated farther inland to the banks of the Ozama River in 1502. Today Santo Domingo is the capital of the Dominican Republic and, because it is based on Renaissance models, the city has a strictly geometric layout with streets in a grid pattern and interspersed with squares such as the Plaza Mayor. The historic center around the Parque Colón features some of the oldest buildings and institutions in America, one example of these being the partially Gothic Catedral de Santa María la Menor from 1541. The oldest university in America, Santo Tomás de Aquino, was founded in 1538 in the Dominican monastery and the ruins of the oldest hospital in the New World, San Nicolás de Bari (1503), are still open to visitors. The viceroy's residence, Alcázar de Colón, exhibits Renaissance influences.

The oldest cathedral in the Americas is Santa María la Menor, which housed Columbus' remains until 1992.

NATIONAL HISTORY PARK – CITADEL, SANS SOUCI, RAMIERS

The early 19th-century buildings of National History Park with the Citadel, the Palace of Sans Souci and the buildings at Ramiers commemorate Haiti's independence from its former colonial power, France. The buildings are symbols of liberty, built by slaves who had gained their freedom.

Haiti occupies the western portion of the island of Hispaniola, the second-largest island in the Greater Antilles. It gained its independence in 1804. The ruins of Sans Souci and Ramiers, together with the La Ferrière Citadel, make up Haiti's National History Park and date from that period. The park covers 25 sq km (10 sq mi) in the north-west of the country close to Cap Haïtien. The driving force behind the buildings was Henri (Christophe) I, a former general who declared himself king here in 1811. The grounds of the Palace of Sans Souci cover around 20 ha (49 acres) amidst an appealing hilly landscape and once accommodated the seat of government, a hospital, and an arsenal. The palace itself was built in 1807 in an eclectic mix of styles; only parts of it survive. The Citadel was built by slaves who had gained their freedom under Henri I and the residential buildings of Ramiers were destroyed after his death.

The cannon balls bear witness to the purpose served by the mighty citadel.

BRIMSTONE HILL FORTRESS NATIONAL PARK

Built in the 18th century, this fortress at the center of the national park on the Caribbean island of St Kitts is one of the best-preserved examples of British military architecture in the New World.

The British colonial powers had already positioned their first guns on the strategically positioned Brimstone Hill by 1690 in order to protect the region from rival powers and privateers who were a constant threat to the highly lucrative sugar trade. Over the course of more than 100 years of slave labor, the fortress had grown into a mighty complex housing more than 1,000 soldiers by the time it was captured by a French fleet in 1782. French rule was short-lived, however, and Brimstone Hill was abandoned in 1851, after which it fell into ruin. The military complex has now been restored and extends over 16 ha (40 acres). It includes a hospital, several ammunition stores and the officers' living quarters. The most majestic fortifications are the Fort George Citadel and the Prince of Wales Bastion, the walls of which are built of volcanic rock up to 2.5 m (8 ft) thick; they were said to be able to withstand fire from enemy ships.

A bird's eye view of the massive Fort George Citadel, which was built with slave labor.

MORNE TROIS PITONS NATIONAL PARK

Morne Trois Pitons Park in Dominica is at the foot of the 1,342-m (4,400-ft) mountain of the same name. It has enchantingly diverse tropical forests and features a variety of volcanic phenomena.

Morne Trois Pitons National Park was established in 1975. The rain forests, cloud forests, lakes and waterfalls within its 70-sq-km (27-sq-mi) area provide an ideal habitat for a variety of animal and plant life. Twenty-one plant species alone have been registered only in this ecologically unique zone. Roughly 150 bird species also inhabit the forests here, among them one type of parrot that is acutely threatened with extinction.

The various volcanic features that can be admired around the still-active Morne Trois Pitons volcano are also of breathtaking beauty and include hot springs, about fifty fumaroles and five active craters. Hot mud bubbles up in one of the park's boiling lakes and the aptly named "Emerald Pool" owes its extraordinary coloration to elemental processes taking place below the surface of the earth. These features make the park an ideal location for studying the geomorphology of our planet.

Fumaroles in the Valley of Desolation (left) and a waterfall at "Emerald Pool" (below).

PITONS NATURE RESERVE

Rising from the sea and connected by a ridge, these two domed volcanic peaks on the Caribbean island of St Lucia both rise above 700 m (2,300 ft) and are known as the Pitons.

This World Heritage Site includes an area of 30 sq km (12 sq mi) at the south-western end of the island near Soufrière. It is composed of two peaks – Gros Piton (770 m, 2,525 ft) and Petit Piton (743 m, 2,440 ft) – as well as the mountain ridge connecting them, a Solfatara field of fumaroles and hot springs, and the adjacent areas of ocean. Up to sixty percent of the underwater region was once covered with coral, but Hurricane Lenny destroyed much of this in 1999. Fortunately, the establishment of no-fishing zones has given the area some relief and the waters around the Pitons are now among the most richly stocked in the Caribbean. The different species recorded include 170 fish, sixty jellyfish, fourteen sponges, eleven echinoderms, fifteen arthropods, and eight annelids. The predominant vegetation on the mainland is tropical rainforest, with small areas of tropical dry forest. Gros Piton is home to 150 plant species (to date); Petit Piton has about 100. Some thirty bird species are also found here, five of which are endemic.

Nobel Prize-winning author Derek Walcott, who is a native of St Lucia, has called these two peaks, which were formed in a volcanic eruption, the "Bosom of the Caribbean".

Colombia

CARTAGENA

This key port city on Colombia's Caribbean coast was once a major hub of the slave trade. The World Heritage Site includes the imposing defensive complex, the port itself and the colonial-era monuments in the Old Town.

Founded in 1533, Cartagena's favorable location on the Caribbean coast saw it quickly become a prospering trading center for silver, gold and slaves. By the mid-16th century, pirate attacks had became more frequent, prompting the city to fortify itself. After the notorious English buccaneer Sir Francis Drake captured Cartagena in 1586, a 12-m-high (39-ft) and, in parts, 18-m-thick (59-ft) countermure was erected. As the largest city wall in the New World, it withstood an attack by the British in the 18th century; a cannonball wedged in the wall of the Santo Toribio church remains as a reminder of the battle.

The mighty fortress walls (top) suffered several attacks in Cartagena's heyday. Arcades and balustrades characterize the façades of colonial-era houses (above).

The Old Town is surrounded by defensive walls and divided into three districts. The stately houses with magnificent main entrances and flower-hung interior courtyards in San Pedro were reserved for the upper class; San Diego was the residential and commercial quarter of the merchants; and the lower classes, predominantly of African origin, lived in Getsemaní. The most prominent buildings include the 16th-century cathedral and the Palacio de la Inquisición.

In addition to the many military buildings, churches also dominate Cartagena's townscape. Pictured here is the façade and bell tower of San Pedro Claver.

HISTORIC CENTER OF SANTA CRUZ DE MOMPOX

From the 16th to the 19th century, Santa Cruz de Mompox was an important trading city on the Rio Magdalena. Even today, entering its well-preserved center feels like travelling back to colonial times.

On the banks of the Río Magdalena some 250 km (155 mi) south of Cartagena is Santa Cruz de Mompox, one of Colombia's oldest and most beautiful colonial-era cities. For a long time it was an important inland port along the trade route to Cartagena. Today, the Río Magdalena flows through a different riverbed and the city has all but lost its economic relevance for the country and the area. Home to Colombia's only attached development in Spanish colonial baroque style, the historic town center is now more like an open-air museum.

Instead of the conventional main square, Mompox's center is formed by three squares connected by the Calle de la Albarrada: La Concepción, San Francisco and Santa Bárbara. Each of these squares has its own 16th-century church, of which Santa Bárbara, with its baroque tower, is the most unusual. Other striking buildings and churches can be found on Calle del Medio.

The city's most unusual building is the octagonal tower of Santa Bárbara, with stucco decorations and a balcony.

LOS KATÍOS NATIONAL PARK

This national park in north-western Colombia on the Panamanian border is composed of low hills, rain forest and swamps. The remote region provides a protected habitat for numerous endangered species and native plants.

This national park covers a total area of 720 sq km (280 sq mi), the eastern section of which includes large parts of swampland around the mouth of the Atrato River on the Gulf of Darién. The western section includes the jagged hill chain of the Serranía del Darién, a beautiful spur of the Western Andes Cordillera. Thanks to plentiful precipitation, which averages 3,000 mm (120 in) a year, extensive areas of swamp and rain forest have flourished energetically; a variety of valuable timber grows here including balsa wood and rubber trees.
The inaccessibility of this primary forest has also assured the survival of its

varied plant life, much of which is endemic. The remoteness has also been a benefit to the animal life here; the forest is home to big cats such as pumas and jaguars, but also to giant anteaters, tapirs, sloths, and various species of monkeys including howlers, capuchins, and brown woolly monkeys. There are also animals in the park that otherwise only occur in Central America such as the turkey-like gray-headed chachalaca.

The bush dog, which is a separate species within the dog family that only lives in Central and South America, has a squat body and lives in this national park.

NATIONAL ARCHAEOLOGICAL PARK OF TIERRADENTRO

The National Archaeological Park of Tierradentro in the Cordillera Central in southern Colombia is crisscrossed by numerous underground tombs whose size and spiral staircases make them unique to South America.

Tierradentro's archaeological park includes several areas of pre-Columbian burial chambers built between the 6th and 10th centuries – Alto del Aguacate, Loma de San Andrés, Alto de Segovia and Alto del Duende – as well as various stone sculptures located in Tablón. The findings most likely date back to an old agricultural civilization that maintained highly developed funerary practices. Their subterranean burial temples were used to store urns, but the remains of bones indicate that there were no uniform burial customs.

Apart from simple chambered tombs, the park also includes larger, semi-circular tombs that are carved out of the rock and accessed via spiral stone staircases. Their walls were up to 12 m (39 ft) wide and painted with red and black geometric figures on a white background; the alcoves housed relief statues. Some of the ceramic urns contained gold jewelry, which suggests precious burial objects.

Geometric patterns and drawings in red, white and black tones adorn the burial chambers of Alto de Segovia.

Colombia

SAN AGUSTÍN ARCHAEOLOGICAL PARK

San Agustín is just south of Tierradentro in southern Colombia and is the most important archaeological site in the country. It contains South America's largest collection of religious monuments and megalith sculptures.

The region around this archaeological site near the headwaters of the Río Magdalena, at the junction between the Eastern and Central Cordilleras, was settled as early as the fifth century BC; simple tombs here with wooden coffins date back to that time. The World Heritage Site includes three excavation sites: San Agustín, which is the largest of the three, Alto de los Õdolos and Alto de las Piedras. In its heyday, the still mysterious civilization living here created numerous chambered tombs as well as tumuli

Monolithic sarcophaguses have also been unearthed in stone chambers.

and grave mounds. Even more impressive are the "Õdolos" characteristic of the San Agustín culture. These human and animal figures made of stone are reminiscent of the statues of gods erected by the Maya in Central America. They include pictures of eagles and snakes, both of which were important sacred animals to the Maya. The anthropomorphic faces with carnivorous fangs possibly depict deities or demons. The culture's decline began in the eighth century and lasted until its inexplicable end in the 15th century. The faces of the 1-m-high (3-ft) stone statues take on more realistic forms. It is presumed that the inhabitants of San Agustín were Central American peoples who came to settle in South America. Peru's Chavín culture, which also disappeared mysteriously, could be another example of this phenomenon.

Around 400 partly painted stone sculptures have been found at the San Agustín archaeological site. Some of the often larger-than-life statues hold a cult item in their hands.

MALPELO NATURE RESERVE

This reserve in the tropical eastern Pacific includes the remote island of Malpelo and about 8,500 sq km (3,200 sq mi) of protected ocean. It is home to a number of endangered marine animals.

The island of Malpelo, which measures just 3.5 km (2 mi) across, is 500 km (310 mi) out in the Pacific off the coast of Columbia. It is part of a marine corridor that connects a series of World Heritage Sites including the Galápagos Islands (Ecuador), Coiba (Panama), and Cocos Island (Costa Rica). The island is actually the tip of the Malpelo Ridge, and underwater mountain range around which the seafloor reaches depths of 3,400 m (11,200 ft).

Due to a varied underwater landscape of high cliffs and vertiginous drops,

Morays have no scales; instead they excrete a toxic slime that protects their bodies.

deep canyons and caves, the waters around Malpelo are a popular spot for divers. The confluence of several ocean currents and the nature of the seabed here have also conspired to create an exceptionally complex and rich ecosystem. The waters are a breeding ground for many marine animals including some 200 species of fish. Sharks are especially numerous and, along with the hammerheads, whale sharks and silky sharks, rare shortnose sawsharks roam the seas here as well. Eagle and manta rays, seahorses, tuna, barracuda, bonitos and snappers live here, and the park is also a refuge for sea turtles and endemic starfish. The island itself is a breeding ground for numerous seabirds including swallow-tailed gulls and Galapagos petrels. The world's largest colony of masked booby — over 40,000 specimens — is also notable.

Many species of fish roam the waters around Malpelo including silky sharks, hammerheads and the spotted eagle ray (from top to bottom).

Ecuador

CITY OF QUITO

Among South America's metropolises, the historic center of Quito, which was built on the ruins of an Inca city, best reflects the character and atmosphere of a Spanish colonial city.

Perched 2,850 m (9,252 ft) above sea level, Quito is not only the second-highest capital city in South America, after La Paz, Peru, but also the oldest. This high-altitude basin surrounded by volcanoes was originally settled by Cara Indians even before the Inca period, but during the Inca Empire it became the second-largest administrative center under the ruler Huayna Cápac. Retreating from the Spanish, the Incas then destroyed this capital of their northern kingdom. Atop its ruins, conquistador Sebastián de Belalcázar founded "San Francisco de Quito" in 1534.

During colonial times, Quito's Old Town was the home of the upper classes. Today it has arguably the greatest concentration of colonial art

Soaring opposite the cathedral at Plaza Grande – also known as Plaza de la Independencia – is the Archbishop's Palace, built around the year 1700.

treasures in South America. The church of San Francisco, erected on the ruins of an Incan palace in the second half of the 16th century, is the largest and oldest church in the city and originates from the so-called "Quito School", which combines influences from Spanish, Italian, Moorish, Flemish and indigenous art.

The cathedral, rebuilt after being severely damaged by an earthquake in 1755, is another magnificent building. Other gems of colonial baroque architecture include the church of Santo Domingo with its impressive Chapel of the Rosary, and the church of La Compañía de Jesús, with its ornate façade.

San Francisco is South America's largest historic architectural complex (top). The interior of the church of La Compañía de Jesús is almost completely covered in gold leaf (right).

HISTORIC CENTER OF CUENCA

The city of Cuenca, situated in a basin in the Andean highlands of southern Ecuador, is one of the best surviving examples of Spanish town planning and architecture in South America.

Surrounded by the mighty summits of the Andes, Ecuador's third-largest city sits at a lofty 2,595 m (8,514 ft) above sea level. Even before the arrival of the Spanish it was an important center for the Cañari Indians and later for the Incas. However, when Gil Ramírez Dáv founded Santa Ana de los Cuatro Ríos de Cuenca here in 1557, the former metropolis of Inca ruler Huayna Cápac was already a ruin, having long since been destroyed and then abandoned. The Spanish designed Cuenca with a grid layout around a central square, Plaza Abdón Calderón, which still forms the heart of the city. The Old Cathedral, with its humble bell tower from 1557, soars towards the heavens here while the New Cathedral just opposite now dominates the townscape. Typical examples of Spanish colonial architecture also include the baroque La Concepción convent, founded in 1599, and the convent of Las Carmelitas Descalzas, completed in 1682. The merging of local and European architectural elements gives the city a unique character and for many locals, the "Athens of Ecuador" is the country's most beautiful city.

Cobblestone streets and pale-colored colonial houses add particular charm to the Old Town.

SANGAY NATIONAL PARK

Sangay National Park is located in the middle of the Ecuadoran Andes. Two active volcanoes add to the particular charm of the landscape, which is a habitat for rare plants and animals.

Sangay is a very remote national park that includes three distinct zones: the volcanic High Andes at elevations of 2,000 to 5,000 m (6,600 to 16,400 ft); the eastern foothills between 1,000 and 2,000 m (3,300 to 6,600 ft); and the alluvial fan that lies at their base. The central uplands are dominated by two active volcanoes, Sangay at 5,230 m (17,160 ft) and Tungurahua at 5,016 m (16,500 ft), and one extinct volcano, El Altar at 5,319 m (17,450 ft). The various vegetation zones change with elevation: subtropical rain forest merges into lower montane rain forest above 2,000 m (6,600 ft), which gives way to wild Páramo grasslands above 4,500 m (14,750 ft). Above 4,800 m (15,750 ft) is a zone of eternal snow. Overall, animal and plant life have benefitted from the isolation here. More than 3,000 plant species have been recorded in the park and the number of bird species is estimated to be from 400 to 500. Many mammals roam the ancient forest including mountain tapirs, giant otters, spectacled bears, pumas, jaguars and ocelots.

This national park offers a dramatic landscape of impressive active volcanoes such as Tungurahua (above) and Sangay (left) with its snowy peak.

Ecuador

Charles Darwin

Charles Robert Darwin (1809–1882) is one of the most prominent naturalists of the 19th century. After completing his studies in theology he embarked on a five-year journey (1831–36) aboard the "Beagle", a research and surveying vessel; the recommendation came from his botany professor, John Stevens Henslow. His travels took him through the Cape Verde Islands and around the eastern and western coast of South America to the Galapagos Islands and Tahiti. He also passed through New Zealand, Mauritius, Cape Town and St Helena. Along the way, the young researcher made countless observations and collected samples of stones, plants and animals.

GALÁPAGOS ISLANDS NATIONAL PARK

The volcanic islands of the Galápagos archipelago present a uniquely living picture of evolution as a result of their isolated situation.

About 1,000 km (620 mi) west of Ecuador in the middle of the Pacific Ocean there is a hotspot where molten magma has been forced through the earth's surface and created a spectacular archipelago of twelve large and over one hundred smaller volcanic islands. The oldest of them are also the furthest east and emerged 2.4 to 3 million years ago; the newest, Fernandina, is only 700,000 years old. Life here is influenced by three great ocean currents, in particular the cold Humboldt, which brings water from the icy polar regions up to the equator. These currents brought life to the Galápagos from tropical and subtropical Central and South America and from the Indo-Pacific Ocean, turning the islands into a melting pot vastly diverse species. Their geographical remoteness then provided plants and animals with the ideal conditions to evolve independently from the rest of the world.

Charles Darwin's visit in 1835 brought international acclaim to the Galapagos. His observations of finches, which were nearly identical save their differently shaped beaks depending on the islands they inhabited, led Darwin to develop important conclusions that eventually led to his groundbreaking theory of evolution. The Galápagos are a paradise for reptiles and birds, but few mammals have made their way here. Most of the animal life on the islands is only found here. Some of the more spectacular residents include the flightless cormorant, the Galápagos land iguana, the marine iguana and the Galápagos giant tortoise. The national park comprises ninety percent of the archipelago's surface area.

The Galápagos giant tortoise is the world's largest living tortoise. It can weigh over 200 kg (440 lb) and live for an estimated 150 years.

Darwin then spent the remainder of his life analyzing the collection, which led to a plethora of groundbreaking discoveries in the areas of geology, botany and entomology. His most notable achievement, however, was the formulation of the modern theory of evolution, which states that the diverse forms and shapes of a species are a result of the varying developments of inherent traits. It justifies the process of natural selection with the differing methods of adaptation to an environment. Darwin held off from publishing his revolutionary theory until 1858, when fellow naturalist Alfred Russel Wallace published some similar ideas. The work "On the Origin of Species" was released the following year; his second work, "The Descent of Man", followed in 1871.

Darwin's studies of the heads and beaks of finches contributed greatly to the development of his theory of evolution. Far left: A portrait of Darwin in his later years.

Marine iguanas warm themselves in the sun. They are the only species of lizard to live exclusively on food from the sea.

Like all of the thirty-five reptile species living on the Galápagos Islands, the Galápagos land iguana is native here.

Green sea turtles can grow to 1.5 m (5 ft) and lay their eggs on the beaches of the Galapagos Islands.

The Sally Lightfoot crab has very few natural enemies, which affords the creature its conspicuous red carapace.

Peru

RÍO ABISEO NATIONAL PARK

In addition to the Páramo grasslands, this national park boasts vast stretches of primary cloud forest that served as a refuge for many plants during the last ice age. Numerous ruins from pre-Columbian times have also been found in the middle of the forest.

In 1983, a national park covering an area of 2,700 sq km (1,050 sq mi) was established on the eastern slope of the Central Cordillera in northern Peru. The sizable reserve was primarily intended to protect the extraordinary flora and fauna found in the local cloud forest. Much of the plant and animal life here is native, among them fifteen species of batrachian (frogs) that call the park home. When the Peruvian yellow-tailed woolly monkey was discovered living here a few years ago it caused a minor scientific sensation – it had been thought to be extinct. The park also offers refuge to the acutely endangered Peruvian guemal and the red howler monkey.

Since 1985, archaeologists have excavated a total of thirty-six building complexes dating from the period of the Inca Empire. They were discovered deep in the dense jungle of the conservation area at elevations between 2,500 and 4,000 m (8,200 and 13,200 ft).

The Río Abiseo National Park is a refuge for a number of rare species including the Andean cock-of-the-rock, the national bird of Peru.

CHAN CHAN ARCHAEOLOGICAL ZONE

The ruins of Chan Chan are all that is left of one of the largest cities in pre-colonial South America. This masterpiece of town planning reflects the advanced political and social structure of the Chimú civilization.

Chan Chan, capital of the mighty Chimú Empire, stretches over an area of 20 sq km (8 sq mi) near present-day Trujillo, Peru, and experienced its heyday in the 15th century. The structures were built with air-dried adobe bricks and clay-cement slabs. In addition to a port, the city also had a sophisticated canal and aqueduct system that brought water from the hinterland. The various districts within the town center, so-called ciudadelas, were surrounded by high walls and had their own temples, residential complexes, storehouses, gardens and cemeteries.

The skillful artisanship of the Chimú is clearly evident in the structural decorations on the ornate adobe walls, in their ceramics, and in their gold and silver trinkets. Many of the death masks and other valuable treasures were stolen by the Spanish, however, leaving only historic descriptions and a few relics to provide, albeit minimal, insight into the real story.

The adobe walls of Chan Chan are adorned with animal reliefs and geometric patterns that can still be clearly distinguished in the Tschudi quarter.

CHAVÍN (ARCHAEOLOGICAL SITE)

Chavín de Huántar in the highlands of northern Peru is a burial site that also gave its name to one of the most influential pre-Columbian cultures in South America. It was known for its architecture and stonemasonry.

The center of the Chavín culture, which experienced its heyday between 1000 and 300 BC, was near the town of Chavín de Huántar at an elevation of 3,200 m (10,499 ft) in the Cordillera Blanca. Its core consisted of the Old Temple, a square pyramidal building with a circular, sunken ceremonial area that was expanded at least twice in its history. The main temple is accessed from the New Temple through a gate flanked by two round columns adorned with reliefs. Its external walls were built with carefully shaped volcanic stone blocks decorated with predatory bird and animal themes. Steps lead down into an underground system of passageways that is home to the "El Lanzón" statue, a 4.5-m-high (15-ft) granite stele depicting a half-human, half-animal creature.

Other important monuments such as the Tello Obelisk and the Raimondi stele can now be found in the Archaeological Museum in Lima. Finds such as textile remains, metal objects and pottery attest to the high standard of artisanry practiced by the city's former inhabitants.

Heads hewn out of stone were typical of the Chavín, who heavily influenced subsequent cultures in South America.

HUASCARÁN NATIONAL PARK

Punctuated by the snowy peaks of the Cordillera Blanca, this national park reaches elevations of 6,000 m (19,700 ft). Its gorges and glacial lakes possess extraordinary natural beauty and are home to many rare plants and animals.

The snow-capped summit of Nevado Huascarán, Peru's highest mountain, towers majestically over the national park of the same name at 6,768 m (22,200 ft). The scenery of the Cordillera Blanca features colossal glaciers, serene mountain lakes, dramatic gorges and raging streams and is a fascinating sight for any visitor. The Huascarán is just one of twenty-seven peaks here that rises above 6,000 m (19,700 ft), and these are flanked by thirty glaciers and over 125 glacial lakes. The average temperature is 3°C but in winter the mercury can dip to -30°C. Nonetheless, robust plants such as the Puya raimondii, a rare cactus species, and the world's largest bromelia, manage to grow here at elevations up to 4,000 m (13,200 ft). Mammals that have adapted handily to the conditions of this bare mountainous world include spectacled bears, pumas, vicuñas, white-tailed deers and Peruvian guemals. Of the 100 or so species of bird living in the park, the puna hawk, the Andean condor and the picaflor, the world's largest hummingbird, are the most spectacular.

The rare Puya raimondii can grow to 10 m (33 ft) in height. Below: Lagunas de Llanganuco at 4000 m (13,500 ft)

SACRED CITY OF CARAL-SUPE

Excavations in Peru's Supe Valley 182 km (113 mi) north of Lima prove that at the time the first pyramids were being built in Egypt a prosperous and highly advanced civilization already existed in Latin America.

Caral, one of the oldest cities in the Americas, lay buried under rubble until 1994 when it was discovered by a team of Peruvian archaeologists. We now know that about 3,000 years before the Common Era as many as 3,000 people were living in Caral, a settlement perched 25 m (82 ft) above the fertile Supe Valley. The city was dominated by six pyramids facing the six lines of sight. Magnificent buildings characterized the upper town while workshops, market places and a series of rather cramped dwellings made up the lower town. The knotted cords systems found beneath one pyramid in Caral prove that "quipu", one of the world's oldest written languages that is communicated using knots, was not developed by the Inca, as previously assumed, but is actually significantly older. The discovery of Caral demonstrates that a very advanced civilization had emerged in Latin America at the same time as those in Mesopotamia, India and Egypt. However, while those sophisticated civilizations had contact with one another, Caral developed on its own.

This well-preserved archaeological site displays a complex urban structure of pyramids, temples, circular plazas, residential homes and burial mounds.

Peru

Francisco Pizarro

Francisco Pizarro was born in 1478 in Trujillo, Extremadura (Spain), the illegitimate son of a Spanish captain. The future conquistador then took part in expeditions in Central America as early as 1510. In 1513 he accompanied Vasco Núñez de Balboa during his crossing of the Isthmus of Panama, which brought them to the Pacific.

Pizarro eventually explored Peru on his own initiative between 1524 and 1527, and was named the Governor and Captain General of Peru just two years later by Emperor Charles V. On 13 May 1531, Pizarro, together with his three half-brothers, landed on the Peruvian coast where they attacked and captured Atahualpa, the

HISTORIC CENTER OF LIMA

In colonial times Lima was the largest and most important city in South America. Fortunately, despite frequent earthquakes, many of the colonial-era buildings have survived.

Lima was founded in 1535 by Francisco Pizarro, known as the Conqueror of Peru, in the fertile valley of the Río Rímac. The city developed quickly due to its coastal location – and the gold and silver the Spanish looted from the defeated Incas. It soon became the most opulent city in the "Gobernación de Nueva Castilla", which was incorporated into the Viceroyalty of Peru in 1542. From 1570 to 1820, the Inquisition was based here in the "City of the Kings" and became a powerful instrument of oppression against indigenous peoples. Also from this time – albeit built by slaves – are the splendid manor houses, monasteries and churches that gave Lima the nickname "Pearl of the Pacific". However, earthquakes (in 1687 and 1746) and battles during the "War of the Pacific" in the late 19th century, severely damage the city's fabric.

The Iglesia de San Francisco, with its Franciscan monastery, was completed in 1672. Its buildings form South America's largest clerical complex from the colonial era. The baroque style prevailed in the early 1700s, which resulted in the construction of edifices such as the large cathedral where Pizarro was buried and the Palacio de Torre Tagle, with Lima's finest carved wooden balconies. The building recalls the way the Andalusian Baroque was influenced by Moorish art.

The Archbishop's Palace and the Government Palace from the 20th century display colonial-era styles. The San Francisco Monastery became a World Heritage Site in 1988, followed three years later by the entire Old Town.

Secular and religious buildings face one another at Lima's central Plaza de Armas. On the right is the cathedral with the Government Palace in the background, and the town hall to the left.

last great ruler of the Incas. Despite enormous ransoms, Pizarro had his hostage executed in 1533 and only managed to defeat the ensuing Inca uprising with the help of recently arrived Spanish troops led by Diego de Almagro. On 15 November 1533, Pizarro invaded the Inca capital of Cuzco. Two years later he founded

Lima, then known as Ciudad de los Reyes. A dispute between Pizarro and Almagro ended with latter's imprisonment and execution in 1538. The ruthless conqueror Pizarro was eventually murdered by some of Diego de Almagro's followers. His mummified corpse is still entombed in Lima's cathedral.

Conqueror of the Inca Empire, Francisco Pizarro is depicted with Cross of St James (far left) in a 16th-century oil painting. The encounter between Pizarro and Atahualpa in Cajamarca in 1532 was initially a peaceful one (mosaic in Cajamarca, left). The guns and horses intimidated the Incas.

The interior of the Iglesia de San Francisco features arched roofs painted with geometric patterns, Sevillian azulejos and domes that recall the Mudejar style.

The Convento de San Francisco houses a 17th-century library with over 20,000 volumes.

In Santo Domingo, Lima's oldest monastery, the beautiful cloister incorporates a lush interior courtyard designed in Sevillan style.

Peru

MACHU PICCHU

Situated on a high mountain ridge, Machu Picchu was rediscovered at the beginning of the 20th century and is arguably the most impressive and best-preserved Inca city ruin. It is also one of the most important archaeological sites in South America.

Hiram Bingham, an American historian, became the first white man to set eyes on this spectacular Inca city in 1911. Drawing on its location beneath Huayna Picchu, "young mountain", he christened the site Machu Picchu, "old mountain". Everything seems mysterious here, hiding amidst tropical mountain forest on the eastern slopes of the Andes and clinging like an eagle's eyrie to a flattened ridge at an elevation of 2,430 m (7,970 ft). The settlement, perched above the Río Urubamba valley, is fascinating not just because of its well-preserved buildings but also because of the unique interplay of architecture and

Machu Picchu is one of the most impressive examples of architecture incorporated into its surrounding environment.

nature – the buildings fit perfectly into the uneven terrain.
There is still speculation today about the importance of this town, which was never recorded or apparently even noticed by the Spanish conquistadors; one theory proposes that it was an attempt by the Incas to colonize the eastern slopes of the Andes. What is certain, however, is that it was built in around 1450 and abandoned only a century later.
The site is divided into two areas: a farmed zone with terraced agricultural land on the mountain's slopes fed by a cunning irrigation system; and an unfortified municipal area consisting of palaces, temples and dwellings. Among the most important monuments are the Round Tower, the Temple of the Sun and the Room of Three Windows.

The sophisticated terrace structure of Machu Picchu is easy to recognize among the ruins (top and middle). The city's buildings were constructed of stone without the use of mortar, including the Temple of Intihuatana, sun god (right).

CUZCO

Cuzco is the most historic city in the Peruvian highlands. The Incas built it as an urban complex serving both religious and administrative purposes but after it was captured by Francisco Pizarro, the Spaniards had their own churches and squares built on the ruins of the Inca structures.

Cuzco is one of the oldest surviving cities in the New World. It is located in a region that was inhabited by agricultural peoples as early as 1000 BC, before becoming the heartland of the mighty Inca Empire 2,000 years later. According to one legend of creation, this city perched at a lofty 3,400 m (11,155 ft) above sea level is said to have been founded around the year 1200 by Manco Cápac, the first mythical Inca ruler. Over the next 300 years, Cuzco developed into the most magnificent of all Inca cities, thus becoming the political, religious and cultural center of the empire.

Many parts of Cuzco's Old Town still display the foundation walls from the Inca era, built virtually without mortar using giant stone blocks.

A majority of the temples and palaces here were erected during the imperial period, which began when Inca king Pachacútec became ruler in 1438. A number of buildings are even said to have been covered with gold and copper plating. Cuzco was conquered and destroyed in 1533 by conquistador Francisco Pizarro, after which missionaries built churches and monasteries on the ruins of the Inca structures to erase the memory of indigenous traditions. The Santo Domingo Convent was erected on the remains of the sun temple, the central sanctuary of the old temple district. For better or worse, the Plaza de Armas has managed to preserve its colonial character. The dome of the Jesuit Church of La Compañía, constructed on the foundation walls of the palace of mighty Inca ruler Huayna Cápac, is one of Peru's finest baroque churches.

A number of buildings were erected on the walls (bottom) of Inca sanctuaries including the cathedral (top) and the Santo Domingo Convent (middle).

Peru

MANÚ NATIONAL PARK

This remote park on the eastern slopes of the Andes towards the Amazon lowlands is a region of superlatives with countless species of native plants and animals. Some indigenous tribes still live here according to their traditional hunting and farming methods.

Peru's second-largest national park covers an area of 15,000 sq km (5,800 sq mi) and includes elevations ranging from 150 to 4,200 m (500 to 13,900 ft). Established in 1973, the park encompasses the entire catchment basin of the Río Manú, a tributary of the Amazon, as well as sections of the Río Alto Madre de Dios basin. The area consists of flood plains, rolling hills and mountains, and the

Hoatzins (top) provide lively background noise in the forest. The emperor tamarin (above) owes its name to its impressive facial decoration.

vegetation ranges from tropical rain and montane forest to grasslands. Still largely undisturbed, it is a true paradise for animals with over a thousand bird species and 200 mammals. Many varieties of parrot live here along with the giant otter, which can reach up to 2 m (7 ft) in length and is threatened with extinction. Even the river terrapin, long since extinct elsewhere, has found refuge here with three-toed sloths. Other typical South American animals found here include the jaguar, the giant armadillo and the coati. Indigenous ethnic groups such as the Machiguenga, Yaminahua and Amahuaca also live undisturbed here.

The rivers here meander through tropical rain forest (top). Blue-headed parrots on a river embankment pick at loamy soil for its mineral content (right).

LINES AND GEOGLYPHS OF NASCA AND PAMPAS DE JUMANA

One of South America's most enigmatic phenomena are the lines and geoglyphs covering an area of some 450 sq km (174 sq mi) around Nasca and in the Pampas de Jumana in the arid coastal region of southern Peru.

The center of the Nasca civilization was approximately 400 km (249 mi) south of present-day Lima in the valley of the Rìo Grande. One of South America's greatest archaeological enigmas was also discovered here: geoglyphs up to 2,000 m (6,562 ft) in length. The first lines were created during the Chavín period from 1000 to 300 BC and were formed by piling stones on top of each other. Most of the drawings, however, are from the Nasca period from 500 BC to AD 500.

The Nasca scuffed off the dark gravel crust leaving the contrasting layers to highlight the contours of the figures. Due to their size, some are only discernible from the air. About seventy figures have been identified as living creatures (birds, insects, plants and humans) while a second group has straight lines and geometric patterns. Their significance is still unclear.

The Nasca lines range from hummingbirds to whales and spiders.

HISTORIC CENTER OF THE CITY OF AREQUIPA

With their archways, vaults, interior courtyards and open spaces, the churches and palaces in the Old Town of Arequipa in southern Peru demonstrate the creativity and inventiveness of the Latin American baroque.

Arequipa, at 2,360 m (7,743 ft) above sea level, was founded by Spanish conquistadors in 1540 and quickly became an important hub in the southern Andes. The focal point here is the arcaded Plaza de Armas whose northern end is formed by the side of the cathedral. Like other buildings in Arequipa, it was severely damaged by an earthquake and rebuilt in a neo-classical style in the 19th century. The Jesuit Church of La Compañía with its ornate façade is one of the most important works of late 18th-century "mestizo-baroque". It is also lavishly

furnished. Other religious buildings from the period between the 16th and 18th centuries include the monasteries and churches of San Francisco, Santa Catalina, Santo Domingo, San Agustín and La Merced. The porches of the about 500 former manor houses built in the 19th century on the site of houses destroyed by earthquakes are also richly decorated.

Plaza de Armas with the cathedral is lovely for a stroll (above). Paintings adorn the walls of Capilla San Ignacio in the Iglesia La Compañía (left).

Bolivia

RUINS OF THE TIWANAKU CULTURE

Tiahuanaco – Tiwanaku in the local Aymara language - was the center of an empire that ruled vast areas of the southern Andes before the Incas.

The ruins of Tiwanaku are roughly 15 km (9 mi) south of Lake Titicaca. In its heyday in the eighth century the city covered 6 sq km (2 sq mi) and was home to some 100,000 people. The ruins of this culture's spiritual and political center are dominated by two enormous pyramid structures – Akapana and Puma Punku – a semi-subterranean temple, and the Kalasasaya temple complex, whose square plan covers roughly 3 ha (7.5 acres) and probably served as an observatory. Towering over the north-west corner is the 3-m-high (10-ft) and 4-m-wide (13-ft) Gate of the Sun, hewn from a stone block that features the relief of an anthropomorphic figure with a puma's snout on the cross-beam. A sophisticated irrigation system and artificial terraces helped the Tiwanaku culture maintain its economic prosperity, which was also reflected in a vast trade network. It was probably a period of drought that forced the settlement's inhabitants to leave their city forever in the first half of the 12th century.

Foundation walls, a gate and some stone figures have been preserved at the Kalasasaya temple complex.

HISTORIC CITY OF SUCRE

Numerous buildings from the 16th century recall the former importance of what is now the constitutional capital of Bolivia. They display an attractive fusion of local and European architectural styles.

After the conquest of Cuzco, the Ciudad de la Plata de Nuevo Toledo was founded in 1538 in the Cordillera Central, and was intended to supply food to the Spanish colony. Thanks to its fertile soil, mild climate and rich silver deposits in the surrounding hills the town quickly prospered and rose up to become the spiritual center of Bolivia. The university, one of the oldest in the Americas, was founded in a Jesuit monastery in 1624. It then became the focal point of the liberal movement, which ultimately led to uprisings against Spanish colonial rule in the early 19th century. The city was named after this movement's leader, Antonio José de Sucre, who later became the first president of Bolivia. With its white buildings constructed between the 16th and 18th century, the Old Town is one of the most beautiful in South America. The Casa de la Libertad, the Palacio de la Glorieta, the former Franciscan monastery and the La Recoleta Museum, the San Felipe Neri convent, the cathedral and a few churches are also worth seeing here.

The San Felipe Neri convent was built in the 17th century. Its opulent furnishings demonstrates the power of the Catholic Church.

CITY OF POTOSÍ

Once Bolivia's largest and richest city, Potosí owes its wealth to the silver ore hidden with the 4,829-m (15,844-ft) Cerro Rico mountain. Two-thirds of the silver extracted in the 17th century came from here.

Hardly any other city in South America recalls the time of the conquistadors like Potosí. Perched at an elevation of 4,000 m (13,124 ft). It was founded at the foot of Cerro Rico mountain after silver veins were discovered there in 1545. Under the colonial yoke of the Spanish, thousands upon thousands of Indians were forced to mine the precious metal in inhumane conditions. The silver was then transported to Lima by llamas and mules and from there onwards to Spain. The city lost its former importance once the silver deposits began declining in the mid-18th century. Today, tin and zinc are mined here.

The alleyways and streets of the city are lined with manor houses featuring coats of arms, colonial-era religious buildings like the cathedrals of La Compañía, San Francisco and San Lorenzo, and the Casa Real de la Moneda mint. They attest to the city's rich history. Apart from the Old Town, the World Heritage Site also includes some historic water management systems and the "Barrios Mitayos" with the humble dwellings of forcibly recruited Indian mineworkers.

The church of San Francisco was built in 1546 and is just one of twenty-two churches in the silver city of Potosí.

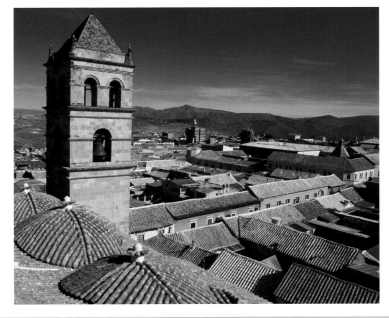

FUERTE DE SAMAIPATA

An enormous rocky outcrop with numerous notches as well as the remains of a settlement attest to the existence of a highly developed pre-Columbian culture in the eastern Andes.

These ruins are perched at an elevation of 2,000 m (6,562 ft) about 100 km (62 mi) south-west of Santa Cruz de la Sierra in the eastern foothills of the Cordillera Oriental. It was once an important religious center that was originally founded by the Mojocoyas in around AD 300. The Incas invaded the complex in the 14th century, developed it into a ceremonial site and secured it with fortifications. After conquering the city, the Spaniards further expanded the forts. The site is about 40 ha (99 acre) in size and consists of two main parts: a giant rocky outcrop, and, south of this, an area containing administrative and residential buildings. The central element is the reddish sandstone massif, which is divided into an upper section, El Mirador, and a 220-m-long (722-ft) and 50-m-wide (164-ft) lower section into which numerous channels, steps, basins and geometric figures have been chiseled. Drawings of snakes and big cats can be clearly distinguished while the area at the base of the rock constituted the ceremonial center, residential district and farmland.

Two parallel channels running in an east-west direction can be made out on the sandstone rocks of Samaipata.

NOEL KEMPFF MERCADO NATIONAL PARK

This national park is one of the largest and most continuous in Bolivia. It is located on the Brazilian border in the western Amazon basin and is home to an incredible variety of plant and animal life.

This park covers 15,000 sq km (5,800 sq mi) of the Huanchaca Plateau and its surrounding lowlands. It ranges in elevation between 200 and 1,000 m (650 and 3,300 ft) and encompasses five separate ecosystems: the tropical rain forest of Amazonia, seasonal floodland savannah, deciduous dry forest and montane forest, areas of thorny scrub forest, and vast expanses of swamps and floodplains. This diverse vegetation is of course home to correspondingly varied plant and animal life. The number of plant species alone in the park has been estimated at around 4,000. Before his brutal murder at the hands of drug smugglers in 1986, Bolivian naturalist Noel Kempff Mercado – after whom the national park is named – had begun recording this vast biosystem. Since then, more than 600 bird and 150 mammals and reptile species have been identified including Gould's toucanet, the hyacinthine macaw, the Amazon river dolphin and the jaguar.

The sandstone and quartzite Huanchaca Plateau is over one billion years old and still covered with dense rain forest.

JESUIT MISSIONS OF THE CHIQUITOS

In the 18th century, Jesuits built several missionary villages in territory belonging to the Chiquito Indians in Bolivia. Their churches have been well preserved and display Catholic architecture fused with local construction methods.

Between 1696 and 1760, Jesuit missionaries built ten so-called "reductions" – settlements where, much like in Paraguay, Brazil and Argentina, they provided Indians with a place to live and converted them to Christianity – in the vast alluvial plains of eastern Bolivia about 200 km (124 mi) northeast of Santa Cruz. They considered the basis of the mission to be the communal nature of everyday life. The language spoken here was predominantly the Indian language known as Chiquito. Life in the mission villages, which also protected the Indians from slave hunters, was characterized by a strict and paternalistic division of labor: the "Chiquitos" tilled the land while Jesuit padres performed the administrative tasks. The communities were in fact very successful economically and the ones that have been best preserved are San Francisco Javier, Concepción, Santa Ana, San Miguel, San Rafael and San José.

The church, usually built of wood, was the focal point of a Jesuit mission. In Concepción, the church comprises three naves painted in mestizo-baroque style.

Chile

HUMBERSTONE AND SANTA LAURA SALTPETER WORKS

The abandoned mine worker settlements in Chile's northern Atacama Desert are silent evidence of a sixty-year industrial period during which saltpeter was mined here.

The world's largest saltpeter districts are located in the drainless basins between the Coastal Cordillera and the High Cordillera in northern Chile. Most of the so-called Chile saltpeter extracted from there was exported and used to manufacture gunpowder, explosives and fertilizers. The industry experienced its boom between 1880 and 1940, before the artificial manufacture of saltpeter led to its collapse. The workers at more than 200 saltpeter works came from Bolivia, Chile and Peru and lived in appallingly poor conditions at the on-site accommodations. Their work conditions were no better either. Over the years, however, they developed their own Pampino culture, which connected the workers from the different countries. The abandoned sites fell into ruin as a result of weathering and pillaging, and are but ghost towns now. Communal and residential buildings in Humberstone and factory complexes in Santa Laura have been preserved.

Rusty machinery, buildings and train cars serve as reminders of the Humberstone factory and railway.

HISTORIC QUARTER OF THE SEAPORT OF VALPARAÍSO

The European emigrants who came to Valparaíso during the 19th century left an indelible mark on this city where hundreds of colorful houses are scattered around the hills above the port.

Valparaíso means "Valley of Paradise". In fact, Chile's second-largest city is in a very picturesque by bay around 120 km (75 mi) west of Santiago, the capital. Behind a narrow coastal strip, the terrain rises quickly in four large terraces and numerous hills. Founded in 1544, the city enjoyed an increasing number of trade relationships between Europe and Chile in the 19th century, predominantly based on the export of wheat, copper and saltpeter. All the ships that rounded the southern tip of South America, Cape Horn, also stopped in Valparaíso. As a result, many Europeans settled here during that time. The wealthy ones, mostly the captains, settled on the steep slopes above town, which were accessed via staircases. Pablo Neruda, who lived in Valparaíso, wrote, "If we have climbed up and down all of Valparaíso's stairs, we have traveled the world". Several funicular railways have since replaced the exhausting climb.

Colorful houses and brightly painted cabins of the "ascensores" give Valparaíso its unique character.

SEWELL MINING TOWN

In 1905, a city was established in the middle of the Andes for the workers at El Teniente, the world's largest underground copper mine. The development and extraction of Chilean raw materials was facilitated by capital from the USA.

Chile's largest copper mine is located near Sewell, about 100 km (62 mi) south-east of Santiago. The El Teniente mine, which is still in operation, was cut into the Andes to a depth of fourteen stories. In the 20th century, the mine operator at the time, Braden Copper Company from the United States, built a city for its workers at an elevation of 2,000 m (6,562 ft) and named it after the company's president, Barton Sewell. The workers' settlement on Cerro Negro mountain is a maze of staircases too steep for vehicles. Two passageways branch into side staircases from the central stairwell, which leads from the train

station to the city. Only via these stairs is it possible to reach the wooden half-timbered houses painted in red, yellow, blue and green. They have copper roofs and were designed in the United States. During its heyday, the city had 15,000 inhabitants who lived in six-bed rooms or family accommodations. It was largely abandoned in the 1970s. The World Heritage Site includes residential homes, a hospital, a Catholic church, a cinema, a theater and a school.

The workers lived in wooden buildings until well into the 1970s.

CHURCHES OF CHILOÉ

The island of Chiloé, south of Puerto Montt, has over 150 wooden churches that combine European architecture with indigenous stylistic elements. They were built in the 17th and 18th centuries.

After Chiloé fell under Spanish colonial rule in 1567, a campaign of proselytization began under Jesuits that was continued by Franciscans even after the Spanish were banished in 1767. The Christianization by the friars saw the emergence of 150 churches, fourteen of which are part of the World Heritage Site. Most of the churches, built predominantly from cypress wood and situated largely in elevated locations near the coast, have a uniform style of construction. The main structure is similar to a cuboid over which a gable roof was placed. A characteristic element of the older wooden churches is the

portico, which adorns the main façade on the tower side. The exterior walls are artistically covered with colorful, interwoven wooden shingles decorated with carvings by local artists. They are made from the wood of the Alerce, a type of larch native to Chiloé. Inside, the wooden churches follow a more European style. The larger ones have three naves and some have ornately painted walls and ceilings. The churches of Achao are particularly colorful.

A colorfully painted portico adorns the wooden church of Chonchi on the island of Chiloé.

RAPA NUI NATIONAL PARK (EASTER ISLAND)

The statues on Easter Island are carved out of tuff and can reach several meters in height. Far out in the middle of the Pacific and just 164 sq km (63 sq mi) in size, the island retains impressive evidence of a lost Polynesian culture.

Located some 3,700 km (2,299 mi) off the South American mainland, and around 4,200 km (2,610 mi) from the Polynesian island of Tahiti, Easter Island is one of the most isolated places on earth. Despite that, it was first settled as early as the year 400 and presumably resettled in the 14th century, when the legendary King Hotu Matua is said to have arrived here with followers from Polynesia. The Polynesians called the island Rapa Nui, or "Large Island". Several hundred "Moai" – tuff sculptures measuring up to 10 m (33 ft) in height – stand tall

on large platforms known as "ahus" and are an impressive testimony to their culture. They are adorned with Rongorongo script, a form of hieroglyphics. The significance of the Moai is not entirely clear. Limited space on the island consistently led to tribal feuds, which culminated in destruction of the sacred sites in 1680.

The purpose of the Moai (left), gigantic tuff figures and heads measuring several meters in height is still a mystery, but they were erected in their hundreds on Easter Island in the Pacific Ocean.

Venezuela

CORO AND ITS PORT

In this city on the Caribbean coast, style elements of Spanish colonial architecture are blended uniquely with those of the Dutch Baroque.

Santa Ana de Coro was founded in 1527 by Juan de Ampíes, who originally developed the city as a trading center. Soon after, however, an ambitious German merchant named Ambrosius Dalfinger landed in Coro and leased it for the Welsers, a wealthy patrician family from Augsburg. The German bankers then ruled here until their right to conquer and settle was terminated in 1546. When the provincial government and bishops' see were later transferred to Caracas, Coro gradually lost its importance. In the 18th century, trade with the Dutch Antilles brought about a welcome economic upswing. The buildings and churches in the Old Town reveal a charming blend of the local mud-brick building style with Spanish Mudéjar architecture and Dutch style elements. The Franciscan church as well as the chapel of the royal hospital are particularly impressive. One of its most attractive squares is the Plaza de San Clemente, on which the cross of San Clemente stands. On an isthmus next to the Caribbean coast is Los Médanos de Coro National Park, which forms another impressive part of the World Heritage Site.

Behind the Plaza de San Clemente are the façade and tower of the Franciscan church.

CIUDAD UNIVERSITARIA DE CARACAS

The Ciudad Universitaria de Caracas was built between 1940 and 1960 and is a masterpiece of modern town planning, architecture and art. Architectural ideals of the early 20th century were realized here in an outstanding manner.

Two main concepts determined the planns for the Ciudad Universitaria in Caracas: on the one hand, it was to create an ambience of a good quality of life; on the other hand, it was to aim at a close fusion of architecture, fine art and sculpture. The design for this gem of modern architecture came from Venezuelan Carlos Raúl Villanueva. The complex, which features a variety of designs, is covered by footpaths that lead between airy halls. These open out to plazas with roofs for shade, the architect's way of dealing with the tropical heat. Works of art are highlights at central points of the ensemble. The most spectacular structures of the University City are the stadium and the aula magna. In the stadium, Villanueva made use of the new possibilities offered by reinforced concrete. The aula magna, in contrast, is an example of the successful fusion of architecture and sculpture. "Clouds" by Alexander Calder are fixed to the ceilings and walls to enliven the appearance.

The concert hall, as seen from the library's balconies.

CANAIMA NATIONAL PARK

The Gran Sabana is one of the world's most beautiful places with mighty plateaus and the world's highest waterfall, Salto Angel. It is also a habitat for innumerable plant species.

In the language of the local Kamarokoto people, Canaima represents a dark deity that has united all evil within itself. By contrast, Venezuela's second-largest national park, covering 30,000 sq km (11,600 sq mi), is a place of overwhelming natural beauty. Located in the south-eastern reaches of the country near the Guyanese and Brazilian borders, this park encompasses the singular landscape of the Gran Sabana. Nestled in amongst the dense vegetation are a host of spectacular waterfalls that crash dramatically into the depths at Salto Angel, Salto Kukenam and the Canaima Lagoon rapids. It is estimated that some 3,000 to 5,000 flowering plants and ferns grow here, many of which are native. In addition to the savannah there is impenetrable montane forest and scrubland. Some unique pioneer vegetation has evolved on the many mesas, with numerous species of carnivorous plants adding to the variety. There is also an impressive diversity of orchid species. Around 550 bird species including hummingbirds and parrots live here with as many species of mammals.

Water from the Río Carrao crashes over a series of parallel cascades into Canaima Lagoon.

HISTORIC INNER CITY OF PARAMARIBO

Thanks to the fusion of indigenous and Dutch construction traditions the historic heart of Paramaribo is a unique architectural ensemble in mainland South America.

Europeans discovered the coast of Guyana at the end of the 15th century. The landscape between the Orinoco and Amazon Rivers is richly blessed with natural resources such as rubber and timber. Over the course of colonization, which began in the 16th and 17th centuries, the Dutch established a trading post on the Suriname River that developed into Paramaribo, the capital of the Republic of Suriname (independent since 1975). Landowners settled here and cultivated sugarcane and tobacco on their plantations. Despite a large fire in 1821, Parama-

ribo now comprises a charming mix of historic buildings from various periods. The many wood constructions in the Old Town were based on local traditions – for example the St Peter and Paul Cathedral. The 19th-century government brick buildings such as the Presidential Palace were more Dutch. Synagogues, mosques and Hindu temples indicate Suriname's diversity.

The court building on Independence Square is one of few stone buildings here. In front of it is a statue of national hero Johan Adolf Pengel standing guard.

CENTRAL SURINAME NATURE RESERVE

This enormous nature reserve encompasses the untouched tropical rain forest of the Guiana Shield and includes an enormous number of plant and animal species, many of which are native to the area.

Over two billion years old and dating back to the Precambrian, the Guiana Shield craton of the north-eastern corner of the South American continental plate is one of the oldest formations on earth. This primeval rain forest covers around 150,000 sq km (58,000 sq mi) and is still largely inaccessible and unexplored. In 1998, Suriname's three most important conservation areas were combined into one colossal area of 16,000 sq km (6,200 sq mi) and renamed the Central Nature Reserve. Among its broad range of landscape formations are table-like mesas, which tower 350 m

(1,150 ft) over the surrounding rain forest. The conservation area has an impressive variety of plant life; 6,000 species have been recorded in the dense forests of the mountains and lowlands. Besides the rain forest, there is also savannah and wetland forest. The animal life on the reserve is extraordinarily diverse: 700 different birds, nearly 2,000 mammals, 150 reptiles, 100 amphibians and nearly 500 fish species have been cataloged.

The nature reserve is home to the Amazon horned frog (top left), the side-necked turtle (top) and the Brazilian tapir (left).

Brazil

CENTRAL AMAZON CONSERVATION COMPLEX

The largest conservation area in the Amazon basin includes Jaú National Park, the Mamirauá and Amanã Nature Reserves, and the Anavilhanas Ecological Station. It is one of the most species-rich places on the planet.

This gigantic rainforest park is about 200 km (125 mi) north-west of Manaus. The heart of the area is Jaú National Park, which covers the complete catchment basin of the Río Jaú up to its confluence with the Río Negro. In 2000, the reserve was inscribed as a World Heritage Site and in 2003 was expanded to more than 60,000 sq km (23,200 sq mi) under the name Complexão de Conservação del Amazonas Central. The Jaú and Negro rivers form a blackwater ecosystem with seasonal water level changes that have nurtured the Igapó inundated forest area. Blackwater rivers are dark in color due to dissolved tannins and organic precipitates; they contain little sediment. Its inhabitants include giant otters, river manatees, South American river turtles and black caimans. The Mamirauá reserve has extensive whitewater flood plains ("várzea") with nutrient-rich soil – whitewater rivers have turbid waters that are rich in light minerals. The conservation area is home to over 450 birds, 300 fish and 120 different mammals including pink and gray river dolphins.

Right: A young woolly monkey.
Below: The Rio Jau estuary from space.

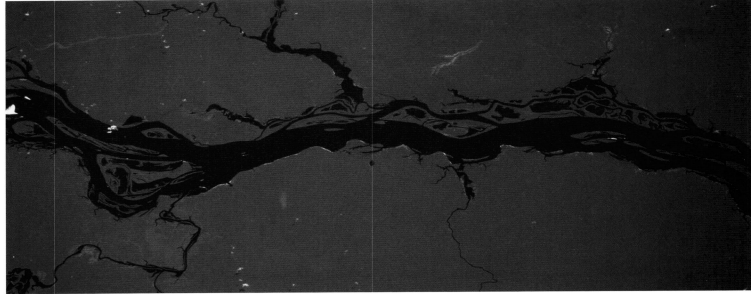

HISTORIC CENTER OF SÃO LUÍS

The historic center of the capital of Maranhão on the north-eastern coast of Brazil boasts a wealth of Portuguese colonial architectural styles that have been adapted for the tropical South American surroundings.

The Portuguese conquered this city as early as 1615, after it had been founded just a few years earlier by the French on the Ilha de São Luís in the Bay of São Marcos. The multilevel façades of many houses lining the roads and lanes of the Old Town, which is laid out on a rectangular grid, are clad in so-called azulejos – colorful, hand-painted tiles. With their many balconies and balustrades, often featuring wrought-iron railings, the buildings look very Portuguese indeed. The inhabitants lovingly refer to their Old Town as Praia Grande or "Great Beach". Stately administrative and governmental palaces such as the Palace of the Lion and the Palácio La Ravardière, attest to the power and the glory of the former colonial rulers. Many of these buildings still house administrative offices while others have been converted into museums. In 1726, the Jesuits built the magnificent Cathedral, which was transferred to the archbishop in 1763. The Carmelite Church (1627) and the Church of Santo Antônio with the Navigators' Chapel (1624) are the oldest churches in the city.

Façades from the colonial period line the lanes of the old town in São Luís, with its characteristic tile-decorated houses.

HISTORIC CENTER OF OLINDA

With its churches, monasteries, colonial buildings and a multitude of groomed gardens, Olinda, near Recife on the north-eastern Atlantic coast, is one of Brazil's most beautiful cities. The town owes its heyday to sugarcane.

Olinda's old town, the "Pearl of Brazilian Baroque", is draped lazily over several palm-tree-covered hills. "O linda situação para uma vila" was how the Portuguese spoke of the "beautiful location for a city" after founding their settlement here in 1535. In the early 17th century, the Dutch conquered the territory in north-eastern Brazil that included Olinda but in 1654, after defeating Dutch colonial troops near Guararapes, the Portuguese reclaimed Olinda for themselves. Many of the buildings destroyed by the Dutch in the 17th century were then rebuilt and enlarged. Thus, most of the buildings preserved today date from the 17th and 18th centuries. Some twenty baroque churches and countless "passos" – the name for small chapels here – attest to the town's importance as a spiritual center along with the Benedictine, Franciscan and Carmelite monasteries like São Francisco and São Bento. The Igreja da Sé, founded in 1537, was home to the first parish in the north-east and has been the cathedral of the archbishopric of Olinda and Recife since 1676.

Fringed by grand palm trees, the Franciscan monastery sits high above Olinda (left). One of the typical alleyways in the city (below).

SERRA DA CAPIVARA NATIONAL PARK

Some of the oldest existing traces of settlement in the Americas can be found in Serra da Capivara National Park in north-eastern Brazil where impressive rock drawings attest to the culture of the original inhabitants.

The earliest traces of human life on the South American continent have been found in the mountainous region of the Serra da Capivara in the Brazilian state of Piauí. In the sizable caves here, prehistoric humans had already discovered fire – proof that South America was populated much earlier than had previously been assumed. According to recent excavations, these original inhabitants lived not only in caves, but also in open settlements out on the savannah. Clay crocks that have been unearthed provide evidence that they were already skilled potters. The most spectacular expression of their culture are the numerous rock drawings, some up to 25,000 years old; most, however, date from the period between 10,000 and 4,000 BC. They depict humans and animals, everyday activities and hunts, providing insight into the lifestyle and imaginary world of these early humans.

The usually red rock drawings mostly depict dancing and hunting scenes as well as humans performing various rituals and ceremonies.

Brazil

HISTORIC CENTER OF SALVADOR DA BAHIA

Magnificent renaissance façades and churches bear witness to the glorious heyday of the former Brazilian capital, now a vibrant center of Afro-Brazilian culture.

In 1501, Italian navigator Amerigo Vespucci came ashore where Salvador da Bahia de Todos os Santos, or "Holy Savior of All Saints Bay", was founded on the Atlantic coast about fifty years later. In fact, between 1549 and 1763, Salvador da Bahia was the first capital of Brazil, and slaves were transported here from the west coast of Africa to work on the extensive sugarcane and tobacco plantations. In 1558, one of the first slave markets in the New World was opened here. Now a museum at the Cafuá das Mercês commemorates that fact. Salvador comprises a Lower Town and an Upper Town that lies 80 m (262 ft)

Next to the colonial buildings in the Pelourinho district is the Igreja de Nossa Senhora do Rosário dos Pretos.

higher up. The port and the business districts were located near the ocean while palaces and churches were perched in the Upper Town. Narrow lanes and steep stairs still connect the two parts of town with each other, but since the end of the 19th century, it has been possible to travel between the Upper and Lower Towns with the help of the Elevador Lacerda, a lift. Salvador's Upper Town is the largest complete district with Renaissance buildings in Brazil where no fewer than 166 churches speak of the glorious heyday of the city. Among the sights are the Cathedral, the Church of São Francisco and the Church of the Carmelite Monastery. Over two-thirds of the inhabitants are descendants of black slaves, which made the town into a melting pot of European and African religions.

The 18th-century baroque Church of São Francisco features a number of impressive gilded carvings.

Salvador is a city of churches. Above, the twin towers of the Igreja do Santíssimo Sacramento peak out over the restored rows of houses in the Upper Town.

One of the most attractive tiled walls in the city can be seen in the cloister of the Franciscan monastery. It was painted in the 18th century, using as a model a collection of allegorical engravings.

The Cathedral of Salvador da Bahia was originally a Jesuit church. Numerous details still indicate this, for example the lavish ceiling of the sacristy, on which the portraits of various brothers of the Jesuit Order can be seen.

Brazil

DISCOVERY COAST ATLANTIC RAIN FOREST RESERVES

The Discovery Coast Atlantic Rainforest Reserves are part of one of the largest and best-preserved ecosystems of its kind, and home to many rare species.

Brazil's Atlantic rain forest extends from the state of Bahía in the north to Río Grande do Sul in the south. Its dense vegetation is largely composed of a 20- to 30-m-high (66- to 100-ft) canopy of trees on which orchids and bromelias grow, but the poor light on the forest floor allows for only sparse undergrowth. The biodiversity and evolutionary history of these forests is of great scientific interest, not least because many of the plant species here are native. Studies have shown that in Bahía, 458 varieties of tree grow in a single hectare. The Discovery Coast boasts eight protected forest and bush reserves, all of which are part of the northern section of the Atlantic rain forest. The Reservas Biológicas of Una and Sooretama, the Reservas Particulares de Patrimônio Natural of Pau Brasil, Veracruz, Linhares, and the three national parks of Pau Brasil, Monte Pascual (named after its highest mountain) and Descobrimento cover an area of more than 1,000 sq km (390 sq mi).

Several sections of the Discovery Coast are still covered with a carpet of dense rain forest; it is home to the world's largest reserves of Brazil nut trees.

CHAPADA DOS VEADEIROS AND EMAS NATIONAL PARKS

Both Chapada dos Veadeiros and Emas National Parks in the state of Goiás are part of the Campos Cerrados, the savannah in central-western Brazil.

Despite its enormous area of about 2,000,000 sq km (770,000 sq mi), the Cerrado is still only Brazil's second-largest ecosystem. And though it has a rather dry climate and arid soil, it still has the greatest biodiversity of any of the country's tropical savannahs. The Cerrado is located in Brazil's highlands, and large portions of the region feature high plateaus punctuated by abrupt ravines and river valleys. The Chapada dos Veadeiros National Park covers a total area of 2,400 sq km (920 sq mi) and includes the highest points of the Cerrado, providing a home for numerous rare species, among them wild deer, mon- keys, and king vultures. A total of forty-five different mammals and 300 birds have been recorded along with about 1,000 butterflies. The Emas National Park, covering a total area of 1,300 sq km (520 sq mi), was named after its population of rheas ("ema" in Portuguese). This grassland expanse with impresive termite hills is also an ideal habitat for giant anteaters.

The Rio Preto, the main river of the Chapada dos Veadeiros, drops 120 m (390 ft) over this waterfall (right). Among the typical plants in this park are the Eriocaulacea sweet grass, also known as "sempre viva" (above).

BRASÍLIA

Brasília, Brazil's futuristic capital, was built from nothing in the 1950s according to the most contemporary principles of town planning. It is located in the middle of the country amidst a treeless savannah.

Brasília was inaugurated in 1960 after only four years of planning and construction. Oscar Niemeyer and Lúcio Costa, the two main architects and top town planners in Brazil at the time, wanted to create a metropolis that kept abreast of contemporary developments: a modern, progressive, functional and yet homogenous city. The decision to move the capital into the country's interior had been made in 1891 and was meant to offset the overly influential coastal states.

On plan, Brasília is laid out in the shape of a flying bird, which is made up of a parabola-shaped main traffic axis and a monumental axis running at right angles to it. The most important government buildings all stand

Three sculptures of angels by Alfredo Ceschiatti are suspended from the ceiling inside the plain circular cathedral.

in a row here. Many of the modern buildings were designed by Oscar Niemeyer and represent architectural masterpieces. For example, the entrance to the Palácio do Itamaraty – the seat of the Ministry of Foreign Affairs – seems to hover above the water. Another outstanding example is the Congresso Nacional. In between the bowl-shaped and cupola-shaped roof constructions of the assembly halls of parliament and the senate are the H-section twin towers of the administrative wing of the national congress; they form a vertical counterpoint. This balance between horizontal and vertical lines is one of Brasília's most important design principles.

The heart of the city is the "Square of the Three Powers", which features the congressional buildings (top), the "Os Candango" sculpture by Bruno Giorgi and the "Pantheon of the Fatherland and Freedom", dedicated to Tancredo Neve (middle). Another building by Oscar Niemeyer is the Cathedral Metropolitana Nossa Senhora Aparecida (below).

Brazil

HISTORIC CENTER OF GOIÁS

The Old Town of Goiás is a typical example of a Portuguese colonial settlement in South America. The architecture in this mining town is perfectly adapted to the climatic, geographical and cultural conditions.

The Portuguese colonial rulers only advanced into the interior of Brazil after settling and securing the vital coastal region with their ships and cannons. In the 16th century, prospectors and so-called Bandeirantes ("followers of the flag") then poured into the territory of the present-day state of Goiás. By the end of the 18th century, the gold rush had reached its zenith, but it was during this time and well into the 19th century that the picturesque historic center of the little town of Goiás developed on the banks of the Vermelho River. It remained the capital of the federal state of the same name until 1937.

The Old Town here features a number of public and private buildings that form a harmonious ensemble. The Portuguese settlers had developed their distinctive architectural style here, using predominantly local materials, mainly wood. The outstanding buildings, aside from the Santana Cathedral and nearly 30 churches, include the Governor's Palace, the Casa de Câmara e Cadeia, the Casa de Fundição, the theater and the barracks.

The charming Igreja da Boa Morte was constructed in 1779 with a pretty gable on the roof. Today it houses a museum of religious art.

HISTORIC TOWN OF OURO PRETO

Brazil's vast gold reserves triggered a gold rush in the little town of Ouro Preto at the end of the 17th century. Today the village enchants with its grandiose baroque and rococo architecture.

The town of Ouro Preto (or "black gold") was also called Vila Rica (or "rich city") for a time and owes its name to the enormous gold deposits nearby. The village was given its municipal charter in 1712 and, as the capital of the Minas Gerais Captaincy (until 1897), it exercised enormous influence on the fate of the country. Many unique and precious baroque churches were built here as well, which became the precursors of the colonial rococo stile. An outstanding example of this is the Igreja de São Francisco de Assis. This and some others, of a total of thirteen pompous church structures, were designed by

Aleijadinho (also known as "Little Cripple", 1730–1814), whose real name was Antônio Francisco da Costa Lisboa and who left his architectural mark on Ouro Preto. The Old Town of Ouro Preto is special due to its simple, original architecture as well as its bridges and fountains. Most of the baroque churches here boast lavish, richly detailed interior furnishings.

The Igreja Nossa Senhora do Carmo majestically dominates the town (above). Inside, magnificently gilded carvings and decorated ceilings speak of the former prosperity of the town and the imagination of its master builders (right).

HISTORIC CENTER OF DIAMANTINA

Gold and diamonds transformed the small town of Diamantina about 200 km (124 mi) north of Belo Horizonte in Minas Gerais. It became a major center of art and trade during the colonial period.

Diamantina has had a turbulent history. After the first diamonds were discovered here in 1731, Arraial do Tijuco, as the settlement was then called, developed into the most important diamond center of the region. Unlike other mining towns, however, Diamantina was controlled directly by the crown from 1771 to 1845. After high-quality diamonds were found in South Africa, however, mining was finished for good here by the early 20th century. In terms of town planning and architecture, Diamantina has been harmoniously integrated into the steep mountain landscape. Among the particularly noteworthy colonial buildings are the houses in the Rua do Burgalhau, the churches Nossa Senhora do Carmo and São Francisco de Assis (both from the second half of the 18th century), the Old Market Hall from 1835, and the Passadiço, a covered blue pedestrian bridge.

Accents in Diamantina are provided by colorful windows, trim and gutters that give a cheerful, buoyant look to the otherwise plain façades of the churches and houses.

SANCTUARY OF BOM JESUS DO CONGONHAS

A highlight of Christian art in Latin America can be found in the Sanctuary of the Good Lord Jesus in Congonhas, where splendid sculptures by Brazilian sculptor Aleijadinho adorn the forecourt and chapels.

The Santuário do Bom Jesus de Matosinhos, which comprises a pilgrimage church and seven chapels dedicated to the Stations of the Cross, lies not far from Ouro Preto, in Congonhas do Campo in Minas Gerais. Hundreds of thousands of pilgrims gather here every year in September. The church, completed in 1772, boasts magnificent rococo-style interior furnishings but the gems of the Santuário are the groups of sculptures in the chapels slightly below the church; they were added in about 1800. These polychrome masterpieces of late-baroque colonial artistry depict Christ's suffering and were created by Aleijadinho and his students. The twelve life-sized figures of the prophets that line the staircase on the church's forecourt are also his work. The sculptures of the artist, who was ravaged by leprosy and scurvy for many years, can easily by classed among the tradition of great European art.

Superb panel paintings and ceiling frescoes in the rococo style adorn the interior of the Bom Jesus Church in Congonhas.

SOUTH-EAST ATLANTIC FOREST RESERVES

The Atlantic rain forests in this reserve have an enormous range of species that is a testament to the evolutionary history of this part of South America.

Brazil's Atlantic rain forests are considered endangered: only seven percent of the original forests remain. A large part of these remnants thrives in the south-eastern section of the country, in the states of Paraná and São Paulo. Large parts of the rain forests in the Discovery Coast reserve in north-eastern Brazil also enjoy World Heritage status. The Atlantic forests grow amidst a stunning landscape that alternates between forested mountains, raging rivers, high waterfalls and shallow swamps. Many rare and endemic plants grow in the twenty-five conservation areas, which together cover an area of 5,000 sq km (1,900 sq mi). In some areas as many as 450 different tree species have been recorded on each hectare, a botanical biodiversity even greater than that found in the Amazon. The animal life in the forest reserves is equally varied, and includes some 120 different mammals (including jaguars, otters and anteaters) as well as about 350 bird species.

Although the upper canopy of the rainforest develops luxuriant foliage, the lack of light on the forest floor means that only sparse vegetation grows here.

Brazil

PANTANAL CONSERVATION AREA

The Pantanal is one of the world's largest freshwater wetlands. It boasts spectacular biodiversity.

The Pantanal wetlands extend across the south-western reaches of Brazil near the borders with Bolivia and Paraguay. From November to April, torrential summer downpours flood the Río Cuiabá and Río Paraguay systems, a low plain three times the size of Costa Rica, and form an enormous, irregular body of water with shallow lakes, swamps and flooded morasses. Four conservation areas here have been inscribed as World Heritage Sites with a combined total area of around 2,000 sq km (770 sq mi). The annual floods function as a natural control mechanism that influence the supply, state, and exchange of groundwater and rainwater. The sediment and nutri-

The green iguana can grow to 130 cm (4.3 ft) and has a distinctive ridgeback that extends all the way to its tail.

ents transported by the floodwater also allow healthy grassland to grow during the drier winter, between the end of April and October, when the water recedes. During these months, Pantanal's unique scenery looks particularly spectacular, steaming in the heat beneath a misty sky. The area stays partially inundated during the dry season, which makes it a refuge for animals. Practically nowhere else in the tropics boasts such a density of animal species, with 650 different birds, 400 fish and eighty mammals. Large sections of the wetlands encroach upon the Cerrado savannah, which is punctuated by trees like the Jatobá, which can get very tall. Acuri palms also form little woods amidst the extensive swamplands.

Water is the basic element of the Pantanal, which features shallow lakes full of plants and rivers that flow through the landscape in meandering arches. The flowers and leaves of the Santa Cruz water lily spread widely across the surface of the water (right).

FERNANDO DE NORONHA AND ATOL DAS ROCAS RESERVES

This island group 500 km (310 mi) north-east of Recife boasts an extraordinary wealth of animal life including dolphins, sharks, sea turtles and many seabirds.

The island reserves of Fernando de Noronha and Atol das Rocas are just a few degrees south of the equator, where the cold waters of the South Atlantic meet warm equatorial currents. Fernando de Noronha, the main island, is a volcanic formation covered in unique island forests and surrounded by a group of twenty-one satellite islands. The Rocas Atoll consists of coral reefs that have formed around the summits of an underwater mountain range. The basins and shallow lagoons of this, the only atoll in the South Atlantic, offer a fascinating natural spectacle at low tide, when a natural aquarium forms. The island reserve also includes a marine conservation area of extraordinary biodiversity. The nutrient-rich coastal waters around the island group teem with tuna, sharks and rare sea turtles such as the loggerhead. Many fish species use it as a spawning and feeding ground. The islands of this South Atlantic archipelago are also the most important staging post for many whales on their annual migrations.

Numerous species of fish make the waters of the archipelago a popular area for diving.

IGUAÇU NATIONAL PARK

Iguaçu Falls sit on the border of three countries – Brazil, Argentina, and Paraguay and are among the biggest and most impressive on earth. This monument is now protected by two parks, one in Brazil and one in Argentina.

You hear these falls long before you see them. First it is a soft gurgling that then quickly swells to a deafening roar. Flanked by dense tropical vegetation, the Iguaçu river – known in Argentina as the Iguazú – is already almost a half a mile wide as it makes the approach to these horseshoe-shaped falls. The foaming masses of water then cross a 2,700-m (9,000-ft) wide rock escarpment and fall into the chasm with seemingly limitless force – a singular natural spectacle where more than 270 individual falls have been counted. The park, which covers a total area of 1,700 sq km (660 sq mi) on the Brazilian side, is also a refuge for many endangered plant and animal species. Parrots and nothuras fly in the shade of the trees, and swifts build their nests in rocky crags between the waterfalls. The luxuriant rain forests are inhabited by ocelots, jaguars, howler monkeys, tapirs, giant anteaters and peccaries, and the now rare giant otter hunts for fish in the troubled waters of the plunge pools.

The Iguaçu approaches the lip of the falls in wide arches before dropping more than 80 m (265 ft) into the depths. Sunlight breaks through the mist and spray and creates magical rainbows.

Brazil / Argentina

JESUIT MISSIONS OF THE GUARANIS

The ruins of settlements established by the Jesuits in southern Brazil and northern Argentina are witnesses of a social experiment that came to a sudden end in the 18th century – when the Jesuits were expelled from South America.

In the early 17th century, the Jesuits were busy establishing what they called "reductions" – mission villages where they settled local Guaraní tribes – in the present-day state of Paraná in Brazil, the Misiones province of Argentina, and later in Paraguay. Padres and indigenous people lived and worked side by side here and tilled the fields together. Thanks to their efficient working methods, the village communities were largely autonomous; at the same time, the settlements served to protect indigenous people from attack by Brazilian

A mighty Jesuit cross rises in front of the church in the Jesuit reduction of São Miguel das Missões in Brazil.

slave traders and exploitative land-owners. The aim of these social institutions, however, was always the conversion and religious reeducation of the indigenous Guaraní people.

Every village comprised a church, a rectory, a school, a hospital, residential houses and storehouses. They were organized in strictly theocratic and paternalistic ways, which is why the villages quickly fell into disrepair after the expulsion of the Jesuits from South America in 1767/68.

The reductions of São Miguel das Missões in Brazil as well as Santa Ana, Nuestra Señora de Loreto and Santa María Mayor in Argentina are today just ruins; only San Ignacio Miní has been restored.

The church of São Miguel das Missões was designed by the Italian Jesuit Gian Battista Primoli (right). Nature has reclaimed many of the ruins including the Santa Ana Mission (top).

JESUIT MISSIONS IN PARAGUAY

The ruins of the Jesuit missions La Santísima Trinidad de Paraná and Jesús de Tavarangue are reminders of the Christianization of the indigenous population in Paraguay.

At the beginning of the 17th century, the Jesuits began to build mission villages for the indigenous people in what is now Brazil and Argentina. Many of these so-called "reductions" were later moved to southern Paraguay where additional ones were founded; the Spanish king had allocated specific territories to the Jesuits there. The Jesuit settlements were small, fortified, fairly uniformly built places in which the Padres lived and worked together with the Guaraní, teaching them important crafts and agricultural techniques. Some of the settlements, for example Trinidad, were actual small towns with solid stone houses in the so-called Guaraní Baroque, a style combining European elements with the design vocabulary of the indigenous peoples. Because the mission villages were established in large numbers, the region was known as the "Jesuit state". Remains of churches, colleges and cemeteries can still be seen in Trinidad de Paraná and in Jesús de Tavarangue.

Of all the Jesuit reductions, Trinidad de Paraná is the best-preserved.

HISTORIC QUARTER OF THE CITY OF COLONIA DEL SACRAMENTO

Located on a small spit of land in the Río de la Plata, this city's turbulent past is reflected in its architecture. The cityscape features a combination of Portuguese, Spanish and post-colonial styles.

Colonia del Sacramento, founded by the Portuguese in 1680, is the oldest European settlement in what is now Uruguay. Its strategic location in the delta of the Río de la Plata led to continuous territorial strife between the Spanish and the Portuguese, which resulted in repeated destruction. The rivalry between the colonial powers did not come to an end until 1828 when the Independent Republic of Uruguay was founded. The Old Town with its low colonial houses, wrought-iron balustrades, quiet plazas and green areas possesses all the charm of colonial-era settlements. Unlike most, however, it is not laid out on a grid, but follows the contours of the terrain. The bastions of San Miguel, San Pedro and Santa Rita, in part still preserved, are now witnesses of Colonia's military past.

Iglesia Matriz from the 17th century is one of the oldest churches in Uruguay. It has been rebuilt several times.

Argentina

QUEBRADA DE HUMAHUACA

This valley in north-western Argentina links the Andes with the lowlands and has been a vital route for the exchange of goods and culture for 10,000 years.

The Río Grande flows through this expansive valley and has carved a deep canyon into the imposing cliffs. Evidence shows that the first hunter-gatherers marked out tracks here as early as 9000 BC; they are still in use today. Also from this time are the engravings and wall paintings in the area's caves. A total of twelve settlements of early farming cultures have been excavated here and date roughly from between 1000 BC to AD 400. Twenty more sites date from the period until 900, when the valley was first used as a trading route. In the pre-Columbian era (900–1450), thirty fortified cities were built here, so-called pucarás. Cultivation on terraces with irrigation systems also began at that time. From 1430 to 1535, the Quebrada de Humahuaca was part of an expansive Inca road system that extended from Chile to Ecuador. In the 16th century, the Spanish conquered the region and built their own villages, towns and churches. During the time of the Independence War, the valley was a key transit route for the army and also became the site of bitter battles. Thanks to the diverse cultural influences, very distinctive traditions developed in the Quebrada that have persisted until the present day.

The Quebrada de Humahuaca broadens out in a wide valley near Maimará.

IGUAZÚ NATIONAL PARK

A national park has also been established on the Argentinian side of the spectacular Iguazú Falls that boasts dense subtropical rain forest and is home to a variety of plant and animal life.

The Iguazú river expands to a width of roughly 3 km (2 mi) at the Brazil-Argentina border, where it reaches the lip of a mighty basalt escarpment and splits into more than 270 cascades and waterfalls before dropping nearly 80 m (265 ft) into the depths. Dense tropical rain forest grows in the red soils of this basalt plateau, where lianas and epiphytes as well as more than 2,000 vascular plant varieties grow inside a national park covering nearly 550 sq km (210 sq mi). Tapirs, giant anteaters, coatis, otters, ocelots and even jaguars roam these remote areas with a number of rain forest primates including black howler monkeys and black hooded monkeys. More than 400 bird species and a wealth of amphibians and reptiles like the endangered broad-snouted caiman, can be found in the the national park as well. The region around Iguazú Falls was declared a national park back in 1934, a move that actually resulted in the relocation of the town of the same name.

The locals call the waterfalls the "Garganta del Diablo" – jaws of the devil. The water plunges down in dozens of cascades along a broad front (right). Even the smallest islands of the Iguazú river are densely overgrown.

ISCHIGUALASTO AND TALAMPAYA NATURAL PARKS

The world's most complete stratified fossil record from the Triassic period lies in these two neighboring nature parks in western Argentina.

The Valle de la Luna, a desert-like valley about 400 km (250 mi) north-west of Córdoba on the Chilean border, was first noted by paleontologists in 1930, but it was not until the 1950s that systematic research began here. The two parks form a continuous area of 2,750 sq km (1,050 sq mi). When the Andes rose from the earth's crust sixty million years ago, they radically changed the environmental conditions that had persisted here for 180 million years. In Talampaya, erosion then shaped dark-brown and green rocks, columns and thin obelisks across a sandy scrubland of brick-red and light-brown earth. Distinct rock strata in steep cliffs and petrified forests in both parks are now like books for geologists and paleontologists, revealing an almost complete evolutionary history of the area stretching back to the Triassic era (245–208 million years ago). Along with dinosaur bones, paleontologists have excavated fossil remains of fifty-five vertebrates, more than 100 plant species and many important pre-Columbian rock paintings.

Water and wind have fashioned a spectacular landscape in the Valle de la Luna.

JESUIT BLOCK AND ESTANCIAS OF CÓRDOBA

One block of houses in Córdoba and several estancias around the city are among the remnants of the Jesuit order's activities in South America.

Starting in 1599, the Jesuits in Córdoba in north-western Argentina constructed a complex of buildings that was to become a center for their missionary work in South America; the Iglesia Compañía de Jesús forms the core of the ensemble. In 1613, the founding of the Colegio Máximo, where the university now resides, heralded a time of prosperity for the city during which several estancias – rural ranches outside a town – were established to ensure economic self-sufficiency and to "civilize" the indigenous population, who had to work in the fields and workshops; it also bound them to the Christian community but gave them a certain degree of economic autonomy. The estancias were part of the reductions in the Jesuit province of Paraguay. Santa Catalina Estancia, built in 1622, was the largest. Caroya Estancia was founded in 1618. Others include Jesús María (1618), Alta Gracia (1643) and La Candelaria (1643). After the expulsion of the Jesuits from South America in 1767/68, the various estancias were privatized.

A richly decorated baroque church towers above the Alta Gracia Estancia.

THE VALDÉS PENINSULA

This peninsula on the mid-Atlantic coast of Argentina is 3,600 sq km (1,390 sq mi) in size and was designated as a World Heritage Site because it is home to an important population of sea mammals in particular.

The Ameghino isthmus is about 30 km (19 mi) long but only 5 to 10 km (3 to 6 mi) wide and connects the largest Argentinian peninsula to the mainland. It is surrounded by waters that are a habitat for several species of marine mammal that breed here every year. The southern right whale, which was hunted almost to extinction and whose populations still decline every year, have since found a safe refuge along the Valdés peninsula. These 14-m (48-ft) giants, which can weigh up to 35 metric tons, congregate here at the beginning of every spring and remain until December. An enormous elephant seal colony also lives in a protected area of the Punta Norte, the northern extremity of the peninsula. These imposing animals are the largest members of the seal family. A colony of sea lions is protected on Cape Punta Delgada which means orcas – also known as killer whales and a natural enemy of the sea lion – of course live here too. There are also Magellan penguins on Valdés, and 180 other bird species, many of which are seabirds.

At several points including Puerto Pirámides, the coast rises steeply to form 100-m (330-ft) cliffs. The seal colonies live at the base of these.

CUEVA DE LAS MANOS, RÍO PINTURAS

Prehistoric rock-art in the "Cave of the Hands" attest to the cultural sophistication of one of South America's earliest societies.

This 24-m-deep (79-ft) and 10-m-high (32-ft) cave is located halfway up the gorge of the Río Pinturas in southern Argentina. It is so named because of the stenciled handprints found here that make up a large part of the spectacular images on the walls. The hunting scenes that are shown are particularly enlightening. Animals are depicted being encircled, lured into a trap and even hunted with stones. Some hunters are shown alone while others are in groups. The paintings were made with natural mineral pigments such as iron oxide, kaolin and manganese oxide.

Thanks to their sheltered position, the strong colors are still preserved today. The images were probably made by the hunter-gatherers who had for a long time inhabited this remote part of Patagonia, before the first European settlers entrenched themselves here in the 17th century. The rock drawings were probably made during three different periods between 8000 BC and AD 1000.

The majority of the rock paintings in the cave on the Río Pinturas are polychrome prints of left hands, which were placed one on top of the other.

Argentina

LOS GLACIARES NATIONAL PARK

The 4,500 sq km (1,800 sq mi) of this national park lie in the heart of the Patagonian Andes near the Chilean border and boast extraordinary scenic beauty including spectacular mountains, glaciers and lakes.

This national park's thirteen glaciers form just a part of the extensive Patagonian ice field, which is composed of forty-seven large glaciers and is the largest continuous mass of ice outside the Antarctic – it covers a total surface area of 15,000 sq km (5,800 sq mi). There are another 200 smaller glaciers that are not directly connected to this ice field. The best-known of these is the Perito Moreno glacier, 30 km (19 mi) long and 5 km (3 mi) wide, which "calves" into Lago Argentino. As one of the few glaciers left in the world that is not retreating, it gradually pushes its terminus out in a kind of peninsula, cutting off a spur of the lake every three or four years. The water level here then rises by up to 30 m (100 ft) and, when the wall of ice can no longer stand the intense pressure, an impressive natural spectacle occurs as the dammed-up water

The terminus of the Perito Moreno glacier towers up to 60 m (200 feet) above Lago Argentino. Large blocks of ice continually break off, crashing into the lake.

ruptures a section of the glacier terminus and floods into the other part of the lake. The Uppsala and Spegazzini glaciers are also a part of this glacial world. The scenic highlights of the granite peaks of Cerro Torre and Monte Fitz Roy, both over 3,000 m (9,900 ft) high are in the northern part of the national park, not far from Lago Viedma. Birds predominate among the animal life in the park; there are some 100 species including condors and the Darwin nandu.

The granite tips of the tallest mountain in the Los Glaciares National Park, Monte Fitz Roy at 3,375 m (11,070 ft), seem to pierce the sky like stone needles.

The cliffs beside the lake have been worn flat by the Perito Moreno glacier.

The first people to settle here called this peak "Chaltén", or smoking mountain.

A breathtaking view from the air over the two tallest peaks in the park: Monte Fitz Roy and Cerro Torre.

Stellar scenes appear when the morning sun glows red on the jagged massif of Cerro Torre and reflects on the surface of Laguna Torre.

Europe

Northern Europe

28° **Jg** 26° **Jh** 24° **Jj** 22° **Jk** 20° **Ka** 18° **Kb** 16° **Kc** 14° **Kd** 12° **Ke** 10° **Kf** 8° **Kg** 6° **Kh** 4° **Kj** 2° **Kk** 0° **La** 2° **Lb** 4° **Ld**

Beerenberg ▲ 2277
Jan Mayen (Nor.)

12

Arctic Circle

66°

N O R W E G I A N

Gláma

13

Breiðafjörður   Húnaflói

S E A

Snæfellsnes

Akureyri

I C E L A N D

64°

REYKJAVÍK
◆ Thingvellir
National Park

1765
Hofsjökull
Herðubreið
1682 ▲

Seyðisfjörður

▲ Hekla
1491
Vatnajökull

Vestmannaeyjar

14

Skaftafell   Hvannadals-
hnúkur
▲ 2119

◆ Surtsey
Höfn

62°

 A T L A N T I C

15

60°
Faroe Islands (DK)
Tórshavn

O C E A N

Ålesund

16
West Norwegian Fjords: Geirangerfjor

Florø

Urnes Stave Ch

Sognefjord

Shetland Islands
58°
West Norwegian Fjords: Nærøyfjord

Lerwick

Bryggen ◆
Bergen

17
Orkney Islands
◆ Heart of Neolithic Orkney
Kirkwall

Hardangerfjord

Thurso
Haugesund

St Kilda ◆   Isle of Lewis
and Harris
Saint Kilda   Stornoway

Ha

Outer Hebrides

Stavanger

North Uist   Ullapool
56°

Northwest Highlands

Boknafjord

South Uist   Skye   Moray Firth
Egersund

UNITED
KINGDOM   N O R T H

Loch
Ness   Inverness   Fraserburgh

Inner Hebrides

Rùm   Peterhead

Ben Nevis
1343

Grampian Mountains

Tiree   Isle of Mull   Aberdeen   S E A

18
Oban
GREAT BRITAIN
Jura   Dundee

0   50   100
km

14° **Kd** 12° **Ke** 10° **Kf** 8° **Kg** 6° **Kh** 4° **Kj** 2° **Kk** 0° **La** 2° **Lb** 4° **Lc** 6° **Ld**

BARENTS SEA

North Cape Kinnaroden
Honningsvåg Båtsfjord
Porsanger- Vardø
halvøya Varanger-
Hammerfest halvøya
Søroya Vadsø Varanger-
Struve fjord
Geodetic Arc

Struve Geodetic Arc

Kirkenes

Alta
Rock Art of Alta
Karasjok Murmansk

Finnmarks-
vidda
Tromsø Struve Geodetic Arc
Inarijärvi Verhnetulomskoe
Inari vdhr
Kautokeino Ivalo
Kola
Andenes Struve Geodetic Arc Peninsula
Harstad Mončegorsk
Hinnøya oz. Imandra
Kandalakša Arctic Circle
White Sea

Svolvær Narvik Torneträsk
Abisko Torneträsk Sodankylä Kovd
Sørvågen Kiruna ozero
Bodø Laponian Area Kolari RUSSIA
Gällivare Struve Geodetic Arc Rovaniemi Pjaozero
Mo i Rana Kuusamo Topozero
Jokkmokk Struve Geodetic Arc Qnežskaja
Struve Geodetic Arc guba
Arjeplog Haparanda Struve Geodetic Arc
Storavan Kemi
Arvidsjaur Church Village of
Vegaøyan: Uddjaure Gammelstad, Luleå
The Vega Archipelago Luleå
Mosjøen Oulu
Tärnaby
Storuman Oulujärvi Kajaani Vyg-
ozero
Skellefteå Segozero
SWEDEN
Vilhelmina Lycksele Nurmes
Åsele Karleby Pielinen
Kokkola Karjalanselkä
Strömsund Umeå Kizhi Pogost
Angermanland Pohjanmaa Kuopio Joensuu Lake Onega
Trøndheimfjord (Österbotten) Petrozavodsk
Trondheim Sollefteå Vaasa FINLAND Orivesi
Storsjön Östersund Örnsköldsvik High Coast/
Kverken Archipelago Hauki-
vesi Lake Ladoga
Røros Mining Town High Coast/ Petäjävesi Old Church Jyväskylä
Røros Kverken Archipelago Struve Geodetic Arc
Medeland Sundsvall Kristinestad Savonlinna
Kristiinankaupunki Verla Groundwood Saimaa
and Board Mill Mikkeli
Sveg Paijänne Lappeenranta
Ljusdal Pori Tampere Lahti Vyborg
Salpausselkä Struve Geodetic Arc
Bollnäs Bronze Age Burial Site Kotka
Lillehammer Rauma of Sammallahdenmäki Tihvin
Old Rauma Saint Petersburg
Hamar Mora Söderhamn Historic Center of Saint Petersburg
Mjøsa Siljan Gävle Turku HELSINKI Struve Geodetic Arc and Related Groups of Monuments
Falun Åbo
Mining Area of the Great Fortress of Suomenlinna
Copper Mountain in Falun Mariehamn Hango
Avesta Uppland Maarianhamina Hanko Gulf of Finland Narva
OSLO Uppsala Struve Geodetic Arc
Torsby Engelsberg Ironworks Norrtälje Historic Monuments of
Västerås Historic Center Novgorod Novgorod and Surroundings
Karlstad Mälaren (Old Town) of Tallinn
Royal Domain of Drottningholm TALLINN oz.Il'men'
Birka and Hovgården STOCKHOLM Struve Geodetic Arc
Örebro Katrineholm Skogskyrkogården ESTONIA Lake Peipus
Nynäshamn Hiiumaa Haapsalu
Larvik Vänern Struve Geodetic Arc
Rock Carvings in Tanum Saaremaa Pärnu Tartu Lake Pskov
Norrköping Pskov Valdayskaya
Lidköping Linköping Kuressaare Vozvyshennost'
Baltic Sea Valga
Västervik Gulf of RUSSIA
Skagen Visby Riga Smiltene Struve Geodetic Arc
Borås Jönköping Hanseatic Town of Visby Gotland Ventspils Velikie Luki
Göteborg Götaland Historic Center of Riga RIGA LATVIA Rezekne
Oskarshamn

NORWAY

11
68°
12
66°
13
64°
14
62°
15
60°
16
58°
17
56°

Central Europe

Orkney Islands
Heart of Neolithic Orkney
Kirkwall
Thurso
N

Haugesund

ATLANTIC
Isle of Lewis
and Harris
Stornoway
Stavanger

St Kilda
Saint Kilda
North Uist
Ullapool
Egersund

OCEAN
South Uist
Skye
Inverness
Moray Firth
Fraserburgh
Peterhead

Rum
Loch Ness
Ben Nevis
1343
Aberdeen
Kristi

Tiree
Isle of Mull
Oban
Grampian Mountains
GREAT

Islay
Jura
Dundee

Giant's Causeway
and Causeway Coast
Glasgow
Edinburgh
Old and New Towns of Edinburgh
NORTH

Londonderry
(Derry)
Kintyre
Arran
New Lanark
Southern Uplands
NORTH

Ulster
North Channel
Carlisle
Frontiers of the Roman Empire
Newcastle upon Tyne
SEA

Sligo
L.Neagh
Belfast
Durham
Durham Castle and Cathedral
B

Portadown
Isle of Man
Cumbrian
Mountains
Middlesbrough
R
German

Connacht
Archaeological Ensemble
of the Bend of the Boyne
Douglas
Studley Royal Park including
the Ruins of Fountains Abbey
Harrogate
I
Bight

Galway
IRELAND
Drogheda
Irish Sea
Blackpool
Saltaire
Leeds
T
A

Mouth of
the Shannon
Leinster
DUBLIN/BAILE ÁTHA CLIATH
Liverpool – Maritime Mercantile City
Holyhead
Liverpool
Manchester
UNITED KINGDOM
Kingston upon Hull
I
N

Limerick
924
Wicklow Mts.
Castles and Town Walls
of King Edward in Gwynedd
Nottingham

Skellig Michael
Carrauntoohil
1038
Killarney
Munster
Pontcysyllte
Aqueduct
and Canal
Derwent
Valley Mills
West Frisian Islands
East Frisian Islan
The Wadden Sea
Ostfriesian

Waterford
Cardigan
Bay
Cambrian Mountains
The Wadden Sea
Groningen
Ir. D.F. Woudagemaal

Cork/
Corcaigh
Saint George's Channel
Ironbridge Gorge
Birmingham
Peterborough
Norfolk
Norwich
Alkmaar
IJsselmeer
Schokland and Surroundings

Skellig Michael
Fishguard
Stratford-u.-A.
Suffolk
Droogmakerij de Beemster
AMSTERDAM
NETHERLANDS
Osn

Blaenavon Industrial Landscape
Blenheim Palace
Cambridge
Defense Line of Amsterdam
Rietveld Schröderhuis

Celtic Sea
Bristol
Channel
Cardiff
Oxford
Westminster Palace,
Westminster Abbey and
Saint Margaret's Church
Harwich
The Hague
Utrecht
Arnhem
Münster

City of Bath
Bristol
Bath
LONDON
Canterbury Cathedral,
St Augustine's Abbey
and St Martin's Church
Rotterdam
Mills at Kinderdijk-Elshout
Zollverein Coal Mine
Industrial Complex in Essen
Dortmu

Cornwall and West Devon Mining Landscape
Stonehenge, Avebury
and Associated Sites
Exeter
Royal Botanic
Gardens, Kew
Maritime
Greenwich
Tower of
London
Canter-
bury
Dover
Strait of Dover
Historic Center
of Brugge
Plantin-Moretus House-
Workshops/Museum Complex
Essen
Cologne
Cathedral
Es

Isles of Scilly
Penzance
Devon
Southampton
South Downs
Portsmouth
Brighton
Dunkerque
Calais
Brugge
Antwerp
Flemish
Béguinages
Gent
Major Town Houses of the
Architect Victor Horta
Düsseldorf
Aachen
Castles of August
and Falkenlust in
Aachen
Cathedral

Plymouth
Cornwall
English Channel
Belfries of Belgium
and France
Ieper
Stoclet House
BRUSSELS
La Grand-
Place
BELGIUM
Bonn
Cologne
Koblenz
C

Cherbourg-
Octeville
Fortifications
of Vauban
St-Vaast-la-Hougue
Dieppe
Picardie
Arras
Tournai
Notre-Dame Cathedral in Tournai
Mons
Charleroi La Louvière and Le Roeulx
Neolithic Flint
Mines at Spiennes
The Four Lifts on the
Canal du Center and
their Environs,
Aachen
Cathedral
Eifel
Westerwa

Le Havre, the City Rebuilt
by Auguste Perret
Le Havre
Amiens
Amiens Cathedral
Fortifications
of Vauban
LUXEMBOURG
Ardennes
Upper Middle
Rhine Valley
Wiesba
Taun

Brest
Fortifications of Vauban
Camaret-sur-Mer
Caen
Rouen
Cathedral of Notre-Dame,
Former Abbey of Saint-Remi
and the Palace of Tau, Reims
Reims
City of Luxemburg:
Old Quarters and Fortifications
Longwy
Fortifications
of Vauban
LUXEMBOURG
Roman Monuments,
Cathedral of St Peter
and Church of
Our Lady in Trier
Mainz

Mont-Saint-Michel
and its Bay
Saint-Malo
Normandie
Seine
Paris, Banks of
the Seine
Châlons-en-
Champagne
Völklingen
Ironworks
Metz
Trier
Völklingen
Ironworks
Kaisers-
lautern
müns
Mannh

Fortifications of Vauban
Rennes
Maine
Palace and Park of Versailles
Versailles
PARIS
Provins, Town of
Medieval Fairs
Provins
Nancy
Place Stanislas,
Place de la Carrière
and Place d'Alliance
in Nancy
Saarbrücken
Speyer
Speyer Cathedral

Lorient
Chartres
Chartres Cathedral
Fontainebleau
Palace and Park
of Fontainebleau
Strasbourg – Grande Île
Strasbourg
Karlsruhe
Baden-
Baden

Le Mans
FRANCE
Moselle
Vosges
Stras-
bourg

Saint-Nazaire
Angers
Chalonnes
Tours
Blois
Orléanais
Orléans
Sully-sur-Loire
Sully-sur-Loire and Chalonnes
Fortifications
of Vauban
Neuf-Brisach
Freiburg

Nantes
The Loire Valley between Sully-sur-Loire and Chalonnes
Loire
Cistercian Abbey of Fontenay
Fortifications
of Vauban
Mulhouse
Basle

Vendée
Bourges Cathedral
Bourges
Vézelay, Church and Hill
Vézelay
Dijon
Besançon
La Chaux-de-Fonds
Le Locle, watchmaking
town planning
Zürich
Conve

Poitiers
Abbey Church of
Saint-Savin sur Gartempe
Saint-Savin-sur-Gartempe
Nevers
From the Great Saltworks of Salins-les-Bains
to the Royal Saltworks of Arc-et-Senans
Arc-et-Senans
BERNE
Old City
of Berne

Fortifications of Vauban
St-Martin-de-Ré
La Rochelle
Poitou
Salin-les-Bains
Neuchâtel
SWITZERLA
A

ATLANTIC OCEAN
Routes of Santiago de
Compostela in France
Lausanne
Lavaux, Vineyard Terraces
Lake Geneva
Geneva
Swiss Alps
Jungfrau-Aletsch
Berner Alpen
Three Castles, Defensive
of the Ma
Town of Bellin

Routes of Santiago de
Compostela in France
Gironde
Angoulême
Limoges
Limousin
Clermont-
Ferrand
Puy de
Sancy
1886
Auvergne
Historic Site of Lyon
Annecy
Rhône
Monte San
Verbania

Fortifications of Vauban
Blaye
Bordeaux, Port of the Moon
Jurisdiction of
Saint-Émilion
Périgueux
Prehistoric Sites and
Decorated Caves
of the Vézère Valley
Saint-Émilion
Massif
Central
Mont
Blanc
Matterhorn
Aosta
Chambéry
Sacri Monti of P
and Lombardy

OSLO

NORWAY

SWEDEN
Avesta
Torsby
Uppland
Engelsberg Ironworks
Uppsala
Mariehamn
Maarianhamina
Hangö
Hanko
Narva

Historic Monuments of
Novgorod and Surroundings

Novgorod

16
58°

TALLINN
Historic Center
(Old Town) of Tallinn

Struve Geodetic Arc

ESTONIA
Lake Peipus

oz.Il'men'

RUSSIA

Karlstad
Västerås
Norrtälje
Mälaren
Royal Domain of Drottningholm
STOCKHOLM
Skogskyrkogården

Örebro
Birka and Hovgården

Nynäshamn

Hiiumaa
Haapsalu

Struve Geodetic Arc

Tartu

Pärnu

Struve Geodetic Arc
Valga
Smiltene

Valdayskaya
Vozvyshennost'

17

Larvik
Katrineholm
Norrköping

Saaremaa
Kuressaare

Lake Pskov
Pskov

Struve Geodetic Arc
Velikie Luki

Skagen
Göteborg
Borås
Jönköping
Lidköping
Linköping
Västervik
Visby
Gotland

Gulf of
Riga

RIGA
Historic Center of Riga

LATVIA

Rezekne

Struve Geodetic Arc

Daugavpils
Polack

Vitebsk

18
56°

Trollhättan
Halland
Vänern
Vättern
Götaland
Småland
Hanseatic Town of Visby

Ventspils

Aalborg
Varberg Radio Station
Varberg
Oskarshamn

Siauliai
Panevėžys

Orsa

Kattegat
Halmstad
Växjö
Kalmar
Öland

Liepaja
Klaipeda
Kurische Nehrung
Curonian Spit

Struve Geodetic Arc
Kaunas
Kernavé Archaeological Site

Struve Geodetic Arc
VILNIUS
Vilnius Historic Center

MINSK

BELARUS

Mahilёv

18

Kronborg Castle
Helsingborg
Naval Port
of Karlskrona
Karlshamn
Karlskrona
Agricultural Landscape of
Southern Öland

LITHUANIA

Sovetsk
Courland
Lagoon

Barysav

Struve Geodetic Arc

Struve Geodetic Arc

19

COPENHAGEN
Roskilde Cathedral
DENMARK

Lund
Malmö
Kristianstad

BALTIC SEA

Kaliningrad

Gulf of
Gdansk

Hrodna
Mir Castle Complex

Architectural, Residential and
Cultural Complex of the
Radziwill Family at Nesvizh

Babrujsk

Dovsk

Sjælland
Ystad
Bornholm (DK)
Rønne

Gdańsk

Białystok
Baranavičy
Salihorsk

Struve Geodetic Arc

52°

Fyn
Vordingborg
Rødbyhavn
Lolland
Falster
Rügen
Stralsund
Pomeranian
Bay

Słupsk
Koszalin
Malbork
Castle of the Teutonic
Order in Malbork
Olsztyn

Masuria

Belovezhskaya Pushcha /
Białowieża Forest

Belovezhskaya Pushcha /
Białowieża Forest

Brest

Pripyat Marshes

Pinsk

Sarny

Struve Geodetic Arc

Masyr

19

Kiel
Wismar
Historic Centers of
Stralsund and Wismar

Schwerin
Neubrandenburg
Mecklenburgische
Müritz
Seenplatte
Szczecin
Bydgoszcz
Toruń
Medieval Town of Toruń

Oder
Vistula
Mazowsze
Podlasie

20

Lübeck
Roland on
ace of Bremen
burg
ide
Elbe

Poznań

Łódź

WARSAW
Historic Center of Warsaw

POLAND

Kovel'
Luc'k

Korosten'
Novohrad-
Volyns'kyj

Žytomyr

20

Palaces and Parks of
Potsdam and Berlin
BERLIN
Berlin Modernism Housing Estates
Potsdam
Museumsinsel

Zielona Góra

Nizina Wielkopolska

Radom
Lublin
Rivne

UKRAINE

50°

Mary's Cathedral and
Michael's Church at Hildesheim
Mines of Rammelsberg and
Historic Town of Goslar
Garden Kingdom of
Dessau-Wörlitz

Cottbus

Zamość
Old City of Zamość

MANY
Quedlinburg
Dessau
Lutherstadt
Wittenberg
Luther Memorials in
Eisleben and Wittenberg
Lutherstadt Eisleben

Muskauer Park /
Park Mużakowski

Lausitz

Świdnica
Wrocław
Centennial Hall in Wrocław

Częstochowa

Małopolska

L'viv
L'viv – the Ensemble
of the Historic Center

Struve Geodetic Arc
Vinnycja

50°

ach
Erfurt
Weimar
Thüringer Wald
Coburg
Bamberg

Leipzig
Görlitz
Dresden
Liberec
Churches of Peace
in Jawor and Swidnica

Katowice
Auschwitz Birkenau: German
Nazi Concentration and
Extermination Camp
(1940–1945)
Oświęcim
Cracow's Historic Center
Cracow

Rzeszów

Wieliczka Salt Mine

Vistula

Struve Geodetic Arc

21

Church, Castle and
wn of Quedlinburg

Muskauer Park

Bauhaus and its Sites in
Weimar and Dessau
Classical Weimar
Chemnitz

Podolian Upland

Vinnycja

21

of Bamberg
Bayreuth
Historic Center of Prague

CZECH REPUBLIC
Hradec Králové

Kutná Hora
PRAGUE
Litomyšl Castle

Holy Trinity
Column in
Olomouc

Kalwaria Zebrzydowska:
the Mannerist Architecture
and Park Landscape Complex
and Pilgrimage Park

Wooden Churches of Southern Little Poland

Bardejov Town Conservation Reserve

L'viv
Struve Geodetic Arc

rzburg Residence with the
rt Gardens and
idence Square
nsbach
Plzeň
Bohemia
Pilgrimage Church of
St John of Nepomuk
at Zelená Hora

Kutná Hora: Historic Town Center
with the Church of St Barbara and
the Cathedral of Our Lady at Sedlec

Olomouc
Gardens and
Castle at Kroměříž

Bardejov
Wooden Churches of the
Slovak part of the
Carpathian Mountain Area

Levoča, Spišský hrad and the
Associated Cultural Monuments

Ivano-
Frankivs'k

Dniester

Kam'janec-
Podil's'kyj

Struve Geodetic Arc

Bamberg
Nürnberg
Frontiers of the
Roman Empire

Historic Center
of Telč
Třebíč
Brno
Tugendhat Villa
in Brno

Vlkolinec
Levoča
Košice

CARPATHIAN

Černivci

Bessarabia

Bukovina

48°

Old Town of Regensburg
with Stadtamhof
Danube
Regensburg
Bayerischer Wald
Český
Krumlov
České
Budějovice
Historic Center of
Český Krumlov

Holašovice Historical
Village Reservation

Jewish Quarter and
St Procopius'
Basilica in Třebíč
Lednice-Valtice
Cultural Landscape

Ružomberok
SLOVAKIA
Caves of Aggtelek Karst
and Slovak Karst

Primeval Beech
Forests of the
Carpathians

Primeval Beech
Forests of the
Carpathians

MOUNTAINS
Bălți
Botoşani
MOLDOVA

Isar
Passau
Linz
Wachau Cultural
Landscape
Danube

Historic Town of Banská
Štiavnica and the Technical
Monuments in its Vicinity

Banská Štiavnica

Tokaj Wine Region
Historic Cultural Landscape

Moldavia

Suceava
Churches of Moldavia

Iaşi

Augsburg
München
Inn
VIENNA
Palace and Gardens
of Schönbrunn
BRATISLAVA

Historic Center
of Vienna

Old Village of Hollókő
and its Surroundings

Miskolc
Tokaj

Satu Mare
Baia Mare

Wooden Churches
of Maramureş

Bistriţa

Piatra-Neamţ

22

gäu
Pilgrimage
Church of Wies
üssen
Zugspitze
2962
Garmisch-
Partenkirchen
Salzburg
Historic Center of the
City of Salzburg
Hallstatt-Dachstein /
Salzkammergut
Cultural Landscape

Semmering
Railway
Mürz-
zuschlag

Fertő / Neusiedler See
Cultural Landscape
Győr

Hollókő

Alföld

Debrecen

Hortobágy National Park
– the "Puszta"

BUDAPEST
Budapest, including the
Banks of the Danube,
the Buda Castle Quarter
and Andrássy Avenue

Kecskemét

Oradea

Cluj-Napoca

Târgu Mureş

Bacău

Siret

46°

TEIN
Inn
Innsbruck
Benedictine Convent of
St John at Müstair
Bolzano
Bozen
The Dolomites
Cortina d'Ampezzo

Hohe Tauern
Grossglockner
3798
Niedere Tauern
Graz
City of Graz–
Historic Center

Fertő /
Neusiedler See
Cultural Landscape

Millenary Benedictine
Abbey of Pannonhalma
and its Natural Environment

Munţii Apuseni

Villages with Fortified
Churches in Transylvania

Historic Center of Sighişoara

Sighişoara

Sfântu Gheorghe

Focşani

tian Railway in
Albula / Bernina
scapes
Trento
Spittal a.d.D.
Karnische Alpen
Klagenfurt
Maribor

Triglav
2864
Drava

HUNGARY

Early Christian
Necropolis of Pécs

Pécs

Szeged

Balaton

Podravina

Arad

Timişoara

Reşiţa

Hunedoara

Sibiu
Dacian Fortresses of
the Orăştie Mountains

Moldoveanu
2544
Carpathian Alps

Brasov

Transylvanian Alps

Braşov

Buzău

23

Garda
Rock Drawings in Valcamonica
Udine
Trieste

Dolomites
Veneto
Archaeological Area and the
Patriarchal Basilica of Aquileia
SLOVENIA
LJUBLJANA
Škocjan Caves

Slavonia

ZAGREB

CROATIA

Osijek
SERBIA

Reşiţa

Târgu Jiu

Monastery of Horezu

Monastery of Horezu

Sibiu

Pitesti

Ploieşti

Slobozia

Southern and South-Western Europe

South-Eastern Europe

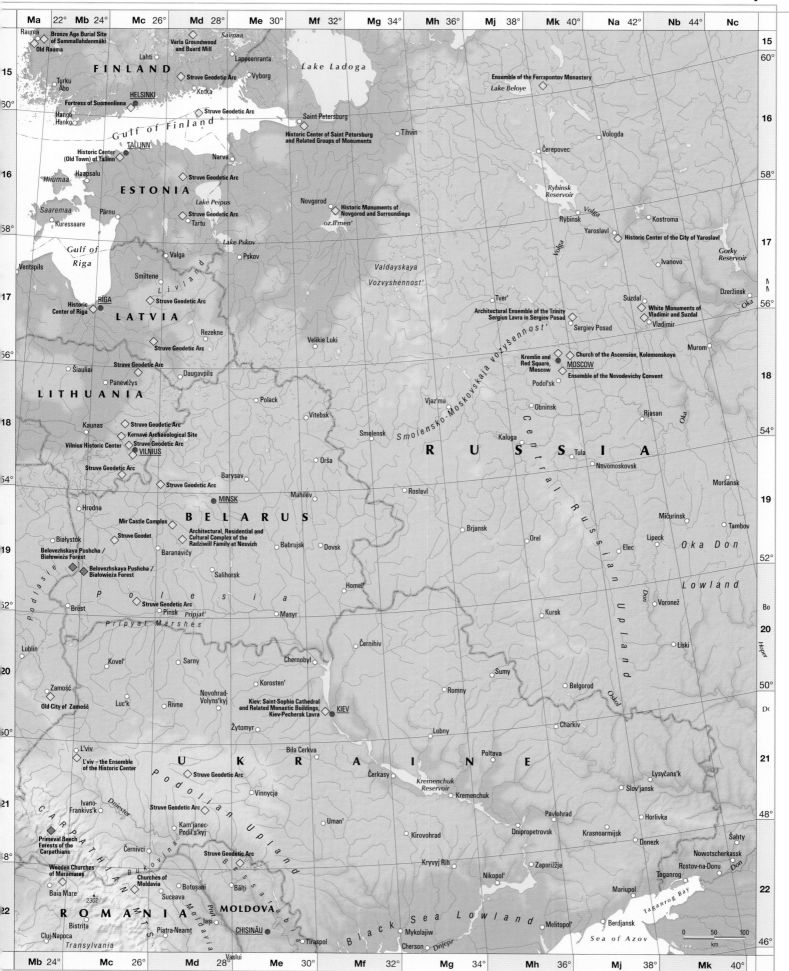

Ma 22° Mb 24° Mc 26° Md 28° Me 30° Mf 32° Mg 34° Mh 36° Mj 38° Mk 40° Na 42° Nb 44° Nc

Rauma
Bronze Age Burial Site of Sammallahdenmäki
Old Rauma
Verla Groundwood and Board Mill
Saimaa
Lappeenranta
Lake Ladoga
Ensemble of the Ferrapontov Monastery
Lake Beloye

15

60°

FINLAND
Lahti
Turku
Åbo
Struve Geodetic Arc
Vyborg
Kotka
HELSINKI
Fortress of Suomenlinna
Hangö
Hanko
Struve Geodetic Arc
Saint Petersburg
Historic Center of Saint Petersburg and Related Groups of Monuments
Tihvin
Vologda
Čerepovec
Rybinsk Reservoir

16

58°

Gulf of Finland
TALLINN
Historic Center (Old Town) of Tallinn
Narva
Hiiumaa
Haapsalu
ESTONIA
Struve Geodetic Arc
Lake Peipus
Novgorod
Historic Monuments of Novgorod and Surroundings
oz.Il'men'
Volga
Rybinsk
Yaroslavl
Historic Center of the City of Yaroslavl
Kostroma
Ivanovo

17

56°

Saaremaa
Pärnu
Kuressaare
Struve Geodetic Arc
Tartu
Lake Pskov
Gulf of Riga
Ventspils
Valga
Pskov
Valdayskaya Vozvyshennost'
Tver'
Architectural Ensemble of the Trinity Sergius Lavra in Sergiev Posad
Suzdal
White Monuments of Vladimir and Suzdal
Dzeržinsk
Oka
Gorky Reservoir

Smiltene
Historic Center of Riga
RIGA
Struve Geodetic Arc
Rezekne
Velikie Luki
Sergiev Posad
Vladimir
Murom

LATVIA
Struve Geodetic Arc
Kremlin and Red Square, Moscow
Church of the Ascension, Kolomenskoye
MOSCOW
Ensemble of the Novodevichy Convent

18

54°

Šiauliai
Struve Geodetic Arc
Daugavpils
Polack
Vitebsk
Vjaz'ma
Smolensk
Podol'sk
RUSSIA
Obninsk
Rjasan
Oka

LITHUANIA
Panevėžys
Kaluga
Tula
Novomoskovsk
Moršansk

Kaunas
Struve Geodetic Arc
Kernavė Archaeological Site
Vilnius Historic Center
Struve Geodetic Arc
VILNIUS
Struve Geodetic Arc
Orša
Roslavl
Central Russian Upland
Mičurinsk
Tambov

19

52°

Struve Geodetic Arc
Barysaw
Mahilëu
Brjansk
Orel
Lipeck
Oka Don Lowland

Hrodna
MINSK
BELARUS
Elec

Białystok
Mir Castle Complex
Struve Geodet
Architectural, Residential and Cultural Complex of the Radziwill Family at Nesvizh
Babrujsk
Dovsk
Kursk
Voronež

Belovezhskaya Pushcha / Białowieża Forest
Baranaviči
Podlasie
Belovezhskaya Pushcha / Białowieża Forest
Salihorsk
Homel'
Don

Brest
P o l e s i a
Struve Geodetic Arc
Pinsk
Pripjat'
Masyr
Liski

20

50°

Lublin
Pripyat Marshes
Sarny
Černihiv
Sumy
Belgorod
Oskol

Kovel'
Korosten'
Romny

Zamość
Old City of Zamość
Luc'k
Rivne
Novohrad-Volyns'kyj
Kiev: Saint-Sophia Cathedral and Related Monastic Buildings, Kiev-Pechersk Lavra
KIEV
Lubny
Charkiv

Žytomyr
UKRAINE
Biła Cerkva
Poltava

21

48°

L'viv
L'viv – the Ensemble of the Historic Center
Struve Geodetic Arc
Čerkasy
Kremenchuk Reservoir
Lysyčans'k
Slov'jansk

Ivano-Frankivs'k
CARPATHIAN
Podolian Upland
Vinnycja
Kremenchuk
Pavlohrad
Horlivka

Struve Geodetic Arc
Uman'
Kirovohrad
Dnipropetrovsk
Krasnoarmijsk
Donezk
Šahty

Primeval Beech Forests of the Carpathians
Kam'janec-Podil's'kyj
Dniester
Černivci
Kryvyj Rih
Zaporižžja
Nowotscherkassk
Rostov-na-Donu
Don

Wooden Churches of Maramureş
Struve Geodetic Arc
Bukovina
Nikopol'
Mariupol
Taganrog

22

46°

Baia Mare
2302
Churches of Moldavia
Botoşani
Bălți
Melitopol'
Berdjansk
Taganrog Bay

ROMANIA
MOLDOVA
Iaşi
CHIŞINĂU
Black Sea Lowland
Sea of Azov

Bistriţa
Piatra-Neamţ
Tiraspol
Mykolajiw
0 50 100 km

Cluj-Napoca
Transylvania
Vaslui
Cherson
Dnjepr
46°

Mb 24° Mc 26° Md 28° Me 30° Mf 32° Mg 34° Mh 36° Mj 38° Mk 40°

North Asia

Lc

SWEDEN
Mo i Rana
Narvik Tromsø
NORWAY
A R C T I

Falun
15°
Sundsvall
Kiruna
Hammerfest
Alta
North Cape

Ld
60°
Umeå
Luleå
Inari
Kirkenes
Franz Josef Land (Rus.)
North Land

Gulf of Bothnia
Vaasa
Kemi
Murmansk
BARENTS SEA

Turku
Åbo
20°
Oulu
Kuusamo

Ma
Tampere
FINLAND
Kola
Peninsula
Novaya Zemlya
Kara Sea

TALLINN HELSINKI
25°
Kuopio

ESTONIA
Saimaa
Lappeenranta
Vyborg
Cultural and Historic Ensemble
of the Solovetsky Islands
White Sea

Narva

Mb
Lake Peipus
Lake Ladoga
Sankt Petersburg
Arhangel'sk
Taymyr

30°
Petrozavodsk
Kizhi Pogost

Novgorod
Historic Monuments of
Novgorod and Surroundings
Lake Onega
gory Byrran Pe

Mc
Lake Beloye
Ensemble of the
Ferrapontov Monastery
Pečora
North Siberian Lo

35°
Tver
Rybinsk
Reservoir
Vologda
Pečora
Vorkuta

Kremlin and
Red Square
Sergiev
Posad

Md
Architectural Ensemble of the Trinity
Sergius Lavra in Sergiev Posad
Uhta
Virgin Komi Forests
1701
plato
Putorana

MOSCOW
White Monuments of
Vladimir and Suzdal
Syktyvkar
U
R
A
L

Ensemble of
the Novodevichy
Convent
Vladimir
40°

Central Siber

Na
Nizhny
Novgorod
Kirov
Ob'
West Siberian

Saransk
Joškar-Ola
Plateau

Kazan
45°

Historic and Architectural
Complex of the Kazan Kremlin
Iževsk
Perm'
Lowland
B

Simbirsk
Nižnjaja Tunguska

Saratov
Ufa
Khanty-Mansiysk
Surgut

Engel's
Volga
Samara
Ufa
Yekaterinburg
Nižnevartovsk

Nb
50°
g.Jamantau
1640
Tjumen
Tobol
Podkamennaja Tunguska
R
U
S

Oral
Čeljabinsk

Orenburg
Kurgan
Irtyš

Ural
Magnitogorsk

Nc
Aktöbe
Saryarka – Steppe and Lakes
of Northern Kazakhstan
Petropavl
Omsk
Enisejsk
Ust-Jlimsk

Embi
Zapadnoe
Krasnojarsk

Bra
Res

Saryarka – Steppe and Lakes
of Northern Kazakhstan
Novosibirsk
Bratsk

55°
45°
Aralsk
ASTANA
Pavlodar
Novokuzneck
Abakan
Angara
Tulun

Aral Sea
Ekibastuz
Barnaul
Eastern Sayan Mountains

Nd
Schesqasghan
Karaghandy
Gorno-Altajsk
Western Sayan Mountains
Kyzyl

Baikonur
KAZAKHSTAN
Semey
Abakan
Enisej

Nukus
Kyzlorda
Öskemen
Irtyš
ALTAI
Khövsgöl
nuur

Turan Lowland
Steppe
Golden Mountains of Altai
Uvs Nuur Basin

Itchan Kala
Betpak Dala
Balkhash
pora Beluha
4506
Uvs nuur

60°
40°
UZBEKISTAN
Turkistan
Lake Balkhash
Zajsan
köli
Khovd

Historic Center of Bukhara
Shymkent
Petroglyphs within the Archaeological
Landscape of Tamgaly
Taldykorgan
Khovd

Oa
Turkmenabat Bukhara
TASHKENT
BISHKEK
CHINA
M O N

Samarkand – Crossroads of Cultures
Orkhon Valley Cultural Landscape

Samarkand
Shakhrisyabz
Almaty
Dzungarian Basin
U

Historic Center of Shakhrisyabz
KYRGYZSTAN
Lake Issyk-Kul

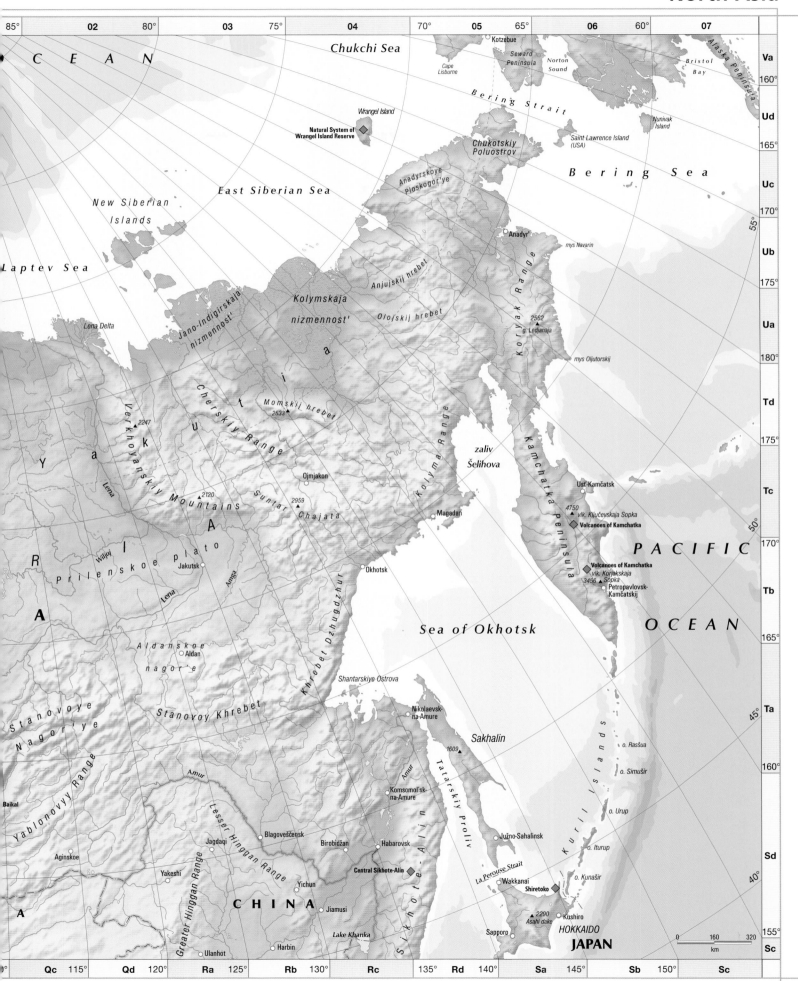

Near and Middle East

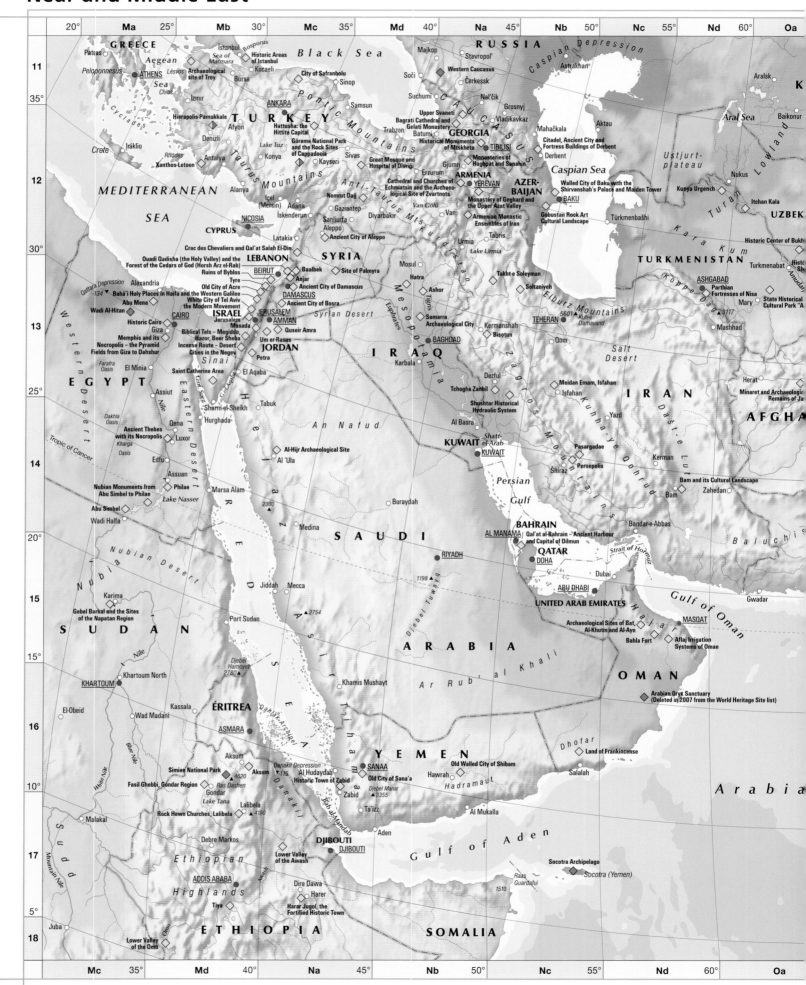

Map labels (top to bottom, left to right):

e Steppe

70° Oc 75° Od 80° Pa 85° Pb 90° Pc 95° Pd 100° Qa 105° Qb 110° Qc

10

MONGOLIA

40°

Hohot

ISTAN

Balkhash

Lake Balkhash

Baotou

Yellow River

Taldykorgan

Dzungarian Basin

Gobi Desert

11

Petroglyphs within the Archaeological Landscape of Tamgaly

Ürümqi

Yinchuan

Yellow River

Mausoleum of Khoja Ahmed Yasawi

BISHKEK

Almaty

7439 Pobedy peak

Korla

Kuruktag

Turpan -154 Turfan Depression

Minghoshan

Mogao Caves

Yellow River

35°

stan

ent

KYRGYZSTAN

Lake Issyk-Kul

Aksu

TARIM BASIN

Qilian Shan

Xining

Lanzhou

Mausoleum of the First Qin Emperor

Qinghai Hu

Xi'an

Fergana Valley Oš

Kashi

Takla Makan Desert

Golmud

12

s of Cultures

Sulaiman-Too Sacred Mountain

TAJIKISTAN

7546 Muztagata

Hotan

Muztag 6973

Qaidam Pendi

Jiuzhaigou Valley Scenic and Historic Interest Area

Huanglong Scenic and Historic Interest Area

ANBE

Pamir

HINDU KUSH

Mount Godwin Austen (K2) 8611

KUNLUN SHAN

Altun Shan

CHINA

Yangtze

Mount Qingcheng and the Dujiangyan Irrigation System

Chengdu

Chongqing

Red Basin

30°

if

6435

Nanga Parbat 8126

Karakorum Range

PLATEAU OF TIBET

Mekong

Sichuan Giant Panda Sanctuaries – Wolong, Mount Siguniang and Jiajin Mountains

Mount Emei Scenic Area, including Leshan Giant Buddha Scenic Area

Dazu Rock Carvings

Leshan

cape and Archaeological a Bamiyan Valley

BUL

Srinagar

Indus

Gongga Shan 7556

13

Buddhist Ruins of Takht-i-Bahi and Neighboring City Remains at Sahr-i-Bahlol

Taxila

ISLAMABAD

Rawalpindi

TRANSHIMALAYA

Lhasa

Historic Ensemble of the Potala Palace, Lhasa

Xichang

Rohtas Fort

Xigaze

Three Parallel Rivers of Yunnan Protected Areas

Lijiang

25°

Fort and Shalamar Gardens in Lahore

Amritsar

Shimla

HIMALAYA

Dehradun

Nanda Devi and Valley of Flowers National Parks

Sagarmatha (Mt. Everest) 8850

BHUTAN

THIMPHU

Brahmaputra

Kaziranga National Park

Old Town of Lijiang

Xiaguan (Dali)

South China Karst

Kunming

Faisalabad

Lahore

Ludhiana

Dhaulagiri 8167

Pokhara

Sagarmatha National Park

Manas Wildlife Sanctuary

3822

Salween

KISTAN

Multan

Red Fort Complex

Qutb Minar and its Monuments, Delhi

NEPAL

Lumbini, the Birthplace of the Lord Buddha

KATHMANDU

Kathmandu Valley

Darjeeling

Mountain Railways of India

Shillong

Imphal

Mekong

VIETNAM

14

Indus

Humayun's Tomb, Delhi

Delhi

Agra Fort

Agra Taj Mahal

Lucknow

Royal Chitwan National Park

Patna

Ruins of the Buddhist Vihara at Paharpur

Mandalay

2704

LAOS

20°

Thar Desert

NEW DELHI

Keoladeo National Park

Fatehpur Sikri

Kanpur

Ganges

Varanasi

BANGLA-

DHAKA

DESH

Chittagong

Bagan

2704

MYANMAR

Shan Plateau

Luang Prabang

Town of Luang Prabang

Archaeological Ruins at Moenjodaro

Jaisalmer

Jodhpur

Jaipur

Jhansi

Tirth Raj Prayag

Mahabodhi Temple Complex at Bodh Gaya

Dhanbad

Ranchi

Khulna

Historic Mosque City of Bagerhat

The Sundarbans

Inle Lake

Chiang Rai

Chiang Mai

THAILAND

15°

Historic Monuments at Makli, Thatta

Udaipur

Bhopal

Buddhist Monuments at Sanchi

Jabalpur

Khajuraho Group of Monuments

Raurkela

Calcutta

Sundarbans National Park

Cox's Bazar

Sittwe (Akyab)

NAYPYIDAW

Historic Town of Sukhothai and Associated Historic Towns

Phitsanulok

Sukhothai

Ahmedabad

Indore

Rock Shelters of Bhimbetka

Raipur

Sandoway

Prome

Champaner-Pavagadh Archaeological Park

Vadodara

Nagpur

INDIA

Narmada

Bhubaneswar

Sun Temple, Konārak

Puri

Puthein (Bessein)

Rangoon

Maula-myaing

Historic City of Ayutthaya

15°

Surat

Diu

Ajanta Caves

Deccan

Thung Yai-Huai Kha Khaeng Wildlife Sanctuaries

Ayutthaya

BANGKOK

Ellora Caves

Daman

Aurangabad

Godavari

1680

Vishakhapatnam

Gulf of Martaban

Tavoy

Chhatrapati Shivaji Terminus

Mumbai

Elephanta Caves

Pune

Sholapur

Western Ghats

Hyderabad

Krishna

Vijayawada

Hua Hin

16

Mergui

Mergui Archipelago

Isthmus of Kra

a

Group of Monuments at Pattadakal

Group of Monuments at Hampi

Nellore

North Andaman

Bay of Bengal

Andaman Islands

Middle Andaman

Panaij

Hospet

Churches and Convents of Goa

Eastern Ghats

Group of Monuments at Mahabalipuram

Chennai

South Andaman

10°

Bangalore

Pondicherry

Port Blair

Little Andaman

Andaman Sea

Mangalore

Mountain Railways of India

Coimbatore

Great Living Chola Temples

Ten Degree Channel

Nicobar Islands

Phuket

17

Laccadive Islands

Palk Strait

Madurai

Jaffna

Little Nicobar

Great Nicobar

SUMATRA

Kochi

Thiruvananthapuram

Sacred City of Anuradhapura

SRI LANKA

Trincomalee

Ancient City of Polonnaruwa

0 160 320 km

Great Channel

Banda Aceh

INDONESIA

5°

18

Ob 70° Oc 75° Od 80° Pa 85° Pb 90° Pc 95° Pd

East Asia

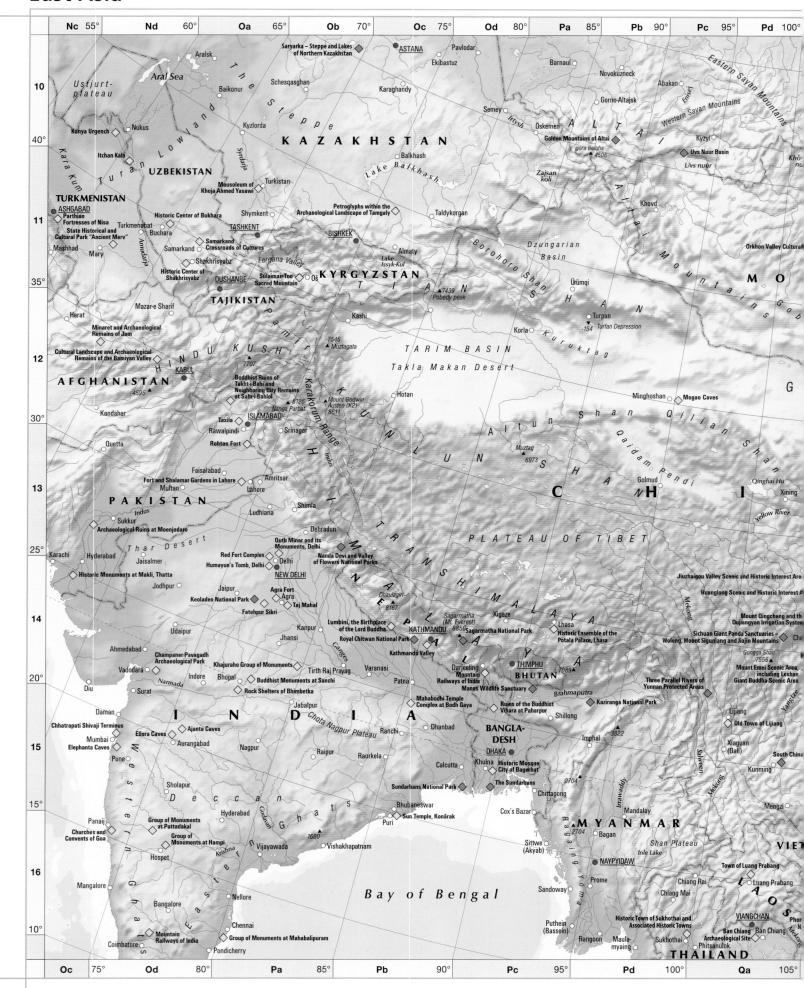

Nc 55° Nd 60° Oa 65° Ob 70° Oc 75° Od 80° Pa 85° Pb 90° Pc 95° Pd 100°

Ustjurt-plateau
Aralsk
Aral Sea
Saryarka – Steppe and Lakes of Northern Kazakhstan
ASTANA
Pavlodar
Baikonur
Schesqasghan
Karaghandy
Ekibastuz
Barnaul
Novokuzneck
Abakan
Eastern Sayan Mountains
Kyzlorda
Semey
Irtysh
Gorno-Altajsk
Western Sayan Mountains
Enisej
Kunya Urgench
Nukus
The Steppe
Turan Lowland
KAZAKHSTAN
Balkhash
Lake Balkhash
Öskemen
Golden Mountains of Altai
gora Beluha 4506
Kyzyl
Uvs Nuur Basin
Uvs nuur
Khövd
Khö nu
Itchan Kala
Kara Kum
UZBEKISTAN
Turkistan
Shymkent
Petroglyphs within the Archaeological Landscape of Tamgaly
Taldykorgan
Zajsan köli
ALTAI
Altai Mountains
MO
TURKMENISTAN
ASHGABAD
Parthian Fortresses of Nisa
State Historical and Cultural Park "Ancient Merv"
Turkmenabat
Mausoleum of Khoja Ahmed Yasawi
Historic Center of Bukhara
TASHKENT
BISHKEK
Almaty
Lake Issyk-Kul
Ürümqi
Dzungarian Basin
Borohoro Shan
Orkhon Valley Cultural
Mashhad
Mary
Buchara
Samarkand – Crossroads of Cultures
Samarkand
Shakhrisyabz
Amudarja
Fergana Valley
KYRGYZSTAN
Os
Sulaiman-Too Sacred Mountain
Pobedy peak 7439
TIAN SHAN
Korla
Kuruktag
Gob
G
Herat
Mazar-e Sharif
Historic Center of Shakhrisyabz
DUSHANBE
Pamir
Kashi
Turpan
-154 Turpan Depression
MO
Minaret and Archaeological Remains of Jam
TAJIKISTAN
7546
Muztagata
TARIM BASIN
Takla Makan Desert
Hotan
Minghoshan
Mogao Caves
Cultural Landscape and Archaeological Remains of the Bamiyan Valley
KABUL
7707
HINDU KUSH
Buddhist Ruins of Takht-i-Bahi and Neighboring City Remains at Sahr-i-Bahlol
8126
Mount Godwin Austen (K2) 8611
Nanga Parbat
Karakorum Range
AFGHANISTAN
4595
K U N L U N   S H A N
Altun Shan
Muztag 6973
Qilian Shan
Qaidam Pendi
Qinghai Hu
C H I N
Kandahar
Taxila
ISLAMABAD
Rawalpindi
Srinagar
Indus
Golmud
Xining
Quetta
Rohtas Fort
Faisalabad
Amritsar
Fort and Shalamar Gardens in Lahore
Multan
Lahore
Ludhiana
Shimla
Dehradun
PLATEAU OF TIBET
Yellow River
PAKISTAN
Indus
Sukkur
Archaeological Ruins at Moenjodaro
Thar Desert
Jaisalmer
Qutb Minar and its Monuments, Delhi
Red Fort Complex
Humayun's Tomb, Delhi
Nanda Devi and Valley of Flowers National Parks
Jiuzhaigou Valley Scenic and Historic Interest Are
Huanglong Scenic and Historic Interest A
Karachi
Hyderabad
Jodhpur
Delhi
NEW DELHI
HIMALAYA
TRANSHIMALAYA
Mount Qingcheng and th Dujiangyan Irrigation System
Historic Monuments at Makli, Thatta
Jaipur
Agra Fort
Agra
Taj Mahal
Keoladeo National Park
Fatehpur Sikri
Kanpur
Dhaulagiri 8167
Lumbini, the Birthplace of the Lord Buddha
KATHMANDU
Sagarmatha (Mt. Everest) 8850
Sagarmatha National Park
Xigaze
Lhasa
Historic Ensemble of the Potala Palace, Lhasa
Sichuan Giant Panda Sanctuaries – Wolong, Mount Siguniang and Jiajin Mountains
Che
Udaipur
Ahmedabad
Champaner-Pavagadh Archaeological Park
Jhansi
Royal Chitwan National Park
Kathmandu Valley
NEPAL
Gongga Shan 7556
Mount Emei Scenic Area, including Leshan Giant Buddha Scenic Area
Vadodara
Indore
Khajuraho Group of Monuments
Tirth Raj Prayag
Varanasi
Darjeeling
Railways of India
THIMPHU
7089
BHUTAN
BRAHMAPUTRA
Manas Wildlife Sanctuary
Three Parallel Rivers of Yunnan Protected Areas
Diu
Narmada
Bhopal
Buddhist Monuments at Sanchi
Patna
Brahmaputra
Kaziranga National Park
Yangtze
Surat
Rock Shelters of Bhimbetka
Mahabodhi Temple Complex at Bodh Gaya
Ruins of the Buddhist Vihara at Paharpur
Shillong
Lijiang
Old Town of Lijiang
Daman
I N D I A
Jabalpur
Chota Nagpur Plateau
Ranchi
Dhanbad
BANGLA-DESH
3822
Imphal
Xiaguan (Dali)
Chhatrapati Shivaji Terminus
Ellora Caves
Ajanta Caves
Nagpur
Raurkela
DHAKA
Historic Mosque City of Bagerhat
South China
Mumbai
Elephanta Caves
Aurangabad
Raipur
Khulna
2704
Chittagong
Kunming
Pune
Sholapur
Deccan
Hyderabad
Sundarbans National Park
The Sundarbans
Cox's Bazar
Mengzi
Godavari
Bhubaneswar
Sun Temple, Konârak
Puri
MYANMAR
Bagan
Mandalay
Irrawaddy
VIET
Panaji
Group of Monuments at Pattadakal
Group of Monuments at Hampi
1680
Vijayawada
Vishakhapatnam
Shan Plateau
Inle Lake
Mekong
Churches and Convents of Goa
Hospet
Krishna
Sittwe (Akyab)
NAYPYIDAW
Town of Luang Prabang
Mangalore
Eastern Ghats
Western Ghats
Bangalore
Nellore
Prome
2704
Sandoway
Ragaing Yoma
Chiang Rai
Luang Prabang
LAOS
Phor N
Mountain Railways of India
Group of Monuments at Mahabalipuram
Chennai
Bay of Bengal
Puthein (Bassein)
Historic Town of Sukhothai and Associated Historic Towns
VIANGCHAN
Coimbatore
Pondicherry
Rangoon
Maula-myaing
Sukhothai
Phitsanulok
Ban Chiang
Ban Chiang Archaeological Site
Mekong
THAILAND

Oc 75° Od 80° Pa 85° Pb 90° Pc 95° Pd 100° Qa 105°

Qb 110°   Qc 115°   Qd 120°   Ra 125°   Rb 130°   Rc 135°   Rd 140°   Sa 145°   Sb 150°   Sc 155°   Sd

RUSSIA

Stanovoye Nagor'ye
Yablonovyy Range
Lake Baikal
Baikal

Ulan-Ude
Aginskoe

Amur
Jagdaqi
Blagoveščensk
Birobidžan
Habarovsk

Komsomol'sk-na-Amure
Amur

Tatarskiy Proliv

Sakhalin

o. Rasšua
o. Simušir

09
45°

ULAN-BATOR

Yakeshi

Yichun

Jiamusi

Central Sikhote-Alin

Južno-Sahalinsk

o. Urup
o. Iturup

Kuril Islands

10

MONGOLIA

Greater Hinggan Range
Lesser Hinggan Range

Harbin
Lake Khanka

Sikhote-Alin

Vladivostok

Manchuria

La Pérouse Strait
Wakkanai
Shiretoko

o. Kunašir

40°

Changchun

2290
Asahi dake
Kushiro

HOKKAIDO

Sapporo
Hakodate

PACIFIC

1609

Baotou
Hohot
Yellow River
Datong
Yungang Grottoes
BEIJING (PEKING)
Mount Wutai
Peking Man Site at Zhoukoudian

Mountain Resort and its Outlying Temples, Chengde
The Great Wall
Chengde
Imperial Tombs of the Ming and Qing Dynasties
Imperial Palaces of the Ming and Qing Dynasties in Beijing and Shenyang
Temple of Heaven: an Imperial Sacrificial Altar in Beijing
Summer Palace, an Imperial Garden in Beijing

Imperial Palaces of the Ming and Qing Dynasties in Beijing and Shenyang
Shenyang

Capital Cities and Tombs of the Ancient Koguryo Kingdom

Complex of the Koguryo Tombs

PYONGYANG

DEMOCRATIC PEOPLE'S REPUBLIC OF KOREA

Donghae

JAPAN

Tsugaru Strait
Aomori
Shirakami-Sanchi

Morioka

HONSHU

Niigata
Sendai
Fukushima

Sea of Japan

OCEAN

11

35°

A
Taiyuan
Pingyao
Ancient City of Ping Yao
Yin Xu
Handan

Xi'an
Mausoleum of the First Qin Emperor

Shijiazhuang
Jinan
Zibo
Qingdao
Mount Taishan
Temple and Cemetery of Confucius and the Kong Family Mansion in Qufu

Longmen Grottoes

Zhengzhou

Yantai
Dalian

Yellow Sea

Changdeokgung Palace Complex
SEOUL
Jongmyo Shrine
Hwaseong Fortress
Haeinsa Temple Janggyeong Panjeon, the Depositories for the "Tripitaka Koreana" Woodblocks

Gochang, Hwasun and Ganghwa Dolmen Sites

REPUBLIC OF KOREA

Daegu
Gwangju
Gyeongju
Gyeongju Historic Areas

Royal Tombs of the Joseon Dynasty
Seokguram Grotto and Bulguksa Temple

Iwami Ginzan Silver Mine and its Cultural Landscape

Korea Strait

Shirame-san
2578
Nikko
Shrines and Temples of Nikko
TOKYO
Fuji-san
3776
Yokohama

Historic Villages of Shirakawa-go and Gokayama

Nagoya

Kyoto
Historic Monuments of Ancient Kyoto
Kobe
Himeji-jo
Osaka
Historic Monuments of Ancient Nara

Buddhist Monuments in the Horyu-ji Area

Sacred Sites and Pilgrimage Routes in the Kii Mountain Range

12

30°

Yellow River
Ancient Building Complex in the Wudang Mountains
Imperial Tombs of the Ming and Qing Dynasties

Three Gorges Dam
Yangtze
Wulingyuan Scenic and Historic Interest Area

South China Karst

Huainan
Hefei
Nanjing
Suzhou
Classical Gardens of Suzhou

Imperial Tombs of the Ming and Qing Dynasties

Shanghai

Hiroshima
Itsukushima Shinto Shrine
Kitakyushu
Fukuoka
Nagasaki

Hiroshima Peace Memorial

SHIKOKU

KYUSHU
Kagoshima

Izu-Shoto

13

25°

Wuhan
Jiujiang
Lushan National Park
Nanchang
Mount Sanqingshan National Park

Mount Huangshan

Hangzhou

Ancient Villages in Southern Anhui – Xidi and Hongcun

Tungting Lake
Changsha
Mount Wuyi

Wuyi Shan

Yakushima
Yakushima

Tokara Islands
Osumi Islands

Satsunan Islands

South China Mountains

Fuzhou

Ryukyu Islands

Okinawa Islands

Gusuku Sites and Related Properties of the Kingdom of Ryukyu
Naha

Tropic of Cancer

14

20°

South China Karst
Guilin

Fujian Tulou
Xiamen

TAIPEI
Taichung

TAIWAN

Kaohsiung

Taiwan Strait

Sakishima Islands

15

Kaiping Diaolou and Villages
Historic Center of Macao
Guangzhou
Macao
Hong Kong

Pearl River

Zhanjiang

Luzon Strait

Beihai
Hainan Strait
Haikou
Hainan Dao
Sanya

South China Sea

Bangui

Baroque Churches of the Philippines
Vigan
Historic Town of Vigan
Banaue

LUZON

PHILIPPINES

Rice Terraces of the Philippine Cordilleras

Philippine Sea

North China Plain

East China Sea

Jeju
Jeju Volcanic Island and Lava Tubes
Jeju-do

0   160   320
km

16

15°

110°   Qc   115°   Qd   120°   Ra   125°   Rb   130°   Rc   135°   Rd   140°   Sa

South Asia

Pd 100° Qa 105° Qb 110° Qc 115° Qd 120° Ra 125° Rb 130° Rc 130°

Taiyuan
Yinchuan
Pingyao
Ancient City of Ping Yao
Handan
Yin Xu

Jinan
Zibo
Qingdao

East China Sea

Nagasaki
Kagoshima
KYUSHU
JAPAN

30°

Qinghai Hu
Xining
Lanzhou

Zhengzhou
Huaiñan

Mausoleum of the
First Qin Emperor

Xi'an

Longmen Grottoes

Mount Taishan
Temple and Cemetery of Confucius
and the Kong Family Mansion in Qufu

Imperial Tombs of the
Ming and Qing Dynasties

Nanjing
Suzhou
Shanghai
Classical Gardens of Suzhou

Yakushima

Tokara Islands

Osumi Islands

Satsunan Islands

13

Yellow River

Jiuzhaigou Valley Scenic
and Historic Interest Area
Huanglong Scenic and Historic Interest Area

C **H** **I** **N** **A**

Ancient Building Complex
in the Wudang Mountains
Imperial Tombs of the
Ming and Qing Dynasties
Wuhan

Hefei

Hangzhou

Mount Huangshan

Ancient Villages in Southern
Anhui – Xidi and Hongcun

25°

Yangtze

Mount Qingcheng and the
Dujiangyan Irrigation System

Chengdu

Three Gorges Dam

Red Basin

Wulingyuan Scenic and
Historic Interest Area

Jiujiang
Lushan National Park
Nanchang
Mount Sanqingshan National Park

Gusuku Sites and Related Properties
of the Kingdom of Ryukyu
Naha

Sichuan Giant Panda Sanctuaries –
Wolong, Mount Siguniang and Jiajin Mountains

Chongqing

Yangtze

Mount Wuyi

Ryukyu Islands

14

Mount Emei Scenic Area, including
Leshan Giant Buddha Scenic Area

Leshan

Dazu Rock
Carvings

South China Karst

Gongga Shan
7556 ▲

Tungting Lake

Changsha

Sakishima Islands

Tropic of Cancer

Three Parallel Rivers of
Yunnan Protected Areas

Guiyang

South China Mountains

Fuzhou

Wuyi Shan

TAIPEI

Taichung

TAIWAN

20°

Lijiang
Old Town of Lijiang

South China Karst
Libo

South China Karst

Guilin

Guangzhou

Xiamen

Kaohsiung

Taiwan Strait

Xiaguan
(Dali)
Kunming

Nanning

Kaiping Diaolou and Villages

Pearl River
Macao
Hong Kong
Historic Center of Macao

Luzon Strait

15

Mengzi

Beihai

Zhanjiang

Philippine Sea

Bangui

Baroque Churches of the Philippines
Vigan
Historic Town of Vigan

LUZON

Mandalay

HANOI

Ha Long Bay

Haiphong

Hainan Strait

Haikou

*Gulf of
Tonkin*

Hainan Dao

Sanya

Rice Terraces of the Philippine Cordilleras
Baguio

15°

MYANMAR

Shan Plateau
Inle Lake

Luang
Prabang
Town of
Luang Prabang

2452

Phong Nha-Ke Bang
National Park

Mt. Pinatubo
1600 ▲
Baroque Churches of the Philippines
MANILA
Mayon
2462 ▲

PHILIPPINES

Catanduanes

16

NAYPYIDAW

Chiang Rai

Chiang Mai

VIANGCHAN

Ban Chiang
Archaeological Site
Ban Chiang

Annam Plateau

Mekong

Complex of Hué Monuments
Hue
Da Nang
Hoi An
Hoi An Ancient Town

*Paracel
Islands*

Mindoro

Samar

Visayas

Historic Town of Sukhothai and
Associated Historic Towns
Sukhothai

Phitsanulok

Khon Kaen

Savannakhét

My Son Sanctuary

L A O S

Panay
Iloilo
Cebu
Cebu

Leyte

Bohol

Butuan

10°

Yangoon

Maula-
myaing

*Gulf of
Martaban*

THAILAND

Ubon
Ratchathani

Pakse

Vat Phou and Associated
Ancient Settlements within
the Champasak Cultural Landscape

Khorat Plateau

Qui Nhon

South China Sea

*Calamian
Group*

Negros

Cagayan
de Oro

Davao

Thung Yai-Huai Kha Khaeng
Wildlife Sanctuaries
Tavoy

Ayutthaya
Historic City of Ayutthaya

BANGKOK

Dong Phayayen-Khao
Yai Forest Complex

Siem Reap

Angkor

Temple of
Preah Vihear

Tonle Sap

VIETNAM

Nha Trang

Spratly Islands

Puerto Princesa Subterranean
River National Park
Puerto Princesa
Palawan

Tubbataha Reefs
Natural Park
Tubbataha Reef

Mt. Apo
2956 ▲

General
Santos

17

Mergui

*Mergui
Archipelago*

Hua Hin

Pattaya

CAMBODIA

PHNOM PENH

Mekong

T.P. Ho Chi Minh
(Saigon)

Sulu Sea

*Zamboanga
Peninsula*
Zamboanga

MINDANAO

Sandakan

Sulu Archipelago

Kep. Sanglhe

man Sea

Phuket

Surat Thani

Isthmus of Kra
Koh Samui

Sihanoukville
(Kompong-Som)

Mui Ca Mau

G. Kinabalu 4095 ▲
Kota Kinabalu
Kinabalu Park

Celebes Sea

Manado

Minahasa

18

Songkhla

Langkawi

Kota Bharu

M A L A Y S I A

BANDAR SERI BEGAWAN
BRUNEI
Miri
Mulu
Gunung Mulu National Park

Sojol
3000

Gorontalo

Tomini
*Teluk
Tomini*

Molucca Sea

0°

bar

George Town
Melaka and George Town, Historic Cities of the Straits of Malacca
Ipoh
Malay Peninsula
Kuantan

Natuna Besar

Kep. Anambas

Kep. Natuna

Kuching

G. Liangpran
2240 ▲

Samarinda

G. Rantemario 3440 ▲

*SULAWESI
(CELEBES)*

3505

Kep. Sula

*Teluk
Tolo*

Banda Sea

19

annel

World Heritage of Sumatra

G. Leuser
3404 ▲

Medan

KUALA LUMPUR

Melaka and George Town, Historic Cities of the Straits of Malacca
Melaka

Johor Bahru

S U M A T R A

Lake Toba

SINGAPORE
SINGAPORE

Singkawang

Pontianak

K A L I M A N T A N

(B O R N E O)

Balikpapan

Masamba

*Teluk
Bone*

Kendari

Mona

Butung

5°

Simeulue

Nias

Kep. Lingga

Natuna Sea

Pekanbaru

Bukittinggi

Tanahmasa

I N D O N E S I A

20

Pd 100° Qa 105° Qb 110° Qc 115° Qd 120° Ra 125°

South-East Asia

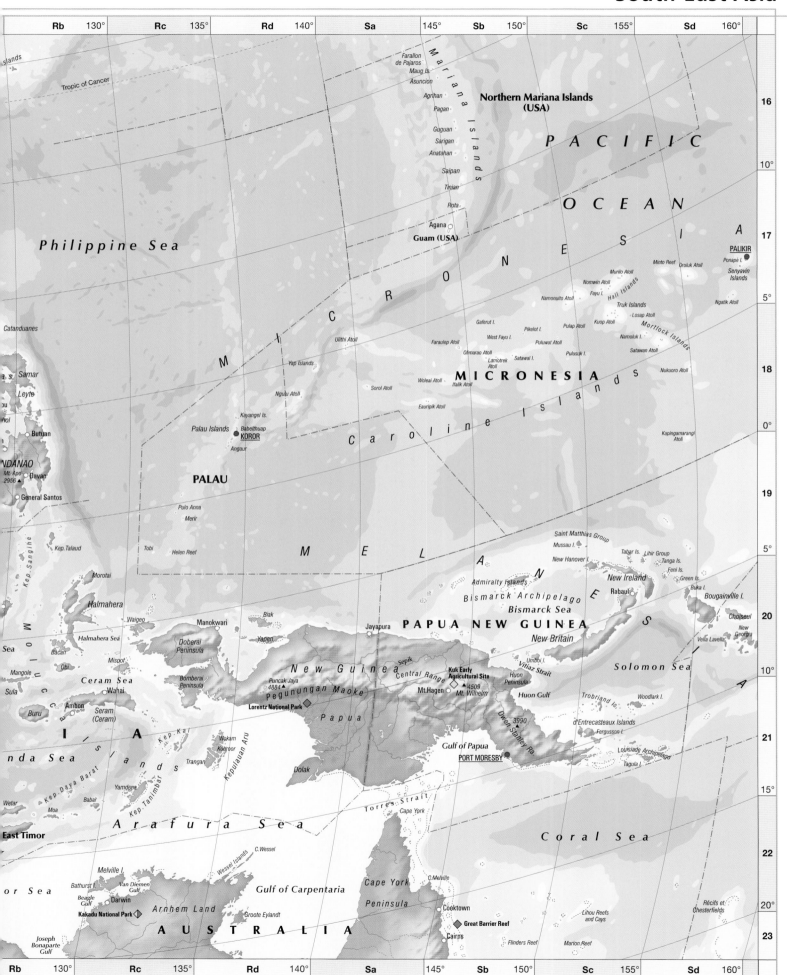

Rb 130°   Rc 135°   Rd 140°   Sa 145°   Sb 150°   Sc 155°   Sd 160°

Tropic of Cancer

16

Farallon de Pajaros
Maug Is.
Asuncion

Agrihan

Pagan

**Northern Mariana Islands
(USA)**

Guguan

Sarigan

Anatahan

P A C I F I C

10°

Saipan

Tinian

O C E A N

Rota

Agana ○

Guam (USA)

17

Philippine Sea

PALIKIR

Ponapé I. ●

Minto Reef   Oroluk Atoll

Senyavin Islands

Murilo Atoll

Nomwin Atoll

5°

Catanduanes

Namonuito Atoll   Fayu I.

Hall Islands

Ngatik Atoll

Truk Islands

— Losap Atoll

Gaferut I.

Pikelot I.   Kuop Atoll

Namoluk I.

Mortlock Islands

Samar

Ulithi Atoll

West Fayu I.   Pulap Atoll

Puluwat Atoll

Namoluk I.

Leyte

Faraulep Atoll

Olimarao Atoll   Satawal I.

Pulusuk I.

Satawan Atoll

Lamotrek Atoll

Nukuoro Atoll

18

○ Butuan

Yap Islands

MICRONESIA

Woleai Atoll   Ifalik Atoll

Sorol Atoll

Nguku Atoll

Caroline Islands

Eauripik Atoll

0°

Kayangel Is.

Palau Islands Babelthuap
KOROR ●

C a r o l i n e   I s l a n d s

Kapingamarangi Atoll

NDANAO
Mt. Apo ▲
2956 ▲   ○ Davao

Angaur

○ General Santos

PALAU

Pulo Anna

19

Merir

Kep. Talaud

Tobi

Helen Reef

M E L A N

Saint Matthias Group

5°

Mussau I. ●

Kep. Sangihe

New Hanover I.

Tabar Is. Lihir Group

Tanga Is.

Feni Is.

Morotai

Admiralty Islands

A

New Hanover I.

Green Is.

Buka I.

Halmahera

Bismarck Archipelago

New Ireland

Bougainville I.

Rabaul ○

Choiseul

20

Waigeo

Biak

Bismarck Sea

N

New Georgia

Manokwari

Vella Lavella

M

Halmahera Sea

Yapen

PAPUA NEW GUINEA

Jayapura

Bacan

Doberai Peninsula

Yapen

New Britain

E

Sea

Obi

Sepik

Umboi I.   Vitiaz Strait

Mangole

Ceram Sea

Misool

New Guinea

Central Range

**Kuk Early
Agricultural Site**

Huon Peninsula

Solomon Sea

10°

Sula   Wahai

Bomberai Peninsula

Puncak Jaya
4884 ▲

Mt. Hagen   ▲ 4509
Mt. Wilhelm

Huon Gulf

Ambon

Pegunungan Maoke

Trobriand Is.

Woodlark I.

Buru

Seram (Ceram)

Lorentz National Park ◇

Papua

d'Entrecasteaux Islands

I   *A*

Kep. Kai

Owen Stanley Ra.
3990

Fergusson I.

n d a   S e a

Wokam

Kotroor

Gulf of Papua

Louisiade Archipelago

21

Kep. Daya Barat

Trangan

PORT MORESBY ●

Tagula I.

Yamdena

Dolak

15°

Kep. Tanimbar

Torres Strait

Wetar

Babar

Cape York

Coral Sea

22

Moa

A r a f u r a   S e a

C. Wessel

or Sea

Melville I.

Wessel Islands

C. Melville

Gulf of Carpentaria

**Cape York
Peninsula**

20°

Bathurst I. Van Diemen Gulf

Arnhem Land

○ Cooktown

*Lihou Reefs
and Cays*

Récifs et Chesterfields

Beagle Gulf   ○ Darwin

Groote Eylandt

Kakadu National Park ◇

◆ **Great Barrier Reef**

Joseph Bonaparte Gulf

AUSTRALIA

○ Cairns

Flinders Reef   Marion Reef

23

Rb 130°   Rc 135°   Rd 140°   Sa 145°   Sb 150°   Sc 155°   Sd 160°

East Timor

M O L U C C A S

Australia, New Zealand

Qc 115°   Qd 120°   Ra 125°   Rb 130°   Rc 135°   Rd 140°   Sa 145°

Arafura Sea

3332 ▲
G.Merapi   Denpasar   Sumbawa   *Flores*   *Torres Strait*
                                                                        Cape York
20   Java   Bali   Lombok   *Timor*   C.Wessel
                        Savu Sea   Kupang   *Wessel Islands*
10° **INDONESIA**   Sumba   Sawu   Roti   Melville I.
                                            Bathurst I.   Van Diemen   Groote Eylandt   Cape York
                        Ashmore   Hibernia Reef   Beagle   Gulf   Peninsula   C.Melville
                        Islands   Cartier I.   Gulf   Darwin   C.Melville
21   **Kakadu National Park** ◇   *Arnhem Land*   Cooktown   Great
     INDIAN OCEAN   Bonaparte Archipelago   Joseph   ◆
                                            Bonaparte   Katherine   *Gulf of Carpentaria*
15°   Gulf   Cairns
                                   Wyndham   Daly Waters   Wellesley Islands   Great
                        Rowley Shoals   L.Argyle   Mornington I.   Wet Tropics of Queensland ◆
                   Derby   *KIMBERLEY*   *Barkly Tableland*   Townsv
                        Broome   *PLATEAU*   936 ▲   **Purnululu National Park** ◆
                                            Halls Creek   *Tanami Desert*   Riversleigh
22   **Australian Fossil Mammal Sites**
                        Port Hedland   (Riversleigh / Naracoorte)
                                        Great Sandy Desert   Tennant Creek
                   Dampier   Mount Isa
20°   North West C.   Black Mtn. ▲
                        Pilbara   L.Mackay   568
                        Hamersley Range   Mt.Liebig   Alice Springs   Barcaldine
                   L.Disappointment   **A U S T R A L I A**   1524
23   Tropic of Capricorn   *Gibson Desert*   **Uluru-Kata Tjuta National Park** ◇   Ayers   Erldunda   *Simpson Desert*   *Great Artesian*
                        Mt.Augustus   Rock ▲   *Basin*
                        1105   L.Carnegie   863   *Musgrave Ranges*   Lake Eyre   *Sturt Stony Desert*
                   Carnarvon   *Basin*   Cunnar
25° Shark Bay   **Shark Bay, Western Australia** ◆   *Great Victoria Desert*   Lake Eyre
                                                                    North
                                                              Coober Pedy   L.Torrens   Lake
                   Mount Magnet   Leonora   Frome
24   Woomera   Broken Hill   Darling
                   Geraldton   *Nullarbor Plain*   Lake   Flinders Ranges
                        Kalgoorlie-   *Eucla Basin*   Gairdner   Port Augusta   **Willandra Lakes Region** ◇
30°   Boulder   Eucla Motels   Eyre   Mildura
                   Norseman   Peninsula   Murray River
                                                              Spencer   Basin
                   Perth   *Great Australian Bight*   Port Lincoln   Gulf   Adelaide   Murray
                        Esperance   C.Spencer
                   C.Naturaliste   Kangaroo I.   **Australian Fossil Mammal Sites** ◆
25°   Archipelago of the   (Riversleigh / Naracoorte)
                        Recherche   Naracoorte   Melbourne   G
                   C.Leeuwin   Albany   Geelong   **Royal Exhibition**
                                                                                         and Carlton Garde
35° **INDIAN OCEAN**   Portland
                                                                        Bass Strait
                                                                    King Island   Flinders

---

Qb 110°   Qc 115°   Qd 120°   Ra 125°   Rb 130°   Rc

                        Christmas-I.   C.York   Devonpo
29   Arnhem   Cape
                   Cocos Is.   Land   York   **Tasmanian Wilderness** ◇   Tasm
20° Madagascar   Mascarene Islands   Peninsula
                   Réunion   Mauritius   *Great Sandy*   **AUSTRALIA**   Hob
                        Desert   *Great Artesian*
30   *Great Victoria*   *Basin*
     INDIAN OCEAN   Desert   Lake Eyre   South
                                                              Darling   East Cape
                        C.Leeuwin   *Nullarbor Plain*   Lord-Howe
                   Amsterdam   *Great*   Murray   Mt.Koszciusko
                   Saint Paul   Australian Bight   2230
40°   Bass Strait   *Tasman*
                                                         Sea
                   Crozet Islands   Tasmania   New Zealand
                                                                                   28
                   Kerguelen Islands
31   **New Zealand Sub-Antarctic Islands**   Auckland Islands
                   Heard and McDonald Islands ◆   Macquarie Island ◆
                        Heard   **Macquarie Island**   Campbell Islands

0   1000   2000
km

60°   Na 80°   Nb 100°   Oa 120°   Ob 140°   Pa 160°   Pb 180°   Rc 135°   Rd 140°   Sa 145°   Sb 1

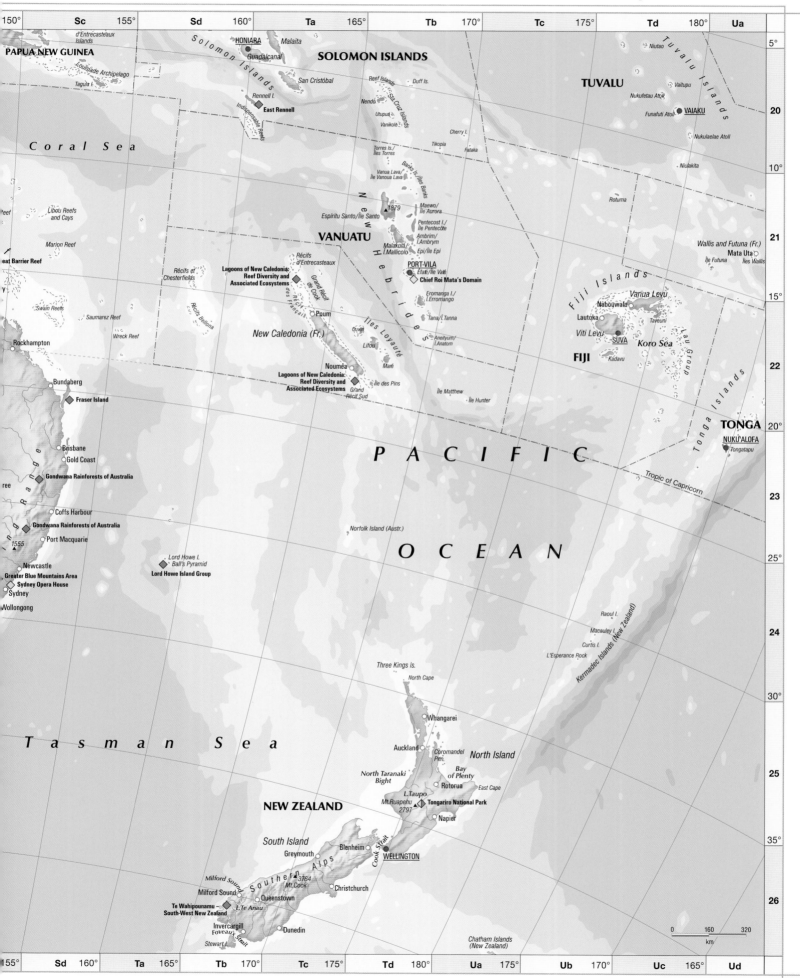

South Pacific Islands

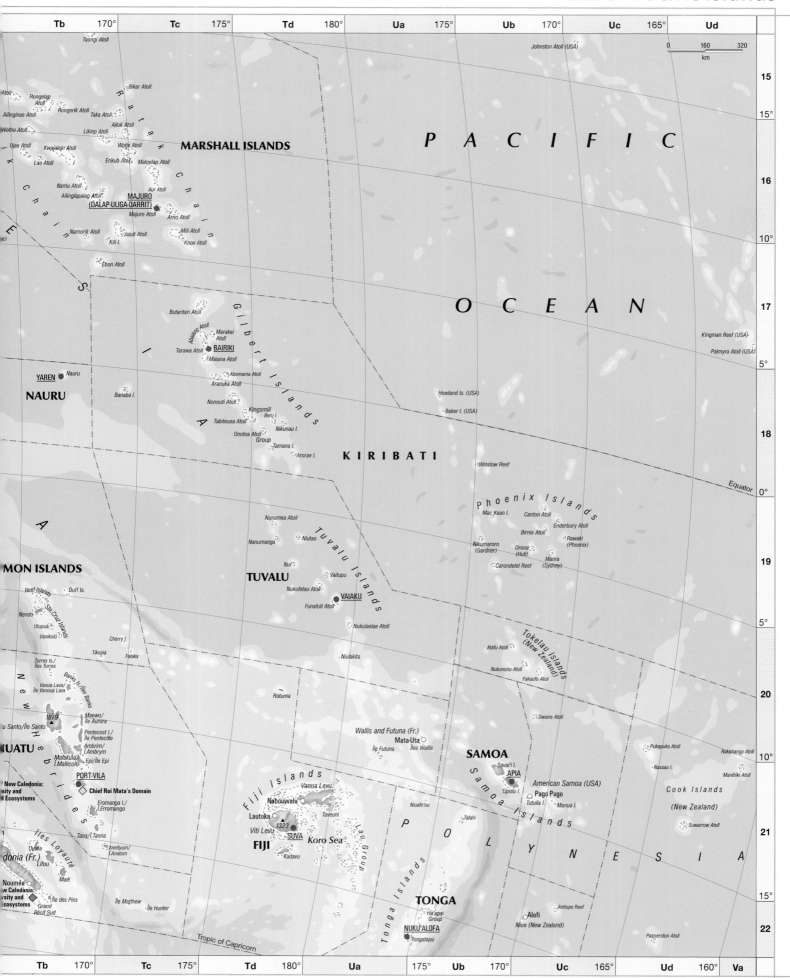

PACIFIC

OCEAN

MARSHALL ISLANDS

Taongi Atoll

Bikar Atoll

Rongelap Atoll
Ailinginae Atoll
Rongerik Atoll
Taka Atoll
Wotho Atoll
Ujae Atoll
Likiep Atoll
Kwajalein Atoll
Wotje Atoll
Lae Atoll
Erikub Atoll
Maloelap Atoll
Namu Atoll
Aur Atoll
Ailinglapalap Atoll
MAJURO
(DALAP-ULIGA-DARRIT)
Majuro Atoll
Arno Atoll
Namorik Atoll
Jaluit Atoll
Mili Atoll
Kili I.
Knox Atoll

Ebon Atoll

Johnston Atoll (USA)

0   160   320
km

Kingman Reef (USA)

Palmyra Atoll (USA)

Butaritari Atoll
Abaiang Atoll
Marakei Atoll
Tarawa Atoll
BAIRIKI
Maiana Atoll
Abemama Atoll
Aranuka Atoll
YAREN
Nauru
NAURU
Banaba I.
Nonouti Atoll
Kingsmill
Beru I.
Tabiteuea Atoll
Nikunau I.
Onotoa Atoll
Group
Tamana I.
Arorae I.

Gilbert Islands

Howland Is. (USA)

Baker I. (USA)

KIRIBATI

Winslow Reef

Phoenix Islands

Mac Kean I.
Canton Atoll
Enderbury Atoll
Birnie Atoll
Nikumaroro
(Gardner)
Orona
(Hull)
Rawaki
(Phoenix)
Carondelet Reef
Manra
(Sydney)

Equator

Nanumea Atoll
Nanumanga
Niutao
Nui
Vaitupu
TUVALU
Nukufetau Atoll
VAIAKU
Funafuti Atoll
Nukulaelae Atoll

Tuvalu Islands

MON ISLANDS

Reef Islands
Duff Is.
Nendo
Santa Cruz Islands
Utupua
Vanikolo
Tikopia
Fataka
Cherry I.

Torres Is./
Îles Torres

Banks Is./Îles Banks
Vanua Lava/
Île Vanoua Lava
1879
Maewo/
Île Aurora
Santo/Île Santo
Pentecost I./
Île Pentecôte
Ambrim/
I.Ambrym
Malakula/
I.Mallicolo
Epi/Île Epi
VANUATU
New Hebrides
PORT-VILA
Chief Roi Mata's Domain
New Caledonia:
sity and
Ecosystems
Eromanga I./
I.Erromango
Tana/I.Tanna
Aneityum/
I.Anatom
Ouvéa
Lifou
donia (Fr.)
Noumêa
New Caledonia
sity and
cosystems
Île des Pins
Grand
Récif Sud
Maré
Île Matthew
Île Hunter

Îles Loyauté

Niulakita

Atafu Atoll

Tokelau Islands
(New Zealand)

Nukunonu Atoll

Fakaofo Atoll

Swains Atoll

Rotuma

Wallis and Futuna (Fr.)
Mata-Uta
Île Futuna
Îles Wallis

SAMOA
Savai'i I.
APIA
'Upolu I.
American Samoa (USA)
Pago Pago
Tutuila I.
Manua Is.

Samoa Islands

Pukapuka Atoll

Rakahanga Atoll

Nassau I.

Manihiki Atoll

Cook Islands
(New Zealand)

Suwarrow Atoll

Fiji Islands
Vanua Levu
Nabouwalu
Lautoka
Taveuni
Viti Levu
1323
SUVA
Koro Sea
FIJI
Kadavu

Niuafo'ou
Tafahi

Lau Group

POLYNESIA

Tonga Islands

TONGA
Ha'apai
Group
NUKU'ALOFA
Tongatapu

Antiope Reef

Alofi
Niue (New Zealand)

Palmerston Atoll

Tropic of Capricorn

North Africa

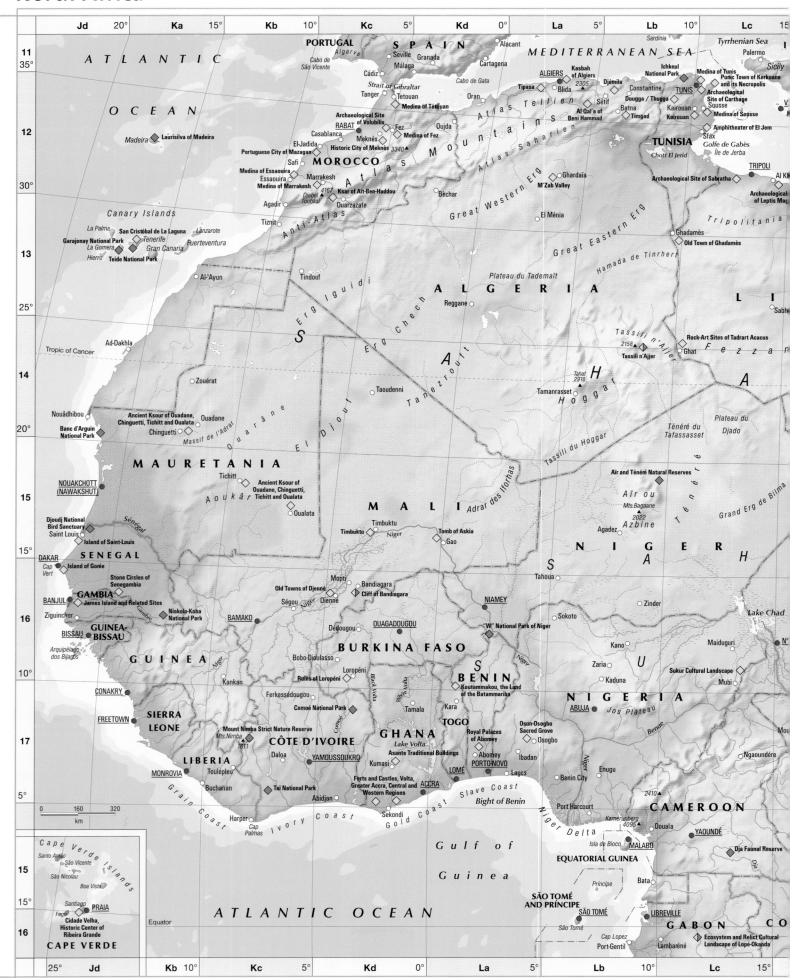

ATLANTIC OCEAN

MEDITERRANEAN SEA

PORTUGAL · SPAIN

Algarve · Cabo de São Vicente · Seville · Granada · Cartagena · Alacant · Sardinia · Tyrrhenian Sea · Palermo · Sicily

Cádiz · Málaga · Cabo de Gata · Tipasa · ALGIERS · Kasbah of Algiers 2305 · Djémila · Ichkeul National Park · Medina of Tunis · Punic Town of Kerkuane and its Necropolis

Strait of Gibraltar · Tanger · Oran · Blida · Sétif · Constantine · Dougga / Thugga · TUNIS · Archaeological Site of Carthage · Sousse

Tetouan · Medina of Tétouan · Al Qal'a of Beni Hammad · Batna · Kairouan · Medina of Sousse

RABAT · Archaeological Site of Volubilis · Fez · Oujda · Timgad · Kairouan · Amphitheater of El Jem

Casablanca · Meknés · Medina of Fez · TUNISIA · Golfe de Gabès · Île de Jerba

El-Jadida · Historic City of Meknés 3340

Portuguese City of Mazagan · Chott El Jerid · TRIPOLI · Al Kh

MOROCCO · Laurisilva of Madeira · Madeira

Medina of Essaouira · Essaouira · Marrakesh · Ghardaïa · Archaeological Site of Sabratha

Safi · Medina of Marrakesh 4167 · Ksar of Aït-Ben-Haddou · M'Zab Valley · Archaeological of Leptis Mag

Djebel Toubkal · Bèchar · Tripolitania

Agadir · Ouarzazate

Tiznit · El Ménia · Great Western Erg

Canary Islands · Anti-Atlas · Great Eastern Erg · Hamada de Tinrherr

La Palma · San Cristóbal de La Laguna · Lânzarote · Ghadamès · Old Town of Ghadamès

Garajonay National Park · Tenerife · Fuerteventura · Plateau du Tademaït · ALGERIA

La Gomera · Gran Canaria · LI

Hierro · Teide National Park · Tindouf

Erg Iguidi · Erg Chech · Reggane · Tassili n'Ajjer 2158 · Rock-Art Sites of Tadrart Acacus · Sabh

Ad-Dakhla · Tassili n'Ajjer · Ghat · Fezza

Tropic of Cancer · Tanezrouft · Hoggar · Fezza

Zouérat · Taoudenni · Tamanrasset · Tahat 2918 · Hoggar · A

Nouâdhibou · Ancient Ksour of Ouadane, Chinguetti, Tichitt and Oualata · Ouadane · Ténéré du Tafassasset · Plateau du Djado

Banc d'Arguin National Park · Chinguetti · Massif de l'Adrar · Ouarâne · El Djouf · Tassili du Hoggar

MAURETANIA · Aïr and Ténéré Natural Reserves

NOUAKCHOTT (NAWAKSHUT) · Tichitt · Ancient Ksour of Ouadane, Chinguetti, Tichitt and Oualata · Aïr ou · Mts.Bagaane · Grand Erg de Bilma

Djoudj National Bird Sanctuary · Aoukâr · Oualata · Azbine 2022 · Ténéré

Saint Louis · Sénégal · Timbuktu · Tomb of Askia · Agadez · NIGER

Island of Saint-Louis · Timbuktu · Niger · Gao · Tahoua

SENEGAL · MALI · Adrar des Iforhas · S A H

DAKAR · Island of Gorée · Mopti · Bandiagara · Zinder · Lake Chad

Cap Vert · Stone Circles of Senegambia · Ségou · Old Towns of Djenné · Dienné · Cliff of Bandiagara · NIAMEY · Sokoto

GAMBIA · James Island and Related Sites · BAMAKO · Kano · Maiduguri

BANJUL · Gambie · Dédougou · OUAGADOUGOU · "W" National Park of Niger · N'

Ziguinchor · Niokolo-Koba National Park · Kano · N I G E R

BISSAU · GUINEA-BISSAU · GUINEA · Bobo-Dioulasso · BURKINA FASO · Zaria

Arquipélago dos Bijagós · Niger · Loropéni · BENIN · Kaduna · Sukur Cultural Landscape

CONAKRY · Kankan · Ruins of Loropéni · Koutammakou, the Land of the Batammariba · Mubi

SIERRA LEONE · FREETOWN · Ferkessédougou · Comoé National Park · Tamala · Kara · ABUJA · Jos Plateau · N I G E R I A

Mount Nimba Strict Nature Reserve · Mts.Nimba 1611 · CÔTE D'IVOIRE · GHANA · TOGO · Osun-Osogbo Sacred Grove · Ngaoundéré

LIBERIA · Daloa · YAMOUSSOUKRO · Lake Volta · Asante Traditional Buildings · Royal Palaces of Abomey · Osogbo · Benue

MONROVIA · Toulépleu · Kumasi · Abomey · Ibadan · Enugu · Benin City

Buchanan · Taï National Park · Forts and Castles, Volta, Greater Accra, Central and Western Regions · PORTO-NOVO · Lagos · Port Harcourt · CAMEROON

Harper · Cap Palmas · Abidjan · ACCRA · LOMÉ · Bight of Benin · Niger Delta · 2410 · Kamerunberg 4095

Grain Coast · Ivory Coast · Sekondi · Gold Coast · Slave Coast · Benin City · Douala · YAOUNDÉ

Gulf of Guinea · Dja Faunal Reserve

Isla de Bioco · MALABO · EQUATORIAL GUINEA

Cape Verde Islands · Príncipe · Bata

Santo Antão · São Vicente · SÃO TOMÉ AND PRÍNCIPE · LIBREVILLE

São Nicolau · Boa Vista · SÃO TOMÉ · GABON · CO

Santiago · PRAIA · ATLANTIC OCEAN · São Tomé

Fogo · Cidade Velha, Historic Center of Ribeira Grande · Equator · Cap Lopez · Port-Gentil · Ecosystem and Relict Cultural Landscape of Lopé-Okanda

CAPE VERDE · Lambaréné

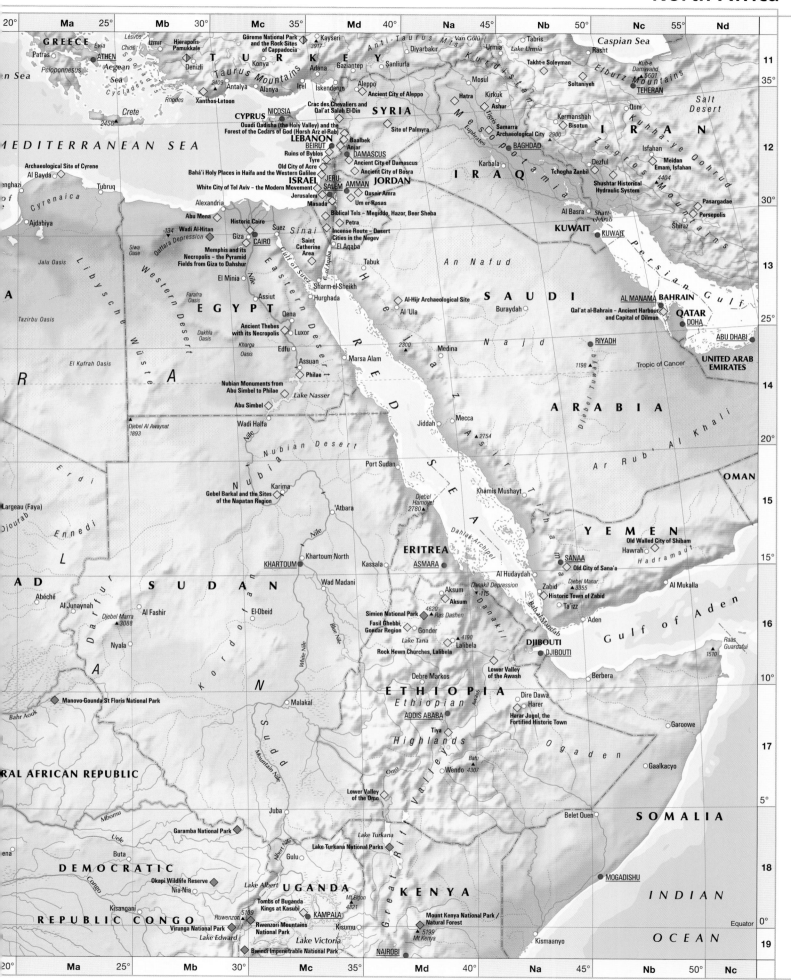

Southern Africa

CAMEROON

SÃO TOMÉ AND PRÍNCIPE
Príncipe
Bata
EQUATORIAL GUINEA

SÃO TOMÉ
São Tomé
LIBREVILLE

GABON
CONGO

Mbandaka
Kisangani

Congo Basin

Ecosystem and Relict Cultural Landscape of Lopé-Okanda

Cap Lopez
Port-Gentil
Lambaréné

DEMOCRATIC

Lac Mai-Ndombe
Ikela

Salonga National Park

BRAZZAVILLE
KINSHASA

REPUBLIC CONGO

Pointe-Noire
Cabinda
Kikwit

Cabinda (Angola)
Matadi

Kananga
Mbuji-mayí

Tshikapa
Kasai

Plateau du Kasai

LUANDA

ANGOLA

Kolwezi

Planalto do Bié
Luena
Zambesi

ZA

Benguela
Huambo

Lubango

Mongu

Barotseland

Namibe

Okavango
Caprivi Strip
Livingstone
Mosi
Victo

ATLANTIC

Sankt Helena (UK)

Ovamboland
Tsodilo
Okavango Delta

Etosha Pan

Grootfontein
Maun

Hereroland

Nationa

Twyfelfontein or /Ui-//aes
Brandberg 2574

Makgadikgadi Pans

Damaraland

Ghanzi

WINDHOEK

BOTSWANA

Walvis Bay
NAMIBIA

GABORONE

Tropic of Capricorn

OCEAN

KALAHARI DESERT

Namaland

Lüderitz
Keetmannshoop

Bechuanaland

Fossil Hominid S
Sterkfontein, Swart
Kromdraai, and En
Jo

Fossil Hominid Sites of Sterkfontein, Swartkrans, Kromdraai, and Environs
Taung
Vre

Richtersveld Cultural and Botanical Landscape
Oranjerivet

Kimberley

Bloemfontein

Namaqualand
Oranjeriver

Upper Karoo

SOUTH AFRICA
D

Cape Floral Region Protected Areas
Great Karoo
2152

Robben Island
Cape Town
Cape of Good Hope
Little Karoo

Port Elizabe

Cape Agulhas

0 160 320
km

Mc 35° Md 40° Na 45° Nb 50° Nc 55° Nd 60° Oa

SOMALIA
● MOGADISHU
INDIAN

18
Equator 0°

fe Reserve
Lake Albert
UGANDA
KENYA
Tombs of Buganda
Kings at Kasubi ◆
Rwenzori Mountains
National Park ▲
◆ KAMPALA
Mt.Elgon
4321 ▲
Mount Kenya National Park /
Natural Forest
▲ 5199
Mt.Kenya
◆ Bwindi Impenetrable National Park
Kisumu
Kismaanyo

OCEAN
19
5°

◆ KIGALI
Bukoba
Musoma
NAIROBI
WANDA
Mwanza
Lake Victoria
Lamu Old Town ◇
Lamu

RUNDI
Serengeti
National Park ◆
*Lake
Natron*
Kilimanjaro
▲ 5895
Malindi
◆ Vallée de Mai Nature Reserve
Praslin
La Digue

UMBURA
Ngorongoro
Conservation Area ◆
Arusha ◆
Kilimanjaro
National Park
Sacred Mijikenda Kaya Forests ◇
Mombasa
Mahé
VICTORIA ●
Amirante Islands

Kigoma
Lake Eyasi
*Masai
Steppe*
Kondoa ●
Tanga
Pemba
SEYCHELLES
5°

rka
TANZANIA
Kondoa Rock-Art Sites ◆
Stone Town of Zanzibar ◆
Zanzibar
Alphonse Group

DODOMA ● ●
Zanzibar
Dar es Salaam ◇
20

Morogoro
Mafia

Sumbawanga
Iringa

ru
Mbeya
Kilawa Masoko
Ruins of Kilwa Kisiwani
and Ruins of Songo Mnara ◇
Aldabra Atoll ● ◎ Aldabra Group
Grande Terre
Atoll de Providence
Farquhar Group

Selous Game Reserve ◆
Lindi
Cosmoledo Atoll
Atoll de Farquhar
10°

Ruvuma
Cabo Delgado
Agalega Is.

Muchinga Mountains
MALAWI
Comoros
MORONI ●
T.Babaomby
Antsiranana ●

MALAWI
● Pemba
COMOROS
Dzaoudzi ●
Mayotte (Fr.)
21

LILONGWE ◆
Chongoni Rock-Art Area ◇
Lake Malawi National Park ◆
Ambanja
▲ 2876
Maromokotro
◆ Rainforests of the Atsinanana

ment
Lago de Cabora Bassa
Island of
Mozambique ◇
Mozambique
Maroantsetra
◆ Rainforests of the Atsinanana
15°

ana Pools National Park,
api and Chewore Safari Areas
Blantyre
Nampula
Mahajanga

HARARE ●
Zambesi
MOZAMBIQUE
◆ Rainforests of the Atsinanana
Cargados Carajos

BABWE
Quelimane
Toamasina
Royal Hill of Ambohimanga ◇
22

Masvingo ●
Great Zimbabwe
National Monument ◆
Beira
Tsingy de Bemaraha
Strict Nature Reserve ◆
*Tsiafajavona
2643* ▲
ANTANANARIVO ●
MAURITIUS
Mascarene Islands

gubwe Cultural Landscape
Morondava
MADAGASCAR
Mas carene Islands
PORT LOUIS ◆ Aapravasi Ghat
I.Rodriguez
20°

arsburg
Limpopo
Morombe
Boby
▲ 2658
◆ Rainforests of the Atsinanana
Saint-Denis
Mauritius
Le Morne Cultural Landscape ◆

*minid Sites of
tein, Swartkrans,
ai, and Environs*
Xai-Xai
Ihosy
Toliara
Réunion (Fr.)
23

Inhambane
Tropic of Capricorn

MAPUTO ●
◆ Rainforests of the Atsinanana
Tôlanaro

◆ MBABANE
*Tanjona
Vohimena*
25°

SWAZILAND

iSimangaliso Wetland Park ◆

amba / Drakensberg Park
Durban
24

INDIAN OCEAN
30°

25

Mc 35° Md 40° Na 45° Nb 50° Nc 55° Nd 60° Oa 65° Ob 70°

Alaska, Canada, Greenland

USA, Central America

Northern South America

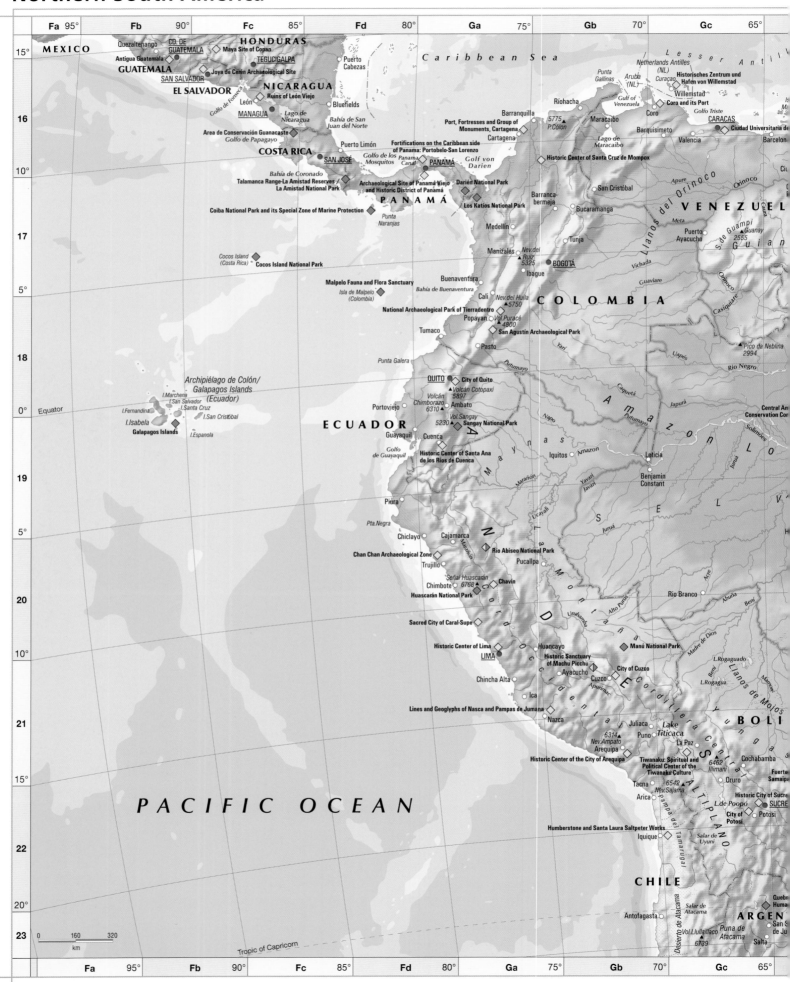

MEXICO

Quezaltenango
CD. DE GUATEMALA
Antigua Guatemala
GUATEMALA
SAN SALVADOR
EL SALVADOR
Joya de Cerén Archaeological Site
Maya Site of Copan
HONDURAS
TEGUCIGALPA
Ruins of León Viejo
NICARAGUA
León
MANAGUA
Golfo de Fonseca
Lago de Nicaragua
Bluefields
Puerto Cabezas

Caribbean Sea

Área de Conservación Guanacaste
Golfo de Papagayo
Bahía de San Juan del Norte
COSTA RICA
SAN JOSÉ
Puerto Limón
Bahía de Coronado
Talamanca Range-La Amistad Reserves / La Amistad National Park
Golfo de los Mosquitos
Panama Canal
PANAMÁ
PANAMÁ
Golf von Darien
Fortifications on the Caribbean side of Panama: Portobelo-San Lorenzo
Archaeological Site of Panamá Viejo and Historic District of Panamá
Darién National Park
Coiba National Park and its Special Zone of Marine Protection
Punta Naranjas
Los Katíos National Park

Port, Fortresses and Group of Monuments, Cartagena
Barranquilla
Cartagena
Ríohacha
Punta Gallinas
Aruba (NL)
Curaçao
Netherlands Antilles (NL)
Willemstad
Historisches Zentrum und Hafen von Willemstad
Coro and its Port
Coro
Golfo Triste
CARACAS
Ciudad Universitaria
Barcelon
Valencia
Barquisimeto
Maracaibo
Gulf of Venezuela
5775 P.Colón
Lago de Maracaibo

Historic Center of Santa Cruz de Mompox
San Cristóbal
Bucaramanga
Barranca-bermeja
Medellín
Manizales
Nev.del Ruiz 5325
Ibagué
BOGOTÁ
Tunja
VENEZUEL
Apure
Orinoco
Llanos del Orinoco
Meta
Puerto Ayacucho
S. de Guampi 2555 Guanay
Guian
Vichada

Cocos Island (Costa Rica)
Cocos Island National Park
Malpelo Fauna and Flora Sanctuary
Isla de Malpelo (Colombia)
Buenaventura
Bahía de Buenaventura
Cali
Nev.del Huila 5750
National Archaeological Park of Tierradentro
Popayán
Vol.Puracé 4800
San Agustín Archaeological Park
Tumaco
Pasto
COLOMBIA
Guaviare
Yari
Casiquiare
Uapés
Rio Negro
Pico da Neblina 2994

Punta Galera
QUITO
City of Quito
Volcán Cotopaxi 5897
Volcán Chimborazo 6310
Ambato
ECUADOR
Vol.Sangay 5230
Sangay National Park
Portoviejo
Guayaquil
Cuenca
Historic Center of Santa Ana de los Ríos de Cuenca
Golfo de Guayaquil
Putumayo
Napo
Iquitos
Amazon
Marañón
Leticia
Central An Conservation Co
Solimões
Amazon
Benjamin Constant
Juruá

Archipiélago de Colón/ Galapagos Islands (Ecuador)
I.Marchena
I.San Salvador
I.Santa Cruz
I.Fernandina
I.Isabela
I.San Cristóbal
Galapagos Islands
I.Española
Equator

Piura
Pta.Negra
Chiclayo
Cajamarca
Chan Chan Archaeological Zone
Trujillo
Rio Abiseo National Park
Pucallpa
Maranón
Ucayali
Yavari
Javari
Juruá
SELV
Montaña
Rio Branco
Abuña
Acre
Beni

Señal Huascarán 6768
Chavin
Chimbote
Huascarán National Park
Sacred City of Caral-Supe
Historic Center of Lima
LIMA
Huancayo
Historic Sanctuary of Machu Picchu
City of Cuzco
Ayacucho
Cuzco
Manú National Park
Chincha Alta
Ica
Madre de Dios
L.Rogaguado
L.Rogagua
Llanos de Mojos
Apurímac
Cordillera Occidental
Cordillera Central

Lines and Geoglyphs of Nasca and Pampas de Jumana
Nazca
Juliaca
Lake Titicaca
Puno
La Paz
BOLI
6314 Nev.Ampato
Arequipa
Historic Center of the City of Arequipa
Tiwanaku: Spiritual and Political Center of the Tiwanaku Culture
6462 Illimani
Cochabamba
Fuerte Samaipa
6542 Nev.Sajama
Oruro
Tacna
Arica
Historic City of Sucre
L.de Poopó
SUCRE
City of Potosí
Potosí
Humberstone and Santa Laura Saltpeter Works
Iquique
Salar de Uyuni
ALTIPLANO
Pampa del Tamarugal

PACIFIC OCEAN

CHILE
Salar de Atacama
Desierto de Atacama
Antofagasta
Vol.Llullaillaco 6739
Puna de Atacama
Quebr Huma
ARGEN
San S de Ju
Salta

Tropic of Capricorn

0 160 320
km

ATLANTIC OCEAN

Ha 55° **Hb** 50° **Hc** 45° **Hd** 40° **Ja** 35° **Jb** 30° **Jc**

15°

.LUCIA
itons Management Area
● BARBADOS
BRIDGETOWN
WN
'INCENT AND THE GRENADINES

16

EORGE'S
DA
Tobago
' OF SPAIN
TRINIDAD
AND TOBAGO

10°

Cuyuni ● GEORGETOWN
GUYANA **Historic Inner City**
of Paramaribo ◇ PARAMARIBO
National Park
10 ▲ Mt. Roraima
Central Suriname
Nature Reserve ◆
SURINAME
Kourou
● Cayenne
W.J. van
Blommesteinmeer
French
Guiana (Fr.)
Maroni
Oiapoque

17

5°

Serra do Tumucumaque
Cabo do Norte
Serra Acara ou Acari
Macapá
Mouths of
the Amazon
Baía
de Marajó
I. de Marajó
Belém

18

Manaus
Amazon
Santarém
Altamira
Represa
de Tucuruí
São Luís
Historic Center of São Luís
Parnaíba
Sobral
● Fortaleza
Atol das Rocas ◆
Brazilian Atlantic Islands:
Fernando de Noronha and
Atol das Rocas Reserves
Ilha Fernando de Noronha (Brazil)

Equator 0°

19

Itaituba
Maraba
Imperatriz
Teresina
Mossoró
Cabo de São Roque
Natal

5°

B R A Z I L
Palmas
Serra da Capivara
National Park ◇
Juazeiro
do Norte
Campina Grande
João Pessoa
Historic Center of the Town of Olinda ◆
Caruaru
Recife
Petrolina

20

Campos Cerrados
Planalto do
Mato Grosso
Barragem de
Sobradinho
São Francisco
Maceió

10°

Cuiabá
Cerrado Protected Areas: Chapada dos ◆
Veadeiros and Emas National Parks
Brasília ◇
Montes
Claros
Vitória da
Conquista
Itabuna
Feira de Santana
Historic Center of Salvador da Bahia ◆
Salvador

21

tional Park
Pantanal
Conservation Area ◆
Taquari
Pantanal
Historic Center of the Town of Goiás ◇
Goiás
BRASÍLIA
Rondonópolis
Goiânia
Pardo
Discovery Coast Atlantic Forest Reserves ◆

15°

Campo Grande
Trés Lagoas
Aracatuba
Pres. Prudente
Ribeirão Preto
São Carlos
Cerrado Protected Areas: Chapada dos ◆
Veadeiros and Emas National Parks
Sertão de Camapuã
Uberlândia
Uberaba
Brazilian
Highlands
Diamantina ◇ 2033
▲ Pico de Itambé
Historic Center of the
Town of Diamantina
Gdor.
Valadares
Belo Horizonte
Ouro Preto
Historic Town of Ouro Prêto ◇
Congonhas ◇ ▲ 2890
Sanctuary of Bom Jesus _Pico da_
do Congonhas _Bandeira_
Vitória

22

Juiz de Fora
Campos
Ilha da Trinidade _Ilha Martim Vaz_
Londrina
Campinas
Taubaté
São Paulo
Rio de Janeiro
Santos

20°

'RAGUAY
Represa de Itaipu
● ASUNCIÓN
Iguaçu National Park ◆
Foz do Iguaçu
Curitiba
Atlantic Forest South-East Reserves ◆
Tropic of Capricorn

23

Ha 55° **Hb** 50° **Hc** 45° **Hd** 40° **Ja** 35° **Jb** 30° **Jc** 25°

Southern South America

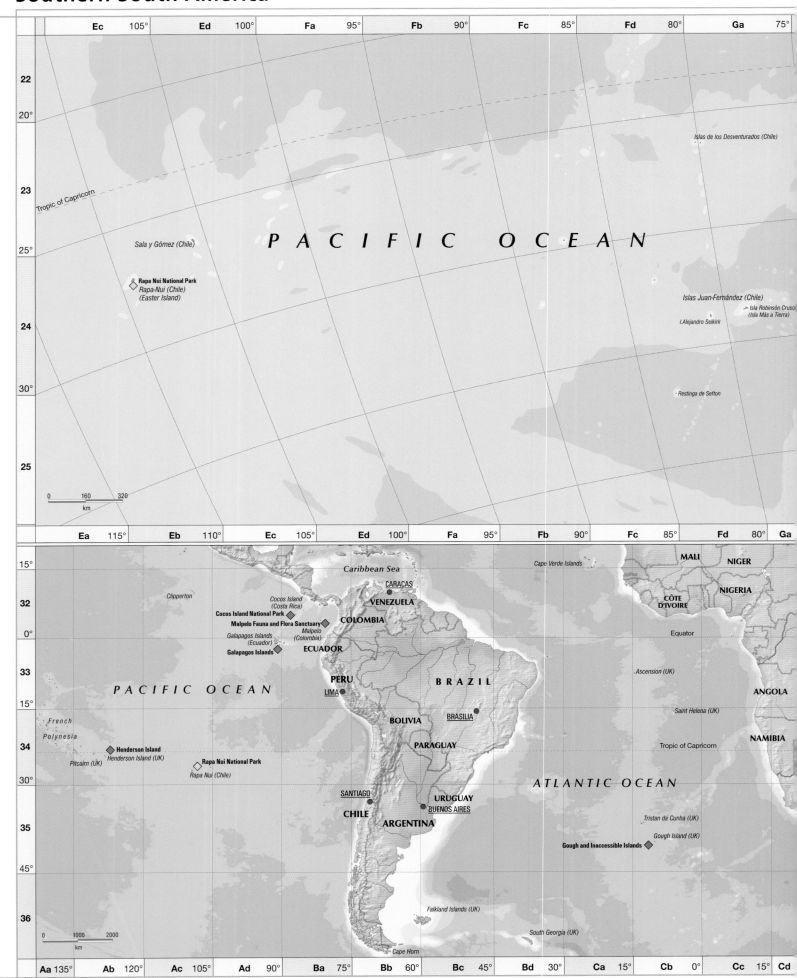

| | Ec | 105° | Ed | 100° | Fa | 95° | Fb | 90° | Fc | 85° | Fd | 80° | Ga | 75° |

PACIFIC OCEAN

Islas de los Desventurados (Chile)

Tropic of Capricorn

Sala y Gómez (Chile)

Rapa Nui National Park
Rapa-Nui (Chile)
(Easter Island)

Islas Juan-Fernández (Chile)

Isla Robinsón Crusoe
(Isla Más a Tierra)

I.Alejandro Selkirk

Restinga de Sefton

0   160   320
km

| | Ea | 115° | Eb | 110° | Ec | 105° | Ed | 100° | Fa | 95° | Fb | 90° | Fc | 85° | Fd | 80° | Ga |

Caribbean Sea

MALI   NIGER

Cape Verde Islands

CARACAS
VENEZUELA

Clipperton

Cocos Island
(Costa Rica)

Cocos Island National Park
Malpelo Fauna and Flora Sanctuary
Galapagos Islands
(Ecuador)

Galapagos Islands

COLOMBIA

Malpelo
(Colombia)

ECUADOR

CÔTE
D'IVOIRE

NIGERIA

Equator

PACIFIC OCEAN

PERU
LIMA

BRAZIL

BRASÍLIA

Ascension (UK)

ANGOLA

French
Polynesia

BOLIVIA

Saint Helena (UK)

Henderson Island
Henderson Island (UK)

Pitcairn (UK)

Rapa Nui National Park
Rapa Nui (Chile)

PARAGUAY

Tropic of Capricorn

NAMIBIA

ATLANTIC OCEAN

SANTIAGO

CHILE

URUGUAY
BUENOS AIRES

ARGENTINA

Tristan da Cunha (UK)

Gough Island (UK)

Gough and Inaccessible Islands

0   1000   2000
km

Falkland Islands (UK)

South Georgia (UK)

Cape Horn

| | Aa | 135° | Ab | 120° | Ac | 105° | Ad | 90° | Ba | 75° | Bb | 60° | Bc | 45° | Bd | 30° | Ca | 15° | Cb | 0° | Cc | 15° | Cd |

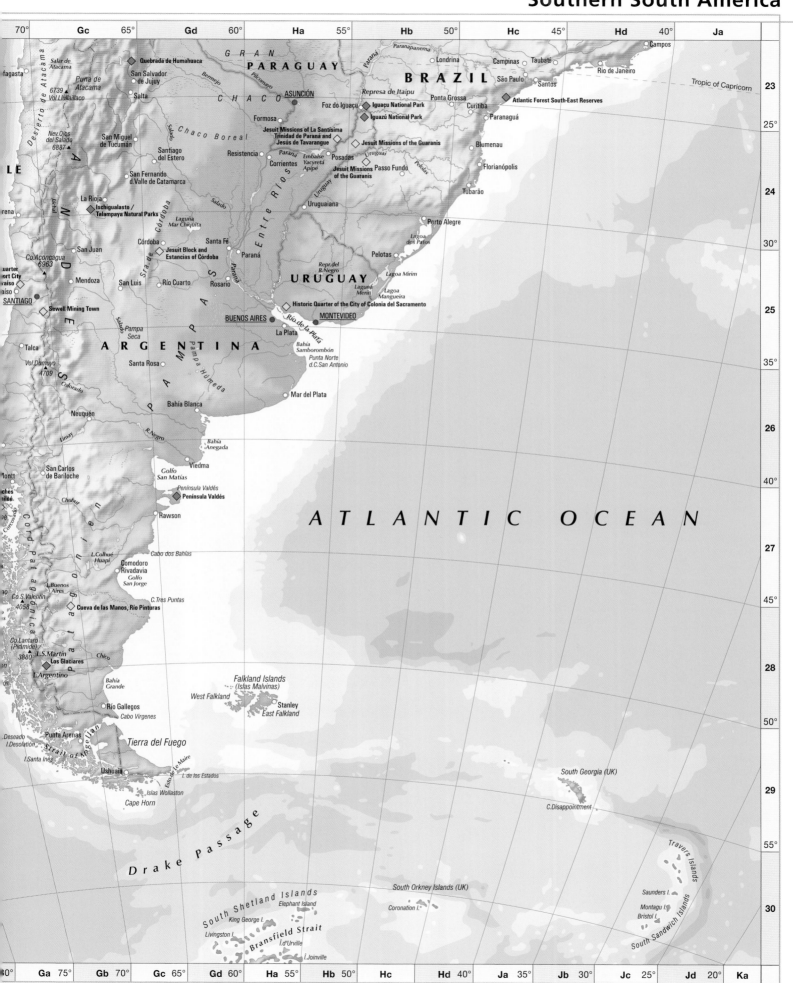

ATLANTIC OCEAN

List of World Heritage Sites – cultural and natural treasures under UNESCO protection

The list of World Heritage Sites comprises 890 monuments in 148 countries. Of these, 689 are cultural sites (C) and 176 are natural sites (N), while twenty-five are part of both cultural and the natural heritage. Transboundary properties are marked "TB" and listed under each country to which they belong. In addition, the year of inclusion in the list as well as any extensions (ext.) of a site are noted. Those monuments that have been deemed to be in serious danger by the UNESCO World Heritage Committee are marked with a red asterisk (*). The first page number (in bold print) refers to the text entry, the second page number to the relevant map, the combination of numbers and letters gives the grid reference for the map.

EUROPE

Iceland

Thingvellir National Park (C, 2004)	10	484 Jk13
Surtsey (N, 2008)	10	484 Jk14

Norway

Struve Geodetic Arc (C, TB, 2005)	124	485 Mb10–11
Rock Art of Alta (C, 1985)	10	485 Mb11
Vegaøyan: The Vega Archipelago (C, 2004)	11	485 Lf13
Røros Mining Town (C, 1980)	11	485 Lf14
Urnes Stave Church (C, 1979)	11	484 Ld15
Bryggen (C, 1979)	12	484 Lc15
West Norwegian Fjords: Geirangerfjord and Nærøyfjord (N, 2005)	14	484 Ld14/15

Sweden

Laponian Area (C, N, 1996)	15	485 Lk12
Struve Geodetic Arc (C, TB, 2005)	124	485 Mb12
Church Village of Gammelstad, Luleå (C, 1996)	15	485 Mb13
Engelsberg Ironworks (C, 1993)	15	485 Lh16
Mining Area of the Great Copper Mountain in Falun (C, 2001)	16	485 Lh15
Rock Carvings in Tanum (C, 1994)	16	485 Lf16
Royal Domain of Drottningholm (C, 1991)	16	485 Lj16
Varberg Radio Station (C, 2004)	17	487 Lg17
Birka and Hovgården (C, 1993)	17	485 Lj16
Naval Port of Karlskrona (C, 1998)	17	487 Lh17
Hanseatic Town of Visby (C, 1995)	18	487 Lk17
Agricultural Landscape of Southern Öland * (C, 2000)	19	487 Lj17
Skogskyrkogården (C, 1994)	19	485 Lk16
High Coast / Kvarken Archipelago (N, TB, 1993, 2006 ext.)	19	485 Lk14/Ma14

Denmark

Ilulissat Icefjord, Greenland (N, 2004)	20	511 Hb05
Roskilde Cathedral (C, 1995)	21	487 Lf18
Jelling Burial Mounds, Runic Stones and Church (C, 1994)	21	487 Le18
Kronborg Castle (C, 2000)	21	487 Lg17

Finland

Struve Geodetic Arc (C, TB, 2005)	124	485 Mb11, Mc14, Md15
Petäjävesi Old Church (C, 1994)	22	485 Mc14
Old Rauma (C, 1991)	22	485 Ma15
High Coast / Kvarken Archipelago (N, TB, 2000, 2006 ext.)	19	485 Lk14/Ma14
Bronze Age Burial Site of Sammallahdenmäki (C, 1999)	22	485 Ma15
Fortress of Suomenlinna (C, 1991)	23	485 Mc15
Verla Groundwood and Board Mill (C, 1996)	23	485 Md15

Estonia

Historic Center (Old Town) of Tallinn (C, 1997)	23	485 Mc16
Struve Geodetic Arc (C, TB, 2005)	124	485 Md16

Latvia

Historic Center of Riga (C, 1997)	24	487 Mb17
Struve Geodetic Arc (C, TB, 2005)	124	487 Mc17

Lithuania

Kernavé Archaeological Site (Cultural Reserve of Kernavé) (C, 2004)	24	487 Mc18
Vilnius Historic Center (C, 1994)	25	487 Mc18
Struve Geodetic Arc (C, TB, 2005)	124	487 Mc18
Curonian Spit (C, TB, 2000)	25	487 Ma18

United Kingdom

St Kilda (C, N, 1986, 2004 u. 2005 ext.)	26	486 Kf17
Heart of Neolithic Orkney (C, 1999)	26	486 Kj16
New Lanark (C, 2001)	26	486 Kj18
Frontiers of the Roman Empire (C, TB, 1987, 2005 and 2008 ext.)	27	486 Kj18
Old and New Towns of Edinburgh (C, 1995)	27	486 Kj18
Durham Castle and Cathedral (C, 1986)	28	486 Kk18
Saltaire (C, 2001)	28	486 Kk19
Liverpool – Maritime Mercantile City (C, 2004)	28	486 Kj19
Blaenavon Industrial Landscape (C, 2000)	28	486 Kj20
Ironbridge Gorge (C, 1986)	29	486 Kj19
Studley Royal Park including the Ruins of Fountains Abbey (C, 1986)	29	486 Kk18
Blenheim Palace (C, 1987)	29	486 Kk20
Derwent Valley Mills (C, 2001)	29	486 Kk19
Westminster Palace, Westminster Abbey and Saint Margaret's Church (C, 1987)	30	486 Kk20
Tower of London (C, 1988)	31	486 Kk20
Royal Botanic Gardens, Kew (C, 2003)	31	486 Kk20
Maritime Greenwich (C, 1997)	31	486 La20
City of Bath (C, 1987)	32	486 Kj20
Cornwall and West Devon Mining Landscape (C, 2006)	32	486 Kh20
Dorset and East Devon Coast (N, 2001)	32	486 Kj20
Stonehenge, Avebury and Associated Sites (C, 1986)	33	486 Kk20
Canterbury Cathedral, St Augustine's Abbey and St Martin's Church (C, 1988)	33	486 La20
Castles and Town Walls of King Edward in Gwynedd (C, 1986)	34	486 Kh19
Pontcysyllte Aqueduct and Canal (C, 2009)	34	486 Kj19
Giant's Causeway and Causeway Coast (N, 1986)	34	486 Kg18
Gough and Inaccessible Islands (N, 1995, 2004 ext.)	35	516 Cb35
Historic Town of St George and Related Fortifications, Bermuda (C, 2000)	35	513 Gd12
Henderson Island (N, 1988)	35	516 Ab34

Ireland

Archaeological Ensemble of the Bend of the Boyne (C, 1993)	36	486 Kg19
Skellig Michael (C, 1996)	36	486 Ke20

Netherlands

The Wadden Sea (N, TB, 2009)	36	486 Lc19
Ir. D.F. Woudagemaal (D F Wouda Steam Pumping Station) (C, 1998)	37	486 Lc19
Schokland and Surroundings (C, 1995)	37	486 Lc19
Droogmakerij de Beemster (Beemster Polder) (C, 1999)	37	486 Lc19
Mills at Kinderdijk-Elshout (C, 1997)	38	486 Lc20
Defense Line of Amsterdam (C, 1996)	38	486 Lc19
Rietveld Schröderhuis (Rietveld Schröder House) (C, 2000)	38	486 Lc19
Historic Area of Willemstad, Inner City and Harbor, Netherlands Antilles (C, 1997)	38	513 Gc16

Belgium

Historic Center of Brugge (C, 2000)	39	486 Lb20
Plantin-Moretus House-Workshops-Museum Complex (C, 2005)	40	486 Lc20
Flemish Béguinages (C, 1998)	40	486 Lb20
Major Town Houses of the Architect Victor Horta (Brussels) (C, 2000)	40	486 Lc20
La Grand-Place, Brussels (C, 1998)	41	486 Lc20
Stoclet House (C, 2009)	41	486 Lc20
Notre-Dame Cathedral in Tournai (C, 2000)	42	486 Lb20
Neolithic Flint Mines at Spiennes (Mons) (C, 2000)	42	486 Lb20
The Four Lifts on the Canal du Center and their Environs, La Louvière and Le Roeuix (Hainault) (C, 1998)	42	486 Lc20
Belfries of Belgium and France (C, TB, 1998, 2005 ext.)	43	486 Lb20

Luxembourg

City of Luxembourg: Old Quarters and Fortifications (C, 1994)	43	486 Ld21

France

Belfries of Belgium and France (C, TB, 2005)	43	486 Lb20
Paris, Banks of the Seine (C, 1991)	44	488 Lb21
Palace and Park of Versailles (C, 1979)	50	488 Lb21
Palace and Park of Fontainebleau (C, 1981)	51	488 Lb21
Amiens Cathedral (C, 1981)	52	488 Lb21
Cathedral of Notre-Dame, Former Abbey of Saint-Remi and the Palace of Tau, Reims (C, 1991)	52	488 Lc21
Chartres Cathedral (C, 1979)	53	488 La21
Bourges Cathedral (C, 1992)	53	488 Lb22
The Loire Valley between Sully-sur-Loire and Chalonnes (C, 2000)	54	488 Kk–Lb22

Mont-Saint-Michel and its Bay (C, 1979)	58	488 Kk21	
Fortifications of Vauban (C, 2008)	58	488 Kk21/Lb21/	
		Lc21/Lc22/Ld21/Ld23/Kk23/Lb24	
Le Havre, the City Rebuilt by Auguste Perret (C, 2005)	59	488 La21	
Provins, Town of Medieval Fairs (C, 2001)	59	488 Lb21	
Place Stanislas, Place de la Carrière and Place d'Alliance in Nancy			
(C, 1983)	59	489 Ld21	
Cistercian Abbey of Fontenay (C, 1981)	60	488 Lc22	
Vézelay, Church and Hill (C, 1979)	60	488 Lb22	
Strasbourg – Grande Île (C, 1988)	61	489 Ld21	
From the Great Saltworks of Salin-les-Bains to the Royal Saltworks of			
Arc-et-Senans, the production of open-pan salt (C, 1982, 2009 ext.)	62	489 Lc22	
Historic Site of Lyon (C, 1998)	62	488 Lc23	
Roman Theater and its Surroundings and the "Triumphal Arch"			
of Orange (C, 1981)	63	488 Lc23	
Pont du Gard (Roman Aqueduct) (C, 1985)	63	488 Lc23	
Arles, Roman and Romanesque Monuments (C, 1981)	63	488 Lc24	
Historic Center of Avignon: Papal Palace, Episcopal Ensemble			
and Avignon Bridge (C, 1995)	64	488 Lc24	
Routes of Santiago de Compostela in France (C, 1998)	66	488 Kk22/La22/	
		Lb23/Lb24	
Abbey Church of Saint-Savin sur Gartempe (C, 1983)	68	488 La22	
Prehistoric Sites and Decorated Caves of the Vézère Valley (C, 1979)	68	488 La23	
Jurisdiction of Saint-Emilion (C, 1999)	68	488 Kk23	
Bordeaux, Port of the Moon (C, 2007)	69	488 Kk23	
Pyrénées – Mont Perdu (C, N, TB, 1997, 1999 ext.)	69	488 Kk24	
Canal du Midi (C, 1996)	69	488 Lb24	
Historic Fortified City of Carcassonne (C, 1997)	70	488 Lb24	
Golf of Porto: Calanche of Piana, Gulf of Girolata,			
Scandola Reserve (N, 1983)	71	489 Le24	
Lagoons of New Caledonia: Reef Diversity and			
Associated Ecosystems (N, 2008)	71	505 Ta22/Tb23	
Germany			
The Wadden Sea (N, TB, 2009)	72	486 Le18/Ld19	
Hanseatic City of Lübeck (C, 1987)	72	487 Lf19	
Town Hall and Roland on the Marketplace of Bremen (C, 2004)	73	486 Le19	
Historic Centers of Stralsund and Wismar (C, 2002)	73	487 Lf19/Lg18	
St Mary's Cathedral and St Michael's Church at Hildesheim (C, 1985)	74	487 Le19	
Collegiate Church, Castle and Old Town of Quedlinburg (C, 1994)	74	487 Lf20	
Mines of Rammelsberg and Historic Town of Goslar (C, 1992)	74	487 Lf20	
Palaces and Parks of Potsdam and Berlin (C, 1990, 1992 and 1999 ext.)	75	487 Lg19	
Museumsinsel (Museum Island), Berlin (C, 1999)	76	487 Lg19	
Berlin Modernism Housing Estates (C, 2008)	76	487 Lg19	
Luther Memorials in Eisleben and Wittenberg (C, 1996)	77	487 Lf20	
Wartburg Castle (C, 1999)	77	487 Lf20	
Bauhaus and its Sites in Weimar and Dessau (C, 1996)	77	487 Lf20	
Garden Kingdom of Dessau-Wörlitz (C, 2000)	78	487 Lg20	
Muskauer Park / Park Mużakowski (C, TB, 2004)	78	487 Lh20	
Classical Weimar (C, 1998)	79	487 Lf20	
Aachen Cathedral (C, 1978)	80	486 Ld20	
Castles of Augustusburg and Falkenlust at Brühl (C, 1984)	80	486 Ld20	
Cologne Cathedral (C, 1996)	81	486 Ld20	
Zollverein Coal Mine Industrial Complex in Essen (C, 2001)	81	486 Ld20	
Upper Middle Rhine Valley (C, 2002)	82	486 Ld20	
Roman Monuments, Cathedral of St Peter and Church of Our Lady			
in Trier (C, 1986)	83	486 Ld21	
Völklingen Ironworks (C, 1994)	83	486 Ld21	
Messel Pit Fossil Site (N, 1995)	83	486 Le21	
Abbey and Altenmünster of Lorsch (C, 1991)	83	486 Le21	
Speyer Cathedral (C, 1981)	84	486 Le21	
Frontiers of the Roman Empire (C, TB, 2005)	84	486/487	
		Le20/Lf21	
Monastic Island of Reichenau (C, 2000)	84	486 Le22	
Maulbronn Monastery Complex (C, 1993)	84	486 Le21	
Würzburg Residence with the Court Gardens and			
Residence Square (C, 1981)	85	487 Le21	
Town of Bamberg (C, 1993)	86	487 Lf21	
Old Town of Regensburg with Stadtamhof (C, 2006)	87	487 Lf21	
Pilgrimage Church of Wies (C, 1983)	87	487 Lf22	
Switzerland			
Convent of St Gall (C, 1983)	88	486 Le22	
Old City of Berne (C, 1983)	89	486 Ld22	
Swiss Alps Jungfrau-Aletsch (N, 2001, 2007 ext.)	90	486 Ld22	
Lavaux, Vineyard Terraces (C, 2007)	91	486 Ld22	
Three Castles, Defensive Wall and Ramparts of the Market Town			
of Bellinzona (C, 2000)	91	486 Le22	
Monte San Giorgio (N, 2003)	91	486 Le23	
La Chaux-de-Fonds / Le Locle, watchmaking town planning			
(C, 2009)	92	486 Ld22	
Benedictine Convent of St John at Müstair (C, 1983)	92	487 Lf22	
Rhaetian Railway in the Albula / Bernina Landscapes (C, TB, 2008)	93	487 Lf22	
Swiss Tectonic Arena Sardona (N, 2008)	93	486 Le22	
Austria			
Historic Center of Vienna (C, 2001)	94	487 Lj21	
Palace and Gardens of Schönbrunn (C, 1996)	98	487 Lj21	
Wachau Cultural Landscape (C, 2000)	99	487 Lh21	
Historic Center of the City of Salzburg (C, 1996)	100	487 Lg22	
Fertö / Neusiedlersee Cultural Landscape (C, TB, 2001)	102	487 Lj22	
Hallstatt-Dachstein / Salzkammergut Cultural Landscape (C, 1997)	102	487 Lg22	
Semmering Railway (C, 1998)	102	487 Lh22	
City of Graz – Historic Center (C, 1999)	103	487 Lh22	
Poland			
Castle of the Teutonic Order in Malbork (C, 1997)	104	487 Lk19	
Medieval Town of Toruń (C, 1997)	104	487 Lk19	
Muskauer Park / Park Mużakowski (C, TB, 2004)	104	487 Lh20	
Centennial Hall in Wrocław (C, 2006)	104	487 Lj20	
Historic Center of Warsaw (C, 1980)	105	487 Ma19	
Cracow's Historic Center (C, 1978)	106	487 Lk20	
Churches of Peace in Jawor and Świdnica (C, 2001)	108	487 Lj20	
Auschwitz Birkenau: German Nazi Concentration and			
Extermination Camp (1940–1945) (C, 1979)	108	487 Lk20	
Kalwaria Zebrzydowska: the Mannerist Architectural and			
Park Landscape Complex and Pilgrimage Park (C, 1999)	108	487 Lk21	
Wieliczka Salt Mine (C, 1978)	109	487 Ma21	
Wooden Churches of Southern Little Poland (C, 2003)	109	487 Ma21	
Old City of Zamość (C, 1992)	109	487 Mb20	
Belovezhskaya Pushcha / Białowieża Forest (N, TB, 1979, 1992 ext.)	109	487 Mb19	
Czech Republic			
Historic Center of Prague (C, 1992)	110	487 Lh20	
Kutná Hora: Historic Town Center with the Church of St Barbara			
and the Cathedral of Our Lady at Sedlec (C, 1995)	112	487 Lh21	
Pilgrimage Church of St John of Nepomuk at Zelená Hora (C, 1994)	112	487 Lg21	
Historic Center of Český Krumlov (C, 1992)	112	487 Lh21	
Holašovice Historical Village Reservation (C, 1998)	113	487 Lh21	
Historic Center of Telč (C, 1992)	113	487 Lh21	
Jewish Quarter and St Procopius' Basilica in Třebíč (C, 2003)	114	487 Lh21	
Litomyšl Castle (C, 1999)	114	487 Lj20	
Holy Trinity Column in Olomouc (C, 2000)	114	487 Lj21	
Tugendhat Villa in Brno (C, 2001)	115	487 Lj21	
Gardens and Castle at Kroměříž (C, 1998)	115	487 Lj21	
Lednice-Valtice Cultural Landscape (C, 1996)	115	487 Lj21	
Slovakia			
Vlkolínec (C, 1993)	116	487 Lk21	
Historic Town of Banská Štiavnica and the Technical Monuments			
in its Vicinity (C, 1993)	116	487 Lk21	
Wooden Churches of the Slovak part of the Carpathian			
Mountain Area (C, 2008)	116	487 Ma21	
Levoča, Spišský Hrad and the Associated Cultural Monuments			
(C, 1993, 2009 ext.)	116	487 Ma21	
Primeval Beech Forests of the Carpathians (N, TB, 2007)	117	487 Mb21	
Bardejov Town Conservation Reserve (C, 2000)	117	487 Ma21	
Caves of Aggtelek Karst and Slovak Karst (N, TB, 1995, 2000 ext.)	117	487 Ma21	

List of World Heritage Sites (by region, country)

Hungary		
Caves of Aggtelek Karst and Slovak Karst (N, TB, 1995, 2000 ext.)	117	487 Ma21
Budapest, including the Banks of the Danube, the Buda Castle		
Quarter and Andrássy Avenue (C, 1987, 2002 ext.)	118	487 Lk22
Fertö / Neusiedlersee Cultural Landscape (C, TB, 2001)	120	487 Lj22
Millenary Benedictine Abbey of Pannonhalma and its		
Natural Environment (C, 1996)	120	487 Lj22
Old Village of Hollókő and its Surroundings (C, 1987)	120	487 Lk22
Tokaj Wine Region Historic Cultural Landscape (C, 2002)	121	487 Ma21
Hortobágy National Park – the "Puszta" (C, 1999)	121	487 Ma22
Early Christian Necropolis of Pécs (Sopianae) C, 2000)	121	487 Lk22
Belarus		
Belovezhskaya Pushcha / Białowieża Forest (N, TB, 1979, 1992 ext.)	122	487 Mc19
Struve Geodetic Arc (C, TB, 2005)	124	487 Mc19
Mir Castle Complex (C, 2000)	122	487 Md19
Architectural, Residential and Cultural Complex of the		
Radziwill Family at Nesvizh (C, 2005)	122	487 Md19
Ukraine		
L'viv – the Ensemble of the Historic Center (C, 1998)	123	491 Mc21
Kiev: Saint-Sophia Cathedral and Related Monastic Buildings,		
Kiev-Pechersk Lavra (C, 1990)	123	491 Mf20
Primeval Beech Forests of the Carpathians (N, TB, 2007)	123	491 Mb21
Struve Geodetic Arc (C, TB, 2005)	124	487 Md21
Moldova		
Struve Geodetic Arc (C, TB, 2005)	124	491 Me21
Russia		
Curonian Spit (C, TB, 2000)	125	487 Ma18
Cultural and Historic Ensemble of the Solovetsky Islands (C, 1992)	125	492 Md06
Kizhi Pogost (C, 1990)	125	492 Md06
Virgin Komi Forests (N, 1995)	125	492 Nd05
Historic Center of Saint Petersburg and Related Groups		
of Monuments (C, 1990)	126	491 Mf16
Struve Geodetic Arc (C, TB, 2005)	124	485 Md15
Ensemble of the Ferrapontov Monastery (C, 2000)	130	491 Mk15
Historic Center of the City of Yaroslavl (C, 2005)	130	491 Na17
Historic Monuments of Novgorod and Surroundings (C, 1992)	130	491 Mf16
Kremlin and Red Square, Moscow (C, 1990)	131	491 Mj18
Ensemble of the Novodevichy Convent (C, 2004)	132	491 Mj18
Architectural Ensemble of the Trinity Sergius Lavra		
in Sergiev Posad (C, 1993)	132	491 Mk17
Church of the Ascension, Kolomenskoye (C, 1994)	132	491 Mj18
White Monuments of Vladimir and Suzdal (C, 1992)	132	491 Na17
Historic and Architectural Complex of the Kazan Kremlin (C, 2000)	133	491 Nb07
Western Caucasus (N, 1999)	133	483 Na10
Citadel, Ancient City and Fortress Buildings of Derbent (C, 2003)	133	483 Nb10
Golden Mountains of Altai (N, 1998)	133	492 Pb08
Uvs Nuur Basin (N, TB, 2003)	134	492 Pc08
Lake Baikal (N, 1996)	134	493 Qb08
Central Sikhote-Alin (N, 2001)	134	493 Rd09
Natural System of Wrangel Island Reserve (N, 2004)	135	493 Ua04
Volcanoes of Kamchatka (N, 1996, 2001, ext.)	135	493 Sd08
Spain		
Route of Santiago de Compostela (C, 1993)	136	488 Kh24
Santiago de Compostela (Old Town) (C, 1985)	138	488 Kf24
Monuments of Oviedo and the Kingdom of the Asturias		
(C, 1985, 1998 ext.)	138	488 Kh24
Tower of Hercules (C, 2009)	138	488 Kf24
Roman Walls of Lugo (C, 2000)	139	488 Kg24
Las Médulas (C, 1997)	139	488 Kg24
Cave of Altamira and Paleolithic Cave Art of Northern Spain		
(C, 1985, 2008 ext.)	139	488 Kh24
Vizcaya Bridge (C, 2006)	140	488 Kj24
Archaeological Site of Atapuerca (C, 2000)	140	488 Kj24
Burgos Cathedral (C, 1984)	140	488 Kj24
San Millán Yuso and Suso Monasteries (C, 1997)	140	488 Kj24
Pyrénées: Mont Perdu (C, N, TB, 1997, 1999 ext.)	141	488 La24

Catalan Romanesque Churches of the Vall de Boí (C, 2000)	141	488 La24
Poblet Monastery (C, 1991)	141	488 La25
Archaeological Ensemble of Tárraco (C, 2000)	141	488 La25
Works of Antoni Gaudí (C, 1984, 2005 ext.)	142	488 Lb25
Palau de la Música Catalana and Hospital de Sant Pau, Barcelona		
(C, 1997)	144	488 Lb25
Old City of Salamanca (C, 1988)	144	488 Kh25
Old Town of Ávila with its Extra-Muros Churches (C, 1985)	145	488 Kh25
Old Town of Segovia and its Aqueduct (C, 1985)	145	488 Kh25
Monastery and Site of the Escurial, Madrid (C, 1984)	145	488 Kh25
University and Historic Precinct of Alcalá de Henares (C, 1998)	146	488 Kj25
Mudejar Architecture of Aragón (C, 1986, 2001 ext.)	146	488 Kk25
Aranjuez Cultural Landscape (C, 2001)	146	488 Kj25
Historic City of Toledo (C, 1986)	147	488 Kh26
Old Town of Cáceres (C, 1986)	147	488 Kg26
Royal Monastery of Santa María de Guadalupe (C, 1993)	147	488 Kh26
Archaeological Ensemble of Mérida (C, 1993)	148	488 Kg26
Rock Art of the Mediterranean Basin on the Iberian Peninsula		
(C, 1998)	148	488 Kk25–26
Historic Walled Town of Cuenca (C, 1996)	148	488 Kj25
La Lonja de la Seda de Valencia (C, 1996)	149	488 Kk26
Palmeral of Elche (C, 2000)	149	488 Kk26
Renaissance Monumental Ensembles of Úbeda and Baeza (C, 2003)	149	488 Kj26
Alhambra, Generalife and Albayzín, Granada (C, 1984, 1994 ext.)	150	488 Kj27
Historic Center of Córdoba (C, 1984, 1994 ext.)	151	488 Kh27
Cathedral, Alcázar and Archivo de Indias in Seville (C, 1987)	152	488 Kg27
Doñana National Park (N, 1994)	154	488 Kg27
Ibiza, Biodiversity and Culture (C, N, 1999)	154	488 La26
San Cristóbal de La Laguna (C, 1999)	154	506 Ka13
Teide National Park (N, 2007)	155	506 Ka13
Garajonay National Park (N, 1986)	155	506 Ka13
Andorra		
Madriu-Perafita-Claror Valley (C, 2004)	155	488 La24
Portugal		
Historic Center of Guimarães (C, 2001)	156	488 Kf25
Historic Center of Oporto (C, 1996)	156	488 Kf25
Alto Douro Wine Region (C, 2001)	156	488 Kg25
Prehistoric Rock-Art Sites in the Côa Valley (C, 1998)	156	488 Kg25
Monastery of Batalha (C, 1983)	157	488 Kf26
Convent of Christ in Tomar (C, 1983)	158	488 Kf26
Monastery of Alcobaça (C, 1989)	158	488 Kf26
Cultural Landscape of Sintra (C, 1995)	158	488 Kf26
Monastery of the Hieronymites and Tower of Belém in Lisbon		
(C, 1983)	159	488 Kf26
Historic Center of Évora (C, 1986)	160	488 Kf26
Landscape of the Pico Island Vineyard Culture (C, 2004)	160	482 Jc11
Central Zone of the Town of Angra do Heroismo in the Azores		
(C, 1983)	161	482 Jc11
Laurisilva of Madeira (N, 1999)	161	482 Ka12
Italy		
Rhaetian Railway in the Albula / Bernina Landscapes (C, TB, 2008)	162	489 Lf22
Church and Dominican Convent of Santa Maria delle Grazie with		
"The Last Supper" by Leonardo da Vinci (C, 1980)	162	489 Le23
Sacri Monti of Piedmont and Lombardy (C, 2003)	162	489 Ld23
Residences of the Royal House of Savoy (C, 1997)	162	489 Ld23
Rock Drawings in Valcamonica (C, 1979)	163	489 Lf23
Crespi d'Adda (C, 1995)	163	489 Le23
City of Vicenza and the Palladian Villas of the Veneto		
(C, 1994, 1996 ext.)	163	489 Lf23
City of Verona (C, 2000)	163	489 Lf23
The Dolomites (N, 2009)	164	489 Lg22
Venice and its Lagoon (C, 1987)	166	489 Lg23
Botanical Garden (Orto Botanico), Padua (C, 1997)	170	489 Lf23
Archaeological Area and the Patriarchal Basilica of Aquileia (C, 1998)	170	489 Lg23
Mantua and Sabbioneta (C, 2008)	170	489 Lf23
Ferrara, City of the Renaissance, and its Po Delta (C, 1995, 1999 ext.)	170	489 Lf23

List of World Heritage Sites (by region, country)

Early Christian Monuments of Ravenna (C, 1996)	171	489 Lg23
Cathedral, Torre Civica and Piazza Grande, Modena (C, 1997)	172	489 Lf23
Genoa: "Le Strade Nuove" and the system of the		
"Palazzi dei Rolli" (C, 2006)	172	489 Le23
Portovenere, Cinque Terre and the Islands (Palmaria, Tino		
and Tinetto) (C, 1997)	172	489 Le23
Piazza del Duomo, Pisa (C, 1987)	173	489 Lf24
Historic Center of Florence (C, 1982)	174	489 Lf24
Historic Center of San Gimignano (C, 1990)	176	489 Lf24
Historic Center of Siena (C, 1995)	176	489 Lf24
Val d'Orcia (C, 2004)	177	489 Lf24
Historic Center of the City of Pienza (C, 1996)	177	489 Lf24
San Marino		
San Marino Historic Center and Mount Titano (C, 2008)	177	489 Lg24
Italy		
Historic Center of Urbino (C, 1998)	178	489 Lg24
Assisi, the Basilica of San Francesco and Other Franciscan Sites		
(C, 2000)	178	489 Lg24
Etruscan Necropolises of Cerveteri and Tarquinia (C, 2004)	179	489 Lf24
Historic Center of Rome, the Properties of the Holy See Enjoying Extraterritorial		
Rights and San Paolo Fuori le Mura (C, TB, 1980, 1990 ext.)	180	489 Lg25
Vatican City (C, 1984)	184	489 Lg25
Italy		
Villa d'Este, Tivoli (C, 2001)	186	489 Lg24
Villa Adriana (Tivoli) (C, 1999)	186	489 Lg25
Historic Center of Naples (C, 1995)	186	489 Lh25
Archaeological Areas of Pompei, Herculaneum and Torre Annunziata		
(C, 1997)	187	489 Lh25
Costiera Amalfitana (C, 1997)	188	489 Lh25
18th-Century Royal Palace at Caserta with the Park, the Aqueduct of		
Vanvitelli, and the San Leucio Complex (C, 1997)	188	489 Lh25
Cilento and Vallo di Diano National Park with the Archaeological sites		
of Paestum and Velia, and the Certosa di Padula (C, 1998)	189	489 Lh25
Castel del Monte (C, 1996)	189	489 Lj25
The Sassi and the Park of the Rupestrian Churches of Matera		
(C, 1993)	189	489 Lj25
The Trulli of Alberobello (C, 1996)	190	489 Lj25
Isole Eolie (Aeolian Islands) (N, 2000)	190	489 Lh26
Archaeological Area of Agrigento (C, 1997)	191	489 Lg27
Late Baroque Towns of the Val di Noto (South-Eastern Sicily) (C, 2002)	191	489 Lh27
Villa Romana del Casale (C, 1997)	192	489 Lh27
Syracuse and the Rocky Necropolis of Pantalica (C, 2005)	192	489 Lh27
Su Nuraxi di Barumini (C, 1997)	192	489 Le26
Malta		
City of Valletta (C, 1980)	193	489 Lh28
Megalithic Temples of Malta (C, 1980, 1992 ext.)	193	489 Lh28
Hal Saflieni Hypogeum (C, 1980)	193	489 Lh28
Slovenia		
Škocjan Caves (N, 1986)	194	489 Lh23
Croatia		
The Cathedral of St James in Šibenik (C, 2000)	194	489 Lh24
Plitvice Lakes National Park (N, 1979, 2000 ext.)	195	489 Lh23
Episcopal Complex of the Euphrasian Basilica		
in the Historic Center of Poreč (C, 1997)	195	489 Lg23
Historic City of Trogir (C, 1997)	195	489 Lj24
Historic Complex of Split with the Palace of Diocletian (C, 1979)	196	489 Lj24
Stari Grad Plain (C, 2008)	196	489 Lj24
Old City of Dubrovnik (C, 1979, 1994 ext.)	197	489 Lk24
Bosnia and Herzegovina		
Old Bridge Area of the Old City of Mostar (C, 2005)	198	489 Lj24
Mehmed Paša Sokolović Bridge in Višegrad (C, 2007)	198	489 Lk24
Serbia		
Studenica Monastery (C, 1986)	199	489 Ma24
Stari Ras and Sopoćani Monastery (C, 1979)	199	489 Ma24
Medieval Monuments in Kosovo * (C, 2004, 2006 ext.)	199	489 Ma24
Gamzigrad-Romuliana, Palace of Galerius (C, 2007)	199	489 Mb24

Montenegro		
Durmitor National Park (N, 1980, 2005 ext.)	200	489 Lk24
Natural and Culturo-Historical Region of Kotor (C, 1979)	200	489 Lk24
Romania		
Wooden Churches of Maramureş (C, 1999)	201	490 Mb22
Villages with Fortified Churches in Transylvania		
(C, 1993, 1999 ext.)	201	490 Mc22
Dacian Fortresses of the Orăştie Mountains (C, 1999)	202	490 Mb23
Historic Center of Sighişoara (C, 1999)	202	490 Mc22
Monastery of Horezu (C, 1993)	202	490 Mb23
Churches of Moldavia (C, 1993)	203	490 Mc22
Danube Delta Biosphere Reservation (N, 1991)	204	490 Me23
Bulgaria		
Srebarna Nature Reserve (N, 1983)	204	490 Md23
Thracian Tomb of Sveshtari (C, 1985)	204	490 Md24
Madara Rider (C, 1979)	204	490 Md24
Ancient City of Nessebar (C, 1983)	205	490 Md24
Rock-Hewn Churches of Ivanovo (C, 1979)	206	490 Md24
Thracian Tomb of Kazanlak (C, 1979)	206	490 Mc24
Boyana Church (C, 1979)	206	490 Mb24
Rila Monastery (C, 1983)	207	490 Mb24
Pirin National Park (N, 1983)	207	490 Mb25
Albania		
Historic Centers of Berat and Gjirokastra (C, 2005, 2008 ext.)	208	490 Ma25
Butrint (C, 1992, 1999 ext.)	208	490 Ma26
Macedonia		
Natural and Cultural Heritage of the Ohrid region		
(C, N, 1979, 1980 ext.)	209	490 Ma25
Greece		
Archaeological Site of Aigai (modern name Vergina) (C, 1996)	210	490 Mb25
Paleochristian and Byzantine Monuments of Thessalonika (C, 1988)	210	490 Mb25
Mount Athos (C, N, 1988)	210	490 Mc25
Meteora (C, N, 1988)	211	490 Ma26
Old Town of Corfu (C, 2007)	211	490 Lk26
Archaeological Site of Delphi (C, 1987)	211	490 Mb26
Acropolis, Athens (C, 1987)	212	490 Mb27
Archaeological Sites of Mycenae and Tiryns (C, 1999)	214	490 Mb27
Sanctuary of Asklepios at Epidaurus (C, 1988)	214	490 Mb27
Archaeological Site of Olympia (C, 1989)	214	490 Ma27
Temple of Apollo Epicurius at Bassae (C, 1986)	214	490 Ma27
Archaeological Site of Mystras (C, 1989)	215	490 Mb27
Delos (C, 1990)	215	490 Mc27
Monasteries of Daphni, Hosios Loukas and Nea Moni of Chios		
(C, 1990)	215	490 Mb26/Md26
Pythagoreion and Heraion of Samos (C, 1992)	215	490 Md27
Historic Center (Chorá) with the Monastery of Saint John "the Theologian"		
and the Cave of the Apocalypse on the Island of Pátmos (C, 1999)	216	490 Md27
Medieval City of Rhodes (C, 1988)	216	490 Me27
Cyprus		
Paphos (C, 1980)	217	490 Mg28
Painted Churches in the Troodos Region (C, 1985, 2002 ext.)	217	490 Mg28
Choirokoitia (C, 1998)	217	490 Mg28
Turkey		
Historic Areas of Istanbul (C, 1985)	218	490 Me25
City of Safranbolu (C, 1994)	222	490 Mg25
Archaeological site of Troy (C, 1998)	222	490 Md26
Hattusha: the Hittite Capital (C, 1986)	222	483 Mc10
Great Mosque and Hospital of Divriği (C, 1985)	222	483 Md11
Göreme National Park and the Rock Sites of Cappadocia (C, N, 1985)	223	483 Mc11
Hierapolis-Pamukkale (C, N, 1988)	223	490 Me27
Xanthos-Letoon (C, 1988)	223	490 Me27
Nemrut Dağ (C, 1987)	223	483 Md11
Georgia		
Upper Svaneti (C, 1996)	224	483 Na10
Bagrati Cathedral and Gelati Monastery (C, 1994)	224	483 Na10
Historical Monuments of Mtskheta * (C, 1994)	225	483 Na10

List of World Heritage Sites (by region, country)

Armenia

Site	Page	Map
Monasteries of Haghpat and Sanahin (C, 1996, 2000 ext.)	226	483 Na10
Cathedral and Churches of Echmiatsin and the Archaeological Site of Zvartnots (C, 2000)	226	483 Na10
Monastery of Geghard and the Upper Azat Valley (C, 2000)	226	483 Nb11

Azerbaijan

Site	Page	Map
Walled City of Baku with the Shirvanshah's Palace and Maiden Tower (C, 2000)	227	483 Nb10
Gobustan Rock Art Cultural Landscape (C, 2007)	227	483 Nb10

ASIA

Syria

Site	Page	Map
Ancient City of Aleppo (C, 1986)	230	494 Md11
Crac des Chevaliers and Qal'at Salah El-Din (C, 2006)	230	494 Md12
Site of Palmyra (C, 1980)	230	494 Md12
Ancient City of Damascus (C, 1979)	231	494 Md12
Ancient City of Bosra (C, 1980)	231	494 Md12

Lebanon

Site	Page	Map
Ouadi Qadisha (the Holy Valley) and the Forest of the Cedars of God (Horsh Arz el-Rab) (C, 1998)	232	494 Md12
Anjar (C, 1984)	232	494 Md12
Ruins of Byblos (C, 1984)	232	494 Md12
Baalbek (C, 1984)	233	494 Md12
Tyre (C, 1984)	233	494 Md12

Israel

Site	Page	Map
Old City of Acre (C, 2001)	234	494 Mc12
Bahá'i Holy Places in Haifa and the Western Galilee (C, 2008)	234	494 Mc12
White City of Tel Aviv – the Modern Movement (C, 2003)	234	494 Mc12
Biblical Tels – Megiddo, Hazor, Beer Sheba (C, 2005)	235	494 Mc12
Masada (C, 2001)	235	494 Md12
Incense Route – Desert Cities in the Negev (C, 2005)	235	494 Mc12

Jerusalem (Site proposed by Jordan)

Site	Page	Map
Old City of Jerusalem and its Walls * (C, 1981)	236	494 Md12

Jordan

Site	Page	Map
Quseir Amra (C, 1985)	238	494 Md12
Um er-Rasas (Kastrom Mefa'a) (C, 2004)	238	494 Md12
Petra (C, 1985)	239	494 Md12

Yemen

Site	Page	Map
Old City of Sana'a (C, 1988)	240	494 Na15
Old Walled City of Shibam (C, 1982)	240	494 Nb15
Historic Town of Zabid * (C, 1993)	240	494 Na16
Socotra Archipelago (N, 2008)	240	494 Nc16

Oman

Site	Page	Map
Archaeological Sites of Bat, Al-Khutm and Al-Ayn (C, 1988)	241	494 Nd14
Aflaj Irrigation Systems of Oman (C, 2006)	241	494 Nd14
Bahla Fort (C, 1987)	241	494 Nd14
Land of Frankincense (C, 2000)	241	494 Nd14

Bahrain

Site	Page	Map
Qal'at al-Bahrain – Ancient Harbour and Capital of Dilmun (C, 2005)	242	494 Nc13

Saudi Arabia

Site	Page	Map
Al-Hijr Archaeological Site (Madâin Sâlih) (C, 2008)	242	494 Md13

Iraq

Site	Page	Map
Hatra (C, 1985)	243	494 Na11
Ashur (Qal'at Sherqat) * (C, 2003)	243	494 Na11
Samarra Archaeological City * (C, 2007)	243	494 Na12

Iran

Site	Page	Map
Armenian Monastic Ensembles of Iran (C, 2008)	244	494 Nb11
Takht-e Soleyman (C, 2003)	244	494 Nb11
Soltaniyeh (C, 2005)	244	494 Nb11
Bisotun (C, 2006)	244	494 Nb12
Meidan Emam, Isfahan (C, 1979)	245	494 Nc12
Tchogha Zanbil (C, 1979)	246	494 Nb12
Shushtar Historical Hydraulic System (C, 2009)	246	494 Nb12
Persepolis (C, 1979)	246	494 Nc13
Pasargadae (C, 2004)	247	494 Nc12
Bam and its Cultural Landscape * (C, 2004)	247	494 Nd13

Kazakhstan

Site	Page	Map
Saryarka – Steppe and Lakes of Northern Kazakhstan (N, 2008)	248	492 Oa08/Ob08
Mausoleum of Khoja Ahmed Yasawi (C, 2003)	248	495 Ob10
Petroglyphs within the Archaeological Landscape of Tamgaly (C, 2004)	248	495 Od10

Uzbekistan

Site	Page	Map
Itchan Kala (C, 1990)	249	494 Oa10
Historic Center of Shakhrisyabz (C, 2000)	249	494 Ob11
Historic Center of Bukhara (C, 1993)	249	494 Oa11
Samarkand – Crossroads of Cultures (C, 2001)	250	495 Ob11

Turkmenistan

Site	Page	Map
Kunya Urgench (C, 2005)	252	494 Nd10
State Historical and Cultural Park "Ancient Merv" (C, 1999)	252	494 Oa11
Parthian Fortresses of Nisa (C, 2007)	252	494 Nd11

Kyrgyzstan

Site	Page	Map
Sulaiman-Too Sacred Mountain (C, 2009)	253	495 Oc10

Afghanistan

Site	Page	Map
Minaret and Archaeological Remains of Jam * (C, 2002)	253	494 Oa12
Cultural Landscape and Archaeological Remains of the Bamiyan Valley * (C, 2003)	253	495 Ob12

Pakistan

Site	Page	Map
Buddhist Ruins of Takht-i-Bahi and Neighboring City Remains at Sahr-i-Bahlol (C, 1980)	254	495 Oc12
Rohtas Fort (C, 1997)	254	495 Oc12
Taxila (C, 1980)	254	495 Oc12
Fort and Shalamar Gardens in Lahore * (C, 1981)	255	495 Oc12
Archaeological Ruins at Moenjodaro (C, 1980)	255	495 Ob13
Historic Monuments at Makli, Thatta (C, 1981)	255	495 Ob14

India

Site	Page	Map
Nanda Devi and Valley of Flowers National Parks (N, 1988, 2005 ext.)	256	498 Pa12
Red Fort Complex (C, 2007)	256	498 Od13
Humayun's Tomb, Delhi (C, 1993)	256	498 Od13
Qutb Minar and its Monuments, Delhi (C, 1993)	257	498 Od13
Fatehpur Sikri (C, 1986)	257	498 Od13
Agra Fort (C, 1983)	257	498 Od13
Taj Mahal (C, 1983)	258	498 Od13
Keoladeo National Park (N, 1985)	260	498 Od13
Manas Wildlife Sanctuary * (N, 1985)	260	498 Pc13
Kaziranga National Park (N, 1985)	260	499 Pc13
Sundarbans National Park (N, 1987)	260	498 Pb14
Chhatrapati Shivaji Terminus (formerly Victoria Terminus) (C, 2004)	261	498 Oc15
Elephanta Caves (C, 1987)	261	498 Oc15
Mahabodhi Temple Complex at Bodh Gaya (C, 2002)	261	498 Pb14
Khajuraho Group of Monuments (C, 1986)	261	498 Od14
Buddhist Monuments at Sanchi (C, 1989)	262	498 Od14
Rock Shelters of Bhimbetka (C, 2003)	262	498 Od14
Champaner-Pavagadh Archaeological Park (C, 2004)	262	498 Oc14
Ajanta Caves (C, 1983)	263	498 Od14
Ellora Caves (C, 1983)	264	498 Od14
Group of Monuments at Pattadakal (C, 1987)	264	498 Od15
Churches and Convents of Goa (C, 1986)	264	498 Oc15
Group of Monuments at Hampi (C, 1986)	264	498 Od15
Sun Temple, Konârak (C, 1984)	265	498 Pb15
Group of Monuments at Mahabalipuram (C, 1984)	265	498 Pa16
Mountain Railways of India (C, 1999, 2005 and 2008 ext.)	265	498 Od16/Pb13
Great Living Chola Temples (C, 1987, 2004 ext.)	265	498 Od16

Bangladesh

Site	Page	Map
The Sundarbans (N, 1997)	266	498 Pb13
Historic Mosque City of Bagerhat (C, 1985)	266	498 Pb14
Ruins of the Buddhist Vihara at Paharpur (C, 1985)	266	498 Pb14

Sri Lanka

Site	Page	Map
Ancient City of Sigiriya (C, 1982)	267	498 Pa17
Sacred City of Anuradhapura (C, 1982)	268	498 Pa17
Golden Temple of Dambulla (C, 1991)	268	498 Pa17
Ancient City of Polonnaruwa (C, 1982)	268	498 Pa17
Sacred City of Kandy (C, 1988)	269	498 Pa17

Site	Page	Code
Sinharaja Forest Reserve (N, 1988)	269	498 Pa17
Old Town of Galle and its Fortifications (C, 1988)	269	498 Pa17
Mongolia		
Uvs Nuur Basin (N, TB, 2003)	270	496 Pc08
Orkhon Valley Cultural Landscape (C, 2004	270	496 Qa09
China		
Capital Cities and Tombs of the Ancient Koguryo Kingdom (C, 2004)	271	497 Rb10
The Great Wall (C, 1987)	271	497 Qd10
Mountain Resort and its Outlying Temples, Chengde (C, 1994)	272	497 Qd10
Peking Man Site at Zhoukoudian (C, 1987)	272	497 Qd11
Imperial Palaces of the Ming and Qing Dynasties in Beijing and Shenyang (C, 1987, 2004 ext.)	273	497 Qd10
Temple of Heaven: an Imperial Sacrificial Altar in Beijing (C, 1998)	274	497 Qd11
Summer Palace, an Imperial Garden in Beijing (C, 1998)	274	497 Qd11
Imperial Tombs of the Ming and Qing Dynasties (C, 2000, 2003 and 2004 ext.)	274	497 Qd10/Qd12
Yungang Grottoes (C, 2001)	274	497 Qc11
Mount Wutai (C, 2009)	275	497 Qc11
Mogao Caves (C, 1987)	275	496 Pd10
Ancient City of Ping Yao (C, 1997)	275	497 Qc11
Yin Xu (C, 2006)	275	497 Qc11
Mount Taishan (C, N, 1987)	276	497 Qd11
Temple and Cemetery of Confucius and the Kong Family Mansion in Qufu (C, 1994)	277	497 Qd11
Longmen Grottoes (C, 2000)	278	497 Qc12
Mausoleum of the First Qin Emperor (C, 1987)	278	497 Qb12
Ancient Building Complex in the Wudang Mountains (C, 1994)	278	497 Qc12
Lushan National Park (C, 1996)	278	497 Qd13
Classical Gardens of Suzhou (C, 1997, 2000 ext.)	279	497 Ra12
Mount Huangshan (C, N, 1990)	279	497 Qd12
Ancient Villages in Southern Anhui – Xidi and Hongcun (C, 2000)	279	497 Qd13
Mount Wuyi (C, N, 1999)	279	497 Qd13
Wulingyuan Scenic and Historic Interest Area (N, 1992)	280	497 Qc13
Dazu Rock Carvings (C, 1999)	280	496 Qb13
Jiuzhaigou Valley Scenic and Historic Interest Area (N, 1992)	280	496 Qa12
Huanglong Scenic and Historic Interest Area (N, 1992)	281	496 Qa12
Mount Qingcheng and the Dujiangyan Irrigation System (C, 2000)	281	496 Qa12
Sichuan Giant Panda Sanctuaries – Wolong, Mount Siguniang and Jiajin Mountains (N, 2006)	281	496 Qa12
Mount Emei Scenic Area, including Leshan Giant Buddha Scenic Area (C, N, 1996)	282	496 Qa13
Three Parallel Rivers of Yunnan Protected Areas (N, 2003)	283	496 Pd13
Old Town of Lijiang (C, 1997)	283	496 Qa13
Historic Ensemble of the Potala Palace, Lhasa (C, 1994, 2000 and 2001 ext.)	284	496 Pc13
South China Karst (N, 2007)	286	497 Qb13
Mount Sanqingshan National Park (N, 2008)	286	497 Qd13
Fujian Tulou (C, 2008)	287	497 Qd13
Kaiping Diaolou and Villages (C, 2007)	287	497 Qc14
Historic Center of Macao (C, 2005)	287	497 Qc14
Nepal		
Kathmandu Valley (C, 1979)	288	498 Pb13
Lumbini, the Birthplace of the Lord Buddha (C, 1997)	289	498 Pa13
Sagarmatha National Park (N, 1979)	289	498 Pb13
Royal Chitwan National Park (N, 1984)	289	498 Pa13
Korea, Democratic People's Republic of		
Complex of the Koguryo Tombs (C, 2004)	290	497 Rb11
Korea, Republic of		
Jongmyo Shrine (C, 1995)	290	497 Rb11
Changdeokgung Palace Complex (C, 1997)	290	497 Rb11
Hwaseong Fortress (C, 1997)	291	497 Rb11
Royal Tombs of the Joseon Dynasty (C, 2009)	291	497 Rb11
Haeinsa Temple Janggyeong Panjeon, the Depositories for the "Tripitaka Koreana" Woodblocks (C, 1995)	292	497 Rb11
Seokguram Grotto and Bulguksa Temple (C, 1995)	293	497 Rb11
Gyeongju Historic Areas (C, 2000)	293	497 Rb11
Gochang, Hwasun and Ganghwa Dolmen Sites (C, 2000)	293	497 Rb11
Jeju Volcanic Island and Lava Tubes (N, 2007)	293	497 Rb12
Japan		
Shiretoko (N, 2005)	294	497 Sa10
Shirakami-Sanchi (N, 1993)	294	497 Sa10
Historic Villages of Shirakawa-go and Gokayama (C, 1995)	294	497 Sa11
Shrines and Temples of Nikko (C, 1999)	295	497 Rd11
Historic Monuments of Ancient Kyoto (Kyoto, Uji and Otsu Cities) (C, 1994)	296	497 Rd11
Historic Monuments of Ancient Nara (C, 1998)	298	497 Rd12
Sacred Sites and Pilgrimage Routes in the Kii Mountain Range (C, 2004)	298	497 Rd12
Himeji-jo (C, 1993)	298	497 Rc12
Itsukushima Shinto Shrine (C, 1996)	299	497 Rc12
Buddhist Monuments in the Horyu-ji Area (C, 1993)	300	497 Rd12
Hiroshima Peace Memorial (Genbaku Dome) (C, 1996)	300	497 Rc12
Yakushima (N, 1993)	300	497 Rc12
Gusuku Sites and Related Properties of the Kingdom of Ryukyu (C, 2000)	301	497 Rc12
Iwami Ginzan Silver Mine and its Cultural Landscape (C, 2007)	301	497 Rb13
Thailand		
Historic Town of Sukhothai and Associated Historic Towns (C, 1991)	302	499 Pd15
Ban Chiang Archaeological Site (C, 1992)	304	499 Qa15
Thung Yai-Huai Kha Khaeng Wildlife Sanctuaries (N, 1991)	304	499 Pd16
Historic City of Ayutthaya (C, 1991)	305	499 Qa16
Dong Phayayen-Khao Yai Forest Complex (N, 2005)	305	499 Qa16
Laos		
Town of Luang Prabang (C, 1995)	306	499 Qa15
Vat Phou and Associated Ancient Settlements within the Champasak Cultural Landscape (C, 2001)	306	499 Qb16
Cambodia		
Temple of Preah Vihear (C, 2008)	307	499 Qa16
Angkor (C, 1992)	308	499 Qa16
Vietnam		
Ha Long Bay (N, 1994, 2000 ext.)	310	499 Qb14
Phong Nha-Ke Bang National Park (N, 2003)	310	499 Qb15
Complex of Hué Monuments (C, 1993)	311	499 Qb15
Hoi An Ancient Town (C, 1999)	311	499 Qb15
My Son Sanctuary (C, 1999)	311	499 Qb15
Philippines		
Historic Town of Vigan (C, 1999)	312	500 Ra15
Rice Terraces of the Philippine Cordilleras * (C, 1995)	312	500 Ra15
Baroque Churches of the Philippines (C, 1993)	312	500 Ra15
Puerto Princesa Subterranean River National Park (N, 1999)	313	500 Qd16
Tubbataha Reefs Natural Park (N, 1993, 2009 ext.)	313	500 Ra17
Malaysia		
Melaka and George Town, Historic Cities of the Straits of Malacca (C, 2008)	314	500 Qa17–18
Kinabalu Park (N, 2000)	314	500 Qd17
Gunung Mulu National Park (N, 2000)	314	500 Qd18
Indonesia		
Tropical Rainforest Heritage of Sumatra (N, 2004)	315	500 Pd18/Qa20
Ujung Kulon National Park (N, 1991)	316	500 Qb20
Borobudur Temple Compounds (C, 1991)	316	500 Qc20
Prambanan Temple Compounds (C, 1991)	316	500 Qc20
Sangiran Early Man Site (C, 1996)	317	500 Qc20
Komodo National Park (N, 1991)	317	500 Qd20
Lorentz National Park (N, 1999)	317	501 Rd19
AUSTRALIA / OCEANIA		
Australia		
Kakadu National Park (C, N, 1981, 1987 and 1992 ext.)	320	502 Rc21
Purnululu National Park (N, 2003)	322	502 Rb22
Shark Bay, Western Australia (N, 1991)	323	502 Qc24
Uluru-Kata Tjuta National Park (C, N, 1987, 1994 ext.)	323	502 Rc24
Wet Tropics of Queensland (N, 1988)	324	502 Sb22

List of World Heritage Sites (by region, country)

Gondwana Rainforests of Australia (N, 1986, 1994 ext.)	324	503 Sc24–25	**Sudan**			
Greater Blue Mountains Area (N, 2000)	324	503 Sc25	Gebel Barkal and the Sites of the Napatan Region (C, 2003)	359	507 Mc15	
Sydney Opera House (C, 2007)	325	503 Sc25	**Mauretania**			
Fraser Island (N, 1992)	325	503 Sc24	Banc d'Arguin National Park (N, 1989)	360	506 Ka14	
Great Barrier Reef (N, 1981)	326	502 Sb22	Ancient Ksour of Ouadane, Chinguetti, Tichitt and Oualata (C, 1996)	360	506 Kb14/Kc15	
Willandra Lakes Region (C, N, 1981)	327	502 Sa25	**Mali**			
Australian Fossil Mammal Sites (Riversleigh / Naracoorte)			Timbuktu (C, 1988)	361	506 Kd15	
(N, 1994)	327	502 Rd22/Sa26	Tomb of Askia (C, 2004)	361	506 Kd15	
Royal Exhibition Building and Carlton Gardens (C, 2004)	327	502 Sb26	Old Towns of Djenné (C, 1988)	361	506 Kd16	
Lord Howe Island Group (N, 1982)	327	503 Sd25	Cliff of Bandiagara (Land of the Dogons) (C, N 1989)	362	506 Kd16	
Tasmanian Wilderness (C, N, 1982, 1989 ext.)	328	502 Sb27	**Niger**			
Macquarie Island (N, 1997)	329	502 Pa31	Aïr and Ténéré Natural Reserves * (N, 1991)	364	506 Lb15	
Heard and McDonald Islands (N, 1997)	329	502 Na31	"W" National Park of Niger (N, 1996)	364	506 La16	
Papua New Guinea			**Cape Verde**			
Kuk Early Agricultural Site (C, 2008)	330	504 Sa20	Cidade Velha, Historic Center of Ribeira Grande (C, 2009)	364	506 Jd16	
Vanuatu			**Senegal**			
Chief Roi Mata's Domain (C, 2008)	330	505 Tb22	Djoudj National Bird Sanctuary (N, 1981)	365	506 Ka15	
Solomon Islands			Island of Saint-Louis (C, 2000)	365	506 Ka15	
East Rennell (N, 1998)	331	504 Ta21	Niokolo-Koba National Park * (N, 1981)	365	506 Kb15	
New Zealand			Island of Gorée (C, 1978)	366	506 Ka16	
Tongariro National Park (C, N, 1990, 1993 ext.)	332	503 Td26	Stone Circles of Senegambia (C, TB, 2006)	368	506 Kb16	
Te Wahipounamu – South-West New Zealand (N, 1990)	334	503 Tb28	**Gambia**			
New Zealand Sub-Antarctic Islands (N, 1998)	335	502 Pb31	Stone Circles of Senegambia (C, TB, 2006)	368	506 Kb16	
			James Island and Related Sites (C, 2003)	368	506 Ka16	
AFRICA			**Guinea**			
Morocco			Mount Nimba Strict Nature Reserve * (N, TB, 1981, 1982 ext.)	368	506 Kc17	
Medina of Tétouan (formerly known as Titawin) (C, 1997)	338	506 Kc11	**Côte d'Ivoire**			
Medina of Fez (C, 1981)	338	506 Kd12	Mount Nimba Strict Nature Reserve * (N, TB, 1981, 1982 ext.)	368	506 Kc17	
Archaeological Site of Volubilis (C, 1997)	339	506 Kc12	Comoé National Park * (N, 1983)	369	506 Kd17	
Historic City of Meknès (C, 1996)	339	506 Kc12	Taï National Park (N, 1982)	369	506 Kc17	
Portuguese City of Mazagan (El Jadida) (C, 2004)	339	506 Kc12	**Burkina Faso**			
Medina of Marrakesh (C, 1985)	340	506 Kc12	Ruins of Loropéni (C, 2009)	369	506 Kd16	
Medina of Essaouira (formerly Mogador) (C, 2001)	341	506 Kc12	**Ghana**			
Ksar of Aït-Ben-Haddou (C, 1987)	341	506 Kc12	Asante Traditional Buildings (C, 1980)	370	506 Kd17	
Algeria			Forts and Castles, Volta, Greater Accra, Central and Western Regions			
Kasbah of Algiers (C, 1992)	342	506 La11	(C, 1979)	370	506 Kd17	
Al Qal'a of Beni Hammad (C, 1980)	342	506 La11	**Togo**			
Tipasa (C, 1982)	342	506 La11	Koutammakou, the Land of the Batammariba (C, 2004)	371	506 La16	
Djémila (C, 1982)	343	506 Lb11	**Benin**			
Timgad (C, 1982)	343	506 Lb11	Royal Palaces of Abomey (C, 1985)	371	506 La17	
M'Zab Valley (C, 1982)	343	506 La12	**Nigeria**			
Tassili n'Ajjer (C, N, 1982)	344	506 Lb14	Osun-Osogbo Sacred Grove (C, 2005)	372	506 La17	
Tunisia			Sukur Cultural Landscape (C, 1999)	372	506 Lc16	
Dougga / Thugga (C, 1997)	346	506 Lb11	**Cameroon**			
Ichkeul National Park (N, 1980)	346	506 Lb11	Dja Faunal Reserve (N, 1987)	372	506 Lc18	
Archaeological Site of Carthage (C, 1979)	346	506 Lc11	**Central African Republic**			
Medina of Tunis (C, 1979)	347	506 Lc11	Manovo-Gounda St Floris National Park * (N, 1988)	372	507 Ma17	
Medina of Sousse (C, 1988)	348	506 Lc11	**Gabon**			
Kairouan (C, 1988)	348	506 Lc11	Ecosystem and Relict Cultural Landscape of Lopé-Okanda (C, N, 2007)	373	508 Lc19	
Punic Town of Kerkuane and its Necropolis (C, 1985, 1986 ext.)	349	506 Lc11	**Congo, Democratic Republic of**			
Amphitheater of El Jem (C, 1979)	349	506 Lc11	Garamba National Park * (N, 1980)	374	507 Mb18	
Libya			Okapi Wildlife Reserve * (N, 1996)	374	509 Mb18	
Archaeological Site of Leptis Magna (C, 1982)	350	506 Lc12	Salonga National Park * (N, 1984)	374	508 Ma19	
Archaeological Site of Sabratha (C, 1982)	350	506 Lc12	Kahuzi-Biega National Park * (N, 1980)	374	508 Mb19	
Archaeological Site of Cyrene (C, 1982)	350	507 Ma12	Virunga National Park * (N, 1979)	375	509 Mb19	
Old Town of Ghadamès (C, 1986)	351	506 Lb13	**Ethiopia**			
Rock-Art Sites of Tadrart Acacus (C, 1985)	351	506 Lc13	Simien National Park * (N, 1978)	376	507 Md16	
Egypt			Aksum (C, 1980)	376	507 Md16	
Wadi Al-Hitan (Whale Valley) (N, 2005)	352	507 Mb13	Fasil Ghebbi, Gondar Region (C, 1979)	377	507 Md16	
Abu Mena * (C, 1979)	352	507 Mb12	Rock Hewn Churches, Lalibela (C, 1978)	378	507 Md16	
Historic Cairo (C, 1979)	353	507 Mc12	Lower Valley of the Awash (C, 1980)	379	507 Na16	
Memphis and its Necropolis – the Pyramid Fields from Giza			Lower Valley of the Omo (C, 1980)	379	507 Md17	
to Dahshur (C, 1979)	354	507 Mc13	Tiya (C, 1980)	380	507 Md17	
Ancient Thebes with its Necropolis (C, 1979)	356	507 Mc13	Harar Jugol, the Fortified Historic Town (C, 2006)	380	507 Na17	
Nubian Monuments from Abu Simbel to Philae (C, 1979)	358	507 Mc14	**Uganda**			
Saint Catherine Area (C, 2002)	358	507 Mc13	Bwindi Impenetrable National Park (N, 1994)	381	507 Mb19	

Rwenzori Mountains National Park (N, 1994)	381	507 Mc18	
Tombs of Buganda Kings at Kasubi (C, 2001)	381	507 Mc18	
Kenya			
Sacred Mijikenda Kaya Forests (C, 2008)	382	509 Md19	
Lamu Old Town (C, 2001)	382	509 Na19	
Lake Turkana National Parks (N, 1997, 2001 ext.)	382	507 Md18	
Mount Kenya National Park / Natural Forest (N, 1997)	383	507 Md18	
Tanzania			
Serengeti National Park (N, 1981)	384	509 Mc19	
Ngorongoro Conservation Area (N, 1979)	386	509 Md19	
Kilimanjaro National Park (N, 1987)	386	509 Md19	
Selous Game Reserve (N, 1982)	386	509 Md20	
Ruins of Kilwa Kisiwani and Ruins of Songo Mnara * (C, 1981)	387	509 Md20	
Stone Town of Zanzibar (C, 2000)	387	509 Md20	
Kondoa Rock-Art Sites (C, 2006)	387	509 Md20	
Zambia			
Mosi-oa-Tunya / Victoria Falls (N, TB, 1989)	388	508 Mb22	
Zimbabwe			
Mosi-oa-Tunya / Victoria Falls (N, TB, 1989)	388	508 Mb22	
Mana Pools National Park, Sapi and Chewore Safari Areas (N, 1984)	389	509 Mb22	
Khami Ruins National Monument (C, 1986)	389	508 Mb23	
Matobo Hills (C 2003)	389	509 Mb23	
Great Zimbabwe National Monument (C, 1986)	389	509 Mc23	
Malawi			
Lake Malawi National Park (N, 1984)	390	509 Mc21	
Chongoni Rock-Art Area (C, 2006)	390	509 Mc21	
Mozambique			
Island of Mozambique (C, 1991)	391	509 Na21	
Botswana			
Tsodilo (C, 2001)	391	508 Ma22	
Namibia			
Twyfelfontein or /Ui-//aes (C, 2007)	391	508 Lc23	
South Africa			
Mapungubwe Cultural Landscape (C, 2003)	392	509 Mb23	
Fossil Hominid Sites of Sterkfontein, Swartkrans, Kromdraai, and Environs (C, 1999, 2005 ext.)	392	508 Ma–Mb24	
Vredefort Dome (N, 2005)	392	508 Mb24	
uKhahlamba / Drakensberg Park (C, N, 2000)	393	509 Mb24	
iSimangaliso Wetland Park (N, 1999)	393	508 Mc24	
Richtersveld Cultural and Botanical Landscape (C, 2007)	394	508 Ld24	
Robben Island (C, 1999)	394	508 Ld25	
Cape Floral Region Protected Areas (N, 2004)	394	508 Ld25	
Madagascar			
Rainforests of the Atsinanana (N, 2007)	395	509 Nb21–23	
Tsingy de Bemaraha Strict Nature Reserve (N, 1990)	395	509 Na22	
Royal Hill of Ambohimanga (C, 2001)	395	509 Nb22	
Mauritius			
Aapravasi Ghat (C, 2006)	396	509 Nd23	
Le Morne Cultural Landscape (C, 2008)	396	509 Nd23	
Seychelles			
Aldabra Atoll (N, 1982)	397	509 Nb20	
Vallée de Mai Nature Reserve (N, 1983)	397	509 Nd19	
THE AMERICAS			
Canada			
Kluane / Wrangell-St Elias / Glacier Bay / Tatshenshini-Alsek (N, TB, 1979, 1992 and 1994 ext.)	400	510 Cd06	
Nahanni National Park (N, 1978)	402	510 Dc06	
Wood Buffalo National Park (N, 1983)	403	510 Eb07	
SGang Gwaay (Anthony Island) (C, 1981)	403	510 Db08	
Canadian Rocky Mountain Parks (N, 1984, 1990 ext.)	404	510 Ea08	
Head-Smashed-in Buffalo Jump (C, 1981)	406	510 Eb09	
Dinosaur Provincial Park (N, 1979)	406	510 Eb08	
L'Anse aux Meadows National Historic Site (C, 1978)	406	511 Ha08	
Gros Morne National Park (N, 1987)	407	511 Ha08	
Miguasha National Park (N, 1999)	408	511 Gc09	

Historic District of Old Québec (C, 1985)	408	511 Gb09	
Rideau Canal (C, 2007)	409	513 Ga10	
Joggins Fossil Cliffs (N, 2008)	409	511 Gd09	
Old Town Lunenburg (C, 1995)	409	511 Gd10	
Waterton Glacier International Peace Park (N, TB, 1995)	410	510 Eb09	
United States of America			
Kluane / Wrangell-St Elias / Glacier Bay / Tatshenshini-Alsek (N, TB, 1979, 1992 and 1994 ext.)	400	510 Cd06	
Waterton Glacier International Peace Park (N, TB, 1995)	410	510 Eb09	
Olympic National Park (N, 1981)	412	510 Db09	
Yellowstone National Park (N, 1978)	412	512 Eb10	
Redwood National and State Parks (N, 1980)	413	512 Dd10	
Yosemite National Park (N, 1984)	413	512 Ea11	
Grand Canyon National Park (N, 1979)	414	512 Eb11	
Chaco Culture (C, 1987)	415	512 Ec11	
Mesa Verde National Park (C, 1978)	415	512 Ec11	
Pueblo de Taos (C, 1992)	415	512 Ec11	
Carlsbad Caverns National Park (N, 1995)	415	512 Ed12	
Statue of Liberty (C, 1984)	416	513 Gb10	
Independence Hall (C, 1979)	416	513 Ga11	
Cahokia Mounds State Historic Site (C, 1982)	416	512 Fb11	
Monticello and the University of Virginia in Charlottesville (C, 1987)	417	513 Ga11	
Mammoth Cave National Park (N, 1981)	417	513 Fc11	
Great Smoky Mountains National Park (N, 1983)	417	513 Fd11	
Everglades National Park (N, 1979)	418	513 Fd13	
La Fortaleza and San Juan National Historic Site in Puerto Rico (C, 1983)	419	513 Gc15	
Hawaii Volcanoes National Park (N, 1987)	419	512 Ab20	
Mexico			
Archaeological Zone of Paquimé, Casas Grandes (C, 1998)	420	512 Ec12	
Whale Sanctuary of El Vizcaino (N, 1993)	420	512 Eb13	
Rock Paintings of the Sierra de San Francisco (C, 1993)	420	512 Eb13	
Islands and Protected Areas of the Gulf of California (N, 2005)	421	512 Eb13	
Historic Center of Zacatecas (C, 1993)	421	512 Ed14	
Agave Landscape and Ancient Industrial Facilities of Tequila (C, 2006)	421	512 Ed14	
Historic Town of Guanajuato and Adjacent Mines (C, 1988)	422	512 Ed14	
Protective town of San Miguel and the Sanctuary of Jesús Nazareno de Atotonilco (C, 2008)	422	512 Ed14	
Historic Monuments Zone of Querétaro (C, 1996)	422	512 Ed14	
Franciscan Missions in the Sierra Gorda of Querétaro (C, 2003)	422	512 Fa14	
Hospicio Cabañas, Guadalajara (C, 1997)	423	512 Ed14	
El Tajin, Pre-Hispanic City (C, 1992)	423	512 Fa14	
Historic Center of Morelia (C, 1991)	423	512 Ed15	
Monarch Butterfly Biosphere Reserve (N, 2008)	423	512 Ed15	
Pre-Hispanic City of Teotihuacan (C, 1987)	424	512 Fa15	
Luis Barragán House and Studio (C, 2004)	426	512 Fa15	
Historic Center of Mexico City and Xochimilco (C, 1987)	426	512 Fa15	
Central University City Campus of the Universidad Nacional Autónoma de México (UNAM) (C, 2007)	427	512 Fa15	
Archaeological Monuments Zone of Xochicalco (C, 1999)	427	512 Fa15	
Historic Center of Puebla (C, 1987)	428	512 Fa15	
Earliest 16th-Century Monasteries on the Slopes of Popocatepetl (C, 1994)	428	512 Fa15	
Historic Center of Oaxaca and Archaeological Site of Monte Albán (C, 1987)	429	512 Fa15	
Historic Monuments Zone of Tlacotalpan (C, 1998)	429	512 Fa15	
Pre-Hispanic City and National Park of Palenque (C, 1987)	430	512 Fb15	
Historic Fortified Town of Campeche (C, 1999)	430	513 Fb15	
Pre-Hispanic Town of Uxmal (C, 1996)	430	513 Fc14	
Pre-Hispanic City of Chichen-Itza (C, 1988)	431	513 Fc14	
Sian Ka'an (N, 1987)	431	513 Fc15	
Ancient Maya City of Calakmul, Campeche (C, 2002)	431	513 Fc15	
Belize			
Belize Barrier Reef Reserve System * (N, 1996)	432	513 Fc15	
Guatemala			
Tikal National Park (C, N, 1979)	432	513 Fc15	

List of World Heritage Sites (by region, country)

Archaeological Park and Ruins of Quirigua (C, 1981)	432	513 Fc15	Historic Sanctuary of Machu Picchu (C, N, 1983)	456	514 Gb21
Antigua Guatemala (C, 1979)	433	513 Fb16	City of Cuzco (C, 1983)	457	514 Gb21
Honduras			Manú National Park (N, 1987)	458	514 Gb21
Río Plátano Biosphere Reserve (N, 1982)	433	513 Fd15	Lines and Geoglyphs of Nasca and Pampas de Jumana (C, 1994)	459	514 Gb21
Maya Site of Copan (C, 1980)	433	513 Fc16	Historic Center of the City of Arequipa (C, 2000)	459	514 Gb22
El Salvador			**Bolivia**		
Joya de Cerén Archaeological Site (C, 1993)	434	513 Fc16	Tiwanaku: Spiritual and Political Center of the Tiwanaku Culture		
Nicaragua			(C, 2000)	460	514 Gc22
Ruins of León Viejo (C, 2000)	434	513 Fc16	Historic City of Sucre (C, 1991)	460	514 Gc22
Costa Rica			City of Potosí (C, 1987)	460	514 Gc22
Area de Conservación Guanacaste (N, 1999, 2004 ext.)	435	513 Fc16	Fuerte de Samaipata (C, 1998)	461	514 Gd22
Cocos Island National Park (N, 1997, 2002 ext.)	435	514 Fc17	Noel Kempff Mercado National Park (N, 2000)	461	515 Gd21
Talamanca Range-La Amistad Reserves / La Amistad National Park			Jesuit Missions of the Chiquitos (C, 1990)	461	515 Gd22
(N, TB, 1983, 1990 ext.)	436	513 Fd17	**Chile**		
Panama			Humberstone and Santa Laura Saltpeter Works * (C, 2005)	462	514 Gc23
Talamanca Range-La Amistad Reserves / La Amistad National Park			Historic Quarter of the Seaport City of Valparaíso (C, 2003)	462	517 Gb25
(N, TB, 1983, 1990 ext.)	436	513 Fd17	Sewell Mining Town (C, 2006)	463	517 Gb25
Coiba National Park and its Special Zone of Marine Protection			Churches of Chiloé (C, 2000)	463	517 Gb27
(N, 2005)	437	513 Fd17	Rapa Nui National Park (C, 1995)	463	516 Ec24
Fortifications on the Caribbean Side of Panama:			**Venezuela**		
Portobelo-San Lorenzo (C, 1980)	437	513 Ga17	Coro and its Port * (C, 1993)	464	514 Gc16
Archaeological Site of Panamá Viejo and Historic District of Panamá			Ciudad Universitaria de Caracas (C, 2000)	464	514 Gc16
(C, 1997, 2003 ext.)	437	513 Ga17	Canaima National Park (N, 1994)	464	515 Gd17
Darién National Park (N, 1981)	437	513 Ga17	**Suriname**		
Cuba			Historic Inner City of Paramaribo (C, 2002)	465	515 Ha17
Old Havana and its Fortifications (C, 1982)	438	513 Fd14	Central Suriname Nature Reserve (N, 2000)	465	515 Ha18
Viñales Valley (C, 1999)	439	513 Fd14	**Brazil**		
Urban Historic Center of Cienfuegos (C, 2005)	439	513 Fd14	Central Amazon Conservation Complex (N, 2000, 2003 ext.)	466	514 Gd19
Trinidad and the Valley de Los Ingenios (C, 1988)	439	513 Ga14	Historic Center of São Luís (C, 1997)	466	515 Hd19
Historic Center of Camagüey (C, 2008)	440	513 Ga14	Historic Center of the Town of Olinda (C, 1982)	467	515 Jb20
San Pedro de la Roca Castle, Santiago de Cuba (C, 1997)	440	513 Ga15	Serra da Capivara National Park (C, 1991)	467	515 Hd20
Archaeological Landscape of the First Coffee Plantations in			Historic Center of Salvador da Bahia (C, 1985)	468	515 Ja21
the South-East of Cuba (C, 2000)	441	513 Ga14	Discovery Coast Atlantic Forest Reserves (N, 1999)	470	515 Ja22
Desembarco del Granma National Park (N, 1999)	441	513 Ga14	Cerrado Protected Areas: Chapada dos Veadeiros and		
Alejandro de Humboldt National Park (N, 2001)	441	513 Ga14	Emas National Parks (N, 2001)	470	515 Hc21/Hb22
Dominican Republic			Brasilia (C, 1987)	471	515 Hc22
Colonial City of Santo Domingo (C, 1990)	442	513 Gc15	Historic Center of the Town of Goiás (C, 2001)	472	515 Hb22
Haiti			Historic Town of Ouro Prêto (C, 1980)	472	515 Hd23
National History Park – Citadel, Sans Souci, Ramiers (C, 1982)	442	513 Gb15	Historic Center of the Town of Diamantina (C, 1999)	473	515 Hd22
Saint Kitts and Nevis			Sanctuary of Bom Jesus do Congonhas (C, 1985)	473	515 Hd23
Brimstone Hill Fortress National Park (C, 1999)	442	513 Gd15	Atlantic Forest South-East Reserves (N, 1999)	473	517 Hc23
Dominica			Pantanal Conservation Area (N, 2000)	474	515 Ha22
Morne Trois Pitons National Park (N, 1997)	443	513 Gd15	Brazilian Atlantic Islands: Fernando de Noronha and Atol das		
Saint Lucia			Rocas Reserves (N, 2001)	475	515 Jb19
Pitons Management Area (N, 2004)	443	513 Gd16	Iguaçu National Park (N, 1986)	475	517 Hb24
Colombia			Jesuit Missions of the Guaranis: San Ignacio Mini, Santa Ana,		
Port, Fortresses and Group of Monuments, Cartagena (C, 1984)	444	514 Ga16	Nuestra Señora de Loreto and Santa Maria Mayor (Argentina),		
Historic Center of Santa Cruz de Mompox (C, 1995)	445	514 Gb17	Ruins of Sao Miguel das Missoes (Brazil) (C, TB, 1983, 1984 ext.)	476	517 Hb24
Los Katíos National Park * (N, 1994)	445	514 Ga17	**Paraguay**		
National Archaeological Park of Tierradentro (C, 1995)	445	514 Ga18	Jesuit Missions of La Santísima Trinidad de Paraná and Jesús		
San Agustín Archaeological Park (C, 1995)	446	514 Ga18	de Tavarangue (C, 1993)	477	517 Ha24
Malpelo Fauna and Flora Sanctuary (N, 2006)	447	514 Fd18	**Uruguay**		
Ecuador			Historic Quarter of the City of Colonia del Sacramento (C, 1995)	477	517 Ha25
City of Quito (C, 1978)	448	514 Ga19	**Argentina**		
Historic Center of Santa Ana de los Ríos de Cuenca (C, 1999)	449	514 Ga19	Quebrada de Humahuaca (C, 2003)	478	517 Gc23
Sangay National Park (N, 1983)	449	514 Ga19	Iguazú National Park (N, 1984)	478	517 Hb24
Galapagos Islands * (N, 1978, 2001 ext.)	450	514 Fb19	Ischigualasto / Talampaya Natural Parks (N, 2000)	478	517 Gc24
Peru			Jesuit Missions of the Guaranis: San Ignacio Mini, Santa Ana,		
Río Abiseo National Park (C, N, 1990, 1992 ext.)	452	514 Ga20	Nuestra Señora de Loreto and Santa Maria Mayor (Argentina),		
Chan Chan Archaeological Zone * (C, 1986)	452	514 Ga20	Ruins of Sao Miguel das Missoes (Brazil) (C, TB, 1983, 1984 ext.)	476	517 Hb24
Chavín (Archaeological Site) (C, 1985)	452	514 Ga20	Jesuit Block and Estancias of Córdoba (C, 2000)	479	517 Gd25
Huascarán National Park (N, 1995)	453	514 Ga20	Península Valdés (N, 1999)	479	517 Gd27
Sacred City of Caral-Supe (C, 2009)	453	514 Ga21	Cueva de las Manos, Río Pinturas (C, 1999)	479	517 Gb28
Historic Center of Lima (C, 1988, 1991 ext.)	454	514 Ga21	Los Glaciares (N, 1981)	480	517 Gb28

In August 2010, the 34th session of the World Heritage Committee of UNESCO convened to inscribe a total of twenty-one new sites to its World Heritage list. Of these, fifteen fall under cultural, five under natural heritage and one is a mixed site belonging to both cultural and natural heritage. The Ngorongoro Conservation Area in Tanzania, which has been included in the World Natural Heritage list since 1979, has also been given recognition for its unique cultural value.

Natural Heritage Sites

China: Red terrigenous sedimentary formations are characteristic of the China **Danxia region** in subtropical south-western China. The spectacular mountain landscape here features steep rock faces, tall pillars and towers, deep canyons and numerous waterfalls..

France: Pitons, Cirques and Remparts of Reunion Island. The tropical island **La Réunion** is a French overseas territory and belongs to the Macarene island group. It is about 800 km (500 mi) east of Madagascar in the Indian Ocean.

Kiribati: The **Phoenix Islands Protected Area** in the South Pacific is the largest marine protection area in the world covering more than 400,000 sq km (154,400 sq mi). It is the only area in the tropics to comprise underwater mountain ranges with peaks up to 5,000 m (16,405 ft) above the sea floor.

Russia: The **Putorana Plateau i**n the Central Siberian Mountains is an untouched natural landscape of extraordinary beauty. Over the course of millions of years, spectacular formations with countless waterfalls up to 100 m (33 ft) in height have emerged along with a number of diverse ecosystems.

Sri Lanka: The **Central Highlands of Sri Lanka** comprises three protected areas: Horton Plains National Park, the Knuckles Range and the Peak Wilderness Sanctuary. The three areas stand out thanks to their extraordinarily rich bio-diversity.

Cultural and Natural Heritage Sites

Tanzania: The **Ngorongoro Conservation Area** has been a World Natural Heritage Site since 1979, but the World Heritage Committee has now chosen to also emphasize the cultural significance of Ngorongoro as an "extraordinary testimony of human evolutionary history ". Of singular importance are the 3.6-million-year-old fossilized human footprints in Laetoli and the excavation sites in Olduvai Gorge.

United States of Americas: The **Papahãnaumokuãkea Marine National Monument** in the Pacific Ocean comprises a group of small islands and atolls extending north-west from Hawaii. With an area of more than 360,000 sq km (138,960 sq mi) it is one of the largest marine nature reserves in the world.

Cultural Heritage Sites

Australia: The **Australian Convict Sites** commemorate the transport of convicts to colonies of the British Empire in the 18th and 19th centuries. The Committee has included a representative selection of eleven penal colonies in the World Heritage list. These are located on the Sydney coast, Tasmania, Norfolk Island and on the west coast near Fremantle.

Brazil: **São Francisco Square in São Cristóvão** is an important testimony to Brazilian colonial history. São Francisco was the focal point of the Old Town with the main headquarters of both civilian and religious entities.rden.

China: The **Historic Monuments of Dengfeng** in "The Centre of Heaven and Earth" represents the multifaceted nature of Chinese cultural history during the entire period between 118 BC and the 20th century. Dengfeng is considered the center of Confucianism and the birthplace of Chan Buddhism.

France: The exceptionally well-preserved **Episcopal City of Albi** on the banks of the Tarn River in south-western France is representative of the architectural and urban history of Europe during the Middle Ages and the Renaissance.

India: The **"Jantar Mantar" in Jaipur** is the most important and best-preserved historic observatory in India. Built in the tradition of Ptolemaic astronomy, it was developed for the observation of planetary movements using just the naked eye.

Iran: The **Ensemble Scheich Safi al-din Khãnegãh and Shrine Ensemble in Ardabil** in north-western Iran is a unique complex of buildings dating from the 16th to the 18th centuries featuring bazaars, public baths and houses as well as religious and public institutions.

Iran: The **Tabriz Historic Bazaar Complex** in north-western Iran is an outstanding example of city architecture that developed as a result of international trade and culture at this crossroads location.

Republic of Korea: The **Historic Villages of Hahoe and Yangdong** from the 14th and 15th centuries represent typical settlements during the reign of the Joseon Dynasty, which followed the ideals of Pungsu Jiri (a Korean version of Feng Shui).

Marshall Islands: The **Bikini Atoll Atomic Bomb Test Area** in the Pacific Ocean is a key location for contemporary history and is of vital international importance. It symbolizes the start of the nuclear age and reminds us of the Cold War.

Mexico: The **Camino Real de Tierra Adentro Historic Trade Route**, also known as the "Silver Route", runs from Mexico City to Texas and New Mexico. From the middle of the 16th century it facilitated the trade in mercury from Europe and silver from the mines of Zacatecas, Guanajuato and San Luis Potosí in Mexico.

Mexico: The **Prehistoric Caves of Yagul and Mitla** in the Central Valley of Oaxaca are valuable testimony to the beginnings of agriculture and of a semi-sedentary lifestyle in Central America.

Netherlands: The **Seventeenth-Century Canal Ring Area of Amsterdam** inside the Singelgracht is representative of urban development and architecture in Amsterdam in the 16th and 17th centuries, when the town was an international center for trade and a hub for scientific and technological exchange..

Saudi-Arabia: The **At-Turaif Quarter in Ad-Dir'iyah** is an extraordinary cultural and architectural relic of the first Saudi state.

Tadjikistan: The **Proto-Urban Site of Sarazm** in the valley of the Serafshan River near the Uzbek border is a unique testimony to the settlement and cultural history of Central Asia from the 4th to the 3rd millennium BC.

Vietnam: The **Imperial Citadel of Thang Long** in present-day Hanoi was constructed in the 11th century by the Lˇ Dynasty as a symbol of the independence of the Dai Viet state.

PICTURE CREDITS

A = Alamy | B = Bilderberg | C = Corbis G = Getty-Images | H = Bildagentur Huber | L = Laif | M = Mauritius Images | p-a = Picture Alliance | Schapo = Bildagentur Schapowalow

Cover: large picture t.: Laif/Redux, large picture c.: Bildagentur Huber/Picture Finder, large picture b.: Laif/hemisphere, small picture t.: Laif/Shabi, small picture c.: Premium, small picture b.: Alamy/John Franham, back cover: Okapia

MONACO BOOKS is an imprint of Verlag Wolfgang Kunth
© Verlag Wolfgang Kunth GmbH & Co.KG, Munich, 2010

For distribution please contact:

Monaco Books
c/o Verlag Wolfgang Kunth, Königinstr. 11
80539 München, Germany
Tel: (+49) 89 45 80 20 23
Fax: (+49) 89 45 80 20 21
info@kunth-verlag.de
www.monacobooks.com
www.kunth-verlag.de

Texts: Natascha Albus, Heike Barnitzke, Catrin Barnsteiner, Gesa Bock, Arno Breckner, Monika Baumüller, Klaus Dammann, Klaus A. Dietsch, Michael Elser, Dietmar Falk, Werner Fiederer, Robert Fischer, Petra Frese, Ute Friesen, Winfried Gerhards, Dr Natalie Göltenboth, Martina Gschließer, Ulrike Köppchen, Dr Steffen Krämer, Ingrid Langschwert, Brigitte Lotz, Angela Meißner, Werner Morgerath, Norbert Pautner, Dr Regina Prinz, Dr Ulrike Prinz, Dr Jürgen Rapp, Ingrid Reuter, André Ruo, Monika Sattrasai, Dr Susanne Scheffler-Gerken, Dr Hans-Wilm Schütte, Ingrid Suvak, Dr Marcus Würmli

Translation: Mike Goulding, Sylvia Goulding, Emily Plank, Katherine Taylor
Editor: Kevin White for bookwise Medienproduktion GmbH, Munich
Coordination: bookwise Medienproduktion GmbH, Munich

Printed in Slovakia